MW01701243

INVESTMENT FUNDAMENTALS

INVESTMENT FUNDAMENTALS

Frederick Amling
The George Washington University

William G. Droms
Georgetown University

The Dryden Press
Harcourt Brace College Publishers

Fort Worth Philadelphia San Diego
New York Orlando Austin San Antonio
Toronto Montreal London Sydney Tokyo

Publisher	Liz Widdicombe
Acquisitions Editor	Rick Hammonds
Project Editor	Amy Schmidt
Production Manager	Marilyn Williams
Book Designer	John Ritland
Copy Editor	David W. Talley
Indexer	Leoni McVey
Compositor	Monotype Composition Company
Text Type	10/12 Caledonia
Cover Image	Sam Samaha

Address for Editorial Correspondence: The Dryden Press, 301 Commerce Street, Suite 3700, Fort Worth, TX 76102.

Address for Orders: The Dryden Press, 6277 Sea Harbor Drive, Orlando, FL 32887. 1-800-782-4479, or 1-800-433-0001 (in Florida).

ISBN: 0-03-047092-7

Library of Congress Catalogue Number: 92-71662

Printed in the United States of America

3 4 5 6 7 8 9 0 1 2 039 9 8 7 6 5 4 3 2 1

The Dryden Press
Harcourt Brace College Publishers

To Nancy, Matthew, Laura Elizabeth, William, Andrew, and Liza Amling

To JoAnn, Courtney, and Justin Droms

The Dryden Press Series in Finance

Amling and Droms
Investment Fundamentals

Berry and Young
Managing Investments: A Case Approach

Boyet
Security Analysis for Investment Decisions: Text and Software

Brigham
Fundamentals of Financial Management
Sixth Edition

Brigham and Gapenski
Cases in Financial Management
Second Edition

Brigham and Gapenski
Cases in Financial Management: Module A
Second Edition

Brigham and Gapenski
Cases in Financial Management: Module B

Brigham and Gapenski
Cases in Financial Management: Module C

Brigham and Gapenski
Financial Management: Theory and Practice
Sixth Edition

Brigham and Gapenski
Intermediate Financial Management
Fourth Edition

Brigham, Gapenski, and Aberwald
Finance with Lotus 1-2-3
Second Edition

Campsey and Brigham
Introduction to Financial Management
Third Edition

Chance
An Introduction to Options and Futures
Second Edition

Clauretie and Webb
The Theory and Practice of Real Estate Finance

Cooley
Advances in Business Financial Management: A Collection of Readings

Cooley and Roden
Business Financial Management
Second Edition

Curran
Principles of Corporate Finance

Evans
International Finance: A Markets Approach

Fama and Miller
The Theory of Finance

Gardner and Mills
Managing Financial Institutions: An Asset/Liability Approach

Gitman and Joehnk
Personal Financial Planning
Sixth Edition

Harrington
Case Studies in Financial Decision Making
Third Edition

Hayes and Meerschwam
Financial Institutions: Contemporary Cases in the Financial Services Industry

Johnson
Issues and Readings in Managerial Finance
Third Edition

Kidwell, Peterson, and Blackwell
Financial Institutions, Markets, and Money
Fifth Edition

Koch
Bank Management
Second Edition

Kohn
Money, Banking, and Financial Markets
Second Edition

Lee and Finnerty
Corporate Finance: Theory, Method, and Application

Maisel
Real Estate Finance
Second Edition

Martin, Cox, and MacMinn
The Theory of Finance: Evidence and Applications

Mayo
Finance: An Introduction
Fourth Edition

Mayo
Investments: An Introduction
Third Edition

Pettijohn
PROFIT+

Reilly
Investment Analysis and Portfolio Management
Third Edition

Reilly
Investments
Third Edition

Sears and Trennepohl
Investment Management

Seitz
Capital Budgeting and Long-Term Financing Decisions

Siegel and Siegel
Futures Markets

Smith and Spudeck
Interest Rates: Principles and Applications

Stickney
Financial Statement Analysis: A Strategic Perspective
Second Edition

Turnbull
Option Valuation

Weston and Brigham
Essentials of Managerial Finance
Tenth Edition

Weston and Copeland
Managerial Finance
Ninth Edition

Wood and Wood
Financial Markets

The Harcourt Brace College Outline Series

Baker
Financial Management

Preface

This book is the result of the authors having engaged in many years of teaching, research, and consulting across a broad spectrum of investment management activities. The book is titled, appropriately, *Investment Fundamentals*, and we believe that a reasonable investment of your time reading this book will provide a solid foundation in all aspects of investment analysis, planning, and management.

Unique Features of the Book

Investment Fundamentals contains several unique features designed to illustrate, summarize, or highlight key investment issues. Each chapter begins with a real-life vignette illustrating the concepts to be presented. Each chapter then ends with a summary of its key "investment management concepts." Many of the lessons we have learned from dealing with individual and institutional investors are summarized in these opening vignettes and closing investment management concepts.

Another interesting feature of this book is the highlighted features scattered throughout that provide short summaries of key concepts related to two leading contemporary investment issues: investment ethics and international investing. In the ethics area, for example, highlighted features discuss the self-regulatory process and securities arbitration, ethical and legal responsibilities of investment managers, insider trading, and corporate raiding. In the international arena, a wide range of topics, such as investments in American Depository Receipts (ADRs), the benefits of international diversification, and the volatility of the Japanese stock market, are highlighted. There are fifteen of these discussions in the book.

All of the chapters introduce financial and investment terms that may be unfamiliar to you. Such new terms are boldfaced in the chapter in which they first appear, and a concise definition of each is included in the margin of the page. This marginal glossary enables you to quickly learn the meaning of new financial terms that will be used repeatedly throughout the book.

Organization of the Subject Matter

Investment Fundamentals is organized to cover all of the major areas of investing. Part I, "Laying the Foundation," covers saving and investing, savings institutions and instruments, and home ownership as a cornerstone investment for individuals. Part II, "Strategy for an Investment Program," contains three chapters, each covering a central area of investing: sources of investment information, securities markets and brokers, and the key topic of risk, return, and asset allocation. Taken together, Parts I and II sketch out the investment landscape and provide a firm foundation upon which to build a solid understanding of the opportunities, risks, and rewards facing investors.

Part III deals with investment analysis and management of the most common types of investment securities. The five chapters in Part III cover the topics of government debt securities, corporate bonds and preferred stock, financial statement analysis, investment opportunities in common stock, and common stock valuation models.

Part IV, "Alternative Investment Opportunities," moves beyond investing in stocks and bonds and into other important categories of investing. The first chapter in this section, "Investment in Real Assets," deals with investing in assets such as real estate, precious metals, and commodities. The next chapter explains the markets for futures and options. The last two chapters explore what are known as "pooled investments," that is, investments that pool money from many investors into one investment vehicle. Together, the two chapters cover mutual funds, closed-end investment companies, and investment-oriented life insurance policies and products.

The final part of the book, "Portfolio Management," contains two chapters. The first explains portfolio theory, investment policy, and risk management; the second deals specifically with individual portfolio management.

Instructional Support Materials

Investment Fundamentals is accompanied by a quality teaching/learning package:

- The *Instructor's Manual*, authored by Stanley Jacobs of Central Washington University, provides answers to the text questions and a test bank that includes true/false and multiple-choice questions.
- A set of videos that supports the end-of-text cases provides auditory and visual reinforcement of the text concepts and heightens students' analytical skills.
- *Investment Analysis on the Personal Computer (IA/PC)*, by James Pettijohn of Southwest Missouri State University, is a menu driven software program that allows students to solve investment problems and computations.
- A special software program called the *Return-to-Risk Maximizer* allows students to construct their own portfolios—using real stock information from over 200 companies—in order to maximize return-to-risk ratios based on their estimates of returns.

As usual, in any undertaking of this size, thanks are owed to many. The lion's share of the typing of this manuscript fell to Jennifer Smith and Anna Shook Ghonim at Georgetown University. Timothy Conklin at The George Washington University also labored long and hard as a research assistant, data analyst, typist, courier between our two campuses, and a source of good cheer. Also, our thanks goes to Elinor Conversano and Amsale Hailu, office managers, for their excellent help, and Jun Lee, Wallid Juni, and Sandy Uno, MBAs and research assistants, at The George Washington University. Charlie Brown, Jean Michael Begin, Larry Carlin, and Timothy Krause, MBA students at Georgetown, also helped research the project.

Mr. Ben G. Baldwin, CLU, ChFC, and Mr. Andrew E. Gross, CLU, ChFC, were most generous with their time and expertise and provided detailed reviews of the insurance chapter. Dr. William Seale at The George Washington University was equally generous with his comprehensive review of the chapter on futures and options. Our respective deans also deserve our thanks for their encouragement over the many years. To Deans F. David Fowler and Benjamin Burdetsky of The George Washington University School of Business and Public

Management, and to Dean Robert S. Parker of the School of Business Administration at Georgetown University, a sincere "thank you" for your support of our efforts.

We would like to thank the following people, who each answered a detailed survey, helped us formulate our ideas, and influenced the final product through their feedback:

Fidelis S. E. Akagha, *Johnson C. Smith University*
Steve Blank, *University of California, Davis*
Lin Bothwell, *Weber State College*
A. J. Carper, *Bob Jones University*
John Clinebell, *University of Northern Colorado*
Carol Denson, *University of Delaware*
A. C. Edwards, *Western Michigan University*
Rupert L. Finley, *Queen's College*
Janean Gardner, *Luther College*
Robert Hartwig, *Worcester State College*
David Heskel, *Bloomsburg University*
Kenneth M. Huggins, *Metropolitan State College*
A. V. Iannucelli, *Roger Williams College*
Gary Jackacky, *Westfield State College*
Arnold Jacobson, *City College of San Francisco*
Elizabeth Joyelland, *North Hennepin Community College*
Winford C. Naylor, *Santa Barbara City College*
Verlyn M. Noring, *Des Moines Area Community College*
J. T. O'Connor, *Worcester Polytechnic Institute*
Toby L. Poplin, *Pfeiffer College*
Ronald Ridgeway, *Rancho Santiago College*
E. Michael Shaffer, *Gwynedd-Mercy College*
Paul Sarmas, *Chapman College*
Al Segars, *University of North Carolina, Charlotte*
Peter Sibbald, *Fullerton College*
Raymond Spudeck, *University of Central Florida*
Robert Stokes, *Belmont Abbey College*
Thomas Till, *Saint Andrew's Presbyterian College*
Charles E. Tychsen, *Northern Virginia Community College*
Dwight Webb, *Salve Regina College*
Richard Yanow, *North Adams State College*

We would like to thank the following people, who prepared detailed reviews during the text's development and who helped us clarify our ideas in order to make *Investment Fundamentals* a better book:

Wayne E. Boyet, *Nicholls State University*
Claire Bronson, *Western New England College*
James D'Mello, *Western Michigan University*
W. Michael Gough, *De Anza College*
Tim Helton, *Joliet Junior College*
Tom Zwirlein, *University of Colorado, Colorado Springs*

A special note of appreciation goes to the professional staff at The Dryden Press. To Mike Roche, Anne Heath, Kathi Early, Amy Schmidt, and Sheryl Nelson, thanks are due for their professionalism and for their contributions to the project. Amy Schmidt's efforts as project editor are particularly appreciated. By phone, fax, and Fed Ex, she managed to track us down with great vigor and good humor and to force us to bring in the manuscript (almost) on time.

Of course, no expression of appreciation is complete without recognizing the very special contribution made by our wives, who have tolerated the trials and tribulations of many books over many years. For their continuing support, we extend our deepest appreciation to Gwen Stewart Amling and JoAnn Gilberti Droms.

Frederick Amling
William G. Droms
Washington, D.C.
June 1993

About the Authors

Dr. Frederick Amling is a professor of finance in the School of Business and Public Management at The George Washington University, where he teaches investment analysis and portfolio management, and a portfolio management seminar to MBA students. Dr. Amling graduated from Baldwin-Wallace College, earned an MBA at Miami University in Oxford, Ohio, and a Ph.D. at the University of Pennsylvania, where he also taught in the undergraduate Wharton School. He was chairman of the finance department at Miami University and dean of the school of business at the University of Rhode Island. He has written three books on investing, including *Investments*, in its sixth edition, and he has co-authored two personal financial planning books with Dr. Droms. Articles by Dr. Amling have appeared in the *Financial Analysts Journal*, *The Wall Street Journal*, *The Wall Street Transcript*, and other journals, magazines, and newspapers.

Dr. Amling serves on the board of several Keystone mutual funds including the Keystone International Fund, and Keystone Precious Metals Holdings Fund, and the Torray Fund, in Washington, D.C. He is president of Amling & Company, Inc., a firm that provides investment advice and valuation estimates for both national and international investors.

Dr. William G. Droms is the John J. Powers, Jr. Professor of Finance and International Business at Georgetown University, where he teaches finance at the MBA and undergraduate levels. He is a graduate of Brown University, holds MBA and DBA degrees from The George Washington University, and is a chartered financial analyst. Dr. Droms is the author or co-author of numerous articles and books, including *The Dow Jones-Irwin Guide to Personal Financial Planning*, *The Life Insurance Investment Advisor*, *The Dow Jones-Irwin Mutual Fund Yearbook*, and *Finance and Accounting for Nonfinancial Managers*. He is an active investment consultant and a director of Baldwin Financial Systems, Inc., a registered investment advisor in the Chicago area that specializes in providing investment management and counseling services to individual investors.

Contents in Brief

Contents in Detail

INVESTMENT FUNDAMENTALS

I

Laying the Foundation

chapter 1

Saving and Investing

The Growth of Assets and Wealth

The authors recently sponsored an investment seminar at George Washington University dedicated to topics of particular interest to individual investors. The three-week seminar featured presentations by a number of prominent investment advisors, attorneys, and tax experts from the Washington, D.C., area, one of whom told how he and his brother had set up a personal investment club right after they graduated from college. The club began with four members—the two brothers and their parents—and gained two new members when the brothers married.

In the first year, each member put $25 per month into a savings account. In the second year the members raised their monthly contributions to $50 each. A few years later they increased the contribution level to its final amount of $100 a month.

When the account had accumulated enough money, the club purchased common stock. All subsequent monthly contributions, plus the interest earned on the savings account and dividends from the stocks, went into the account to fund more stock purchases whenever the balance would cover a reasonable number of shares.

The club members kept making contributions for 12 years. It wasn't always easy to put aside money to invest, but they always found a way to do it. Personal needs were great and they could easily have spent the money instead of saving it. Still, they stuck to their plan.

At the end of 12 years, the club members stopped making monthly contributions. Several years later a lump-sum contribution of $10,000 from another source was added to the account. The club is still operating today after nearly 40 years, the value of its portfolio having reached $1,700,000. Its single most profitable investment was the purchase of approximately $4,000 worth of Wal-Mart stock a little over 10 years ago that has grown in value to $600,000.

The success of this family's financial discipline and long-range planning is evidence that wealth can be created through fairly modest investments over long periods of time. Today the founding members' grandchildren have set up their own investment club and are contributing $25 per month.

Introduction

Perhaps hundreds or even thousands of high school and college graduating classes have been treated to the time-honored advice: Work hard and save your money. The advice is good and will continue to be so. In order to reach your financial goals enabling you to purchase a new stereo, make a down payment on your first car, or buy your dream home or condominium, you will need to save money first. If you ever plan to open your own business, you will need your savings dollars to get you started. From the small goals we set as children, such as buying new video games, to the larger goals we set as adults, such as preparing for retirement, we all need to save for the future.

In this book, we will suggest going beyond saving to plan for the investment of your hard-earned savings. We will examine the need for saving and investing, the financial prerequisites that must underlie an investment program, the role of permanent housing in investment planning, and the techniques used by successful investors. We will explore the background of strategic investment planning, including the structure and operations of the securities markets, how to design and maintain a personal investing information system, and the risks and returns available in the securities markets. We will also discuss how to evaluate investments in all types of securities, from the safest U.S. government securities to the riskiest opportunities in the options and futures markets. Along the way, we also will discuss investing in real estate, gold and silver, collectibles, mutual funds, and investment-oriented life insurance products. Finally, we will explain the techniques of portfolio management, including investment timing, market conditions analysis, and long-term investment planning for retirement.

Saving money to fund an investment program requires a good deal of perseverance and a willingness to do without current consumption in order to provide for future wants and needs. After a long, disciplined effort to build savings, you certainly will want to invest these funds wisely. An **investment** may be defined as the purchase of an asset that will provide income or future capital growth, or both. For example, a U.S. Treasury bond pays income in

investment: Purchase of an asset that will provide income, future capital growth, or both.

the form of semiannual interest payments, which the bondholder may spend for current consumption or reinvest to provide still more income in the future.

This book will show you how to maximize wealth and achieve **financial independence** through successful investing. Financial independence does not necessarily imply great wealth; rather it requires that you make maximum use of your income, whatever its level. Achieving financial independence means keeping your expenses from exceeding your income, including the necessary monthly budget item of saving a reasonable portion of income for investment, so that by retirement age, if not earlier, you can support a satisfactory lifestyle free of financial worries. These may sound like modest goals, but many people never achieve them because they pay insufficient attention to their investment strategies.

financial independence: Living within one's income, saving and investing a reasonable portion of this income, and, by retirement age or earlier, being able to support a satisfactory lifestyle free from financial worries.

Following the principles of disciplined savings and successful investing, you can build up significant personal wealth and achieve financial independence. The dollar value of your personal wealth obviously will depend on the level and stability of your income. On even a moderate income, however, you can build a significant nest egg if you save and invest small amounts of money over long periods of time.

Investment Objectives

The main investment objective is to increase wealth over time. This begins with saving and then proceeds to investing accumulated savings. The first goal of saving is to establish an emergency fund; then come short-term financial goals such as accumulating a down payment on a new car or a first home. Investment goals, on the other hand, should be oriented toward the long term. This allows the investor to assume more risk than would be acceptable in a savings program. In return for increased risk, you can earn a higher rate of return on investments than you normally would earn on a savings account.

Common stocks, for example, have been shown to be more profitable than most other investments, but they are also riskier because their principal values vary more. Over long periods of time these variations average out to provide relatively high rates of return compared to other alternatives, so that, over the past 20 years, common stock returns have averaged slightly over 10 percent per year, compared to about 5 percent per year earned in savings accounts.

As savings dollars accumulate, at some point they will reach an amount that will fund investments that are more profitable than a savings account, yet not so risky that all your judiciously saved money could disappear. Two things happen as savings build. First, the saver achieves a goal of saving enough to invest, often realizing how a small amount of money, saved on a regular basis, can grow into a significant sum for investing. Second, increasing wealth and income inevitably brings increases in federal income taxes. A savings account that paid $5\frac{1}{2}$ percent interest is now offering as little as

4 percent after deducting federal income taxes, and even less after state income taxes. Net return declines when ordinary income and, therefore, the tax rate, rise.

To maximize wealth, investors look for investments that offer high rates of return after taxes without undue risk. But what investments? They might choose **common stocks,** as mentioned earlier, which are securities that represent ownership shares in the corporations that issue them. If so, how do they select among all the available stocks? Where do they buy the stocks? Where do they obtain information on which to base a purchase decision, and do they have to pay for this information?

common stocks: Securities issued by corporations that represent ownership shares in those corporations.

Perhaps **bonds** seem more attractive than stocks. When corporations (or other entities) issue bonds, they borrow money from investors to help finance operations. In return for the purchase price of the bond, the issuer pays interest to the bondholder and repays the principal when the bond matures. When, where, and how do investors buy them? Maybe **Treasury bills** (short-term debt securities issued by the U.S. government) will pay a higher interest rate for the amount of risk. Should an investor buy gold? Why not invest in diamonds, silver, gold coins, or in real estate?

bonds: Debt securities issued by corporations and governments that wish to borrow money; the issuer pays interest to the bondholder and repays the principal amount at maturity.

Treasury bills: Short-term debt securities issued by the U.S. Treasury.

If **inflation,** a period of generally rising prices, becomes a problem, **real assets** such as precious metals or real estate may provide better returns than securities. Finally, how will these individual investments fit into an overall retirement or other investment program and contribute to achievement of financial goals? Such a barrage of questions may leave you feeling too confused, uncertain, and afraid to risk your money, but failure to do anything virtually guarantees that you will lose ground to inflation.

inflation: A condition of generally rising prices.

real asset: A tangible asset such as real estate or precious metals.

Prices have been known to rise at a higher rate than the rates of return on some investments, eroding the **purchasing power** of investment dollars since those dollars buy fewer goods and services at the higher prices. Even a high 10 percent rate on a saving certificate yields a loss with a 10 percent inflation rate after deducting taxes on the interest income from the certificate. The investor who was not familiar with better investments or who was afraid to take risks would lose money on such a deal.

purchasing power: The quantity of goods or services that can be purchased with a given amount of money; inflation erodes purchasing power.

Fear due to lack of information should not, however, be mistaken for risk. Fear of committing to an investment does not affect the actual possibility of a loss on that investment.

In this chapter we will suggest some questions you should answer in attempting to put your savings into more profitable investments. We will discuss the risks of these investments along with the financial conditions that should precede consideration of more risky investments.

The Search for Investments: The Investment Process

Investors can choose from a broad array of investment opportunities. They can invest in corporate securities, buying bonds or common stock issued by a corporation. A bondholder receives a fixed amount of interest periodically, along with the return of the principal amount invested at the bond's maturity. Bonds do not participate in earnings, but interest payment is guaranteed and paid before any stock dividends can be paid. Owners of common stock are said to have **equity,** that is, an ownership interest, in the issuing company. If the company prospers and earnings increase, its owners, that is, its common stockholders, share in its profits and in the increases in its value. If the company should fail, and some do, then these owners may lose all or part of their investments.

equity: A security that represents an ownership interest in a business.

Investors may also purchase **preferred stock,** which is something of a hybrid, with characteristics of both bonds and common stock. Like common stock, preferred stock is an equity investment that pays **dividends** to its owner. Dividends on preferred and common stock are cash payments to stockholders that represent shares of the corporation's profits. Preferred dividends must be paid before any common dividends can be paid and they are higher than common stock dividends for most corporations. These two advantages over common stock are offset by the disadvantage that, like bond interest payments, preferred stock dividends generally are fixed in amount and do not rise as the company grows, as common stock dividends generally do.

preferred stock: A hybrid security that is an equity, but pays a fixed amount of income in the form of dividends.

dividends: Cash payments made by corporations to owners of preferred and common stock in the corporation.

Investors in corporate securities also can buy **convertible bonds** or **convertible preferred stock.** These securities add an important feature to straight bonds or preferred stock: The owner can convert them into shares of common stock. If the company prospers and its common stock price rises, convertible owners can participate in this success by converting their fixed-payment securities to common equity shares.

convertible bonds: Corporate bonds that can be converted into shares of common stock.

convertible preferred stock: Preferred stock that can be converted into shares of common stock.

Any basic economics book explains how individuals' investments in productive capital encourage wealth formation and growth in the national economy. The collective savings and investments of individuals and businesses provide absolutely essential funds to pay for the assets growing businesses need, and this growth determines the success of the capitalist economy. In spite of its weaknesses, the capitalist system is more likely to benefit the individual than any other economic system in the history of the world. Even the totalitarian communist governments of the world have begun to adopt the basic concepts of our free enterprise system to get their domestic economies moving again.

The individual investor can participate in the growth and prosperity of the U.S. economy by investing in the securities markets. All of the data show that, over long periods of time (decades, if not each individual year), common stocks have paid greater returns than bonds and savings accounts, and stocks have beaten inflation. More importantly, even a small investor can share in the growth of the economy by investing small amounts of money over long periods of time. If you invest for the long term in a diversified group of securities, you will prosper financially, and at the same time you will help our economic system work even better. Long-term investments help to create new jobs and new economic opportunities.

You need to prepare yourself before undertaking an investment program, however. **First,** you must understand the general risks associated with all kinds of investments. **Second,** your financial position must be secure enough to accept these risks. **Third,** you must know what kinds of investments are available, the return and risk characteristics of each kind of investment, and the part each will play in your investment program. **Fourth,** you must have accurate information that is easily and cheaply obtained. **Fifth,** you must understand the principles of portfolio management. **Sixth,** you must understand the marketplace where securities are bought and sold. **Seventh,** you must know how to analyze investments and derive reasonable values for them. All this might seem a difficult task, but a little work over a period of time can transform a beginner into an informed, and wealthy, investor.

Reading this book is a good first step toward becoming an informed investor. The remainder of this chapter will deal with the first two aspects of an investment program, understanding the risks associated with investment and assessing the investor's financial ability to undertake those risks.

Investment Risks

Most investors prefer to avoid risk. They dislike the idea of losing money. All investments involve risks, however, so an investor must understand the nature of these risks and attempt to minimize them. The overall investment objective is to earn the maximum rate of return that is possible without assuming more risk than the investor can tolerate.

Inflation

Inflation was public enemy number 1 in the 1970s and early 1980s, and investors still fear the threat that the purchasing power of their investment dollars will diminish by the time they receive them. This threat is known as **purchasing power risk.** Simply stated, it is the risk that invested money will earn a rate of return that falls short of the rate of inflation.

purchasing power risk: The risk that invested money will earn a lower rate of return than the inflation rate.

Inflation has posed a very difficult problem during recent decades. The annual rate of price increases in the United States is commonly measured by changes in the **consumer price index (CPI),** a statistical measure compiled monthly by the Bureau of Labor Statistics of the U.S. Department of Labor that shows the percentage increase in prices paid by U.S. consumers. The inflation rate rose from 3.3 percent in 1972 to 11.0 percent in 1974 at the height of the OPEC oil embargo. It dropped to the 2- to 3-percent level for most of the 1980s, then picked up somewhat again. By the early 1990s inflation was in the 4 percent range.

consumer price index (CPI): A statistical measure calculated monthly by the U.S. Department of Labor's Bureau of Labor Statistics to show the rate of increase in prices paid by U.S. consumers.

One way to beat inflation is to purchase real assets or common stocks that increase in price along with the increase in the general price level. Real estate, the real asset most commonly owned by individuals, has been a good hedge against inflation except for brief periods of recession when prices stabilized or declined. Gold coins and gold bullion, another real asset that is widely held by individuals, also has been a good anti-inflation investment.

Diamonds have done well during periods of high inflation as have some stamps and antiques.

Many groups of common stocks have done well during inflationary periods, and the long-run return on common stock investments, in general, has substantially outpaced the inflation rate. Chapters 10 and 11 will explore techniques for selecting stocks that will perform well enough to beat inflation.

Business Failure

Business failure is another risk that investors face. In its absolute form, this is the threat of loss of all funds invested in a business that fails completely. The threat of loss of earnings per share is a relative business risk. In general, **business risk** can be defined as the risk that a company's earnings will decline. This shows up in financial data as a reduction or too much variation in **earnings per share (EPS),** which is the company's total earnings during the year divided by the weighted average number of shares outstanding during the year. The earnings per share figure represents the claim that each share of stock has on the earnings of the company.

business risk: The risk of an earnings decline in a company in which money is invested.

earnings per share: A corporation's total annual after-tax earnings divided by the weighted average number of shares of common stock outstanding.

business cycle: Periods of expansion and contraction (prosperity and recession) in a nation's economic activity.

Business risk affects investor expectations. If a company's earnings disappoint investors, they may sell their stock, pushing its share price lower. Therefore, a drop in a company's sales and earnings per share may force the market price of its shares dramatically downward. The earnings in some cyclical industries rise and fall with the **business cycle,** which is the alternation of periods of expansion and contraction (prosperity and recession) in business activity. Automobile companies' earnings vary widely with the business cycle because auto sales drop dramatically during periods of recession and boom during expansions. Investors expect the auto companies' earnings per share to vary with the business cycle.

Companies with growing or stable earnings are more attractive to conservative investors than companies with fluctuating earnings. Generally, investors are willing to pay a higher price for a dollar of earnings that they expect to be stable or to grow at a constant rate per year than they will pay for a dollar of earnings that may fluctuate uncertainly. Even stable companies' earnings may not grow as expected, eroding the stock price and the investor's wealth. No common stock is immune from business risk.

The best protection from business risk is careful analysis of companies in which one plans to invest. This analysis requires evaluation of the company's future earnings, the price behavior of its stock, and the character of its earnings growth. You will learn how to do this in Chapters 10 and 11. Business risk usually affects investments in common stocks most directly, but it may also affect the price behavior of preferred stock and lower-quality corporate bonds.

Market Risk

The prices of common stocks and other securities react to events that are unrelated to earnings or dividend changes. The ownership of stock stimulates strong emotions. Security prices are susceptible to the psychology of the marketplace, whether it is rational or irrational. News events such as a report on the rate of inflation, war or peace in the Middle East, the death of a prominent politician, drought in the West, a storm in the Midwest, or a labor strike, all have their momentary and long-term effects on stock prices. These events are usually unpredictable, and when they occur the marketplace responds with fluctuations in stock prices. This **market risk** is normal. Prices vary within much higher ranges than most people suspect. This suggests the possibility of high returns from well-timed moves, but it suggests high risks, as well.

market risk: Fluctuations in the prices of common stocks and other securities caused by changes in general market conditions rather than by actions of a particular company.

The magnitude and directions of short-term changes in stock prices are almost impossible to predict. These short-term price movements are said to be random in character, that is, independent and unpredictable, giving rise to the **random walk hypothesis,** which is widely accepted by stock market analysts. Over a period of time, however, stocks generally increase in value and their prices tend to vary around levels determined by the companies' earnings and dividends.

random walk hypothesis: The hypothesis that short-term changes in security prices are random and unpredictable.

The problem facing an investor is that the market could move in a direction opposite of what is expected. This could result in a loss if you suddenly must sell your investments. The only way to protect yourself is to be able to hold your investment position and not sell in a weak market.

Interest Rate Risk

When the general level of interest rates in the economy changes, the prices of individual bonds change, too. Increasing interest rates cause decreasing bond prices and falling interest rates boost bond prices. This causes **interest rate risk,** the risk of loss of principal because of changes in the general level of interest rates. The level of interest rates affects common stocks indirectly, as well, since higher interest rates increase the returns on competing investments forcing higher common stock yields. Increasing stock dividend yields generally are associated with decreasing stock prices.

interest rate risk: The risk of loss of principal due to changes in the general level of interest rates.

An investor must estimate the direction of interest rates to reduce risk. For example, an investor who purchased a 10-percent, 20-year bond for $1,000 would lose money over a 1-year period if yields were to rise to 12 percent. The 10-percent bond would pay a fixed amount of $100 per year over its life, while new $1,000 bonds issued to yield 12 percent would pay $120 per year. To induce another investor to buy the 10-percent bond, the bondholder would have to accept a price that would make $100 a year interest plus the $1,000 maturity value in 19 years yield the same 12 percent return available elsewhere in the market. This price is approximately $853, a $147 loss on the initial price of the bond. Therefore, as yields in the market rise, prices on previously issued bonds drop. As yields fall, outstanding bond prices rise.

To prevent a substantial loss one must carefully analyze the trends in interest rates. If rates are expected to increase, invest in short-term securities.

If rates are high and expected to fall, purchase long-term bonds. The investor in the example above could avoid any loss by holding the bond until prices recovered, but the fact remains that even fixed-income securities fluctuate in value. Despite their assured interest payments, they are not riskless. We will examine techniques of investing in debt securities in detail in Chapters 7 and 8.

Strategic Planning for Investing

In order to accept the risks associated with any investment, you must be in a strong financial position. The stronger you are financially, the greater your ability to profit by intelligent investment management and diversification.

To assess your financial strength, you must take stock of your assets and liabilities. You need to know what you own and what you owe. The simplest tool for this evaluation is a personal balance sheet summarizing your assets, liabilities, and net worth. Analysis of your balance sheet will indicate whether you can really accept investment risks.

Financial Prerequisites to Investing

Before committing funds to investments, you should satisfy several prerequisites: (1) You should have adequate life insurance; (2) you should assess your home ownership position; (3) you should have only modest consumer debt, if any; (4) you should have money set aside for an emergency; and (5) you should have enough money to commit to investment to make it profitable and economical. You must also have a plan of how to accumulate funds for investment on a regular schedule.

Adequate Life Insurance One important prerequisite for investment is adequate life insurance. The main purpose of life insurance is to replace income needed to support dependents that would be lost if the insured should die. Cash value life insurance also provides a savings investing vehicle. The amount of life insurance that would be considered adequate will vary from person to person. Chapter 15 shows how to evaluate your life insurance needs and opportunities.

Home Ownership For most people, the purchase of a home is the largest single investment they ever make. In an inflationary economy, home ownership provides a substantial inflation hedge. Even at lower inflation rates the economics of housing favor the owner. Done properly and within your income, home ownership can be a very attractive investment. It will allow you to improve your financial well-being in the long run and give you enjoyment and satisfaction. In investment planning, it is important that your housing needs be carefully evaluated before you invest in securities. You should buy a house you can afford. Start small and then move up as your income grows. This will help you maximize your net worth in the long run. Planning for home ownership is explored in detail in Chapter 3.

consumer installment purchases: Purchases of consumer goods and services using charge accounts or credit cards that spread payment over several months or even years, often charging high interest rates.

Minimal Installment Debt Keep **consumer installment purchases,** purchases made on charge accounts or credit cards, to a minimum. Installment credit usually is very expensive, and interest charges of 18 to 20 percent or even more are not at all uncommon. You cannot expect to increase your net worth borrowing money at 18 to 20 percent while putting your excess cash to work to earn 9 percent. In no case should monthly consumer debt payments exceed 20 percent of net monthly income after taxes. In most cases 10 percent of monthly net income is a better guide. With a net income of $3,000 a month, you should not spend more than $300 to $600 a month for installment debt. If you limit installment debt, you will be in a much better position to invest, and you can do so with less risk.

Adequate Emergency Fund Before investing you should have adequate savings that can serve as an emergency fund. Such savings can provide for temporary needs or finance purchases of business or personal assets when attractive opportunities arise. Such a reserve can solve financial problems before they occur without difficulty.

The amount of ready cash you need is determined in part by your habits. Some people think they do not need much cash because they can rely on personal loans from a commercial bank. Relying on such credit lines might be dangerous because high interest rates might make it impossible to obtain a loan at a reasonable price. Under these conditions an adequate emergency reserve can be a lifesaver.

The size of your emergency fund should be based on your income, your other assets, and your attitude about financial security. As a general rule, you should have between three and six months' after-tax income set aside. The funds can serve productive uses earning interest in a savings account at a commercial bank, a mutual savings bank, or a savings and loan association. If the amount is sufficiently large, it can be invested in United States government bonds or tax-exempt municipal bonds. Any savings vehicle for emergency funds should be a **liquid investment,** that is, an investment which is immediately convertible into cash.

liquid investments: Investments that can be converted to cash quickly and inexpensively.

Money to Invest With the life insurance, home ownership, and emergency fund questions resolved, you can turn your attention to investments in securities and other productive assets. Many people wonder, however, where they will get money to invest. They often don't have any money to invest and seem to spend every cent they make, and they don't foresee any change in this situation in the future.

The solution for this problem begins with commitment. You must truly want to become financially secure. Without commitment to a serious investment program, you will never reach the objective of financial independence. As in other fields, success comes from work. Once you are committed to the goal, you are well on the way to achieving it, and an early start will help you reach your goal sooner.

The second step toward financial independence is saving. To accumulate funds to invest, you must save something from current income. Without saving, you will never achieve your goal. The more you save, the sooner you will reach your goal. Saving is not easy. Every dollar of after-tax income seems to expand opportunities for current consumption. One person might covet clothing, a new Gucci handbag, or a Rolex watch; another may want a new BMW or Mercedes. Spending your money on these items might make you look like a millionaire, but unless you save to meet your goal you won't ever really become a millionaire.

Think like an investor. Spend as much income as you can on items that will increase in value and keep consumption to a minimum. Houses tend to remain stable or increase in value, judging from housing prices over the past 50 years; rental payments are gone forever. A delightful dinner at a five-star restaurant is certainly enjoyable, but it does not add to your wealth. Buying antiques instead of new furniture is a good way to save while consuming, because antiques often increase in value, whereas new furniture tends to depreciate. In general, seek to spend your money on assets that will increase in value.

Over the past four decades, long-term stock investments have provided excellent rates of return. As mentioned earlier, houses have increased steadily in price over the past 50 years. Long-term bonds and mortgage investments have provided high compounded returns of the kind that can build into substantial sums of capital. Savings accounts or **money market funds,** mutual funds that invest in short-term debt securities, can serve as a repository for money until enough accumulates for investment, but the rates are really too low to build capital.

money market funds: Mutual funds that invest in short-term debt securities.

The commitment to financial independence and the savings discipline that makes this goal achievable must continue over a period of time. If you commit to the goal, save a regular portion of your income, and think like an investor, you will reach your investment goals in time. Time and the magic of compound interest are the most important allies in the quest for investment success.

The Impact of Income Taxes

Effective investment planning requires familiarity with the tax environment and its effect on your investment income and growth of capital. Throughout this book, the tax aspects of different investments will be discussed along with their other characteristics. For the present, however, it is important that you recognize that most investment income is subject to both federal and state income taxes, just as wage and salary income is subject to taxation by state and federal governments (and sometimes by city governments, as well). The impact of these income taxes can critically influence planning for the spending or reinvestment of investment income. Exhibit 1.1 shows the current federal income tax rates for individuals.

capital gains and losses: Gains and losses resulting from the sale or other disposal of capital assets such as real estate or investment securities.

ordinary income: Taxable income from sources such as salaries or wages.

short-term capital gains (losses): Capital gains (losses) on assets owned for 6 months or less.

long-term capital gains (losses): Capital gains (losses) on assets owned for more than 6 months.

Investors must pay special attention to the tax treatment of **capital gains and losses,** profits (or losses) from the sale or other disposal of capital assets such as real estate or investment securities. These gains and losses are taxed under different rules than **ordinary income** like salaries and wages. Capital gains and losses are taxed at the same rates as ordinary income, except that they are subject to a maximum tax rate of 28 percent. Although they are taxed at the same rates, current tax law still makes a distinction between **short-term capital gains (losses)** and **long-term capital gains (losses).** Long-term gains or losses result from changes in value of assets held for more than six months; short-term gains and losses result from changes in value of assets held for less than 6 months.

net capital gain: The amount by which capital gains exceed capital losses.

net capital loss: The amount by which capital losses exceed capital gains.

To determine the amount of capital gains income on which you owe tax, you deduct capital losses from capital gains. If you have a **net capital gain** (gains exceed losses), you must pay tax at your normal rate on that amount. If you have a **net capital loss** (losses exceed gains), you can deduct the loss from ordinary income, subject to one important limitation. You may not deduct more than $3,000 in net capital losses in any one year. You can carry any net capital losses in excess of $3,000 forward and deduct them from ordinary income in future years.

Consider a concrete example of capital gain and loss treatment. Suppose in one year you had $5,000 in capital gains and $9,000 in capital losses. You could offset the entire $5,000 in capital gains with $5,000 in capital losses, leaving a net capital loss of $4,000. Of this $4,000 loss, you could deduct $3,000 in the current year and carry forward the additional $1,000 net loss to offset your next year's taxable income. In the first year, you could deduct a total of $8,000 from taxable income: $5,000 to offset the capital gain on which you would otherwise have had to pay taxes and $3,000 more, which would reduce your taxable ordinary income.

international investing: Investing in stocks and bonds of non-U.S. corporations and governments.

global investing: Investing in a broadly diversified portfolio of securities issued both within and outside the United States.

emerging markets: Relatively new securities markets in newly industrializing nations that have established formal securities markets.

The Global Marketplace

Investment opportunities are not confined to the United States. Industrialized countries around the world offer profitable investment opportunities. The term **international investing** generally refers to investing in the stocks and bonds of corporations and governments located outside the United States. The term **global investing** generally covers a broadly diversified range of securities issued by both U.S. and non-U.S. corporations and governments. Sophisticated international investors are beginning to invest in so-called **emerging markets,** that is, relatively new securities markets outside the major industrialized nations, especially in newly industrializing nations with formal securities markets. The fledgling markets in Eastern Bloc coun-

EXHIBIT 1.1

Individual Income Tax Rate Schedules, 1991

FILING STATUS	TAXABLE INCOME BRACKET[a]	TAX RATE[b]
Unmarried (other than surviving spouses and heads of households)	Less than $20,350	15%
	$20,350 to $49,300	28
	Over $49,300	31
Married filing joint return, and surviving spouses	Less than $34,000	15
	$34,000 to $82,150	28
	Over $82,150	31
Married filing separate returns	Less than $17,000	15
	$17,000 to $41,075	28
	Over $41,075	31
Unmarried head of household	Less than $27,300	15
	$27,301 to $70,450	28
	Over $70,450	31

[a] Taxable income equals income after deducting amounts allowed for exemptions and standard or itemized deductions.

[b] Maximum rate for capital gains is 28%.

tries such as Poland, Hungary, and Czechoslovakia are examples of very new emerging markets. A new market that currently handles only local trades is emerging in Russia.

Most investors should consider holding at least some international securities among their assets. Presently, U.S. securities account for approximately 35 percent of the dollar value of the world's investments. It makes sense to look beyond U.S. borders at the other 65 percent of the world's markets. A

perspective on **INTERNATIONAL INVESTMENTS**

Mexican Tesobonos: 8.24 percent, 28-day, Short-term Money Market

Americans were faced with low interest rates when they purchased short-term money market funds or U.S. Treasury bills in the early 1990s. In fact they received less than 5 percent, which was half of what they had received in the late 1980s. One international alternative was the 28-day, short-term, Mexican Tesobonos. They were indexed to the U.S. dollar, so there was no exchange rate risk with the peso. As they mature in 28 days, the notes may be rolled over until they might be needed for other uses. The rates fluctuate with money market rates and they are guaranteed by the Mexican government. In mid-1992 the rate of 8.25 percent was twice the rate that could be earned on short-term U.S. Treasury bills.

EXHIBIT 1.2

Selected Examples of Investment Alternatives

TYPE OF INVESTMENT	INVESTMENT OBJECTIVE	RISK
Short-term Debt Investments		
Bank money market deposit accounts	Income	Purchasing power
Treasury bills	Income	Purchasing power
Treasury notes	Income	Purchasing power
Federal agency notes	Income	Purchasing power
Money market mutual funds	Income	Purchasing power
Certificates of deposit	Income	Purchasing power
Commercial paper	Income	Purchasing power
Long-term Debt Investments		
Treasury bonds	Income	Interest rate
Federal agency bonds	Income	Interest rate
Corporate bonds	Income	Interest rate, Business
Convertible corporate bonds	Income	Interest rate, Business
Bond mutual funds	Income	Interest rate, Business

This is by means an exhaustive list of all investments available to individuals. It is meant only to providing some examples of the types of assets in which individuals commonly invest.

The list here and on the next page is by no means an exhaustive list of all investments available to individuals. It is meant only to provide some examples of the types of assets in which individuals commonly invest.

recent study undertaken at George Washington University indicated an optimal proportion of international securities holdings for most investors of approximately 30 percent.[1]

This is no magic number, of course; 30 percent may not be the correct proportion for everyone at all times, nor can anyone guarantee that international diversification will ensure success in an investment program. The important point is that international investing should be considered as part of an overall strategy. Later this text will describe a composite group of international equities that has been more profitable, and also more risky, than U.S. stocks during the 1980s. The sizes of the international markets, however, seem to demand attention to foreign sources of profitable investment opportunities.

Knowledge of Investment Alternatives

You must understand the types of investment securities available in order to choose among them. It is important to know the expected return and risk characteristics of each investment you consider making to support intelligent investment decisions. This requires knowledge about the amount

Selected Examples of Investment Alternatives *(continued)*

TYPE OF INVESTMENT	INVESTMENT OBJECTIVE	RISK
Tax-exempt Investments		
Municipal bonds	Income	Interest rate, Business
Municipal bond mutual funds	Income	Interest rate, Business
Equity Securities		
Preferred stock	Income	Interest rate, Business
Convertible preferred stock	Growth, Income	Business, Market
Common stock	Growth, Income	Business, Market
Common stock mutual funds	Growth, Income	Business, Market
Real Asset Investments		
Real estate	Growth, Income	Business
Precious metals	Growth	Market

of expected return, the time period you expect to hold the investment, and the variability of return, or the risk of the investment. Also, return and risk characteristics do change, and successful investing requires anticipating these changes along with correctly analyzing a range of future events.

Exhibit 1.2 summarizes some investment alternatives, starting with low-risk debt investments and ending with uncertain investments in equity securities and real assets such as houses and precious metals. An investor must become knowledgeable about these investment alternatives since they are the building blocks of any investment program. Few people invest in all of these different types of securities, but it is good to know about all available options. All of these securities will be discussed in detail in the following chapters.

Overview of the Book

This book is organized into five major sections. Part I, Laying the Foundation, begins with this introductory chapter on the growth of assets and wealth. Chapter 2 lays out the basic knowledge about savings institutions and instruments you need to establish your base of secure savings before moving ahead to investments with higher return and risk levels. Chapter 3 deals with home ownership as a cornerstone investment.

Part II, Strategy for an Investment Program, provides the background you need to devise a strategic investment plan to maximize your wealth over the long run. The three chapters in this part deal with sources of investment information, the operations of securities markets and brokers, and the interrelated topics of risk, return, and asset allocation.

Part III, Securities Investments, deals with investing in stocks and bonds. Chapter 7 covers government debt securities, and Chapter 8 considers corporate bond and preferred stock investments. Chapter 9 presents techniques for understanding and analyzing corporate financial statements. Chapter 10 explores the principles of investing in the stock market, and Chapter 11 discusses stock valuation models.

Part IV, Alternative Investment Opportunities, includes four chapters that deal with alternative investment products. Chapter 12 discusses such real assets as real estate, precious metals, collectibles, and art. Chapter 13 considers futures and options. Chapter 14 explains investment opportunities in mutual funds and closed-end investment companies. The final chapter in this section, Chapter 15, deals with a relatively new choice: investment-oriented life insurance.

Finally, Part V, Portfolio Management, discusses techniques for managing an investment portfolio. Chapter 16 deals with portfolio theory and risk management. Chapter 17 examines the techniques necessary to manage a portfolio effectively.

SUMMARY

The main objective of this book is to show you how to maximize wealth and achieve financial independence through successful investing. Financial independence means, first, learning to live within your income, then saving and investing a reasonable portion of this income so that by retirement age or earlier you will be free of financial worries and able to support a satisfactory lifestyle.

Your main investment objective should be to increase your wealth over time. This requires saving first, and then investing accumulated savings. Savings help you work toward short-term financial goals, while investments help you work toward long-term goals. A long-term orientation toward investing will allow you to take more risk in your investment program than in your savings program in order to seek a higher long-run rate of return.

Investors have a broad array of investment opportunities available to them. This book will provide the foundation of information that must underlie an investment program. It will explain the risks associated with investing and how to assess the ability to assume those risks. It will describe the kinds of investments that are available, including return and risk characteristics and the part that each can play in an investment program. It will show how to set up an investment information system and teach the principles of successful investment and portfolio management. It will explore the organization of the securities markets and reveal how to analyze and value investments.

There are risks associated with all investments. The best overall investment objective is to earn the maximum possible rate of return that is consistent with the risk an investor is willing to accept. The major components of risk include purchasing power risk, business risk, market risk, and interest rate risk. To accept the risks associated with investing requires a strong financial position. The financial prerequisites to investing include adequate life insurance, evaluation of home ownership needs, minimal installment debt, and an adequate emergency fund.

Effective investment planning requires familiarity with the tax environment and its effect on investment income and capital growth. Most investment income is subject to both federal and state taxes. The treatment of capital gains and losses is a special concern for investors who may be taxed on profits from the sale of investments.

Attractive investment opportunities are not confined to the United States. Investment planning requires a global look at the securities markets since U.S. securities comprise less than half of the dollar value of the world's securities. At least one major study has shown that U.S. investors should invest about 30 percent of their assets in securities issued outside the United States.

Reading this book is an important first step toward successful investing and, ultimately, financial independence.

INVESTMENT MANAGEMENT CONCEPTS

1. Financial independence requires that you make maximum use of your income, whatever its level.

2. Wealth grows from productive assets; your main investment objective should be to increase your wealth over time, first by saving, and then by investing your accumulated savings.

3. Savings are productive assets, but savings grow relatively slowly.

4. Investments are productive assets that grow at a faster rate than savings, but they generally are more risky.

5. Some personal assets, such as housing, can be productive, as well.

6. Most personal assets, such as clothing and automobiles, are not productive; these assets depreciate in value over time.

7. Think carefully about what you want for your personal investment goals and plan carefully to reach these goals over time.

8. Small amounts of money saved and invested over a long period of time will pave the way for financial security.

9. There are risks associated with all investments; successful investors understand the nature of these risks and attempt to minimize them.

10. You should meet the financial prerequisites to investing before embarking on an investment program so that you will be financially able to look at your investment program from a long-term perspective.

REVIEW QUESTIONS

1. Describe in your own words what the term *financial independence* means to you as an investor.

2. What is the impact of inflation on your long-term investment planning?

3. What major factors should you be aware of before undertaking an investment program?

4. Define *purchasing power risk*.

5. What is market risk and how does it differ from the risk of business failure?

6. How does interest rate risk affect the prices of stocks and bonds?

7. Briefly describe the five financial prerequisites to investing and explain why it is important to meet these prerequisites.

8. What is the difference between ordinary income tax and capital gains tax?

9. Why is it important for you to consider investing in securities issued outside the United States?

10. Is there an optimal proportion of your portfolio that should be invested in securities issued outside the United States?

SELF-CORRECTING PROBLEM

Richard and Carolyn are a young couple who have been married about $1\frac{1}{2}$ years. They live in a rental apartment outside Minneapolis for which they pay $750 per month rent. They both work and try to save about 10 percent of their combined income each month; they both carry adequate company-subsidized life and health insurance. They have been very careful in their use of credit cards and consumer installment debt, although they do have a small car loan for the compact car they bought last year.

They incur the normal expenses of a professional couple. They like to travel, and they eat in restaurants often due to their heavy work schedules. Nevertheless, they successfully met their savings objectives and are now thinking about beginning a systematic investment program. If you were serving as their advisor in this process, what steps would you advise them to take to begin their investment program?

Answer to Self-Correcting Problem

Richard and Carolyn should first be sure they meet the financial prerequisites for investing. It appears that consumer installment debt is not a problem for them and their insurance needs appear to be met. They also have done well in their savings program. The only real question is whether they want to consider investing their savings in a home before they get involved in other investments. If they are more comfortable at this stage in their lives living in a rented apartment, they may well want to defer this purchase and build an investment nest egg for the eventual purchase of a home. Assuming they want to go ahead with an investment program, they should decide what kinds of risks they will be willing to accept and let their risk tolerance guide their investment policy. Since they are both young and have no children to support, they probably can accept somewhat more risk, within reason, in pursuit of higher returns. They should plan a program heavily oriented toward common stocks. At this point, their most important objective will be to set up a system by which to learn about investing, and this should be their next step. Once they begin to feel confident, they can venture out into the stock market. For now, however, they should keep their money in short-term bank certificates of deposit, a bank money market deposit account, or a money market fund.

SELECTED READINGS

Amling, Frederick. *Investments: An Introduction to Analysis and Management*, 6th ed. Englewood Cliffs, N.J.: Prentice-Hall, 1989.

Amling, Federick, and William G. Droms. *The Dow Jones-Irwin Guide to Personal Financial Planning*, 2d ed. Homewood, Ill.: Dow Jones-Irwin, 1986.

Droms, William G., ed. *Implementing and Managing a Global Investment Practice*. Charlottesville, Va.: Association for Investment Management and Research, 1991.

Randall, Carter, with William Gianopulos. *Up on the Market with Carter Randall: Wisdom, Insights, and Advice from a Lifetime on Wall Street*. Chicago: Probus Publishing, 1992.

Solnik, Bruno. *International Investments*, 2d ed. Reading, Mass.: Addison-Wesley, 1991.

chapter 2

Savings Institutions and Savings Instruments

A young couple named John and Ann recently attended an investment planning seminar sponsored by a major brokerage firm. During the course of the seminar, they complained that they could not seem to save a significant amount of money for investment because their living expenses consumed every penny they made. One might not be surprised to hear this from people at the low end of the pay scale or from young couples with growing families, but John and Ann, it turned out, were the classic "yuppie" couple and were also "dinks" (double income, no kids).

As John and Ann walked out of the building with their broker, May, she noticed their new BMW 735 sedan parked across the street. They told May that in addition to a loan on the car and a second loan on their other car (a Mercedes 190), they also had run up fairly large balances on their gold credit cards from various vacation trips, clothes buying sprees, and dining outings in some of the city's best restaurants. John and Ann realized that when they got their paychecks, they were so busy trying to figure out how they could pay for what they had already purchased, there was no time or budget space to plan for the best use of their financial resources.

May advised them to give some serious thought to changing their spending patterns and establishing savings objectives. That night the couple went through their old check stubs and charge slips and were startled to discover how much money "slipped through their fingers" every month for luxury purchases. They then set up a budget for themselves and limited the amount of money they would spend each month on clothing, traveling, and dining out. They also decided to take the rather radical step of selling the BMW and buying a less expensive car, reducing their debt payments every month. When they finished rearranging their financial priorities, they found that they could expect to save about $350 per month of their combined incomes. They planned to put this money in a savings account until they accumulated a large enough sum to meet with their broker and talk to her about long-term investing.

Young professionals can change their consumption patterns in order to save. But think of the typical employees earning less. If you ask people in this group to save and invest $25 a month, you're really asking them to give up a dinner out, a movie, or a new T-shirt. Saving for this group is a sacrifice.

One company offered its employees options to buy stock in the company at below-market prices. Many workers decided to forego the stock options for a fatter monthly paycheck. Unfortunately, at the end of 20 years of investing in the stock, they would have been far better off buying the stock than spending the money. The authors of this book strongly urge middle-income earners, as well, to take the saving and investment route.

Introduction

To accumulate savings either for long-term financial goals or short-term desires, you need to spend less than you earn. Your savings also protect you against loss of income due to unemployment or illness, and they may allow you to take advantage of a bargain price on something you have always wanted, should a good deal suddenly appear.

Some people neglect saving, thinking that their incomes will increase in the future, making it easier to do so at that time. As your income increases, however, so does your need for ready cash to meet growing expenditures. Most people tend to spend more over time to accommodate inflation and to support rising standards of living. Your **liquidity needs** also will increase with your income. Liquidity needs include the need to hold some savings for normal, daily transactions, as a reserve fund for emergencies, and to allow you to take advantage of unexpected opportunities such as a particularly attractive investment. Savings can provide an important reserve when monthly cash outflow exceeds inflow

liquidity needs: The need to hold savings for normal day-to-day transactions, for emergencies and to take advantage of unexpected opportunities.

Saving requires discipline and a focus on the future. You might think of saving as a battle between current and future needs. By giving up some current income, you can accumulate savings that will provide for future needs. Many people neglect to save simply because they have never taken the time to plan for their financial future and set saving and investment objectives for themselves. Some may feel that they don't need to save because they have ready access to easy credit via charge cards to meet emergency expenses; the credit doesn't seem so convenient, though, when the bills arrive with interest charges that take painful bites out of future monthly budgets. Saving can keep you out of this trap, and it doesn't have to be drudgery. It does require that you invest some time and effort to set clear financial objectives and then exercise some self-discipline to meet them.

This chapter will examine the reasons you should systematically save part of your income, show you how to set and meet savings objectives, and describe the important characteristics of the main financial institutions and instruments that savers generally use.

Establishing a Savings Plan

To establish a savings plan, you must recognize the simple, but important distinction between saving and investing. Your savings account provides a pool of funds to meet short-term cash shortages or to avoid a financial emergency, such as illness that could keep you from working. Because of this short-term time horizon, your primary savings objective should be safety and liquidity. You want to be sure that your money is available when you need it, and you want to minimize the possibility of losing the principal. The interest earned on savings, although important, should be considered as secondary to the need for safety and liquidity.

investment capital: Money available for long-term investment.

In comparison to savings objectives, investment objectives have longer-term time horizons. You should invest money for which you do not expect to have any immediate need. In short, **investment capital** is money put away for the long term. Liquidity is a much lower priority with investment capital. Long-term investing allows you to take more risk to achieve a higher return, because later gains can make up for possible losses. The main objective of an investment strategy is to earn the highest possible return within an acceptable level of risk.

Reasons for Saving

Emergency Fund One of the primary purposes of saving is to amass a pool of emergency funds to prevent financial disaster from an unexpected illness, a sudden unanticipated expense such as a major auto repair, or a period of unemployment. An emergency fund can prove to be invaluable when unexpected expenses pop up, and it can relieve the panic brought on by a sudden period of unemployment. A lay off becomes less threatening when you know that you can still meet your financial obligations and search for another job calmly. As a senior executive in an industry well-known for sudden firings commented, "In this business your bankbook is your best friend!"

Specific Purpose Most people also save for some specific purpose at some time. You may wish to accumulate money for a down payment on a house, for example, or for a car or a boat or a special vacation. Whatever the reason, a short-term savings goal is appropriate and can become part of a long-term investment plan.

Liquidity People often save to meet various liquidity needs. A savings account can be the key to making your monthly budget work when you anticipate a monthly cash outflow that will exceed your cash income. For example, additional expenses during end-of-year holiday periods can throw the most carefully planned budgets out of balance. Savings can be a source of temporary funds to keep the monthly budgets in balance at such times. You also may want to build up money in liquid savings for investment later.

Low Cost of Funds Savings dollars are often the least expensive source of funds to purchase a high-cost item, such as a new car or color TV set. Also, the accumulated interest on savings can help foot the bill for such a purchase. Consider an example of how this works. Suppose you want to buy a new Chevy Cavalier you see advertised in your local newspaper. The ad states that the car can be purchased for $499 down and $249 a month for 48 months. The fine print reveals that the cash price of the car is $9,175; this is the price that you would pay if you could pay cash for the car. On the **extended payment terms,** however, you would pay a total of $12,451 (the $499 down payment plus $249 per month times 48 months). The cost difference of $3,276 (between the $12,451 extended payment price and the $9,175 cash price) represents the cost of credit, in this case about 18 percent per year.

extended payment terms: Credit terms for the purchase of an expensive good as opposed to cash payment at the time of purchase.

If you have enough money in savings to pay cash for the car, you can avoid both high interest charges and a fixed monthly payment obligation. Of course, you will give up the future interest earnings on your savings account, but this is a good exchange for avoiding the much higher interest charges on credit. The $249 monthly payment represents the payment on a loan of $8,676 ($9,175 cash price of the car less the $499 down payment). Compare the option of paying on that loan to paying cash and depositing $249 a month into a savings account earning 6 percent interest. In 4 years, monthly deposits of $249 would accumulate to $13,470, including total deposits of $11,952 ($249 times 48) plus 4 years of interest totalling $1,518. Your ending balance of $13,470 should be enough to buy your next new car for cash, with some money left over. A later section of this chapter, The Magic of Compound Interest, will show you how to calculate these interest earnings.

Establishing Savings Objectives

The first step in a savings plan should be to establish saving objectives. The first objective will be to accumulate an emergency fund. A conventional rule of thumb calls for a savings account balance equal to 3 to 6 months' after-tax income to meet this need. Whatever the specific amount, the important point is to set definite upper and lower limits on your emergency fund. A pool of 3 months' after-tax income should provide an adequate cushion for any sudden emergency. To this sum you may want to add an additional month's after-tax income to meet any liquidity needs. You can think of this additional month's income as a source of periodic short-term loans you make to yourself.

Few people will need more than 6 months' after-tax income in an emergency fund. Any funds accumulated above this level should be invested to earn a higher rate of return. Since they are not needed for any likely current expense, these excess funds can be invested. Even people that hold as much as 6 months' income in an emergency fund should consider investing part of that fund in more permanent investments.

Meeting Savings Objectives

Once you establish savings objectives, you must begin to work toward meeting them. Obviously, you cannot save 3 or 4 months' income overnight. Someone starting a first job who has little or no savings to begin with will have to save for some time to accumulate this amount. As an initial objective, you should try to save 5 to 10 percent of after-tax income toward this goal. At that rate it would take 2 to 4 years to accumulate a substantial emergency fund, assuming a zero beginning balance. By that time your savings habits should be firmly entrenched, and you can then invest additional savings for the long run. Investors who are really committed to meeting their savings objectives should consider saving 20 percent of after-tax income.

pay-yourself-first: Paying money into your savings account before paying any other bills or obligations.

Pay Yourself First Most successful savers adopt a **pay-yourself-first** policy. They pay their savings accounts before any other bills or obligations, simply depositing 5 to 10 percent of each paycheck into a savings account on each pay day. Other expenses become secondary to savings objectives. People who fail to meet savings goals generally do the opposite—they pay themselves last. After covering all of their other expenses, if any money remains they put it in savings. Few who follow this policy find much money left for saving at the end of the month. A popular saying describes this policy: "I throw all my cash at the ceiling. Whatever sticks goes into my savings account."

automatic savings plan: A specified amount of money deducted each month from your paycheck or checking account and automatically transferred into a savings account.

Savings Discipline One of the most effective ways of enforcing self-disciplined saving is to participate in some sort of **automatic savings plan** in which a specified amount of money from each paycheck or from a checking account is transferred each month into a savings account. Many employers offer such plans. Because this money never shows up in net pay, employees seldom miss it. Systematic saving through some type of automatic plan is probably the most effective way to enforce saving discipline.

Many banks also offer automatic savings plans. An account holder can designate the transfer of a fixed sum of money automatically each month from a checking account to a savings account. In this way the bank can help enforce the pay-yourself-first policy, deducting money for savings before

EXHIBIT 2.1

Nominal versus Effective Rates of Interest

Nominal Rate = 6 Percent

COMPOUNDING PERIODS	BEGINNING BALANCE	ENDING BALANCE	EFFECTIVE RATE
Annual	$1,000	$1,060.00	6.00%
Semiannual	1,000	1,060.90	6.09
Quarterly	1,000	1,061.36	6.14
Daily	1,000	1,062.70	6.27

you spend it for anything else. This kind of plan will keep your savings account growing systematically to meet your objectives. Whatever techniques you use to save, the most important point is to work toward your goals systematically.

The Magic of Compound Interest

nominal rate: The stated rate of interest paid on a savings account.

effective rate (effective annual yield): Annualized rate of return taking into account the earnings of interest on interest.

compound interest: Payment of interest on interest in a savings account.

If you save money in a bank or money market fund, you need to consider the number of times per year that your interest is paid and reinvested. Money market funds typically reinvest interest daily. Bank savings accounts and certificates of deposit typically compound interest annually, quarterly, monthly, or daily, depending on the type of account and the bank's policy. The stated rate of interest on an account balance is the **nominal rate.** The rate the account actually earns at the end of the year, taking compounding into account, is the **effective rate** or **effective annual yield.** The effective rate reflects the payment of interest on previously paid interest.

A simple example will illustrate the difference between the two rates. Exhibit 2.1 shows the effect of this **compound interest** on a $1,000 account at a nominal rate of 6 percent. When interest is compounded annually, the effective rate equals the nominal rate. With semiannual compounding, the effective rate increases to 6.09 percent. The reason for this is simple. Semiannual compounding pays 3 percent interest (one-half the annual interest rate) for each 6-month period. At the end of the first 6 months, the account balance would total $1,030. At the end of second 6 months, the account earns 3 percent interest on this $1,030 balance, giving an ending balance of $1,060.90 for an effective return of 6.09 percent. The magic of compound interest is that you earn interest on your principal and then you earn interest on your interest.

The more often interest is compounded, the higher the effective rate of interest becomes. Quarterly compounding increases the effective rate in the

EXHIBIT 2.2

Growth of Savings of $2,000 per Year

YEARS SAVED	INTEREST RATE 8%	10%	12%	14%
1	$ 2,160	$ 2,200	$ 2,240	$ 2,280
2	4,333	4,420	4,509	4,599
3	6,679	6,862	7,050	7,243
4	9,214	9,548	9,896	10,257
5	11,951	12,503	13,083	13,693
6	14,907	15,753	16,653	17,610
7	18,100	19,329	20,652	22,076
8	21,547	23,262	25,130	27,166
9	25,271	27,588	30,146	32,969
10	29,293	32,346	35,763	39,585
11	33,636	37,581	42,055	47,127
12	38,327	43,339	49,101	55,725
13	43,394	49,673	56,993	65,526
14	48,865	56,640	65,832	76,700
15	54,774	64,304	75,732	89,438
16	61,156	72,735	86,820	103,959
17	68,049	82,008	99,239	120,514
18	75,492	92,209	113,147	139,386
19	83,532	103,430	128,725	160,900
20	92,214	115,773	146,172	185,425

above example to 6.14 percent. Daily compounding increases the effective rate to 6.27 percent. This is an increase of just over one-quarter of 1 percent per year with no additional risk or effort.

A few simple calculations can illustrate the dramatic effect of systematic saving with compound rates of return over long periods of time. Exhibit 2.2 shows the growth of annual deposits of $2,000. The magic of compound interest turns these systematic deposits into very large sums over long periods of time. Over 20 years, $2,000 per year will grow to $115,773 if the accumulating balance earns a 10 percent after-tax rate of return. After 30 years, the amount would grow to $332,161—not bad for a total deposit of only $60,000 ($2,000 per year for 30 years). An after-tax return of 10 percent per year is high and would be difficult to achieve, but is not outside the realm of possibility.

Exhibit 2.3 shows the growth of a $10,000 account at various rates of return. Few traditional savings media pay rates of return much over 8 to

Growth of Savings of $2,000 per Year *(continued)*

YEARS SAVED	INTEREST RATE 8%	10%	12%	14%
21	$ 101,592	$ 129,350	$ 165,713	$ 213,385
22	111,719	144,286	187,598	245,259
23	122,656	160,714	212,110	281,595
24	134,469	178,786	239,563	323,018
25	147,226	198,664	270,311	370,241
26	161,005	220,530	304,748	424,075
27	175,885	244,584	343,318	485,445
28	191,956	271,042	386,516	555,408
29	209,312	300,146	434,898	635,165
30	228,057	332,161	489,085	726,088
31	248,302	367,377	549,776	829,740
32	270,166	406,114	617,749	947,904
33	293,779	448,726	693,879	1,082,610
34	319,282	495,598	779,144	1,236,176
35	346,824	547,158	874,641	1,411,240
36	376,570	603,874	981,598	1,610,814
37	408,696	666,262	1,101,390	1,838,328
38	443,391	734,888	1,235,557	2,097,694
39	480,862	810,376	1,385,824	2,393,371
40	521,331	893,414	1,554,122	2,730,443

10 percent. To earn the 12 to 14 percent rates illustrated, you would have to move your savings into some higher risk investments such as common stocks.

rule of 72: Dividing the effective annual rate of return into 72, the result is the approximate number of years it takes for money to double.

Rule of 72 Assuming, however, that you could earn a 12 percent effective annual return on an investment portfolio, your $10,000 would grow to $31,058 after 10 years, $96,463 after 20 years, and nearly $300,000 after 30 years. Your original investment just about doubles in the first 6 years, and it doubles again about every 6 years after that. This illustrates the **rule of 72,** which states that if you divide the effective annual rate of return into 72, the result is the approximate number of years it will take for an investment to double. Dividing 12 percent into 72 indicates that your money will double approximately every 6 years. At 8 percent, it takes about 9 years for your money to double; at 18 percent, it takes about 4 years. The rule of 72 is a handy shortcut for estimating the future growth of capital at various rates of return.

EXHIBIT 2.3

Growth of a $10,000 Savings Account

YEARS SAVED	INTEREST RATE 8%	10%	12%	14%
1	$ 10,800	$ 11,000	$ 11,200	$ 11,400
2	11,664	12,100	12,544	12,996
3	12,597	13,310	14,049	14,815
4	13,605	14,641	15,735	16,890
5	14,693	16,105	17,623	19,254
6	15,869	17,716	19,738	21,950
7	17,138	19,487	22,107	25,023
8	18,509	21,436	24,760	28,526
9	19,990	23,579	27,731	32,519
10	21,589	25,937	31,058	37,072
11	23,316	28,531	34,785	42,262
12	25,182	31,384	38,960	48,179
13	27,196	34,523	43,635	54,924
14	29,372	37,975	48,871	62,613
15	31,722	41,772	54,736	71,379
16	34,259	45,950	61,304	81,372
17	37,000	50,545	68,660	92,765
18	39,960	55,599	76,900	105,752
19	43,157	61,159	86,128	120,557
20	46,610	67,275	96,463	137,435

Savings Institutions

A variety of savings institutions will establish savings accounts. Commercial banks, savings and loan associations, mutual savings banks, and credit unions offer a number of services in addition to savings accounts. This section will examine these institutions' roles in a savings program.

Commercial Banks

Commercial banks are by far the most popular savings institutions among American consumers. Commercial banks provide most of us with day-to-day personal financial services. They offer checking and savings accounts, personal and commercial loans, and an array of other consumer financial

Growth of a $10,000 Savings Account *(continued)*

YEARS SAVED	INTEREST RATE			
	8%	10%	12%	14%
21	$ 50,338	$ 74,002	$ 108,038	$ 156,676
22	54,365	81,403	121,003	178,610
23	58,715	89,543	135,523	203,616
24	63,412	98,497	151,786	232,122
25	68,485	108,347	170,001	264,619
26	73,964	119,182	190,401	301,666
27	79,881	131,100	213,249	343,899
28	86,271	144,210	238,839	392,045
29	93,173	158,631	267,499	446,931
30	100,627	174,494	299,599	509,502
31	108,677	191,943	335,551	580,832
32	117,371	211,138	375,817	662,148
33	126,760	232,252	420,915	754,849
34	136,901	255,477	471,425	860,528
35	147,853	281,024	527,996	981,002
36	159,682	309,127	591,356	1,118,342
37	172,456	340,039	662,318	1,274,910
38	186,253	374,043	741,797	1,453,397
39	201,153	411,448	830,812	1,656,873
40	217,245	452,593	930,510	1,888,835

Federal Deposit Insurance Corporation (FDIC): A U.S. government corporation that insures deposits in federally chartered banks and savings and loans. The maximum FDIC insurance in any one institution is $100,000 and is a full faith and credit obligation of the United States government.

services. Nearly all commercial banks are insured by the **Federal Deposit Insurance Corporation (FDIC).** The FDIC insures any type of deposit in a commercial bank up to a maximum of $100,000 for all accounts in the same name at any one bank. For example, you might have two separate savings accounts and one checking account with a bank. The total amount of money deposited in all three accounts would be insured by the federal government up to $100,000. This insurance provides a federal government guarantee that you will not lose your money (or your interest) if the bank should go bankrupt. This is obviously a very important guarantee. You should not even consider depositing money in a bank not insured by the FDIC.

Joint account holders can extend the $100,000 insurance limit by establishing accounts under different family names. A married couple could establish accounts under three names, one under each person's name separately and one under both of their names jointly, and each account would be insured for $100,000 for a total of $300,000 of federal deposit insurance.

Passbook and Statement Accounts You may already be familiar with a regular savings account offered by a commercial bank. This is often called a **passbook account.** You can open it with almost any amount of money. (Some banks may set a minimum opening deposit, but it is usually very small, normally $10 or less.) This type of savings account normally requires no prior notice or waiting period for withdrawal. Technically, banks have a legal right to demand 30 days' notice of withdrawal, but they seldom exercise the right. Thus, a passbook account is a highly liquid form of savings, and federal insurance makes it, and all other insured commercial bank accounts, a very safe way to save.

passbook account: A savings account with a bank or other financial institution where deposits, withdrawals, and interest are kept track of in a passbook.

The primary disadvantage of passbook accounts is their low interest rates. When you open a passbook savings account, you should obtain information about other types of savings accounts that offer higher interest rates. Nearly all banks offer saving plans that pay higher interest rates than passbook accounts pay.

One common savings vehicle in addition to, or instead of, a passbook account is a **statement savings account.** This is essentially the same as a passbook account except that you do not use a passbook for your records. Instead, the bank sends you a periodic statement of your transactions and balances. With a passbook account, your passbook serves as the record of your account so the bank does not send you a statement.

statement savings account: A savings account where deposits, withdrawals, and interest are accounted for by a monthly statement mailed to the account owner.

NOW Accounts and Automatic Transfer Accounts Negotiable order of withdrawal (NOW) accounts are relatively new offerings of financial institutions. A **NOW account** functions as a checking account that pays interest. Actually, a NOW draft is not the legal equivalent of a check, but, rather, a negotiable order to withdraw money from your savings account. Still, it looks just like a check, and it is accepted nearly everywhere as being equivalent to a check.

NOW account: Negotiable Order of Withdrawal account paying interest and functioning as a checking account.

NOW accounts were first available in Massachusetts and New Hampshire. In the mid-1970s they were authorized for the rest of New England and New York. Finally, the Depository Institutions Deregulation and Monetary Control Act of 1980 authorized all insured U.S. commercial banks, savings and loans, mutual savings banks, and credit unions to offer NOW accounts.

The act also continued authority for **automatic transfer accounts.** These accounts offer automatic transfers from a savings account to a checking account. Whenever a check is presented for payment, the bank automatically transfers money from your savings account to cover the check. In effect, you can keep your checking account at a zero balance and achieve the equivalent of an interest-bearing checking account.

automatic transfer account: An account that links a non-interest-paying checking account with a savings account paying interest. The checking account is kept at a zero balance, with money automatically transferred from savings when a check is presented for payment.

The chief disadvantage of an automatic transfer account is its low interest rate if the average account balance falls below $1,000 to $1,500. Each individual plan differs, so it is not possible to generalize about rates. If your bank offers such a plan, read about it carefully. You may actually be better off keeping your savings and checking accounts separate, with your savings earning a higher rate of interest than the combined savings–checking plan and your checking account balance earning no interest. Which option is better for you depends on your particular situation and the terms offered by your bank.

Money Market Deposit Account (MMDA): Checking accounts that pay interest rates competitive with money market mutual funds.

super NOW account: Special type of NOW acount that pays higher interest than a regular NOW account.

MMDAs and Super NOWs On December 14, 1982, banks and savings and loan associations began offering insured deposit accounts that paid interest rates that were competitive with yields from money market mutual funds. These accounts, called **money market deposit accounts (MMDAs),** are checking accounts that pay interest rates comparable to yields on short-term debt instruments such as Treasury bills and commercial paper. In January 1983, banks and other thrift institutions introduced **super NOW accounts,** which paid higher interest rates than NOW accounts.

One of the most attractive features of an MMDA is that it is federally insured. The nationwide savings and loan crisis of the late 1980s underscores the importance of insurance on deposits. An unattractive feature of an MMDA is its transaction restrictions, which are normally more confining than those of a money market mutual fund, a competing savings vehicle described later in this chapter. A minimum deposit of $2,500 generally is required to open an MMDA account, although some banks will accept lower opening deposits. Most MMDAs require the saver to maintain this minimum balance to avoid the interest paid being reduced to the passbook rate. Money market mutual funds, on the other hand, normally pay market competitive interest rates, even on balances that fall below the minimum opening amount. MMDAs also have more restrictive check writing policies. Most banks allow only three checks per month for a minimum of $500 each on the account. Additional withdrawals can be made in person at the bank.

Super NOW accounts generally are less restrictive than MMDAs, most requiring $1,000 minimum balances. They allow unlimited check writing and most pay interest at higher rates than MMDAs. Some institutions impose fees for checks written, overdrafts, stop payment orders, and other transactions, and fees vary widely among institutions.

certificate of deposit: A bank deposit account that requires money to be left on deposit for a specified minimum amount of time.

Certificates of Deposit Commercial banks also offer a number of time deposit accounts that require depositors to leave money on deposit for some minimum period of time. The accounts are commonly called **certificates of deposit** or CDs. A CD normally offers a higher interest rate than passbook or other savings accounts, but withdrawing money before the time limit triggers substantial interest penalties. Certificates are available with maturity dates ranging from 90 days to 8 years, and sometimes longer. Longer maturities normally offer higher rates of return, but they are also less liquid.

variable-rate CD: A CD that offers a variable interest rate rather than a fixed interest rate over the life of the CD.

Certificates of deposit traditionally have offered fixed rates of interest over the terms of the deposits. In recent years, however, banks and other thrift institutions have begun to offer **variable-rate CDs,** which protect both the bank and the depositor against widely fluctuating interest rates of the kind experienced during the 1970s and 1980s. Instead of being fixed over the life of the CD, the variable-rate CD's interest rate reflects changes in market interest rates. The rate is typically linked to some widely reported interest rate, such as the yield on 5-year Treasury bonds. When the linked rate rises, the interest rate on the CD rises as well, saving the consumer from losing out on a low-rate investment in a time of rising rates. When rates fall, the CD's interest rate falls, relieving the bank from the burden of paying high rates on older CDs.

The choice of a fixed-rate versus a variable-rate CD depends on your expectations for future interest rates. At the time of purchase, variable-rate CDs generally offer lower interest rates than fixed-rate CDs. This difference is the price you pay for protection against rising rates. If you think rates will rise in the future, you should opt for a variable-rate CD. If you think they will fall, then look for a fixed-rate CD.

Unfortunately, predicting future interest rates is a very difficult and imprecise task. If you are buying a CD with a relatively short maturity, say three to four years or less, you cannot go too far wrong with a fixed-rate CD. On the other hand, if you are buying a long maturity instrument, you should carefully consider investing in a variable-rate CD. Exhibit 2.4 illustrates returns that were available on a variety of CDs, including jumbo CDs (CDs over $1 million), nationwide mid-year of 1991.

savings club plan: An account like a Christmas club or vacation club that has a payment book specifying required dates for deposits to be made into the account.

Savings Clubs In addition to regular accounts and certificates of deposit, many commercial banks also offer **savings club plans** such as Christmas clubs and vacation clubs. When you enroll in this type of plan, the bank gives you a payment book full of coupons indicating the required payment dates for your club. Depositors typically make payments every 2 weeks; at the end of a year a depositor will have made 25 payments. The bank will then send a check for the amount deposited plus interest. Christmas clubs normally require you to make the first payment in October and the last payment the following September so the amount saved will be available in time for Christmas shopping.

The primary advantage of such a club account is that it forces savers to exercise self-discipline. The payment book serves as a constant reminder to make payments on time and aids you in reaching your savings goal. The primary disadvantage is that the interest rate paid on a club plan is fairly low. Most people who use club plans find that the benefit of forced saving outweighs the sacrifice of a lower interest payment. Because the amounts involved are relatively small, the sacrifice in interest is quite modest. However, a well-disciplined saver may not need a club savings plan.

Savings and Loan Associations

mutual savings and loan association: A savings and loan association owned by its depositors.

Savings and loan associations (S&Ls) may be either mutual or corporate associations. The **mutual savings and loan association,** the most common form of association, is owned by the depositors, who are the association's legal shareholders. Interest the mutual S&L pays on deposits is considered to be a dividend paid to shareholders. The dividends are treated as interest for

EXHIBIT 2.4

Top Savings Deposit Yields Nationwide

Money Market Account

Institution	Location	Telephone No.	Min. Deposit	Recent % Rate	Effect. % Yield
Standard Pacific	Nwprt Bch,CA	(800)325-7283	10000	6.25 (CD)	6.54
Chevy Chase FSB	ChevCh,MD	(800)825-9000	20000	6.30 (CM)	6.49
Imperial Thrift	Burbank,CA	(818)842-2000	15000	6.25 (CD)	6.45
Perpetual Svgs Bk	Alexandria,VA	(800)422-6546	2500	6.25 (CD)	6.45
Valley Federal	Van Nuys,CA	(818)904-3000	10000	6.25 (CM)	6.45

Six-Month CDs

Institution	Location	Telephone No.	Min. Deposit	Recent % Rate	Effect. % Yield
Imperial Thrift	Burbank,CA	(818)842-2000	2000	6.50 (CM)	6.70
Gateway Svgs Bank	Oakland,CA	(415)268-8108	1000	6.37 (CM)	6.56
Independence Fed	Washington	(202)626-0430	500	6.40 (CQ)	6.56
Bankeast	Manchestr,NH	(800)992-0286	10000	6.35 (CM)	6.54
State Bank	New Hyde Pk,NY	(516)437-1000	2500	6.30 (CM)	6.50

Rates are the highest yields on six types of accounts offered by federally-insured banks and savings associations nationwide. Yields are based on the stated rate and compounding method in effect Friday and are subject to change. Six-month CD yields assume reinvestment of principal and interest at the same rate for an additional six months.

One-Year CDs

Institution	Location	Telephone No.	Min. Deposit	Recent % Rate	Effect. % Yield
Imperial Thrift	Burbank,CA	(818)842-2000	2000	6.80 (CM)	7.02
Lasalle Bk Lk Vu	Chicago	(312)880-1505	2500	6.80 (CQ)	6.98
Independence Fed	Washington	(202)626-0430	500	6.65 (CQ)	6.82
1st Deposit Natl	Tilton,NH	(800)821-9049	10000	6.58 (CD)	6.80
Gateway Svgs Bank	Oakland,CA	(415)268-8108	1000	6.60 (CM)	6.80

2½-Year CDs

Institution	Location	Telephone No.	Min. Deposit	Recent % Rate	Effect. % Yield
Citibank, S.D.	Sioux Falls	(800)248-4669	2500	7.27 (CD)	7.64
Lasalle Bk Lk Vu	Chicago	(312)880-1505	2500	7.35 (CQ)	7.56
Western Financial	Irvine,CA	(800)333-2627	1000	7.25 (CD)	7.52
Imperial Thrift	Burbank,CA	(818)842-2000	2000	7.25 (CM)	7.50
Key Bank USA	Albany,NY	(800)872-5553	5000	7.25 (CM)	7.50

(CC) Compounded continuously
(CD) Compounded daily
(CM) Compounded monthly
(CQ) Compounded quarterly
(CSA) Compounded semiannually
(CA) Compounded annually
(SI) Simple interest

Five-Year CDs

Institution	Location	Telephone No.	Min. Deposit	Recent % Rate	Effect. % Yield
San Francisco Fed	San Francisco	(800)733-3348	10000	8.00 (CM)	8.30
Hamilton Federal	Brooklyn,NY	(718)833-4300	500	7.75 (CM)	8.18
MBNA America	Wilmingtn,DE	(800)345-0397	2500	7.85 (CD)	8.17
Pioneer S&L	Whitestone,NY	(718)746-6500	2500	7.75 (CM)	8.17
Metropolitan Bank	Leesburg,VA	(703)777-3848	1000	7.90 (CQ)	8.14

90-Day Jumbo CDs

Institution	Location	Telephone No.	Min. Deposit	Recent % Rate	Effect. % Yield
Poughkeepsie Svgs	Poughkpsie,NY	(914)431-6100	100000	6.45 (SI)	6.65
Dartmouth Bank	Manchestr,NH	(800)888-1152	100000	6.50 (SI)	6.50
Independence Fed	Washington	(202)626-0430	50000	6.45 (SI)	6.45
Ameribanc	Alexandria,VA	(703)768-7020	100000	6.38 (SI)	6.38
Santa Barbara Fed	Santa Barb,CA	(800)556-2323	90000	6.15 (CM)	6.37

SOURCE: *Barron's*, August 5, 1991, p. 133. Reprinted by permission of *Barron's*,

corporate savings and loan association: An S&L organized as a regular corporation and owned by the shareholders of the corporation.

tax purposes, however. **Corporate savings and loan associations** are organized like any other corporation and pay interest on savings just like commercial banks do. The depositor should care little whether S&Ls are mutual or corporate organizations. As the lines distinguishing commercial banks from S&Ls continue to blur with continuing deregulation, S&Ls appear more and more like banks to their customers. In fact, many depositors do not really differentiate between the two and most consumers who use S&Ls for savings, checking, and borrowing refer to the S&L as "my bank."

Unlike bank interest, dividends paid by a mutual S&L are not guaranteed. The association pays these dividends out of operating profits, and the board of directors can legally reduce them if necessary. As a practical matter, however, S&L dividends are almost never reduced; they are virtually guaranteed. Interest paid by a corporate association is guaranteed.

Savings and loan associations are the second most popular type of savings institution. Historically, savings and loan associations existed primarily to provide financing for the housing industry, but recent legal changes have allowed S&Ls to make some consumer loans in addition to housing loans. Savings and loans offer essentially the same selection of savings plans as commercial banks. Passbook accounts, statement savings accounts, NOW accounts, super NOWs, MMDAs, and certificates of deposit are available.

Most savings and loans are federally insured by the Federal Deposit Insurance Corporation under the same terms as commercial banks. The insurance funds for banks and S&Ls are separate, although both insurance programs are administered by the FDIC and both are backed by the full faith and credit of the U.S. government. In some states, savings and loan associations may choose not to join the FDIC and obtain insurance through private, state-sponsored insurance associations. Even in states that allow private insurance, however, federally insured associations are available and preferable to private insurance. You should open an account only at a federally insured savings and loan association.

Mutual Savings Banks and Federal Savings Banks

Mutual savings banks enjoy limited popularity in the United States, operating mainly in New York and New England. Outside New England, there are a few mutual savings banks in Pennsylvania, New Jersey, Washington, Indiana, and Minnesota. These institutions are chartered as banks rather than S&Ls, but they operate much like mutual savings and loan associations. Along with S&Ls, mutual savings banks fall into the broad category of **thrift institutions,** that is, financial institutions that take in deposits and provide a broad array of loans and other services to individuals and businesses. Mutual savings banks offer savings plans similar to those of banks and S&Ls, and their deposits are insured by the FDIC.

thrift institution: Generic term referring to a financial institution such as a bank, savings and loan, and credit union that takes in deposits and makes loans.

Federal savings banks are federally chartered as banks to operate much like corporate savings and loan associations. Like S&Ls, they have emphasized saving and lending for housing in the past, but now they act very much like banks. Recently, many former savings and loan associations have drawn up new charters as federal savings banks to avoid the stigma that resulted from the S&L bailout that began in the late 1980s and will probably continue through the 1990s. The last section of this chapter, dealing with the Financial Institutions Reform, Recovery, and Enforcement Act of 1989, describes the bailout problem in more detail.

Credit Unions

Credit unions are mutual associations of people sharing some common interest or characteristic, often a common place of employment. For example, membership in one of the world's largest credit unions, the Navy Federal Credit Union headquartered in Washington, D.C., is open only to civilian and military employees of the U.S. Navy. Many private firms and other organizations sponsor credit unions.

The main purpose of a credit union is to provide a cooperative association where members can invest their savings and obtain low-cost consumer loans. A new member can open an account at a credit union by buying shares, usually in $5 units. The member can normally redeem shares immediately by selling them back to the credit union. The credit union pays dividends on shares out of its earnings. The board of directors, which is elected by the members, is responsible for overseeing the operation of the credit union.

National Credit Union Association (NCUA): An association that provides U.S. government–guaranteed insurance for deposits in credit unions.

Deposits in federal credit unions are insured up to $100,000 by the **National Credit Union Association (NCUA).** Dividends and the safety of members' principal balances depend upon the successful operation of the credit union. The bankruptcy rate for credit unions is much higher than the rate for banks, S&Ls, and mutual savings banks, so you should not save at any credit union not insured by the NCUA.

In addition to the accounts described in the discussions of banks and S&Ls, credit unions offer share draft accounts. Share draft accounts function just like NOW accounts at commercial banks, savings and loans, and mutual savings banks.

Selection Criteria

The main criteria for selecting a savings institution should be convenience, cost, and service. Shop for an account with reasonable costs and compare alternatives based upon the number of checks you expect to write each month. You should also consider the convenience of the institution's location. Finally, you should give some weight to the range of other services competing institutions offer. Regardless of the type of institution at which you choose to save, you should make absolutely certain that your account is federally insured.

Other Savings Media

In addition to the financial institutions discussed above, three additional savings media should be described here: U.S. savings bonds, life insurance, and money market mutual funds.

U.S. Savings Bonds

U.S. savings bond: An interest-paying debt security sold to the general public in small denominations by the U.S. Treasury.

U.S. savings bonds are debt securities sold to the general public in small denominations by the U.S. Treasury. These bonds are among the safest investments available because they are backed by the full faith and credit of the U.S. government. The United States government offers two types of savings bonds for purchase by individuals: Series EE and Series HH bonds. These replaced the old Series E and Series H bonds in January 1980.

Series EE bond: A U.S. savings bond sold at one-half of the face value that pays a variable interest rate.

Series EE savings bonds are sold at one-half their face value and pay a variable interest rate keyed to the average rate of interest on 5-year U.S. Treasury bonds over the period the saver owns the savings bond. If you hold the bond for 5 years or longer, savings bonds guarantee a minimum rate of interest of 6 percent. If you hold the bond less than 5 years, you will receive a lower rate of interest. The interest rate on a Series EE bond may exceed 6 percent, depending upon the returns on Treasury bonds. The interest reduction for bonds held for less than 5 years changes from time to time. Any financial institution that sells savings bonds can provide information about current rates.

Series EE bonds are sold in minimum units of $50. You can buy a $50 bond for $25 and redeem it for $50 in approximately 12 years if it earns the minimum 6 percent interest. Series EE bonds must be held for a minimum of 6 months before they can be cashed.

Series HH bond: A U.S. savings bond sold in minimum denominations of $500 that pays interest semiannually.

Series HH savings bonds are current income bonds. They may be purchased in minimum denominations of $500 and pay interest semiannually. Series HH bonds have 5-year maturities and may be subject to interest penalties if cashed prior to maturity. HH bonds may be purchased only in exchange for Series E or Series EE bonds worth $500 or more. HH bonds are offered by the Treasury as a means of providing steady and safe income to savers who have accumulated money through Series EE bonds that pay no current interest. By "rolling" your Series EE bonds into HH bonds, you can continue to enjoy the safety of U.S. government–guaranteed securities while you earn semiannual interest payments.

Savings bonds can be purchased and redeemed at any federally insured commercial bank, S&L, or mutual savings bank. Many employers' payroll savings plans offer options for systematic Series EE bond purchases. This type of plan can provide very helpful savings discipline for people who find setting aside current income difficult. In fact, the forced saving aspect of savings bond deduction plans is the bond's primary attraction to many people.

Savings bonds offer a number of other advantages. Because principal and interest payments are fully guaranteed by the federal government, they are the safest possible means of saving. If a bond is lost or stolen, it can be replaced easily through a bank. Savings bonds also offer some tax advantages, providing income that is exempt from state and local taxes. You also can defer the federal income tax on a Series E or EE bond until you cash it. Finally, if you buy Series HH bonds with your Series E or EE bonds, you can defer the federal income tax due on your Series E or EE bonds until the HH bonds are redeemed.

One final tax advantage is available to savers who use EE bonds to save for a college education for themselves or for their children. For individuals who qualify, interest on college savings is exempt from federal income tax. To qualify for the interest exclusion, the EE bonds must be issued after December 31, 1989, to individuals who are at least 24 years old. The interest may be exempt from taxes on bonds redeemed in a year in which the owner pays tuition and fees that are equal to or greater than the total redemption proceeds (principal and interest). To qualify for the exemption, the bondholder must pay tuition and fees to eligible institutions including colleges, universities, technical institutes, and vocational schools. If the bondholder pays tuition and fees that total less than the value of the bonds cashed, the interest exemption is proportional to the bonds' value that was used for tuition and fees. The amount of the exemption is also subject to income limitations. No interest exemption is allowed for single taxpayers with taxable incomes over $55,000 or married taxpayers filing jointly with taxable incomes over $90,000. (These income levels are adjusted for inflation every year.) A full exemption is allowed for single taxpayers with less than $40,000 in taxable income and married taxpayers filing jointly with less than $60,000 in taxable income. Between these upper and lower limits, a partial exemption is allowed.

Savings bonds also have some disadvantages. For one, the 6-month waiting period before cashing a Series EE bond reduces its liquidity. In addition, the potential interest penalty on bonds cashed prior to maturity is an obvious disadvantage. Finally, before buying a Series EE bond, you should carefully compare its interest rate to rates available from other alternatives.

Life Insurance

Certain types of life insurance policies have built-in savings features. Whole life, universal life, or variable life policies build cash values over the years. These types of policies, called **cash-value life insurance policies,** bundle life insurance together with savings. The advantages and disadvantages of these policies are explained in detail in Chapter 15, which is devoted entirely to life insurance.

cash-value life insurance policy: A life insurance policy that offers both life insurance and a savings feature.

Money Market Mutual Funds

money market mutual fund: A mutual fund that invests solely in short-term debt instruments such as Treasury bills, bank certificates of deposit, and short-term corporate debt.

Money market mutual funds have grown enormously in recent years. As mentioned in Chapter 1, these are mutual funds that invest solely in short-term debt instruments such as Treasury bills, bank certificates of deposit, and short-term corporate debt. Many people consider these funds an excellent place to keep all or part of their savings. A list of money market mutual funds obtained from *The Wall Street Journal* is shown in Exhibit 2.5. *The Journal* lists over 400 funds, which represents truly phenomenal growth since 15 years ago fewer than a dozen funds were operating, managing a few billion dollars. Today, money market funds manage more than $450 billion and are a major component of the mutual fund industry.

average maturity: The average time it takes for investments owned by a money market fund to be repaid with interest.

Money market fund managers take different investment approaches, and some take more risks than others. The least risky funds invest solely in U.S. government securities and maintain very short **average maturities.** Average maturity is the average time that it takes for investments owned by a fund to be repaid with interest. Money market funds typically maintain average maturities of 30 to 60 days. More risky funds may invest solely in corporate securities and maintain relatively long average maturities.

Nearly all major mutual fund families offer one or more money market funds. Large fund families typically offer one fund investing solely in government securities and another investing in both government and corporate securities. The large national brokerage firms also offer no-load money market funds. (A no-load fund is a mutual fund you can buy without paying a commission to the brokerage firm.) Money market funds expose savings to absolutely minimal risk. In addition, their other characteristics make them appealing to savers as well as investors: stability, liquidity, and high interest rates.

Price stability and liquidity go hand-in-hand with money market funds. During periods of rapidly fluctuating interest rates, long-term debt instruments fluctuate widely in price. A $1,000 corporate bond issued 10 years ago with a 6-percent interest rate is no longer worth $1,000 because new bonds of similar risk are currently paying in the neighborhood of 8 to 10 percent interest, depending on market conditions. To sell one of the old 6 percent bonds, the bondholder would have to accept a price that was reduced far enough to make the investment pay the same overall yield that competing securities were offering, that is, the current market rate. The reverse is also true; a 10-percent bond initially sold for $1,000 will go up in price if interest rates decline.

Changing interest rates have much less impact on the prices of the short-term debt instruments that money market funds buy. The price of a Treasury bill that comes due in 40 days, for example, changes much less than a longer-term security for a given change in interest rates, because it is certain to be redeemed for its face value in a few weeks, and the short-term outlook for interest rates is much more certain than the outlook over a period of years. This price stability of the underlying securities is one of the great appeals of money market funds.

EXHIBIT 2.5

Sample Listing of Money Market Mutual Funds

MONEY MARKET MUTUAL FUNDS

The following quotations, collected by the National Association of Securities Dealers Inc., represent the average of annualized yields and dollar-weighted portfolio maturities ending Wednesday, July 31, 1991. Yields don't include capital gains or losses.

Fund	Avg. Mat.	7Day Yld.	e7Day Yld.	Assets
AALMny	80	5.21	5.34	215
AARP HQ	53	5.33	5.47	362
AIM MM	23	5.15	5.28	109
AMA TrP	83	4.59	4.70	18
AMA PrP	73	4.85	4.97	108
AMEV	42	5.33	5.47	131
ASO Pr	51	5.37	5.52	307
ASO US	34	5.33	5.47	344
ActAsGv	53	5.26	5.40	602
ActAsMny	51	5.54	5.69	3801
AlexBwn	37	5.43	5.58	1162
AlxBTr	49	5.20	5.33	646
AlgerMM	81	6.10	6.29	158
AlliaCpRs	65	5.40	5.55	1948
AliaGvR	65	5.15	5.28	1461
AlliMny	69	5.42	5.57	1272
AlturaPr	42	5.42	5.57	202
AlturUS	47	5.27	5.41	60
AmAAdMM	86	6.23	6.43	852
AmCRes	45	5.12	5.25	427
AmExDDiv	82	5.54	5.69	17100
AmExGv	82	5.48	5.63	3639
AExpM	50	5.35	5.49	56
AmNatl	19	5.18	5.35	27
AmPerCsh	82	5.69	5.85	104
AmPerTrs	18	5.34	5.48	108
ArchFd	33	5.19	5.32	790
AMF St Lq	13	5.37	5.51	128
AutCsh	45	5.63	5.79	1271
AutGvt	35	5.52	5.67	2808
AutGvCs	40	5.49	5.64	227
Babson	49	5.16	5.29	78
BedfdGv	36	5.30	5.44	329
BdfdMM	49	5.22	5.35	757
BellAtl	55	5.23	5.36	14
BenhGvAg	54	5.63	5.79	1170
BlnchGv	53	5.09	5.22	33
WmBlrRdy	41	5.44	5.59	401
BostCo	87	5.56	5.71	268
BostGvt	80	5.30	5.44	88
BullBDlr	84	5.15	5.28	75
Bradfd	58	5.20	5.33	609
CBC Cn Pr	90	5.58	5.74	146
CBC Cn Tr	34	5.41	5.56	579
CIMCO	39	4.97	5.09	12
CalvSoc f	44	5.25	5.39	202
CapCash	18	5.52	5.67	2
CapitolMM	63	5.70	5.86	24
CapPrsv	52	5.24	5.38	3388
CapPre II	1	5.13	5.26	494
CardGvt	25	5.05	5.18	589
Carillon	36	5.30	5.44	52
Carnegie	18	5.15	5.29	126
CascdCs	59	5.28	5.42	162
CshAcctGv	8	5.10	5.23	30
CshAset	46	5.62	5.78	338
CashEqv	44	5.23	5.37	3759
CshEqGv	19	5.28	5.42	3276
CashMgt	24	5.38	5.53	2214
CshTrGv	38	5.24	5.37	644
CshTrPr	44	5.26	5.39	582
CshTrTreas	35	5.15	5.28	755
CshTrII	42	5.15	5.29	79
Centn Csh	41	5.00	5.13	123
CentnGv	57	5.29	5.43	535
Centen	42	5.36	5.51	566
ChchCsh	49	5.55	5.70	231
CignCsh	61	5.12	5.18	97
CigMM h	64	5.11	5.24	132
ColonlMMT	48	5.14	5.27	64
ColDln f	39	5.37	5.51	791
ComSens	46	4.97	5.09	89
Comp NJ Tx	48	3.97	4.05	34
CompCs	48	5.62	5.78	394
CompUS	60	5.47	5.62	748
CmpCshMM	27	5.02	5.15	221
CnstgCs	27	5.60	5.76	58
CnstgUS	37	5.35	5.49	158
CoreFd	66	5.77	5.94	494
CoreTr a	57	[illegible]		
CortldGn				

Fund	Avg. Mat.	7Day Yld.	e7Day Yld.	Assets
FstCshMM	24	5.80	5.96	109
FstCshAmTr	48	5.35	5.49	108
FstFdAmGv	1	5.31	5.45	146
FstFdMM	24	5.50	5.65	186
FstFdAmTr	48	5.14	5.27	48
FtInvCs f	30	4.96	5.07	277
FtPraMM	34	5.34	5.48	429
FtPraGv	7	4.93	5.05	785
FtVarG f	51	5.36	5.51	343
FlexFd	63	5.86	6.03	279
Founders	35	5.02	5.19	107
FountSCP	38	5.70	5.86	213
FountSq	35	5.65	5.81	242
FrkMny	21	5.24	5.37	1445
FrkFdl b	1	4.99	5.12	179
FrnkGvt	13	5.70	5.86	119
FrnkIFT	20	5.76	5.93	231
FrkIFTGS	1	5.61	5.76	349
FreeCsh	50	5.29	5.43	1159
FreeGv	57	5.15	5.28	317
FremntMM	60	5.72	5.89	6
FdTrMny	56	5.41	5.37	54
GT Mny	82	4.98	5.11	80
GW Glob	68	5.94	6.12	96
GW Gv	64	5.29	5.43	60
Gab OC DP	40	5.53	5.68	206
Gab OC Mgr	38	5.10	5.23	4
Gab OC UST	56	5.42	5.57	184
GalaxyGv	21	5.67	5.84	359
GalxyMM	53	5.69	5.85	427
GalaxTr	56	5.65	5.81	189
GnGvSec	64	5.69	5.85	476
GnMMkt	89	5.56	5.71	716
GSILFd f	52	5.70	5.87	1721
GSILGv f	37	5.57	5.72	2609
GSILMM f	37	5.78	5.95	1693
GSILPO f	49	5.73	5.89	3511
GSILTr f	38	5.51	5.67	2059
GvInvTr	35	4.88	4.99	140
GradCshR	56	5.29	5.43	654
GradUS	57	5.12	5.25	35
GrdCsFd	29	5.43	5.58	357
GrdCsMg	27	5.24	5.38	48
HTInsgtCs	56	5.52	5.67	206
HTInsgtGv	79	5.46	5.61	152
HanvCsh	44	5.46	5.61	203
HanvGov	63	5.44	5.59	299
Harbor	53	5.34	5.48	54
HatterasPr	60	5.62	5.78	172
HatterasTr	50	5.41	5.55	87
HelmsPr	52	5.54	5.70	747
HelmsUS	54	5.35	5.49	356
HrtgCsh	42	5.27	5.39	910
HiMrkDv	55	5.47	5.62	422
HiMrkUS	48	5.22	5.36	105
HiMrkUST	67	5.07	5.20	284
HYCT	16	5.52	5.67	20
HilrdGovt	64	5.20	5.33	229
HorznPr	65	6.24	6.43	1295
HorznTr	56	5.78	5.94	2716
Hummer	33	5.25	5.39	192
IDS CshM	31	5.22	5.35	1656
IDS PLA	27	5.47	5.62	159
IMGLiq	85	5.35	5.50	112
IndCaGv	31	4.96	5.09	290
IndCaMM	47	5.12	5.26	309
IndOnPr	60	5.53	5.69	370
IndOnUS	62	5.40	5.55	125
InfnAlGv	25	5.34	5.48	51
InfCCR	74	5.22	5.35	184
InfinPeg	59	6.15	6.33	186
InfnAlPr	49	5.32	5.45	33
InstCsh	51	5.95	6.13	217
InstFd	56	5.49	5.64	10
InstGov	15	5.86	6.03	143
Invesco	32	5.85	6.02	246
InvCshRsv	51	5.05	5.22	20
InvCshGv	20	5.51	5.66	46
IvyMny	16	5.04	5.17	21
JanMS Gov	31	4.96	5.09	290
JanMS MM	47	5.12	5.26	309
JHanCshM	54	5.21	5.35	260
KemperGvt	20	5.63	5.79	1129
KemperM	44	5.63	5.79	7572
KeyLqd	47	4.87	4.99	360
KidPeGv	40	5.16	5.29	545
KidPePr	44	5.30	5.44	1051
LandUSTr	43	5.52	5.67	307
LehPFdT	44	5.99	6.17	89
[illegible]	45	5.97	6.15	[illegible]

Fund	Avg. Mat.	7Day Yld.	e7Day Yld.	Assets
MdInInst	47	5.78	5.95	67
Mon&ManPr	37	5.26	5.40	119
MonManGvt	33	4.62	4.73	25
MonMMgt f	45	5.18	5.31	179
MonMkTrst	44	5.65	5.81	943
MonitorGvT	52	5.39	5.53	61
MonitorMMT	48	5.57	5.72	301
MonitorUST	56	5.46	5.61	146
MS Mony	60	5.64	5.80	586
MutlOmah	54	5.12	5.25	229
NCC Govt	37	5.36	5.51	1
NCC MM	23	5.39	5.54	19
NYL Inst	57	5.70	5.87	131
NatwMM	44	5.40	5.55	599
NeubCsh	57	5.36	5.50	277
NeubGvt	68	5.13	5.26	254
NEMMkt	59	5.48	5.63	1147
NEUSGvt	69	5.56	5.71	91
Newton	44	5.66	5.82	251
Nicholas	31	5.56	5.71	144
OldeMM	76	5.00	5.13	103
OldePrem	88	6.14	6.34	223
OppMoney	39	5.48	5.63	977
OvidExMM	49	5.41	5.55	258
PNC Prm	44	5.57	5.72	616
PNC Gvt	41	5.50	5.65	154
PcHrzTr	56	5.46	5.60	2716
PcHrzPr	65	5.92	6.09	1143
Pacifica	39	5.49	5.64	141
PacificGv	68	5.46	5.61	181
ParagTr	42	5.64	5.80	289
ParkPr	54	5.66	5.82	704
ParkUS	49	5.27	5.41	340
ParkCsh	29	5.05	5.18	66
Phonix	62	5.33	5.47	169
PionrCs	38	5.07	5.20	84
PionUS	37	5.26	5.40	27
PiprMM	63	5.27	5.41	1225
PiprUS	66	5.18	5.31	198
PortGv	32	5.33	5.48	67
PortInstMn	56	5.58	5.73	188
PortMM	45	5.60	5.75	622
PortUS	38	5.40	5.55	207
PortUSFed	42	5.34	5.48	48
Prem US	43	5.52	5.67	108
PrimeCsh	37	5.47	5.62	356
PrincorCash	49	5.45	5.60	262
PrvMut	33	4.75	4.86	45
PruCdGvt	63	5.51	5.67	424
PruCdMny	53	5.64	5.79	2470
PruSMM	63	5.52	5.67	257
PruGvt	61	5.54	5.70	1212
PruTr	75	5.32	5.46	281
PruMart	63	5.60	5.76	7774
PruInMM	66	5.86	6.03	511
PruInGov	60	5.24	5.38	52
PutDDiv	70	5.37	5.51	775
PW Cash	49	5.57	5.72	4576
PW MstrM b	55	4.23	4.32	43
PW RMA	51	5.55	5.71	4339
PW Retr	65	5.39	5.54	2141
PW RM US	49	5.41	5.56	946
QuestCsP	52	5.24	5.37	1146
QustCsG	71	5.27	5.41	143
RNC Liq	67	5.25	5.39	70
RegisDSI	59	5.49	5.64	213
RenaisGvt	29	5.33	5.48	70
RenaisMM	30	5.43	5.58	404
ReserveFd	42	5.07	5.20	1789
ReserveFd Gvt	45	4.97	5.10	795
RetirGv	50	4.65	4.76	52
RiversdeCap	45	6.23	6.42	165
RdSqMM	53	5.72	5.88	898
RdSqUS	34	5.55	5.70	455
Rshmre	32	5.18	5.31	128
RshFGI	58	5.10	5.23	788
SBK MMFT	21	5.35	5.49	52
SBK TMMFT	22	5.23	5.36	141
SBSF MM	88	5.65	5.81	22
SEI LqTr	53	5.66	5.82	2240
SEI LqGv	56	5.60	5.75	488
SEI LqPr	45	5.71	5.88	1824
SEI LqCl	42	5.62	5.78	53
SEI LqTII	53	5.57	5.73	81
SEI CsFd	49	5.39	5.54	172
SEI CsGv	51	5.74	5.90	475
SEI CsMM			[illegible]	390
SE[illegible]				

Fund	Avg. Mat.	7Day Yld.	e7Day Yld.	Assets
TwCntCs	39	5.32	5.47	1063
UMB Fed	48	5.55	5.70	220
UMB Prim	51	5.51	5.66	210
USFG Cs	54	4.88	5.00	69
USAA Mutl	72	5.76	5.93	1006
UnionInv	53	5.73	4.07	244
US Tr Am	82	5.19	5.33	44
US TreSec	60	5.07	5.20	177
US TreCs	39	5.48	5.63	76
UST Gvt	38	5.63	5.79	615
UST Mny	30	5.72	5.89	528
UST Treas	32	5.22	5.36	131
UtdCshM	54	5.52	5.68	572
UtdGvt	77	5.76	5.93	28
ValLin	79	3.92	4.00	477
VnEckUS a	56	4.27	4.36	43
VanKmpMM	84	4.98	5.10	35
VangFdl f	50	5.67	5.83	2029
VangPr f	49	5.80	5.97	14039
VangUST	46	5.43	5.58	2012
VantgCsh	37	5.37	5.52	1174
VantgGvt	32	5.28	5.41	302
VisnMM	50	5.28	5.41	92
VisnTr	37	5.11	5.24	75
VistaUS	40	5.26	5.40	382
WPG Sht	47	5.09	5.22	85648
WebsCshR	45	5.31	5.45	2171
WestcrCs	80	5.81	5.98	148
WestcrGv	46	5.21	5.35	94
WestcrPr	22	5.22	5.36	104
WestcrTr	46	5.37	5.51	142
WoodGv	66	5.49	5.65	299
WoodMM	47	5.57	5.73	802
WorkAsets	58	5.14	5.27	245
WrightMgd	38	5.35	5.48	33
ZweigGvt	51	5.38	5.52	140
Tax Exempt:				
ASO TxEx	34	3.68	3.75	25
AT OhioTx	41	4.08	4.16	257
ActAstTx	63	4.02	4.10	1376
AlxB TF	47	3.81	3.88	256
AlliaTax	66	3.86	3.93	893
AllTxCal	69	3.68	3.75	115
AllTxNY	90	3.82	3.89	69
AlturTF	21	4.41	4.51	39
AmExCal	62	3.90	3.98	667
AmExTxDD	63	4.17	4.26	3136
AmExNY	66	4.06	4.14	498
AExpTF	61	4.01	4.09	16
ArchFd	56	3.72	3.79	144
AtlasCA	72	4.11	4.20	42
BdfdTxFr	44	3.62	3.68	213
BedfordNY	49	3.12	3.17	32
BenCAMu	51	4.66	4.77	118
BenCaTF	50	3.68	3.74	374
BenNaTF	49	4.22	4.31	100
BostonCo	45	4.00	4.08	173
CBC Cn Nat	82	3.86	3.93	30
CBCCnNY	60	3.62	3.69	71
CIGNATx	46	3.66	3.73	42
CignTE CT	50	3.97	4.05	27
CalDaly	83	3.87	3.94	82
CalMM	61	3.85	3.93	125
CalMuCs	48	4.18	4.26	60
CalTF	85	4.04	4.12	79
CalvTxFr	45	4.79	4.91	1336
ClvTF CA	22	4.57	4.68	263
ClvTF NJ	75	5.01	5.14	47
CapTFB	42	3.81	3.88	5
CardTx	20	3.94	4.01	96
CarnegTx	42	4.13	4.21	250
CashEq	41	4.01	4.09	1154
CshTrMunl	48	4.12	4.20	413
CsTrIIMun	41	4.27	4.36	53
Centn CA	2	3.75	3.82	34
CentenTx	24	4.08	4.16	802
ColTEx	15	3.79	3.86	29
CompTx	72	4.20	4.29	121
CmpCshTx	70	3.82	3.89	49
cnstgTF	35	4.04	4.12	24
ConnDly	59	3.57	3.63	178
Core TF	70	4.44	4.61	55
CortldTx	49	4.15	4.24	195
CounslNY	61	3.42	3.48	72
DallTx c	25	4.35	4.45	760
DWSrNY	75	3.35	3.40	80
DWSears	58	3.97	4.05	875
DWSrCal	72	3.92	3.99	352
[illegible]Tax	82	3.80	3.87	58
[illegible]	82	3.68	3.75	336
[illegible]		4.25	4.34	[illegible]

Fund	Avg. Mat.	7Day Yld.	e7Day Yld.	Assets
HanvTF	52	3.91	3.99	129
HattTERtl	50	4.13	4.21	39
Helmsmn	48	4.24	4.33	174
HiMrkCal	71	3.86	3.93	146
HiMrk	49	4.17	4.26	59
HorznTE	38	4.39	4.48	412
IDS Tx c	54	3.67	3.74	139
IMG TE	73	3.60	3.67	25
IndCaTF	52	3.87	3.95	81
IndOnMIMn	90	3.99	4.07	33
InstTF	59	4.57	4.68	68
Invesco	27	4.72	4.84	56
JanMS TF	52	3.87	3.95	81
KmprMM	42	4.22	4.31	789
KiddrPeaTx	61	3.98	4.06	703
KidP CalT	62	3.50	3.56	202
KidPe CT	66	3.43	3.49	47
KidP NJ	60	4.34	4.44	37
KidPE NY	60	4.11	4.19	38
LehPMCa	36	4.05	4.13	508
LehPMNY	56	3.62	3.69	339
LehPMCs	38	4.31	4.40	362
LehPMu	41	4.03	4.11	853
LndmkNY	56	3.68	3.75	614
LdmkTxFr	46	4.05	4.13	193
LaurlTE	55	4.25	4.34	134
LebentNY	79	3.91	3.99	44
LegMTE	45	3.76	3.83	186
LexingTx c	53	4.04	4.12	55
LqdGrTx	46	4.02	4.10	53
Losanv TF	45	4.02	4.10	117
MngdTF	56	4.03	4.11	124
MarinTx	39	3.82	3.89	95
MarinNY	60	3.56	3.62	89
MktMstTE	23	3.94	4.02	173
McDld	46	3.83	3.90	113
MLCMA Cal	60	4.03	4.11	102
MLCMA CT	58	3.71	3.78	146
ML CMAMI	58	4.00	4.08	174
MLCMA NY	66	3.62	3.69	591
ML CMA NC	60	4.03	4.11	102
ML CMAOH	81	4.06	4.14	147
MLCMA TE	83	4.05	4.13	7968
ML CMA MA	75	3.96	4.04	96
ML CMA NJ	67	3.72	3.79	322
ML CMA PA	71	4.02	4.10	204
ML Inst TE	64	4.27	4.36	358
MichDly	36	4.09	4.17	107
MdwstGrp	61	4.28	4.37	48
MdwOHTF	78	4.07	4.15	211
MS Muni	72	3.80	3.87	172
MnyMgt	64	4.44	4.54	77
MonitorTFT	53	3.71	3.78	68
NCC TE	31	4.12	4.20	4
NeubBMu	42	3.99	4.07	169
NETxEx	60	4.03	4.11	73
NJ Mu Ins	62	4.07	4.15	41
NYDlyTF	72	4.09	4.18	195
NYMuniCT	47	4.30	4.39	215
NuvCal	53	4.09	4.18	515
NuvnMas	36	4.15	4.24	86
NuvNY	49	4.05	4.13	42
NuvTxEx	76	4.33	4.42	2098
NuvnTFRs	39	4.15	4.23	450
OppTECsh	20	3.88	3.96	24
OvrExp	50	3.92	4.00	305
PNC Tx	49	3.88	3.95	95
PcHorCA	36	4.11	4.19	105
PacHorz	41	4.24	4.32	100
PWRMA CA	68	3.51	3.57	281
PWRMA NY	66	3.51	3.57	115
PW RM Tx	63	3.74	3.81	1233
ParkTF	47	3.91	3.99	139
PiperTF	85	4.00	4.08	140
PorticoTE	61	3.97	4.04	22
PrincrTE	47	3.80	3.87	58
PruCdTx	64	4.01	4.09	764
PruCA	52	3.69	3.76	352
PruNJ	81	4.37	4.47	113
PruNY	57	3.64	3.70	238
PruTax	73	3.88	3.95	698
PutCA	79	3.56	3.63	68
PutNY	64	3.55	3.62	64
PutTE	69	4.08	4.16	103
QuestCs	54	3.83	3.90	108
RsrvConn	45	3.42	3.48	221
ResrvInt	64	3.91	3.98	348
ResrvNY	72	3.54	3.60	146
RdSqTE	[illegible]		[illegible]	247
RshFT[illegible]				[illegible]

SOURCE: *The Wall Street Journal*, August 1, 1991 p. C25. Reprinted by permission of *The Wall Street Journal*,

Money market funds maintain constant share values of $1. If you buy 1,000 shares today for $1,000, you know that you will be able to sell those shares 1 week, 1 month, or 1 year from today for $1,000. The interest is compounded daily (although normally paid monthly) and automatically reinvested in the fund. If the market value of a fund's assets changes due to fluctuating interest rates, the change in value is added to or deducted from the net asset value of the fund. Not all funds follow this **marking to market** system exactly, but the net result of the various systems funds follow is approximately the same.

marking to market: The system by which changes in the market value of a fund's assets are added to or deducted from the net asset value of the fund every day.

Money market funds offer instant liquidity to shareholders. In addition to withdrawing funds by mail, telephone, or wire transfer, you can write checks against your money market account balance. Some funds impose minimum limits on the amounts of checks, often $250 to $500. You normally continue to earn interest on your money until checks clear.

Interest earnings on money market funds roughly follow inflation. Prior to the deregulation of the banking industry, money market funds prospered through their ability to offer much higher interest rates than banks. As federal control over bank interest rates has diminished, the funds have lost this advantage except on balances falling below prescribed minimums.

An investor in money market funds should be concerned primarily with safety and yield. Insured bank money market deposit accounts are safer because they are federally insured. The choice between money market mutual funds and bank money market deposit accounts will depend on their relative yields, on the need for check-writing flexibility, on the importance to the saver of federal insurance, and on the size of account. For long-term investors, bank funds may seem preferable if their yields are competitive.

Discount Brokerage Services and Cash Management Accounts

In recent years, the deregulation of the financial services industry has led to increased competition among banks and brokerage firms for consumer accounts. **Brokerage firms** are corporations that buy and sell stocks, bonds, and other securities on behalf of their customers. In the late 1970s and early 1980s most major brokerage firms began offering money market mutual funds that competed very successfully with banks for consumers' savings. Following the high inflation of the 1970s, consumers became concerned about the relatively low interest rates on bank savings accounts. In response to this concern, brokerage firms began offering money market funds. As these offerings became successful, the brokerage firms began to supplement their services by offering **cash management accounts.** These accounts combined traditional brokerage accounts with money market fund accounts by automatically transferring any cash balances in the brokerage account to a money market fund. Since the money market account offered a much higher rate of interest than that available from banks, these accounts rapidly grew in popularity with both investors and savers.

brokerage firms: Corporations that buy and sell stocks, bonds, commodities, and other securities on behalf of their customers.

cash-management account: A brokerage account that combines a traditional brokerage account with a money market fund by automatically transferring any cash balances in the brokerage account into the money market fund.

perspective on **ETHICS**

The U.S. Savings and Loan Scandal

During the late 1980s and early 1990s, the United States was rocked by an unprecedented financial scandal in the savings and loan industry. The costs of cleaning up the scandal are estimated to run as high as $500 billion, making it by far the most expensive financial scandal in history. As *Fortune* magazine observed in its November 5, 1990, issue, "Though yet perceived only in hazy outline, today's S&L fraud dwarfs every previous carnival of white-collar crime in America."

Although the vast majority of savings and loan officers and directors operated their institutions with honesty and integrity, widespread abuses occurred during the "debt decade" of the 1980s, and the cleanup of the industry by the federal government will almost certainly extend well into the 1990s. In a report to Congress in 1988, the Federal Home Loan Bank Board (FHLBB) cited fraud and insider abuse as the most pernicious of all factors leading to the insolvency of thrift institutions. (The term "insider" in normal business usage generally refers to an officer or director of a corporation or an individual who owns 10 percent or more of the corporation's stock.) The FHLBB defined fraud and insider abuse as follows:

"... individuals in a position of trust in the institution or closely affiliated with it have, in general terms, breached their fiduciary duties; traded on inside information, usurped opportunities or profits; engaged in self-dealing; or otherwise used the institution for personal advantage. Specific examples of insider abuse include loans to insiders in excess of that allowed by regulation; high-risk speculative ventures; payment of exorbitant dividends at times when the institution is at or near insolvency; payment from institution funds for personal vacations, automobiles, clothing, and art; payment of unwarranted commissions and fees to companies owned by a shareholder; payment of 'consulting fees' to insiders or their companies; use of insiders' companies for association business; and putting friends and relatives on the payroll of the institution."

Testifying before the Congress, Frederick D. Wolf, Assistant Comptroller General of the Government Accounting Office, outlined the responsibilities of officers and directors to establish adequate internal control systems. These are the types of controls that most managers and director do in fact follow and are a good guide to the ethical and legal responsibilities of thrift managers. As described in Mr. Wolf's testimony:

"... thrift management is responsible for creating an environment which encourages safe and sound operations and reduces the potential for insider fraud and abuse. Management is also responsible for developing policies and procedures, including a system of internal controls, designed to foster sound practices, to comply with laws and regulations, and to protect the institution against insider abuse, fraud, and other crimes. Further, directors should ensure that management is aware of applicable laws and regulations and develops a system to implement and monitor compliance. Managers are also under a duty to avoid behaving in a manner which places their own personal interests above the interests of the bank. When management does not foster an environment conducive to safe and sound practices and compliance with laws and regulations, the thrift becomes vulnerable not only to fraud and insider abuse, but also to other unsafe practices ..."

As may be inferred from the above testimony, the real bottom line is that "good ethics is good business." The thrift crisis showed us that sloppy and dishonest banking procedures led inevitably to thrift failures and then to investigations, indictments, convictions, and bankers serving time in jail for their transgressions. The huge losses in the savings and loan industry clearly illustrate why illegal and unethical activities ultimately lead to disaster for the businesses and individuals involved.

United States General Accounting Office testimony, *Failed Thrifts*, 22 March 1989, Rep. GAO/T-AFMD-89-4.

In response to the competition from brokerage firms, banks introduced money market deposit (MMDA) accounts, and many large banks began to add security brokerage services. Nearly all of these bank-owned brokerage firms offer discount commission rates; that is, they generally charge lower commissions than a full-service security brokerage firm would.

Many banks offer cash management accounts to their customers, as well, combining brokerage accounts with MMDA accounts. Any idle balances in brokerage accounts from such sources as dividend and interest payments or security sales are automatically transferred to customers' MMDA accounts to earn money market rates.

The Financial Institutions Reform, Recovery, and Enforcement Act of 1989

The current federal deposit insurance system for commercial banks and savings and loans has resulted from the most sweeping financial bailout effort in U.S. history. During the second half of the 1980s, savings and loans in the United States began failing at an alarming rate. This high failure rate was brought about by numerous factors, the most important of which was the virtual collapse of real estate values in some parts of the country at a time when S&Ls were aggressively promoting and financing real estate deals. As property values and rentals declined, many properties could not generate enough cash to pay principal and interest payments on time; loans went into **default.** Savings and loans that had overextended their mortgage portfolios found themselves repossessing properties that had come to be worth less than the amount of the loans they had secured.

default: Failure to make interest or principal payments on a debt obligation.

A second major cause of widespread S&L failures was the unprecedented volatility of interest rates during the 1980s, coupled with the deregulation of the financial services industry. Many savings and loans were paying more to attract deposits than they were earning on their portfolios of old, low-interest real estate loans. Widespread **writedowns** (reducing the value of the collateral for a loan on the books of the lender) and **writeoffs** (declaring the value of the collateral as zero and removing the loan from the S&L's list of assets) forced many S&Ls into bankruptcy. Many institutions further aggravated their financial problems by losing even more money speculating in the bond and real estate markets. Finally, considerable fraud and mismanagement in the industry contributed further to losses.

writedown: Reducing the value of the collateral for a loan on the books of the lender.

writeoff: Declaring the value of an asset as worthless and removing it from the books of the lender.

The net result was that the government agency that insured savings and loans, the Federal Savings and Loan Insurance Corporation, did not have enough money to cover depositors' insured losses. To restore stability to the thrift industry and protect depositors up to the maximum federal insurance, Congress passed the Financial Institutions Reform, Recovery, and Enforcement Act of 1989 (FIRREA). Former President Bush signed FIRREA into law on August 9, 1989.

To an individual saver, probably the most important aspect of this law was its reaffirmation of the full-faith-and-credit commitment of the United States government to stand behind depositors' savings balances up to the $100,000 per account. The federal insurance of banks and savings associations was consolidated and placed under the control of the FDIC, abolishing the Federal Home Loan Bank Board and the Federal Savings and Loan Insurance Corporation. In the 1990s, banks and savings associations are now insured by the same agency, the FDIC.

The most important effect of FIRREA on the overall economy is its establishment of a new banking regulatory structure. The 1989 act was the most comprehensive revision of federal banking laws that had occurred since the Great Depression of the 1930s. It provided the regulatory structure under which hundreds of insolvent savings associations were closed or merged with healthy banks or savings associations. As a consumer, you can remain confident that your deposits in federally insured financial institutions are safe.

SUMMARY

You must save to meet your financial goals. In establishing your savings plan, you need to understand clearly the difference between savings and investment. Because of the short-term time horizon of your savings account, your primary savings objective should be to earn the highest possible return that is consistent with minimal risk.

Along with this objective, another major objective of saving should be to establish an emergency fund equal to 3 to 6 months' after-tax income. You may also want to save for additional specific purposes or to provide for liquidity needs. To meet your savings objectives, you should follow a pay-yourself-first policy, saving 5 to 10 percent of your after-tax income.

Commercial banks are by far the most popular savings institutions used by American consumers. Savings and loan associations are the next most popular. Mutual savings banks and credit unions claim a much smaller share of consumers' savings. These institutions offer a variety of savings plans, including passbook accounts, statement savings accounts, MMDAs, NOW accounts, super NOWs, certificates of deposit, and club accounts. Many people also use U.S. savings bonds, cash-value life insurance, and money market mutual funds as savings media.

The manner in which interest is computed on your account and the number of compounding periods play a major role in determining the actual dollars of interest paid. An account that compounds interest daily and pays from day of deposit to day of withdrawal will pay the most annual interest for a given interest rate.

INVESTMENT MANAGEMENT CONCEPTS

1. You must save to reach financial independence.
2. Establish your savings objectives to first meet your liquidity and emergency needs.

3. Save 5 to 10 percent of each paycheck to develop a habit of thrift.
4. Pay yourself first.
5. Select the federally insured savings institution that offers the highest yield.
6. You may want to save by investing in U.S. savings bonds through a payroll deduction plan.
7. Life insurance and money market funds offer additional ways to save.
8. The way in which interest is compounded on your savings account is important.
9. Select a savings account that pays the highest interest from day of deposit to day of withdrawal.
10. A checking account at a full-service bank may offer advantages.
11. Select a checking account that gives you moderate cost, convenience, and service.

REVIEW QUESTIONS

1. Why should you save?
2. Why do you need to reserve part of your current income to pay for future expenses?
3. What are some of the objectives of saving?
4. How can you devise a plan to meet your savings objectives?
5. What is a pay-yourself-first savings plan?
6. What is an automatic savings plan?
7. How much should you plan to save for an emergency fund?
8. Explain the difference between a savings account at a commercial bank, savings and loan, mutual savings bank, or federal credit union.
9. What is a certificate of deposit?
10. What are NOW and super NOW accounts?
11. What is an MMDA account?
12. What is meant by "the magic of compound interest"?
13. How do banks calculate interest on savings accounts?
14. What services does a full-service bank offer?
15. Are service charges generally the same at all banks?

SELF-CORRECTING PROBLEMS

1. John and Carla have saved $2,500 toward the down payment on a house they expect to be able to buy their first house in about 5 years and therefore want to invest their $2,500 in a CD for that time. They have located a

federally insured savings and loan association in their community that pays very competitive interest rates. The only problem they face is whether they should buy a fixed-rate or a variable-rate CD.

A 5-year, fixed-rate CD currently offers 8.25 percent interest, compounded quarterly. A variable-rate CD offers an initial rate of 7.85 percent, also compounded quarterly. The interest rate on the variable-rate CD changes every 6 months to follow the rate on newly issued 5-year Treasury bonds. Principal withdrawals from the variable-rate CD are allowed without penalty when the interest rate changes. As another alternative, they could buy a 1-year CD and simply roll it over every year (that is, reinvest the proceeds each year when the CD matures by buying another 1-year CD). Such 1-year CDs currently offer an interest rate of 7.65 percent, compounded monthly.

a. What is the effective annual yield on each of the CDs?

b. Discuss the factors John and Carla should consider when they make this choice.

c. In which CD would you advise them to invest?

2. Using Exhibits 2.2 and 2.3, answer the following questions:

a. If you invested $2,000 per year for the next 20 years and earned a rate of return of 12 percent per year on your money, how much would your investments be worth at the end of 20 years?

b. Suppose you got your first job after college at the age of 22 and decided that you would work until age 60 (or for 38 years), then retire and live off your company pension, Social Security, and your investments. To do this, you decide that you will invest $2,000 per year ($167 per month) for the next 38 years. How much money would you have in your investment fund at the end of this time if your investment fund earned 12 percent per year?

c. If you invested $10,000 today at 8 percent, how much would your investment be worth 10 years from now, 20 years from now, and 30 years from now?

Answer to Self-Correcting Problems

1. a. The 5-year, 8.25 percent fixed-rate CD, with interest compounded quarterly, pays 8.25 percent divided by 4 quarters, or 2.0625 percent per quarter, and 1.020625^4 equals 1.0851, or an 8.51 percent effective annual yield.

The variable-rate CD, with its rate of 7.85 percent compounded quarterly, pays 7.85 percent divided by 4 quaerters, or 1.9625 percent per quarter, and 1.019625^4 equals 1.0808, or an 8.08 percent effective annual yield at its current rate.

The 1-year CD, with 7.65 percent interest compounded monthly, yields 7.65 percent divided by 12 months, or 0.6375 percent per month, and 1.006375^{12} equals 1.0792, or a 7.92 percent effective annual yield.

b. The most important factor that John and Carla should consider is their time horizon. If they are very certain that they will not need this money before 5 years pass, then the 5-year CD offers a good value. Obviously, the interest rate also is important, but being locked up for 5 years to pick up 0.43 percent per year additional interest on $2,500 is too much risk for the additional return.

c. Emergencies can easily arise during such a long period of time, and John and Carla should probably not leave most of their savings subject to early withdrawal penalties. The variable-rate CD offers a better rate than the 1-year certificate and it is also flexible, so it is their best option. They also should check on two-year CDs to see if they could get a better deal than the variable rate CD.

2. a. $146,172 (from Exhibit 2.2)

b. $1,235,557 (from Exhibit 2.2)

c. $29,293 in 10 years, $92,214 in 20 years, and $228,057 in 30 years (from Exhibit 2.3). Note the impact of compound growth: Your investment is 2.9 times larger in 10 years, 9.2 times larger in 20 years, and 22.8 times larger in 30 years. If you invested $40,000 at age 30, it would be worth nearly $1 million by age 60 (4 × $228,057 = $912,228).

SELECTED READINGS

Barth, James R. et al. *The Thrift Industry under Siege*. New York: Ballinger, 1988.

Board of Governors of the Federal Reserve System. *Alice in Debitland*. Washington, D.C.: Federal Reserve Board, 1984. (Free copies available on request from Publication Services, Division of Support Services.)

Krefetz, Gerald. *All about Savings*. New York: Wiley, 1987.

Shilling, Dana, and John Hancock Financial Services. *Real Life, Real Answers: Earning, Saving, Investing, and Enjoying—a Realistic Guide to Managing Your Money*. New York: Arbor House, 1988.

Stigum, Marcia, and Frank Fabozzi. *The Dow Jones-Irwin Guide to Bond and Money Market Investments*. Homewood, Ill.: Dow Jones-Irwin, 1988.

chapter 3

Home Ownership

A Cornerstone Investment

Betsy and Jean, two sisters, recently graduated from college. They shared a rented apartment in the suburbs of Minneapolis, Minnesota, but they decided that they both would prefer to live in the city rather than commute from the suburbs to their jobs downtown. As they looked at the costs of rental apartments in town, they thought that they might benefit financially if they pooled their savings and purchased a small townhouse or condominium together. Rather than paying rent each month for use of the apartment, they would jointly own a piece of real estate that would increase in value over time and help them build their personal net worth.

After consulting with a real estate agent, Betsy and Jean spent their next four weekends looking at properties in their price range that were located near both of their offices, eventually settling on a $140,000 townhouse. They had to make a down payment of 10 percent, or $14,000, and pay $5,000 to cover a variety of legal fees and taxes associated with the transfer of real estate. Thus they had to invest $19,000 of their savings in the initial purchase. They also arranged a long-term mortgage on the property in the amount of $126,000. The monthly payments on this loan, including both principal and interest plus real estate taxes and insurance on the property, totaled $1,400, or $700 each. They could rent a comparable townhouse for about $400 per month less, but they expected this additional $400 monthly expenditure to bring returns in the form of increases in the value of the property in the future. They also could deduct interest and real-estate taxes from their incomes.

Based on past data, Betsy and Jean expected the value of their property to increase by about 5 percent per year over the long run, or about $7,000 per year, based on its $140,000 price. They did not expect the property's value to rise every year (in fact, recent experience has shown that in some years property values may actually decline), but they knew that over any recent 5- or 10-year period, property values have increased. Over the next 5 years an average increase in value of 5 percent per year would result in a total gain of nearly $40,000 in value. If they should decide to sell the townhouse at that time, they would share a very nice gain. In the meantime, they would enjoy an attractive living environment and be free from worries about rent increases or landlords' whims. If their circumstances should change due, for example, to a career move or marriage, they could rent the townhouse to help with the mortgage payment while watching it increase in value. All in all, this arrangement looked like both a good investment and a good living arrangement for Betsy and Jean.

Introduction

Most people wonder at one time or another whether it is better to buy a home or to rent. Even in today's changeable economic environment, the answer is simple and direct. It is almost always better to own than to rent, though owning might be more expensive in the short run. Support for this simple and direct answer requires a discussion of the many financial advantages of home ownership, including tax advantages and protection against inflation. Additionally, home ownership offers emotional stability and security. This chapter will consider all of these factors.

The purchase of a home is the largest and most important financial transaction most people ever make. Home ownership probably will add the most money to a person's total wealth of any long-term investment, while it provides the greatest personal enjoyment. To make certain that you get your money's worth, however, you must understand the process of buying a home, including selection criteria, buying mechanics, obtaining down payment money, and financing. Finally, you also must understand what you must spend to live in your home and maintain it. Reading this chapter is a good first step toward the understanding you need to be certain you get the largest benefit possible from this most important financial transaction.

Why Buy a Home?

There are many good financial reasons to seriously consider buying a home. The major financial benefits of home ownership include the strengths of real estate as an inflation hedge, preferential tax treatment of ownership expenses, stability of costs, and forced savings. Planned carefully, including keeping costs in line with income, home ownership can serve as a critical cornerstone of a personal investment portfolio.

A Home As an Inflation Hedge

Inflation alone makes home ownership extremely attractive. Housing prices in most U.S. metropolitan areas have risen dramatically since the end of World War II. During the 1970s and 1980s, especially, prices rose explosively. A typical, moderately priced, good-quality, single-family home with three or four bedrooms might have cost approximately $60,000 to $80,000 10 years ago, depending upon its location. Today the same home would cost just about twice that much—$120,000 to $160,000—in most areas of the country. In some major metropolitan areas such as Boston, Los Angeles, or Washington, D.C., the price would have nearly tripled! Housing price increases have generally slowed dramatically during the last few years, but past downturns have only postponed later increases in housing prices.

Exhibit 3.1 shows the increase in the average price of a single-family home from 1980 to the beginning of 1990. The average price of a new home has risen from approximately $62,500 in 1980 to just over $120,000 in 1990, a 100-percent increase in 10 years. The rate of increase in the average price for an existing home, while not quite as high, still shows a substantial jump of approximately 65 percent from just over $60,000 to just under $100,000 during this period. Clearly, housing prices have risen dramatically, making home ownership a good **inflation hedge,** that is, an asset the value of which has increased faster than the rate of inflation. Owning a house can protect the purchasing power of your assets from diminishing due to general increases in prices.

inflation hedge: An asset that increases in value faster than the rate of inflation.

People looking at today's housing prices raise several typical questions:

Will housing prices increase forever?

Can I afford to take the risk of home ownership after such a dramatic rise in the prices?

Certainly these questions indicate concern for the future. The economy has seen periods of recession in housing before, and it will see them again. Yet, housing downturns have generally been brief after which prices resumed their upward march. Some concern for future declines is warranted, but chances are that the prices of houses, both old and new, will continue to rise

EXHIBIT 3.1

Average Price of a One-Family Home

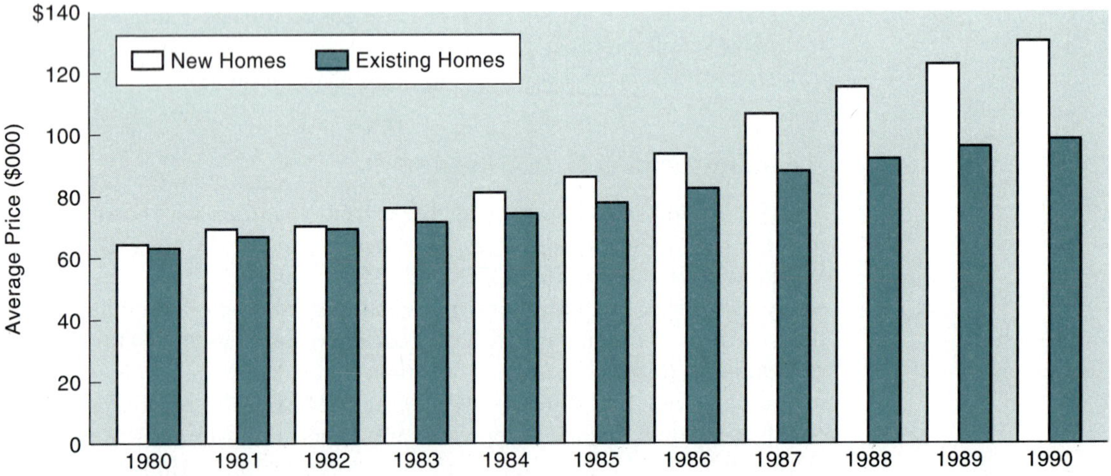

SOURCE: Bureau of the Census, *Construction Reports*, series C–25, C–27.

over the long run because our ever-growing need for shelter and the scarcity of desirable land create inflationary pressures that will continue to force housing prices upward, as they have in the past.

Exhibit 3.2 projects the expected future prices of new and existing homes at a rate of increase of 5 percent per year through the end of the century. This forecast of a 5-percent annual increase in housing prices through the 1990s seems quite reasonable, perhaps even conservative, in light of increases of approximately 7 percent annually that occurred during the 1980s. At this rate of increase, the average price of a new home in the United States will approach $200,000 in 1999 and the average price of an existing home will be around $150,000.

These reasonable estimates suggest that purchasing a home will provide both an inflationary hedge and a way to build capital and net worth. Net worth increases both as the home's value increases and as the owner pays down the mortgage. Payments on the mortgage reduce the balance of the loan and increase the owner's **home equity** in the home, that is the difference between its value and the principal balance of the mortgage, which represents the lender's claim against the home.

home equity: The difference between the market value of a home and the balance still owed on the mortgage.

EXHIBIT 3.2

Future Home Prices with 5 Percent Inflation

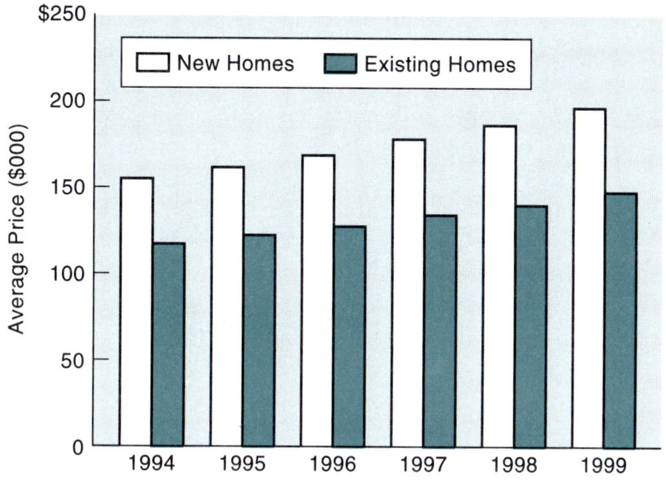

Tax Advantages of Home Ownership

after-tax cost of housing: The cost of mortgage payments minus the tax reduction from deducting mortgage interest and real estate taxes paid from taxable income.

Another financial reason for buying a home is the tax break it brings you. The federal government allows you to deduct the interest you pay on your mortgage from taxable income, giving you a lower **after-tax cost of housing.** Interest on the mortgage is also deducted on state income tax returns. In addition, you can deduct real estate taxes you pay from taxable income. Many people begin to itemize their income tax deductions only after they buy homes to take advantage of these substantial tax write-offs. These tax reductions can make home ownership very worthwhile.

For example, if you were to purchase a $125,000 home, putting $25,000 down and taking out a $100,000 mortgage at 10 percent interest, your interest payments in the first year would total slightly less than $10,000. Your real estate taxes would vary depending on your area of the country, but a figure of $1,200 is reasonable. If you were in the 28 percent federal income tax bracket, the deductions for mortgage interest and real estate taxes would save you about $3,100 in federal income taxes. If your state levies an income tax, these deductions would reduce that bill, as well.

Taxes weigh heaviest on unmarried, middle-income taxpayers who do not own homes. A single person pays about one-third more than a married couple in taxes for the same income. Also, few single people buy houses;

most rent, missing out on deductions that could reduce their income taxes substantially. A single, middle-income taxpayer should certainly consider the tax benefits of home ownership.

The government gives another tax break to homeowners aged 55 and over. Current tax law allows them a one-time exclusion from capital gains tax of up to $125,000 in capital gains on the sale of a home that is the taxpayer's primary residence. The **capital gains tax** is the income tax due on profits from the sale of a capital asset such as a home.

capital gains tax: Income tax due on profits from the sale of a capital asset such as a home.

An example will show how this exclusion works. Suppose Bob and Shirley, both over the age of 55, sell their primary residence for $175,000 after living there for 25 years. They originally paid $35,000 for the house, so they would have a capital gain of $140,000 ($175,000 – $35,000, ignoring transaction costs for simplicity). Current law would tax this gain at the same rate as the owners' other income, but after taking the $125,000 exclusion, they would pay taxes on only $15,000 of the gain ($140,000 – $125,000). If they were in the 28 percent federal tax bracket, the exclusion would save them $35,000 in federal income taxes.

Stable Costs

Another financial advantage of home ownership is not as direct as the tax advantage. Principal and interest payments are constant over the lives of most mortgages, which gives home ownership another important advantage since it keeps the amount the owner pays monthly for housing constant. Property taxes do generally increase over time, but they usually represent only a small portion of housing costs. Rent on a house or an apartment, on the other hand, will almost certainly increase over time. Therefore, you tend to reduce fluctuations in long-term housing costs by buying rather than renting.

In recent years lenders have introduced mortgages with interest rates that change with market rates. Principal and interest payments on a variable-rate mortgage do not remain constant because they increase whenever mortgage rates increase. However, almost all of these mortgages specify interest rate caps that state maximum interest rates over the life of a loan. Thus, even if rates go up, the cost of a variable rate mortgage may still be more stable than the cost of renting. Also, if interest rates were to decrease, the mortgage payment would decrease, as well. A later section of this chapter explains mortgage financing in more detail.

Savings Discipline

Real estate ownership brings another financial benefit by forcing the owner to save. You will probably spend a greater percentage of your income for housing if you buy a home than if you rent. Also, if you own your own home, you are likely to put more money into furnishings, decorations, landscaping, and other improvements. Many buyers tend to stretch their budgets to buy the homes of their dreams, but even those who spend more to own a home than they would spend for rent end up using their money to increase their net worth. Net worth increases because the value of the property increases over time due to inflation, and due to the owner's improvements to the property. Paying down the mortgage balance also increases net worth.

Risk of Home Ownership

Wherever there are rewards, there are also risks, and home ownership is no exception to this rule. Buying a home requires a very large financial commitment that may restrict your ability to afford other things, such as a nice car or an interesting vacation. Some people may not be able to afford home ownership early in life and some may simply want to avoid responsibility for large house payments and other costs of ownership. A home is also a very **illiquid investment** that is both expensive and time consuming to sell to convert the investment into cash. If you buy a home and then change your mind about home ownership, it may take several months to sell the home and escape the commitment. You have to prepare financially for this liquidity risk.

illiquid investment: An investment, such as a home, that requires expensive and time-consuming procedures to convert into cash.

Home ownership also brings the risk of price fluctuation. Although home prices generally have risen over long periods of time, they also have declined in some years. In the early 1990s, for example, home prices generally declined in most areas of the United States. Someone who purchased a home in 1989 and then decided to sell it in 1990 may have had to sell the home for less than the price paid for it. Additionally, as this chapter will explain later, a home purchase and sale can involve high settlement costs and brokers' commissions. If you own a home for only a short period of time, these costs may consume all of your profits from the sale, or even bring you a net loss on the investment. Someone who expects to live in one place for only a short period of time would probably be better off renting than buying.

Financing a Home Purchase

Before you start looking for a home to buy, you should ask yourself how much you can afford to pay. A clear answer to this question will save a lot of time and effort. Essentially this question raises three subordinate issues. First, how much money do you have available as a down payment? Second, how much income can you devote to mortgage loan payments? Finally, what interest rate does the mortgage require and how many years do you have to repay the loan? All these factors will influence how much you can afford to spend on a house.

mortgage loan: A long-term loan made for the purpose of buying property, which serves as collateral for the loan.

collateral: An asset pledged as security for a loan; if the borrower does not make payments on time, the lender may seize the asset and sell it to pay off the loan.

foreclosure: The legal process by which a lender takes control of property pledged as collateral and sells it to pay off the loan.

A **mortgage loan** is a long-term loan made for the purpose of buying property, which serves as **collateral** for the mortgage. With the property as collateral, the lender has the right, through the legal process of **foreclosure,** to take control of the property and sell it to pay off the mortgage loan, should the borrower fail to make payments on time or otherwise default on the terms of the mortgage.

Generally, a larger down payment allows a buyer to afford a bigger and better house. Second, a higher income and a greater proportion available for mortgage payments after other debt payments allows the buyer to afford a more expensive home. Third, a lower interest rate on the mortgage allows the buyer to afford a larger mortgage for a given monthly payment, and therefore a more expensive home.

Mortgage Amount and Income Level

Some detailed financial data will help you understand a bit more about the financial requirements of paying the principal and interest on a home. Exhibit 3.3 indicates the size of the mortgage and the price of the home a buyer could afford at various income levels. This table's first column lists annual income figures in $6,000 increments, from $18,000 up to $84,000. It translates these totals to monthly income figures in the second column. The third column shows the proportion of monthly income available for payment of principal and interest based on the conventional guideline that principal and interest payments should not exceed 25 percent of gross income (income before taxes and other deductions). In some locations these figures might be high because, in addition to principal and interest, monthly payments must include deposits for real estate taxes and property insurance premiums on the property. **Property insurance premiums** cover the cost of insuring the property against loss from fire or other damage. The owner must also pay for electricity, heating, maintenance, water, sewage, telephone service, and other expenses. Even though the figures in the third column of Exhibit 3.3 only approximate the amount of money available for principal and interest payments, they can serve as a guide to the size of mortgage a given income level can support.

property insurance premiums: Periodic payments to insure property against loss from fire or other types of damage.

The mortgage payments in Exhibit 3.3 are based on a 30-year mortgage at 10, 12, 14, and 16 percent, assuming a 20 percent down payment. The figures in the percentage columns represent the mortgage amounts that each level of principal and interest payments can support. If you earn $24,000 per year, you have $500 a month available for principal and interest, which allows you to afford a mortgage of $56,946. Notice the dramatic effect of increases in the interest rate on the amount of mortgage a given monthly payment will buy. At 12 percent, a $500 monthly principal and interest payment will support a mortgage of $48,592; at 14 percent, the same payment will support $42,192; at 16 percent, it supports only $37,340. As the interest rate rises, the value of the house a given buyer can afford declines.

EXHIBIT 3.3

How Much Home Can You Afford?

ANNUAL INCOME	MONTHLY INCOME	INCOME AVAILABLE FOR PRINCIPAL AND INTEREST	MORTGAGE YOU CAN AFFORD				PRICE OF HOME YOU CAN AFFORD (80% mortgage)				DOWN PAYMENT REQUIRED (20% down payment)			
			10%	12%	14%	16%	10%	12%	14%	16%	10%	12%	14%	16%
$18,000	$1,500	$ 375	$ 42,711	$ 36,444	$ 31,644	$ 28,005	$ 53,388	$ 45,555	$ 39,555	$ 35,007	$10,677	$ 9,111	$ 7,911	$ 7,002
24,000	2,000	500	56,948	48,592	42,192	37,340	71,184	60,740	52,740	46,676	14,236	12,148	10,548	9,336
30,000	2,500	625	71,825	60,740	52,740	46,675	88,980	75,925	65,925	58,345	17,795	15,185	13,185	11,670
36,000	3,000	750	85,422	72,888	63,288	56,010	106,776	91,110	75,110	70,014	21,354	18,222	15,822	14,004
42,000	3,500	875	99,659	85,036	73,826	65,346	124,572	106,295	92,296	81,683	24,913	21,259	18,459	16,338
48,000	4,000	1,000	113,896	97,184	81,384	74,681	142,368	121,480	105,480	93,352	28,472	24,296	21,096	18,672
54,000	4,500	1,125	128,133	109,332	94,932	81,016	160,164	136,665	118,666	105,021	32,031	27,333	23,733	21,006
60,000	5,000	1,250	142,370	121,480	105,480	93,351	177,960	151,850	131,850	116,690	35,590	30,370	26,370	23,340
66,000	5,500	1,375	156,607	133,628	116,028	102,686	195,756	167,035	145,035	128,359	39,149	33,407	29,007	25,674
72,000	6,000	1,500	170,844	145,776	136,576	112,021	213,552	182,220	158,220	140,028	42,708	36,444	31,644	28,007
78,000	6,500	1,625	185,081	157,924	137,124	121,356	231,351	197,405	171,405	151,697	46,270	39,481	34,281	30,341
84,000	7,000	1,750	199,318	170,072	147,672	130,691	249,147	212,590	184,590	163,366	49,829	42,518	36,918	32,675

Since the 30-year mortgage represents 80 percent of the value of the home, with the other 20 percent coming from the down payment, the next question is how much home a given mortgage amount will buy. With $500 a month available for principal and interest payments, Exhibit 3.3 shows that a buyer who makes a 20 percent down payment can afford a house valued at $71,184 when interest rates are at 10 percent. The same buyer could afford a $60,740 house when rates were at 12 percent, a $52,740 house at 14 percent, and only a $46,676 house at 16 percent. Again, a higher mortgage interest rate reduces the value of the house you can afford.

The data in Exhibit 3.3 clearly demonstrate the impact of high interest rates on buyers' ability to finance and buy homes. This problem has become enormous during periods of dramatic increases in interest rates. In the early 1980s mortgage interest rates increased from 12 percent to approximately 16 percent, a 33-percent increase in the cost of mortgage money. An increase of this size dramatically reduces how much house a buyer can afford at a given income level. Conversely, in the early 1990s, mortgage interest rates declined to below 8 percent, increasing the amount of mortgage buyers could carry at a given income level.

While increasing interest rates make mortgages much more expensive, higher rates also put downward pressure on housing prices. Because buyers can afford less, prices tend to decline. On the other hand, declining interest rates tend to support increasing housing prices.

The discussion of how much a given buyer can afford suggests that someone who wanted to buy a more expensive house would have to make a larger down payment, find a mortgage at a lower interest rate, or increase his or her income. If your income seems likely to increase, as is common, you should try to stretch to reach a more expensive house that will be appropriate for later, higher income levels. This process of **growing into a house** saves the trade-up time needed to buy a small house first and then move up to a larger one, and it saves the effort and expense of moving. Whatever your inclination, though, at a reasonable income level, you may well be able to afford to buy some kind of house or condominium. You will almost always benefit from buying something you can afford and selling later, that is, moving up, than simply saving money for the house of your dreams. By jumping into home ownership, you will learn to adapt your lifestyle and your budget to this investment while you build up home equity. This addition to your net worth will ultimately allow you to afford that dream house.

growing into a house: Buying a more expensive house than you really can afford at the time of purchase with the expectation of "growing into" the mortgage as your income increases over time.

If you wait until you save the down payment on an expensive home, you may never catch up to the price increases on it. For example, it may take you 5 years to save $20,000 for the down payment on a $100,000 house, but at the end of that time the same house may well be selling for $125,000. You will then need a $105,000 mortgage on the home that sold for only $100,000 when you first started saving for the down payment! One way to avoid this inflation trap is to find a way to accumulate a down payment money as quickly as possible.

Sources of Down Payment Money

The difficulty of obtaining money for a down payment is always a problem, but it is especially critical when housing prices are rising rapidly. Even though housing price increases slowed in the 1990s, prices are still high relative to incomes, requiring high down payments. Every future home owner must face this very real, very frustrating problem. There is just no easy solution.

Once they own homes, many buyers are pleasantly surprised by increases in their equity and net worth due to increases in housing prices. By selling, they convert their equity to down payment money for a new house, and go on building net worth in a new location. Most prospective home owners who are trying to save money to buy a first house secure money for the down payments through diligent saving and planning. Besides savings, down payment funds may come from gifts, loans, second trusts, or what some call "sweat equity."

Savings Most home buyers obtain down payment money through regular savings. This can be difficult for young people who have not been working long; it is difficult to save $14,000 to $15,000 at any income level, but worse if you earn a low salary in an entry-level job. A prospective home buyer who saves 10 percent of a $24,000 annual gross salary will take over 5 years to save $14,000 for a down payment. A two-income household can accelerate this savings process, but regardless of income level, it is important to plan ahead and save systematically for home ownership and other goals.

Gifts Gifts represent another source of down payment cash. Many young people buy their first houses using money given by their parents to make the down payment. Under the Internal Revenue Code, each parent may give up to $10,000 a year to each child without paying a gift tax. Such a gift could benefit the parents, as well, by reducing their estate for tax purposes.

second trust (second mortgage): A loan against the equity in a property that is second in seniority to the primary mortgage (first mortgage); in the event of foreclosure, the first mortgage must be paid off before the second mortgage is paid.

Second Trusts The seller of a house, whether an individual or a builder, may provide another source of down payment funds through a second trust. A **second trust** (also called a **second mortgage**) is a loan against the value of a house that is second in seniority to the primary mortgage; it is paid off over a shorter period of time than the mortgage. Being second in seniority means that if the owner fails to make the payments and the mortgage holders foreclose on the property and sell it to repay their mortgages, the first mortgage must be paid off completely before the second mortgage holder receives any funds.

A young couple who had only $10,000 available for a down payment would have a 10 percent down payment on a $100,000 house instead of the required 20 percent. To sell the house, the owner might accept a second trust loan for the remaining $10,000 with the buyers' equity in the house as collateral for this loan. The buyers would then pay off the loan, normally in 3 to

7 years. A second trust may give a buyer an opportunity to own a house, paying down the mortgage and the second trust to the seller as salaries increase over time. Of course, not every seller is willing to accept a loan in place of down payment money.

Sweat Equity Sweat equity is another way to earn down payment money. In one form of sweat equity, the builder of the house allows the buyer to do some work to complete the house. This adds to the value of the house without increasing the builder's costs, and it builds the buyer's equity or ownership. For example, a builder may include an allowance of $5,000 for painting and landscaping labor in the price of the house. The buyer who does the painting and landscaping earns the $5,000; it becomes part of the equity in the house as well as substituting for down payment cash.

You can also earn sweat equity on an existing house that needs a substantial amount of work. The mortgage lender may be willing to make a loan on the finished value of the improved house rather than on its value before renovation. You find a house in need of substantial repair, move in, and make improvements that increase its value. The financial institution making the loan recognizes this increase in value as part of your equity, reducing the down payment money you need to obtain the loan.

These are several ways in which you can come up with down payment money and get over this major hurdle for young people buying a first house. Once you have purchased your first home, you can sell it to convert your equity to down payment money for your next home. Coming up with the initial down payment is the all-important first step. If you consider each of the many ways to do this, you can probably obtain a down payment if you really want to buy a house or condominium.

Sources of Real Estate Mortgages

Buying a house requires familiarity with the individuals and businesses that make mortgage loans. A list of sources of mortgage loans would include savings and loan associations, commercial banks, mutual savings banks, mortgage banks, private individuals, and home sellers. In other words, the people with whom you do business as a savings depositor can probably provide a loan to buy a home.

It is a good idea to check as many sources as possible when shopping for a mortgage loan. Depending on the area of the country and the competitiveness of the local lending market, mortgage interest rates may vary widely among various lending institutions. Since a mortgage loan represents a very long-term commitment—usually 20 or 30 years—even a small difference in interest rates can add up to a large dollar amount over the life of the loan.

Savings and Loan Associations

Savings and loan associations are one of the most important sources of mortgage funds in the United States, accounting for as much as one-third of the total mortgage debt outstanding. As the largest source of conventional first mortgages on one- to four-family houses, S&Ls tend to concentrate their loans in the communities where they are located, and they generally have the most liberal lending policies. A local savings and loan is a good first stop when shopping for a first or second mortgage.

Commercial Banks

Traditionally, commercial banks have not been a major source of mortgage loans; their primary role has been to make relatively short-term loans, and they have been able to extend only a limited amount of mortgage credit. However, in recent years, commercial banks have become a more important source of mortgage money. Commercial banks are also a source of construction money for people building houses themselves, or for members of the building industry. Banks provide short-term loans to initially construct a building, then some other source supplies the long-term mortgage money to pay off the bank construction loan.

Mutual Savings Banks

As mentioned in Chapter 2, mutual savings banks are most common in New England and the mid-Atlantic region. They emphasize savings and making mortgage loans, and they are not limited to one particular region, but they can make loans outside the states in which they are headquartered. Mutual savings banks' mortgage interest rates may be lower than those of savings and loan associations. They depend mainly on individual savings as sources of mortgage money.

Mortgage Banks

Mortgage bankers obtain capital from equity investors and borrowing, which they in turn lend to people who wish to finance homes, businesses, shopping centers, and other real estate ventures. Mortgage bankers really serve as intermediaries between persons needing loans and investors needing returns on their investment capital. Mortgage bankers might work as loan correspondents to life insurance companies, mutual savings banks, or pension funds. Normally they originate loans and then service them for lenders or owners. They may be good sources of mortgage money in a particular market.

Private Individuals

Private individuals who are selling property sometimes finance the sale by making a mortgage loan to a potential buyer. A seller who has no immediate need for the proceeds from the sale of a house may be willing to make a mortgage loan to the purchaser. In essence, the purchaser gives the owner what is called a **purchase money mortgage.** This is a private financing arrangement in which the buyer makes principal and interest payments to the seller just as he or she would to any lending institution. The seller holds a first mortgage on the property, which reverts back to the seller if the buyer defaults. This is not a regular, dependable source of funds, but owners sometimes take back mortgages on their properties when they want to sell at a time when mortgage money is scarce.

purchase money mortgage: A private financing arrangement that allows buyers to pay principal and interest to sellers just as they would to financial institutions.

In addition, a buyer may be able to assume the seller's existing mortgage. As long as the buyer meets credit requirements, the seller also may take a second trust for part of the down payment, allowing a buyer to come up with only 10 percent or even less as a down payment. The buyer assumes the old mortgage, often along with the responsibility for paying off a second trust. Sometimes these types of financing arrangements can be made without any down payment, depending upon the amount of the seller's equity.

Real Estate Mortgage Financing

Most people tend to think of mortgage payments as fixed monthly amounts that pay off the principal over time, but this wasn't always so. U.S. mortgage holders during the 1920s and 1930s did not reduce the amounts of their mortgage loans; they simply paid interest on their mortgage amounts. When their debts matured, they were required to pay off the principal in a lump sum or borrow the same amount again. This meant that many people never repaid their mortgage debts. When these mortgage loans matured and the borrowers didn't have the money, they lost their homes, especially when unscrupulous lenders, primarily individuals, would not allow them to refinance. To stop lenders from seizing people's homes to satisfy maturing mortgage obligations, the Federal Housing Administration established a direct loan reduction schedule that specified mortgage payments that included repayment of both principal and interest until the mortgage debt was satisfied. The idea of fixed payments has been with us since the beginning of this FHA program in the United States.

A search for home financing reveals many different types of mortgages available in the marketplace. A borrower should carefully compare the various mortgage lenders and the different types of loans they make. This section will review the most common types of mortgage loans available to individuals. Beginning with conventional financing, it will review VA and FHA financing, several variable-rate mortgage options, various creative financing techniques, and the use of home equity credit lines after home purchases. It will also discuss how and why the availability of mortgage money may vary from time to time.

Conventional Mortgages

conventional mortgage: A traditional mortgage made by a financial institution, which assumes the risk of loss if the buyer fails to meet the obligations of the loan.

A **conventional mortgage** is the traditional mortgage made by most financial institutions. The financial institution assumes the risk of loss should the homeowner fail to make payments on the mortgage. To protect its interests, the lender usually requires a 20 percent down payment. As discussed earlier in this chapter, the property then acts as collateral for the loan. Most conventional loans are made for terms of 15, 20, or 30 years, with 30-year financing the most popular option.

private mortgage insurance: Insurance that protects the lender from loss due to default by the borrower; if the lender forecloses on the property, but does not recover enough money to pay off the loan, the insurance policy pays the difference.

PITI: The total of a monthly mortgage payment composed of principal, interest, real estate taxes, and insurance.

escrow account: An account in which monthly payments for taxes and insurance are accumulated, to be paid as the costs fall due.

A conventional lender may require a down payment less than 20 percent, but in almost every such case, the lender will require the borrower to pay an extra fee to cover **private mortgage insurance,** which insures the lender against default by the borrower. If the lender has to foreclose on the property and the foreclosure sale does not generate enough money to repay all of the loan balance, the mortgage insurance company then pays the lender the missing amount.

The monthly payment on a mortgage has four major components: principal, interest, taxes, and insurance (summed up in the acronym **PITI**). In addition to collecting payments on principal and interest, nearly all lenders also collect a monthly sum sufficient to pay annual real estate taxes and property insurance on the house. The lender accumulates these monthly deposits by the borrower in an **escrow account,** from which it draws funds to make annual insurance and real estate tax payments on the house as they fall due. The escrow system assures the lender that these payments will be made on time so its interest in the property will be protected against damage or seizure for unpaid taxes. The lender makes an accounting for the escrow account to the borrower each year. On a $120,000 house with a $100,000 mortgage, the monthly escrow payments for taxes and insurance may amount to $200 a month or more. This is a major commitment that should be taken into account when taking out a mortgage.

Exhibit 3.4 shows the principal and interest payments on a $100,000 mortgage. The payment amounts depend on the interest rate and the number of years over which the mortgage is paid, or its term. A lower rate and a longer term make for lower monthly payments. A 30-year loan for $100,000 at 8 percent, for example, would require monthly principal and interest payments of $734. The same 30-year loan at 12 percent would require monthly payments of $1,029.

Reducing the repayment term increases the monthly payment, but, because the loan is paid off more rapidly, the borrower pays less interest and the sum of the total payments is lower. Look, for example, at the 10 percent column in Exhibit 3.4. A 10-year loan would cost $1,322 per month, while a 30-year loan would cost $876 per month. However, the 10-year loan requires

EXHIBIT 3.4

Monthly Payments on a $100,000 Mortgage

	INTEREST RATE				
YEARS	8%	9%	10%	11%	12%
10	$1,207	$1,267	$1,322	$1,378	$1,435
20	836	900	965	1,032	1,101
30	734	805	876	952	1,029

only 120 payments (10 years × 12 months) while the 30-year loan requires 360 payments (30 years × 12 months). The 120 payments of $1,322 on the 10-year loan total $158,640; the 360 payments of $876 on the 30-year loan total $315,360—a difference of $156,720! Most new home buyers, however, take out 30-year loans because they cannot afford the higher payments on 10-year loans. If you can afford the higher payments, they make good, long-term sense.

Variable-Rate Mortgages (VRMs)

High real estate prices and interest rates on mortgage loans have driven principal and interest payments out of the reach of many young families. Within the last 10 years lenders have developed new kinds of mortgages to solve this problem. The new type of loan allows the buyer to pay less in the early stages of the mortgage and more later when a rising income makes higher payments affordable.

Another change has come about because some lenders have lost substantial sums of money to increases in interest rates on mortgages. Borrowers favor mortgages with fixed interest rates because their payments increase only when taxes or insurance fees rise. As interest rates continue to rise, however, borrowers are reluctant to commit to long-term loans at high fixed rates. They don't want to lock themselves into 30-year mortgages at interest rates in excess of those likely to prevail in a few years. To answer this concern, mortgage lenders have developed **variable-rate mortgages (VRMs)** with interest rates that fluctuate with changes in market interest rates. The rate on a VRM, and therefore the mortgage payment, changes automatically to follow market interest rates. If long-term interest rates rise, the VRM payments rise, and payments fall if rates decline. It makes sense for borrowers to pay more when interest rates rise and less when they fall.

variable-rate mortgage (VRM) or adjustable-rate mortgage (ARM): A mortgage with an interest rate, and, therefore, a monthly payment, that fluctuates with changes in market interest rates.

Variable-rate mortgages are often marketed under the name **adjustable-rate mortgages (ARMs).** An ARM is just a type of VRM, as is the **graduated-**

graduated-payment mortgage (GPM): A mortgage with an interest rate, and therefore a monthly payment, that increases over time to a predetermined fixed rate.

payment mortgage (GPM). A GPM is very similar to an ARM except that its interest rate increases over time to some predetermined fixed rate. For example, a 30-year GPM might start with an interest rate of 7.0 percent, then increase in five annual steps to a fixed rate of 11.5 percent.

The VRM has advantages and disadvantages. Its primary advantage is its lower initial interest rate as compared to a fixed-rate loan, which allows people to borrow more money when interest rates are high. If rates stay high, the initial interest rate will increase. When rates decline, principal and interest costs for mortgage repayment also decline. Without VRMs, people who buy houses at a time of high interest rates would want to use short-term financing, arranging permanent mortgages when rates come down to reasonable levels.

The primary disadvantage of the VRM is the possibility that the interest rate and monthly payments will increase with market interest rates in the future. To protect borrowers from this risk, most VRMs specify maximum interest rates that can be charged in the future. A VRM with an initial rate of 8 percent, for example, might specify a maximum rate of 13 percent regardless of how high rates may rise in the future. Since nearly all VRMs offer initial interest rates that are lower than the interest rates on fixed-term loans, their interest rates are virtually certain to increase in the first few years of their terms. Someone who finances a house purchase with a VRM should plan to meet these increasing payments in the future.

It may seem logical to start with a low rate and increase it over time since most people's incomes increase over time. Thus, the borrower's income should probably keep pace with the increasing mortgage payments. This brings a benefit in qualifying for a loan since the lending institution qualifies a buyer for a loan amount by comparing the monthly payment on the mortgage amount to the borrower's monthly income. Most lenders will allow payments in the neighborhood of 27 to 29 percent of gross monthly income. Since the payments on a VRM are lower than those on a fixed-rate mortgage in the early years, the borrower can qualify for a higher loan amount on a VRM than on a fixed-rate mortgage.

The annual interest rates on most VRMs are linked to some widely published index, such as the Treasury bill or Treasury bond rate. A VRM with a rate of "Treasury bill plus 3 points" would charge interest at a rate 3 percent above the Treasury bill rate. In early 1993 the Treasury bill interest rate was about 3.4 percent. The rate on the example VRM would then be 6.4 percent. The interest rate in the first year of the loan would probably have been less than 6.0 percent, rising over four or five years to follow the rate to which it is tied.

VA and FHA Mortgages

Veterans can take advantage of a special government program to help finance house purchases: Department of Veterans Affairs (DVA) financing, known as a VA loan. Such a loan charges an interest rate somewhat below the market rate on conventional loans. Congress created VA financing after World War II as a benefit to veterans, to provide inexpensive money for house purchases at a time when such money was not available. The DVA does not make loans itself; it partially guarantees loans made by lending insituations. The VA guarantee of repayment of a portion of the loan lends it additional security. The current maximum guarantee is 60 percent of the outstanding loan balance up to a maximum of $25,000; it has been raised periodically from the original maximum guarantee following World War II of $4,000 in response to inflation.

The ultimate security for a VA loan lies in the value of the property that serves as collateral for the loan. The VA guarantee effectively provides extra collateral for the loan. Ordinarily VA mortgages cover 90 to 95 percent of the value of the property, particularly on lower-priced properties. The maximum VA-guaranteed loan amount currently available is $135,000. Historically, VA loans have been attractive, despite a large burden of administrative work involved in obtaining them. Sometimes money is not available for VA loans because the conventional mortgage rate is substantially higher than the rate established for VA loans. Lenders may not be willing to make VA loans if they cannot earn a rate of return comparable to what they earn on other mortgages.

The Federal Housing Administration administers a similar home financing program that allows nonveterans to borrow money at attractive rates from specified lenders that operate under conditions established by the FHA. Essentially, the FHA program combines the first and second mortgage, and it adds a system of mortgage insurance. In this way FHA supplies money to repay the lender in case a buyer defaults on an FHA loan.

Borrowers pay the cost of the FHA loan program. The FHA charges them an insurance premium of 0.5 percent of the unpaid loan balance to pay expenses and cover possible losses. Under an FHA contract you can take out a mortgage loan from any of the types of lending institutions previously discussed. Your mortgage will require a smaller down payment and allow repayment over a longer term at a lower interest rate than a conventional mortgage would allow. However, an FHA loan requires more red tape than a conventional loan. Also, money may not be readily available under FHA loans because the interest limit on FHA loans, like that on VA loans, often is below the market rate of interest charged for conventional loans.

Creative Financing

creative financing: Techniques that allow a buyer to purchase a property with little or no money down.

Much of our discussion of obtaining down payment money reflects **creative financing** techniques. Real estate professionals use this term to describe techniques to purchase real estate with little or no money down. For an example of creative financing, a buyer might purchase a $120,000 home with a $95,000 first mortgage entirely with borrowed money. First, the buyer assumes the $95,000 9 percent, 30-year mortgage, taking responsibility for payments of $765 per month. To come up with the additional $25,000, a creative buyer might borrow the required 10-percent down payment ($12,000) against a commercial bank line of credit requiring payments of $260 per month, with interest at the going rate. The seller would then take back a $13,000 second trust note requiring a $130 monthly payment of interest only for 5 years at 12 percent, with the principal repayment of $13,000 due at the end of the 5 years. (The repayment of the principal in a lump sum at the end of the loan term is called a **balloon payment.**) The buyer now owns the house, having spent none of his or her own money. He or she simply needs the income to support a $120,000 debt. The buyer also needs to plan to accumulate the $13,000 balloon payment on the second trust. This is the rub in creative financing—you can get so creative that you go broke!

balloon payment: A loan arrangement that requires minimal payments approximately equal to the monthly interest due, with all of the principal due in one lump sum (the balloon) at the end of the loan term.

Real estate buyers use may different creative financing techniques. Exhibit 3.5 summarizes 15 of them. Creative financing can be particularly helpful during periods of high interest rates and tight money.

Home Equity Loans

Once you own a home, your equity will grow over time as the value of the home increases and you pay your mortgage down. This equity can work for you as collateral for a **home equity loan** if you need to borrow money for some purpose. A home equity loan has a major advantage compared to other types of consumer loans because you normally can deduct its interest payments from your taxable income (although there are limits on the total amount of home equity interest you can deduct). Congress eliminated the deduction for interest on other types of consumer loans as of 1990. In addition to its tax advantages, a home equity loan generally offers a lower rate of interest than other types of consumer debt because the home equity loan is secured by a second mortgage against your home, which is strong collateral.

home equity loan: A credit line secured by the equity in the borrower's home.

Depending on your equity position, you may be able to borrow more on a home equity credit line than on other forms of credit. Lenders typically grant credit lines worth up to 80 percent of an owner's equity, and some institutions will lend as much as 90 or 95 percent of equity. Home equity credit lines have one important risk to consider, though. Since the loan is secured by a second mortgage note, if you fail to make the payments, the lender can foreclose on your home to satisfy the loan. Many consumers use home equity loans to finance major expenses such as automobile purchases or college costs. The home equity line of credit supplies such needs conveniently and at a lower after-tax interest cost.

The Hunt for Mortgage Money

A prospective buyer venturing into the marketplace to buy a house must search vigorously for the best source of financing. Professional real estate brokers can provide valuable guidance in this search, including up-to-date reports detailing who is making mortgage loans at what rates and in what

EXHIBIT 3.5

Summary of Creative Financing Techniques

TYPE	DESCRIPTION	CONSIDERATIONS
Fixed-rate mortgage	Fixed interest rate, usually long-term; equal monthly payments of principal and interest until debt is paid in full.	Offers stability and long-term tax advantages; limited availability. Interest rates may be higher than other types of financing. New fixed rates are rarely assumable.
Flexible-rate mortgage	Interest rate changes are based on a financial index, resulting in possible changes in monthly payments, loan term, and/or principal. Some plans have rate or payment caps.	Readily available. Starting interest rate is slightly below market, but payments can increase sharply and frequently if index increases. Payment caps prevent wide fluctuations in payments, but may cause negative amortization. Rate caps, while rare, limit amount total debt can expand.
Renegotiable-rate mortgage (rollover)	Interest rate and monthly payments are constant for several years; changes possible thereafter. Long-term mortgage.	Less frequent changes in interest rates offer some stability.
Balloon mortgage	Monthly payments based on fixed interest rate; usually short-term; payments may cover interest only, with principal due in full at term end.	Offers low monthly payments, but possibly no equity until loan is fully paid. When due, loan must be paid off or refinanced. Refinancing poses high risk if rates climb.
Graduated-payment mortgage	Lower monthly payments rise gradually (usually over 5 to 10 years), then level off for duration of term. With flexible interest rate, additional payment changes possible if index changes.	Easier to qualify for. Buyer's income must be able to keep pace with scheduled payment increases. With a flexible rate, payment increases beyond the graduated payments can result in additional negative amortization.
Shared-appreciation mortgage	Below-market interest rate and lower monthly payments in exchange for share of profits on a specified date or when property is sold; many variations.	If home appreciates greatly, total cost of loan jumps. If home fails to appreciate, projected increase in value may still be due, requiring refinancing at possibly higher rates.
Assumable mortgage	Buyer takes over seller's original, below-market rate mortgage.	Lowers monthly payments. May be prohibited by due-on-sale clause in original mortgage. Not permitted on most new fixed-rate mortgages.
Seller take-back	Seller provides all or part of financing with a first or second mortgage.	May offer a below-market interest rate; may have a balloon payment requiring full payment in a few years or refinancing at market rates, which could sharply increase debt.

Wraparound	Seller keeps original low-rate mortgage. Buyer makes payments to seller, who forwards portion to the lender holding original mortgage. Offers lower effective interest rate on total transaction.	Lender may call in old mortgage and require higher rate. If buyer defaults, seller must take legal action to collect debt.
Growing-equity mortgage (rapid-payoff mortgage)	Fixed interest rate, but monthly payments may vary according to agreed-upon schedule or index.	Permits rapid payoff of debt because payment increases reduce principal. Buyer's income must be able to keep up with payment increases.
Land contract	Seller retains original mortgage. No transfer of title until loan is fully paid. Equal monthly payments based on below-market interest rate with unpaid principal due at loan end.	May offer no equity until loan is paid. Buyer has little protection if conflict arises during loan.
Buy-down	Developer (or third party) provides an interest subsidy, which lowers monthly payments during the first few years of the loan. Can have fixed or flexible interest rate.	Offers a break from higher payments during early years. Enables buyer with lower income to qualify. With flexible-rate mortgage, payments may jump substantially at end of subsidy. Developer may increase selling price.
Rent with option	Renter pays "option fee" for right to purchase property at specified time and agreed-upon price. Rent may or may not be applied to sales price.	Enables renter to buy time to obtain down payment and decide whether to purchase. Locks in price during inflationary times. Failure to take option means loss of option fee and rental payments.
Reverse-annuity mortgage (equity conversion)	Borrower owns mortgage-free property and needs income. Lender makes monthly payments to borrower, using property as collateral.	Can provide homeowners with needed cash. At end of term, borrower must have money available to avoid selling property or refinancing.
Zero-rate and low-rate mortgage	Appears to be completely or almost interest free. Large down payment and one-time finance charge, then loan is repaid in fixed monthly payments over short term.	Permits quick ownership. May not lower total cost (because of possibly increased sales price). Doesn't offer long-term tax deductions.

SOURCE: *The Mortgage Money Guide*, Federal Trade Commission, Division of Credit Practices, 6th and Pennsylvania Avenue NW, Washington, D.C. 20580.

points: Mortgage interest paid in advance at the time of settlement; 1 point equals 1 percent of the face value of the mortgage.

maximum amounts, and whether or not they are charging points. **Points** are important to anyone going into the mortgage market because they add a given amount to the borrower's interest cost in the form of a lump sum paid at the time of settlement, that is, when the sale transaction is concluded. One point is simply 1 percent of the face value of the loan. If the lender charges 1 point, the borrower must pay a fee of 1 percent of the loan value ($10 per $1,000) to obtain the loan.

An example will clarify how points work. Assume that a lender is willing to make a mortgage loan at 9 percent with 2 points. If you borrow $90,000, you will have to pay $900 for each point, for a total of $1,800. That $1,800 represents an additional interest cost in the first year so it actually increases the rate of interest you pay. Lenders receive points to increase their interest income on loans in markets where money is tight and interest rates do not really reflect market rates.

In addition, a lender may charge points to avoid usury limits imposed by state governments while still earning market interest rates. If the government imposed a 12 percent interest rate ceiling while market mortgage rates were 13 percent, the lender would be unwilling to lend. Since the lender cannot charge the 13 percent market rate, it will make no loans, so the buyer cannot buy, the seller cannot sell. The lender can get around this difficulty by charging enough points to bring the rate up to 13 percent, at which point it becomes profitable to lend again, while the loan contract still lists the legal interest rate of 12 percent. Some states have insisted on maintaining a maximum limit on mortgage interest rates. In addition, some states have refused to allow any charges for points. When points are charged, they usually are deductible from taxable income as mortgage interest.

Finding an Affordable Home

Having saved your down payment money, assessed the size of mortgage you can afford, and located a good financing source, your next step is to find a house you can afford. A professional real estate broker can put you in touch with prospective sellers. As a basic guide, you should look for a house or condominium in the best location you can afford. A quality property in a good location is your best chance for making both a valuable investment and for living comfortably. Search for a house that is close to transportation and shopping and one that is energy-efficient. You also should consider the costs of getting to work and the costs of maintaining the house.

House Hunting Information

The search for a desirable house in a good location at the right price begins in the weekly real estate section of a local newspaper. Professional real estate brokers and individual sellers advertise in newspapers to list houses offered for sale and tell when the houses are open for viewing. Besides information about particular houses for sale, newspapers can give invaluable insight into life in the areas they cover.

A second source of information is a relationship with a professional real estate agent in your area. This person can explain the real estate market and give straightforward, inside information about the pros and cons of various areas, along with an objective idea of what a particular buyer can afford. The broker can then get the buyer started looking at houses that meet his or her needs.

The search for information, and ultimately for the best house to buy, takes time. Still, investing the time to read newspapers, tour neighborhoods, and ask questions will lead the buyer to a desirable property in a good area for living, working, and playing.

The Role of the Real Estate Agent

After extensive reading and contemplation, the buyer determines an affordable price range and a desirable area where this amount will buy a good house. The real estate agent can then lead him or her to suitable properties that are offered for sale. After learning as much as possible about them, the buyer settles on the one he or she wants to buy. An understanding of the relationships among the parties in the transaction can help simplify the sometimes complex process of completing the purchase.

The list of parties begins with the agent, whose job is to sell the house for the owner. The agent represents the owner and receives a commission only if he or she sells the house. Still, the agent will try to answer questions thoroughly and honestly since he or she wants the transaction to satisfy both buyer and seller. After all, today's home buyer is tomorrow's seller, and the agent also would like to earn a commission on future transactions.

To sell a house, the agent will try to explain in detail its qualities and strengths. When a home owner lists a property for sale with a brokerage firm, he or she fills out a **listing sheet** that provides all the information a buyer would want to know about the house including its asking price, operating expenses, school district, and similar details. The listing sheet for a single-family house amounts to an agreement between the owner and broker that the owner signs to authorize the agent to represent him or her. Most agents are associates of licensed real estate brokers. These associates are professionals engaged in the business of selling houses for home owners.

listing sheet: A list prepared by a real estate agent that lists information about a house offered for sale, such as the asking price, number of bedrooms, square feet of floor space, and school district in which it lies.

The Asking Price—Making an Offer

Among many other details, the listing agreement specifies the asking price for a house, whether or not a mortgage exists on the property, and the rate of interest on any mortgage. The agent has a responsibility to sell the house as soon as possible at a good price. The asking price normally is established based on the sale of recent comparable properties called "comps." The agent helps the owner establish this price to reflect the market values of similarly situated houses in the same market at the same time. Still, all prices are subject to negotiation, depending on competitive conditions in the market at the time, the availability of funds, and the urgency of the seller's desire to sell and the buyer's desire to buy.

The Sales Commission

commission: The fee the seller of a house pays to the real estate broker equal to some percentage of the sales price, commonly 5 or 6 percent.

The seller pays the agent or broker a fee, referred to as a **commission,** for selling a house. Commissions typically range from 5 to 6 percent of the selling price, depending upon the region. An agent who sells a $100,000 home earns a commission of $5,000 to $6,000; actually, this amount is divided among the selling broker, his or her associate (if any) who actually sells the house, and the listing broker and associate. In a typical real estate transaction, the listing broker receives 20 percent of the commission and the selling broker and associate divide the remaining 80 percent. Out of a $6,000 commission, normally $1,200 goes to the lister, and the selling broker and associate divide $4,800.

The Sales Contract

sales contract: The legal document that specifies the terms of sale of a property.

earnest money or good-faith money: A deposit the buyer offers with a sales contract.

An offer on a house must satisfy certain formal rules, including that it be in writing. The real estate agent helps the borrower complete a **sales contract** which the agent presents formally to the owner for acceptance or rejection. A deposit called **earnest money** or **good-faith money** must accompany the sales contract. When the seller accepts the sales contract, the earnest money is deposited in an escrow account, where it accrues interest until the date of settlement when it is credited toward the buyer's down payment.

Sales contract provisions vary, but most include some characteristic details. Suppose a buyer has $25,000 in savings and earns $36,000 a year; this person finds a desirable house with an asking price of $105,000. The buyer's income would support a 10 percent mortgage of $85,422 according to Exhibit 3.3. A 20 percent down payment on the $105,000 house would total $21,000, which the buyer can afford, leaving a mortgage of $84,400. The numbers look good for the purchase.

After reexamining the house to be sure it suits him or her, the buyer asks the agent if the $105,000 asking price is firm. Generally, sellers list their houses at prices that are higher than the final prices they are willing to accept. Most buyers expect to negotiate final selling prices and it is normally a good idea to make an initial offer for less than the asking price if the market is not too competitive. If the owner does not accept this offer, the buyer can offer more in subsequent negotiations. The buyer in the example offers $100,000 for the house, putting down earnest money with the intention of supplying the rest of the money at the settlement. **Settlement** is the formal resolution of the real estate transaction during which ownership of real estate passes from seller to buyer.

settlement: The legal process by which ownership of real estate passes from seller to buyer.

To continue the example, suppose the seller accepts an offer of $100,000. The sales contract specifies the property changing hands and the total sales price upon which the parties have agreed. It states the amount and terms of the earnest money deposit and the down payment the buyer will pay at settlement, which together total $20,000 (20 percent of the purchase price). The contract specifies that the buyer will obtain a first trust mortgage at a certain interest rate to finance the remaining $80,000, and it states how much the buyer will pay monthly to retire the debt. Ordinarily, if the buyer has already arranged financing and knows the exact interest rate the mortgage lender will charge, the contract will specify this rate. In a rapidly changing mortgage market it might be prudent to state in the contract the intention of arranging the best possible financing within a given period of time. Usually an addendum to the contract affirms that the entire contract is subject to the availability of mortgage money at an interest rate not to exceed a certain maximum amount. This nullifies a contract if the buyer cannot obtain proper financing, after which the real estate agent must return the earnest money deposit and the transaction is not completed.

The part of the contract concerned with financing describes a traditional first trust mortgage. If a second trust mortgage will supply part of the purchase price, assuming this is agreeable to the first mortgage lender, the contract will describe the second mortgage, as well. If the buyer will assume the seller's existing mortgage, or if the seller is accepting a second trust, the contract specifies these conditions.

Next the contract describes the type of first mortgage loan to be placed against the house, calling for a conventional, FHA, or VA loan. The contract also notes any settlement fees that will be due and which party is obligated to pay them.

The sales contract specifies the title the buyer will receive to the property and the name of the buyer to whom this title will be conveyed. This is followed by a settlement date, which is usually determined by the seller, but may be decided by negotiation between buyer and seller. Ordinarily, an interval of 45 days between signing the contract and settlement is adequate, provided the purchaser can obtain the necessary financing. As a rule, the seller gives the purchaser ample opportunity to make suitable financial arrangements to raise the money to buy the house.

A specific sales contract may contain other provisions dealing with special conditions or details, usually in addenda. A buyer is well-advised to include an addendum making the contract subject to inspections for insect damage, structural integrity, and the condition of mechanical systems. Such a provision nullifies the contract if any part of the house, including the heating and plumbing systems, the sewage or septic system, the foundation, or the structural parts are defective. This addendum assures the buyer that the house is in good working order, preventing problems when, as has happened all too often, a buyer pays the purchase price and moves in, only to be stuck two weeks later with a bill for expensive repairs.

Obtaining a Mortgage

Getting the seller's signature on a sales contract that states the buyer's terms may take a day or two. The buyer then applies to a financial institution for a loan, which requires both a copy of the sales contract and a credit information sheet.

The real estate agent generally asks the buyer to fill out a credit information sheet before submitting an offer to the seller. This is not a loan application, but simply summarizes the buyer's finances, giving the real estate associate some idea of his or her creditworthiness. Among the details requested on a credit information sheet are the borrower's name, age, address, with an indication of how long he or she has lived at that address, dependents, employer, base salary plus any bonuses and other income. If the buyer's spouse works, the sheet will ask for his or her employer and salary and other income. On the sheet, the buyer should also list debts and obligations including present rent (or another mortgage along with any equity in that property), installment payments on automobile loans or other consumer loans, and any child support or alimony payments as well as payments resulting from lawsuits. References and brief balance sheets also are required.

Complete and accurate information on the credit information sheet gives the agent some idea of the buyer's ability to live up to the terms of the contract. Failing to provide this information may cause the seller to reject the contract for credit reasons before the bank ever becomes involved.

To obtain mortgage financing, the buyer fills out a mortgage application that asks for much the same information as the agent's credit information sheet. The lender is especially interested in the monthly income the buyer will have available to pay principal, interest, taxes, and insurance (PITI) on the property. The mortgage lender will also want a complete history of the buyer's financial and work experience.

This suggests a piece of advice. Before trying to buy a house, one should reduce payments on automobile loans, charge accounts, and other consumer loans to a minimum. This leaves the maximum possible income to satisfy a mortgage commitment. A higher income after subtracting payment obligations increases the amount the lender will lend.

After receiving the loan application and all its supporting documents, the lender will send an appraiser to examine the property. The appraiser's report tells the lender that the property offered as collateral for the loan is worth more than the amount of the loan, which means that the lender can recover its loan balance by selling the property should the borrower default. Once the lending institution approves the loan, it sends a loan commitment to the buyer to allow the purchase to be completed; then the real estate agent, in consultation with the buyer and seller, will establish a settlement date. After the final inspection and formality of settlement, the buyer becomes a home owner.

Settlement Costs

Congress strengthened settlement procedures when it passed the Real Estate Settlement Procedures Act of 1974 (RESPA), which was amended in 1975. This act established a procedure for settling, or closing, transactions on one- to four-family residential properties with the aim of providing all consumers with more information about settlement fees in a more timely fashion. **Settlement fees** include such costs as transfer taxes, document preparation fees, title examination and insurance, real estate taxes, and other costs. Settlement fees may run as high as 3 to 4 percent of the cost of the property. RESPA requires that buyers be notified about all of these settlement costs in detail.

settlement fees: The costs imposed for settling a real estate transaction, including attorney's fees, transfer taxes, document preparation fees, a title insurance premium, and other costs.

In addition, the federal Truth in Lending Act requires that the lender supply at closing a statement of the total interest to be paid on the loan over its term. For example, a \$100,000 loan at 10 percent for 30 years requires 360 monthly payments of \$877.50. The borrower will pay out a total of \$315,900, of which \$100,000 goes to repay the principal and \$215,900 pays for interest. Some unsuspecting buyers may panic when they see how much interest they actually pay, but they should remember a few things: (1) they will have jobs during this time; (2) as big as the sum of interest seems, they will be able to make their monthly payments; (3) they will be able to deduct the interest from taxable income, reducing tax payments; and (4) the value of the property will probably increase, and they will get the money back later when they sell. This should calm some of the panic over the commitment the buyer makes at settlement time.

The three main components of settlement fees are real estates taxes, title insurance premiums, and miscellaneous transfer costs. If the lender charges points, the borrower must also pay this total at closing. The details vary, but the main idea is that a home buyer must be prepared to pay the costs of settlement and points in addition to the down payment, though they are sometimes hidden in the negotiations to buy a house. On a \$100,000 home purchase, settlement costs plus points may range from \$3,000 to \$5,000 or even higher.

Don't Lose Your Home!

Some people purchase homes, but suddenly find that they cannot keep up with payments on the principal and interest. Perhaps they become ill and unable to work or unemployed or have large, unexpected expenses. What are the options in this situation? A home owner who cannot pay a mortgage should open up an honest dialogue with the lender to explain the cause of the trouble, indicate all the resources available to pay the loan, and work out some way to repay the debt. This person should make every effort to demonstrate that he or she intends to fulfill the obligation.

One valuable solution is available for an FHA or conventional mortgage holder. The lender may be willing to forego payments temporarily until the borrower can overcome the difficulties that prevent prompt payment. The term of the mortgage would be extended over a longer period to accommodate the period of missed payments, but eventually the borrower can retire the debt.

Some may be tempted to borrow more money to make up missed mortgage payments. This would only increase their indebtedness and make the situation more difficult in the long run. A borrower should not hire an outsider for representation, but deal directly with the lender's staff. More detailed advice is available in a federal government pamphlet, "Having Problems Paying Your Mortgage?" available from Publications Distribution, Room B258, Department of Housing and Urban Development, Washington, D.C. 20140. Any HUD field office can provide this information, as well.

SUMMARY

This chapter has examined several advantages of owning a home: (1) Its increasing value acts as a hedge against inflation; (2) the deductibility of interest and real estate tax payments reduces income tax payments; (3) the sizes of most mortgage payments remain fixed while other costs go up; and, (4) home ownership is a form of forced savings that adds more to net worth than do most other investments.

The house a particular buyer can afford depends on the amount of income he or she can devote to home ownership, the level of interest rates, and the total of his or her other financial obligations. Mortgage lenders have income-based formulas for calculating the largest mortgage a buyer can afford. Most lenders will allow maximum monthly payments (including principal, interest, taxes, and insurance) of 27 to 29 percent of gross income. Higher down payments increase the value of the house a buyer can afford, as do lower interest rates. Interest rates around 12 percent will reduce the value of the house a buyer can afford compared to interest rates around 8 or 10 percent.

One of the biggest obstacles to buying a house is finding down payment money. It can come through savings, gifts, second trusts, and through the buyer's labor in a sweat equity deal. In some cases, deals can be arranged with little or no money for down payments in an arrangement referred to as creative financing. In addition to the down payment, the buyer must pay settlement fees in cash when the home purchase transaction is closed.

A second major obstacle concerns mortgage money. Mortgage loans generally come from savings and loan institutions, commercial banks, or mortgage banks. A borrower can take a creative view of financing a home, but complete knowledge about the implications of financing techniques is critical. In addition to conventional mortgages, some buyers may qualify for VA and FHA mortgages and variable-rate mortgages. Variable-rate mortgages offer lower interest rates and lower monthly payments in their early years than normal, fixed-rate loans.

A real estate agent can help a serious buyer locate a suitable and affordable home. Remember, however, that although the agent strives to meet the needs of both buyer and seller, the agent is legally the seller's representative. The agent earns a commission, paid by the seller, only when the buyer purchases the house.

The major expense of home ownership is the monthly payment for PITI, or principal, interest, taxes, and insurance. Most of this monthly payment will cover interest and property taxes in the early years of the loan; these costs are deductible from taxable income, making the payments less expensive than they first appear by reducing tax payments. The home owner must also pay maintenance and operating costs.

Over the years, the value of a home will generally increase to exceed the amount of money invested in it. Thus, home ownership increases an owner's net worth over time. Even if prices do not rise, equity increases as the mortgage is paid down.

INVESTMENT MANAGEMENT CONCEPTS

1. Unless you plan to live in a location for a fairly short period of time, you are almost always better off owning a home rather than renting.

2. Home ownership helps you build your net worth since the value of a home increases with inflation and as the owner pays down the mortgage.

3. The tax deduction allowed for home mortgage interest and real estate taxes is the single most important tax break for most American taxpayers.

4. Home ownership offers more stable and predictable housing costs than long-term renting.

5. It is a good idea to buy as much home as you can afford.

6. Consider creative financing alternatives if conventional financing is not available.

7. Be very cautious of variable-rate financing and make certain that any variable-rate mortgage imposes a cap that limits the interest rate over the life of the loan.

8. It generally is not necessary to offer full price for a house; most sellers set their asking prices above the minimum they will accept to leave room to negotiate the final price.

9. A home owner who has trouble meeting mortgage payments should communicate directly with the lender as soon as possible to work out a solution. It is always better to contact the lender before missing a payment rather than after.

REVIEW QUESTIONS

1. What are the major advantages of home ownership?
2. Why is home ownership an important cornerstone investment?
3. How can a home function as an inflation hedge?
4. What determines the amount of money you can afford to spend for a house?
5. Where can you obtain the down payment to buy a house?
6. Where can you obtain mortgage money?
7. Explain the special features of a VA or FHA mortgage.
8. Do VA or FHA loans have any disadvantages?
9. Explain how you might find out about houses that are available for sale.
10. Should you always offer the asking price in writing a sales contract for a house?
11. Explain the major features of a sales contract for a house.
12. What costs must be paid at settlement?
13. What is RESPA and how does it help the purchaser of a house?
14. Explain a home's operating costs.
15. If you get into financial trouble, what should you do to avoid losing your home?

SELF-CORRECTING PROBLEMS

1. Jane and Mack, both 29 years old, are a married couple with two children. They want to buy a house to meet their family needs. Both parents work full time, earning a combined annual income of $52,000. They pay $235 per month on an automobile loan. In addition, they have total monthly charge account payments of $75.

Jane and Mack have located a house selling for $110,000. The annual real estate taxes amount to 1.4 percent of its value, and operating costs come to about $1,800 per year. Jane and Mack have accumulated $22,000 for a down payment.

a. What down payment will Jane and Mack need for this house, assuming a 30-year conventional mortgage at 10 percent interest with a 20 percent down payment?

b. If Jane and Mack cannot cover the full down payment and settlement fees required with their $22,000, where can they obtain the additional money they need?

c. What is your estimate of the settlement fees on the house?

d. What is the total cash that will be required at settlement?

e. What will the monthly mortgage payment be?

f. Can Jane and Mack afford to buy this house?

2. a. Estimate the average price of a new home in 1995, assuming 5 percent inflation per year above 1990 levels.

   b. How much would you need for a down payment on this house with a 20 percent down loan?

   c. What mortgage balance would you need to buy this house if you made a 20 percent down payment?

   d. Estimate your monthly payments and the total of payments over the lives of 10-year, 20-year, and 30-year loans in the amount in item c. at a 10 percent interest rate.

Answers to Self-Correcting Problems

1. a. $22,000

   b. Because the down payment will require their entire savings of $22,000, they will not have enough cash to pay the down payment, any points, and settlement fees. However, they probably will not pay the full $110,000 asking price (unless they are in a particularly active real estate market featuring many buyers competing for scarce houses). Therefore, their down payment of 20 percent of the final sales price will probably be less than $22,000.

   They have many good options at this point. First, they could tap their emergency savings fund for the additional money they need to cover settlement fees and points. Second, they could make an offer asking the seller to take back a second trust for $5,000 to $10,000 as part of the deal. Third, they could make a full-price offer contingent on the seller paying all settlement cost and points. Fourth, they could shop around for a loan requiring only 10 percent down; they probably could find such a loan, but would have to pay a higher interest rate through the imposition of a special mortgage insurance premium to protect the lender's collateral interest.

   c. Using the textbook estimate of 3 to 4 percent, settlement fees should run approximately $3,300 to $4,400. The midpoint of this range, $3,800, is a reasonable estimate.

   d. Assuming they buy the house at $105,000, find a 10-percent down loan or get the seller to take a second mortgage for 10 percent of the selling price, and pay 1 point, their cash outlay will total $15,350: $10,500 for the down payment + $3,800 for settlement costs + $1,050 for points. This will leave them approximately $7,000 cash from their initial $22,000, which should cover any expenses of moving into the house and all the things new homeowners need (a lawn mower, garbage cans, more furniture, etc.), and still leave some money for emergencies.

   e. They pay $105,000 for the house less the $10,500 down payment, leaving a $94,500 balance for their 10 percent, 30-year loan. Dividing the figure from Exhibit 3.4 by 100 to get the payment per thousand dollars of principal, their monthly payment will be $828 per month (94.5 thousands × $8.76 per thousand).

   f. Yes; Exhibit 3.3 indicates that they can afford $1,000 to $1,125 per month in principal and interest payments.

2. a. Approximately $160,000 (from Exhibit 3.2)

   b. $32,000

   c. $128,000

d. Using Exhibit 3.4: 10-year loan payment is $1,692, total of payments is $203,040; 20-year loan payment is $1,235, total of payments is $296,400; 30-year loan payment is $1,121, total of payments is $403,560.

SELECTED READINGS

Adler, Bill, Jr. *The Home Buyer's Guide*. New York: Simon & Schuster, 1984.

Brown, R. E. *Buy Smart! The Complete Homebuyer's Guide to Residential Evaluation*. New York: McGraw-Hill, 1987.

Brueggeman, William B., Leo D. Stone, and Jeffrey D. Fisher. *Real Estate Finance*, 8th ed. Homewood, Ill.: Richard D. Irwin, 1988.

Buying and Selling a Home: How to Profit from Your Real Estate Transactions, rev. ed. Washington, D.C.: Kiplinger Publishers, 1987.

Department of Housing and Urban Development. *Having Problems Paying Your Mortgage?* Washington, D.C.: U.S. Government Printing Office, current edition.

Department of Housing and Urban Development. *Settlement Costs: A HUD Guide*. Washington, D.C.: U.S. Government Printing Office, current edition.

Miller, Peter G. *The Common-Sense Mortgage: How to Cut the Cost of Home Ownership by One Hundred Thousand Dollars or More*. New York: Harper & Row, 1987.

Minton, Robert. *Banking on Your Home: A Consumer's Guide to Home Equity Loans*. Homewood, Ill.: Dow Jones-Irwin, 1986.

National Association of Home Builders. *Buying a New Home: A Step-by-Step Guide*. Washington, D.C.: NAHB, 1986

National Association of Home Builders. *The Current Housing Situation*. Washington, D.C.: NAHB, current edition.

II

Strategy for an Investment Program

chapter 4

Sources of Investment Information

Long before he won an Academy Award for his performance in *Rainman*, Dustin Hoffman played the title role in a classic film, *The Graduate*. The character was a young man from an affluent background who had just graduated from college and was searching for direction in his life. Concerned parents, friends, and relatives all offered advice, to which the young man listened with detachment. At a party, one well-meaning guest sidled up to him with drink in hand and said, simply, "plastics," implying the word conveyed some critical meaning. The guest then moved on, leaving a perplexed young man to ponder his future. Though the plastics industry may have offered guaranteed prosperity, the puzzled young man needed much more information than a single word could convey before he could make a career decision of the kind the guest imagined. The well-meaning advisors assumed certain conclusions about the nature of the young man's decision rather than offering him basic information on which to base his own conclusions.

A second story can illustrate another kind of information error people make, particularly in deciding about investments. In a conversation overheard in a Washington, D.C., elevator, one young businessman told his friend, "I just bought 100 shares of Super Computer common. A friend told me about it. I think it's going to be a good investment!"

The second man asked, "What does the company make?"

"I don't know," answered the first man, "but it looks like a great stock!"

"I'm going to get some of it myself," his friend decided. This appalling display of ignorance is an excellent example of how investment decisions should *not* be made. The stories remind us that investors must be informed in order to make good investment decisions. Even complete information and knowledge cannot make all investments successful, but knowledge will help to keep mistakes to a minimum.

Introduction

Many years ago the slogan of the New York Stock Exchange was "Investigate Before You Invest." This advice was intended to encourage the public to obtain as much information as possible before purchasing common stock as an investment. An investor considering purchasing shares in any firm should investigate:

1. The quality of the firm's management
2. Its current financial condition
3. The quality of its product or service
4. Its productivity
5. The soundness of its capital structure
6. The expected growth rate for its profits
7. The expected growth rate for its earnings and dividends per share
8. The expected rate of return and risk on the investment

This kind of critical information cannot be conveyed in a single, brief word in the style parodied in *The Graduate*, yet many people make decisions, including investment decisions, based on similarly limited information. Investors must investigate and obtain extensive data to make good investment decisions. Such a process requires, first, research into sources of information. Each investor must develop a productive, easy-to-use, low-cost information system that satisfies his or her lifestyle goals and investment needs.

What Is an Investment Information System?

Investors buy assets they think will provide future income and growth of principal. These assets include common stocks, which represent shares of ownership of a company; bonds, which represent long-term borrowing by companies or governments; and money market securities, which represent short-term borrowing by businesses and governments. Investors need to know what these assets are, where they are traded, and where to obtain information about them.

marketplace: A place where buyers and sellers exchange securities.

In general terms, securities are traded in a **marketplace,** a place where buyers and sellers exchange assets. The marketplace may have a single physical location or it may consist of an international computer network. Purchasers can buy securities directly from issuers (for example, buying a Treasury bill or bond directly from the United States Treasury) or they can buy them through brokerage firms, which buy and sell securities on behalf of clients. We will discuss the markets and brokers in greater detail in the next chapter.

Most investors receive much of their information about the marketplace through daily financially oriented newspapers such as *The Wall Street Journal* and the business sections of local newspapers, through weekly financially oriented magazines such as *Barron's* and *Business Week*, and through monthly business magazines such as *Money, Forbes*, and *Fortune*. Together, these sources are called the **financial press.**

financial press: Newspapers, magazines, and broadcast media outlets that publish financial news.

The marketplace transmits new information to the investor remarkably efficiently. Academic research on the stock market has verified this premise and codified it as the **efficient market hypothesis (EMH),** which suggests that all information that might affect a security's price reaches the marketplace and investors so quickly, easily, and cheaply that it is immediately reflected in the prices of all financial assets. An investor could benefit from an information advantage only by knowing the kind of inside information about a company that is generally limited to its officers and directors. It is, however, illegal to trade securities to profit from such information.

efficient market hypothesis (EMH): The premise that information about securities reaches the marketplace quickly and cheaply, and all security prices fully reflect all information.

An astute stock analyst or professional investment manager can certainly benefit from special knowledge gained by correctly interpreting publicly available information, but, usually, by the time information is reported in the financial press, everybody knows about it and it no longer gives any special advantage. Thus, if your broker or a friend gives you a hot tip about a security, you can be sure that the information has already been widely disseminated. This doesn't mean that you should ignore your broker or friends, but you must put the information they provide in perspective.

In addition to publications, radio and TV programs bring a constant flow of business information. In particular, cable TV stations, CNN and CNBC, provide extensive financial information. Such sources facilitate immediate access to information about financial matters. Within minutes, millions knew about the stock market's crash on October 19, 1987, and its declines in October 1989 and August 1990. By tapping into the flow of data in the financial press, an investor can become a fully informed participant in the efficient investment marketplace.

To take full advantage of this valuable opportunity, each investor must develop a personal **investment information system.** This could mean reviewing literally hundreds of periodicals, but a more limited effort will yield good results. You can develop a workable investment information system that will keep you informed and still leave time to enjoy the fruits of your profitable investments.

investment information system: An organized set of procedures to gather and evaluate information about investments.

Your Investment Information System

You probably don't think of playing your favorite game or sport as systematic. If you were to write down what you do when you engage in these activities, however, you would be describing systems. For example, if you were to decide to improve your golf game, you might follow this set pattern:

Take a golf lesson every two weeks

Practice your golf lesson three times each week for one hour each time

Read a book on the lesson for 10 minutes each day

Play golf competitively with friends at least twice each week

Work out in the gym at least twice or three times each week

Similar goals can help you become an informed investor. One goal is to develop a simple information system that suits your lifestyle. It must be organized to produce results; it must be effective to keep you informed about your investments; it must keep costs low in terms of both dollars and time spent.

Goals of an Investment Information System

The primary goal of an investment information system is to establish and improve an investor's results. To do this, the system should help the investor find investments that offer the highest rates of return at any given risk level. **Rate of return** is the income from an investment plus any price appreciation or minus any price decline as a percentage of the investment's purchase price. **Risk** is the variability of return.

rate of return: A measure of the investor's gain from an investment, found by dividing the income from the asset plus any gain or minus any loss by the asset's price.

risk: The variability of rate of return.

In order to discover profitable investments that expose the investor to minimal risk, the investor must decide what he or she wants from an investment and the desired timing of these benefits. A younger investor, for example, may look for assets that will increase in value over time to build a foundation for financial independence. This type of investor will put aside small amounts of money regularly, which will accumulate to become larger sums that can fund purchases of assets that will appreciate in value.

In short, the major focus of an investment information system is to identify and gather a continuous stream of information about investment opportunities that might suit a particular investor. This is no open-ended search for investment information, but rather a goal-oriented process that helps the investor find and exploit good opportunities.

Start with *The Wall Street Journal*

The Wall Street Journal is widely acknowledged as an excellent source of information for investors. The newspaper presents this information in three sections. The first section teaches the investor to read between the lines of regular news stories, summarizing world events from an investor's point of view. The second section, "Marketplace," reports on companies' activities, successes, and failures. The third section, "Money & Investing," deals directly with securities and the markets in which they trade.

The information on the next few pages, taken from the Educational Edition of *The Wall Street Journal*, gives a step-by-step guide to getting the information you need from the *Journal*. Following this approach a step at a time, you can become an informed investor. As you read this material, keep a copy of the *Journal* in front of you to follow along.

HOW TO READ BETWEEN THE LINES

The First Section

Basic reading for all businesspeople. The top business and economic stories of the day, along with international news, opinions, and politics.

STEP 1

Look at **What's News,** the second and third columns from the left on the front page. Here you'll find a quick summary of the day's national and international and business news—a preview of the Journal's contents.

Each paragraph in the left-hand column, headed "Business and Finance," summarizes a major business, economic, or financial news story. (At the bottom, you'll also find the major market indexes, just for convenience.) And each paragraph tells you where to go in the Journal to get the complete story. You can pick out the highlights in a few moments, or read in depth when you have the time.

News briefs in the column headed "World-Wide" cover important national and international news. If there is an expanded story elsewhere in the Journal we tell you right where to find it.

More people read What's News than any other single feature in the Journal. No wonder. Even if that's all you have time for in the Journal that day, you'll be better informed than if you'd read the average daily newspaper cover to cover.

STEP 2

Take a quick glance at the **Today's Contents** index, underneath What's News. It's the quickest way to discover the other important stories and features in that day's Journal.

STEP 3

Now go to columns one and six for the Journal's "leaders." Every day, these two well-known columns range wide to cover business, social, and management trends; in-depth looks at the industries, companies, cities, and countries; profiles of businesspeople and political leaders; and extensively researched investigative pieces. Whether covering breaking news or summing up developments others have missed, they're the premier stories that day's Journal has to offer.

STEP 4

Column four is headed each day with a performance graph of a major economic indicator. Wall Street Journal graphs and charts like this one help reduce bewildering statistical information to precise, easy to read visuals.

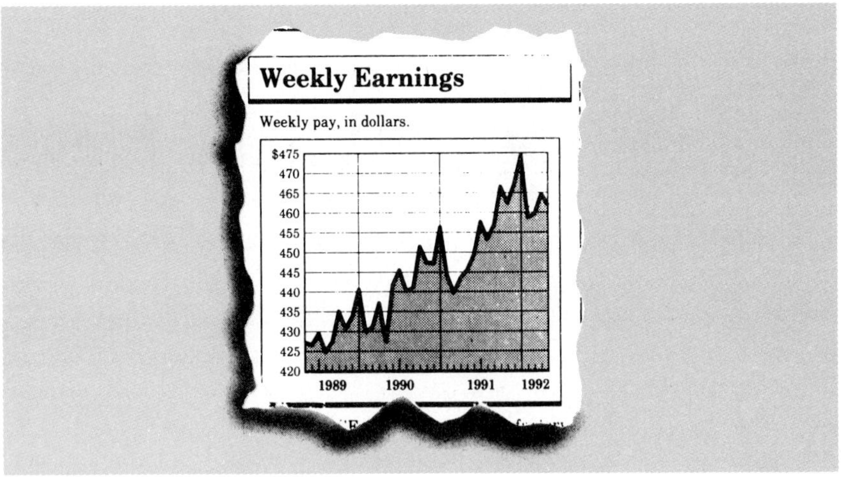

STEP 5

Below the graph you'll find a special-interest daily column. An offbeat feature that's just a bit out of the business mainstream, it's typically entertaining, always insightful.

STEP 6

Column five—the second from the right—brings you one of the Journal's five well-known weekly front-page newsletters. On Mondays, it's a commentary on the economic climate; on Tuesdays, labor; Wednesday, taxes. On Thursdays, the emphasis is on developments in business. And on Fridays we report on national government in the Washington Wire.

STEP 7

Flip to page A2, where the lastest economic news is anchored on the **Economy** page. Inflation and unemployment, government announcements, forecasts, Federal Reserve policy—here is wehre the Journal helps its readers make sense of every day's flood of economic indicators and statistics.

STEP 8

If you have time, look through the rest of the first section. You'll find the in-depth stories behind the news briefed in What's News. Each day, more than 400 Journal reporters keep their ears to the ground for late-breaking developments in business, finance, politics, and international affairs. Their findings appear in this section every morning as vital, authoritative news. If you're pressed for time, just scan the headlines.

STEP 9

You may want to pause at the day's **Industry Focus,** which often appears in this section. In these stories the Journal assesses the fortunes of a particular industry or company. One day it might be cars, the next day cable television—wherever there's an emerging trend that Journal readers need to know about.

STEP 10

Near the back of the section you'll find two facing pages devoted to international reports from the Journal's foreign bureaus. Here is where the Journal anchors news of important foreign companies and business trends, as well as overseas political and economic news. Scan these pages daily and watch the global economy take shape.

STEP 11

On the next to last set of facing pages in this section we run our **Leisure & Arts** coverage. It's eclectic, award-winning criticism and news on everything from music to sports, from film to books.

STEP 12

The two facing pages at the end of the section are our editorial pages, where Wall Street Journal editors express their opinions about the current state of business, politics, and world affairs. You'll also find the views from a wide range of distinguished guest columnists, and letters from the Journal's unusually articulate readers.

STEP 13

Finally, flip the section over. The back page is devoted to **Politics & Policy**—the news made in Washington and on the campaign trail, and how it affects the country as a whole, the world of business, and you.

Marketplace (Second Section)

How companies compete, how consumers respond. And a closer look at some important topics that affect everyone in business.

STEP 1

Start at the left side of the first page with the front-page column. Each day it's devoted to the latest trends in a variety of fast-changing areas, providing quick information in a series of short summaries. The topics include real estate, design, business travel, managing, demographics, regional economies—even "Shop Talk," the Journal's inside look at corporate life.

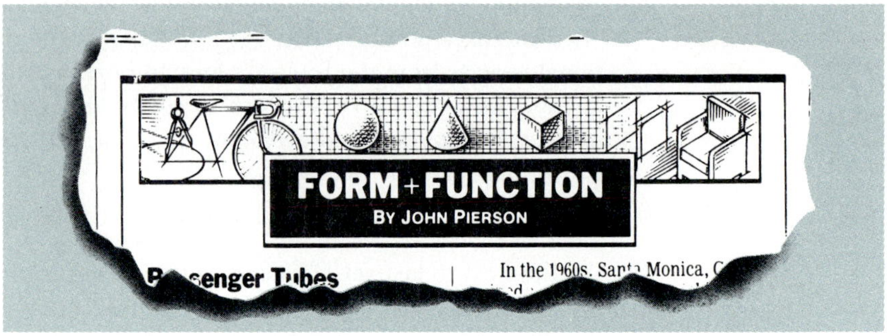

STEP 2

Just below these columns, you'll find the "orphan." It's typically an amusing, slightly off-center story held to some eight short paragraphs, making it a quick, entertaining read.

STEP 3

The rest of the "second front" (page B1) deals with a wide variety of business trends and news. However, they are written from a different perpective than similar stories in the first section. Often they'll focus on the changing marketplace for goods and services—and how companies themselves are responding. Others will address you as a consumer, not just as a businessperson, with thoughts and insights on how the news might affect you personally. There's always something here of interest.

STEP 4

There's one more important Journal index to check every day, on page B2. It's called the **Index to Businesses,** and sooner or later, you'll be glad you used it.

The Index to Businesses lists the companies that play significant roles in the day's business news, and tells you the pages where each company's story appears. And within each Journal news story, the first time the company is mentioned it appears in boldface type, so you can find it more easily. If there are companies you need to follow each day, the Index to Businesses means you'll never miss a story.

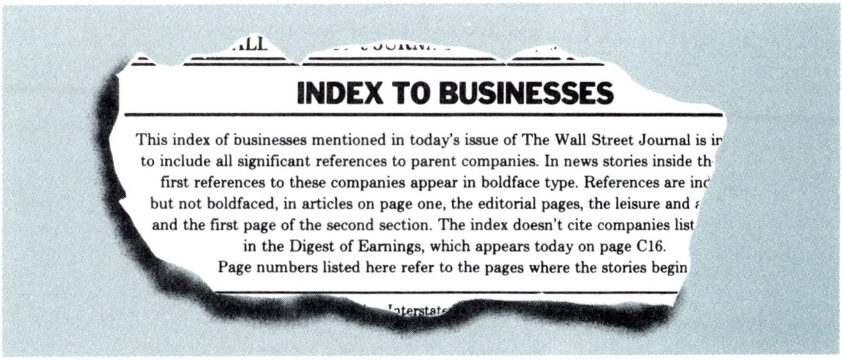

STEP 5

On the same page, you'll find **Enterprise,** devoted to the fast-growing, fast-changing world of smaller companies. How they manage, how they succeed, why they fail—if you see yourself as an entrepreneur, "Enterprise" will head you in the right direction.

STEP 6

Further on in the section, keep up with the future by taking a look at the page (or pages) headed **Technology.** Daily, it organizes in one place the Journal's coverage of the companies and discoveries that are at the forefront of modern technology. Computers, biotechnology, advanced healthcare, robotics—catch the latest developments here, before they're history.

TECHNOLOGY

s, JVC Set Venture to Make
or Large-Screen Televisions

commercial endeavors and reduce its reliance on military contracts.
In the latest teaming with the Japanese consumer products powerhouse known as JVC, Hughes also has converted a technol-

IBM
PC S
By S

STEP 7

Turn the page again, and scan the **Marketing & Media** coverage. Similar in format to Technology, it's where you'll find news affecting the major consumer marketing companies, ad agencies, and the media.

MARKETING AND MEDIA

SING / By JOANNE LIPMAN

oversy Propels Several Ads
p 10 List for '91 Campaigns

African guerrilla grasping a

STEP 8

Next in the section, a daily page devoted to **The Law**—but by no means written exclusively for lawyers. It will give anyone a more thorough understanding of the cases and issues that shape business decision making.

STEP 9

Further on in the section, you'll find **Who's News.** This is where the Journal profiles new and established business leaders, and details changes in corporate managements.

STEP 10

The back pages of the section usually carry the Journal's classified advertising. (Tuesdays and Wednesdays are the principal days for employment ads.) Whether you're looking for a job or just sizing up the market, The Wall Street Journal's classified ads are the place to see. And be seen.

Money & Investing (Third Section)

A comprehensive, easy-to-navigate guide to the stock market and every market that affects America's businesses—and your finances, as well.

STEP 1

The first two left-hand columns on the front page are the fastest way yet to check yesterday's market activity: the **Markets Diary.** It charts the movements of five major markets: stocks, interest rates, bonds, currencies, and commodities. All designed so you can take it in at a glance.

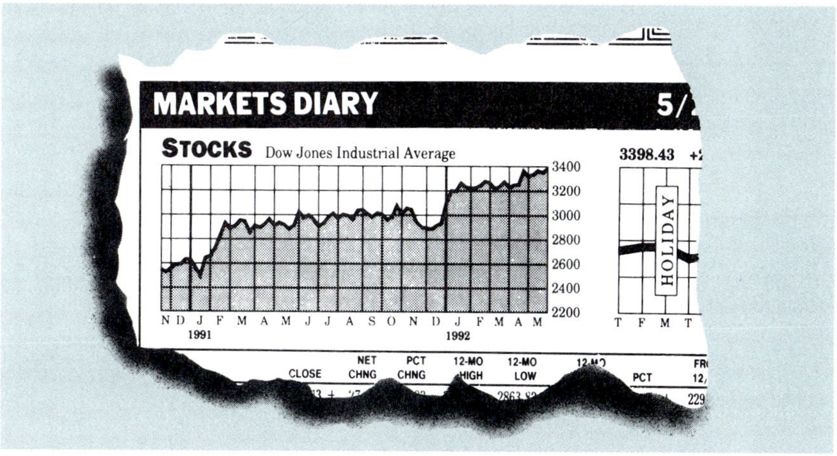

Underneath, the "Investment Insight" also uses graphs and tables, but this column highlights a particular trend of interest in a market, or a relationship between markets. An ongoing course in market-watching.

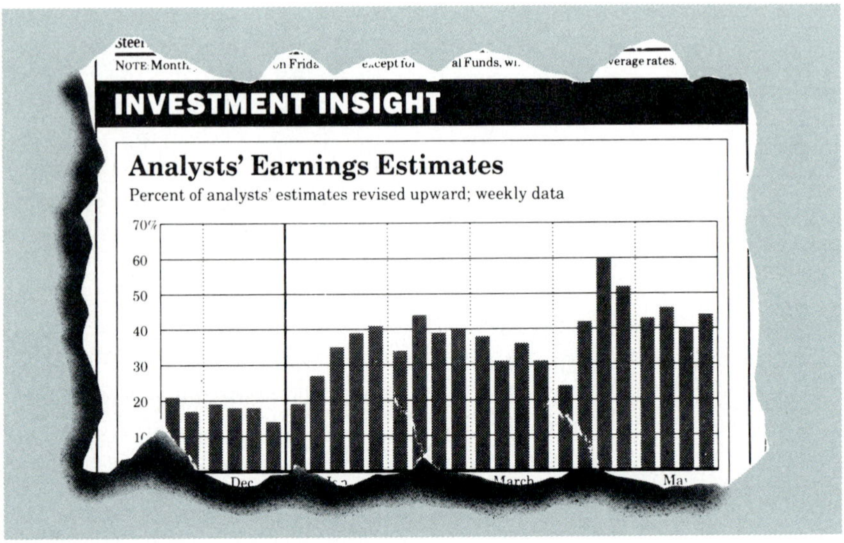

STEP 2

Also on the front page, check the daily markets story, which summarizes the previous day's developments in all the markets. The stock market often moves in response to what's going on in other markets, and this feature gives you a quick understanding of what forces drove yesterday's trading.

STEP 3

Now move on to **Your Money Matters,** also on the front page of this section every day. This is the Journal's renowned personal-finance and investing column. Read it if you have money to invest. Read it if you don't, and you may have some soon.

STEP 4

On the rest of the front page, look for the day's major market stories: important news about the previous day's stock-market activity, expert opinion on what's happening and why. At the top of the page, you'll find a concise index that highlights other important stories and statistics inside.

STEP 5

Turn to page C2 for a closer look at the stock markets. You'll find "Abreast of the Market" and "Heard on the Street," two of America's most influential investment columns. (They may begin on the front section when the news warrants it.) "Abreast" gives you a concise summary of all the major investment markets, citing causes and quoting experts. "Heard" comments on specific companies and industries: mergers, acquisitions, new-product introductions, stock splits, and more. To the right of these two columns, the Stock Market Data Bank summarizes the most important daily stock-market measures in a clean, easy-to-read format.

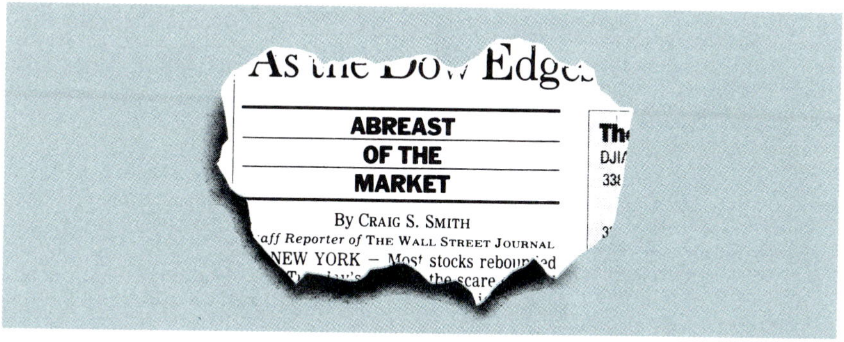

STEP 6

On page C3, coverage of the stock market continues with graphs of the famous Dow Jones averages and the opening page of the New York Stock

Exchange quotes. You don't have to be an investor to spend time with this page and those that follow: Journal readers apply this daily financial data to business decisions ranging from marketing to mergers, and buyouts to borrowing. (To learn how to read and use the data, you'll want to read "Understanding Financial Data" [in the Educational Edition of The Wall Street Journal].)

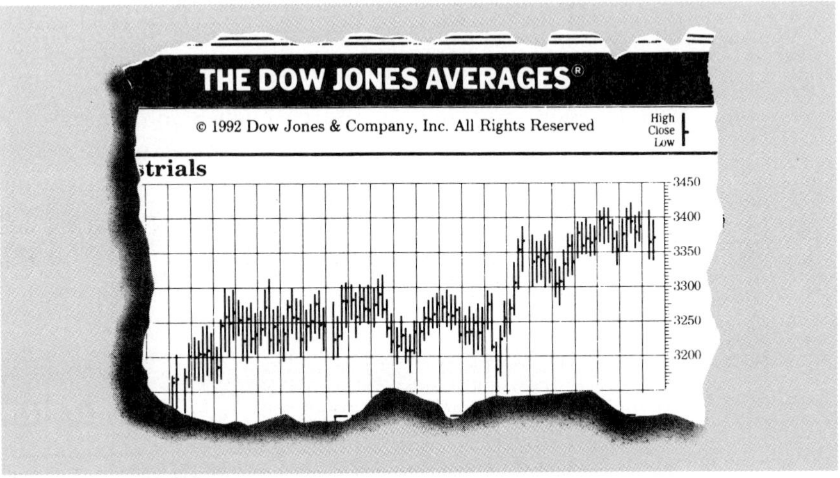

STEP 7

If you have time, page through the rest of the **Money & Investing** section. It's organized in the same order every day, with stock-market quotations and stories near the beginning of the section, and mutual funds at the end. In between, you'll find international stocks and foreign currencies, commodities, and the bond and credit markets; futures and options quotations run near their related markets. And Journal news stories and columns on a particular market always run near the related statistics, so it's easy to refer to the quotations themselves when you need to.

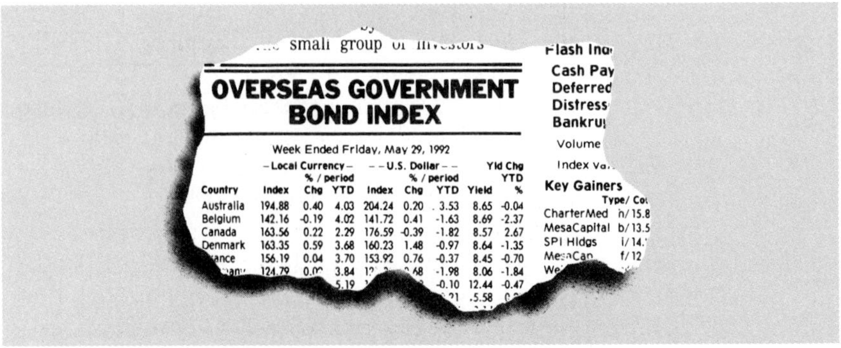

OVERSEAS GOVERNMENT BOND INDEX

Week Ended Friday, May 29, 1992

	–Local Currency–			– –U.S. Dollar– –				Yld Chg
		% / period			% / period			YTD
Country	Index	Chg	YTD	Index	Chg	YTD	Yield	%
Australia	194.88	0.40	4.03	204.24	0.20	3.53	8.65	-0.04
Belgium	142.16	-0.19	4.02	141.72	0.41	-1.63	8.69	-2.37
Canada	163.56	0.22	2.29	176.59	-0.39	-1.82	8.57	2.67
Denmark	163.35	0.59	3.68	160.23	1.48	-0.97	8.64	-1.35
[illegible]ance	156.19	0.04	3.70	153.92	0.76	-0.37	8.45	-0.70
[illegible]	124.79	[illegible]	3.84	[illegible]	[illegible]	-1.98	8.06	-1.84
[illegible]	[illegible]	[illegible]	5.19	[illegible]	[illegible]	-0.10	12.44	-0.47
[illegible]	[illegible]	[illegible]	[illegible]	[illegible]	[illegible]	[illegible]	5.58	[illegible]

Cash Pay
Deferred
Distress
Volume
Key Gainers

STEP 8

Most people start out as investors by buying shares in mutual funds, and on the last two pages in the section we gather the latest mutual fund quotations and news. And for a snapshot of which funds are doing particularly well, check the Mutual Fund Monitor, a daily analysis of the best and worst performing funds in a particular investment category.

Basic Information Needs

Wise investors keep up regularly with several types of basic information to help them make effective investment decisions. Important topics include the U.S. and global economies, the outlooks for various industries, and the prospects of individual companies.

National Economy First, the investor needs information about the general business climate in the United States and abroad. Expectations for strong growth and little inflation throughout the economy, such as occurred between 1986 and mid-1990, can imply good times and growing profits for individual businesses. These conditions could make investments in common stocks or high-interest bonds especially attractive. On the other hand, expectations for inflation followed by a business recession may make investments in short-term government securities or money market funds more appropriate while discouraging investments in common stock and long-term bonds.

Other kinds of world events can affect an investor's decisions, as well. When Iraqi troops invaded Kuwait in late 1990 and the United States and other nations responded by sending troops to defend Saudi Arabia, few investors wanted to hold large investments in common stocks, fearing a declining market. In the short run, the conflict drove oil prices upward and caused a great deal of economic uncertainty. After the conflict was quickly resolved, however, the stock market enjoyed a major boom, generating an annual return of approximately 30 percent.

Of course, you can and should bet on more than one horse. With an uncertain economic outlook, it may be best to divide your money between stocks and less risky investments like bonds and money market funds. This decision about how to allocate available funds among various types of investments, called the *asset allocation decision*, will be discussed in detail in Chapter 6. The important point here is the effect of information about general economic conditions on an individual investor's decisions.

Many sources can yield information about the national economy and general business conditions. These include local newspapers, *The Wall Street Journal*, *Barron's*, *Forbes*, *Fortune*, and the Sunday *New York Times*.

Many local newspapers publish weekly business magazine supplements, which can be valuable resources.

One particularly informative and readily available source is the *Business Week* Index found in *Business Week* magazine. Exhibit 4.1 shows a sample of the index. Notice that it lists both individual production indexes for classes of products and a composite production index that consolidates results for the individual classes. Annual changes in the consolidated production index indicate which way the economy is moving. For example, the production index indicated weakness in April and May 1992. Annual increases in the production indexes for autos, lumber, and paper indicated strengthening areas in the economy.

The leading indicators index increased in April 1992, following a rise in stock prices. This gave another sign of strength. Also, lower bond yields and higher business failures suggested future problems in the economy.

Production data is only one example of important information, though. The foreign exchange index indicates that the dollar weakened during the previous year against the Japanese yen from a ratio of 139 yen to the dollar to 132. Since fewer yen would buy a dollar compared to a year earlier, the dollar became weaker. This made products purchased with yen cheaper, but it also reduced the value in yen of previously purchased U.S. government bonds. The Japanese consumer could buy American products at better prices, but the Japanese investor suffered a loss, all because of the declining value of the dollar. These relationships make exchange rates important pieces of information for the investor to track.

Information about rising prices is critical for investors in the stock and long-term bond markets. Usually inflation means higher interest rates, which puts downward pressure on stock and bond prices. The exhibit shows that prices declined, which is favorable for stock prices. The monthly economic indicators of industrial prices supported the notion that inflation was not a problem. A pickup in the economy was evidenced by monthly economic indicators such as increases in construction spending and manufacturer's shipments.

The monetary indicators showed weakness and constraint in declines in banks' business loans, free reserves, and nonfinancial commercial paper. When business loans and free reserves decline, business activity in general declines. Money supply, M1, increased, but is a low-powered supply of money, and not indicative of money growth strength.

Money market rates, the interest rates on short-term borrowing, declined from the previous year, suggesting weak demand for loans and/or stimulus from the federal government to provoke economic expansion. Continued low interest rates would tend to stimulate the economy over time. Therefore, the prevailing interest rates were a stimulus to the economy, foreshadowing the eventual economic recovery. Even the best investment information system can send contradictory signals when the economic picture is muddy.

EXHIBIT 4.1

General Economic Data

BusinessWeek Index

PRODUCTION

Change from last week: −0.6%
Change from last year: 4.7%

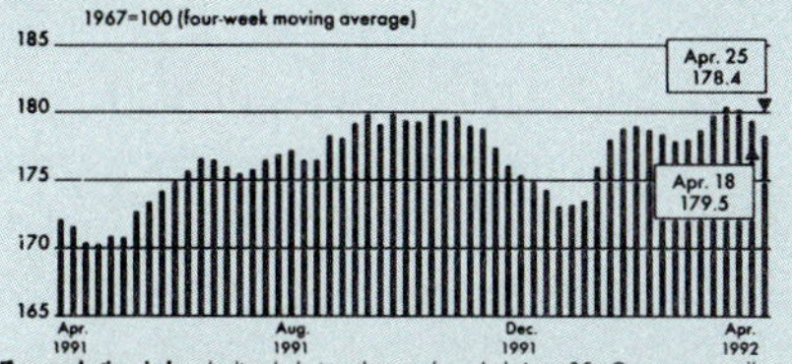

The production index declined during the week ended Apr. 25. On a seasonally adjusted basis, output of trucks, autos, crude-oil refining, paperboard, and rail-freight traffic increased. Electric power and paper production were down, while coal and lumber output were unchanged from the previous week. Before calculation of the four-week moving average, the index dropped to 177.4 from 177.8. But some of that decline likely reflects plant closings for the Easter holiday.

LEADING

Change from last week: 0.1%
Change from last year: −1.4%

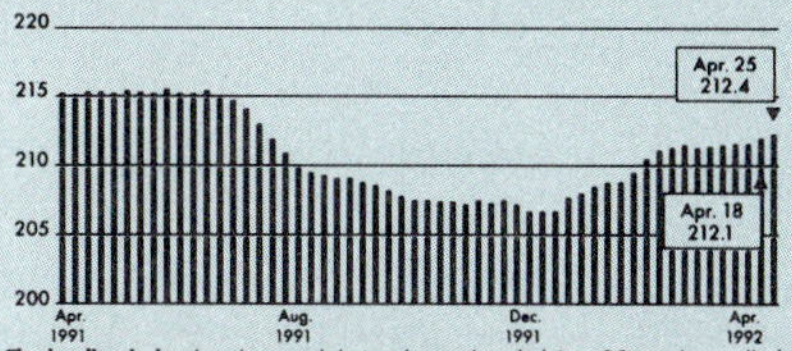

The leading index barely moved during the week ended Apr. 25, as almost all of the indicators retraced the gains posted in the previous week. On the negative side were lower stock prices, higher bond yields, slower growth rates for materials prices and real estate loans, and an increase in the number of business failures. Growth in M2 was unchanged. Before calculation of the four-week moving average, the index dropped to 212.2 from 213.1.

PRODUCTION INDICATORS

	Latest week	Week ago	% Change year ago
STEEL (5/2) thous. of net tons	1,792	1,827#	13.6
AUTOS (5/2) units	130,519	107,022r#	12.8
TRUCKS (5/2) units	86,149	75,811r#	10.3
ELECTRIC POWER (5/2) millions of kilowatt-hours	51,854	50,969#	1.3
CRUDE-OIL REFINING (5/2) thous. of bbl./day	13,234	13,420#	−0.9
COAL (4/25) thous. of net tons	18,207#	18,337	−3.4
PAPERBOARD (4/25) thous. of tons	817.1#	809.2r	7.7
PAPER (4/25) thous. of tons	769.0#	776.0r	0.8
LUMBER (4/25) millions of ft.	499.6#	502.9	0.7
RAIL FREIGHT (4/25) billions of ton-miles	20.2#	19.7	8.0

Sources: American Iron & Steel Institute, Ward's *Automotive Reports*, Edison Electric Institute, American Petroleum Institute, Energy Dept., American Paper Institute, WWPA[1], SFPA[2], Association of American Railroads.

LEADING INDICATORS

	Latest week	Week ago	% Change year ago
STOCK PRICES (5/1) S&P 500	411.41	410.17r	8.8
CORPORATE BOND YIELD, Aaa (5/1)	8.37%	8.33%	−5.2
INDUSTRIAL MATERIALS PRICES (5/1)	97.7	97.5	0.7
BUSINESS FAILURES (4/24)	453	420	10.2
REAL ESTATE LOANS (4/22) billions	$400.7	$401.8r	−3.1
MONEY SUPPLY, M2 (4/29) billions	$3,444.1	$3,443.1r	1.9
INITIAL CLAIMS, UNEMPLOYMENT (4/22) thous.	404	404	−19.2

Sources: Standard & Poor's, Moodys, *Journal of Commerce* (index: 1980=100), Dun & Bradstreet (failures of large companies), Federal Reserve Board, Labor Dept. CIBCR seasonally adjusts data on business failures and real estate loans.

MONTHLY ECONOMIC INDICATORS

	Latest month	Month ago	% Change year ago
CONSTR. SPENDING (Mar.) annual rate, billions	$419.9	$413.3r	4.5
12 LEADING INDICATORS COMPOSITE (Mar.) index	147.9	147.6	4.5
MANUFACTURERS' INVENTORIES (Mar.) billions	$372.9	$372.8r	−3.4
MANUFACTURING SHIPMENTS (Mar.) billions	$243.9	$241.7	6.6

Sources: Census Bureau, Commerce Dept.

FOREIGN EXCHANGE

	Latest week	Week ago	Year ago
JAPANESE YEN (5/6)	132	134	139
GERMAN MARK (5/6)	1.63	1.66	1.73
BRITISH POUND (5/6)	1.79	1.77	1.72
FRENCH FRANC (5/6)	5.50	5.58	5.86
CANADIAN DOLLAR (5/6)	1.20	1.19	1.15
SWISS FRANC (5/6)	1.50	1.52	1.47
MEXICAN PESO (5/6)[3]	3,065	3,066	2,997

Sources: Major New York banks. Currencies expressed in units per U. S. dollar, except for British pound expressed in dollars.

MONETARY INDICATORS

	Latest week	Week ago	% Change year ago
MONEY SUPPLY, M1 (4/20)	$945.7	$939.8r	12.4
BANKS' BUSINESS LOANS (4/22)	287.0	288.4r	−10.4
FREE RESERVES (4/29)	1,009	1,033r	−4.5
NONFINANCIAL COMMERCIAL PAPER (4/22)	145.1	145.4	−4.4

Sources: Federal Reserve Board (in billions, except for free reserves, which are expressed for a two-week period in millions).

PRICES

	Latest week	Week ago	% Change year ago
GOLD (5/6) $/troy oz.	336.700	335.700	−5.7
STEEL SCRAP (5/5) #1 heavy, $/ton	94.00	92.00	−1.1
FOODSTUFFS (5/4) index, 1967=100	203.3	199.9	−1.0
COPPER (5/2) ¢/lb.	103.8	103.7	−6.7
ALUMINUM (5/2) ¢/lb.	60.5	62.3	−2.3
WHEAT (5/2) #2 hard, $/bu.	3.92	4.10	32.9
COTTON (5/2) strict low middling 1-1/16 in., ¢/lb.	56.53	54.27	−31.0

Sources: London Wednesday final setting, Chicago market, Commodity Research Bureau, *Metals Week*, Kansas City market, Memphis market.

MONEY MARKET RATES

	Latest week	Week ago	Year ago
FEDERAL FUNDS (5/5)	3.77%	3.50%	5.79%
PRIME (5/6)	6.50	6.50	8.50
COMMERCIAL PAPER 3-MONTH (5/5)	3.93	3.96	5.92
CERTIFICATES OF DEPOSIT 3-MONTH (5/6)	3.84	3.91	5.91
EURODOLLAR 3-MONTH (5/2)	3.95	4.04	5.98

Sources: Federal Reserve Board, First Boston

#Raw data in the production indicators are seasonally adjusted in computing the BW index (chart); other components (estimated and not listed) include machinery and defense equipment.
1=Western Wood Products Assn. 2=Southern Forest Products Assn. 3=Free market value NA=Not available r=revised NM=Not meaningful

SOURCE: *Business Week*, May 18, 1992, p. 6. Reprinted by special permission, copyright © 1992 by McGraw-Hill, Inc.

Recognizing the need for good information, several prominent companies provide economic and business data as their primary product. Exhibit 4.2 shows a summary of a *Quarterly Economic Review* published by one such firm, Value Line. The main body of the report reviews in detail the outlook for the U.S. economy, including a six-quarter estimate for the major economic variables as well as a five-year annual forecast. The full text of a *Quarterly Economic Review* is too extensive to be reproduced here, but you might obtain a copy of a current report to learn what information it offers.

gross domestic product (GDP): A narrower measure of economic activity than GNP that redefines net exports to exclude some categories of international income earnings.

gross national product (GNP): A measure of economic activity that represents the total value of goods and services produced in the economy, including consumption, investment, government expenditures, and net exports (exports minus imports).

The summary forecasts a weak U.S. economy with **gross domestic product (GDP),** a narrow measure of goods and services produced in the economy, increasing at an annual rate of only 2 percent in 1992, following a 0.7 percent decline in 1991. This 2 percent rate is the real rate of economic growth, that is, the growth rate in terms of current dollars minus the inflation rate. Notice the inflation rate estimate of 3.2 percent in 1992 as measured by the consumer price index. This rate of inflation is a decrease from the 4.2 percent rate in 1991. New economic analysis emphasizes gross domestic product replacing **GNP (gross national product),** which measures the broadest dollar amount of goods and services produced by the U.S. economy in a given year. Notice in Exhibit 4.2 that the unemployment rate was expected to increase to 7.1 percent in 1992, up from 6.7 percent in 1991, a clear signal of weakness. The Treasury bill rate was projected to decline and the 30-year Treasury bond rate was projected to remain flat in 1992.

All of this information about the general economy predicted only slow growth, or no growth, in corporate profits, with higher interest rates and higher inflation for 1991. At the time of publication, the Dow Jones Industrial Average, an index of stock-market activity, had declined from a high near 3,000 to around 2,450.

Taken all together, this information suggested that investors should make commitments to stocks or long-term bonds very selectively. The individual investor should carefully examine the kinds of data about the U.S. economy we have reviewed in order to form conclusions about personal investing plans.

Unfortunately, data from publications, services like Value Line and other sources, rely on estimates and projections that may turn out to be incorrect. Still, investors must make estimates, revising them as necessary, on which to base decisions about investment of funds.

Industry Information After assessing the outlook for the economy as a whole, the investor must review the growth prospects for companies grouped into industries. Financial information services provide two of the best sources of this information. Standard & Poor's publishes *Industry Surveys* and *Outlook,* and Value Line produces industry reports to complement its reports on the overall economy. The U.S. Department of Commerce anually publishes its own industry data in the *Industrial Outlook.* Fortunately, all of these publications are generally available in the business section of

EXHIBIT 4.2

Value Line Economic Forecast

Value Line's estimates of sales and earnings growth for individual companies are derived by correlating sales, earnings, and dividends to appropriate components or subcomponents of the National Income Accounts (Gross Domestic Product, Capital Spending, etc.), presented below. A more detailed forecast appears periodically in *Selection & Opinion.*

HYPOTHESIZED ECONOMIC ENVIRONMENT
3 TO 5 YEARS HENCE

The hypothesized 1995-97 economic environment into which earnings are forecast is as follows: Unemployment will average 6.1% of the national labor force compared to 6.7% in 1991. There will be no major war in progress at that time. Manhour productivity per worker will be expanding about 1.7% per year. Price inflation will continue. Prices as measured by the broad-based GDP deflator will advance about 3.7% per year on the average. The corporate income tax rate will be around 34%.

Long-term interest rates on high-grade corporate bonds are projected to be about 8.7% in the years 1995-97. We expect the Federal Reserve Board to pursue expansionary policies except in years in which the economy is clearly overheating or when balance of payments considerations govern. Based on these assumptions, the Gross Domestic Product will average $7861 billion in the years 1995-97, a level 38% above the 1991 total of $5674 billion.

Things may turn out differently. But in the absence of knowledge of the future, we use the above assumptions, which appear to be the most plausible. Thus we are able to apply a common economic environment to all stocks for the purpose of measuring relative growth potentiality.

THESE ARE THE NATIONAL INCOME SERIES TO WHICH VALUE LINE SALES, EARNINGS AND DIVIDEND ESTIMATES ARE CORRELATED

ANNUAL STATISTICS	1981	1982	1983	1984	1985	1986	1987	1988	1989	1990	1991	1992*	1993*	1995-97*
Gross Domestic Product ($Bill.)	3031	3150	3405	3777	4039	4269	4540	4900	5244	5514	5674	*5935*	*6334*	*7861*
Real GDP ($Bill. 1987)	3843	3760	3907	4149	4280	4404	4540	4719	4837	4885	4850	*4945*	*5103*	*5653*
Consumer Spending ($Bill.)	1926	2059	2258	2460	2667	2851	3052	3296	3518	3743	3889	*4075*	*4367*	*5481*
Capital Spending ($Bill.)	410	414	400	469	504	492	498	545	571	587	550	*566*	*623*	*785*
Industrial Production (1987=100)	85.7	81.9	84.9	92.8	94.4	95.3	100.0	105.4	108.1	109.2	107.1	*109.3*	*114.4*	*128.8*
Housing Starts (Mill. Units)	1.10	1.06	1.70	1.77	1.74	1.81	1.63	1.49	1.38	1.21	1.01	*1.33*	*1.36*	*1.42*
Total Car Sales (Mill. Units)	8.5	8.0	8.2	10.4	11.0	11.4	10.2	10.6	9.9	9.3	8.2	*8.9*	*9.9*	*10.4*
Personal Savings Rate (%)	8.8	8.6	6.8	8.1	6.5	6.0	4.3	4.4	4.4	5.1	5.2	*5.3*	*5.3*	*5.0*
National Unemployment Rate (%)	7.5	9.7	9.6	7.5	7.2	7.0	6.2	5.5	5.3	5.5	6.7	*7.1*	*6.6*	*6.1*
AAA Corp. Bond Rate (%)	14.2	13.8	12.0	12.7	11.4	9.0	9.4	9.7	9.3	9.3	8.8	*8.5*	*8.8*	*9.1*
30-Year Treasury Bond Rate (%)	13.4	12.8	11.2	12.4	10.8	7.8	8.6	9.0	8.4	8.6	8.1	*8.0*	*8.4*	*8.7*
3-Month Treasury Bill Rate (%)	14.0	10.6	8.6	9.5	7.5	6.0	5.8	6.7	8.1	7.5	5.4	*4.3*	*5.2*	*6.2*
ANNUAL RATES OF CHANGE														
Real GDP	1.8	-2.2	3.9	6.2	2.7	2.9	3.1	3.9	2.5	1.0	-0.7	*2.0*	*3.2*	*3.7*
GDP Price Deflator	10.0	6.2	4.1	4.4	3.2	2.7	3.1	3.9	4.4	4.1	3.7	*2.6*	*3.4*	*3.8*
Consumer Price Index	10.4	6.1	3.2	4.4	3.1	1.9	3.7	4.1	4.8	5.4	4.2	*3.2*	*4.3*	*4.5*

QUARTERLY ANNUALIZED RATES	1991				1992*				1993*			
	1st	2nd	3rd	4th	1st*	2nd*	3rd*	4th*	1st*	2nd*	3rd*	4th*
Gross Domestic Product ($Bill.)	5589	5653	5709	5747	*5822*	*5879*	*5972*	*6067*	*6172*	*6270*	*6392*	*6500*
Real GDP: ($Bill. 1987)	4824	4841	4863	4872	*4887*	*4923*	*4964*	*5005*	*5041*	*5078*	*5126*	*5166*
Consumer Spending ($Bill.)	3828	3868	3916	3942	*3984*	*4035*	*4104*	*4176*	*4250*	*4324*	*4406*	*4489*
Capital Spending ($Bill.)	560	555	547	537	*543*	*560*	*573*	*587*	*601*	*614*	*630*	*647*
Industrial Production (1987=100)	105.8	106.4	108.2	108.0	*108.2*	*108.8*	*109.5*	*110.8*	*112.4*	*113.7*	*115.2*	*116.3*
Housing Starts (Mill. Units)	0.92	1.00	1.04	1.09	*1.31*	*1.33*	*1.38*	*1.31*	*1.32*	*1.33*	*1.39*	*1.40*
Total Car Sales (Mill. Units)	8.0	8.2	8.3	8.3	*8.6*	*8.8*	*9.0*	*9.2*	*9.5*	*9.8*	*10.0*	*10.2*

*Estimated

SOURCE: Value Line Investment Survey, May 8, 1992, p. 1,150.

a public library. Spending some time reading these publications helps you invest your money as wisely as possible.

Exhibit 4.3 shows a Value Line report on the growth prospects for the restaurant industry. Value Line generates these industry composite statistics by summing the sales of the companies it has identified as industry participants. Standard & Poor's would have a different list and a different total, and Department of Commerce figures would differ from both Value Line's and S&P's. These variations suggest that the information reflects potentially flawed human judgments, rather than a completely reliable summary

EXHIBIT 4.3

Industry Growth Data
*Composite Statistics: Restaurant Industry**

1986	1987	1988	1989	1990	1991		93–95E
9,435.8	10,410	11,557	12,775	***14,025***	***15,580***	Sales ($millions)	***21,250***
20.7%	20.6%	21.2%	21.4%	***21.5%***	***21.7%***	Operating margin	***22.8%***
451.3	514.3	591.5	645.7	***730***	***810***	Depreciation ($millions)	***1,090***
709.5	794.8	964.9	1,041.2	***1,145***	***1,300***	Net profit ($millions)	***1,955***
44.0%	41.7%	37.8%	36.9%	***37.0%***	***37.0%***	Income tax rate	***36.9%***
7.5%	7.6%	8.3%	8.2	***8.2%***	***8.3%***	Net profit margin	***9.2%***
d166.7	d363.9	d481.9	d574.1	***d530***	***d522***	Working capital ($millions)	***d325***
2,883.3	3,248.6	4,372.6	5,153.7	***5,710***	***5,770***	Long-term debt ($millions)	***7,075***
4,384.2	5,015.1	4,944.8	5,289.7	***5,975***	***6,865***	Net worth ($millions)	***10,285***
11.7%	11.4%	12.2%	12.2%	***12.0%***	***11.5%***	Percentage earned total capital	***12.0%***
16.2%	15.8%	19.5%	19.7%	***19.5%***	***19.0%***	Percentage earned net worth	***19.5%***
13.2%	12.7%	12.9%	16.9%	***13.0%***	***12.5%***	Percentage retained to common equity	***13.0%***
20%	20%	17%	17%	***18%***	***17%***	Percentage of all dividends to net profits	***16%***
19.5	19.8	13.9	15.0	***Bold figures are***		Average annual P/E ratio	***14.0***
1.32	1.32	1.15	1.14	***Value Line***		Relative P/E ratio	***1.15***
1.0%	1.0%	5.6%	1.1%	***estimates***		Average annual dividend yield	***1.0%***

**d* indicates a deficit in working capital.

SOURCE: Value Line Industry Surveys.

of industry conditions. The investor should view such data as relative indicators of likely conditions and not all-inclusive, definitive pictures of all industries. With that warning firmly in mind, we can proceed to consider some information about the restaurant industry.

The sales data indicate expansion from about $14.0 billion in 1990 to $15.6 billion in 1991. This indicates an 11.09 percent increase in industry sales with a real growth rate of 6.69 percent after adjustment for the 4.40 percent inflation expected in 1991. This growth appears extremely strong in an economy that is growing at an overall rate of 1.0 percent. Further, Value Line expects industry sales to expand from $15.6 billion in 1991 to $21.3 billion from 1993 to 1995, an increase of 36.4 percent for the period. This increase far outpaces the expected growth of the U.S. economy. Other data indicate improving profit margins in the restaurant industry, bringing higher net profits, and a stable income tax rate.

At this point, the industry analysis should focus on the sales or revenue growth for the industry rather than reviewing the full range of information available. The investor should study the sales growth rates for a variety of industries to find those that appear to have the best chances for future growth; companies in these industries should offer the best investment opportunities. We will examine other industry data later in a different context, but at this stage of the analysis the investor should be seeking industries that appear to offer attractive investments.

For a brief example of this kind of comparison, note that revenue in the industrial services industry was expected to grow only 5.9 percent from 1990 to 1991, with total growth in revenues through 1995 of 22.2 percent. This was substantially below the rate of growth of the restaurant industry. In the absence of any other information, an investor might favor investment opportunities in the restaurant industry over those in industrial services due to strong expected future growth in restaurants.

Company Information After assessing prospects for the general economy and identifying strong industries within it, the investor needs to gather information of a third type: information about specific companies and the stocks and bonds they have issued that are available in the securities markets. News reports about individual companies and listings of their securities' prices appear in a broad range of daily and weekly local and national newspapers, including *The Wall Street Journal*, *Barron's*, and *USA Today*. The *Financial Times* is an especially good source of information about foreign companies and securities.

Financial information services publish extensive information about individual companies. The business sections of most public libraries offer *Moody's Handbook*, Standard & Poor's *Stock Reports*, and Value Line company reports. Exhibit 4.4 shows an example of a Value Line report on the company Microsoft. The publishers update these kinds of reports regularly. The following text explains the terms in the report. Comments about specific features correspond to the matching letters in the exhibit.

EXHIBIT 4.4

Value Line Company Report

A B BB C D

MICROSOFT OTC-MSFT	RECENT PRICE 123	P/E RATIO 34.6 (Trailing: 40.5 Median: NMF)	RELATIVE P/E RATIO 2.07	DIV'D YLD Nil	VALUE LINE 2124

F **TIMELINESS** (Relative Price Performance Next 12 Mos.) **1** Highest

SAFETY **3** Average

AA (Scale: 1 Highest to 5 Lowest)

BETA 1.35 (1.00 = Market)

G **1995-97 PROJECTIONS**

	Price	Gain	Ann'l Total Return
High	165	(+35%)	*8%*
Low	110	(-10%)	*-3%*

Y **Insider Decisions**

	A	M	J	J	A	S	O	N	D
to Buy	0	0	0	0	0	0	0	0	0
Options	0	0	7	1	4	6	2	3	1
to Sell	1	3	12	11	11	11	2	6	3

X **Institutional Decisions**

	2Q'91	3Q'91	4Q'91
to Buy	106	140	144
to Sell	110	77	79
Hld's(000)	49583	55245	56157

	1986	1987	1988	1989	1990	1991	Target Price Range 1995 1996 1997
High:	8.5	26.4	23.5	29.8	53.8	112.0	
Low:	3.5	7.9	15.1	15.3	28.0	48.7	

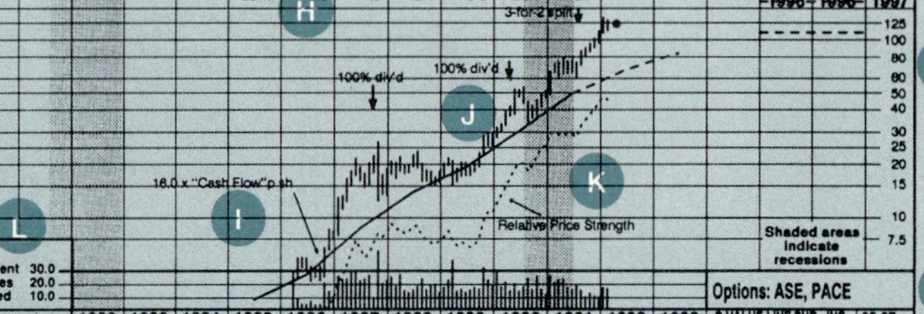

Z Options: ASE, PACE

Microsoft was founded in 1975 as a partnership between William Gates and Paul Allen. Mr. Allen temporarily ended his ties with the company in April of 1985. He now owns 16.2% of Microsoft's stock and serves as a member of the Board of Directors.

Microsoft was incorporated in 1981, and an initial public offering was held in March of 1986 at a price of $5.25 a share.

M

1982	1983	1984	1985	1986	1987	1988	1989	1990	1991	1992	1993	© VALUE LINE PUB., INC.	95-97
.20	.39	.76	1.09	1.29	2.19	3.67	4.91	6.94	10.58	*14.85*	*18.80*	Sales per sh[A]	*31.50*
--	--	--	.21	.29	.54	.87	1.19	1.91	3.09	*4.20*	*5.25*	"Cash Flow" per sh	*8.60*
.03	.05	.12	.17	.26	.47	.74	1.01	1.56	2.47	*3.55*	*4.50*	Earnings per sh[B]	*7.25*
--	--	--	--	--	--	--	--	--	--	*Nil*	*Nil*	Div'ds Decl'd per sh	*Nil*
--	--	--	.05	.09	.37	.44	.55	.93	1.52	*.95*	*1.00*	Cap'l Spending per sh	*1.20*
.07	.11	.24	.42	.91	1.51	2.33	3.43	5.39	7.75	*11.95*	*17.55*	Book Value per sh	*34.50*
123.88	128.21	127.56	129.20	153.12	158.14	160.99	163.76	170.55	174.23	*180.00*	*186.00*	Common Shs Outst'g[C]	*190.50*
--	--	--	17.7	19.5	19.8	25.2	17.8	19.9	22.6	*Bold figures are Value Line estimates*		Avg Ann'l P/E Ratio	*19.0*
--	--	--	1.44	1.32	1.32	2.09	1.35	1.48	1.46			Relative P/E Ratio	*1.45*
--	--	--	--	--	--	--	--	--	--			Avg Ann'l Div'd Yield	*Nil*
24.5	50.1	97.5	140.4	197.5	345.9	590.8	803.5	1183.4	1843.4	*2675*	*3500*	Sales ($mill)[A]	*6000*
21.2%	21.3%	29.9%	31.6%	33.7%	38.9%	34.4%	33.2%	37.1%	39.4%	*40.0%*	*39.0%*	Operating Margin	*38.0%*
--	--	--	3.5	5.8	7.6	16.0	24.2	46.3	75.8	*75.0*	*90.0*	Depreciation ($mill)	*150*
3.5	6.5	15.9	24.1	39.3	78.1	123.9	170.5	279.2	462.7	*685*	*890*	Net Profit ($mill)	*1485*
37.3%	41.4%	43.3%	43.7%	40.5%	42.4%	32.6%	32.0%	32.0%	31.0%	*32.0%*	*32.0%*	Income Tax Rate	*32.0%*
14.3%	12.9%	16.3%	17.2%	19.9%	22.6%	21.0%	21.2%	23.6%	25.1%	*25.6%*	*25.4%*	Net Profit Margin	*24.8%*
--	--	21.5	41.5	118.5	166.4	227.8	310.1	533.1	735.1	*1435*	*2455*	Working Cap'l ($mill)	*5505*
--	--	.4	--	1.9	2.0	--	--	1.9	--	*Nil*	*Nil*	Long-Term Debt ($mill)	*Nil*
8.3	14.6	30.7	54.4	139.3	239.1	375.5	561.8	918.6	1350.8	*2150*	*3265*	Net Worth ($mill)	*6575*
42.3%	44.3%	51.0%	44.3%	27.8%	32.4%	33.0%	30.3%	30.4%	34.3%	*32.0%*	*27.5%*	% Earned Total Cap'l	*22.5%*
42.3%	44.3%	51.7%	44.3%	28.2%	32.6%	33.0%	30.3%	30.4%	34.3%	*32.0%*	*27.5%*	% Earned Net Worth	*22.5%*
42.3%	44.3%	51.7%	44.3%	28.2%	32.6%	33.0%	30.3%	30.4%	34.3%	*32.0%*	*27.5%*	% Retained to Comm Eq	*22.5%*
--	--	--	--	--	--	--	--	--	--	*Nil*	*Nil*	% All Div'ds to Net Prof	*Nil*

W **CAPITAL STRUCTURE as of 12/31/91**

Total Debt $18.4 mill. **Due in 5 Yrs** $18.4 mill.

LT Debt Nil

Leases, Uncapitalized $14.9 mill.

Pension Liability None - No defined benefit pension plan.

Pfd Stock None

Common Stock 176,197,000 shs. (100% of Cap'l) as of 10/31/91

V

CURRENT POSITION ($MILL.)	1990	1991	12/31/91
Cash Assets	449.2	686.3	976.0
Receivables	181.0	243.3	259.2
Inventory (FIFO)	55.6	47.1	58.0
Other	34.1	51.8	58.4
Current Assets	719.9	1028.5	1351.6
Accts Payable	51.0	85.9	137.9
Debt Due	6.5	19.5	18.4
Other	129.3	188.0	200.9
Current Liab.	186.8	293.4	357.2

U

ANNUAL RATES of change (per sh)	Past 10 Yrs.	Past 5 Yrs.	Est'd '89-'91 to '95-'97
Sales	--	48.0%	*27.0%*
"Cash Flow"	--	52.0%	*27.0%*
Earnings	--	56.0%	*27.5%*
Dividends	--	--	*Nil*
Book Value	--	60.0%	*35.5%*

Fiscal Year Ends	QUARTERLY SALES ($ mill.)[A] Sep.30	Dec.31	Mar.31	Jun.30	Full Fiscal Year
1989	176.4	209.9	197.0	220.2	803.5
1990	235.2	300.4	310.9	336.9	1183.4
1991	369.4	460.5	486.9	526.6	1843.4
1992	580.5	681.9	*690*	*722.6*	*2675*
1993	*750*	*875*	*925*	*950*	*3500*

T

Fiscal Year Ends	EARNINGS PER SHARE[A B] Sep.30	Dec.31	Mar.31	Jun.30	Full Fiscal Year
1989	.22	.28	.24	.27	1.01
1990	.29	.42	.41	.44	1.56
1991	.47	.61	.65	.74	2.47
1992	.75	.90	*.92*	*.98*	*3.55*
1993	*.95*	*1.10*	*1.15*	*1.30*	*4.50*

S

Cal-endar	QUARTERLY DIVIDENDS PAID Mar.31	Jun.30	Sep.30	Dec.31	Full Year
1988	NO CASH DIVIDENDS BEING PAID				
1989					
1990					
1991					
1992					

N **BUSINESS:** Microsoft Corp. is one of the three largest independent makers of personal computer software. Systems software & languages (36% of 1991 sales) include *MS-DOS* (by far the most widely used operating system for IBM PCs and compatibles), *Windows*, *XENIX*, and *LAN Manager*. Applications software (51%) includes word processing, spreadsheet and other business programs. *Microsoft Mouse*, other hardware and books (13%). R&D: 13% of sales. Foreign sales were 47% of sales and 46% of pre-tax profits in 1991. Has 8,225 employees and 12,115 stockholders. Insiders own 54.1% of stock. Chairman and C.E.O.: William H. Gates. Inc.: DE. Address: One Microsoft Way, Redmond, WA 98052-6399. Telephone: 206-882-8080.

O **Microsoft is soaring from success to success.** Sales of the *Windows* graphic user interface (GUI) are holding up well. More important, as the *Windows* installed base grows, it pulls through sales of Microsoft's applications programs that are tailored to take advantage of *Windows'* capabilities. An upgraded version of the GUI that is more reliable and manages memory better should boost sales further starting in the last quarter of fiscal '92 (ends June 30th). And a revamped *Excel* spreadsheet program, also expected to debut in the June quarter, should lift that product's already impressive sales. Looking further out, by the end of calendar 1992 Microsoft likely will unveil its next generation *Windows New Technology*, which not only improves the product's functionality for individuals, but also will move the company solidly into the growing client-server field. We think these efforts, and a continuing stream of product upgrades, will keep sales and earnings on an upward trajectory through the middle of the decade.

Microsoft shares have been rising too. And the equity is top-ranked for year-ahead relative price performance. However, the issue's recent price appears to discount the earnings gains we project for the next 3 to 5 years. Too, the issue's high multiple makes it vulnerable should the company's earnings momentum slow. What's more, the equity could be especially volatile during the next several months, since . . .

P **The Apple lawsuit is moving forward.** Apple has sued Microsoft, claiming that *Windows* infringes on Apple's *Macintosh* interface. Papers filed in the case indicate that Apple thinks that *Windows* may have cost it over $4 billion. Microsoft has filed motions seeking the dismissal of the litigation, and all parties are scheduled to file all replies and motions by March 20th. After that, the judge will decide which, if any, of the claims should be dropped, and whether a trial, which could start by this summer, should be held. There is no way to predict an outcome, but it seems unlikely that any award would approach the full amount of damages claimed by Apple. In any event, Microsoft shares are likely to react to news on the legal front until the issue is decided.

George A. Niemond *March 13, 1992*

R (A) Fiscal year ends June 30th. (B) Primary earnings. Excludes nonrecurring loss: '87, 10c.

Next earnings report due mid-April.

(C) In millions, adjusted for stock splits and dividends.

Q

Company's Financial Strength	A+
Stock's Price Stability	30
Price Growth Persistence	90
Earnings Predictability	95

SOURCE: Value Line Ratings and Reports, March 13, 1992. Copyright © 1992 by Value Line Publishing, Inc. Used by permission.

Value Line Company Report

A Recent Price gives the price nine days prior to publication of the report.

B P/E Ratio gives the most recent price divided by the sum of earnings per share for the most recent six months and estimated earnings per share for the following six months.

C Relative P/E Ratio divides the stock's current P/E ratio by the median P/E ratio for all stocks under Value Line review.

D Dividend Yield estimates cash dividends to be declared in the following 12 months divided by the recent price.

E Target Price Range estimates the range over which Value Line expects the stock to trade over the following three to five years. This range is highlighted on the price chart and shown numerically in the box labeled "1995–97 Projections" at the left of the price chart.

F Timeliness and Safety show Value Line's ranks (1–Highest to 5–Lowest) for the stock on these attributes. Timeliness refers to expected stock price performance relative to stocks in general. Safety measures the stock's price stability and the company's financial strength.

G 1995–97 Projections, as discussed above.

H High and low figures give the stock's highest and lowest prices for the year.

I This figure gives Value Line's report of earnings plus depreciation (cash flow) for the company multiplied by a number selected to correlate the stock's three- to five-year projected price with the firm's projected cash flow.

J The ratio chart plots monthly price ranges of the stock on a logarithmic scale to show percentage changes in true proportion. This chart shows a $1 move in a $10 stock as equivalent to a $10 move in a $100 stock.

K Relative Price Strength describes the stock's past price performance as compared to the Value Line Composite Average of 1,700 stocks. The Timeliness Rank usually predicts the future direction of the stock's trend.

L This figure gives the number of shares traded monthly as a percentage of the total shares outstanding.

M Statistical milestones reveal significant long-term trends in two ways. (1) The upper series records per-share results. (2) The lower series records company performance. Note that the statistics for 1992 and 1993 are estimated, as are the average figures for 1995 to 1997. Value Line revises these estimates to reflect future developments. The weekly Summary & Index calls attention to such revisions.

N This summary gives a condensed description of the business.

O This section is a 400-word report on recent developments and prospects, which Value Line issues quarterly on a preset schedule.

P The concluding paragraph of the report usually provide a summary and outlook.

Q Value Line indexes represent the company's financial strength, price stability, price growth persistence, and earnings predictability.

R Footnotes explain a number of things, such as the way earnings are reported, whether fully diluted or on a primary or average shares outstanding basis.

S Quarterly Dividends Paid reflect actual payments. The total of dividends paid in four quarters may not equal the figure shown in the annual series on dividends declared since dividends declared at the end of a year are paid in the first quarter of the following year.

T Quarterly Earnings shown are earnings per share. (Estimates appear in bold type.) Quarterly sales figures report gross sales.

U This figure gives the annual rate of change per share for sales, cash flow, earnings, dividends, and book value, with actual data for past results and estimates of future performance.

V Current Position evaluates current assets, current liabilities, and other components of working capital.

W Capital Structure data indicate the firm's long-term debt and equity position, showing the percentage of capital in debt, preferred stock, and common stock.

X This section reports decisions to buy or sell the stock made during the previous five quarters by the biggest institutions including banks, insurance companies, mutual funds, investment advisers, internally managed endowments, and pension funds with over $70 million in equity holdings. It also shows how many shares these institutional investors hold.

Y The record of Insider Decisions reflects trading in the stock by corporate officers as reported to the SEC a month or more after execution.

Z The Options section indicates whether options are listed on the stock, and on what exchange they are most actively traded.

AA Here is the core of the report's advice. This shows how Value Line ranks the stock for timeliness, safety, and beta (which indicates the stock's sensitivity to fluctuations in the market as a whole). Microsoft's 1.35 rating indicates the stock is 35 percent more volatile than the market as a whole. (A rating of 1 indicates a volatility *on par* with the market as a whole.)

BB P/E Median gives a rounded average of four values from the middle of the range of the stock's average annual price–earnings ratios over the previous 10 years.

Standard & Poor's Stock Reports Standard & Poor's provides another excellent source of information in its *Stock Reports*, an example of which appears in Exhibit 4.5. As with the Value Line report, the following text will

EXHIBIT 4.5

Standard & Poor's Stock Report

A

AmVestors Financial Corp.

B NASDAQ Symbol AVFC (Incl. in Nat'l Market)

Price	D Range	E P-E Ratio	F Dividend	G Yield	H S&P Ranking	I Beta
C Jan. 22'92	1991-2					
$3\frac{1}{8}$	$3\frac{1}{2}$-1	7	None	None	B-	NA

Summary

J **AmVestors Financial is the holding company for American Investors Life Insurance Co., which primarily sells single-premium deferred annuities. Following a net loss in 1990 that reflected reduced premium income and greater investment losses, results were profitable in the first nine months of 1991.**

Business Summary

K AmVestors Financial Corporation is the holding company for American Investors Life Insurance Co., which principally sells single-premium deferred annuities. The company offers its insurance products in 46 states and the District of Columbia through about 15,000 licensed agents and brokers. The company does not intend to seek admission in New York. As of September 1986, the company disposed of, through assumption and coinsurance reinsurance treaties, about 75% of its nonparticipating ordinary life insurance. During 1989, AmVestors executed a coinsurance agreement that reinsured 90% of the risk on its block of single-premium whole life policies written prior to 1989.

L

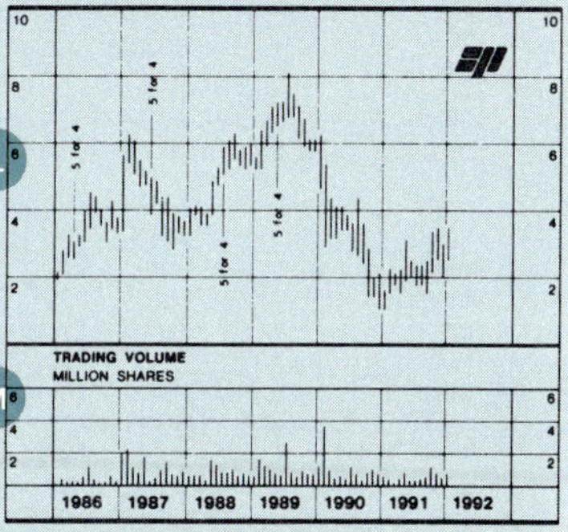

M

Revenues from principal products in recent years were as follows:

N	1990	1989
Single-premium whole life ...	1%	19%
Single-premium deferred annuities	88%	66%
Single-premium immediate annuities	8%	12%
Other life	1%	2%
Other annuity	2%	1%

During 1990, AmVestors continued its emphasis on the marketing of single-premium life and annuity insurance products through independent life insurance agents and brokers. The company currently markets eight fixed-benefit single-premium deferred annuity (SPDA) plans. These annuities provide various competitive interest guarantees, tax-deferred accumulation of interest, guaranteed cash values and a choice of guaranteed income options on the selected maturity date. A flexible-premium deferred annuity (FPDA) and single-premium immediate annuities (SPIAs) are also available.

During 1984's fourth quarter, AmVestors introduced SPDAs, which accounted for 95% of its annuity production in 1990. SPIAs and FPDAs accounted for the remainder of annuity production. An SPDA contract generally involves the tax-deferred accumulation of the single premium, at interest rates revised periodically by the company until the maturity date, when the policyowner generally can elect to defer the maturity date or can elect to apply the policy value under one of various annuity payout options available.

O **Important Developments**

Jan. '92— AmVestors issued 172,000 shares of $2 Series B convertible preferred stock for a total stated value of $4.3 million to Financial Securities Fund, L.P. in exchange for a 25.03% equity position in the fund, a nonpublicly traded limited partnership that invests primarily in undervalued securities of financial institutions and other financial services companies. Additionally, the company said that it expected earnings for 1991 to exceed $0.60 a share.

Next earnings report expected in late March.

P **Per Share Data ($)**

Yr. End Dec. 31	**1990**	**1989**	**[1]1988**	**1987**	**1986**	**1985**	**1984**	**1983**
Tangible Bk. Val.	**1.18**	2.71	3.20	2.43	1.75	1.34	1.41	NA
Oper. Earnings[2]	**NA**	NA	NA	0.27	0.19	d0.19	0.22	0.09
Earnings[2]	**d1.29**	d0.31	[3]0.58	0.18	0.30	d0.04	0.21	0.13
Dividends	**0.20**	0.18	0.145	0.123	0.098	0.081	0.078	0.073
Payout Ratio	**NM**	NM	25%	68%	33%	NM	38%	57%
Prices—High	**$6\frac{1}{4}$**	$8\frac{1}{8}$	$6\frac{1}{4}$	$6\frac{1}{4}$	$4\frac{5}{8}$	$2\frac{7}{8}$	$3\frac{1}{2}$	$3\frac{3}{8}$
Low	**1**	$5\frac{1}{4}$	$3\frac{1}{4}$	$2\frac{3}{4}$	$2\frac{5}{8}$	$1\frac{3}{4}$	$2\frac{5}{8}$	$2\frac{1}{2}$
P/E Ratio—	**NM**	NM	11-6	24-10	24-14	NM	16-12	36-26

Data as orig. reptd. Adj. for stk. divs. of 25% May 1989, 25% Jul. 1988, 25% Jun. 1987, 25% Apr. 1986, 5% Mar. 1985, 5% Mar. 1984, 5% Mar. 1983. **1.** Refl. acctg. change. **2.** Bef. spec. items of +0.04 in 1986, +0.01 in 1983. **3.** Ful. dil.: 0.50. NM-Not Meaningful. NA-Not Available. d-Deficit.

Q Standard OTC Stock Reports
Vol. 58/No. 14/Sec. 6

R **February 3, 1992**

S Standard & Poor's Corp.
25 Broadway, NY, NY 10004

EXHIBIT 4.5

Standard & Poor's Stock Report *(continued)*

3125M **AmVestors Financial Corporation**

T **Income Data (Million $)**

Year Ended Dec. 31	Life Ins. In Force	Premium Income Life A & H	Premium Income Cas./Prop.	Net Invest. Inc.	Total Revs.	Net Bef. Taxes	Net Oper. Inc.	[2]Net Inc.	% Return On Revs.	% Return On Assets	% Return On Equity
1990	**455**	**9**	**Nil**	**132**	**116**	**d14.1**	**NA**	**d17.7**	**NM**	**NM**	**NM**
1989	479	15	Nil	113	119	3.5	NA	d4.5	NM	NM	NM
[1]1988	506	8	Nil	75	82	7.6	NA	6.6	8.0	0.8	14.9
1987	604	226	1.45	35	263	5.0	4.53	3.7	1.4	0.9	10.8
1986	530	134	1.47	15	150	1.5	1.35	2.1	1.4	0.8	8.9
1985	1,200	46	0.83	5	52	d1.1	d1.12	d0.2	NM	NM	NM
1984	1,472	20	1.67	2	24	NM	1.31	1.2	0.1	0.1	NA
1983	1,580	12	0.04	2	14	0.4	.0.50	0.7	2.5	1.1	NA

U **Balance Sheet Data (Million $)**

Dec. 31	Cash & Equiv.	[3]Premiums Due	Investment Assets [4]Bonds	Investment Assets Stocks	Investment Assets Loans	Total	% Invest. Yield	Deferred Policy Costs	Total Assets	Debt	[5]Common Equity
1990	**35.9**	**1.21**	**1,445**	**0.79**	**Nil**	**1,458**	**10.2**	**118**	**1,623**	**33.6**	**17.3**
1989	49.6	0.91	1,124	1.23	Nil	1,135	11.0	91	1,282	31.6	40.2
1988	39.9	0.67	901	1.30	Nil	916	9.8	74	1,039	31.1	41.2
1987	17.0	0.90	591	1.20	3.20	606	6.9	33	660	10.7	47.2
1986	11.3	1.38	327	1.84	2.47	333	6.7	15	364	10.0	38.3
1985	3.5	0.59	101	3.81	3.58	110	6.7	12	129	Nil	7.9
1984	0.9	1.50	33	3.77	2.36	41	NA	10	57	Nil	8.3

Data as orig. reptd. **1.** Refl. acctg. change. **2.** Bef. spec. items. **3.** Accts. & notes receiv. **4.** Fixed maturities, incl. short-term inv. **5.** Incl. conv. pfd. aft. 1985. d-Deficit. NA-Not Available. NM-Not Meaningful.

V **Review of Operations**

For the nine months ended September 30, 1991, total revenues were $120,819,000, up 53%, year to year, primarily reflecting higher investment income and the recording of net investment gains, against net investment losses. Investment income benefited from greater average invested assets, which resulted from increased SPDA premiums. Pretax income contrasted with a deficit and, after taxes of $783,000, versus $2,117,000, net income was $4,105,000 ($0.30 a share), against a loss of $19,685,000 ($1.43).

W **Share Earnings ($)**

Quarter:	1991	1990	[1]1989	1988
Mar.	0.15	0.06	0.10	0.12
Jun.	0.09	0.04	0.02	0.11
Sep.	0.06	d1.48	0.12	0.15
Dec.		0.09	d0.55	0.13
		d1.29	d0.31	0.58

X **Dividend Data**

Prior to omission in November 1990, dividends on the common had been paid each year since 1967.

Y **Finances**

In September 1991, AmVestors substantially completed a significant restructuring of its bond portfolio through the disposal of approximately $188 million (par value) of below-investment-grade bonds. The restructuring also involved the sale of $250 million of investment-grade bonds.

AmVestors realized net losses of $24.3 million on its bond portfolio in 1990. As of September 30, 1991, the company's total unrealized bond losses were $25,453,000, compared with $81,527,000 at year-end 1990. The portfolio of below-investment-grade bonds was reduced to 10% at September 30, 1991, from 21% at December 31, 1990, and 35% at 1989 year-end. In 1990, AmVestors ceased making new investments in "junk" bonds.

As a result of a conversion offer concluded on June 1, 1989, substantially all of the company's 8½% subordinated debentures due 2012 were converted into 2,394,486 AmVestors common shares. During 1988, $10,353,000 of the debentures had been converted into 2,310,749 common shares.

Z **Capitalization**

Notes Payable: $35,064,000 (9/91).

Common Stock: 14,004,701 shs. (no par).
Institutions hold about 20%.
Shareholders of record: About 6,200 (12/90).

Options: To purchase 1,716,878 shs. at $1.94 to $5.50 ea. (9/91).

d-Deficit.

AA **Office**—415 Southwest 8th Ave., P.O. Box 2039, Topeka, KS 66601-2039. **Tel**—(913) 232-6945. **Chrmn, CEO & CFO**—R. W. Laster Jr. **Pres**—M. V. Heitz. **Secy**—L. F. Hammes. **Dirs**—J. Q. Adams Jr., J. L. Andersen, R. G. Billings, W. E. Cooper, M. V. Heitz, R. W. Laster Jr., R. R. Lee, R. R. Peake. **Transfer Agent & Registrar**—Commerce Bank & Trust, Topeka. **Incorporated** in Kansas in 1986. **Empl**—71.

 S. Q. Gallagher

explain the S&P Stock Report for AmVestors Financial Corp., with specific comments keyed to the exhibit through letter designations.

A Gives the name of the company.

B Gives the company's stock symbol. Most NASDAQ and OTC symbols include four letters, while New York Stock Exchange symbols include three letters.

C States the common stock's price in dollars per share on the date of the report.

D Shows the range over which the price per share varied during the period indicated.

E Gives the stock's current price–earnings ratio, calculated by dividing the price in C by the previous year's annual earnings per share.

F Reports the dividend in dollars per share paid during the current year.

G Divides the dividend by the price in C.

H Gives S&P's ranking for the stock, which is based on the historical growth and stability of earnings and dividends over the previous 10 years. S&P awards seven grades: A+, A, and A− indicate above-average stocks; B+ is average; B, B−, and C are below average. The notation *NR*, for no ranking, indicates a stock that lacks sufficient historical data or does not fit well in the ranking process. A rank of D signifies a company in reorganization. Note that S&P's ranks do not anticipate future performance, nor do they measure quality. A high rank is not tantamount to an opinion that the stock is a good investment or to a recommendation to buy it. Investment decisions require thorough analysis to assess future prospects; a security's performance has no effect on you before you own it.

I Lists the beta of the stock, which measures the variability of its price in relation to the variability of the market as a whole, as mentioned above.

J The summary briefly reviews the company's recent performance.

K The Business Summary describes the company and its operations.

L The graph depicts the range over which the stock's price varied over the period indicated.

M Shows the volume of shares traded monthly.

N The table indicates the proportion of its revenues the company has earned from its principal products.

O Comments about new developments in the company.

P The table gives per-share data going back several years, including book value, operating earnings, earnings, and dividends, along with the dividend payout ratio, high and low prices, and price–earnings ratio. The book value per share is the net worth of the company divided by the number of common shares outstanding. Operating earnings reflect income before security transactions for financial companies; earnings reflect income after security transactions. Dividends represent payments to shareholders. The payout ratio is the percentage of earnings per share paid out to common shareholders.

Q Indicates whether the stock is traded over the counter, on the American Stock Exchange, or the New York Stock Exchange.

R Gives the date of the report.

S Names the source of the report with its address.

TU Summarize the company's income and balance sheet information for several years. The income data include total revenues or sales, net income from operations, net income after taxes, profit as a percentage of revenues, and return on assets and equity. The kinds of information presented here vary for different companies. The balance sheet data review the company's assets and liabilities, identified by type and amount, including total assets, debt, and common equity.

V Reviews company operations and results, including current changes in revenues, total assets, operating expenses, and total earnings.

W Reports on the trend of quarterly earnings per share for a few years.

X Details dividend declarations and distribution.

Y Discusses the company's financing operations.

Z Summarizes the company's capital structure, reporting total debt and notes payable, common stock, retained earnings, shares of stock outstanding, number of shareholders, and the proportion of the outstanding shares that are owned by financial institutions.

AA Gives the address of the company and names its officers and directors, and its transfer agent and registrar.

Standard & Poor's updates all of the data in its Stock Reports in a timely fashion. This and similar kinds of information about specific companies should help the investor to keep up with the fortunes of interesting firms in a dynamic market.

The Basic Information System

The investor should be able to build an excellent personal investment information system by combining several of the components mentioned above, including a range of publications supplemented by investment information service resources that are available without cost at a public library. The basic system should start with *The Wall Street Journal* and *Business Week* plus the Sunday *New York Times*. Subscriptions to these publications represent an expenditure of about $300 a year. If this cost is too high at the beginning of your investment program, just stick with your local newspaper and read the rest at the library. You'll be visiting there regularly anyway to review

Value Line company reports and Standard & Poor's data in Stock Reports, Industry Surveys, and *Outlook*. These sources can form the foundation of an excellent information system.

Whatever the particular sources of information, the search for investments follows a **top down plan.** In this approach to investing, you begin by hunting for information about the future outlook for the economy as a whole. When you become confident that the market environment will be favorable, you look for industries that show strong growth prospects, and then you identify the companies that are **competitive leaders** within the best industries. These companies' securities will generally give the investor the highest return for his or her money.

top down plan: A method of identifying attractive investments that begins with analysis of the economy as a whole, then proceeds to analyze industry data, and finally, to review company performance.

competitive leaders: The most efficient and profitable companies in an industry.

In addition to the mountains of printed investment information that is available, modern investors have access to a new, and potentially invaluable source of information. The rapid spread of personal computer technology has brought huge volumes of data and extremely flexible tools for reviewing that data within the reach of just about everyone. PC-based services can supplement a system using publications and information services, ease the burden of complex calculation and data-handling requirements, and even give access to brokers' trading systems after the investor arrives at a decision. These services have become integral parts of many investors' information systems, and they will surely become more important in coming years.

Personal Computer-Based Information Systems

Dow Jones News/Retrieval Service

If you are willing to pay the price, the Dow Jones News/Retrieval Service can provide a constant stream of news and financial information 24 hours a day, 365 days a year to your personal computer (assuming it is equipped with a modem). The price can be high. A standard membership costs $29.95 per location for a start-up fee, with an annual fee of $18, which is waived the first year. The start-up fee includes three hours of connect time within 90 days of receipt of the password. After that, the user pays a per-minute charge for time connected to the system; standard service outside prime service hours costs from $0.20 to $1.76 per minute. Corporate and Blue Chip membership connect time rates are lower, but membership fees are higher. For this expenditure, you get access to a wide array of information of many kinds, including information on topics ranging from the apparel market to the Supreme Court.

Value Line's Value/Screen Plus

Value/Screen Plus is an easy-to-use database derived from Value Line's *Investment Survey* that allows the investor to analyze investment performance over time of some 1,600 stocks. Value Line provides this information

EXHIBIT **4.6**

Value/Screen Plus Variables

Ratings and Estimates	
Timeliness rank	Price stability index
Safety rank	Beta
Financial strength rating	Current earnings per share
Industry code	Current dividend
Industry rank	Technical rank

Market Data	
Recent price	Price/book value
52-week high price	13-week percentage price change
52-week low price	26-week percentage price change
Current P/E ratio	Market value ($millions)
Current yield (%)	Options listing

Historical Measures	
Sales ($millions)	Last quarter earnings per share
Percentage return on net worth	12-month percentage change in earnings per share
Percentage retained to common equity	5-year earnings per share growth
Book value per share	5-year dividend growth
Debt as percentage of capital	5-year book value growth

Growth Projections	
Estimated percentage change in earnings per share quarter 1	Projected earnings per share growth
Estimated percentage change in earnings per share quarter 2	Projected dividend growth
Estimated percentage change in fiscal year	Projected book value growth
Projected 3–5 year appreciation (%)	Projected 3–5 year average return

SOURCE: Value/Screen Plus instruction manual, p. 1.3. Copyright © 1992 by Value Line Publishing, Inc. Used by permission.

EXHIBIT 4.7

Ad for Schwab Equalizer

SOURCE: © & ® Charles Schwab & Co., Inc. (PPP) 1992. All Rights Reserved. THE EQUALIZER® IS A REGISTERED TRADEMARK OF CHARLES SCHWAB & CO., INC. Courtesy of Charles Schwab & Co., Inc.

on two diskettes as frequently as once per week. (Most investors use quarterly data.) The investor specifies an acceptable range of values for each variable and Value/Screen Plus identifies the stocks that meet the specified criteria. Exhibit 4.6 provides a list of the 38 variables for which Value/Screen Plus can select.

The Equalizer

The Equalizer from discount brokerage service Charles Schwab & Company provides news, company information, and research reports, just as other services do. In addition, it offers portfolio management assistance and even allows the investor to make trades. Exhibit 4.7 shows the Equalizer software package.

Brokers As Information Sources

Brokerage firms offer investors more than mere access to securities exchanges. One of their most important roles is to provide information. Brokers send monthly statements to their retail clients to verify holdings and transactions. In addition, they can provide information about a company or security upon request, and many supply unsolicited information they think might be interesting from time to time. The investor pays for this information in transaction commissions and other fees, so he or she should take full advantage of it. Few retail clients have access to the substantial volumes of research data that brokers supply to their institutional clients, but an individual investor to whom such information is available could certainly benefit from it.

All of this assumes, of course, that the investor wishes to make his or her own decisions rather than agreeing to invest money at the direction of the broker. This also assumes that the information is available free or relatively cheaply. (Most brokerage firms cover the cost of providing information in the transaction commissions they charge.) Using the broker as a source of information, rather than simply letting the broker invest your money, can make you a bit more independent.

SUMMARY

Effective investing takes time and knowledge. Published sources provide much of the necessary knowledge and information; you must supply the time, beginning by developing your personal investment information system. Analyze how you work and think, and find investment information sources to fit your needs. This search starts in *The Wall Street Journal;* read it regularly, noting any information that may affect your investment goals. *The*

Journal contains a wealth of information about the economy in general, particular industries, and individual companies. You might wish to start a file about each company you are considering for investment.

To identify the best securities in which to invest, follow the top down plan. First, look for forecasts for the economy as a whole in *The Journal*, *Business Week*, Value Line reports, and Standard & Poor's *Outlook*. When a favorable economic climate seems likely, look for information about performance of various industries. S&P's *Industry Survey* and Value Line reports will help you find the best prospects. Finally, you want to identify the companies that are competitive leaders in strong industries, based on information in Standard & Poor's *Stock Reports* and Value Line company reports.

During good economic times, the common stock of the most efficient, profitable companies in growing industries will provide the best rates of return for a given level of risk. Through diligence and persistence, you can develop a powerful investment information system through which to spot excellent investment opportunities.

INVESTMENT MANAGEMENT CONCEPTS

1. All investors must inform themselves about their available opportunities before making investment decisions.

2. A personal investment information system will make it easier to identify and track investments and keep up with changes.

3. Understanding the types of available information and the best sources of each type can lead toward informed investing.

4. The flow of information keeps securities markets efficient, assuring investors of security prices that fully reflect company performance.

REVIEW QUESTIONS

1. Why is it important to know where to look for investment information?

2. What is an investment information system?

3. What is the purpose of an investment information system?

4. What basic types of information does an investor need about the economy?

5. What type of information does the investor need about individual industries?

6. What information does the investor need about companies within an industry?

7. Future earnings and dividends are important to the investment decision. Explain where information of this type can be obtained.

8. Explain what information about the general economy can be obtained from Value Line reports and Standard & Poor's *Outlook*.

9. What industry information can be obtained from Value Line industry reports and Standard & Poor's Industry Surveys?
10. What information can be obtained about companies from Value Line company reports and Standard & Poor's *Stock Reports?*
11. What important attributes of a company should an investor examine?
12. Explain the part brokers play in the investment information process.

SELF-CORRECTING PROBLEM

Suppose that a classmate in your computer science class suggested that Microsoft common stock would be a good investment. To satisfy yourself that your classmate's judgment is correct, you might ask a few questions about the stock.

What is its price?

Where is it listed?

What dividend does it pay?

Does the firm have much debt?

Is it, in general, a good company?

Will the company's earnings grow in the future?

Purchased at its current market price, what annual rate of return will the stock provide?

Exhibit 4.4 represents a sample page for Microsoft Corporation from the Value Line *Investment Survey: Ratings and Reports.* To verify your classmate's good opinion of Microsoft common stock, find answers to these questions in the Value Line report. Does Microsoft stock look like a good investment?

Answer to Self-Correcting Problem

The price of the stock is 123.

It is listed in the OTC market under the symbol MSFT.

The company pays no dividend on the stock.

The company's $18.4 million total debt is low in comparison to its net worth of $1,350.8 million in 1991.

One of the three largest independent makers of personal computer software, Microsoft produces the most popular operating system software packages in the personal computer market, including MS-DOS, OS/2, and Windows. It is certainly a good company.

Microsoft's earnings per share are expected to grow 27.5 percent between 1995 and 1997.

Its annual average rate of return is estimated to be between 7 and −3 percent for the period 1993 to 1995.

On the surface Microsoft Corporation is a dominant company in the computer software field. At a price of 123 per share, however, it offers a very low annual average return for the period 1995 to 1997. Although the company is strong, the stock doesn't seem to be a very profitable investment.

Confronting your classmate with your analysis, you learn that she based her favorable opinion of the stock on a conversation she overheard between two professors. An effective information system can give you critical protection from potentially bad investments!

SELECTED READINGS

Burgauer, James. *The Do-It-Yourself Investor*. Chicago: Probus Publishing, 1987.

Frumkin, Norman. *Guide to Economic Indicators*. Armonk, N.Y.: M. F. Sharpe, 1990.

Levine, Sumner N., ed. *The 1991 Business One–Irwin Business and Investment Almanac*. Homewood, Ill,: Business One–Irwin, 1991.

O'Hara, Frederick M., and Robert Sicigano. *Handbook of United States Economic and Financial Indicators*. Westport, Conn.: Greenwood Press, 1985.

In addition to the books listed above, investors can find useful information about investments from many sources, including the periodicals listed below.

Federal Government Sources

Periodic reports on the national economy, Bureau of Economic Analysis, Washington, D.C.

Federal Reserve Bulletin, Board of Governors of the Federal Reserve, Washington, D.C.

Survey of Current Business, U.S. Department of Commerce, Washington, D.C.

Business Conditions Digest, Bureau of the Census, U.S. Department of Commerce, Washington, D.C.

Private Publications

Barron's
Business Week
Dun's Review and Modern Industry
Financial World
Forbes
Fortune
Money
Nation's Business
New York Times
The Wall Street Journal

Investment Services

Moody's Investors Service

Standard & Poor's Corporation

Publications include *Outlook, Stock Survey, Stock Reports, Stock Guide, Basic Analysis, Current Analysis*, and *Outlook and Earnings Forecaster*.

Value Line

Institutional Brokers Estimate System (IBES)

chapter 5

Security Markets and Brokers

The authors' first experience with a broker who bought and sold shares was with an investment club formed by a group of professors in a business school. Each member of the club contributed $10 as an initial investment and then contributed $10 per month. With 20 members in the club, the total monthly contribution was $200. At the end of the first year, with interest earnings added, the investment fund totalled $2600. After five years the total amount contributed by the members reached $12,200. Each member, therefore, had paid in $610.

When the club was dissolved at the end of the five-year period, each person received $960. The gain was $350 per member.

The $350 gain might not seem like much; however, the average annual rate of return for each of the five years in the investment period was over 20 percent. This was an excellent return. At the time Treasury bills yielded 6.0 percent, long-term government bonds provided the investor with a yield of 8.0 percent, and mortgages on residential houses were at the 9.5 percent level. This background sets the stage for the main point of the story, which is about the services provided by a broker.

The first item of business after meeting with the broker was filling out the agreement form between the broker and the Oxford Investment Club. Next was to identify the person who would be authorized to trade for the club. The goals of the club were also indicated: growth and income. Then the agreement was signed by the authorized agent of the club—the president—and the club was in business. The next step was to give the broker the check for $200 and decide where to invest the club's money. Because the club's $200 was not enough to buy stock, it was held in the club's brokerage account until sufficient funds were available.

The club members provided the investment recommendations, while the broker provided the place to keep the money and the securities and provided the club members with monthly reports. In spite of the fact that a minimum of almost 6 percent commission was paid on small trades, the fees were not onerous because the club traded shares infrequently.

As the fund grew, the members became bolder and ventured into the new issue market. Today it is referred to as IPOs, or initial public offerings. When a new issue came up, the broker called, and let the president know about it. If there were an interest indicated, on a preliminary basis, the broker would hold 100 or 200 shares for the club. The president of the club was in touch with the broker weekly. When the new issue came to market, the broker would send a prospectus—a red herring prospectus, which was preliminary information in the same form as a final prospectus. At that point the club would either buy or decline to buy the shares. Of course, these new issues were discussed in *The Wall Street Journal* so that all the members knew about them before they went public.

During one of their monthly meetings, the club members discussed an IPO in a company called Polychrome, based on information obtained from the broker. The president called the broker the next day and ordered the purchase of 100 shares of Polychrome. A few weeks later, the president called the broker to find out about Polychrome. The broker said, "I bought you 100 shares at the initial offering price of $8.00 a share. It's now trading at $16.00." This was the most profitable speculative investment the club ever made. The club members earned a 100 percent return on their investment in only a few weeks' time.

The broker quickly told the president that the next time he had a "dog or cat" (a nickname for unpopular IPOs) to sell, that the club better be a buyer. "Let me think about that," said the president; "I'll get back to you." The club members were happy about the success of the investment, but they did not care for the broker's attitude about buying dogs. They decided that they did not wish to be involved with speculative stocks of poor quality. Therefore, they thought it best to find a broker who would be more attuned to their investment goals. The moral of this story is that even if you are making money, you might have the wrong broker to suit your needs.

Introduction

Securities are bought and sold just like any other product or service. Someone who wants to buy a new suit goes to a clothing store. A full-service store will provide alterations, extend credit, and stand behind its products, but its price might be higher than a discount store for similar or identical merchandise. The discounter, however, would provide alterations only at additional cost, and its selection of colors, sizes, and designs would be limited. The investor faces a similar choice among brokerage firms that can give access to the same securities, but offer different ranges of services and charge different commissions.

The retail salesperson might advise the clothes buyer about style, price, and fit; a securities broker does similar things to provide investors what they want. The retail store is the marketplace for the clothing purchaser, the place where buyers and sellers arrange transactions through the assistance of the retail salesperson, who receives a salary, and possibly a commission on each sale, as compensation. The securities marketplace resembles the clothing store in many ways. Investors arrange stock or bond transactions on securities exchanges through brokers, who receive commission income for their effort.

securities exchange: Marketplace where investors' representatives trade listed securities.

stock broker: A person who buys and sells securities on behalf of investors for a commission.

We will examine the operations of the various **securities exchanges** toward the end of the chapter. First, we will consider the investor's relationship with the **stock broker,** who is the intermediary between the exchange and the investor.

Life with Your Broker

To gain insight into the investor–broker relationship, we interviewed several brokers. The following investment professionals offered information and advice:

William Raiford, Vice President, Shearson, Lehman, Hutton and Company, Washington, D.C.

John Cleveland, Vice President and Office Manager, Kidder, Peabody, Washington, D.C.

William Craig, Vice President, Kidder, Peabody, Cleveland

Elliott Benson, Vice President and Director of Retail Investment Research, Ferris Baker Watts, Washington, D.C.

Robert Randal, Vice President, Paine Webber, Washington, D.C.

Virtually all of these professionals suggested a similar procedure for selecting a broker. Begin by interviewing the broker, providing details about your complete financial background and your investment goals. Friends, bankers, and business associates can recommend candidates for you to interview. Parents and relatives are a good source of information about brokers. Many people have friends who are brokers; knowledge of the character and capabilities of such a person can speed up and simplify the process of searching for a broker.

All of the brokers we interviewed suggested meeting with the brokers on your list, along with their office managers, at their offices. In the meeting, explain what you want from your investments, your attitude toward risk, and what role you want the broker to play in your investment decisions. Ask the broker what services you could expect and how these services would be provided. After the interviews, possibly with the help of the office manager, you can determine whether the broker would suit your needs. Personality is important, and you will know after the interview whether you like the broker and can work with him or her. If not, the office manager may well be able to suggest another member of the office staff that would be more suitable.

Selecting a broker is a lot like selecting a doctor or dentist. You usually seek recommendations from family and friends, based on which you meet several doctors and talk to them. It takes time, but the interview answers the critical question of whether you like this person. After interviewing your candidates, you decide, and you reevaluate your decision in the course of your relationship with the professional you choose.

Pointers on Selecting a Broker

The following summary provides a few more detailed pointers to help you select a broker:

1. Seek recommendations from family, friends, bankers, and businesspeople you know.
2. Interview the recommended brokers to determine whether their personalities and methods of operation suit your investment objectives. Ask them what types of stocks or bonds they would recommend to you and how frequently they would suggest that you trade. If you want to make long-term investments in high-quality securities, you don't want a broker who likes to make frequent trades involving risky stocks or bonds.
3. Make certain that the broker has adequate experience in both up and down markets.
4. Try to verify the impression of the broker's honesty and integrity that you got from the person who recommended him or her.
5. Make certain that the broker knows your goals and how you wish to achieve those goals.
6. Make certain that the broker can execute your orders quickly and also cheaply.

Throughout your search, watch for these overriding qualities: experience, honesty and integrity, and eagerness to help you make sound financial decisions and implement them economically.

perspective on **ETHICS**

The Self-Regulatory Process and Securities Arbitration

The Securities and Exchange Commission (SEC) has primary responsibility for regulating the nation's securities markets. Some of the regulatory duties of the SEC are delegated to what are known as self-regulatory organizations (SROs), such as the New York Stock Exchange, the American Stock Exchange, and the National Association of Securities Dealers. These SROs, subject to the supervision of the SEC, operate and regulate their respective markets. They also promulgate and enforce ethical standards for participants in these markets. One of the SRO's ethical responsibilities is to administer securities arbitration forums, which are subsidized by the broker-dealer member firms of the SROs.

Arbitration forums exist to arbitrate disputes that arise between broker-dealers and their customers and offer a valuable and inexpensive alternative to litigation in the event of a dispute. Most broker-dealers require, as a condition of opening an account, that individual investors agree to use arbitration in the event of a dispute between the investor and the firm. Cases involving small dollar amounts (less than $10,000) may be settled by a single arbitrator, while larger cases go before a panel of three arbitrators, with one member chosen from the securities industry and two public members from outside the industry. Small cases can even be settled by mail.

Disputes between investors and their brokers arise from a variety of disagreements, but most often involve allegations of unsuitable investments, churning (excessive trading in order to earn more commissions for the broker), fraud, and unauthorized trading. Lack of suitability is the most common cause of such disputes. Unsuitability complaints generally allege that a particular investment strategy or transaction was excessively risky and therefore unsuitable based on the investment objectives, age, income, wealth, or other characteristics of the customer bringing the charges. In one case in New York, for example, a couple living on the income from a family trust fund moved the funds from a bank to a brokerage account where their broker invested their money in high-risk futures and options trading. When the bulk of the trust funds were lost to commissions and trading losses, the couple took the broker to arbitration to seek return of the money on the grounds that these investments were obviously unsuitable. The arbitrators agreed and the broker and his firm had to reimburse the couple.

There has long been controversy about whether arbitration panels, because they are sponsored by the industry SROs, are biased in favor of the industry. However, a recent study by the General Accounting Office (GAO) found that "analysis of statistical results of decisions in arbitration cases at both industry-sponsored and independent forums showed no indication of a pro-industry bias in decisions at industry-sponsored forums."

The two most likely alternatives to industry-sponsored arbitration forums are to submit to arbitration by an independent arbitrator, most often via the American Arbitration Association, or to begin formal court proceedings (litigation). Litigation is very expensive and time-consuming and may result in literally years of appeals. All things considered, arbitration seems to offer many advantages to individual investors who have a dispute with their brokers. The many advantages of arbitration were summarized succinctly in *Fortune* magazine (1991 Investors Guide edition, pp. 202–208) by Lloyd S. Clareman, a New York attorney who has represented investors both in arbitration and litigation:

> "Arbitration today offers more advantages than disadvantages to aggrieved investors. A dissatisfied customer who might not otherwise have thought of suing, or who would have shunned the prospect of getting involved in arduous litigation, can now contemplate going to a reasonably evenhanded arbitration in which all he needs to do is file a complaint and then show up for the hearing. To learn how to initiate action, he can just call the arbitration department of any of the exchanges or other organizations specified in his customer's agreement. . . . Suing your broker has never been easier. With arbitration it is fast and simple. There can be no war of attrition in which the deep-pocketed corporation, through artful court maneuvers, can outlast the customer's depleted resources or his patience."

SOURCE: General Accounting Office, *Securities Arbitration* (May 1992). Lloyd S. Clareman, "1991 Investors Guide," *Fortune*, 202–208.

Selecting a Brokerage Firm

Most investors meet brokers first and then learn about the firms where these professionals work. Still, you select a brokerage firm in much the same way that you select a broker, beginning by asking friends, relatives, bankers, and businesspeople about which firms are considered the best.

You must choose whether to do business with a regional firm or a national firm. Many investors like to deal with members of their local communities. They think these people give them better service and more attention. Other investors like the bigger, national firms that provide more extensive (though not necessarily better) research, among other benefits.

Regional or national, you want a firm that satisfies the following guidelines:

1. Seek a firm that has a reputation for quality and integrity.
2. Make certain that the firm has adequate research facilities and offers a broad range of services in all security markets.
3. Look for a profitable firm with a strong balance sheet. The investment information services profiled in Chapter 4 follow many brokerage firms. Moody's, Standard & Poor's, and Value Line can provide a great deal of valuable information about the financial condition and earnings outlook for a publicly traded brokerage firm.
4. Verify that the firm can execute orders promptly and efficiently.

Remember that the broker and the firm serve the investor. A diligent search will identify an investment professional and a brokerage firm that will work quickly, efficiently, and economically to do the best job for you. This requires that they understand and respect you and your goals and objectives.

Getting Started—Opening a Brokerage Account

Opening a brokerage account is much like opening a checking account. You begin by filling out a form like the one in Exhibit 5.1. Accurate information on this form will help the broker to better assess and serve your needs.

In filling out the form, you tell the broker a lot about yourself, including your age, financial background, net worth, goals, and objectives. Based on this information, the broker recommends appropriate investments. Part of the broker's responsibility is to know the client to be sure recommended investments meet the client's needs.

Most of the information requirements of the new account form are self-explanatory, but a few items need some explanation. In Item 2 you provide your name and address. If more than one person owns the account, the form must specify ownership terms. *Jt Ten* indicates that account holders will be joint tenants with rights of survivorship. Each tenant has the right to deal in securities in the account. *Ten by Ent* stands for "tenants by entirety," in which, should one account holder, or tenant, die, the other owns the entire account. *Ten in Comn*, for "tenants in common," means that if one tenant should

EXHIBIT 5.1

New Brokerage Account Form

Kidder, Peabody & Co.
INCORPORATED

NEW ACCOUNT REQUEST

1. ACCOUNT NO. (OFFICE) (ACCOUNT) R.R. NO. (R.R. NO.)

2 ACCOUNT NAME AND MAILING ADDRESS
☐ MR.
☐ MRS.
☐ MISS
☐ MS.
STATE ZIP CODE

☐ JT TEN
☐ TEN BY ENT
☐ TEN IN COMM
☐ UGTMA
☐ COM PROP

3 I.R.S. NO.

4. EACH MUST BE ANSWERED — YES NO
A. U.S. CITIZEN?
B. CHARGE FULL N.Y. STATE TRANSFER TAX? (ONLY INDIVIDUAL N.Y. STATE NONRESIDENTS MAY CLAIM LOWER TAX.)
C. K.P. EMPLOYEE OR RELATION? (SEE 18D BELOW)
D. IN-HOUSE DISCRETIONARY ACCT.? (SEE 21 BELOW)
E. ATTAINED AGE OF MAJORITY?

5. DISPOSITION OF INCOME
4 HOLD IN REGULAR ACCOUNT
ACCUMULATE IN INCOME ACCOUNT, AND
5 SPECIAL HANDLING — 6 HOLD IN INCOME ACCT
7 REMIT QUARTERLY — 8 REMIT MONTHLY

5B. SPECIAL REMIT ADDRESS

6 DISPOSITION OF SECURITIES
A TRF&SHIP — 2 SHIP & DP-RP N.Y.
B TRF&HOLD — 3
C STREET NAME — 4 DRAFT
D DEL. FREE — 5 DP N.Y.
0 SHIP & DP — 6 DP N.Y.-RP N.Y. (OUT OF TOWN REGION ONLY)
1 DRAFT-RP N.Y. — 0 DP N.Y.-RP N.Y. (N.Y. REGION ONLY)
IF CODE IS 0 OR 6 LINE 8A MUST BE COMPLETED

6A. SHIP BRANCH OR DELIVER BANK

6B. TRANSFER NAME, DELIVER NAME OR OTHER INSTRUCTIONS

7A. INSTITUTIONAL CREDIT CODE — % RATE — 7B. ACCT. PROFILE NUMBER

8A. FINS NO. –

INTERNAL ACCOUNT

INTERESTED PARTY 1
2
3

9 NUMBER OF DUPLICATE CONFIRMS REQUIRED

9A DUPLICATE CONFIRM MAIL ADDRESS, IF OTHER THAN ACCOUNT NAME

10 NUMBER OF DUPLICATE STATEMENTS REQUIRED

10A DUPLICATE STATEMENTS MAIL ADDRESS IF OTHER THAN DUPLICATE CONFIRM NAME

THE QUESTIONS BELOW ARE IMPORTANT UNDER THE "KNOW YOUR CUSTOMER" RULE AND THEREFORE MUST BE ANSWERED IN FULL. IF TRUSTEE, EXECUTOR, GUARDIAN, OR CUSTODIAN IS INVOLVED, INFORMATION SHOULD REFER TO SAME

16A RESIDENCE IF DIFFERENT FROM MAILING ADDRESS AND, IF CORPORATION ACCOUNT, NATION OF INCORPORATION IF NOT U.S.A. *

(B) NAME AND ADDRESS OF EMPLOYER — (F) AGE — (G) MARRIED — (H) NO. DEPENDENTS
(C) RESIDENCE TEL. NO.
(D) BUSINESS TEL. NO.
(E) POSITION — (I) DOES NASD FREE RIDING RULE APPLY TO CUSTOMER — YES NO
(J) SPOUSE'S NAME — (K) SPOUSE'S EMPLOYER — (L) POSITION

17 BANK AND LOCATION — (A) SAVINGS / SPECIAL CHECK / REGULAR CHECK — (B) APPROX. BAL. $ — (C) NAME OF OFFICER CONTACTED

18A HOW LONG HAVE YOU KNOWN CUSTOMER? — MOS. YEARS — 18B NAME & K.P. ACCOUNT NO. OF CUSTOMER INTRODUCING ACCOUNT IF APPLICABLE

18C DOES K.P. EMPLOYEE OR RELATION HAVE ANY DIRECT OR INDIRECT INTEREST IN THIS ACCOUNT? — YES NO — 18D IF QUESTION 4C OR 18C ANSWER IS "YES", GIVE NAME OF EMPLOYEE AND RELATION TO CUSTOMER

19 INITIAL TRADE BUY SELL — QUANTITY — DESCRIPTION — PRICE — 20. DOES INITIAL TRADE REQUIRE OPENING MARGIN OR OPTION ACCOUNT WITH COMPLETED DOCUMENTS ON HAND? — YES NO

21A TO YOUR KNOWLEDGE WILL THERE BE ANY TRADING AUTHORITY CONNECTED WITH THIS ACCOUNT? — YES NO — IF ANSWER IS "YES", PLEASE WRITE IN NAME OF AGENT

21B RELATIONSHIP OF AGENT TO CUSTOMER. IF AGENT ANOTHER K.P. CUSTOMER, GIVE ACCOUNT NO.

21 BACKGROUND OF AGENT — (C) IS AGENT EMPLOYEE OF K.P. — (D) REGISTERED INVESTMENT ADVISOR — (E) ATTORNEY — (F) OTHER

22(A) REMARKS OR SPECIAL INSTRUCTIONS (ANY INVESTMENT OBJECTIVE IDENTIFIED EXPLICITLY BY THE CUSTOMER MUST BE RECORDED)

SOURCE OF ACCOUNT: ☐ REFERRAL ☐ ADVERTISING ☐ COLD CALL

22(B) ARE YOU LICENSED TO DO BUSINESS IN STATE OF CUSTOMER'S RESIDENCE? YES ☐ NO ☐ — 22(C) DEPOSIT $ — BRANCH MANAGER INITIAL IF DEPOSIT IS WAIVED

SIGNATURE OF REGISTERED REPRESENTATIVE — SIGNATURE OF BRANCH MANAGER — MONTH DAY YEAR

IMPORTANT IF THIS REQUEST IS NOT ACCEPTABLE, OR NOT SUBMITTED PROMPTLY, FURTHER TRANSACTIONS MAY BE REFUSED.
* IF ALIEN, IT IS ESSENTIAL WE HAVE RESIDENT OR INCORPORATION ADDRESS TO MAKE APPROPRIATE FEDERAL WITHHOLDING.

BRANCH

SOURCE: Kidder, Peabody & Co., Inc. Reprinted by permission.

die, the predetermined percentage of the account owned by that tenant passes to his or her estate.

UGTMA indicates an account under the Uniform Gifts to Minors Act or the Uniform Transfer to Minors Act. These acts accommodate gifts of securities to minors, who cannot legally own shares in their own names. State laws define a minor as someone below the age of either 18 or 21. The brokerage house might impose its own restrictions on accounts owned by those under 21 years of age.

Com Prop indicates community property ownership of the account. Some states, California for one, have enacted community property laws that direct that a married person owns a one-half interest in any asset that his or her spouse owns.

Item 5 on the new account form gives instructions for the disposition of income in the account. The simplest arrangement is to retain any investment income from interest or dividend payments in the account. The broker will invest this income in a money market fund until the investor withdraws it or reinvests it in other securities.

Item 6 specifies the disposition of the security certificates. Many investors like to keep their own securities, though this requires safekeeping facilities and sending them through the mail between the brokerage and the investor to accommodate trades. It is easier to keep the assets in **street name,** which means that the broker holds the actual securities, while the investor receives all the information, dividends, and interest that the company owes the security owner. This eliminates the inconvenience of physical safekeeping of the securities.

street name: Registering one's personal investments in the name of the broker having custody of the investments.

Securities held in your account at a brokerage firm are insured by the **Securities Investors Protection Corporation (SIPC),** a nonprofit organization of broker-dealers created by an act of Congress in 1970, against loss due to financial failure of the firm or inability of the firm to meet its financial obligations to its customers. SIPC's financial resources consist of approximately $600 million of member contributions, a $500 million line of credit with a consortium of banks, and a backup line of credit of up to $1 billion with the U.S. Treasury. Each account at a firm that is a member of SIPC is insured against losses of up to $500,000 worth of cash and securities, although insurance of cash is limited to $100,000. Obviously, SIPC cannot insure against loss in market value of securities, but it does provide important protection against losses due to business failures by brokerage firms. You should never consider allowing a brokerage firm that is not a member of SIPC to hold your securities for safekeeping or in street name. If your account exceeds $500,000, most brokerage firms have insurance available over and above SIPC limits. The leading discount broker, Charles Schwab & Co., for example, automatically provides all accounts with an additional $2,000,000 of account insurance at no cost to the customer through the Aetna Casualty and Surety Company. Additional insurance above the $2.5 million limit can be purchased by customers if needed.

Security Investors Protection Corporation (SIPC): A nonprofit broker organization created by an act of Congress that insures investors' brokerage accounts against losses due to failure of the firm holding the securities to meet its financial obligations to customers.

Several additional items of information requested are worth noting. Item 19, for example, specifies the initial transaction for the account. Item 20 asks whether the initial trade requires a margin account or option account. A margin account is a credit account through which the investor borrows money from the brokerage firm to buy shares. **Margin** is the percentage of the dollar amount of a transaction that the investor must pay in cash to buy securities; the brokerage lends the balance of the purchase price. In effect, you pledge the securities as collateral for the loan to buy them. The Federal Reserve Board establishes margin requirements, that is, the portion of a security's purchase price an investor can borrow, in an effort to maintain orderly conditions in the financial markets. Currently, the Fed has set the margin requirement for stocks at 50 percent and bonds at 30 percent. A beginning investor probably will not need a margin account, but this is one service the brokerage can offer.

margin: The cash deposited when financing part of a securities purchase with a loan from a brokerage firm.

An investor who needs to open a margin or option account must fill out additional forms. An **option** gives the investor the right to buy or sell a security, as a later chapter will discuss.

option: A right to buy or sell a security at a fixed price for a limited period of time.

Items 21A, B, and C specify the authorization the investor gives the broker to trade shares for his or her account. Most investors should not authorize the broker to make his or her investment decisions. This is particularly important to beginning or novice investors, who should look for long-term investments rather than strings of get-rich-quick trades. Excessive trading is often unprofitable after brokerage costs for transactions are deducted from the proceeds from trades. Also, individual investors should make their own decisions to buy or sell securities rather than passing this responsibility to the broker.

Item 22A is extremely important for the investor. This is where you state your investment goals, your willingness to take risks, and the types of investments you want to make. In this space, for example, you might tell the broker you will call when you want to make a trade, rather than having the broker call you to suggest trades. This preserves your right to make your own decisions. Spend some time preparing these instructions; it will pay off in the future.

The Broker's Role—Buying and Selling Securities

Investors purchase bonds, shares of common and preferred stock, and many other types of securities through brokers, paying commissions for the trades they make. You could conceivably buy or sell securities yourself, if you could find a buyer. First, however, a broker or banker would have to guarantee that the owner of the securities could legitimately sell them. Also, finding a buyer on your own is not easy. The broker can identify another investor who wants to buy exactly what you want to sell much more cheaply and efficiently on one of the recognized securities exchanges. These and

EXHIBIT 5.2

Comparative Brokerage Commissions

	COMMISSION ON							
	50 SHARES		100 SHARES		200 SHARES		1,000 SHARES	
BROKER	$20 STOCK	$75 STOCK	$20 STOCK	$75 STOCK	$20 STOCK	$75 STOCK	$20 STOCK	$75 STOCK
Burke Christensen & Lewis	$25	$25	$25	$25	$ 50	$ 50	$116	$225
Charles Schwab & Co.	35	67	51	85	68	107	122	209
Heartland Securities	24	24	31	31	46	46	126	126
Pacific Brokerage	25	25	25	25	25	25	78	78
Royal/Grimm & Davis	30	38	32	40	38	50	90	110
Merrill Lynch	50	95	71	97	115	194	356	708

As full-service brokerage commissions rise, investors who don't need the advice of a firm like Merrill Lynch can save by using discount brokers, but discounters' rates differ widely, as the table shows.

SOURCE: *Fortune*, March 16, 1987, p. 112.

other practical obstacles make securities trading a job for professionals, despite the fees they charge for completing your transactions.

Transaction Costs

commission: The fee received by a broker for executing an investor's transaction.

The cost of buying and selling securities can be substantial. Brokers charge **commissions** based on the dollar amount of each transaction and the number of shares involved. They take smaller percentages for trades with larger dollar amounts, as shown in Exhibit 5.2, which is a partial schedule of typical commission fees for 50- to 1,000-share orders. Before May 1, 1975, all members of the New York Stock Exchange charged standard commissions. Since then the Securities and Exchange Commission has required them to negotiate commissions, which has reduced this cost considerably.

round lot: The usual increment for trading stock, 100 shares.

Commissions vary for round-lot and odd-lot stock transactions. A **round lot** is a block of 100 shares; a block of fewer than 100 shares is called an

odd-lot fee: A fee charged by a brokerage in addition to the commission for a transaction involving fewer than 100 shares.

odd lot. A broker will charge an **odd-lot fee** of ⅛ to ¼ of a point ($.125 to $.25) per share in addition to the usual commission for any transaction involving fewer than 100 shares. To buy 10 shares of a stock selling for $75 per share, you might pay a commission of $25, including the odd-lot fee; this transaction cost amounts to 3.33 percent of the transaction's value. You could buy 100 shares of the same stock for approximately $85, or 1.13 percent; and for a 1,000-share purchase, your commission would be approximately $210, or 0.28 percent. You can keep brokerage costs to a minimum by trading in round lots and large dollar amounts.

Other Costs of Buying and Selling Besides the commission and perhaps an odd-lot fee, a broker will charge an SEC fee of $0.01 for each $500 of the transaction's value. This fee helps to finance the Securities and Exchange Commission (SEC), the primary regulatory body for the securities industry.

Sellers must pay small amounts in New York state taxes on proceeds from trades on the New York Stock Exchange. Mail and registry fees are paid when shares are sent through the mail.

underwriting fee: A commission charged for purchase of an initial public offering that is implicit in the security's price.

The buyer of a security at an initial public offering (IPO) pays an **underwriting fee** rather than a commission. The broker sells the security for a bit more than the issuing company receives for it. The difference, or spread, between the selling price and what the issuer receives is the broker's compensation for marketing the security. The investor's confirmation slip for the trade and monthly statement will show only the price he or she paid for the security with no commission indicated, but the price includes an implicit selling fee. Investors must not be fooled into thinking that they pay no commissions for IPOs.

Transaction costs consume funds that could otherwise pay for purchases of valuable assets. As Exhibit 5.3 shows, they can become a significant drain on the net worth of the investor who disregards them. You should plan trades with these costs in mind.

Discount Brokerage Firms

discount brokerage firm: A firm that executes investors' securities transactions for lower commissions than traditional brokerage firms charge.

In recent years, many large discount brokerage firms have emerged to compete with traditional firms. **Discount brokerage firms** can charge lower commissions than traditional brokerage firms because they keep their costs of operating lower by providing less research information and investment counseling. In fact, most discount firms provide only one service—they execute investors' orders upon request. If you gather information yourself and make investment decisions on your own, a discount brokerage can save you some money. The advisory services of traditional brokerage might be worth their price, though. Exhibit 5.2 compares fees for discount brokerage firms to those of the full-service Merrill Lynch.

EXHIBIT 5.3

Brokerage Fees for Various Types of Investments

How Much Will That Cost?

What a broker or financial adviser earns on a $10,000 investment

MUTUAL FUNDS	
Closed-end fund (new offering)	$400 - $900
Mutual fund (open-end)	$400 - $850
Closed-end (secondary market)	$200 - $250
Money market fund	$0
No-load fund (not sold by broker)	$0

STOCKS	
Penny stocks, thinly traded OTC	$200 - $1,000+
Common (initial offering)	$300 - $600
Common stock	$200 - $250

BONDS	
Municipal and corporate:	
(long-term)	$200 - $500+
(short-term)	$ 50 - $100
Treasury bills, notes, bonds	$ 50

OTHER	
Limited partnerships	$400 - $825
Annuities, life insurance (single premium)	$400 - $800
Unit investment trust, Initial offering:	
(long-term)	$400 - $500
(short-term)	$100 - $300

SOURCE: *The Wall Street Journal*, June 25, 1991, p. C1. Reprinted by permission of *The Wall Street Journal*, © 1991 Dow Jones & Company, Inc. All rights reserved worldwide.

Principles of Effective Securities Transactions

The primary goal for procedures to buy and sell securities is to keep order execution efficient and to minimize transaction costs. Keeping the following principles in mind will promote achievement of that goal:

1. Trading larger blocks of shares reduces commission rates.
2. Commission rates are lower for trades with larger dollar values.
3. Brokers reduce their charges as you do more business with them.
4. Discount brokerages usually charge less for small trades than traditional brokerages.

Mechanics of Trading Securities

Giving Orders

market order: An order to buy or sell a security at its market price as soon as possible.

limit order: An order to buy or sell a security at a specific price.

stop order: An order to buy or sell that becomes a market order when the stock price meets or exceeds a stated level.

To trade securities, you must learn how to communicate with your broker. The simplest, most direct way to make a securities transaction is to enter a **market order.** This simply tells the broker to buy or sell a certain number of shares immediately at the existing market price. Brokerage industry regulations require the broker to sell at the highest price or buy at the lowest price available in the market when an order is given.

Another type of order, a **limit order,** instructs the broker to trade a security when it reaches a specific price. For example, you might enter a limit order to buy one round lot of General Motors (GM) at 42 when the stock's current price was 47. If the price of GM were to decline to 42, the broker would buy 100 shares for you. If the price did not decline to 42, your order would remain unfilled. A broker can have difficulty filling such an order in a dynamic market when prices are changing rapidly.

A **stop order** becomes a market order when the price meets or exceeds a stated level. You might enter a stop order to sell a stock you own (called a sell stop) if its price drops to or below a certain minimum level at which you no longer want to own it. If the price falls to or below the specified level, the stop order becomes a market order and the broker sells your stock at the best available price. Thus your sale may occur at or below the stop price. If the stock never drops to your stated minimum, the order remains unfilled.

A Typical New York Stock Exchange Trade

To summarize the discussion of the mechanics of trading securities, consider an example. Suppose that you have determined that the outlook for the economy as a whole is bright, and your search for investments that will offer the best returns has led you to investigate the restaurant industry, with special attention to the fast-food segment. Your analysis has revealed that the industry is expected to grow faster than the national economy, but it is a hotly competitive industry led by McDonald's, Kentucky Fried Chicken, Burger King, Wendy's, and Hardee's. In addition, a host of other companies compete, including Sizzler, Taco Bell, Arthur Treacher's Seafood, and Long John Silver's, along with smaller chains and local competitors.

Your analysis suggests that McDonald's is a good buy at about $30 a share. Although its growth has slowed, the company is introducing new products and building new stores, one of them in Moscow, and it plans further international expansion. A newspaper report states that McDonald's earnings increased about 11 percent last year and it controlled 18.7 percent of sales in the near-$70 billion U.S. fast-food industry. After careful thought and thorough analysis, you decide to buy 100 shares of McDonald's.

You call your broker at Kidder, Peabody and Co., Inc. and place a market order to buy 100 shares of McDonald's. The Kidder, Peabody broker

EXHIBIT 5.4

Brokerage Order Form

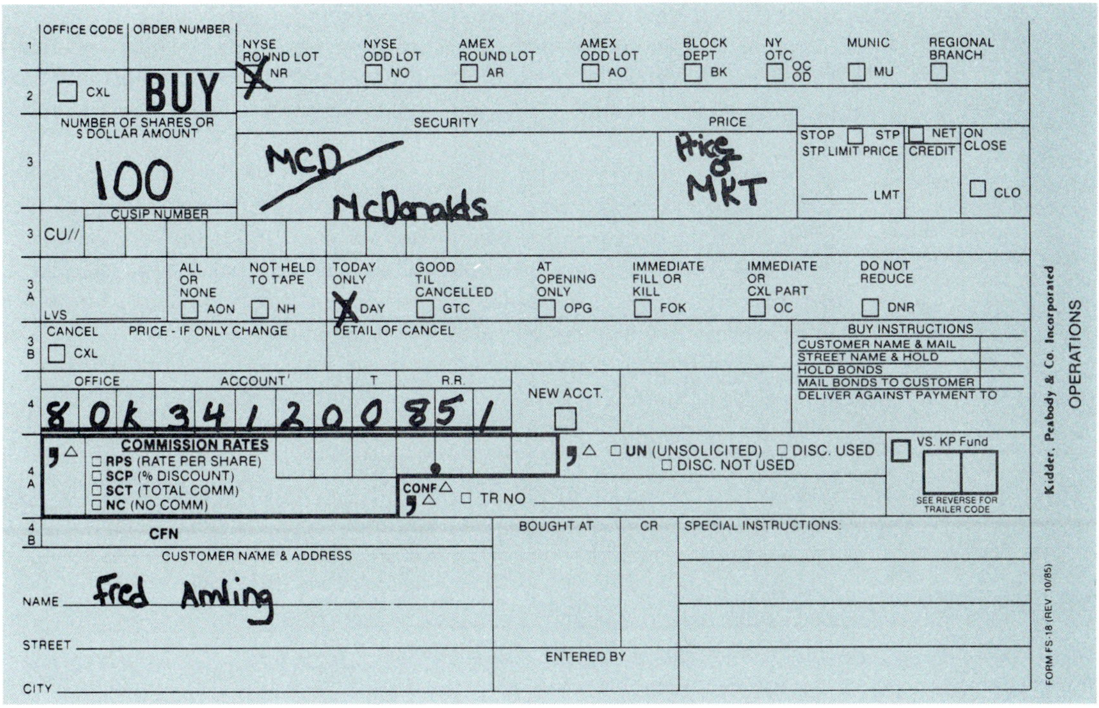
OFFICE CODE | ORDER NUMBER
NYSE ROUND LOT NR (X) — NYSE ODD LOT NO — AMEX ROUND LOT AR — AMEX ODD LOT AO — BLOCK DEPT BK — NY OTC OC OD — MUNIC MU — REGIONAL BRANCH
CXL — BUY
NUMBER OF SHARES OR $ DOLLAR AMOUNT: 100
SECURITY: MCD McDonalds
PRICE: Price MKT
STOP — STP — STP LIMIT PRICE — LMT — NET CREDIT — ON CLOSE — CLO
CUSIP NUMBER — CU//
LVS — ALL OR NONE AON — NOT HELD TO TAPE NH — TODAY ONLY DAY (X) — GOOD TIL CANCELLED GTC — AT OPENING ONLY OPG — IMMEDIATE FILL OR KILL FOK — IMMEDIATE OR CXL PART OC — DO NOT REDUCE DNR
CANCEL CXL — PRICE - IF ONLY CHANGE — DETAIL OF CANCEL
BUY INSTRUCTIONS: CUSTOMER NAME & MAIL — STREET NAME & HOLD — HOLD BONDS — MAIL BONDS TO CUSTOMER — DELIVER AGAINST PAYMENT TO
OFFICE — ACCOUNT — T — R.R.: 8 0 k 3 4 1 2 0 0 8 5 1
NEW ACCT.
COMMISSION RATES: RPS (RATE PER SHARE) — SCP (% DISCOUNT) — SCT (TOTAL COMM) — NC (NO COMM)
UN (UNSOLICITED) — DISC. USED — DISC. NOT USED
VS. KP Fund — SEE REVERSE FOR TRAILER CODE
CONF — TR NO
CFN — BOUGHT AT — CR — SPECIAL INSTRUCTIONS:
CUSTOMER NAME & ADDRESS
NAME Fred Amling
STREET
CITY
ENTERED BY
Kidder, Peabody & Co. Incorporated — OPERATIONS
FORM FS-18 (REV 10/85)

SOURCE: Kidder, Peabody & Co., Inc. Reprinted by permission.

fills out a buy order form like the one shown in Exhibit 5.4, stating the number of shares to be purchased, the name and stock symbol of the company, and the price desired (or the market price). The order form also indicates the type of order, in this case a day order, which must be exercised upon receipt. Your broker passes the order form to Kidder, Peabody's operations department, which routes copies for internal record keeping and sends the original to the trading desk, where a brokerage employee wires the order via the firm's New York office to the floor of the New York Stock Exchange where the stock is listed and traded.

DOT system: The NYSE's computerized Designated Orders Turnaround system which automates securities transactions.

The New York Stock Exchange's **Designated Orders Turnaround (DOT) system** numbers the trade and transmits it to the post where McDonald's shares are traded. Since your order is for less than 5,000 shares, the computer system automatically matches it with a corresponding order to sell 100 shares of McDonald's; larger orders are presented to the crowd gathered at the trading post for prompt execution. The price you pay is determined in the on-going auction at the trading post when your order is executed. The order is reported on the tape at that price and the buy price is then reported back to your broker.

This complicated process takes only a matter of seconds to complete, thanks to the New York Stock Exchange's computer automation of the trading process and systems for the direct transmission of orders and completed transaction information between the stock exchange's trading post and brokers' offices. In 1984 the NYSE launched its Super DOT 250 system to further improve its operations.

trade confirmation: A written statement from a broker verifying execution of an investor's order.

Your broker will probably call you soon after you place the order to tell you the exact price you paid, and will send you a **trade confirmation** statement detailing this price, the commission for your trade, and the settlement date. The settlement date is the date when you must pay for the shares you purchased (and when the seller will receive cash for the shares he or she sold), usually five trading days after the trade date.

A sample trade confirmation statement appears in Exhibit 5.5. It confirms the purchase of 100 shares of McDonald's Corporation on October 2, 1989, for a price of $29\frac{3}{4}$ for a total transaction value of $2,975. This trade involved a commission of $61.33 and a service charge of $2.00 to cover the costs of processing the trade. This transaction must be settled by October 10, 1989. The investor's money market fund account held sufficient cash to pay for the McDonald's stock. Had the account not held enough money, the investor would have sent a check for $3,038.33 to the broker at Kidder, Peabody who took the order. The standardized trade confirmation form also shows the name and address of the account holder and those of the broker. It is extremely important that the investor review each piece of information in the confirmation report to verify the accuracy and appropriateness of these details. If the form contains an error, it should be reported to the broker immediately.

A Typical NASDAQ Trade

Not all stocks are listed on a securities exchange like the New York Stock Exchange. Those that are not listed are traded over the counter via a computer network that connects brokerage firms. The network, maintained by the National Association of Securities Dealers (NASD), is called the NASD Automated Quotations (NASDAQ) system. An example will show how this system works.

The *Washington Post* recently quoted a closing price of 14 for shares of Hechinger, a supplier of building materials for do-it-yourself consumers. After following the company for a period of time, you know the shares have sold as high as 26, and recently they have sold between 18 and 20. Company management charted a new direction for the company to cater to the home-improvement market. Although the company's current stock price is weak compared to its recent performance, you consider the company attractive

EXHIBIT 5.5

Trade Confirmation

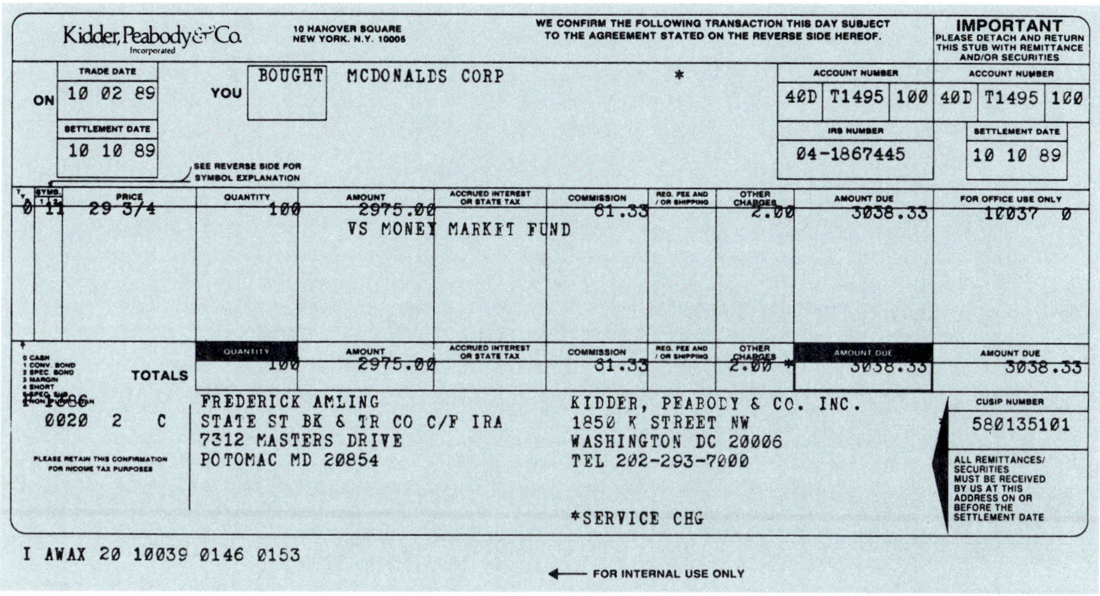

Kidder, Peabody & Co. Incorporated
10 HANOVER SQUARE NEW YORK, N.Y. 10005
WE CONFIRM THE FOLLOWING TRANSACTION THIS DAY SUBJECT TO THE AGREEMENT STATED ON THE REVERSE SIDE HEREOF.
IMPORTANT PLEASE DETACH AND RETURN THIS STUB WITH REMITTANCE AND/OR SECURITIES

ON TRADE DATE 10 02 89 — YOU BOUGHT MCDONALDS CORP *
SETTLEMENT DATE 10 10 89
SEE REVERSE SIDE FOR SYMBOL EXPLANATION
ACCOUNT NUMBER 40D T1495 100 — ACCOUNT NUMBER 40D T1495 100
IRS NUMBER 04-1867445 — SETTLEMENT DATE 10 10 89

TY	SYMB.	PRICE	QUANTITY	AMOUNT	ACCRUED INTEREST OR STATE TAX	COMMISSION	REG. FEE AND / OR SHIPPING	OTHER CHARGES	AMOUNT DUE	FOR OFFICE USE ONLY
0	11	29 3/4	100	2975.00		61.33		2.00	3038.33	10037 0
				VS MONEY MARKET FUND						
TOTALS			100	2975.00		61.33		2.00 *	3038.33	AMOUNT DUE 3038.33

0 CASH 1 CONV. BOND 2 SPEC. BOND 3 MARGIN 4 SHORT 5 SPEC. SUB 6 NON-...
F1566
0020 2 C
PLEASE RETAIN THIS CONFIRMATION FOR INCOME TAX PURPOSES

FREDERICK AMLING
STATE ST BK & TR CO C/F IRA
7312 MASTERS DRIVE
POTOMAC MD 20854

KIDDER, PEABODY & CO. INC.
1850 K STREET NW
WASHINGTON DC 20006
TEL 202-293-7000

*SERVICE CHG

CUSIP NUMBER 580135101
ALL REMITTANCES/SECURITIES MUST BE RECEIVED BY US AT THIS ADDRESS ON OR BEFORE THE SETTLEMENT DATE

I AWAX 20 10039 0146 0153
← FOR INTERNAL USE ONLY

SOURCE: Kidder, Peabody & Co., Inc. Reprinted by permission.

for long-term investment. You call your broker at Ferris Baker Watts and ask for a price quote.

While you wait on the phone, the broker punches the stock symbol for Hechinger stock (Hech A) into a stock quotation terminal. The screen responds with a table of prices showing a current NASDAQ price of Bid $12\frac{1}{4}$ Ask $12\frac{3}{8}$. This means that the highest price any buyer is currently willing to pay, the bid price, is $12\frac{1}{4}$. The lowest price any seller is willing to accept, the ask price, is $12\frac{3}{8}$. The broker tells you the stock is offered at $12\frac{3}{8}$.

You give the broker a limit order to buy 100 shares if the price declines to $12\frac{1}{4}$. The broker agrees to place the order and call you when it is executed. The broker then fills out a buy order form for one round lot at a limit price of $12\frac{1}{4}$, indicating that the order is GTC, i.e., good 'til canceled. If the ask price remains above $12\frac{1}{4}$, you will not purchase the shares, and the order will remain in effect until you cancel it or until the ask price falls back to $12\frac{1}{4}$.

The broker keeps part of the form and takes the rest of it to the trader across the room. The trader telephones the order to the New York OTC brokerage that handles Hechinger stock. Here is the first major difference between over-the-counter trading and trading on listed exchanges; recall that

EXHIBIT 5.6

Monthly Account Statement

Kidder, Peabody Investor Account

Statement Period: Sep 29 - Oct 26, 1989 **Page 1 of 4**
Account Number: 40D-T1495-100 Tax ID Number: 04-1867445

GE Financial Services

Your registered representative
JOHN G. CLEVELAND
1850 K STREET NW
WASHINGTON DC 20006 (202) 293-7000

To:
FREDERICK AMLING
STATE ST BK & TR CO C F IRA
7312 MASTERS DRIVE
POTOMAC MD 20854

Copies sent to:
STATE ST BK & TR CO CUST FBO

October Portfolio Balance Sheet

FREDERICK AMLING

	(A) Previous Month	(B) Added Purchases	(C) Subtracted Sales	(D) Changes in Portfolio Value	(E) Current Month	(F) % of Portfolio
Cash and Money Market Funds	4,272.92	75.32	3,038.33		1,309.91	10.3%
Equities	8,850.00	3,038.33	0.00	-538.33	11,350.00	89.7%
Net Worth of Portfolio	**$13,122.92**				**$12,659.91**	**100.0%**

Change In Net Worth (G)

Previous Month	13,122.92
Portfolio Performance	-463.01
Net Flow Into Account	0.00
Current Month	12,659.91

Kidder, Peabody Investor Account

Statement Period: Sep 29 - Oct 26, 1989 **Page 2 of 4**
Account Number: 40D-T1495-100 Tax ID Number: 04-1867445

Balances

Cash and Money Market Funds	(H) Opening Balance	(I) Net Activity	(J) Closing Balance	(K) Dividends This Month	(L) Dividends This Year	(M) Current Yield%	(N) Annual Yield%
Cash	0.00	0.00	0.00				
Webster Cash Reserve Fund	4,272.92	-2,963.01	1,309.91	15.32	225.38	8.09	8.38
Total	4,272.92		1,309.91				

Equities (O)	(P) ......Last Month....... Quantity	Market Value	(Q) ....This Month........... Quantity	Price	Market Value	(R) Current Yield	(S) Est. Annual Income
MCDONALDS CORP	0	0.00	100	31.250	3,125.00	0.99	31.00
SCHLUMBERGER LTD	200	8,850.00	200	41.125	8,225.00	2.91	240.00
Total					11,350.00		

Transactions

Purchases And Sales (T)		Quantity	Price	Amount	Accrued Interest
	Stocks Purchased				
10 10 89 Purchased	MCDONALDS CORP VS MONEY MARKET FUND	100	29 3/4	3,038.33	
	Total Stocks Purchased			3,038.33	

R - Reportable for accrued interest

Monthly Account Statement *(continued)*

Kidder, Peabody Investor Account

Statement Period: Sep 29 - Oct 26, 1989 Page 3 of 4
Account Number: 40D-T1495-100 Tax ID Number: 04-1867445

Transactions (Continued)

Dividends and Interest (U)		Quantity	Amount
10/06/89 Dividend	SCHLUMBERGER LTD	200	60.00
Total			60.00

Cash and Money Market Funds (V)	Price Per Share	No. of Shares	Added	Subtracted	Balance	Total Dividends
Kidder, Peabody Webster Cash Reserve Fund						
Opening Balance					4,272.92	
98/91/10 Share Dividend	1.00	15	15.32			15.32
10/09/89 Share Purchase	1.00	60	60.00			
10/10/89 Share Sale	1.00	3,038		3,038.33		
Closing Balance					1,309.91	15.32
Total Money Market Funds			75.32	3,038.33	1,309.91	15.32
Cash			0.00	0.00	0.00	
Total Cash and Money Market Funds			75.32	3,038.33	1,309.91	

Information

Tax Information (W)	Subject To IRS 1099 Reporting This Period	Subject To IRS 1099 Reporting This Year	Not Subject To IRS 1099 Reporting This Period	Not Subject To IRS 1099 Reporting This Year	Total This Period	Total This Year
Earnings						
Cash Dividends From Equities			60.00	180.00	60.00	180.00
*Money Market Fund Dividends			15.32	225.38	15.32	225.38
Total Earnings			75.32	405.38	75.32	405.38

An (*) indicates that our agent bank will be reporting that category of income or taxes withheld (if applicable)

Kidder, Peabody Investor Account

Statement Period: Sep 29 - Oct 26, 1989 Page 4 of 4
Account Number: 40D-T1495-100 Tax ID Number: 04-1867445

Information (Continued)

Cash (X)	Opening Balance	Added	Subtracted	Closing Balance
Opening Balance	0.00			
Securities Sold Purchased			3,038.33	
Dividends And Interest		60.00		
Money Market Transactions		2,978.33		
Closing Balance				0.00

Open Orders (Y)		Quantity	Type of Order	Order Price	Current Price
08/25/89 Sell	SCHLUMBERGER LTD	100.00	Limit	50.00	41.12

SOURCE: Kidder, Peabody & Co., Inc. Reprinted by permission.

the order for the NYSE stock went to the exchange trading post for that stock. In New York the OTC broker calls up HECH A on the computer screen and finds a current ask price of $12\frac{1}{4}$. A push of the trade button on the broker's terminal completes your trade. The trader at the New York brokerage reports back to the Ferris Baker Watts office where you placed your order to confirm the sale, and your broker calls you to inform you of your purchase. You receive a confirmation statement much like the one in Exhibit 5.5 in the mail within the next few days and pay by the settlement day.

Monthly Account Report

Each month, the brokerage sends the investor an account statement similar to the Investor Account form from Kidder, Peabody in Exhibit 5.6. The first page of the monthly account statement summarizes the status of the account.

A Previous month's account balance broken down into cash plus money market funds and equities (another term for common stocks). This column also lists the total net worth, or value, of the portfolio, or list of securities.

B New purchases since the previous month. The investor added $75.32 to the cash balance and $3,038.33 to equities. (This represents the purchase of the McDonald's stock discussed above.)

C Sales and other subtractions. The investor transferred $3,038.33 from cash and money market funds to pay for the McDonald's stock.

D Changes in portfolio value. The figure reflects a loss of $538.33 in the value of the stocks in the equity component of the account.

E Current month's account balance broken down into cash plus money market funds and equities. These figures are found by adding purchases and other additions to the previous month's balance, then subtracting sales and other fees.

F Proportions of the account balance in the equities and cash and money market fund components, by percentages.

G Change in net worth shows the previous month's balance of $13,122.92 minus $463.01, the result of the $538.33 loss on the equities plus cash income of $75.32, for a new balance for the current month of $12,659.91.

The second page of the account statement shows how the money market funds and equities balances have changed, including summaries of transactions.

H Cash balance at the beginning of the month of zero and a balance in the Webster Cash Reserve Fund, a money market fund, of $4,272.92.

I Withdrawal of $2,963.01 from the Webster Cash Reserve Fund.

J Closing balance for the cash and money market fund component, after the withdrawal and any cash additions, plus dividends.

K Dividends of $15.32 from the Webster Cash Reserve Fund.

L Dividends on the money market fund for the year amounting to $225.38.

M Current yield, in percent, found by dividing the dollar amount of the dividend by the price paid for the money market fund investment.

N Annual yield, in percent, allowing for compounding of the monthly returns.

O Equities, or common stock, owned, including 200 shares of Schlumberger, Ltd. and the newly purchased McDonald's stock.

P Previous month's market value of $8,850 for the Schlumberger stock. The investor did not own the McDonald's shares during the previous month so this column shows a zero value for that stock.

Q Current market value of stock owned. Schlumberger declined to a value of $8,225. With the $3,125 value of the McDonald's stock, the equities have a total value of $11,350.

R Current yield on each stock.

S Estimated annual income from each stock.

T Transactions, purchases and sales, made during the month. The investor purchased the 100 shares of McDonald's stock October 10 1989, at a price of $29\frac{3}{4}$ for a total cost of $3,038.33.

The third page of the account statement completes the transaction information and summarizes the investor's income from the account for tax returns and other purposes.

U Dividend of $60 received on October 6, 1989, from Schlumberger.

V Breakdown of the cash balance, in this case zero, and the money market fund balance.

W Summary of income received on the account. This information will help the investor complete income tax returns.

The fourth page of the account statement completes the information for the cash component of the account and lists open orders.

X Summary of cash transactions. To a zero opening balance the investor added $60 from dividends and interest and $2,978.33 from the sale of holdings of the Webster Money Market Fund. The investor then transferred $3,038.33 to pay for the 100 shares of McDonald's stock.

Y Open orders. This shows a limit order placed on August 25, 1989, to sell 100 shares of Schlumberger at $50.00 a share. On the date of the account statement, Schlumberger was selling for $41.12. This limit order

EXHIBIT 5.8

Dollar Volume of Equity Trading in Major World Markets: 1991

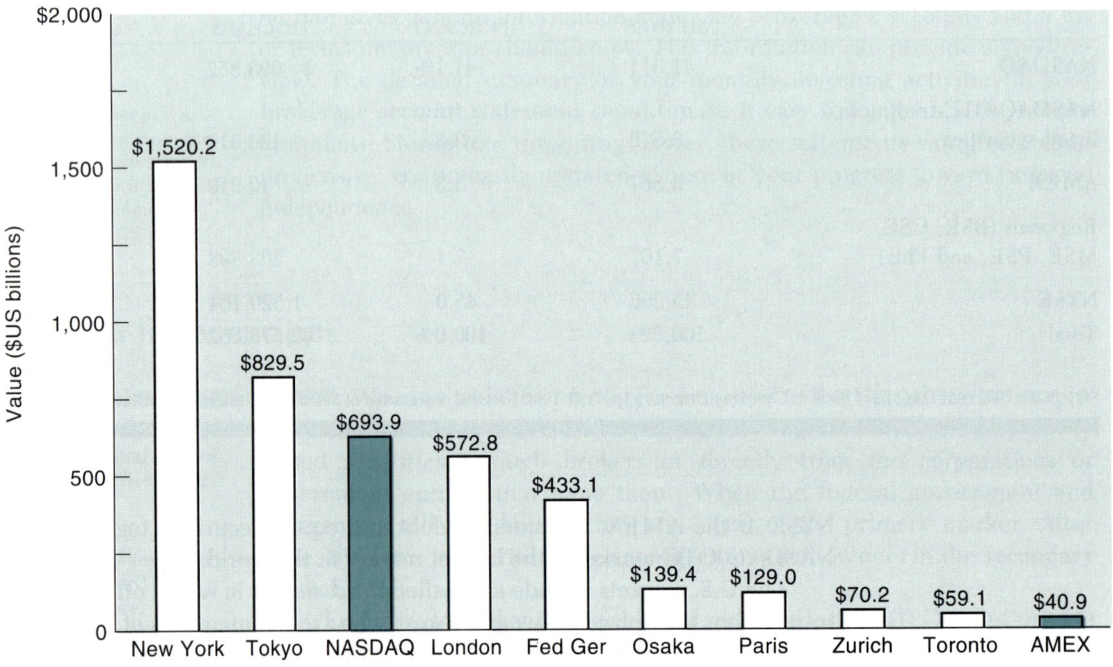

SOURCE: *1992 NASDAQ Fact Book & Company Directory*, p. 13.

of capital. The exhibit shows that the NASDAQ system is a larger market for foreign securities than the New York Stock Exchange.

Exhibit 5.10 shows a sample of price quotes for U.S. securities from *The Wall Street Journal*. Exhibit 5.11 shows quotes from markets outside the United States.

Where Will Your Broker Execute Your Trades?

Your broker will buy and sell securities for your account in the market that offers the best price at the time. Electronic technology for information transmission makes this a simple matter. Today's market presents buying and selling opportunities 24 hours a day, with trading following the sun around the globe.

EXHIBIT 5.9

NASDAQ Trading in ADRs and Foreign Securities Issues: Share Volume and Dollar Volume: 1986–1991

	AMERICAN DEPOSITORY RECEIPTS			FOREIGN SECURITIES		
	ISSUES	SHARE VOLUME (millions)	DOLLAR VOLUME ($millions)	ISSUES	SHARE VOLUME (millions)	DOLLAR VOLUME ($millions)
1991	83	2,182.8	$16,969.6	185	1,143.7	$10,700.4
1990	87	2,219.2	21,313.1	184	841.6	7,069.9
1989	92	1,800.1	17,391.1	194	879.9	5,888.4
1988	96	1,078.4	9,903.8	196	1,498.0	4,672.0
1987	97	1,822.1	18,864.6	204	1,111.0	8,465.0
1986	88	1,576.1	20,026.5	178	826.7	4,859.1

ADR Share Volume and Issues—NASDAQ, NYSE, and AMEX: 1991

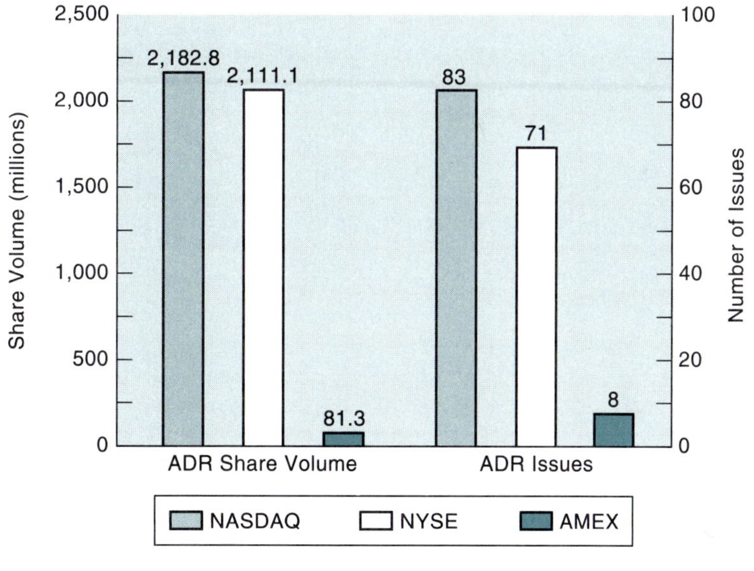

SOURCE: *1992 NASDAQ Fact Book & Company Directory*, pp. 14, 15.

perspective on **INTERNATIONAL INVESTMENTS**

The Fall of the Nikkei Average

Reversing the trend of the 1980s, U.S. stocks have outperformed their Japanese counterparts for the past two years by 80 percent. Whether this trend will continue or reverse yet again remains to be seen, and analysts are divided over where and when and how much. According to a *U.S. News and World Report* article ("Appreciating Japan's Market," February 24, 1992), few analysts expected the Nikkei index, the Japanese equivalent of the Dow Jones averages, to fall below 20,000; many even expected the market to reverse itself and show gains to anywhere from a conservative 25,000 to an optimistic 28,000 within the year. Kenneth Courtis, senior economist for Deutsche Bank Capital Markets in Tokyo, stated in a *Fortune* article ("The Falling Tokyo Stock Market: Things Could Get 'Very Dicey' in the U.S.," February 24, 1992) that he expected the index to fall to 17,000 before hitting bottom. He also stated he would become a buyer at 18,000 to 19,000. When the Nikkei closed at 18,559.71, Charles Elliott, a London-based Japan strategist for Goldman Sachs and Company, recommended in *USA Today* that individual investors begin buying in the Japanese market. However, in the same article, Barton Biggs, chairman of Morgan Stanley Asset Management, warned that the Nikkei could fall to 15,000, or another 20 percent, and he expected Japanese stocks to underperform their other market counterparts for a decade.

Despite the plummeting Nikkei, *U.S. News and World Report* revealed that mutual funds which invested solely in Japanese stocks tended to do better than the index. One such fund, the Merrill Lynch Pacific, had an 18.2 percent gain despite the drop in stock prices. Analysts recommended mutual funds as the best way to invest in Japanese stocks. This is a good way to diversify an American portfolio because the two markets rarely move in tandem.

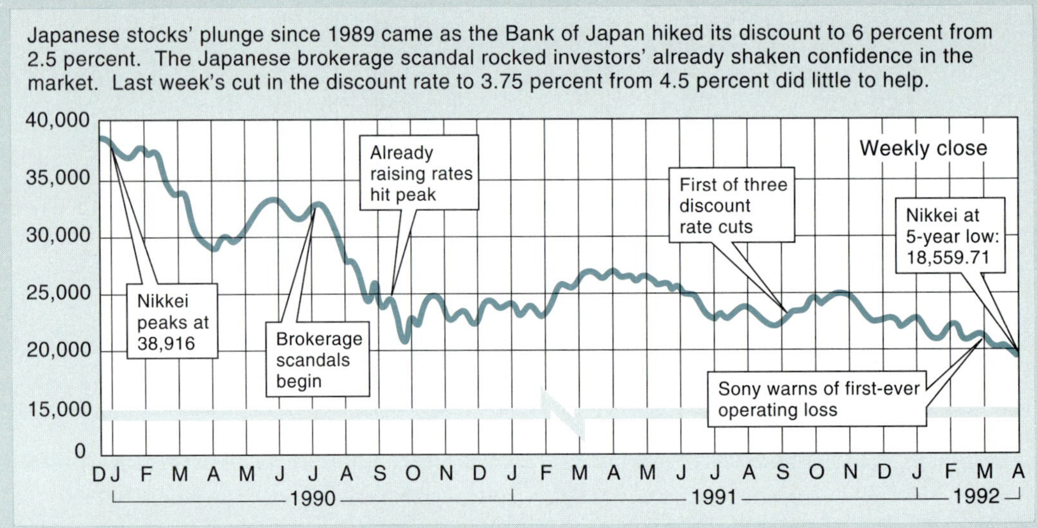

SOURCE: "Nikkei Average Goes South," *USA Today*, April 6, 1992, p. 48. Copyright 1992. Graph reprinted with permission.

EXHIBIT 5.10

Stock Market Quotations

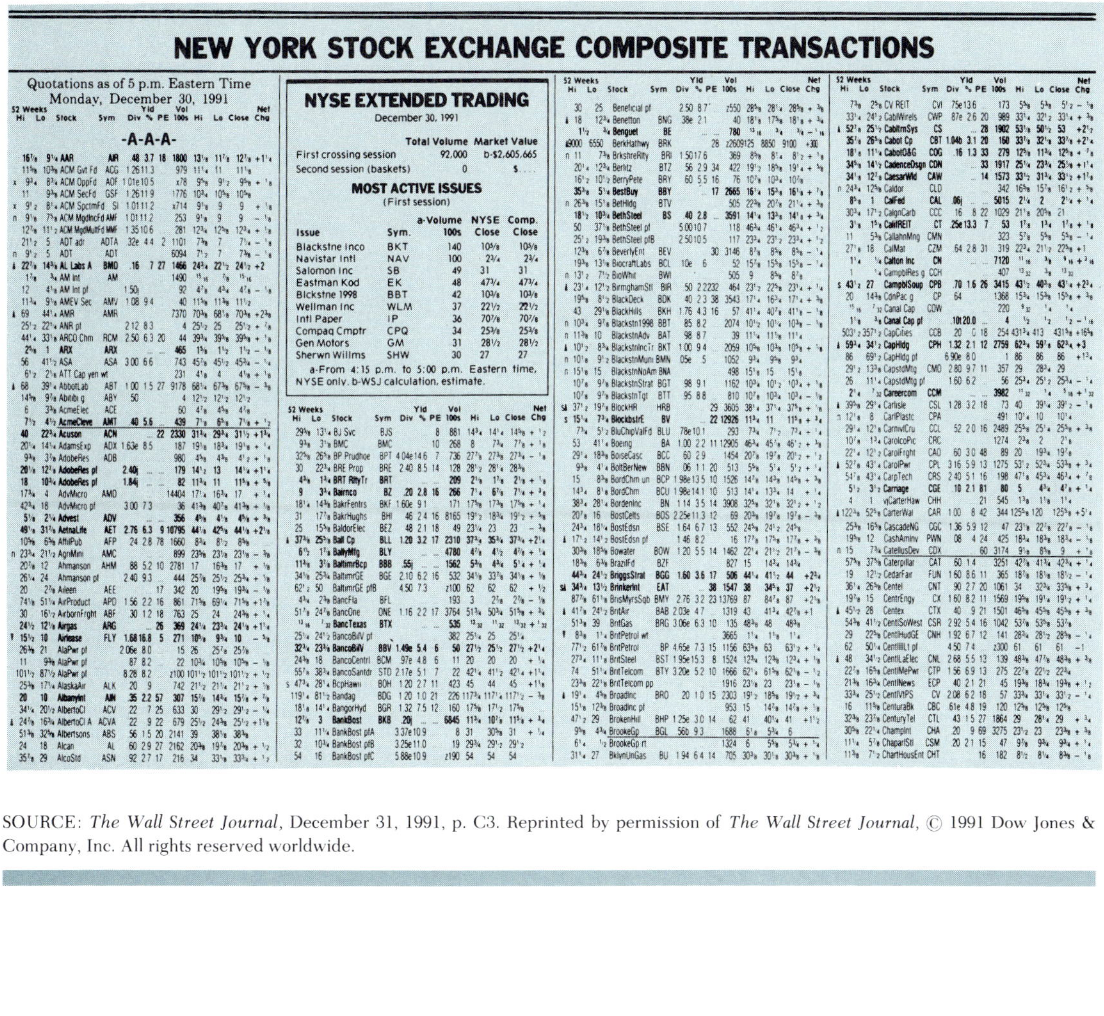

NEW YORK STOCK EXCHANGE COMPOSITE TRANSACTIONS

Quotations as of 5 p.m. Eastern Time
Monday, December 30, 1991

NYSE EXTENDED TRADING

December 30, 1991

	Total Volume	Market Value
First crossing session	92,000	b-$2,605,665
Second session (baskets)	0	$....

MOST ACTIVE ISSUES
(First session)

Issue	Sym.	a-Volume 100s	NYSE Close	Comp. Close
Blackstne Inco	BKT	140	10 5/8	10 5/8
Navistar Intl	NAV	100	2 3/4	2 3/4
Salomon Inc	SB	49	31	31
Eastman Kod	EK	48	47 3/4	47 3/4
Blckstne 1998	BBT	42	10 3/8	10 3/8
Wellman Inc	WLM	37	22 1/2	22 1/2
Intl Paper	IP	36	70 7/8	70 7/8
Compaq Cmptr	CPQ	34	25 3/8	25 3/8
Gen Motors	GM	31	28 1/2	28 1/2
Sherwn Willms	SHW	30	27	27

a-From 4:15 p.m. to 5:00 p.m. Eastern time, NYSE only. b-WSJ calculation, estimate.

SOURCE: *The Wall Street Journal*, December 31, 1991, p. C3. Reprinted by permission of *The Wall Street Journal*, © 1991 Dow Jones & Company, Inc. All rights reserved worldwide.

Market Regulation

blue sky law: State law regulating sales of securities within state borders.

States' **blue sky laws** regulate trading in securities within state borders. The Securities and Exchange Commission (SEC) regulates securities trading nationally. The SEC has jurisdiction over companies with relatively large asset bases and large numbers of shareholders and shares outstanding. Investors gain some protection from the Security Investor Protection Act and other laws, but their best protection comes from their knowledge of the broker and the brokerage firm, and of the companies whose securities they trade.

EXHIBIT 5.11

Price Quotes on Foreign Securities

FOREIGN MARKETS

Monday, December 30, 1991

TOKYO
(in yen)

	Close	Prev. Close
ANA	1310	1300
Aiwa	1210	1210
Ajinomoto	1360	1340
Alps Elec	1220	1150
Amada Co	895	895
Ando Elec	1500	1500
Anritsu	1170	1170
Asahi Chem	694	690
Asahi Glass	1160	1130
Bank of Tokyo	1520	1470
Bk of Yokohama	1260	1240
Banyu Pharm	1270	1270
Bridgestone	1030	1020
Brother Ind	515	525
C. Itoh	615	595
CSK	3630	3590
Canon Inc	1410	1400
Canon Sales	2870	2830
Casio Computer	1280	1260
Chubu Pwr	3190	3110
Chugai Pharm	1230	1200
Citizen Watch	813	795
Dai Nippon Print	1460	1440
Dai-ichi Kangyo	2410	2310
Daiei	1110	1090
Daiichi Seiyaku	1690	1630
Dainippon Pharm	1560	1520
Daiwa House	2010	1990
Daiwa Securities	1190	1130
Eisai	1690	1710
Ezaki Glico	1440	1410
Fanuc	4210	3930
Fuji Bank	2500	2410
Fuji HI	389	399
Fuji Photo Film	2780	2770
Fujisawa Pharm	1500	1480
Fujitsu	800	814
Furukawa Elec	590	585
Green Cross	1100	1030
Haseko	777	777
Hirose Elec	3330	3290
Hitachi Cable	800	800
Hitachi Credit	1430	1410
Hitachi Ltd	912	890
Hitachi Maxell	1620	1580
Hitachi Metals	979	988
Hitachi Sales	718	708
Honda Motor	1510	1450
Hosiden Elec	1290	1300
Hoya	2050	2030
IHI	566	556
Ind Bank Japan	3220	3090
Intec	2260	2280
Isetan	2930	2920
Isuzu	369	359
Ito-yokado	4330	4300
Iwatsu Elec	580	580
JAL	980	955
JEOL	790	785
JUSCO	1700	1640
Japan Aviat El	725	735
Japan Radio	2580	2460
Jujo Paper	598	577
KDD	12400	11700
Kajima	1400	1340
Kandenko	2900	2850
Kansai Elec	2900	2850
Kao Corp	1220	1220
Kawasaki Hi	558	532
Kawasaki Steel	357	350
Kinki Elec Con	2450	2380
Kirin	1340	1300
Kobe Steel	415	415
Kokusai Elec	2690	2650
Kokuyo	2800	2720
Komatsu Ltd	749	727
Konica	770	735
Kubota	637	622
Kumagai Gumi	756	732
Kuraray	1200	1150
Kureha Chem	590	583
Kyocera	3950	3800
Kyowa Hakko	1280	1270
Kyushu Matsushit	2750	2750
Lion	645	645
Makino Milling	815	810
Makita Elec	1840	1820
Marudai Food	1040	1050
Marui	1800	1750
Matsushita Com	2360	2360
Mats' Elec Ind	1450	1400
Mats' Elec Wrks	1300	1300
Mazda	520	488
Meiji Seika	830	812
Minolta	545	537
Misawa Homes	1620	1600
Mitsubishi Bank	2590	2560
Mitsubishi Corp	1300	1260
Mitsubishi Elec	577	560
Mitsubishi Real	1380	1340
Mitsubishi Hi	696	664
Mitsubishi Kasei	505	506
Mitsubishi Matl	540	530
Mitsubishi Trust	1750	1640
Mitsubishi Whse	1470	1470
Mitsui Mar&Fire	970	962
Mitsui Real	1490	1430
Mitsui TaiyoKobe	1800	1750
Mitsui & Co	758	731
Mitsukoshi	1200	1160
Mochida Pharm	2200	2000
NCR Japan	1080	1050
NEC	1200	1140
NGK Spark	740	731
NIFCO	1340	1330
NKK	339	331
NSK	560	563
NTN	615	590
NTT	734000	728000
Nihon Unisys Ltd	1690	1690
Nikko Securities	859	853
Nikon Corp	895	875
Nintendo	11700	11500
Nippon Chemi-con	724	700
Nippon Columbia	700	695
Nippon El Glass	1930	1860
Nippon Express	820	805
Nippon Hodo	2970	2940
Nippon Meat	1890	1870
Nippon Mining	535	537
Nippon Oil	900	889
Nippon Sanso	570	570
Nippon Shinpan	1110	1100
Nippon Steel	375	358
Nissan Motor	632	671
Nissin Food	2540	2430
Nitsuko	747	740
Nomura Securities	1620	1570
OKK	690	690
Obayashi Corp	830	818
Odakyu Railway	980	935
Oji Paper	825	800
Oki Elec Ind	600	569
Okuma Corp	1060	1010
Olympus Optical	1340	1310
Omron	1660	1610
Ono Pharm	4840	4800
Onoda Cement	643	618
Onward	1730	1630
Orient Corp	970	950
Pioneer Electron	3440	3400
Renown	620	615
Ricoh Co	640	630
Royal Co	1450	1450
Ryobi	530	535
Secom	6000	5920
SMK	636	630
Sankyo Co	2620	2570
Sanrio	1930	1920
Sanwa Bank	2240	2130
Sanyo Elec	518	497
Sapporo Brewery	1220	1220
Sekisui House	1400	1380
Seven-eleven	8350	8290
Sharp	1320	1250
Shimizu Corp	1260	1230
Shin-etsu Chem	1490	1480
Shionogi	928	910
Shiseido	1720	1680
Showa Denko	404	400
Skylark	2070	2060
Sony	4100	4030
Sumitomo Bank	2120	2020
Sumitomo Chem	470	465
Sumitomo Corp	1040	1020
Sumitomo Elec	1110	1070
Sumitomo Marine	985	958
Sumitomo Metal	350	346
Sumitomo Realty	1010	975
Sumitomo Trust	1470	1380
Suzuki Motor	611	622
TDK	4000	3980
Taisei Corp	863	857
Taisho Pharm	2080	2030
Taiyo Yuden	818	795
Takeda Chem	1310	1280
Tanabe Seiyaku	1130	1100
Teijin	509	510
Toho Co	16700	16900
Tokio Mar&Fire	1290	1250
Tokyo Denki Kom	1660	1680
Tokyo Elec Power	3540	3460
Tokyo Electron	2260	2200
Tokyo Gas	583	565
Tokyo Style	1420	1400
Tokyu Corp	853	851
Tonen Corp	1630	1620
Toppan Print	1370	1340
Toray	636	609
Toshiba	635	608
Toto	1710	1680
Toyo Seikan	3980	3940
Toyobo	469	450
Toyoda Mach	702	706
Toyota Motor	1500	1450
Tsugami	597	586
Uny	1430	1430
Ushio	757	763
Wacoal	920	930
Yamaha	1590	1540
Yamaichi Sec	736	718
Yamanouchi Phm	2870	2840
Yamatake-Hnywl	1440	1410
Yamato Transport	1210	1200
Yamazaki Baking	2030	2010
Yasuda Fire	880	866
Yokogawa Elec	1050	1050

LONDON
(in pence)

	Close	Prev. Close
Albert Fisher	69	68
Allied-Lyons	595	596
Argyll Group	276	276
Arjo Wiggins	237	237.5
Assoc Brit Fds	464	463
BAA plc	524	523
Barclays	369	377
Bass	979	989
BAT Indus	511	600
Blue Circle	216	217
BOC Group	589	598
Boots	426	428
Borland	4200	4200
Bowater Indus	650	649
BPB Indus	126	127
British Aero	317	320
British Airwys	226	225
British Gas	259	261
British Pete	279	277
British Steel	66.5	67.5
British Telcom	326	328
BTR	381	382
Burmah Castrol	466	473
Cable&Wireless	584	583
Cadbury Schwp	418	420
Charter Cons	499	504
Coats Viyella	164	163
Commercial Un	464	465
Courtaulds	468	467
Dixons	197	192
Dowty Group	143	138
Eng Ch Clay	472	468
Fisons	311	293
Forte	228	265
GEC	198.5	199
Genrl Accidnt	437	440
GKN	281	283
Glaxo Hldgs	813	819
Granada	189	189
Grand Metrop	856	856
Guardian Royal	111	114
Guinness	493	503
Hanson PLC	194	201
Hawker Sidley	729	729
Hillsdown	162	173
Imp Chem Ind	1134	1123
Johnson Mathy	319	312
Kingfisher	467	471
Ladbroke Grp	230	225
Land Secrs	445	453
LASMO	221	227
Legal & Genl	363	365
Lloyds Bank	380	385
Lonrho	151	154
Lucas	113	114
Marks&Spencer	268	271
MEPC	394	400
Midland Bank	210	212
Nat Wstmn Bk	272	275
NFC	225	224
P & O	424	424
Pearson	675	673
Pilkgtn Bros	134	132
Prudential	236	236
Racal Elect	49	48
Rank Org	573	560
Reckit&Colman	623	624
Redland	431	428
Reed Intl	515	513
Reuters	1013	999
RMC	525	524
Rolls Royce	125	125
Royal Insur	231	233
RTZ Corp	457	463
Stchi&Stchi	11.75	11.25
J Sainsbury	365	363
Sears	90	92
Sedgwick Grp	207	209
Shell Trnspt	482	483
Siebe plc	504	508
Smithkln Bchm	853	823
Smith&Nephew	138.5	137.25
Std Chartrd	409	412
Storehouse	85	87
Sun Alliance	272	274
Tarmac	113	111
Tate & Lyle	395	396
Tesco	217	215
Thorn EMI	734	743
Trafalgar Hse	120	121
TSB Group	117	119
Ultramar	254	265
Utd Biscuits	386	387
Unilever	876	871
Vodafone	361	356
Warburg	504	508
Wellcome	1066	967
WPP Group	44	36

South African Mines
(in U.S. dollars)

	Close	Prev. Close
Bracken	0.38	0.38
Deelkraal	2.00	2.00
Doornfontein	0.68	0.68
Durban Deep	6.50	6.50
E. Rand Gold	2.06	2.06
E. Rand Prop	2.81	2.81
Elandsrand	7.69	7.69
Elsburg	0.98	0.98
Grootvlei	1.40	1.45
Harmony	6.15	6.10
Hartebstftn	4.55	4.65
Impala Pltm	13.19	13.19
Kinross	13.62	13.62
Leslie	0.93	0.93
Libanon	0.93	0.93
Loraine	1.30	1.03
Randfontein	5.06	5.12
Rustenburg	18.19	18.19
Southvaal	19.50	19.50
Stilfontein	1.05	1.05
Unisel	2.75	2.75
West Areas	1.65	1.65
Winkelhaak	10.00	10.25

MILAN
(in lire)

	Close	Prev. Close
Banca Com	3660	3625
Benetton	10675	10505
Ciga	1715	1623
CIR	1682	1637
FIAT Com	4675	4549
FIAT Pref	3220	3131
Generali	28300	27700
Mediobanca	13650	13290
Montedison	1208	1173
Olivetti Com	2460	2407
Olivetti NC	1890	1851
Pirelli Co	4270	4230
Pirelli SpA	1095	1070
Rinascente	6180	5945
RAS	20100	19596
Saipem	1620	1610
SIP	1346	1330
Snia	1080	1035

HONG KONG
(in Hong Kong dollars)

	Close	Prev. Close
Bank E Asia	24.30	23.70
Cathay Pacific	9.85	9.65
Cheung Kong	19.60	19.30
China L & P	23.10	22.80
Dairy Farm	9.60	9.60
Hang Seng Bk	38	37.25
HK Electric	13.60	13.50
HK Land	9.25	9.20
HK Telecom	8.10	8.15
HSBC Hldgs	35.75	35.25
Hutchsn Whmp	14.50	14.50
Jardine Mathsn	39	38.75
Sun Hung Kai	23	22.50
Swire Pacific	23	22.60
Wharf Holdings	11	10.80

STOCKHOLM
(in krona)

	Close	Prev. Close
AGA	300	297
Asea	279	280
Astra	600	585
Atlas Copco	240	238
Electrolux	218	216
Ericsson	108	111
SE Bank	52	50
Skanska	145	135
SKF	94	94
Volvo	315	310

PARIS
(in French francs)

	Close	Prev. Close
Accor	640	635
Air Liquide	695	679
Alcatel Alstm	556	547
BSN-Gervais	999	997
Carrefour	2315	2280
Club Med	420	417
Dassault Avitn	307	312
Elf Aquitaine	392	390.5
Euro Disneyld	142.3	138.1
Generale Eaux	2022	1998
Hachette	146.3	135.9
Havas	432	420.1
Imetal	239.5	234
Lafarge Coppe	323.5	323
LVMH	4134	4027
Machines Bull	26	24.5
Matra	172	168.6
Michelin	120	119.8
L'Oreal	748	735
Paribas	308.8	307.6
Pernod Ricard	1233	1205
Peugeot	585	578
Saint Gobain	428.9	423
Sanofi	1045	1040
Schneider	560	552
Soc Generale	461	460
Source Perrier	1198	1220
Suez	280.2	277.5
Thomson CSF	151.8	151.8
Total Francais	962	946

AMSTERDAM
(in guilders)

	Close	Prev. Close
ABN Amro	42	41.80
Aegon	119.10	119.20
Ahold	77.80	77.10
Akzo	133.40	132.50
AMEV	51.60	50.10
Buhrmn-Tett	41.50	41
DSM	89.70	90.60
Elsevier	99	99.80
Fokker	29.60	29.60
Gist-Brocades	32.30	32.10
Heineken	156.50	155.70
Hoogovens	43.70	44.10
Intl Ndrlndn Gr	45.70	45.60
KLM	40.30	41.40
KNP	47.50	46.20
Nedlloyd	55.60	55
Oce-van Grntn	61.90	61
Pakhoed Hldg	42.40	41.80
Philips	29.20	29.70
Robeco	93.20	92.50
Rodamco	56.80	56.90
Rolinco	95	93.90
Rorento	69.70	69.20
Royal Dutch	142	141.40
Unilever	175.70	173.70
VOC	40.30	40.10
VNU	69.50	69.50
VRG-Group	46.90	46
Wessanen	79.90	78.60
Wolters Kluwer	60.70	60.30

BRUSSELS
(in Belgian francs)

	Close	Prev. Close
Arbed	3200	3250
BBL	3240	3200
Bekaert	9130	9140
Delhaize	8410	8120
Electrabel	4820	4750
GIB	1200	1200
Gevaert	6400	6320
Gen de Bnque	5960	5990
Petrofina	10900	10825
Soc Gen Belg	1840	1800
Solvay	11725	11500

MEXICO
(in pesos)

	Close	Prev. Close
Alfa A	28200	27700
Apasco A	10250	10250
Bimbo 1	12000	12000
Bimbo 2	12000	12000
Cemex B	45000	43600
Cifra B	3800	3750
Cifra C	3590	3490
Femsa B	13000	13000
Gcarso A1	35000	35000
Kimber A	48100	48100
Maseca B2	2350	2300
Tamsa	27400	26600
Ttolmex B2	21600	21200
Vitro NVO	76000	76000

FRANKFURT
(in marks)

	Close	Prev. Close
AEG	198.5	198.8
Allianz	2098	2062
Asko	630	616
BASF	219.7	217.7
Bayer	277.5	276
Byr Vereinsbk	404.5	401.5
BMW	472.5	471
Commerzbank	247.5	246.5
Continental	207	203
Daimler Benz	742	735.5
Degussa	291	282.5
Deutsche Bank	671	666
Dresdner Bank	326.8	324
Henkel	519	517
Hochtief	965	945
Hoechst	223.9	218.5
Karstadt	630	621
Kaufhof	434	430
Linde	681	679
Lufthansa	161.5	160
Mannesmann	245.5	245
MAN	340.5	337.5
Metallges	385.5	382
Munchen Ruck	2250	2240
Nixdorf	182.5	184.5
Porsche	537	532
RWE	385.8	382.1
SEL	447	446
Schering	767.8	756.5
Siemens	624.9	622
Thyssen	201.2	199.8
Veba	356.8	355.5
VEW	217.5	218
Volkswagen	301.5	295.4

SYDNEY
(in Australian dollars)

	Close	Prev. Close
Amcor	6.69	6.58
ANZ Group	4.68	4.65
Ashton	1.30	1.30
Boral	3.38	3.40
Bougainville	0.61	0.63
Brambles Inds	18.42	18.22
Brokn Hill Prp	13.40	13.10
Burns Philp	3.40	3.40
Coles Myer	12.12	12.10
Comalco	3.60	3.55
Centrl Norsemn	0.35	0.35
CRA	11.74	11.56
CSR	4.70	4.71
Foster's	1.84	1.82
Gld Mns Kalgo	0.79	0.80
Goodman	1.58	1.53
Leighton	1.28	1.23
Mayne Nickless	8.50	8.50
MIM Holdings	2.14	2.10
Nat Aust Bnk	7.86	7.84
News Corp	14.34	14
Normdy Poseidn	1.12	1.12
Nrth Brk Hill	2.40	2.37
Orbital Engine	3.95	4.05
Pacific Dunlop	5.51	5.53
Pancontinental	0.82	0.82
Renison Gldflds	4.77	4.72
Santos	2.93	2.91
S Pac Pete	0.40	0.40
TNT Ltd	1.51	1.48
Western Mining	4.59	4.49
Westpac	4.47	4.42
Woodside	3.87	3.85

SWITZERLAND
(in Swiss francs)

	Close	Prev. Close
Alusuisse	900	900
Brown Boveri	3250	3220
Ciba-Geigy br	3190	3130
Ciba-Geigy reg	2980	2940
Ciba-G ptc ctf	2840	2820
CS Holding	1740	1720
Hof LaRoch br	4080	4090
Roche div rt	2610	2590
Nestle bearer	8720	8690
Nestle reg	8600	8550
Nestle ptc ctf	1675	1665
Sandoz	2460	2430
Sulzer	425	430
Swiss Bnk Cp	302	293
Swiss Reinsur	2550	2480
Swissair	720	705
UBS	3610	3590
Winterthur	3560	3540
Zurich Ins	4320	4300

SOURCE: *The Wall Street Journal*, December 31, 1991, p. C8. Reprinted by permission of *The Wall Street Journal*,

Measures of the Markets

Many people talk about the behavior of the stock market as if it were a single, unified entity. Clearly, however, the market is made up of a wide range of individual stocks. It is impossible to evaluate the behavior of all these stocks separately to assess the performance of the market as a whole. Instead, we need a single, easily understandable measure to indicate the direction of the overall market. To meet this need, investment professionals have developed various market indexes.

Dow Jones Averages: Four statistical averages of individual securities' prices intended to represent trends in the overall market.

Exhibit 5.12 shows charts of the daily changes in the most famous of these indexes, the **Dow Jones** Industrial. Transportation, and Utility **Averages,** for a six-month period. Note that the lists of companies included in the indexes change periodically and their prices change from day to day. The exhibit also shows the volume of shares traded and the hourly prices for each day of the previous week. These index data give the investor some indication of the behavior of the overall market for comparison with the results for individual securities. *Barron's* gives complete information about the Dow Jones averages on a weekly basis.

History of the Dow Jones Averages The name of the Dow Jones averages comes from Charles Henry Dow, cofounder in 1882 of Dow Jones & Company, the publisher of *The Wall Street Journal* and *Barron's*. Charles Dow's first stock average appeared on July 3, 1884, in a publication distributed by Dow Jones called the *Customer's Afternoon Letter*. The Dow is the oldest continuous price index of the U.S. stock market. Because of its history and familiarity, the Dow ranks as the most widely used indicator of stock market action.[1]

Dow Theory: A method of assessing the direction of the market based on the Dow Jones Industrial and Transportation Averages.

Dow, a journalist and market analyst, attempted to discern trends in the daily movement of stock prices, ultimately developing the **Dow Theory** of the movement of stock prices based on the behavior of ocean tides, waves, and ripples. Dow was concerned not with the daily price changes, which he likened to little ripples, but with larger, longer-term movements that he compared to waves and the tide. As the tide rises, each successive wave makes a new high, falls back, and then makes another new high. When the tide turns, each wave falls short of the previous high, moves back, and then surges again, each time failing to reach the previous high.

Dow developed the Dow Jones Industrial Average (DJIA) and the Dow Jones Transportation Average (DJTA) to indicate the trend in the tide of stock prices. He found that the primary movement of the market lasts from one to two and one-half or three years, sometimes longer. Downward trends, called *bear markets*, tend to be shorter than rising trends, called *bull markets*.

Secondary trends in the market, the waves, move in the opposite direction to the primary trend, or tide, and last from three weeks to three months. The secondary trends usually lose from one-third to two-thirds of the previous gain in a rising market, and they gain back the same proportions of previous losses in a falling market.

EXHIBIT 5.12

Charts of the Dow Jones Averages

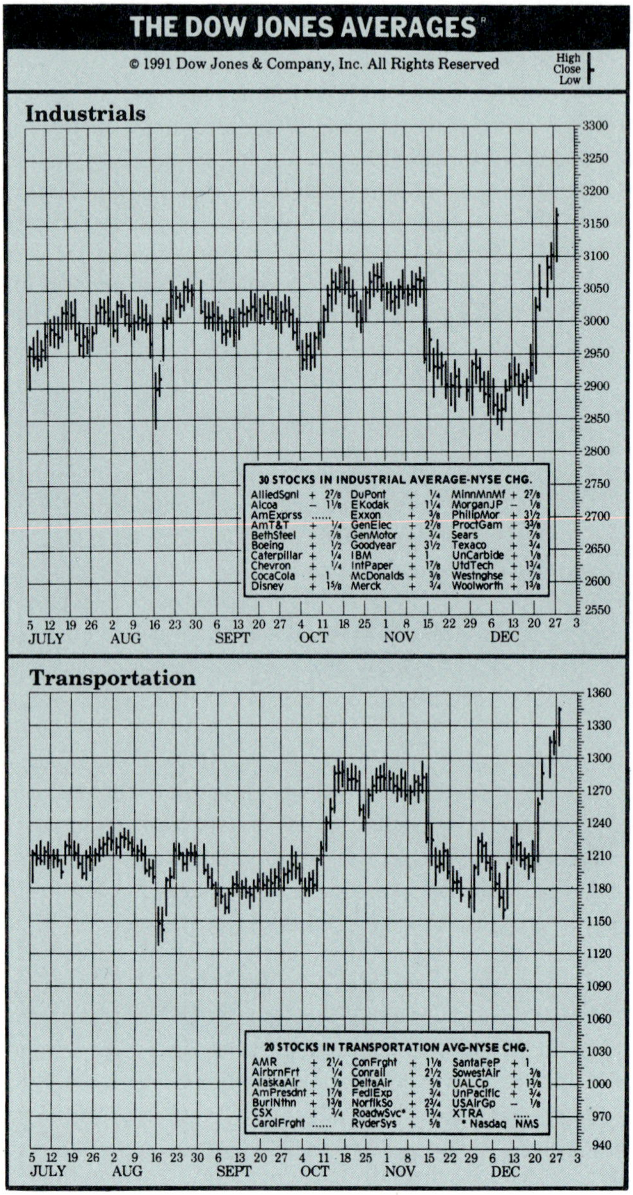

SOURCE: *The Wall Street Journal*, December 31, 1991, p. C11. Reprinted by permission of *The Wall Street Journal*, © 1991 Dow Jones & Company, Inc. All rights reserved worldwide.

Charts of the Dow Jones Averages *(continued)*

Utilities

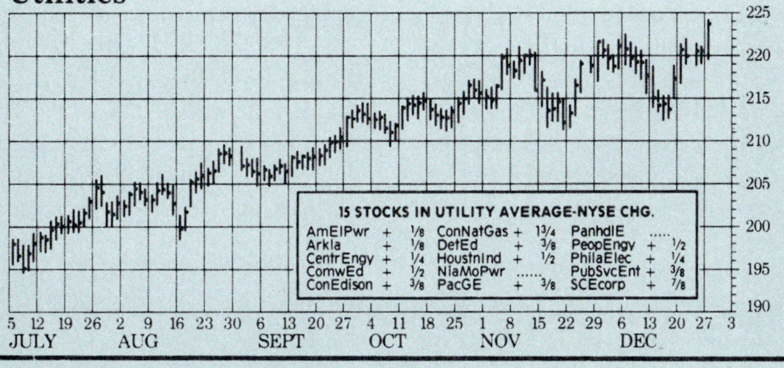

NYSE Volume (9:30 a.m. to 4 p.m. EDT)

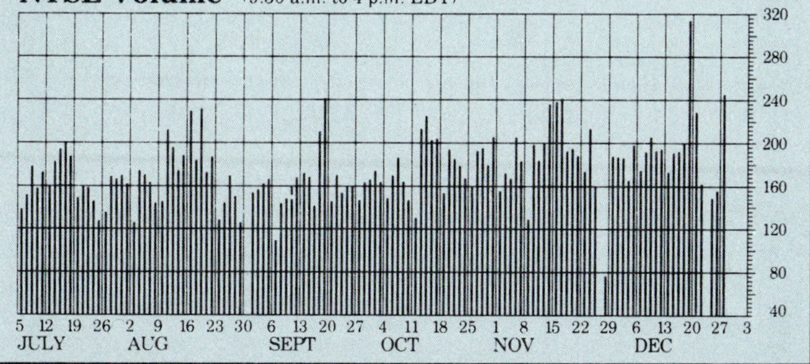

Following are the Dow Jones averages of INDUSTRIAL, TRANSPORTATION and UTILITY stocks with the total sales of each group for the period indicated.

DATE	OPEN	10 AM	11 AM	12 NOON	1 PM	2 PM	3 PM	CLOSE	CH	%	HIGH*	LOW*	VOLUME
30 INDUSTRIALS													
Dec 30	3102.64	3108.68	3111.36	3134.17	3139.98	3148.26	3144.90	3163.91	+ 62.39	+ 2.01	3174.64	3090.79	27,906,100
Dec 27	3085.20	3095.04	3087.21	3085.87	3096.38	3095.48	3095.93	3101.52	+ 18.56	+ 0.60	3121.65	3063.73	19,099,400
Dec 26	3051.88	3061.72	3057.25	3065.07	3062.16	3073.35	3080.05	3082.96	+ 31.98	+ 1.05	3101.97	3036.23	16,419,800
Dec 24	3031.31	3037.34	3045.39	3076.25	3054.79	....	....	3050.98	+ 28.40	+ 0.94	3087.88	3015.65	21,210,800
Dec 23	2929.79	2938.06	2939.85	2944.77	2957.07	2971.60	2989.04	3022.58	+ 88.10	+ 3.00	3037.57	2919.05	31,628,300
20 TRANSPORTATION COS.													
Dec 30	1316.89	1317.45	1320.44	1326.42	1328.48	1330.53	1330.53	1344.92	+ 30.08	+ 2.29	1347.35	1311.10	5,211,800
Dec 27	1316.89	1316.70	1312.22	1309.60	1310.35	1313.15	1311.66	1314.84	− 0.18	− 0.01	1325.67	1302.88	2,554,800
Dec 26	1286.43	1292.04	1289.05	1294.28	1296.71	1305.87	1309.42	1315.02	+ 28.96	+ 2.25	1320.07	1281.76	2,808,900
Dec 24	1266.07	1265.70	1276.16	1295.96	1286.43	....	....	1286.06	+ 28.03	+ 2.23	1300.26	1261.77	3,508,800
Dec 23	1208.15	1208.33	1217.30	1223.84	1228.33	1234.68	1240.47	1258.03	+ 51.00	+ 4.23	1264.01	1204.04	5,013,400
15 UTILITIES													
Dec 30	220.58	220.71	220.58	221.27	221.96	222.27	222.21	223.71	+ 3.19	+ 1.45	224.27	219.52	3,974,100
Dec 27	220.39	220.33	220.39	219.95	220.08	219.52	220.27	220.52	....	....	221.14	219.02	2,024,100
Dec 26	220.14	219.83	220.02	220.02	220.08	220.08	220.21	220.52	+ 0.57	+ 0.26	221.52	218.77	2,241,100
Dec 24	220.71	220.71	220.52	220.58	220.14	....	....	219.95	− 0.76	− 0.34	222.02	218.95	2,409,300
Dec 23	217.70	217.70	218.14	218.77	219.33	219.83	220.08	220.71	+ 3.38	+ 1.56	221.46	216.70	4,104,800
65 STOCKS COMPOSITE AVERAGE													
Dec 30	1128.88	1130.36	1131.56	1138.25	1140.47	1142.92	1142.18	1150.77	+ 22.68	+ 2.01	1154.00	1124.22	37,092,000
Dec 27	1125.14	1127.08	1124.40	1123.15	1125.60	1125.69	1125.97	1128.09	+ 3.78	+ 0.34	1135.39	1116.23	23,678,300
Dec 26	1110.55	1113.73	1112.21	1115.12	1115.16	1119.74	1122.09	1124.31	+ 14.18	+ 1.28	1130.22	1105.14	21,469,800
Dec 24	1101.68	1102.84	1106.94	1118.26	1111.15	....	....	1110.13	+ 12.24	+ 1.11	1122.78	1096.09	27,128,900
Dec 23	1064.19	1065.94	1068.85	1071.94	1076.01	1080.95	1086.17	1097.89	+ 33.29	+ 3.13	1103.02	1060.21	40,746,500

Averages are compiled daily by using the following divisors: Industrials, 0.559; Transportation, 0.669; Utilities, 1.997; Composite, 2.707.

*Averages of the highs and lows reached at any time during the day on the primary market by the individual stocks.

EXHIBIT 5.13

Computation of Dow Jones Averages

The original method of computation was elementary arithmetic. When there were 12 stocks, the prices were added together and the total divided by 12. When there were 20, the sum was divided by 20.

But the divisor is *not* 30 for the industrials or 20 for the transportation index or 15 for the utilities. Why not?

The answer is that the divisor is changed from time to time to maintain the historical continuity of the average. The most frequent reason for such an adjustment is a stock split. When the market price of a company's shares advances to a point where the company believes it is losing its appeal for individual investors, the stock often is split by, for example, issuing one new share for each share currently outstanding (two-for-one). Other things being equal, each share of stock is then worth half the earlier price.

Such stock splits by companies included in the average would produce distortions if the new price was simply substituted for the old one. Here is an example: Assume three stocks selling at $5, $10 and $15. Their average price is $10. Now the $15 stock is split three-for-one, which would make the new shares sell for $5. Nothing has happened to the value of an investment in these shares, but the average of their prices now is $6.67—an obvious distortion in comparison with the earlier average.

An adjustment must be made to compensate so that the "average" will remain at $10. This can be done in different ways. The method used to compute the Dow Jones Averages is to change the divisor, the number divided into the total of the stock prices.

In this case the new divisor would be 2 instead of 3 and the new figure would be used in subsequent computations of the average. Here is the formula to calculate a new divisor:

$$\frac{\text{Former Divisor}}{\text{Former Total Value}} = \frac{\text{New Divisor}}{\text{New Total Value}}$$

SOURCE: "The Dow Jones Averages: A Nonprofessional's Guide," revised edition, Educational Service Bureau, Dow Jones & Co., Inc. Reprinted by permission.

How do you recognize a bull market? When the Dow Jones Industrial and Transportation Averages rise, fall back, and rise again to new highs, they indicate a rising tide. When the Dow Jones averages fall, rise again without penetrating the previous highs, and then fall again to new lows, the tide is falling.

Unfortunately, the Dow Theory cannot really predict the future. It indicates the direction in which the market is moving, but you can never be really certain that the next market change will follow the previous pattern. Toward the end of 1990 a bear market was in full swing after a bull market had lost momentum in the middle of the year. Many people expected the Dow Jones Industrial Average to fall back to around the 2,100 level, to rise again after the end of the recession that began in 1990 and the Persian Gulf war. Instead, a bullish rally disrupted the bearish pattern at the end of the year. For a more complete discussion of the Dow Theory, with references, see pages 566 to 571 in *Investments, An Introduction to Analysis and Management*, sixth edition, by Frederick Amling.

Computation of Dow Jones Averages *(continued)*

The evening before the split takes place, after the average has been worked out for publication the same way as on preceding days, the Statistical Department of The Journal makes a theoretical calculation. The same stock prices are added up but the stock that is about to split is included as if the split had already taken place ($5 + $10 + $5 = $20). This total, or 20, is divided by the actual average previously calculated, or 10. The result is the new divisor, or 2, and it is used until another adjustment is needed. Such adjustments are made not only for stock splits, but also for stock dividends and to accommodate a change in the roster of companies in the average, for example, after a merger that eliminates 1 of the 30.

Over the more than 50-year history of the 30-stock average, the divisor has changed many times, mostly downward. This explains why the "average" can be reported as, for example, 1,000 while no single stock in the average is even close to that level in price. And it also explains the wide movements of the average in comparison to stock prices. With a divisor of 2, for example, an increase of $1 in the price of each of the 30 stocks produces a 15-point increase in the average.

In fact, the use of the term "average" is justified only by long usage. More accurately, it is an index or indicator.

Each day's change in each stock average is published by Dow Jones not only in points, but also in percentages. The purpose of doing this is to stress the fact that the use of a divisor other than 30 doesn't in any way affect the percentage change as long as the divisor remains the same. The published percentage figure reflects more accurately than any other just how the market for the 30 stocks moved.

Current divisors are published daily by The Journal and weekly by Barron's. They may be found with other statistics of the averages with the chart in the newspaper and in Barron's Market Laboratory section. Other related statistics include the dividend yield and price-earnings ratio of the averages.

Stock Selection for the Dow The editors of *The Wall Street Journal* determine which stocks' prices to include in the Dow Jones averages. The lists change from time to time to keep the Dow "aimed at tracking underlying trends over a period of time."[2] Such changes are infrequent and usually result from mergers. Some changes are made to enhance the accuracy with which the Dow represents the market.

The 30 Dow Jones Industrial Average stocks represent the broad stock market and the diversity of American industry. These are major competitors in their industries whose stock is widely held by both individual and institutional investors. These 30 stocks account for about 25 percent of the value of all stocks traded on the New York Stock Exchange. Exhibit 5.13 shows how the Dow Jones averages are computed.

Other Market Indexes

Exhibit 5.14 shows a table from *The Wall Street Journal* that lists results for other stock market indexes. After the Dow, the second most widely followed

EXHIBIT 5.14

Quotations for Market Indexes

STOCK MARKET DATA BANK 4/23/92

MAJOR INDEXES

HIGH	LOW (†365 DAY)		CLOSE	NET CHG	% CHG	†365 DAY CHG	% CHG	FROM 12/31	% CHG
DOW JONES AVERAGES									
3366.50	2863.82	30 Industrials	3348.61	+ 9.84	+ 0.29	+ 427.57	+14.64	+ 179.78	+ 5.67
1467.68	1129.06	20 Transportation	1375.75	+ 32.14	+ 2.39	+ 205.62	+17.57	+ 17.75	+ 1.31
226.15	195.17	15 Utilities	208.38	+ 0.57	+ 0.27	− 1.00	− 0.48	− 17.77	− 7.86
1195.42	1028.33	65 Composite	1185.21	+ 10.39	+ 0.88	+ 138.27	+13.21	+ 28.39	+ 2.45
396.64	343.91	Equity Mkt. Index	386.80	+ 1.54	+ 0.40	+ 32.40	+ 9.14	− 5.10	− 1.30
NEW YORK STOCK EXCHANGE									
231.84	202.10	Composite	226.16	+ 0.74	+ 0.33	+ 18.66	+ 8.99	− 3.28	− 1.43
290.02	253.72	Industrials	282.40	+ 0.78	+ 0.28	+ 22.28	+ 8.57	− 3.42	− 1.20
102.27	87.76	Utilities	96.92	+ 0.36	+ 0.37	+ 5.06	+ 5.51	− 5.21	− 5.10
212.02	166.15	Transportation	204.75	+ 4.89	+ 2.45	+ 33.52	+19.58	+ 2.88	+ 1.43
177.72	147.12	Finance	173.93	+ 0.39	+ 0.22	+ 21.10	+13.81	+ 1.25	+ 0.72
STANDARD & POOR'S INDEXES									
420.77	368.57	500 Index	411.60	+ 1.79	+ 0.44	+ 32.35	+ 8.53	− 5.49	− 1.32
499.27	438.51	Industrials	487.07	+ 1.71	+ 0.35	+ 36.94	+ 8.21	− 5.65	− 1.15
362.50	277.02	Transportation	353.55	+ 10.35	+ 3.02	+ 69.28	+24.37	+ 12.09	+ 3.54
155.70	133.52	Utilities	145.75	+ 0.94	+ 0.65	+ 4.75	+ 3.37	− 9.41	− 6.06
35.14	28.77	Financials	34.92	+ 0.13	+ 0.37	+ 4.64	+15.32	+ 0.82	+ 2.40
154.74	119.18	400 MidCap	140.53	− 0.26	− 0.18	+ 16.19	+13.02	− 6.06	− 4.13
NASDAQ									
644.92	473.08	Composite	576.05	− 2.18	− 0.38	+ 80.02	+16.13	− 10.29	− 1.75
741.92	523.54	Industrials	628.99	− 4.35	− 0.69	+ 74.05	+13.34	− 39.96	− 5.97
632.09	522.07	Insurance	594.35	− 3.45	− 0.58	+ 35.49	+ 6.35	− 6.74	− 1.12
413.20	317.36	Banks	413.20	+ 1.53	+ 0.37	+ 83.35	+25.27	+ 62.64	+ 17.87
285.0[illegible]	208.31	Nat. Mkt. Comp.	254.73	− 0.99	− 0.39	+ 35.87	+16.39	− 5.01	− 1.93
296.32	207.84	Nat. Mkt. Indus.	251.39	− 1.77	− 0.70	+ 30.18	+13.64	− 16.40	− 6.12
OTHERS									
418.99	356.79	Amex	386.26	− 0.09	− 0.02	+ 22.06	+ 6.06	− 8.79	− 2.23
266.85	228.21	Value-Line (geom.)	252.48	+ 0.12	+ 0.05	+ 11.32	+ 4.69	+ 3.14	+ 1.26
212.61	167.00	Russell 2000	194.71	− 0.29	− 0.15	+ 20.12	+11.52	+ 4.78	+ 2.52
4121.28	3529.97	Wilshire 5000	3976.66	+ 10.88	+ 0.27	+ 344.31	+ 9.48	− 64.45	− 1.59

†-Based on comparable trading day in preceding year.

SOURCE: *The Wall Street Journal*, April 24, 1992, p. C2. Reprinted by permission of *The Wall Street Journal*,

index is the Standard & Poor's 500 Index. Some indexes reflect movements in specific markets for stocks; the NYSE Index, NASDAQ Index, and AMEX Index all indicate changes in those individual markets. The Value Line Index shows composite changes in all companies followed by Value Line. The

Russell 2000 represents the performance of 2,000 companies followed by The Frank Russell Company, and the Wilshire 5,000 represents 5,000 companies followed by the Wilshire Group in California. Together, these indexes can give the investor a good idea of the trend in prices in the overall stock market.

S&P 500 Index Changes in higher-priced securities can affect some indexes (like the Dow) more than identical percentage changes in lower-priced securities. The S&P 500 Index corrects for this distortion by weighting its sample of securities by their total market values. Exhibit 5.15 describes the mechanics of calculating the index.

Exhibit 5.16 provides a graphic view of the Standard & Poor's 500 Index over the period June 1990 to May 1992. Notice that the index rose from 360 to about 418 for a gain of 16.1 percent. The S&P 500 then declined in 1990 to the 325 level for a 7.1 percent loss.

Exhibit 5.16 also shows the performance of the Russell 2000 Index of smaller company stocks. It rose from 162 to 192 in 1992, posting an 18.5 percent gain. This shows that all segments of the stock market do not move at the same rate. The big-capitalization stocks purchased by institutional investors increased approximately two-thirds as much as the smaller company stocks in the Russell 2000 Index.

You may well find bargains among the smaller companies that will yield large gains when other investors discover them and bid up their prices, but you run the risk that those other investors will fail to see the light, leaving your stock unappreciated. The contradictory idea that you should buy only the big companies has its own flaws, however. Often risk-averse investors bid up the prices of large, well-known companies to a point where the securities do not provide adequate rates of return. Whatever your investment strategy, you must evaluate the prospects for your investments carefully.

Exhibit 5.17 lists the industries represented among the 500 stocks of the S&P 500 Index. The industrial category accounts for the largest single group of industries, 67. Four of the industries are in transportation, nine are in the financial category, and three fall under utilities. The index is dominated by companies in the industrial category, which reflects the characteristics of the U.S. stock market as a whole.

Refer back to Exhibit 5.14. The table lists the percentage changes of the market indexes for the previous 12 months and for the period between December 31, 1991, and the date the exhibit appeared in the paper. Notice that the Dow Jones 30 Industrials had gained 5.67 percent since the end of 1991. The S&P 500 declined 1.32 percent, and the NASDAQ Composite declined 1.75 percent over the same period. This shows that the smaller companies, as indicated by the NASDAQ Composite, suffered more than the bigger companies in the market decline.

EXHIBIT 5.15

Calculation Methodology for the S&P 500

Step 1. The Base Period as of December 30, 1988

STOCK	SHARE PRICE (in dollars)	NUMBER OF COMMON SHARES OUTSTANDING (millions)	MARKET VALUE ($millions)
A	$20	50	$ 1,000
B	30	100	3,000
C	40	150	6,000
Total			10,000

NOTE: Base Period Value = $10 billion = 10.

Step 2. Index Values as of January 3, 1989 (Day 1)

STOCK	SHARE PRICE (in dollars)	NUMBER OF COMMON SHARES OUTSTANDING (millions)	MARKET VALUE ($millions)
A	$22	50	$ 1,100
B	33	100	3,300
C	44	150	6,600
Total			11,000

$$\text{Index} = \frac{11{,}000{,}000{,}000.00}{10{,}000{,}000{,}000.00} = 1.10 \times 10 = 11$$

Thus, the formula for calculating the S&P 500 is:

$$\frac{\text{Sum of shares outstanding} \times \text{Price for period 1}}{\text{Sum of shares outstanding} \times \text{Price for base period}} \times 10$$

Statistically, the formula for the base-weighted aggregative index is:

$$\text{Index} = \frac{\Sigma P_1 Q_1}{\Sigma P_0 Q_0} \times 10$$

where P_1 represents the current market price, P_0 the market price on the base period, Q_1 the number of shares currently outstanding, and Q_0 the number of shares outstanding in the base period. Σ is the Greek letter sigma, which always indicates addition, or the sum of, and in this instance indicates the addition of all the market values of the individual companies comprising the group.

Calculation Methodology for the S&P 500 *(continued)*

Understanding how the S&P 500 is calculated can become quite involved. The basic formula for the 500 seems rather straightforward, but the maintenance process is very complicated and tedious. Therefore, this part of the discussion will deal only with the formula and some simple concepts in constructing the index. The maintenance process, including adjustments to the base divisor, is a separate subject and will follow.

In its simplest form, the 500 is a basket of a weighted average of stock prices and common shares outstanding. The value of the basket is regularly compared to a starting point, or base period. To make the numbers easier to work with, they are adjusted to a scale with ten as an initial index value.

An example of how the 500 is calculated can be demonstrated by using a three-stock sample. The table illustrates the process. First, a starting point is selected and the initial value of the three-stock index is set equal to ten.

Taking Stock A's share price of $20 and multiplying it by its total common shares outstanding of 50 million in the base period provides a market value of $1 billion. This calculation is repeated for Stocks B and C with the resulting market values of $3 billion and $6 billion, respectively.

The three market values are added up, or aggregated, and set equal to ten to form the base period value. All future market values will be compared to the base period market value in indexed form.

Note on Day 1 of the new index that the prices of the three stocks have each increased by 10 percent. By multiplying through and aggregating the market values (Step 2) the three-stock sample's value has increased by 10 percent. The final step is to divide the Period 1 market value by the base period market value and multiplying the resulting number by 10.

Completing the Period 1 computation yields an index value of 11. The index value has increased by 10 percent, which is the same as the increase in market value. But note how much simpler it is to work with index numbers versus actual market values. In the case of the 500, it would prove rather cumbersome trying to manipulate and interpret a basket with a market value in excess of $2 trillion. A 500 index value in the area of 300 makes much more sense.

Now, the actual formula for the 500 can be explained and interpreted. In statistical terminology, the 500 utilizes a modified "base-weighted aggregative" expressed in relatives with the average market value for the current 1941 to 1943 base period set equal to ten. The table displays the formula.

The 500 calculation at any time involves the same multiplication of share prices and common shares outstanding for each of the 500 component stocks. The aggregate market value is divided by the base value and multiplied by 10 to arrive at the current index number.

A current index number of 300 means that the market value for the 500 is 30 times greater than it was during the base period ($300 \div 10 = 30$). It would mean that a portfolio of stocks that exactly replicated the 500's weighting scheme would have increased 3,000 percent in value versus the initial 1941 to 1943 investment.

SOURCE: Standard & Poor's Corporation, "S&P 500 1989 Directory," 1989, pp. 10–12. Adapted with permission.

EXHIBIT 5.16

S&P 500 and Russell 2000 Performance

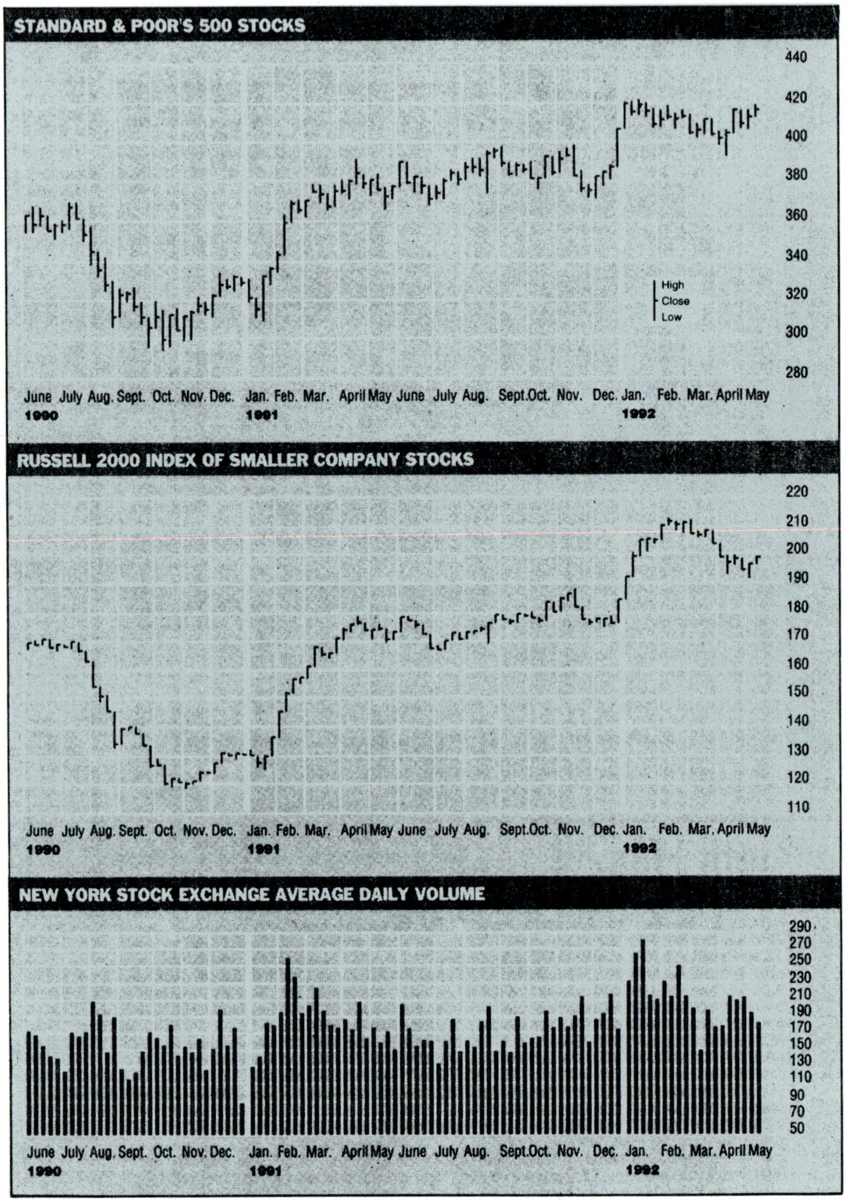

SOURCE: *The New York Times*, May 10, 1992. Copyright © 1992 by the The New York Times Company. Reprinted by permission.

EXHIBIT 5.17

Standard & Poor's 500 Industry Groups

INDUSTRIALS

Aerospace/Defense
Aluminum
Automobiles
Auto Parts—After Market
Heavy Duty Trucks and Parts
Beverages—Alcoholic
Beverages—Soft Drinks
Broadcast Media
Building Materials
Chemicals
Chemicals Diversified
Coal
Commercial Services
Communication—Equipment/Manufacturing
Computer Software and Service
Computer Systems
Conglomerates
Containers—Metal and Glass
Containers—Paper
Cosmetics
Electrical Equipment
Electronics—Defense
Electronics—Instrumentation
Electronics—Semiconductors
Engineering and Construction
Entertainment
Foods
Food Wholesalers
Gold
Hardware and Tools
Homebuilding
Health Care Diversified
Health Care Miscellaneous
Drugs
Hospital Management
Medical Products and Supplies
Hotel—Motel
Household Furnishing and Appliances
Household Products
Leisure Time
Machinery Tools
Machine Diversified
Manufactured Housing
Manufacturing Diversified
Metals Miscellaneous
Miscellaneous
Office Equipment and Supplies
Oil and Gas Drilling
Oil Domestic Integrated
Oil International Integrated
Oil Well Equipment and Services
Paper and Forest Products
Pollution Control
Publishing
Publishing—Newspapers
Restaurants
Retail—Department Stores
Retail—Drugstores
Retail—Food Chains
Retail—General Merchandise Chains
Retail—Specialty
Shoes
Steel
Textile Apparel Manufacturing
Textile Products
Tobacco
Toys

TRANSPORTATIONS

Air Freight
Airlines
Railroads
Truckers

FINANCIALS

Money Center Banks
Major Regional Banks
Other Major Banks
Life Insurance
Multiline Insurance
Property Casualty
Savings and Loans
Personal Loans
Financial Miscellaneous

UTILITIES

Electric Companies
Natural Gas
Telephone

SOURCE: Standard & Poor's Corporation, "S&P 500 1989 Directory," 1989, p. 62. Reprinted by permission.

Rate of Return for Market Indexes

Recall that you find an investment's rate of return by summing the percentage return from interest or dividend income and the percentage return from its annual price change. A similar calculation using data for the market indexes yields a benchmark figure for the return provided by the market as a whole. To estimate the rate of return on a market index, just add the annual percentage dividend return to the percentage price increase. Over long periods of time, average annual market returns have been approximately 8 to 11 percent, which is not a bad rate of return. The S&P 500's average annual return was just over 15 percent for the decade of the 1980s, indicating that this was an excellent decade for stock owners.

Market Price Quotations

To gather data for individual security return calculations, you have to be able to read price quotations. This is not as difficult as it may appear at first. Exhibit 5.18 is a sample of New York Stock Exchange price quotations from *The Wall Street Journal.* The following text explains each data item in the exhibit. This is the key to interpreting the wealth of information contained in this small space.

The left-most columns are labeled "52 Weeks, Hi Lo." They give the stock's high and low prices for the previous 52 weeks, excluding the latest trading day. The prices are quoted in dollars per share.

The column labeled "Stock" gives the abbreviated name of the company. These abbreviations require considerable interpretation. "Sara Lee," for example, is the abbreviation for the Sara Lee Corporation. If no other notation appears after the firm name, the quotation reports data on the firm's common stock. Various notations indicate other classes of securities or conditions, each of which later chapters discuss in detail. *Pf* and *Pr* indicate preferred stock. *A*, *B*, and *D* following *Pf* or *Pr* refer to the particular stock series. *Wt* indicates a warrant. *Rt* is the abbreviation for right. Unit shares of stock are indicated by *un*. The symbol *wi* means when issued, indicating a classification of stock that can trade in conditional transactions, final execution of which depends upon the eventual completion of planned stock issues. Other symbols appear in this column from time to time; they are defined in the Footnotes box that is printed near the price quotations.

The "Sym" column shows the stocks' ticker symbols. These one- to three-letter designations are the best way to identify a stock in financial information systems and computer databases, among other information sources. It is a good idea to learn to recognize the symbols of the stocks you want to follow. AT&T's symbol, for example, is *T*. CNN and other television stations that air the delayed trading tape for trades on the New York Stock Exchange and the NASDAQ system will show this symbol together with prices at which the stock is traded.

EXHIBIT 5.18

Sample Stock Price Quotations

NEW YORK STOCK EXCHANGE COMI

52 Weeks Hi	Lo	Stock	Sym	Div	Yld %	PE	Vol 100s	Hi	Lo	Close	Net Chg
4⅛	1¼	PatheComm	PCC		...	...	170	2⅞	2¾	2¾	− ⅛
3⅞	2	PatrickPete	PPC		...	...	440	3	2¾	2⅞	+ ⅛
10	8⅛	PatrDivFd	PDF	.80	8.2	...	333	9¾	9⅝	9¾	+ ¼
11⅝	9⅝	PatrDivFdII	PDT	.90	8.1	...	285	11⅛	11	11⅛	...
17½	13⅝	PatrSelDiv	DIV	1.65	9.9	...	238	16⅝	16⅜	16⅝	+ ⅛
2¼	11/16	Patten	PAT		...	25	110	1⅞	1¾	1¾	...
27⅛	22¼	PennCentral	PC	.80	3.0	16	550	26¾	26½	26⅝	...
60¼	47⅛	Penney JC	JCP	2.64	4.5	17	2842	59½	58⅞	59⅛	+ ⅝
53	42½	PennP&L	PPL	3.10	6.3	12	814	49⅝	49⅛	49⅛	− ½
63	50	PennP&L pf		4.40	7.4	...	z20	59½	59½	59½	− ½
105	95¼	PennP&L pf		8.60	8.3	...	z50	103¼	103¼	103¼	− ¼
106¾	92	PennP&L pr		8.40	8.2	...	z200	103	102	103	+1½
104	88	PennP&L pr		8.00	8.0	...	z70	100⅛	100⅛	100⅛	...
106	95½	PennP&L pr		8.70	8.4	...	z300	103	103	103	...
▼ 76½	51¼	Pennzoil	PZL	3.00	5.9	29	678	51⅞	51	51¼	−1
28¼	22⅛	PeopEngy	PGL	1.76	6.9	12	526	26½	25⅝	25⅝	− ⅝
19⅞	10⅜	PepBoys	PBY	.13	.7	30	3188	19⅞	19¼	19¼	...
35¾	27	PepsiCo	PEP	.48	1.6	23	16196	31⅝	30½	30¾	−1
▲ 34⅝	25	PerkElmer	PKN	.68	1.9	24	3911	36	34¼	35⅛	+ ⅞
20½	14⅞	PerkFamR	PFR	1.30	6.4	14	111	20½	20¼	20⅜	+ ⅛
4¾	3¾	PermRltyTr	PBT	.51e	12.4	7	211	4⅛	4	4⅛	...
11	5¾	PerryDrug	PDS		...	17	415	10⅝	10¼	10¼	...
23¾	15⅛	Pet Inc	PT	.18e	.8	23	4819	22¼	21⅝	21⅝	− ⅜
25⅜	18⅜	PetrieStrs	PST	.20	.9	137	370	24¼	23	23¼	− ¾
29	24⅝	PeteRes	PEO	2.15e	8.0	...	204	27¼	26¾	26¾	− ⅝
x 19⅞	17¼	PeteRes pf		1.57	8.1	...	x48	19⅝	19¼	19⅜	+ ¼
s 87	49⅝	Pfizer	PFE	1.48	2.1	33	14255	72¼	69⅝	70¼	−1½
8	[illegible]	[illegible]					303	7	[illegible]	[illegible]	

52 Weeks Hi	Lo	Stock	Sym	Div	Yld %	PE	Vol 100s	Hi	Lo	Close	Net Chg
35⅞	28⅝	StJoePaper	SJP	.20	.6	47	67	35⅜	35	35¼	+ ⅛
34¾	27⅝	StJoeL&P	SAJ	1.72	5.2	13	64	33	32⅜	32⅞	+ ⅜
75¾	57⅛	StPaulCos	SPK	2.72	3.7	8	453	73⅛	72½	72⅞	+ ¼
7¾	2⅛	vjSalant	SLT		...	...	25	6⅛	6⅛	6⅛	+ ⅛
37⅞	32¾	SallieM pf		2.50	6.6	...	200	37⅝	37⅝	37⅝	− ¼
76	48¼	SallieM	SLM	1.00	1.5	19	1213	68⅜	67¼	67¼	−1
14¼	12⅛	SalomonFd	SBF	1.70e	12.0	...	857	14⅛	14	14⅛	+ ¼
37	20¾	Salomon	SB	.64	2.2	8	3522	30½	29¾	29¾	− ¼
26⅜	20¾	Salomon pf		2.37	9.2	...	90	25⅞	25½	25¾	+ ⅛
46⅛	36½	SanDieGE	SDO	2.80	6.4	12	311	43¾	43¼	43½	− ⅛
6½	4¾	SanJuanBsn	SJT	.45e	8.4	13	143	5⅜	5¼	5⅜	+ ⅛
28½	26¼	Santandr pf		2.66	9.5	...	162	27⅞	27¾	27⅞	...
33⅜	13⅛	Sanifill	FIL		...	20	232	18¾	18⅜	18⅜	− ½
27	16	SaAnitRlty	SAR	1.36	7.1	18	65	19¼	19	19¼	...
4⅜	2⅜	SaFeEPtrs	SFP	.40	12.3	...	65	3¼	3⅛	3¼	...
16¾	7	SantaFeEngy	SFR	.16e	1.8	30	1192	8⅞	8⅝	8¾	− ¼
14⅛	7	SantaFePac	SFX	.10e	.8	22	11142	12½	11⅞	12⅛	+ ¼
36⅝	27⅛	SaFePacPipe	SFL	2.80	8.3	11	155	33⅞	33⅛	33¾	+ ⅝
58⅛	34⅛	SaraLee	SLE	1.00a	2.0	17	3708	51¾	49½	50⅛	−1½
29½	25⅝	SavnhEP pfA		2.37	8.5	...	5	28	28	28	+ ¼
8¼	4½	Savin pfA		1.50	25.5	...	55	6¼	5⅞	5⅞	...
4	**⅞**	**Savin pfB**			...	...	**450**	**2¾**	**2**	**2¼**	**− ¼**
5	**1**	**Savin pfD**			...	...	**25**	**2½**	**2¼**	**2⅜**	**− ⅜**
n 9½	**1¾**	**Savin**	**SVB**		...	...	**2658**	**7**	**4½**	**5⅛**	**−1⅞**
44⅜	34⅞	SCANA	SCG	2.62	6.3	9	334	41⅞	41	41½	+ ⅜
n 30¾	18	Scherer	SHR		...	...	375	27⅛	26½	26½	− ¾
68	46¼	ScheringPl	SGP	1.32	2.3	19	8827	58⅜	56⅝	56⅝	−1¼
[illegible]	[illegible]	Schlumbgr	SLB						59⅝	59⅞	−1[illegible]

52 Weeks Hi	Lo	Stock
43	34⅛	TexUtil
7⅝	3⅞	Texfiln
40¼	28⅞	Textro
6¼	4½	Thack
11¼	7½	ThaiCa
22⅜	14⅝	ThaiFd
47½	30⅛	ThermoL
21¼	13⅝	Thiokol
65¼	50⅜	ThomBet
14¾	9⅞	ThomInd
19½	9½	ThomsAr
25⅛	9½	ThorInd
18½	9⅞	Tidewtr
57½	41¼	Tiffan
15⅜	7¼	Tim'
x 125	77¾	Ti'
49¼	41⅛	T
53⅝	36⅜	T
36⅞	25½	T
30	21	Ti
▼ 31⅛	18½	Tip
4⅞	2½	Titai
11½	8¼	Titan
n 6⅝	4	ToddSi
15⅞	7½	Tokheim
29½	26⅛	ToledoEc
26¼	23¾	ToledoEd
		[illegible]doEd

SOURCE: "How to Read Stock Market Quotations," revised edition, Educational Service Bureau, Dow Jones & Company, Inc. Reprinted by permission.

The column labeled "Div" indicates the annual dividends each stock pays per share, in dollars. Often, letters follow dividend quotations. The meanings of these letters are explained in the Footnote box. The "Yld %" column gives the stocks' dividend yields as percentages of their prices. This figure represents the return an investor can expect from dividends on each share of stock. It is found by dividing the price of the share of stock into the dollar amount of the dividend per share.

The "PE" column reports the stocks' P/E, or price–earnings ratios, found by dividing their earnings per share for the most recent four quarters into their current prices per share. For example, if a company's stock sells for $40 per share and it earned $3.00 per share over the previous year, its

EXHIBIT 5.19

NASDAQ Price Quotations

NASDAQ BID & ASKED QU

Stock & Div	Sales 100s	Bid	Asked	Net Chg.
-A-A-A-				
ACSEn	85	1 5/8	1 3/4	− 1/16
AFP	90	1 7/16	1 1/2	+ 1/16
APA s	48	8 1/4	8 1/2	...
ASK Cp	270	21/32	23/32	− 1/16
ATC	327	2 7/8	3 1/16	− 1/8
ATC wt	75	1 1/4	1 11/16	...
Acclaim	109	3 3/16	3 1/4	...
Aclm wtA	40	1 1/2	1 11/16	− 1/16
Acl wtB	3	1 1/8	1 1/4	...
AckCm h	103	6 1/2	7	...
ActnSt s	6196	3/4	7/8	− 1/8
Adelph h	6	26 1/2	26 3/4	...
AdNMR	62	3 1/4	3 1/2	...
A NMR wt	100	2 1/2	2 3/4	...
AdvPr	668	1 1/2	1 11/16	+ 1/8
AdPrd un	4	7 1/4	7 1/2	+ 1/2
Advatex	8	2 5/8	2 7/8	...
Aeroson	10	1 5/8	1 3/4	...
AirInt	142	3 5/16	3 7/16	− 3/16
Alcide	627	2 5/8	2 11/16	+ 1/16
Alpha1	81	1 3/8	1 1/2	− 1/4
AlsFrm	10	1 1/2	1 19/32	
Amribc	[illegible]	10	10[illegible]	

Stock & Div	Sales 100s	Bid	Asked	Net Chg.
FahnVin	89	1 11/16	1 7/8	+ 1/16
FalcLt g 5.75e	2079	25 1/8	25 3/8	− 3/8
FamShp	155	1 1/2	1 3/4	− 3/8
FamSh pf .20	25	2	2 3/8	− 3/8
FastCm	65	1 1/16	1 3/16	− 1/16
FidlMd	167	1	1 1/16	..
50-Off	39	5 1/8	5 5/16	.
Filmstr	539	2 11/16	2 13/16	+ 1/8
Flm wt90	200	21/32	23/32	+ 1/32
Flmst wt91	300	21/32	23/32	+ 1/32
FinlInd	2	6 1/2	8	...
Fd SVP s	330	1 15/16	2 3/16	+ 1/16
Firplce	5	15/16	1 1/8	...
FAmHlt	20	3	3 1/8	...
FtCarIn .50	1	30	31 1/2	...
FtMed	60	1 7/8	2 1/8	...
FNtOh	53	1 3/4	2 1/4	...
FUtdSv .30	12	10 1/4	10 3/4	..
FishBu	580	2 3/8	2 1/2	+ [illegible]
FishTrn	30	7/8	1	..
Fisons .78e	302	18 7/8	19	− [illegible]
FltAer	12	6 1/32	6 1/4	+ 1/32
Florfx	10	1 3/8	1 7/16	...
[illegible]nd .16				

SOURCE: "How to Read Stock Market Quotations," revised edition, Educational Service Bureau, Dow Jones & Company, Inc. Reprinted by permission.

P/E ratio is 13.3. The P/E ratio helps the investor appraise the value of the shares. A high P/E ratio relative to the overall market and the stock's previous history suggests investor confidence in the company and the stock; a low P/E suggests risk and a lack of confidence.

The "Vol 100s" column indicates the number of 100-share trades for the day. A value of 424 in this column would mean that 42,400 shares of stock traded that day. A *z* preceding the number means that the number reports the actual number of shares traded. Stocks with large volume surges compared with their usual trading ranges are underlined.

The "Hi," "Lo," and "Close" columns report stocks' high, low, and closing prices for the day. The "Net Chg" column gives the difference between the day's closing price and that from the previous day. If one of these prices represents a new 52-week high or low, a small up or down arrow appears to the far left of the stock's listing. The new record will be reflected in the stock's 52-week high–low range on the following day. If the closing price is up or down more than 5 percent from the previous day's close, the entire listing for the stock is boldfaced.[3]

Exhibit 5.19 provides a sample of NASDAQ Bid and Asked Quotations. The "Stock & Div" column lists company names and dividends. The dividend figures are annualized rates with notations similar to those in New York Stock Exchange quotations. Exceptions are covered in the footnote. As in the NYSE quotations, the "Sales 100s" column reports the number of round lots traded, with *z* indicating actual numbers of shares. The "Bid" and "Asked" columns list the highest bid and asked prices for shares of stock as of 4 p.m. on the previous trading day. The "Net Chg" column gives the change in bid prices from the previous day's bid figures.[4]

How Profitable Is the Stock Market?

Exhibit 5.20 lists the annual rates of return of the DJIA and the S&P 500 Index from 1979 to 1989. These rates of return were based on the indexes' gains or losses in price for each year. For example, subtracting the 1979 price from the year-end 1980 price gives the annual gain for 1980. Adding the dividends paid by stocks in the indexes during 1980 gives their annual dollar gains for 1980. Dividing these annual dollar gains for 1980 by the 1979 prices gives the annual rates of return, or **total rates of return,** for 1980. (Some use the total return terminology because total return includes capital gains, rather than just the dividends, which would give current returns.)

total rate of return: The rate of return found by dividing the sum of capital gains and dividends by the initial price of an investment.

In spite of some years of negative rates of return, the average rates of return earned on both market indexes between 1979 and 1989 were quite substantial. This leads to the conclusion that the stock market has been quite profitable over time in spite of the variability of the annual rates of return. Over long periods of time the stock market, as measured by the rate of return on the S&P 500, has been more profitable than investments in either Treasury bills or long-term government bonds.

What about Risk?

Investing in the stock market involves more risk than T-bills or bonds, as well, but how much riskier? The variability of the market's annual rate of return over time is a good measure of its risk. Variability is measured by the standard deviation of past annual returns, found by averaging the annual

EXHIBIT 5.20

Returns and Risks of the DJIA and S&P 500

DJIA

	PRICE	CAPITAL GAIN/LOSS	DIVIDENDS	DOLLAR RETURN	PERCENTAGE RETURN
1979	$ 838.74	33.73	50.98	$ 84.71	10.52%
1980	963.99	125.25	54.36	179.61	21.41
1981	875.00	(88.99)	56.22	(32.77)	−3.40
1982	1,046.54	171.54	54.14	225.68	25.79
1983	1,258.64	212.10	56.33	268.43	25.65
1984	1,211.57	(47.07)	60.63	13.56	1.08
1985	1,546.67	335.10	62.03	397.13	32.78
1986	1,895.95	349.28	67.04	416.32	26.92
1987	1,938.83	42.88	71.20	114.08	6.02
1988	2,168.57	229.74	79.53	309.27	15.95
1989	2,440.06	271.49	92.13	363.62	16.77
Mean rate of return		16.32%			
Standard deviation of return		11.07%			

S&P 500

	PRICE	CAPITAL GAIN/LOSS	DIVIDENDS	DOLLAR RETURN	PERCENTAGE RETURN
1979	103.00	6.98	5.43	12.41	12.92%
1980	118.80	15.80	5.99	21.79	21.16
1981	128.10	9.30	6.45	15.75	13.26
1982	119.70	(8.40)	6.82	(1.58)	−1.23
1983	160.40	40.70	6.99	47.69	39.84
1984	160.50	0.10	7.35	7.45	4.64
1985	186.80	26.30	7.75	34.05	21.21
1986	236.30	49.50	8.16	57.66	30.87
1987	286.80	50.50	8.58	59.08	25.00
1988	270.50	(16.30)	9.34	(6.96)	−2.43
1989	328.85	58.35	10.50	68.85	25.45
Mean rate of return		17.34%			
Standard deviation of return		12.71%			

returns for a period of years and calculating the standard deviation of these returns from the average. The standard deviation for the DJIA for the period between 1979 and 1989 was 11.1 percent. The standard deviation for the S&P 500 Index was 12.7 percent.

This suggests that the two stock market indexes had similar risk, which makes sense. Note, however, that any money you invest in common stocks will be at risk through price variation. If you cannot face the thought of your precious dollars diminishing while you watch, you should look for more stable types of investments.

SUMMARY

The investor needs to know how securities are bought and sold. Knowledge of how stocks are traded will help you understand the dynamics of the pricing process and take some of the mystery out of securities transactions.

Selecting a broker is just as important to your financial health as selecting a doctor or a dentist is for your physical well-being. Select a broker and a brokerage firm that can give you the service you want to meet your investment objectives and needs. You need to understand the reports the broker will send, how to place an order, and what fees the broker will charge to maximize the benefits from your money. The simple process of opening a brokerage account starts the communication between customer and broker. This gives the broker hard facts about your resources, investment goals, and attitude toward risk, all of which guide his or her efforts on your behalf.

You need to know about the markets where securities are traded to track your investments and to make certain they continue to perform as expected. Placing orders for trades requires awareness of specialized terminology and the effects of each type of order. Understanding the global marketplace for securities opens new opportunities for investment profits.

Investors use several measures to gauge the level and performance of the stock market. Knowledge of the history and characteristics of the Dow Jones Industrial Average and other market indexes helps you use these measures to evaluate conditions in the market.

The stock market has indeed been profitable over long periods of time, outperforming both short-term and long-term bonds. During the 1980s, the market indexes provided average annual compound rates of return of over 15 percent.

Annual returns on common stock investments vary widely, however, in spite of their long-term profitability. Investors must expect variations in their annual rates of return, which we measure by the standard deviation of annual returns. If you can accept losses in some years to earn excellent returns over time, then you will be happy investing in common stocks.

INVESTMENT MANAGEMENT CONCEPTS

1. Select an experienced broker whom you like, who shares your values, and who works at a reputable brokerage firm.
2. Understand every part of the account application form you fill out.
3. Try to minimize transaction costs.
4. Know what information appears in the monthly account statement.

Know how to calculate your gains and the rate of return on a stock and the market as a whole.

REVIEW QUESTIONS

1. Where is the best place to start to look for a broker?
2. What type of experience do you want your broker to have?
3. Why should the broker know your goals and objectives?
4. What do you want to know about the broker's character and philosophy?
5. What type of brokerage firm should you choose?
6. Why is it a good idea to review each item on the application form when opening an account with a broker?
7. What is the most important part of the form?
8. What is the broker's first job?
9. What is the best type of order to give to your broker and why?
10. How can you minimize your brokerage commissions?
11. Will your broker execute your orders personally on the floor of the exchange? Explain.
12. Explain the difference between placing an order on the NYSE and through the NASDAQ system.
13. What is the broker's confirmation statement?
14. Why is it important to understand every detail of your monthly brokerage account statement?
15. What is the primary market for securities?
16. What is the secondary market for securities?
17. What are the main secondary markets in the United States?
18. Where in the world are securities traded?
19. Besides the United States, what are the three next-largest securities markets by country?
20. What is an American depository receipt (ADR)?
21. How are securities markets regulated?
22. Are investors protected against losses due to firm failure or fraud when they hold securities in street name with a broker?
23. What are the Dow Jones Industrial averages and how were they started?
24. How is the Dow Jones Industrial Average computed?
25. What information is found in *The Wall Street Journal* about stock prices?
26. What is the Standard & Poor's 500 Index?
27. How do you calculate the rate of return earned on the stock market indexes?

28. Has the S&P 500 Index indicated a profitable market overall?
29. Has the DJIA indicated a profitable market?
30. Have the S&P 500 Index and the DJIA indicated a risky market?

SELF-CORRECTING PROBLEMS

1. *The Wall Street Journal* reports that AT&T closed yesterday at 37.
   a. What was the price paid for a share of stock?
   b. How much would you pay for a round lot?
2. What commission would you expect to pay to buy 100 shares of AT&T at 37?
3. If you bought 500 shares of AT&T at 37, what would the total cost of your stock be?
4. What commission would you pay on a purchase of 500 shares of AT&T at 37?
5. The DJIA closed at 3,007.16 on September 9, 1991, and a 2,985.69 on September 13, 1991.
   a. What was the gain or loss or loss on the market between these dates?
   b. What was the rate of return?

Answers to Self-Correcting Problems

1. a. $37 share
   b. $3,700
2. Between $45 and $75 depending on the broker (based on Exhibit 5.2)
3. $18,500 (500 × 37)
4. Probably around $185, depending on the broker (based on Exhibit 5.2)
5. a. 3,07.16 − 2,985.69 = 21.47
   b. 21.47/3,0017.16 = 0.714 percent loss

SELECTED READINGS

Amihud, Yakov, et al. *Market Making and the Changing Structure of the Securities Industry*. Lexington, Mass.: Lexington Books, 1985.

Introduction to Brokerage Operations Department Procedures. New York: New York Institute of Finance, 1988.

Koehler, David. *Winning with Your Stockbroker in Good Times and Bad*. Chicago: Longman, 1988.

Scott, David L. *How Wall Street Works: The Basics & Beyond*. Chicago: Probus Publishing, 1991.

Teweles, Richard J., and Edward S. Bradley. *The Stock Market*. New York: John Wiley & Sons, 1987.

Weiss, David M. *After the Trade Is Made: Processing Securities Transactions*. New York: Prentice-Hall, 1986.

chapter 6

Risk, Return, and Asset Allocation

Joan Cahill, a 46-year-old junior college mathematics teacher, faced a dilemma. Her husband died suddenly, leaving her to nurture their family alone with the help of a large sum of cash from life insurance policies. Having no investment experience, Joan attended a seminar led by the authors to learn how to put the life insurance proceeds to work for her and her children.

"I have two major worries about investing the insurance money," Joan said. "First, my current salary from teaching is not enough to pay all of the costs of raising the kids and running the house, so I need investment income to help pay current expenses. But I also need investments that will grow in value in the future to pay for the children's college costs and to provide for my retirement. I really need both growth and income."

Joan's late husband had told her that common stocks provided the best investment returns, in spite of their high risk. A review of the couple's monthly brokerage account statements for the previous two years made her doubt this advice, however, since her husband's extremely speculative trading had failed to produce the kind of results that his enthusiasm had led her to expect. The risks her money would face in the stock market made Joan extremely apprehensive and rather reluctant to invest her nest egg there.

To achieve both growth and a reliable stream of income, Joan Cahill needed to resolve what investment analysts commonly refer to as the *asset allocation decision*. She had to choose assets in which to invest and allocate proportions of her portfolio for investment in assets from each category. This choice depended upon the amount of risk Joan was willing to accept, her needs for growth and income, and a number of other factors. Her investment advisors worked to guide her through this process to develop a plan for the most productive investment of her capital.

Over the course of the next year, with her advisors' help, Joan fashioned such a plan and invested her money in a diversified portfolio designed to meet both her current and future needs. This asset allocation process is the real heart of investment planning for both individuals and institutions.

Introduction

Long-term investment planning requires a balance between the conflicting desires for the highest possible returns and the smallest possible variation in returns. If you're too conservative, you may pass up golden opportunities; on the other hand, taking unreasonable risks could seriously deplete (or even completely consume) your capital.

Risk and return are inseparable companions in the financial marketplace. Virtually all investments that offer higher rates of return require investors to take more risks. Stock market investors, for example, generally earn about double the average rates of return that bank savings accounts pay over long periods of time. However, everyone knows that stock prices rise and fall, and it is possible to lose money in the stock market. This risk is the price investors pay for their higher returns.

This does not imply, however, that taking more risks guarantees earning higher returns. If you put all of your capital into one extremely risky company just before it goes bankrupt, you will probably lose all of your money. To avoid this kind of disappointment, one of the first lessons stock market investors learn (or should learn) is to spread their investments among a reasonably large number of individual companies in different industries. That way, profits on successful investments can make up for losses on the failures.

Investors also learn not to put all of their money into investments of a single type. Investment capital should be spread around (the term in financial circles is *diversified*) among different kinds of investments such as bank deposits, money market instruments, bonds, common stocks, and other assets. This way, if stocks are having a bad year, bonds or real estate may perform well enough to make up for the disappointing stock returns.

This chapter explores the topic of asset allocation as an aid to investment decision making. The chapter begins with a discussion of quantitative measures of investment return and risk and then presents a simple asset allocation technique developed by one of the authors that has been widely used by investment counselors in bank trust departments, insurance companies, accounting firms, and brokerage companies. This simple "model" can be used by individual investors to plan their investment portfolios. The next section presents historical data that summarize the returns and risks investors have experienced with different classes of investments. Finally, the chapter concludes with an explanation of the concepts of compound interest and present value; these ideas form the basis for intelligent comparisons of investment and savings options.

Measurements of Investment Risks and Returns

Chapter 2 introduced the concept of compound interest and explained the difference between nominal yield and effective annual yield on funds deposited in a savings account. It is easy to calculate the effective annual yield on a savings account that pays interest at regular intervals. Cash flows from other classes of investments are often not as regular as those from savings accounts, however, and the market values of these investments also may fluctuate. This complicates the essential work of comparing returns among investments of different types.

total return: Effective annual yield on an investment, taking into account both changes in principal value and cash flows such as dividends paid on stocks or interest paid on bonds.

To state returns on investments in a way that allows direct comparisons, you must calculate their annual total returns. **Total return** can be defined most conveniently as the effective annual yield on an investment, taking into account both changes in principal value and cash flows, such as dividends on stocks or interest on bonds. This notion of return was mentioned earlier in the text as the reward for investing.

Quantitative Return Measures

Calculation of the total return on an investment is conceptually simple, but the math can get complicated. Fortunately, we can use an approximating formula to estimate the correct value sufficiently accurately for most practical purposes, at least for time periods of one year or less. For a one-year period, this formula calculates total return as the annual capital gain or loss on the investment plus the annual cash payments the investment provides from interest or dividends, all divided by the beginning price of the investment, as follows:

$$\frac{P_1 - P_0 + CF_1}{P_0}$$

where

P_0 = asset's beginning-of-year market price

P_1 = asset's end-of-year market price

CF_1 = cash flow received from dividends or interest

As an example, assume that an investor bought 100 shares of AT&T common stock at the beginning of the year at a price of $26.00 per share. By the end of the year the stock's price had increased to $30.00 per share, and during the year AT&T's directors decided to pay a dividend of $1.20 per share on the stock. To find the total return on the investment using the previous formula, first subtract $26.00 from $30.00 to determine the year's capital gain, $4.00. Adding the $4.00 capital gain to the $1.20 dividend gives a total dollar return of $5.20 per share. Dividing this dollar return by the original investment of $26.00 results in a total percentage return of approximately 20 percent.

The 20 percent figure is approximate because it does not reflect the timing of the dividend payment; it implicitly assumes that the company paid the dividend at the end of the year. If it paid the dividend earlier in the year, perhaps quarterly or semiannually, the stockholder could have reinvested it in more stock or some other income-earning asset.

Similarly, the above total return formula does not account for the timing of the rise in the stock price. If this increase occurred early in the year, the stockholder could have decided to reinvest the gain, either by continuing to hold the stock, hoping for further price increases, or selling the stock to take the gain in cash to fund the purchase of another asset. The formula implicitly assumes that any change in value occurs at the end of the year. In fact, the values of most investments fluctuate throughout the year, but this price fluctuation and the problem with the timing of dividend payments affect the total return on one stock for one year only minimally. The formula yields a satisfactory approximation of true total return on one asset for one year.

To calculate returns over a number of years, however, or the total return on a portfolio of securities, you need a more accurate calculation. Small estimation errors compound as you generate return figures for many individual assets over time. To calculate portfolio returns, the **time-weighted rate of return,** also called the **linked rate of return,** is the generally accepted standard in the investment industry.

time-weighted (linked) rate of return: Holding period return between all periods of cash contributions to or withdrawals from a portfolio.

The most precise measurement of a portfolio's time-weighted return is its **holding period return (HPR)** between cash contributions or withdrawals. The formula to find HPR for an asset is:

holding period return (HPR): The beginning value of an investment portfolio plus all income and capital changes during a period, all divided by the beginning value of the investment; equal to 1 plus the decimal equivalent of the percentage total return on the investment.

$$HPR_t = \frac{I_t + C_t + P_t}{P_t}$$

where:

HPR_t = holding period return for period t

I_t = income payments received during period t

C_t = capital changes during period t

P_t = principal value of investment at beginning of period t

If you apply the HPR formula to the AT&T example above, assuming the dividend is paid at the end of the period, it will give the same answer as the total return formula, since the formulas are algebraically equivalent under these conditions. The holding period return for the example is calculated as follows:

$$\text{HPR} = \frac{\$1.20 + \$4.00 + \$26.00}{\$26.00}$$

$$\text{HPR} = \frac{\$31.20}{\$26.00} = 1.20$$

The answer from the HPR formula appears different until you recognize that it takes the form of 1 plus the total return. To convert the HPR figure to a total return figure, you simply subtract 1 from the HPR to leave a decimal, 0.20, which you multiply by 100 to get a percentage, 20 percent. Equivalent to total return for the period under consideration, this value is called the **holding period yield (HPY).**

holding period yield (HPY): An indicator of rate of return for a given holding period equal to the holding period return minus 1.

To see why the approximate formula does not yield an exact return, reconsider the AT&T stock, but assume now that the company paid its dividend in four installments of $0.30 at the end of each quarter rather than in a lump sum at the end of the year. Further, assume that the value of the stock increased by $1.00 each quarter so that it was worth $27.00 at the end of the first quarter, $28.00 at the end of the second quarter, and so forth. The four quarterly HPRs would be calculated as follows:

$$\text{HPR}_1 = \frac{\$0.30 + \$1.00 + \$26.00}{\$26.00} = 1.050$$

$$\text{HPR}_2 = \frac{\$0.30 + \$1.00 + \$27.00}{\$27.00} = 1.048$$

$$\text{HPR}_3 = \frac{\$0.30 + \$1.00 + \$28.00}{\$28.00} = 1.046$$

$$\text{HPR}_4 = \frac{\$0.30 + \$1.00 + \$29.00}{\$29.00} = 1.045$$

Note that the quarterly HPR declines each quarter as the dividend payment and capital gain remain constant, and as the value of the beginning investment increases. The HPR declines because the investor earns the same dollar return on an increasing dollar investment as the price of the stock increases. Earning $1.30 ($0.30 dividend plus $1.00 capital gain) on a $26.00 investment in the first quarter gives a 5.0 percent rate of return, but earning the same $1.30 on an investment worth $27.00 (the value of the stock at the end of the first quarter) gives a 4.8 percent return.

To convert the four quarterly HPRs into a single, annual HPR, multiply the four quarterly HPRs together. This gives an annual HPR of 1.203, which converts to a holding period yield of 20.3 percent. This represents the true return on the investment for the period under study more accurately than the total return formula's result of 20.0 percent. The difference comes from quarterly compounding as the stockholder reinvests dividends. This gives an effective annual yield value equivalent to that derived from the calculation in Chapter 2 of effective annual yields on savings accounts with quarterly compounding of interest. Although the difference here is small, the principle is extremely important when calculating returns for large portfolios, containing hundreds of securities.

The HPR formula never gives a negative value since the lowest possible number from any set of cash flows is zero. This does not mean that you cannot measure the holding period returns on losing investments, though. An HPR value below 1.0, when converted by subtracting 1 and multiplying by 100 as explained above, can give a negative percentage for the holding period yield. A holding period return of 0.95, for example, would convert to a holding period yield of -5.0 percent.

By eliminating negative outputs, the HPR formula allows investors to calculate the arithmetic mean and geometric mean of a series of HPRs. These statistics give important indications of long-term investment performance. The **arithmetic mean (A)** is the simple arithmetic average of a series of HPRs; it measures the average annual return. The **geometric mean (G)** measures the average annual compound rate of return; it is calculated by taking the *n*th root of a geometric (or multiplied) series of individual HPRs. For example, given three annual HPRs of 1.095, 1.162, and 0.962, the arithmetic and geometric means would be found as follows:

arithmetic mean return (A): Simple arithmetic average of a series of holding period returns or holding period yields.

geometric mean return (G): Average annual compound rate of return on an investment calculated by taking the *n*th root of a geometric (multiplied) progression of a series of holding period returns.

$$A = \frac{1.095 + 1.162 + 0.962}{3} = 1.073$$

$$G = \sqrt[3]{1.095 \times 1.162 \times 0.962} = 1.070$$

The arithmetic mean HPR provides the best estimate of the amount of cash return an investor would have per dollar of original investment at the end of one holding period. The arithmetic mean would be a good response if someone asked, based on a series of annual HPRs, what is your best guess about the HPR for a single year. The geometric mean, on the other hand, gives a single value for the average annual compound return over time on an original investment if all cash flows were reinvested. Most investors are more often interested in average annual compound returns than arithmetic mean returns.

As shown in the AT&T example, given HPRs for subperiods within a year, you can find an annual HPR by multiplying the subperiod HPRs together. Cash flows from large portfolios occur frequently and often irregularly, and HPR calculations have to reflect both cash income from investments and contributions to or withdrawals from the principal balance. To get a theoretically correct figure, the portfolio manager should calculate an HPR for every subperiod within a year during which a cash flow occurs, and then convert the large number of individual-period HPRs to an annual HPR. As a practical matter, however, you can estimate an annual HPR by calculating monthly HPRs and converting them to an annual figure, in effect assuming that all cash flows occur at the end of the month. This method generally provides a satisfactory approximation, although a computerized record-keeping system can allow exact calculation, which is preferable.

Quantitative Risk Measures

standard deviation: A statistical measure of variability around the mean or average value of a distribution of numbers.

As mentioned, you can properly evaluate investment returns only in relation to the risk taken to achieve them. Risk is commonly measured in terms of standard deviation about the mean annual total return. This measure of total risk can be applied to virtually any investment. As noted earlier, **standard deviation** measures the dispersion of individual values in a series about the mean for the total series. A higher standard deviation of return relative to the mean return indicates greater risk.

Essentially, standard deviation defines the range about the mean return within which individual-period returns fall most of the time. Based on statistical theory, an investor can expect the return on an investment in any one year to fall within one standard deviation above or below the long-term mean return on that investment approximately 68 percent of the time. The return can be expected to fall within two standard deviations above or below the mean approximately 95 percent of the time, and within three standard deviations of the mean 99.5 percent of the time. The percentage change represented by one standard deviation depends upon the variability of the returns on the investment over time.

Consider, for example, the riskiness of common stocks. Most estimates of stock returns show that a broadly diversified portfolio of common stocks should return approximately 10 percent per year over long periods of time (20 years or more), with a standard deviation of approximately 20 percent per year. This means that 68 percent of the time, one would expect the return in any single year to lie between −10 percent (the mean return of 10 percent minus one standard deviation of 20 percent) and +30 percent (the mean return plus one standard deviation). This range reflects the rather wide variations in common stock returns, but stockholders earn their high long-term returns precisely for accepting this variability. In comparison, long-run returns on intermediate- to long-term government bonds average 4.5 to 5 percent per year, with a standard deviation of approximately 5 percent per year. Government bonds offer much less risk than common stocks, but they pay much lower returns.

Measuring risk in terms of the standard deviation of return is a central concept in investment theory. At this point, it is sufficient to understand what *standard deviation* means and how it is used to measure risk. Chapter 10 explains in detail how to calculate standard deviation and how to use it to evaluate a particular security's risk.

EXHIBIT 6.1

Average Annual Total Return and Risk on Securities, 1926–1990

Series	Geometric Mean	Arithmetic Mean	Standard Deviation
Common Stocks	10.1%	12.1%	20.8%
Small Company Stocks	11.6	17.1	35.4
Long-Term Corporate Bonds	5.2	5.5	8.4
Long-Term Government Bonds	4.5	4.9	8.5
Intermediate-Term Government Bonds	5.0	5.1	5.5
U.S. Treasury Bills	3.7	3.7	3.4
Inflation	3.1	3.2	4.7

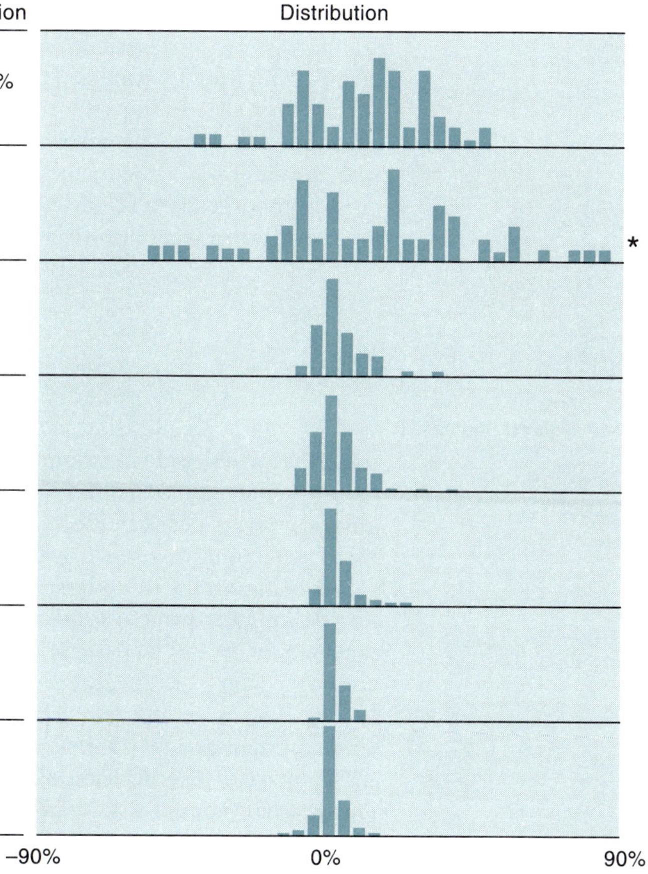

* The 1933 Small Company Stock Total Return was 142.9 percent.

SOURCE: *Stocks, Bonds, Bills, and Inflation, 1991 Yearbook*™ (Chicago: Ibbotson Associates, Capital Market Research Center, 1991). Annually updates work by Roger G. Ibbotson and Rex A. Sinquefield. All rights reserved.

Ibbotson Associates provides long-term data that are widely used in the investment community to measure historical returns and risks.[1] To give you an idea of the relative riskiness of various types of investments, Exhibit 6.1 presents the geometric means, arithmetic means, and standard deviations from 1926 to 1990 for inflation and the returns on six classes of investments:

U.S. Treasury bills (the shortest-term government debt securities with maturities of not less than one month), intermediate-term government bonds, long-term government bonds, corporate bonds, all common stocks, and stocks of small-capitalization companies.

liquidity risk: Risk of inability to liquidate an investment promptly without loss of principal.

As important as this measure of risk is, the individual investor must watch for kinds of risk that the standard deviation of total returns cannot measure. Chief among these are **liquidity risk,** the chance that one might be unable to sell an investment promptly without loss of principal, and the risk of incurring a loss within a particular holding period. The risk of a single-period loss also is important to investors in the stock market, because experience shows that stocks' higher long-run returns as compared to bonds come at the price of incurring losses during some years. The asset allocation model proposed here attempts to encompass all of these risks and balance them against return objectives.

Portfolio Asset Allocation

Many people know exactly what they want in an investment: something that will double in value in six months with no risk. Of course, no such investment exists. To achieve the best risk–return combination that *is* available, you must begin by developing a consistent attitude toward risk. This takes you a long way toward setting portfolio return objectives.

It is important to understand that there is no such thing as a risk-free investment. Investment capital cannot avoid risk. Even in choosing to leave your money in the bank or buy Treasury bills, you would face serious purchasing power risk since these investments' after-tax returns generally fail to keep pace with inflation. These "risk-free" options almost guarantee loss of investment capital purchasing power.

As part of the decision about where to invest your capital, you must decide what types of risk you are willing to accept and in what amounts. The asset allocation process should help you make this decision and then go on to assess and meet your needs for income, liquidity, and long-run total return. The overall objective of asset allocation should be to generate the highest possible long-run rate of return available from investments that are compatible with the investor's risk tolerance and income and liquidity needs.

asset allocation decision: Selection of the types of assets in which to invest and the percentage of the portfolio to invest in each type of asset.

Investment professionals refer to the choice among available investment options as the **asset allocation decision.** This means the investor must select assets in which to invest and allocate the appropriate percentage of available capital to each type of asset. The asset allocation decision is the single most important influence on the long-term results of an investment plan.

In a widely quoted study, Brinson, Hood, and Beebower devised a means to test the performance contribution of three activities in the investment management process: investment policy (asset allocation), market timing, and security selection.[2] They found that investment policy dominates market timing and security selection, explaining 94 percent of the variation in total return for 91 large U.S. pension plans. In short, the impact of the allocation of capital among chosen asset classes totally overwhelms the impacts of what particular securities an investor owns within each asset class. Within the conventional asset classes, for example, the decision to invest 70 percent of a portfolio in a broadly diversified group of common stocks or common stock mutual funds has a far more important impact on long-run performance than the selection of the individual stocks or funds. This is an important point for all investors to remember.

Asset Allocation Techniques

Three broad techniques for asset allocation are generally recognized.[3] Strategic asset allocation focuses on long-range policy decisions to determine the appropriate normal asset mix. Tactical asset allocation changes the asset mix based on market predictions to exploit superior market predictions through such techniques as sector rotation or market timing. Dynamic asset allocation reacts to changing market conditions by making relatively frequent changes in the asset mix with the goal of combining downside protection with upside participation. Tactical asset allocation and dynamic asset allocation techniques normally are employed within the context of overall investment policy set by strategic asset allocation; they amount to variations on the theme laid out in strategic asset allocation.

The most common technique for strategic asset allocation in both theory and practice has been the Markowitz optimization model for portfolio selection.[4] We can group the Markowitz model and its adaptations with the Capital Asset Pricing Model (CAPM) developed by William Sharpe to form the basis of **Modern Portfolio Theory (MPT)**. (Markowitz and Sharpe were awarded Nobel Prizes in 1990 for this work.) For the present, we will summarize the lessons learned from these theories and defer detailed discussion to Chapter 16.

Modern Portfolio Theory (MPT): A body of theory pioneered in 1952 by Harry Markowitz to combine investments into portfolios to produce the highest possible rate of return at every risk level, measuring risk by standard deviation of annual returns.

The lessons learned from MPT are the foundation for any serious effort to develop a formal asset allocation model. The earlier discussion followed the lead of the Markowitz portfolio selection model by defining risk in terms of standard deviation of expected future return. The Markowitz model shows that investors can optimize their risk–return positions by investing in what Markowitz called efficient portfolios. An **efficient portfolio** is the portfolio that provides the highest possible return at each risk level. This quantifies the relationship between return and risk in the form of a tradeoff curve showing how return increases with rising risk. To support the asset allocation decision, the Markowitz model shows optimal combinations of assets based on expected future returns, standard deviations of returns, and correlations of returns for different asset classes.

efficient portfolio: A portfolio that provides the highest return at a given risk level or, alternatively and equivalently, the lowest risk for a given return level.

To understand the use of the Markowitz model, it is helpful to think about the impact of correlations among returns in various asset categories on portfolio diversification. Recall that the correlation coefficient measures the degree to which the returns on two assets move together. If one moves one unit in the same direction for every one-unit move of the other, they are said to be perfectly positively correlated; their correlation coefficient is +1.0. If they move the same amount but in exactly opposite directions, they are perfectly negatively correlated, with a correlation coefficient of −1.0. If the changes in one asset's returns bear no relationship at all to changes in the returns on the other, the correlation coefficient is 0.0. The "magic of diversification" is that if assets with low correlation coefficients are grouped together into portfolios, the overall variability of the portfolio is decreased.

Consider an extreme case where two assets both have average annual returns of 10 percent, annual standard deviations of 20 percent, and a correlation coefficient of −1.0. This correlation coefficient means that changes in the return on one asset exactly offset changes in the return on the other. Both average 10 percent per year, but when one is up the other is down by the same amount. Combining equal amounts of the two assets would give a portfolio with an average return of 10 percent per year with a standard deviation of zero. Each individual asset would have up years and down years, but the two taken together would earn 10 percent every year.

Of course, perfect negative correlation does not happen in the real world, but pairs of asset classes do have correlation coefficients of less than 1.0, and some even have negative values. An asset allocation optimization model based on the Markowitz theory identifies combinations of assets that yield the maximum expected return at each level of standard deviation. The graph of all these points shows the efficient frontier, that is, the range of asset combinations that make up efficient portfolios with various risk–return characteristics. The Markowitz model is described in detail in Chapter 16.

institutional portfolio: A portfolio held by an institutional investor, such as a bank, pension fund, or insurance company.

Most professional managers of large **institutional portfolios** like pension funds and university endowments use some variation of the Markowitz model to make optimal asset allocation decisions, arranging their asset holdings to position themselves along the efficient frontier. Locating the efficient frontier is actually the easiest part of the exercise. A mathematical model can be built to incorporate constraints on such factors as the allowable asset categories, the maximum and minimum proportions for each asset, cash yield requirements, and so forth. Once such a model defines the efficient frontier, the more difficult question is where to position the portfolio along the efficient frontier—at the high-risk/high-return end, the low-risk/low-return end, or somewhere in the middle.

There is a solid theoretical answer to this question, but practical applications are rather scarce. In theory, fund managers should determine the shapes of their indifference curves, that is, the plots that indicate the amount of additional return they would require to accept each additional increment of risk. Theoretically, every investor can graph a series of curves to represent the combinations of risk and return to which he or she is indifferent. For example, an investor might be equally satisfied with an 8 percent return with 12 percent standard deviation or an 11 percent return with 20 percent standard deviation. The yield increase of 3 percent between these two alternatives is this investor's price of risk; this investor requires 3 percent more return to accept 8 percent more standard deviation. Given a map of indifference curves, the investor should locate the point at which his or her highest indifference curve runs tangent to the efficient frontier.

Not surprisingly, given the complex mathematics involved, very few investors attempt to do this, but the concept does provide some guidance for the asset allocation decision.

In sum, the efficient frontier is easy to identify. Unfortunately, however, plots of indifference curves are subjective, posing serious difficulties for the rigorous application of the theory. In the final analysis, placing a portfolio along the efficient frontier is more an art than a science.

Investment Asset Categories

To build a portfolio, the investor must select investments from a virtually unlimited array of possibilities. To simplify this enormous task, the investor can place his or her individual asset allocation choices in the context of similar choices made by most investors by grouping available assets into three classes: money market instruments, fixed-income securities, and equity investments. These three categories of investments offer different patterns of **risk–return tradeoffs** to meet different investor needs and objectives.

risk–return tradeoff: A shorthand expression of the inverse relationship that commonly holds between risk and return; a higher return almost always requires the investor to accept more risk.

Money market instruments are short-term, interest-bearing debt certificates such as U.S. Treasury bills, short-term bank certificates of deposit, and short-term corporate debt agreements. Individuals generally purchase these assets through investments in money market mutual funds or deposits in bank money market deposit accounts. Such investments offer extreme safety of principal, immediate liquidity, and rates of return that rise and fall with inflation. To obtain these advantages, money market investors bear purchasing power risk since, over long periods of time, after-tax returns from these instruments generally fail to match the inflation rate. This is the price money market investors pay for safety and liquidity.

money market instrument: A short-term interest-bearing debt certificate such as a Treasury bill, short-term certificate of deposit, or bankers' acceptance.

Fixed-income investments, such as corporate or government bonds and mortgage-backed securities, generally offer high current yields and excellent protection of principal, assuming the investor buys only high-quality securities. Liquidity covers a moderate range, from virtually instantaneous marketability for widely traded U.S. Treasury bonds to the slower market for corporate bonds. Additionally, high-quality, long-term bonds offer an excellent hedge against **deflation,** or periods of falling prices and interest rates. Bonds thrive in such conditions such as these since they increase in value as interest rates fall.

fixed-income investment: A security that represents a debt that requires fixed, periodic interest payments by the issuer to the security owner plus return of principal at maturity.

deflation: A decline in the general price level; the opposite of inflation.

In return for high yields and deflation protection, fixed-income securities subject the investor to interest rate risk. Recall from Chapter 1 that interest rate risk results from the inverse relationship between interest rates and bond prices. During periods of increasing interest rates, bond prices decline.

From 1978 to 1981, for example, high interest rates forced bond values down so far that total returns on bonds (changes in capital value plus interest earnings) were negative for all four years. Total returns were so dismal that one famous Wall Street economist was quoted as saying, "Every bond bought during the last 40 years is now being held at a loss!" Bonds subsequently staged a spectacular recovery, surging over 40 percent when rates fell during 1982.

equity investment: An investment such as common stock or real estate that gives the investor an ownership interest in an asset.

Equity investments, such as common stocks and real estate, offer the best opportunity for long-term capital gains. This characteristic has made them the classic hedges against inflation since their values generally rise faster than the general price level over long periods of time as the economy expands. To gain this protection from rising prices, the equity investor must accept the highest risk of the three classes of investments as measured by fluctuations in principal values.

Based on past experience, equity investors must prepare themselves financially and psychologically for the near certainty that their holdings will decline in value in some years. In fact, historical data show that, although common stocks provide the highest long-run rates of return overall, they lose money about one-third of the time.

Portfolio Allocation Scoring System (PASS)

As mentioned earlier, Modern Portfolio Theory provides the formal theoretical framework for the quantitative asset allocation models used by the managers of most institutional portfolios, such as pension funds and university endowments. Individual investors, however, must evaluate risk in a more complex and subtle way that goes beyond the simple standard deviation of expected future returns. Developing an appropriate asset allocation strategy requires a realistic assessment of the type and magnitude of risk the investor is able and willing to accept in light of the rate of return the investor wants to earn. To illustrate these concepts, Exhibit 6.2 presents the Portfolio Allocation Scoring System (PASS).[5] This system can provide a rough outline of an asset allocation strategy for an individual investor.

The PASS system asks you to score yourself on a 1-to-5 scale on seven important return and risk objectives. A high score suggests that you should orient your portfolio toward equity investments; a low score indicates that your portfolio should lean toward fixed-income investments and money market instruments. The PASS system essentially develops a kind of aggressiveness index, since higher scores reflect more aggressive return objectives and correspondingly high risk tolerances.

To use PASS, simply circle the number under the column that best describes the importance of each investment objective to you. After responding to each statement, add up the total value of all the numbers you circled and use this score to determine your diversification guidelines, given in the lower

EXHIBIT 6.2

Portfolio Allocation Scoring System

	STRONGLY AGREE	AGREE	NEUTRAL	DISAGREE	STRONGLY DISAGREE
1. Earning a high long-term total return that will allow my capital to grow faster than the inflation rate is one of my most important investment objectives.	5	4	3	2	1
2. I would like an investment that allows me to defer taxation of capital gains and/or interest to future years.	5	4	3	2	1
3. I do not require a high level of current income from my investments.	5	4	3	2	1
4. My major investment goals are relatively long-term.	5	4	3	2	1
5. I am willing to tolerate sharp up and down swings in the return on my investments in order to seek a higher return than would normally be expected from more stable investments.	5	4	3	2	1
6. I am willing to risk short-term losses in return for a potentially higher long-run rate of return.	5	4	3	2	1
7. I am financially able to accept a low level of liquidity in my investment portfolio.	5	4	3	2	1

Portfolio Allocation Models

TOTAL SCORE	MONEY MARKET INSTRUMENTS	FIXED-INCOME SECURITIES	EQUITY INVESTMENTS
30–35	10%	10%	80%
22–29	20	20	60
14–21	30	30	40
7–13	40	40	20

SOURCE: William G. Droms, "Investment Asset Allocation for PFP Clients," *Journal of Accountancy* (April 1987).

section. The PASS system statements are structured to award 5 points for a response of "strongly agree" and 1 point for a response of "strongly disagree." A "neutral" response scores 3 points.

The first three statements measure return objectives. Strong agreement that you need to earn a high long-term total return so your capital will grow faster than the inflation rate results in a score of 5. If this objective is not at all important to you, you would strongly disagree with the statement and score 1 point for this statement. Remember that this is not an exam; a high score is best only if it most closely matches *your* attitudes toward risk and return. It is important that investors answer these questions carefully and thoughtfully.

The second statement deals with the importance of deferring taxation on capital gains and/or interest; opportunities to defer taxes are generally associated with equity investments. The third statement assesses the extent to which you need the portfolio to generate current income. A lower current income requirement allows you to orient the portfolio toward more aggressive long-term capital gains.

The last four statements on the PASS system survey deal with your time horizon, fluctuations in total return, the probability of realizing losses in some years, and liquidity needs. These statements measure four different aspects of your risk tolerance. More willingness to tolerate these kinds of risk are reflected in a higher PASS score, suggesting a stronger portfolio orientation toward equities.

The highest possible PASS score of 35 means that you strongly agreed with all of the statements on the form. This indicates a set of risk and return objectives that you could best meet by allocating nearly all of your capital to equity investments such as common stocks. Even with a PASS score of 35, your portfolio should combine 10 percent money market instruments and 10 percent fixed-income securities with the high 80 percent proportion of common stock.

The lowest possible PASS score of 7 would result from strongly disagreeing with all of the statements about your investment return and risk objectives. With this score, PASS suggests that you invest only 20 percent of your assets in equity investments, allocating 40 percent of your remaining capital to money market instruments and 40 percent to fixed-income securities. A PASS score between the extremes suggests that you should allocate your portfolio among the three asset classes in some intermediate proportion.

Obviously, the PASS system provides only a rough guideline for portfolio allocation. It is not meant to be a fail-safe, mechanical system to meet all of an individual investor's planning needs. The PASS score does, however, provide a very useful approximation of your optimal portfolio, based on which you can begin to turn your personal return and risk objectives into an action strategy. The system also forces you to explicitly recognize the tradeoff between risk and return and come to grips with your own **risk–return preferences** and income needs.

risk–return preference: The amount of risk an investor is willing to accept in pursuit of increasing investment returns.

EXHIBIT 6.3

Post-World War II Investment Returns, 1946–1990

	AVERAGE ANNUAL COMPOUND RETURN	YEAR-END 1990 CUMULATIVE WEALTH INDEX
Consumer prices	4.5%	$ 725
U.S. Treasury bills	4.9	861
Corporate bonds	5.1	938
Common stocks	11.4	12,878

[a]Cumulative wealth index represents the ending value of $100 invested at the beginning of the period indicated.

SOURCE: *Stocks, Bonds, Bills, and Inflation, 1991 Yearbook* ™ (Chicago: Ibbotson Associates, Capital Market Research Center, 1991).

EXHIBIT 6.4

Investment Returns, 1970–1990

	AVERAGE ANNUAL COMPOUND RETURN	YEAR-END 1990 CUMULATIVE WEALTH INDEX
Consumer prices	6.3%	$361
U.S. Treasury bills	7.7	475
Corporate bonds	9.0	611
Common stocks	11.2	929

[a]Cumulative wealth index represents the ending value of $100 invested at the beginning of the period indicated.

SOURCE: *Stocks, Bonds, Bills, and Inflation, 1991 Yearbook* ™ (Chicago: Ibbotson Associates, Capital Market Research Center, 1991).

Historical Return and Risk Characteristics

Historical data are useful to illustrate the risk–return implications of asset allocation decisions. One of the best sources of this data is Ibbotson Associates. Exhibit 6.3 shows the average annual compound rates of return on three types of investments over the period from 1946 to 1990, along with the value at the end of that period of a theoretical $100 investment made at the beginning of the period. Exhibit 6.4 shows the same information for the period between 1970 and 1990.

The data for both the post-World War II period and the more recent period reinforce the hypothesis of a long-term risk–return tradeoff in the financial markets. As you take increasing risk, moving from the most secure investments in Treasury bills to the most risky investments in common stocks, your return also increases. From 1946 to 1990, common stocks provided an average annual compound rate of return nearly two and one-half times higher than Treasury bills. Recall from Exhibit 6.1 that the long-term standard deviation of stock returns is over six times higher than that of Treasury bills. This risk–return tradeoff relationship has also held in more recent years. Between 1970 and 1990, common stocks earned an average annual compound rate of return of approximately 11.2 percent compared to 9.0 percent for corporate bonds and 7.7 percent for T-bills. Inflation averaged 6.3 percent over this period.

Besides comparing returns on the classes of assets, the data also allow us to assess the assets' performance against inflation. Apparently, the commonly expressed goal of beating inflation was easily achievable (before allowing for taxes). A **continuous investment** in Treasury bills would have provided a long-run return slightly greater than the rate of inflation during any of the time periods measured. For a modest increase in risk over T-bills' levels, e.g., investing in a money market mutual fund that holds CDs, commercial paper, and bankers' acceptances, your pretax returns will almost certainly outpace inflation over the long run with minimal risk. After deducting taxes, however, returns from T-bills and money market funds should not be expected to keep pace with inflation; neither of these investments will give after-tax growth rates for capital above the inflation rate. As noted earlier, this is the price you pay for safety and liquidity.

continuous investment: Money left invested over a period of time without withdrawal of capital.

Besides returns on assets of different classes, historical data can also illustrate the implications of asset allocation choices and provide a basis for estimating expected future returns on different portfolios. Exhibits 6.5 and 6.6 show returns from different asset allocation decisions over the periods from 1946 to 1990 and 1970 to 1990. The T-bill data represent the performance of the entire asset class of money market instruments; corporate bonds represent the fixed-income security class, and common stocks (measured by the Standard & Poor's 500 index) represent the equity investments. The **cumulative wealth index** data in the far right columns of these exhibits illustrate the accumulated value at the end of each period of an investment of $100 in the proportions indicated made at the beginning of each period.

cumulative wealth index: The ending value of an investment of a given sum of money in a given asset for a specified period of time.

The exhibits show that a portfolio of 10 percent T-bills, 10 percent corporate bonds, and 80 percent common stocks would have earned an average annual compound rate of return of approximately 10.1 percent between 1946 and 1990. By comparison, an **income-oriented portfolio** consisting of 40 percent T-bills, 40 percent corporate bonds, and 20 percent common stocks would have earned a return of approximately 6.3 percent over the same period. If these past returns represent reasonable estimates of future long-run returns, you can use these data as a rough guide to future return expectations for your own portfolio. If your assessment of future conditions leads you to doubt that these historical data provide a reasonable estimate, you can choose data from some other historical period that more closely matches current conditions or substitute your own return expectations. The data in

income-oriented portfolio: An investment portfolio whose primary objective is to generate high levels of current income.

EXHIBIT 6.5

Historical Returns of Representative Asset Allocations, 1946–1990

TREASURY BILLS	CORPORATE BONDS	COMMON STOCKS	PERCENTAGE TOTAL RETURN	CUMULATIVE WEALTH INDEX[a]
10%	10%	80%	10.1%	$7,593
20	20	60	8.8	4,449
30	30	40	7.6	2,701
40	40	20	6.3	1,563

[a]Cumulative wealth index represents the ending value of $100 invested at the beginning of the period indicated.

SOURCE: *Stocks, Bonds, Bills, and Inflation, 1991 Yearbook* ™ (Chicago: Ibbotson Associates, Capital Market Research Center, 1991).

EXHIBIT 6.6

Historical Returns of Representative Asset Allocations, 1970–1990

TREASURY BILLS	CORPORATE BONDS	COMMON STOCKS	PERCENTAGE TOTAL RETURN	CUMULATIVE WEALTH INDEX[a]
10%	10%	80%	10.6%	$830
20	20	60	10.1	754
30	30	40	9.5	673
40	40	20	8.9	599

[a]Cumulative wealth index represents the ending value of $100 invested at the beginning of the period indicated.

SOURCE: *Stocks, Bonds, Bills, and Inflation, 1991 Yearbook* ™ (Chicago: Ibbotson Associates, Capital Market Research Center, 1991).

the exhibits show that the proportions in which you can trade risk for return hold up with dramatic consistency, and thus these kinds of estimates can provide a reasonable basis for assessing the long-term return implications of asset allocation decisions.

Individual investors can base their asset allocation decisions on this risk–return tradeoff concept to select individual assets from the three major categories: money market instruments, fixed-income securities, and equity investments. This gives them a systematic way to incorporate many subjective impressions of risk and return, leading to a method of rational planning for individual investors. Employing such a method, the investor can implement the two central lessons of Modern Portfolio Theory—that expected return can increase only at the cost of increases in risk and that investors should diversify to reduce risk.

Time Value of Money

Following investment industry practice, the return data presented in this chapter expressed long-run rates of return as average annual compound rates of return. Similarly, Chapter 2 compared yields on savings accounts expressed as effective annual yields. Understanding these kinds of return comparisons among savings and investing opportunities requires knowledge of the concepts of compound interest, present value, and the time value of money. The remainder of this chapter will acquaint you with the mathematical tools you need to master these concepts.

Compound Interest

compound interest: Payment of interest on accumulated previous interest payments in addition to the principal amount.

The term **compound interest** reflects the effect of multiplying a growing principal amount by a constant rate of interest, yielding an actual return over time above that implied by the stated rate of interest. The compound interest formula is the basis for all time-value-of-money calculations. This equation expresses the value of a sum of money left on deposit or invested for a given period of time at a given rate of interest, as follows:

$$V_n = P(1 + i)^n$$

where:

V_n = value at the end of n years

P = principal amount deposited or invested

i = interest rate per year

n = number of years

The derivation of this compound interest formula is actually quite simple. Exhibit 6.7 shows the value of $100 at the end of each of four years after being invested at the beginning of year 1 to earn interest at 6 percent compounded annually. The value of the $100 investment at the end of year 1 is equal to $100 multiplied by 1.06 (1 plus the decimal equivalent of the 6 percent interest rate, or 0.06) raised to the first power.

At the beginning of the second year, the new principal value of $106 will earn interest at 6 percent, so the value of the $100 investment at the end of the second year is $106 times 1.06, or $112.36. Notice that multiplying $106 by 1.06 is the same as multiplying $100 by 1.06, then multiplying the result by 1.06, which equals $100 times 1.06^2. This process continues through the fourth year, when the ending value of the original investment is $126.25, which is equal to $100 times 1.06 to the fourth power:

EXHIBIT **6.7**

Investment Growth at 6 Percent

YEAR	BEGINNING VALUE	INTEREST	ENDING VALUE	COMPOUND INTEREST FACTOR
1	\$100.00	\$6.00	\$106.00	$\$100(1.06) = \$106.00$
2	\$106.00	\$6.36	\$112.36	$\$100(1.06)(1.06) = \$100(1.06)^2 = \$112.36$
3	\$112.36	\$6.74	\$119.10	$\$100(1.06)(1.06)(1.06) = \$100(1.06)^3 = \$119.10$
4	\$119.10	\$7.15	\$126.25	$\$100(1.06)(1.06)(1.06)(1.06) = \$100(1.06)^4 = \$126.25$

$$\begin{aligned} V_n &= \$100 \times 1.06 \times 1.06 \times 1.06 \times 1.06 \\ &= \$100 \times 1.06^4 \\ &= \$100 \times 1.2625 \end{aligned}$$

In the general case, if interest compounds for n years, the \$100 investment will grow to \$100 times 1.06^n.

rule of 72: Dividing the rate of annual compound interest into 72 yields the approximate number of years required for money invested at that rate to double.

Rule of 72 If the investment is left to compound for 12 years, its ending value will be \$100 times 1.06^{12} or \$100 times 2.012, which equals \$201.20, or approximately double the amount originally invested. This illustrates the **rule of 72,** which states that dividing the compound rate of interest into 72 gives an estimate of the number of years required to double the original investment. Dividing 6 into 72 indicates that it takes approximately 12 years for an investment to double in value if it earns interest at 6 percent compounded annually.

Compound Interest Tables Calculations of compound interest over long periods of time can become tedious. To simplify this work, compound interest tables like the one in Exhibit 6.8 are commonly available. To use the table, find the compound interest factor at the intersection of the column that represents the appropriate interest rate and the row that represents the number of years over which the total will be compounded; then multiply this factor by the number of dollars in the original principal amount. For example, to find the amount to which \$1,500 would grow if invested at 8 percent to compound for 12 years, you would look up the compound interest factor in the 8 percent column and the 12 years row, or 2.518. You would multiply this factor by 1,500 to find the answer, \$3,777. This shows that \$1,500 would grow to \$3,777 if invested at 8 percent for 12 years.

EXHIBIT **6.8**

Sample Compound Interest Factors, Compound Value of $1.00

	INTEREST RATE (*i*)						
PERIOD	2%	4%	6%	8%	10%	12%	14%
1	1.020	1.040	1.060	1.080	1.100	1.120	1.140
2	1.040	1.082	1.124	1.166	1.210	1.254	1.300
3	1.061	1.125	1.191	1.260	1.331	1.405	1.482
4	1.082	1.170	1.262	1.360	1.464	1.574	1.689
5	1.104	1.217	1.338	1.469	1.611	1.762	1.925
6	1.126	1.265	1.419	1.587	1.772	1.974	2.195
7	1.149	1.316	1.504	1.714	1.949	2.211	2.502
8	1.172	1.369	1.594	1.851	2.144	2.476	2.853
9	1.195	1.423	1.689	1.999	2.358	2.773	3.252
10	1.219	1.480	1.791	2.159	2.594	3.106	3.707
11	1.243	1.539	1.898	2.332	2.853	3.479	4.226
12	1.268	1.601	2.012	2.518	3.138	3.896	4.818
13	1.294	1.665	2.133	2.720	3.452	4.363	5.492
14	1.319	1.732	2.261	2.937	3.797	4.887	6.261
15	1.346	1.801	2.397	3.172	4.177	5.474	7.138
16	1.373	1.873	2.540	3.426	4.595	6.130	8.137
17	1.400	1.948	2.693	3.700	5.054	6.866	9.276
18	1.428	2.026	2.854	3.996	4.560	7.690	10.575
19	1.457	2.107	3.026	4.316	6.116	8.613	12.056
20	1.486	2.191	3.207	4.661	6.728	9.646	13.743

Semiannual and Other Compounding Periods If interest is compounded more than once a year, perhaps semiannually, quarterly, monthly, or even daily, then a simple adjustment to the compound interest formula will accommodate the change:

$$V_n = P\left(1 + \frac{i}{m}\right)^{nm}$$

where:

m = number of times per year that interest is compounded

As this formula indicates, if interest is compounded more often than annually, you simply divide the interest rate by the number of times per year that the interest is compounded (m) and then raise the interest factor (1 plus the decimal equivalent of the interest rate) to the power nm, the product of the number of years over which interest will be compounded (n) times the number of compounding periods per year (m). For example, if the interest rate is 8 percent per year compounded semiannually, the value of $100 left to compound for two years is:

$$V_n = P\left(1 + \frac{i}{m}\right)^{nm}$$

$$V_2 = \$100\left(1 + \frac{0.08}{2}\right)^{2 \times 2}$$

$$= \$100(1 + 0.04)^4$$

$$= \$100(1.04)^4 = \$100(1.170)$$

$$= \$117.00$$

If the same amount is left for the same period at the same rate, compounded quarterly:

$$V_2 = \$100\left(1 + \frac{0.08}{4}\right)^{2 \times 4}$$

$$= \$100(1.02)^8 = \$100(1.172)$$

$$= \$117.20$$

Compounded monthly, the same figures yield:

$$V_2 = \$100\left(1 + \frac{0.08}{12}\right)^{2 \times 12}$$

$$= \$100(1.00667)^{24} = \$100(1.181)$$

$$= \$118.10$$

Notice that compounding interest more often increases the ending value (or terminal value) of the investment without increasing the amount invested, the time period over which it is invested, or the interest rate at which it is invested.

The tables can still provide help when interest is compounded more often than annually. You simply find the compound interest factor for the relevant number of periods (which is the product of the number of years times the number of periods per year) and the interest rate per period (which is the annual rate divided by the number of periods per year). For example, to find the value of $100 after two years at 8 percent per year, compounded quarterly, take the interest factor for eight periods (two years times four compounding periods per year) at 2 percent (8 percent annual rate divided by four compounding periods). Exhibit 6.8 gives a factor of 1.172, so $100 will grow to $117.20 over the two-year period.

To complete the discussion of compound interest, we can extend the preceding calculations to find an effective annual interest rate. Since more frequent compounding gives a higher terminal value for the same principal amount, time period, and interest rate, it also gives a higher effective rate of return. Adding interest more often means that the original investment earns interest on the accumulated interest more often, returning more to the investor for the same investment.

To calculate this effective rate of return, you simply subtract 1 from the one-year compound interest factor for a given periodic interest rate and number of compounding periods per year. To find the effective annual rate of return for the preceding problem, find the one-year compound interest factor for 2 percent per period over four periods, and then subtract 1 (since this represents the original principal), as follows:

$$\begin{aligned} i_E &= (1 + 0.02)^4 - 1 \\ &= 1.0824 - 1 \\ &= 0.0824 = 8.24 \text{ percent} \end{aligned}$$

where:

$$i_E = \text{effective annual rate of return}$$

This gives an effective annual rate of return for 8 percent per year compounded quarterly of 8.24 percent. In other words, 8 percent per year compounded quarterly provides the same return as 8.24 percent per year compounded annually. (This assumes, of course, that all the principal plus the accumulating interest is left to compound for the entire year.) To convert the equation above to a general formula, the effective annual interest rate is found as follows:

$$i_E = \left(1 + \frac{i}{m}\right)^{mn} - 1$$

Present Value

present value: The value today of a sum of money to be received in the future, given the interest rate at which money in hand today can be invested.

time value of money: The concept that a dollar received in the future is less valuable than a dollar in hand today, which can be invested to increase in value in the future.

Present value, a key concept in finance, is closely related to compound interest. The present value of a dollar represents the value now of a given sum of money to be received in the future, if money in hand today can be invested at a given interest rate. This reflects the fact that a dollar received in the future is less valuable than a dollar in hand today, which can be invested to grow to more than a dollar in the future. Present value calculations provide a simple means of quantifying this **time value of money** by using the reciprocal of the compound interest formula.

The present value formula may be derived directly from the compound interest formula introduced earlier. If we let r equal the rate at which money currently in hand may be invested (this is directly comparable to i in the compound interest formula), the present value of a dollar may be found as follows:

$$V_n = PV(1 + r)^n$$

$$PV = \frac{V_n}{(1 + r)^n}$$

$$PV = V_n\left[\frac{1}{(1 + r)}\right]^n$$

where:

PV = present value of the amount V_n to be received n periods in the future

r = discount rate per period

discount rate: The rate of return used to calculate present value, indicating the rate at which money in hand can currently be invested.

discounted present value (discounted cash flow): Alternative terms for present value.

The rate at which money currently in hand may be invested, r, is referred to as a **discount rate** rather than an interest rate. The present value formula uses the rate of return currently available to "discount" future dollars back down to their lower current, or present, values. This explains terms such as **discounted present value** or **discounted cash flow** by which people refer to sums of cash to be received in the future.

A simple example will make the concept clearer. Suppose you want to know the value today, or the present value, of $1,500 to be received eight years from now if money in hand can be invested at 10 percent. You can answer this question using the present value formula. Simply solve the following equation:

$$PV = V_n\left[\frac{1}{(1 + r)}\right]^n$$

$$= \$1{,}500\left[\frac{1}{1.10^8}\right]$$

$$= \$1{,}500(0.467) = \$700.50$$

The present value of $1,500 to be received eight years from now given a 10 percent discount rate is $700.50. Stated another way, an investment of $700.50 today will grow at an interest rate of 10 percent to be worth $1,500 a the end of eight years. To confirm this answer, refer to the compound interest table in Exhibit 6.6 (with allowance for rounding errors):

$$V_n = P(1 + i)^n$$

$$= \$700.50(1.10)^8$$

$$= \$700.50(2.144)$$

$$= \$1{,}501.87$$

As for compound interest factors, tables listing present value factors are commonly available. These present value factors are nothing more than the

EXHIBIT **6.9**

Sample Present Value Factors, Present Value of $1.00

	DISCOUNT RATE (r)						
PERIOD	2%	4%	6%	8%	10%	12%	14%
1	0.980	0.962	0.943	0.926	0.909	0.893	0.877
2	0.961	0.925	0.890	0.857	0.826	0.797	0.769
3	0.942	0.889	0.840	0.794	0.751	0.712	0.675
4	0.924	0.855	0.792	0.735	0.683	0.636	0.592
5	0.906	0.822	0.747	0.681	0.621	0.567	0.519
6	0.888	0.790	0.705	0.630	0.564	0.507	0.456
7	0.871	0.760	0.665	0.583	0.513	0.452	0.400
8	0.853	0.731	0.627	0.540	0.467	0.404	0.351
9	0.837	0.703	0.592	0.500	0.424	0.361	0.308
10	0.820	0.676	0.558	0.463	0.386	0.322	0.270
11	0.804	0.650	0.527	0.429	0.350	0.287	0.237
12	0.788	0.625	0.497	0.397	0.319	0.257	0.208
13	0.773	0.601	0.469	0.368	0.290	0.229	0.182
14	0.758	0.577	0.442	0.340	0.263	0.205	0.160
15	0.743	0.555	0.417	0.315	0.239	0.183	0.140
16	0.728	0.534	0.394	0.292	0.218	0.163	0.123
17	0.714	0.513	0.371	0.270	0.198	0.146	0.108
18	0.700	0.494	0.350	0.250	0.180	0.130	0.095
19	0.686	0.475	0.331	0.232	0.164	0.116	0.083
20	0.673	0.456	0.312	0.215	0.149	0.104	0.073

reciprocals of the compound interest factors introduced earlier. A sample present value factor table is presented in Exhibit 6.9.

annuity: A stream of cash flows of a fixed amount received periodically for some number of periods into the future.

present value of an annuity (A_n): The lump-sum value today of an annuity of a specified amount for a given time period, assuming money in hand can be invested at a given interest rate.

Present Value of an Annuity The present-value-of-an-annuity concept extends the concept of the present value of a dollar. In finance, an **annuity** is a constant series of receipts (or payments) that are received (or paid) at the end of each year for some number of years into the future. The **present value of an annuity (A_n)**, then, is the present value at a given discount rate, r, of a stream of future cash receipts of a fixed amount received at the end of each year for some number of years into the future.

For example, the present value of a future stream of three annual, end-of-year receipts of $100 given a discount rate of 6 percent is found, using discount factors from Exhibit 6.10, as follows:

EXHIBIT **6.10**

Sample Present Value Annuity Factors, Present Value of an Annuity of $1.00 per Period

	DISCOUNT RATE (*r*)						
PERIOD	2%	4%	6%	8%	10%	12%	14%
1	0.980	0.962	0.943	0.926	0.909	0.893	0.877
2	1.942	1.886	1.833	1.783	1.736	1.690	1.647
3	2.884	2.775	2.673	2.577	2.487	2.402	2.322
4	3.808	3.630	3.465	3.312	3.170	3.037	2.914
5	4.713	4.452	4.212	3.993	3.791	3.605	3.433
6	5.601	5.242	4.917	4.623	4.355	4.111	3.889
7	6.472	6.002	5.582	5.206	4.868	4.564	4.288
8	7.325	6.733	6.210	5.747	5.335	4.968	4.639
9	8.162	7.435	6.802	6.247	5.759	5.328	4.946
10	8.983	8.111	7.360	6.710	6.145	5.650	5.216
11	9.787	8.760	7.887	7.139	6.495	5.938	5.453
12	10.575	9.385	8.384	7.536	6.814	6.194	5.660
13	11.348	9.986	8.853	7.904	7.103	6.424	5.842
14	12.106	10.563	9.295	8.244	7.367	6.628	6.002
15	12.849	11.118	9.712	8.559	7.606	6.811	6.142
16	13.578	11.652	10.106	8.851	7.824	6.974	6.265
17	14.292	12.166	10.477	9.122	8.022	7.120	6.373
18	14.992	12.659	10.828	9.372	8.201	7.250	6.467
19	15.678	13.134	11.158	9.604	8.365	7.366	6.550
20	16.351	13.590	11.470	9.818	8.514	7.469	6.623

$$
\begin{aligned}
A_n &= \$100(0.943) + \$100(0.890) + \$100(0.840) \\
&= \$100(0.943 + 0.890 + 0.840) \\
&= \$100(2.673) \\
&= \$267.30
\end{aligned}
$$

In other words, the present value of an annuity of $100 per year for three years is equal to the present value of $100 received one year from now plus the present value of $100 received two years from now plus the present values of $100 received three years from now. This is mathematically equivalent to summing the present value factors for each of the three years and multiplying the sum by the amount of the constant annual receipt, that is, the annuity.

EXHIBIT 6.11

Illustrative Annuity Schedule

	YEAR		
	1	2	3
Beginning balance	$267.30	$183.34	$ 94.34
Annual interest at 6 percent	16.04	11.00	5.66
Subtotal	$283.34	$194.34	$100.00
Annual withdrawal	(100.00)	(100.00)	(100.00)
Ending balance	$183.34	$ 94.34	$ 0.00

Once again, tables of present value annuity factors are readily available. These tables simply sum the individual years' present value factors for given numbers of years. To calculate these factors directly, you could use the following equation:

$$A_n = R\left[\frac{1}{(1+r)}\right] + R\left[\frac{1}{(1+r)^2}\right] + \cdots + R\left[\frac{1}{(1+r)^n}\right]$$

$$= R\left[\frac{1}{(1+r)} + 1 + (1+r)^2 + \cdots + \frac{1}{(1+r)^n}\right]$$

$$= R\,\frac{\left[1 - \frac{1}{(1+r)^n}\right]}{r}$$

where

A_n = present value of an annuity

R = amount of future receipts

r = discount rate

n = number of years

The simple example presented at the beginning of this section found the sum of a three-year annuity of $100 to be $267.30, given a 6 percent discount rate. One way to interpret this result is to state that $267.30 represents the amount of money that you would have to invest today at 6 percent to be able to withdraw $100 at the end of each year for the next three years before exhausting the investment. Exhibit 6.11 illustrates this process.

compound value of an annuity (S_n): The reciprocal of the present value of an annuity; the cumulative lump-sum value of a given annuity at the end of the series of payments.

Compound Value of an Annuity The **compound value of an annuity (S_n)** is the reciprocal of the present value of an annuity. Formally stated, the compound value of an annuity is the ending value of a series of constant payments made at the end of each year for a specified number of years that earn a given rate of interest per year. In general terms, the compound value of an annuity may be found as follows:

$$S_n = P(1 + i)^{n-1} + P(1 + i)^{n-2} + \cdots + P(1 + i) + P(1)$$
$$= P[(1 + i)^{n-1} + (1 + i)^{n-2} + \cdots + (1 + i) + 1]$$
$$= P\left\{\frac{[(1 + i)^n]}{i} - 1\right\}$$

where:

S_n = compound sum of annuity

P = principal amount deposited each year

i = interest rate

n = number of years

Note from this formula that each deposit compounds for one year less than the remaining number of years in the annuity. The first deposit earns interest for n − 1 years, the second deposit for n − 2 years, and so forth. The last deposit earns no interest at all. The annuity formula is set up this way because it assumes that deposits are made at the end of each year. For example, the ending value of an investment of $100 at the end of each year for four years will be as follows:

$$S_4 = \$100(1 + i)^{n-1} + \$100(1 + i)^{n-2} + \$100(1 + i)^{n-3} + \$100(1 + i)^{n-4}$$
$$= \$100(1.06)^3 + \$100(1.06)^2 + \$100(1.06)^1 + \$100(1.06)^0$$
$$= \$100(1.191) + \$100(1.124) + \$100(1.06) + \$100(1)$$
$$= \$100(1.191 + 1.124 + 1.060 + 1.000)$$
$$= \$100(4.375)$$
$$= \$437.50$$

In sum, the compound value of an annuity formula addresses this question: If I invest a constant amount of money at the end of each year at a given interest rate, what total sum will I have accumulated at the end of a given number of years? Once again, tables of compound value annuity factors like that in Exhibit 6.12 are commonly available to aid calculations.

Few people regularly use compound interest and present value tables to solve time-value-of-money problems. Even relatively inexpensive hand-held

EXHIBIT 6.12

Sample Compound Value Annuity Factors, Sum of an Annuity of $1.00 per Period

	INTEREST RATE						
PERIOD	2%	4%	6%	8%	10%	12%	14%
1	1.000	1.000	1.000	1.000	1.000	1.000	1.000
2	2.020	2.040	2.060	2.080	2.100	2.120	2.140
3	3.060	3.122	3.184	3.246	3.310	3.374	3.440
4	4.122	4.246	4.375	4.506	4.641	4.770	4.921
5	5.204	5.416	5.637	5.867	6.105	6.353	6.610
6	6.308	6.633	6.975	7.336	7.716	8.115	8.536
7	7.434	7.898	8.394	8.923	9.487	10.089	10.730
8	8.583	9.214	9.897	10.637	11.436	12.300	13.233
9	9.755	10.583	11.491	12.488	13.579	14.776	16.085
10	10.950	12.006	13.181	14.487	15.937	17.549	19.337
11	12.169	13.486	14.972	16.645	18.531	20.655	23.044
12	13.412	15.026	16.870	18.977	21.384	24.133	27.271
13	14.680	16.627	18.882	21.495	24.523	28.029	32.089
14	15.974	18.292	21.051	24.215	27.975	32.393	37.531
15	17.293	20.024	23.276	27.152	31.772	37.280	43.842
16	18.639	21.825	25.673	30.324	35.950	42.753	50.980
17	20.012	23.698	28.213	33.750	40.545	48.884	59.118
18	21.412	25.645	30.906	37.450	45.599	55.750	68.394
19	22.841	27.671	33.760	41.446	51.159	63.440	78.969
20	24.297	29.778	36.786	45.762	57.275	72.052	91.025

calculators will solve most compound interest and present value problems quickly and easily. More complex annuity problems can be programmed on nearly all business and scientific calculators rather easily. Common personal computer spreadsheet packages also can be used to solve any class of time-value-of-money problem without much difficulty. Compound interest and present value tables have rapidly become an anachronism; they are shown here only to illustrate the concepts.

Time Value of Money in Personal Decision Making

One can find a useful personal application of the techniques just described in the job of planning for a child's college expenses. Assume that a parent wishes to provide $15,000 per year for four years for an infant's college tuition in 18 years. (Given current college tuition levels and rates of inflation, $15,000 may be a low estimate!) The parent wishes to accumulate a lump sum sufficient to make these four annual payments of $15,000 beginning 18 years from now by making annual installment payments at the end of each of the next 17 years and then making the first withdrawal at the end of the 18th year. Finally, assume that the annual payments are invested to earn an average effective annual rate of return of 12 percent.

The parent faces two simple problems that can be solved using the formulas for the sum of annuity and present value of annuity just described. First, the parent must determine the lump sum needed to pay out $15,000 per year for four years. The parent must then determine how much money to deposit each year for the next 17 years in order to accumulate this lump sum.

To solve the first problem, adapt the present-value-of-annuity formula to give the following equation (using present-value-of-annuity factors from Exhibit 6.10):

$$A_n = R\left\{\frac{\left[1 - \frac{1}{(1+r)^n}\right]}{r}\right\}$$

$$\begin{aligned} A_4 &= \$15{,}000\left\{\frac{\left[1 - \frac{1}{(1.12)^4}\right]}{0.12}\right\} \\ &= \$15{,}000(3.037) \\ &= \$45{,}555 \end{aligned}$$

This shows that a lump sum of $45,555 is required to pay out $15,000 per year for four years. A quick computational check shows why this is so (with allowance for rounding error):

	YEAR			
	1	2	3	4
Beginning balance	$45,555	$36,022	$24,345	$13,386
Interest at 12 percent	5,467	4,323	3,041	1,606
Subtotal	$51,022	$40,345	$28,386	$14,992
Annual withdrawal	(15,000)	(15,000)	(15,000)	(14,992)
Ending balance	$36,022	$24,345	$13,386	0

Proceeding to the second part of the problem, the question becomes: Given that $45,555 must be accumulated over the next 17 years, what annual deposit is required to accumulate this lump sum? To solve this problem, the compound-value-of-an-annuity formula must be used as follows (using a compound-value-of-an-annuity factor from Exhibit 6.12):

$$S_n = P\left\{\frac{[(1+i)^n - 1]}{i}\right\}$$

$$45{,}555 = P\left\{\frac{[(1.12)^{17} - 1]}{0.12}\right\}$$

$$P = \frac{\$45{,}555}{48.884}$$

$$= \$932$$

The solution to the problem shows that the parent must deposit \$932 at the end of each year for the next 17 years in order to accumulate a lump sum of \$45,555, from which \$15,000 may be withdrawn each year for the following four years. Of course, a different interest rate will give a different answer. At a lower interest rate, the parent would have to accumulate a larger lump sum, which would require larger annual deposits; at a higher interest rate, the parent would have to accumulate a smaller lump sum, and could make lower annual deposits.

In the chapters that follow, the time-value-of-money concepts learned here will help you to compare various investment opportunities. These concepts also will underlie an understanding of the all-important topics of stock and bond valuation.

SUMMARY

Long-term investment planning requires a balance between pursuing the highest possible returns and trying to minimize the variability of return. Taking more risk does not necessarily lead to higher rates of return, however, so one of the first lessons successful investors learn is to diversify their investments among a number of asset categories and a number of individual securities within each asset category.

The total return on an investment can be defined as its effective annual yield, including both income payments and changes in principal value, assuming reinvestment of cash flows. The investor can base return figures on an approximate formula for total return or an exact calculation of holding period return. The time-weighted rate of return, also known as the linked rate of return, is the generally accepted standard in the investment industry.

Investors can measure risk quantitatively by the standard deviation of returns about the average annual total return. This measure of risk can be applied to virtually any investment and measures the dispersion about the mean of total annual returns: A higher standard deviation indicates higher risk. Most estimates of stock market returns show that broadly diversified portfolios of common stocks return approximately 10 percent per year over long periods of time with a standard deviation of approximately 20 percent per year.

Selecting among available investment options is the heart of the asset allocation decision. The investor selects both the kinds of investment assets in which to invest and the percentage of the portfolio to allocate to each type of investment asset. For most portfolios, the asset mix is the single most important determinant of long-term investment performance. The Portfolio Allocation Scoring System (PASS) introduced in this chapter can help you make these decisions.

The three generic categories of investments, in increasing order of risk and return, are money market instruments, fixed-income securities (bonds), and equity securities (stocks and other ownership assets, such as real estate). These asset categories offer advantages (returns) and disadvantages (risks).

Money market instruments offer the highest degree of safety, the highest degree of liquidity, and a return roughly commensurate with inflation over the long run. The major risk of money market investing is long-term exposure to purchasing power risk.

Fixed-income investments offer high current yields, moderate liquidity, good protection of principal value, and excellent protection against deflation. These investments are subject to interest rate risk.

Equity investments offer the best opportunity for long-term growth of capital; they are the classic hedges against inflation. Total returns for equity investments fluctuate more than returns for the other classes, with losses in some years virtually inevitable. Equities also have the greatest exposure to business risk and market risk. Historical risk and return data show that higher long-run rates of return are accompanied by higher fluctuation in total return as measured by the standard deviation of annual returns.

Understanding return comparisons among savings and investment opportunities requires knowledge of the concepts of compound interest, present value, and the time value of money. The compound interest formula is the basis for all time-value-of-money calculations. The present value formula is simply the reciprocal of the compound interest formula: The present value of a dollar is the current worth of a sum of money to be received in the future if money in hand today can be invested at a given rate of return. Present value calculations quantify the relationship between time and money, stating the margin by which an amount received in the future is less valuable than the same amount in hand today. This concept assumes that money in hand today will be invested at some positive rate of return.

An annuity is a series of constant receipts (or payments) of cash, received (or paid) at the end of each year for some number of years into the future. The present value of an annuity is the present value of such a stream of future cash receipts of a fixed amount received at the end of each year for some number of years into the future, at a given discount rate. The compound sum of an annuity is the reciprocal of the present value of an annuity. It is the ending value of a series of constant payments, made at the end of each year for a specified number of years, that earn a given rate of return per year.

The mathematics that underlie compound interest calculations illustrated in this chapter will be applied in valuing investment opportunities and estimating potential rates of return in future chapters. It is important to grasp these basics firmly before moving on to the next chapter.

INVESTMENT MANAGEMENT CONCEPTS

1. Investment planning must strike a balance between pursuit of the highest possible return and minimal risk.

2. Seek the highest possible return at each risk level.

3. Investment return is best measured by calculating the time-weighted holding period return.

4. Investment risk is measured quantitatively through calculation of the standard deviation about the means total return.

5. Total returns in the stock market over long periods of time normally average about 10 percent per year with a standard deviation of about 20 percent per year.

6. Asset allocation requires selection of the kinds of investment assets in which to invest and the proportion of the portfolio to invest in each asset category.

7. The best way to minimize risk is through broad diversification across asset categories and among assets within each category.

8. Selection of the asset mix is the single most important determinant of long-term investment performance.

9. Historical return and risk data show that higher levels of investment in stocks lead to higher returns and higher risks; higher levels of investment in bonds and money market instruments lead to lower returns and lower risk.

REVIEW QUESTIONS

1. Will taking more risk always guarantee that you will earn a higher return on your investment?

2. Why should investment portfolios be diversified?

3. How is total return on an investment calculated?

4. Define exactly a holding period return.

5. What is the difference between a holding period return and a holding period yield?

6. What is the difference between the arithmetic mean return and the geometric mean return on an investment over a period of time?

7. Define standard deviation of return and explain how investors use the statistic.

8. What is the asset allocation decision?

9. Explain this statement: There is no such thing as a risk-free investment.

10. How do bonds provide a hedge against deflation?

11. Why are common stocks regarded as an inflation hedge?

12. Summarize the advantages and disadvantages of investing in money market instruments.

13. What are the major advantages of investing in bonds?

14. What do historical return and risk data tell us about the risk–return tradeoff hypothesized by Modern Portfolio Theory?

15. Describe the derivation of the compound interest formula.

16. What is the relationship of present value to compound interest?

17. What is an annuity?

18. Define the present value of an annuity and the compound sum of an annuity.

SELF-CORRECTING PROBLEMS

1. What would be the value of $2,500 invested at 8 percent compounded annually after five years?

2. If the same $2,500 were invested at 8 percent compounded quarterly, how much would it be worth in five years?

3. What is the present value of $9,000 to be received nine years from now if money in hand can be invested at 12 percent?

4. What is the present value of an annuity of $1,000 per year for the next nine years if money in hand can be invested at 12 percent?

5. Why is the answer to Question 4 greater than the answer to Question 3?

6. Suppose that you can choose between receiving $25,000 in a lump sum now or $4,000 per year for each of the next ten years. Which should you select if money in hand can be invested at 8 percent?

7. You expect to retire next month at the age of 70. Upon retirement, you expect to convert all of your assets (except for a condominium in Miami that you own debt-free) into cash, which you will then invest in a tax-free municipal bond fund yielding 6 percent. You intend to use the proceeds of this fund for two purposes:

   a. To provide a lump sum of $150,000 needed to enter a home for aged executives ten years from now on the off chance that you live to be 80. This fund will be designated the hedge fund. If you do not live to collect the hedge fund, it will be passed on to your heirs along with the condo in Miami.

   b. To provide a ten-year annuity to supplement your retirement plan income while you live in Miami for the next ten years.

Assuming you currently have $350,000 available, how much of an annuity can you establish after allowing for the $150,000 needed to enter the home?

Answers to Self-Correcting Problems

1. $\$2{,}500(1.08)^5 = \$2{,}500(1.469) = \$3{,}672.50$
2. $\$2{,}500(1.02)^{20} = \$2{,}500(1.486) = \$3{,}715.00$
3. PV = $\$9{,}000[1/(1.12)^9] = \$9.000(0.361) = \$3{,}249$
4. PV = $\$1{,}000\{1 - [1/(1.12)^9]/0.12\} = \$1{,}000(5.328) = \$5{,}328$
5. Although both Problems 3 and 4 provide $9,000 in a nine-year period, Problem 4 provides the money faster. Early-year cash flows can be reinvested and earn additional interest until the ninth year is reached.
6. PV of $4,000 per year = $\$4{,}000\{1 - [1/(1.08)^{10}]/0.08\} = \$4{,}000(6.710) = \$26{,}840$

$4,000 per year is preferred at an 8 percent discount rate. At a 10 percent discount rate, the $25,000 lump sum would be preferred: $4,000(6.145) = $24,580; $25,000 invested at 10 percent could provide a ten-year annuity of 4,068.35: $25,000 = R(6.145), R = $25,000/6.145 = $4,068.35

7. a. Hedge fund:

$$V_n = P(1 + i)^n$$
$$\$150{,}000 = P(1.06)^{10}$$
$$P = \$150{,}000/1.791$$
$$P = \$83{,}752$$

b. Cash remaining = $350,000 − $83,752 = $266,248. Available annuity:

$$A_n = R\{1 - [1/(1 + r)^n]/r\}$$
$$\$266{,}248 = R(7.360)$$
$$R = \$266{,}248/7.360$$
$$= \$36{,}175$$

SELECTED READINGS

Arnott, Robert, and Frank J. Fabozzi, editors. *Asset Allocation: A Handbook of Portfolio Policies, Strategies, and Tactics*. Chicago: Probus Publishing, 1988.

Bayston, Darwin, editor. *Serving the Individual Investor*. Homewood, Ill.: Dow Jones-Irwin/Institute of Chartered Financial Analysts, 1988.

Brinson, Gary P., L. Randolph Hood, and Gilbert L. Beebower. "Determinants of Portfolio Performance." *Financial Analysts Journal*, July/Angust 1986, pp. 39–44.

Droms, William G., editor. *Asset Allocation for the Individual Investor*. Homewood, Ill.: Dow Jones-Irwin/Institute of Chartered Financial Analysts, 1987.

Droms, William G. "Investment Asset Allocation for PFP Clients." *Journal of Accountancy*, April 1987, pp. 114–118.

Ellis, Charles D. *Investment Policy: How to Win the Loser's Game*. Homewood, Ill.: Dow Jones-Irwin, 1985.

Gibson, Roger C. *Asset Allocation: Balancing Financial Risk*. Homewood, Ill.: Dow Jones-Irwin, 1990.

Joehnk, Michael D., editor. *Asset Allocation for Institutional Portfolios*. Homewood, Ill.: Dow Jones-Irwin/Institute of Chartered Financial Analysts, 1987.

Sharpe, William F. "Integrated Asset Allocation." *Financial Analysts Journal*, September/October 1987, pp. 25–32.

Speidell, Lawrence S., Deborah H. Miller, and James R. Ullman. "Portfolio Optimization, A Primer." *Financial Analysts Journal*, January/February 1989, pp. 22–30.

III

Securities Investments

chapter 7

Government Securities

One sunny April afternoon, Mrs. Frances Maguire stopped by to visit her banker at the Key Bank in Albany, New York. Mrs. Maguire, a retired secretary, had a certificate of deposit maturing at the end of April and wanted to talk to the branch manager about rolling over her CD into a new CD.

Like many retirees living on a fixed income, Mrs. Maguire relied on income from her savings to supplement her social security payments and her pension from the local school system, where she had worked for 33 years. Over the course of the years that Mrs. Maguire and her husband lived and worked, they had managed to save about $150,000 in addition to the rights that had accrued under their respective pension plans. Unfortunately, Mr. Maguire had died about ten years after the couple had retired, and Mrs. Maguire now lived in an apartment in a retirement community in Saratoga, New York. She had made many new friends in this community and lived a comfortable life relatively free from financial worries.

The branch manager, Mr. John Diamond, welcomed Mrs. Maguire into his office. John was an old friend and classmate of Mrs. Maguire's oldest son, who also lived in the Albany area. John looked up Mrs. Maguire's CD on his computer and after a pause, said: "Well, Mrs. Maguire, I guess I've got good news and bad news. The good news is that the CD you bought here five years ago for $20,000 has been paying you $1,900 interest per year, which is a current yield of 9.5 percent. But the bad news is that interest rates have come down dramatically over the past five years. New CDs from the bank are only paying 6.2 percent right now. That works out to only $1,240 a year on a new $20,000 CD. On the one hand, that's quite a drop, but the reason for the drop is that inflation and interest rates have come down so far over the past five years. The interest rate is still ahead of the inflation rate, but is just not as high as it used to be."

"Well," said Mrs. Maguire, "that is disappointing news, but I can see the reasons for the lower interest rates, and I certainly do like the lower inflation rate. When you have to rely mostly on a pension and social security to support yourself like I do, those high inflation rates can be downright scary. But is there anything I can do to get a higher interest return without taking a lot of risk?"

John thought about this for a minute and then said, "Mrs. Maguire, I know you have not done any investing in the past, but I think you should consider investing in some bonds. Our bank, like most banks these days, has a brokerage subsidiary. We could invest your money in some bonds issued by New York State. Not only will this give you a higher return than our CDs, but you will not have to pay state or federal income tax on the bonds. What would you think about that idea?"

"To tell you the truth," said Mrs. Maguire, "I would have to think that over for a while. Are there any other options?"

"Well, yes, there are," said John. "We also could offer you some U.S. Treasury bonds. These bonds offer absolute safety because they are full faith and credit obligations of the U.S. government. We also can invest in bonds issued by several U.S. government agencies that offer a little higher return than straight Treasury bonds. I have a brochure you can read that describes investing in Treasury and municipal bonds. Perhaps you should read it before your CD matures, and we can get together again."

"Thanks, John, I will do that," said Mrs. Maguire. "I will call you next week to set up another appointment and we'll see about taking my first 'plunge' into investing!"

Introduction

The U.S. Treasury, representing the federal government, along with state and local governments, issue debt securities to finance their operations, promising to make periodic interest payments and to repay the principal invested. Investors group these securities into three categories: U.S. Treasury issues, U.S. government agency issues, and municipal issues, which include bonds issued by states, cities, and other local government units.

U.S. Treasury issues are the safest possible investments, backed by the financial integrity of the United States government. In investment termi-

full faith and credit obligation: A Treasury bill, note, or bond that is backed by the full faith and credit of the United States government.

nology, they are said to be **full faith and credit obligations** of the United States. The federal government issues these securities in three forms, Treasury bills, Treasury notes, and Treasury bonds, which differ in their times to maturity. Treasury bills mature within 1 year after they are issued. Treasury notes mature in from 1 to 10 years. Treasury bonds mature anywhere from 10 years to as long as 30 years after issue.

Some U.S. government agencies such as the Government National Mortgage Association and the Federal Farm Credit Bank also issue notes and bonds. These bonds are backed by the creditworthiness of the issuing agencies, which makes them extremely secure, and they pay interest at higher rates than Treasury issues.

State, municipal, and local governments issue the third class of government obligations, municipal notes and bonds. Risk levels on these securities vary, but the interest they pay is exempt from federal income tax.

This chapter will examine the important characteristics of these three classes of government debt securities. It will also explore the term structure of interest rates, that is, the relationship between the time a bond remains outstanding and its yield. Finally, we will examine the fundamentals of bond valuation, applying the time value of money principles discussed in Chapter 6.

Short-Term U.S. Government and Agency Securities

Just like a business, the U.S. government must borrow to pay for its activities. The U.S. Treasury is the agency that handles the job of financing the government's debt. It borrows money from investors and pays interest, and repays principal from income tax receipts and other sources. Some say it spends too much, since officials know that investors will eagerly buy the securities it issues, resulting in interest payments that are a growing national burden.

Treasury Bills

Treasury bills: Short-term (less than one year term to maturity) debt obligations of the U.S. Treasury.

Whether or not the government can justify the growth in federal expenditures and debt, it has financed the bulk of this debt by issuing **Treasury bills.** It sells these Treasury bills primarily to commercial banks, other financial institutions, foreign investors, and an ever-growing number of individual investors.

risk-free security: A security that has no risk of default.

Investors, especially individuals, are becoming more interested in T-bills as they are sometimes called, for several reasons. First, they offer extreme safety as full faith and credit obligations of the United States government. This guarantee and their short maturities, which minimizes risk from changes in interest rates over time, make T-bills the worldwide standard for a **risk-free security.** Second, T-bills are highly liquid, that is, investors can easily convert them into cash. Finally, income from Treasury bills is exempt from state and local income taxes. These powerful advantages induce investors of many classes to own these top-quality securities.

Treasury bills do have disadvantages, though. Their yields are fixed only for their limited lives. (Most mature 91 days after issue). Yields on different issues have fluctuated widely in the past. Treasury bill yields were as low as 3 percent in 1963, for example, and over 15 percent in 1981. In early 1992, 91-day T-bills yielded approximately 3.0 percent.

A second disadvantage for the individual investor is the $10,000 minimum purchase requirement with additional amounts available in $5,000 increments. This puts T-bills out of reach for an investor who has only a few hundred dollars, or even a few thousand dollars, to invest.

The cheapest way to buy Treasury bills is by mail from the U.S. Treasury. Upon receiving payment, the Treasury makes an entry in its books to show ownership of a T-bill and sends a statement to the purchaser to confirm ownership. When the T-bill matures, the investor can collect its $10,000 face value from a Federal Reserve Bank or a commercial bank acting as agent for the Treasury. If the investor wants to reinvest the proceeds without paying a commission, the Treasury will send the person a check for the difference between the **par value** of the matured T-bill ($10,000) and the purchase price of the new T-bill.

par value: Face or stated value of an investment security.

If an investor is not in a position to buy directly from the Treasury, the next least expensive source for T-bills is the secondary market, that is, commercial banks or brokerage firms. This normally involves a fee of approximately $35. If the selling bank or brokerage holds the securities in safekeeping, it imposes an additional charge of as much as $35 for custodian fees. These charges can reduce the total yield on a single Treasury bill significantly.

After issue, of course, the Treasury or Federal Reserve Banks will not redeem Treasury bills until they mature. Before maturity, they can be sold only in the secondary market through brokers or commercial banks. In spite of these disadvantages, Treasury bills provide the investor with a short-term, liquid investment of excellent quality.

discount: A security, such as a Treasury bill, that is sold at a discount from face value and pays full face value at maturity.

Treasury Bill Yields Treasury bills are sold at a **discount.** This means that the investor receives no separate check for interest; instead, he or she buys the T-bill for a price below its maturity value, then realizes interest income at maturity in the amount of the difference between the purchase price and the maturity value. If you bought a 91-day Treasury bill with a $10,000 maturity value for $9,850, you would earn the $150 difference as interest income. To find the approximate annual rate of return, divide the amount of the interest ($150) by the principal you invested ($9,850) and then multiply by 4, since there are approximately four 91-day periods in a year.

$$(\$150/\$9{,}850) \times 4 = 1.523 \times 4 = 6.091 \text{ percent}$$

The time value of money discussion in Chapter 6 indicates, however, that the effective rate of return on the T-bill is actually higher than 6.091 percent when you take compounding into account. The \$150 interest income represents a return for one quarter (91 days) of 1.523 percent (\$150/\$9,850 = 0.01523). To apply the compound interest equation, you need to add 1.0 to 0.01523 and raise this quarterly compound interest factor to the fourth power, since you earn this return four times in a year, to obtain the annual compound interest factor of 1.0623. You then convert the compound interest factor to a percentage yield by subtracting 1.0 and multiplying by 100, giving the effective annual return of 6.23 percent.

Yield quotations for Treasury bills appear in *The Wall Street Journal* and many other leading newspapers in tables like the one in Exhibit 7.1. Notice that these quotes show yields and not prices because T-bills are traded on a discount basis. Trading on a discount basis means that T-bills are traded based on their annualized percentage discount from face value.

A little practice will help you to understand how to read Treasury bill quotes. The column in Exhibit 7.1 headed "Maturity" indicates the date when each security matures. "Days to Mat." gives the number of days until each T-bill matures. For example, the bill that matured on March 5, 1992 (look for "Mar 05 '92" about halfway down the list) matured 92 days after the quote appeared. The "Bid" column lists the yield for each T-bill from its **bid price,** that is, the price at which a dealer is willing to buy the security. The "Asked" column represents the yield based on the **asked price,** the price at which a dealer is willing to sell. The dealer is willing to buy the March 5, 1992, Treasury bill at a price that would provide a yield of 4.39 percent; the dealer is willing to sell a T-bill from the same issue at a price to yield 4.37 percent.

bid price: The price at which a dealer is willing to buy a security.

asked price: The price at which a dealer is willing to sell a security.

The next column, headed "Chg.," indicates the change in each issue's asked yield since the previous trading day. The yield on the March 5, 1992 T-bill changed by +0.03 percent. The last column, "Ask Yld.," gives the true bond equivalent yield if an investor pays the asked price. The true **bond equivalent yield** is the effective annual rate of return based on a 365-day year. The March 5, 1992, bill offers an annualized yield of 4.49 percent.

bond equivalent yield: The effective annual rate of return on a T-bill or other discount security assuming a 365-day year and semiannual compounding.

basis point: A unit for yield measurements equal to one-hundredth of 1 percent; there are 100 basis points in 1 percent.

To find the discounted purchase price of a Treasury bill worth \$10,000 at maturity, subtract the discount rate in basis points times the days remaining to maturity times \$0.0027778 from the \$10,000 maturity value. One **basis point** equals one-hundredth of 1 percent; there are 100 basis points in 1 percent. The number \$0.0027778 represents the value of one basis point in dollars per day for a \$10,000 Treasury bill. For example, refer again to the March 5, 1992, Treasury bill issue, which was selling at an asked discount rate of 4.37 percent on December 3, 1991. First, convert the discount rate to basis points. Multiply the number of basis points (437) by the number of days remaining to maturity (92), and multiply the result by \$0.0027778. Subtract the final result from the T-bill's maturity value (\$10,000) to find its price on the day in question.

$$\begin{aligned}\text{Purchase price} &= \$10{,}000 - (437 \times 92 \times \$0.0027778) \\ &= \$10{,}000 - \$111.68 \\ &= \$9{,}888.32\end{aligned}$$

EXHIBIT 7.1

Representative Treasury Bill Yields

TREASURY BILLS

Maturity	Days to Mat.	Bid	Asked	Chg.	Ask Yld.
Dec 05 '91	1	4.55	4.45	+0.41	4.52
Dec 12 '91	8	4.17	4.07	+0.04	4.14
Dec 19 '91	15	4.12	4.02	+0.03	4.08
Dec 26 '91	22	3.98	3.88	+0.05	3.95
Jan 02 '92	29	4.04	3.94	+0.02	4.02
Jan 09 '92	36	4.19	4.15	+0.04	4.24
Jan 16 '92	43	4.22	4.18	+0.02	4.26
Jan 23 '92	50	4.26	4.22	+0.01	4.32
Jan 30 '92	57	4.28	4.24	−0.01	4.34
Feb 06 '92	64	4.33	4.31	−0.01	4.42
Feb 13 '92	71	4.35	4.33	+0.01	4.43
Feb 20 '92	78	4.36	4.34	+0.01	4.45
Feb 27 '92	**85**	**4.38**	**4.36**	**+0.03**	**4.48**
Mar 05 '92	92	4.39	4.37	+0.03	4.49
Mar 12 '92	99	4.39	4.37	+0.02	4.50
Mar 19 '92	106	4.39	4.37	+0.02	4.50
Mar 26 '92	113	4.37	4.35	+0.02	4.48
Apr 02 '92	120	4.41	4.39	+0.01	4.53
Apr 09 '92	127	4.40	4.38	....	4.52
Apr 16 '92	134	4.40	4.38	−0.01	4.53
Apr 23 '92	141	4.41	4.39	−0.02	4.54
Apr 30 '92	148	4.40	4.38	....	4.53
May 07 '92	155	4.42	4.40	+0.01	4.56
May 14 '92	162	4.41	4.39	....	4.55
May 21 '92	169	4.42	4.40	+0.01	4.57
May 28 '92	**176**	**4.41**	**4.39**	**+0.01**	**4.56**
Jun 04 '92	183	4.38	4.36	+0.01	4.53
Jul 02 '92	211	4.42	4.40	−0.01	4.58
Jul 30 '92	239	4.43	4.41	−0.02	4.59
Aug 27 '92	267	4.44	4.42	−0.02	4.61
Sep 24 '92	295	4.41	4.39	−0.02	4.59
Oct 22 '92	323	4.44	4.42	−0.02	4.63
Nov 19 '92	351	4.44	4.42	−0.01	4.64

SOURCE: *The Wall Street Journal*, December 3, 1991. Reprinted by permission of *The Wall Street Journal*,

You can compare the bond equivalent yield for a 91-day Treasury bill to the yields on other bonds or investments that pay interest compounded semi-annually. Once you know the discount rate (use the asked discount rate), you can easily calculate the annualized compounded yield. The bond equivalent yield is essentially the same calculation that we did earlier to find the effective annual return. To avoid using an equation, simply check the yield quote in *The Wall Street Journal*.

Investors' Uses of Treasury Bills Investors find Treasury bills attractive when they yield more than typical passbook savings accounts and certificates of deposit or other short-term investments. Historically, T-bill yields have been slightly above the inflation rate, providing reasonable rates of return for risk-free securities. They also can provide a defensive haven for funds under conditions of rising interest rates when long-term yields are expected to increase.

Treasury bills also provide a haven from an uncertain stock market. To avoid losses from an expected decline in common stock prices, investors can sell stocks and invest the proceeds in Treasury bills. In this manner Treasury bills can be a profitable and liquid reserve for funds awaiting commitment to other investments.

Treasury bills' major advantage is their high quality. Secure in the knowledge that your funds are safe, you can turn your focus to yield. Quotes in *The Wall Street Journal*, however, indicate only approximate market prices, yields, or discounts at any given time. Actual trades at the Federal Reserve Bank or through an agent in the secondary market establish the exact discount rate and yield.

Probably the best way to learn the current yield is to call a customer representative of a brokerage house or an officer of a commercial bank who can provide that information along with the costs of the transaction. If it is not convenient to buy directly from the Treasury or a Federal Reserve Bank, a broker or commercial bank can complete the transaction.

Short-Term Government and Agency Securities

Under certain conditions, other securities issued by the U.S. government and its agencies can function like short-term T-bills. When a U.S. Treasury note or bond or a government agency bond reaches its final year before maturity, it can serve the same investing goals as a short-term security. The characteristics of U.S. Treasury and agency bonds are discussed in the next section.

Long-Term Government and Agency Securities

The U.S. Treasury issues Treasury notes and bonds to finance the general operations of the federal government. Individual U.S. government agencies issue **agency bonds** to finance their specific projects and activities. You may have heard of issues from such agencies as the Federal National Mortgage Association (Fannie Mae) and the Federal Farm Credit Bank. Unlike Treasury bills, which sell at a discount, these securities sell at face value when issued and pay interest semiannually by one of two methods.

agency bond: A debt security issued by an agency or organization of the U.S. government to finance its projects or operations.

bearer bond: A bond that has no registered owner and pays interest or principal upon demand to the holder of the appropriate coupon.

registered bond: A bond that is registered on the issuer's records in the name of the purchaser with no interest payment coupons attached.

nominal rate: The stated interest rate for a bond at issue, expressed as a dollar amount or a percentage of face value.

coupon rate: The nominal rate of interest stated as a percentage of face value.

current yield: A nominal interest payment in dollars divided by the current market price of the bond.

When an interest payment is due on a **bearer bond,** the bondholder detaches a coupon that comes with the security and presents it to any commercial bank that acts as an agent for the U.S. Treasury. A **registered bond,** on the other hand, is listed on the issuer's records in the name of the buyer. The issuer simply makes interest payments to that person as they fall due.

The interest rate a bondholder will earn is fixed at the time the bond is issued, stated as a **nominal rate,** which is commonly specified either in dollars of interest paid per $1,000 bond or as a percentage of the $1,000 face value. When the interest rate is expressed as a percentage of face value, however, it is more frequently called the **coupon rate.** A $1,000 bond with an $80 nominal interest payment has an 8 percent coupon rate and a yield to maturity of 8 percent.

At issue, the current yield of the bond is also 8 percent. The **current yield** on a bond is its nominal interest payment in dollars divided by its current market price. If interest rates should rise after the bond's issue, its price would drop enough to keep its total return in line with the higher returns available on newly issued bonds. In effect, a new purchaser would earn the same fixed-dollar interest on a smaller-dollar investment, and therefore a higher current yield, than someone who had held the bond since its issue. While the current yield rises and falls, however, the nominal rate and the coupon rate remain set for the life of the bond. The variability in market price due to changes in interest rates, defined in Chapter 1 as interest rate risk, is one of the risks you accept when you purchase any fixed-income security.

Long-Term Notes and Bonds

Long-term government securities are as safe as T-bills in terms of their credit quality, but their prices fluctuate more. When interest rates are high, some people invest heavily in federal debt securities to seize the opportunity to lock in relatively high interest rates on these superior quality bonds. Under normal circumstances long-term government notes and bonds sell at higher yields than Treasury bills to compensate investors for their greater interest rate risk. Since the quality of such securities is uniform, the only real variable to affect the investor's choice is the yield, which depends on the time remaining before maturity.

default: Failure to pay interest or principal when due.

Unlike Treasury securities, agency bonds vary somewhat in quality, at least in theory, since they are only indirectly guaranteed by the government of the United States. This gives these securities somewhat lower credit ratings, and therefore higher yields, than Treasury bonds and other full faith and credit obligations of the U.S. government. Historically, however, these securities have been considered moral obligations of the U.S. government. They have paid interest on time and have not **defaulted,** that is, failed to make payments as promised. This creates the opportunity to earn a higher yield than Treasury bonds of the same maturity with only a minimal increase in default risk.

Exhibit 7.2 lists quotations on Treasury bonds and notes as found in *The Wall Street Journal*. The table lists bond and note issues in order of maturity date, giving much the same information as the T-bill quotes in Exhibit 7.1. Coupon interest rates are listed in the left-most column. At about the middle of the listing, for example, a row begins "$8\frac{3}{4}$ Oct 97n." These bonds will pay interest at $8\frac{3}{4}$ percent of their par, or face, values of $1,000 and mature in October 1997. The table quotes bid and asked prices in **points** and 32nds of a point. One point equals 1 percent of the $1,000 par value or $10. One 32nd of one point, therefore, equals $10 divided by 32, or $0.3125. The bid price of 109:12 for the October 1997 issue indicates a bid price of $109\frac{12}{32}$ points, or 109 times $10 ($1,090) plus $\frac{12}{32}$ times $10 ($3.75) or a total price of $1,093.75. The asked price, quoted as 109.14, works out to a dollar price of $1,094.375.

point: A unit in a bond price quotation equal to 1 percent of the par value of $1,000, or $10.

As before, the asked price is the price at which dealers are willing to sell these bonds and the bid price is the price at which they are willing to buy them. Dealers earn the difference between the bid and asked prices, called the **spread,** as their profit. This compensates them for providing an orderly and liquid bond market in which institutions and individuals may trade with confidence.

spread: The difference between a dealer's bid and asked prices, which represents dealer profit.

The last column in the table lists the bonds' annualized yields, 6.77 percent for the October 1997 issue. This figure gives the effective annual rate of return; it is comparable to the bond equivalent yield on a Treasury bill and annual total return on other types of securities.

The minimum Treasury bond purchase is usually either 5 or 10 bonds, giving a total face value of $5,000 or $10,000. In addition, the investor must pay a commission charge for secondary market transactions. Brokers or commercial banks generally handle these trades for fees of $30 to $50. The commission per bond declines as the number of bonds traded in a single transaction increases.

The October 1997 $8\frac{3}{4}$ percent bond issue was trading at a **premium** over its par value, that is, its price was higher than its face value. To understand why, consider that this bond was issued several years ago and it has been trading in the secondary market for a while. (Such issues are called **seasoned bonds.**) If the Treasury followed its usual practice with the issue that matures in October 1997, it probably issued the bonds in October 1967 with 30-year maturities, setting the coupon rate at $8\frac{3}{4}$ percent at that time. Since then, interest rates have declined and, in the reverse of the scenario discussed earlier, the bond price has increased to keep the issue's total return comparable to returns available on newly issued bonds with lower coupon rates. This flip side of interest rate risk would provide original investors who sold their October 1997 bonds in 1992 with a capital gain over what they paid for the bonds, in addition to semiannual interest payments. Of course, if they hold the bonds to maturity, they would receive only the face value of the bonds.

premium: A price above face value.

seasoned bond: A bond trading in the secondary market after issue.

EXHIBIT 7.2

Yields on U.S. Treasury Bonds and Notes

TREASURY BONDS, NOTES & BILLS

Monday, December 2, 1991

Representative Over-the-Counter quotations based on transactions of $1 million or more.

Treasury bond, note and bill quotes are as of mid-afternoon. Colons in bid-and-asked quotes represent 32nds; 101:01 means 101 1/32. Net changes in 32nds. n-Treasury note. Treasury bill quotes in hundredths, quoted on terms of a rate of discount. Days to maturity calculated from settlement date. All yields are to maturity and based on the asked quote. Latest 13-week and 26-week bills are boldfaced. For bonds callable prior to maturity, yields are computed to the earliest call date for issues quoted above par and to the maturity date for issues below par. -When issued.

Source: Federal Reserve Bank of New York.

U.S. Treasury strips as of 3 p.m. Eastern time, also based on transactions of $1 million or more. Colons in bid-and-asked quotes represent 32nds; 101:01 means 101 1/32. Net changes in 32nds. Yields calculated on the asked quotation. ci-stripped coupon interest. bp-Treasury bond, stripped principal. np-Treasury note, stripped principal. For bonds callable prior to maturity, yields are computed to the earliest call date for issues quoted above par and to the maturity date for issues below par.

Source: Bear, Stearns & Co. via Street Software Technology Inc.

GOVT. BONDS & NOTES

Rate	Maturity Mo/Yr	Bid	Asked	Chg.	Ask Yld.
7 5/8	Dec 91n	100:08	100:10	....	3.25
8 1/4	Dec 91n	100:09	100:11	− 1	3.43
11 5/8	Jan 92n	100:25	100:27	− 1	4.02
8 1/8	Jan 92n	100:19	100:21	....	3.83
6 5/8	Feb 92n	100:11	100:13	− 1	4.47
9 1/8	Feb 92n	100:27	100:29	....	4.40
14 5/8	Feb 92n	101:29	101:31	− 2	4.42
8 1/2	Feb 92n	100:29	100:31	....	4.31
7 7/8	Mar 92n	101:02	101:04	....	4.28
8 1/2	Mar 92n	101:08	101:10	....	4.31
11 3/4	Apr 92n	102:18	102:20	− 1	4.34
8 7/8	Apr 92n	101:23	101:25	....	4.38
6 5/8	May 92n	100:29	100:31	− 1	4.40
9	May 92n	101:30	102:00	....	4.42
13 3/4	May 92n	104:02	104:04	....	4.33
8 1/2	May 92n	101:27	101:29	....	4.51
8 1/4	Jun 92n	102:01	102:03	....	4.51
8 3/8	Jun 92n	102:03	102:05	....	4.53
10 3/8	Jul 92n	103:12	103:14	− 1	4.64
8	Jul 92n	102:04	102:06	....	4.59
4 1/4	Aug 87-92	98:10	99:10	+ 1	5.26
7 1/4	Aug 92	101:22	101:26	+ 1	4.59
7 7/8	Aug 92n	102:03	102:05	....	4.71
8 1/4	Aug 92n	102:11	102:13	....	4.71
8 1/8	Aug 92n	102:14	102:16	....	4.65
8 1/8	Sep 92n	102:22	102:24	+ 1	4.68
8 3/4	Sep 92n	103:06	103:08	....	4.68
9 3/4	Oct 92n	104:05	104:07	+ 1	4.71
7 3/4	Oct 92n	102:18	102:20	....	4.76
7 3/4	Nov 92n	102:21	102:23	....	4.78
8 3/8	Nov 92n	103:08	103:10	+ 1	4.76
10 1/2	Nov 92n	105:07	105:09	+ 1	4.74
7 3/8	Nov 92n	102:14	102:16	+ 1	4.76
7 1/4	Dec 92n	102:15	102:17	+ 1	4.80
9 1/8	Dec 92n	104:14	104:16	+ 1	4.78
8 3/4	Jan 93n	104:05	104:07	+ 1	4.82
7	Jan 93n	102:10	102:12	+ 1	4.87
4	Feb 88-93	96:29	97:29	− 5	5.83
6 3/4	Feb 93	102:03	102:07	+ 3	4.82
7 7/8	Feb 93	103:10	103:14	+ 1	4.89
8 1/4	Feb 93n	103:25	103:27	+ 1	4.91
8 3/8	Feb 93n	103:30	104:00	+ 2	4.90
10 7/8	Feb 93n	106:25	106:27	+ 1	4.93
6 3/4	Feb 93[illegible]	[illegible]	[illegible]	[illegible]	4.94
7 1/[illegible]	[illegible]	[illegible]	[illegible]	[illegible]	[illegible]

Rate	Maturity Mo/Yr	Bid	Asked	Chg.	Ask Yld.
8 1/2	Jul 97n	108:06	108:08	+ 12	6.71
8 5/8	Aug 97n	108:24	108:26	+ 11	6.74
8 3/4	Oct 97n	109:12	109:14	+ 14	6.77
8 7/8	Nov 97n	110:01	110:03	+ 15	6.78
7 7/8	Jan 98n	105:03	105:05	+ 15	6.83
8 1/8	Feb 98n	106:09	106:11	+ 13	6.85
7 7/8	Apr 98n	105:00	105:02	+ 14	6.88
7	May 93-98	101:03	101:11	+ 3	6.02
9	May 98n	110:23	110:25	+ 12	6.90
8 1/4	Jul 98n	106:29	106:31	+ 14	6.92
9 1/4	Aug 98n	112:01	112:03	+ 14	6.96
7 1/8	Oct 98n	101:10	101:12	+ 14	6.87
3 1/2	Nov 98	98:15	99:15	+ 10	3.59
8 7/8	Nov 98n	110:05	110:07	+ 15	6.99
8 7/8	Feb 99n	110:04	110:06	+ 14	7.05
8 1/2	May 94-99	105:17	105:25	....	5.93
9 1/8	May 99n	111:13	111:15	+ 17	7.11
8	Aug 99n	104:31	105:01	+ 15	7.14
7 7/8	Nov 99n	104:07	104:09	+ 15	7.16
7 7/8	Feb 95-00	103:00	103:04	+ 8	6.77
8 1/2	Feb 00n	107:24	107:26	+ 16	7.22
8 7/8	May 00n	109:28	109:30	+ 13	7.28
8 3/8	Aug 95-00	105:03	105:07	+ 11	6.76
8 3/4	Aug 00n	109:00	109:02	+ 14	7.32
8 1/2	Nov 00n	107:13	107:15	+ 14	7.35
7 3/4	Feb 01n	102:15	102:17	+ 11	7.37
11 3/4	Feb 01	128:27	128:31	+ 11	7.36
8	May 01n	104:05	104:07	+ 13	7.37
13 1/8	May 01	139:02	139:06	+ 18	7.31
7 7/8	Aug 01n	103:16	103:18	+ 13	7.35
8	Aug 96-01	104:17	104:21	+ 10	6.83
13 3/8	Aug 01	141:02	141:06	+ 13	7.36
7 1/2	Nov 01n	101:08	101:10	+ 13	7.31
15 3/4	Nov 01	158:04	158:08	+ 20	7.38
14 1/4	Feb 02	148:05	148:09	+ 16	7.42
11 5/8	Nov 02	130:24	130:28	+ 17	7.45
10 3/4	Feb 03	124:11	124:15	+ 15	7.48
10 3/4	May 03	124:18	124:22	+ 15	7.50
11 1/8	Aug 03	127:18	127:22	+ 12	7.52
11 7/8	Nov 03	133:21	133:25	+ 14	7.54
12 3/8	May 04	138:08	138:12	+ 12	7.56
13 3/4	Aug 04	149:23	149:27	+ 13	7.57
11 5/8	Nov 04	132:18	132:22	+ 16	7.61
8 1/4	May 00-05	104:17	[illegible]	[illegible]	7.50
12	May 05	[illegible]	[illegible]	[illegible]	[illegible]
10 3/4	Au[illegible]	[illegible]	[illegible]	[illegible]	[illegible]

Mat.	Type	Bid	Asked	Chg.	Bid Yld.
Nov 99	np	55:21	55:25	+ 8	7.48
Feb 00	ci	54:14	54:18	+ 6	7.53
Feb 00	np	54:09	54:14	+ 8	7.56
May 00	ci	53:14	53:18	+ 9	7.53
May 00	np	53:08	53:12	+ 8	7.57
Aug 00	ci	52:13	52:17	+ 9	7.54
Aug 00	np	52:09	52:13	+ 9	7.57
Nov 00	ci	51:13	51:17	+ 9	7.55
Nov 00	np	51:10	51:14	+ 9	7.57
Feb 01	ci	49:26	49:30	+ 3	7.69
Feb 01	np	49:28	50:00	+ 9	7.68
May 01	ci	48:27	48:31	+ 3	7.70
May 01	np	48:27	48:31	+ 9	7.70
Aug 01	ci	47:30	48:02	+ 3	7.70
Aug 01	np	47:30	48:02	+ 9	7.70
Nov 01	ci	46:31	47:04	+ 2	7.71
Feb 02	ci	45:15	45:19	+ 2	7.85
May 02	ci	44:18	44:22	+ 2	7.86
Aug 02	ci	43:21	43:25	+ 3	7.87
Nov 02	ci	42:23	42:28	+ 3	7.89
Feb 03	ci	41:19	41:23	+ 3	7.96
May 03	ci	40:24	40:28	+ 3	7.97
Aug 03	ci	39:30	40:03	+ 4	7.97
Nov 03	ci	39:04	39:08	+ 4	7.98
Feb 04	ci	38:03	38:07	+ 3	8.04
May 04	ci	37:11	37:16	+ 3	8.04
Aug 04	ci	36:20	36:24	+ 3	8.04
Nov 04	ci	35:27	36:00	+ 2	8.05
Nov 04	bp	35:27	36:00	+ 2	8.05
Feb 05	ci	35:01	35:05	+ 3	8.08
May 05	ci	34:11	34:15	+ 3	8.08
May 05	bp	34:15	34:19	+ 3	8.05
Aug 05	ci	33:21	33:25	+ 3	8.08
Aug 05	bp	33:25	33:30	+ 3	8.05
Nov 05	ci	33:00	33:04	+ 3	8.08
Feb 06	ci	32:03	32:07	+ 2	8.14
Feb 06	bp	32:08	32:12	+ 3	8.10
May 06	ci	31:13	31:17	+ 2	8.15
Aug 06	ci	30:25	30:29	+ 2	8.15
Nov 06	ci	30:05	30:10	+ 1	8.15
Feb 07	ci	29:14	29:18	+ 3	8.18
May 07	ci	28:25	28:29	+ 3	8.20
Aug 07	ci	28:06	28:10	+ 3	8.20
Nov 07	ci	27:20	27:24	+ 3	8.20
Feb 08	ci	27:00	27:04	+ 3	8.22
May 08	ci	26:12	26:16	+ 3	8.24
Aug 08	ci	25:26	25:30	+ 3	8.25
Nov 08	ci	25:08	25:12	+ 3	8.26
Feb 09	ci	24:21	24:25	+ 3	8.28
May 09	ci	24:05	24:09	+ 3	8.28
Aug 09	ci	23:21	23:25	+ 2	8.28
Nov 09	ci	23:06	23:10	+ 2	8.28
Nov 09	bp	22:24	22:28	+ 2	8.39
Feb 10	ci	22:19	22:23	....	8.31
May 10	ci	22:05	22:09	....	8.31
Aug 10	ci	21:22	21:26	....	8.31
Nov 10	ci	21:08	21:12	....	8.31
Feb 11	ci	20:25	20:29	+ 2	8.32
May 11	ci	20:12	20:16	+ 2	8.32
Aug 11	ci	19:31	20:02	+ 3	8.32
Nov 11	ci	19:18	19:21	+ 3	8.32
Feb 12	ci	19:04	19:08	+ 1	8.33
May 12	ci	18:24	18:27	+ 2	8.33
Aug 12	ci	18:11	18:15	+ 1	8.33
Nov 12	ci	18:00	18:03	+ 2	8.33
Feb 13	ci	17:16	17:20	+ 1	8.36
May 13	ci	17:05	17:08	+ 1	[illegible]
[illegible]	ci	16:26	[illegible]	[illegible]	[illegible]

SOURCE: *The Wall Street Journal*, December 3, 1991. Reprinted by permission of *The Wall Street Journal*,

EXHIBIT 7.3

Yields on U.S. Government Agency Issues

GOVERNMENT AGENCY & SIMILAR ISSUES

Monday, December 2, 1991

Over-the-Counter mid-afternoon quotations based on large transactions, usually $1 million or more. Colons in bid-and-asked quotes represent 32nds; 101:01 means 101 1/32.

All yields are calculated to maturity, and based on the asked quote. * -- Callable issue, maturity date shown. For issues callable prior to maturity, yields are computed to the earliest call date for issues quoted above par, or 100, and to the maturity date for issues below par.

Source: Bear, Stearns & Co. via Street Software Technology Inc.

Federal Home Loan Bank

Rate	Mat.	Bid	Asked	Yld.
7.00	12-91	100:04	100:08	2.82
11.40	12-91	100:13	100:21	0.63
6.05	1-92	100:07	100:09	4.04
6.75	1-92	100:09	100:11	4.30
7.00	1-92	100:10	100:14	3.91
5.43	2-92	100:06	100:08	4.25
6.25	2-92	100:11	100:13	4.35
8.35	2-92	100:25	100:29	4.19
11.45	2-92	101:15	101:19	4.17
6.55	3-92	100:18	100:20	4.44
7.10	3-92	100:23	100:27	4.27
8.85	3-92	101:08	101:12	4.26
10.00	3-92	101:20	101:24	4.17
8.15	4-92	101:12	101:16	4.27
8.30	4-92	101:13	101:17	4.34
9.65	4-92	101:30	102:02	4.33
11.70	4-92	102:23	102:27	4.36
8.60	5-92	101:25	101:29	4.52
9.15	5-92	102:02	102:08	4.33
8.40	6-92	102:00	102:04	4.48
8.45	6-92	102:03	102:07	4.36
8.25	7-92	102:07	102:11	4.51
8.38	7-92	102:09	102:13	4.53
5.63	8-92	100:21	100:23	4.59
8.60	8-92	102:22	102:26	4.58
10.35	8-92	103:30	104:04	4.47
5.68	9-92	100:23	100:25	4.67
8.25	9-92	102:18	102:24	4.72
5.55	10-92	100:21	100:23	4.71
8.00	10-92	102:20	102:24	4.81
8.15	10-92	102:24	102:28	4.81
10.85	10-92	105:00	105:04	4.90
7.65	11-92	102:15	102:19	4.89
8.00	11-92	102:29	103:01	4.77
8.80	11-92	103:19	103:23	4.84
11.10	11-92	105:24	105:30	4.78
7.38	12-92	102:10	102:14	4.99
7.95	12-92	103:01	103:07	4.81
[illegible]	12-92	104:01	[illegible]	[illegible]
9.60	2-94	108:01	108:07	5.61
12.00	2-94	112:20	113:00	5.69
7.58	3-94	104:00	104:02	5.67
7.58	4-94*	101:05	101:09	6.97
7.28	4-94	103:16	103:20	5.63
7.42	4-94*	101:07	101:11	6.80
8.50	4-94	106:06	106:12	5.61
9.55	4-94	108:14	108:20	5.64
7.20	5-94	103:11	103:15	5.68
7.50	6-94	104:01	104:05	5.73
8.60	6-94	106:20	106:26	5.70
8.63	6-94	106:22	106:28	5.70
8.30	7-94	106:00	106:06	5.74
6.70	8-94	102:07	102:09	5.78
8.60	8-94	106:30	107:04	5.73
6.58	9-94	102:02	102:06	5.72
8.30	10-94	106:21	106:27	5.70
5.89	11-94	100:14	100:18	5.68
8.20	11-94	106:04	106:10	5.86
8.05	12-94	105:28	106:02	5.86
8.40	1-95	107:00	107:06	5.86
8.60	2-95	107:23	107:31	5.85
7.88	3-95	105:07	105:09	6.09
9.00	3-95	108:21	108:29	5.99
7.90	4-95*	101:12	101:16	7.38
8.88	6-95	108:12	108:20	6.14
10.00	6-95	111:27	112:03	6.16
10.30	7-95	113:13	113:21	6.06
7.95	12-95*	104:22	104:26	6.58
9.50	12-95	111:02	111:10	6.30
8.10	3-96	105:23	105:31	6.49
9.80	3-96	112:00	112:08	6.49
7.75	4-96	104:17	104:25	6.48
8.25	5-96	106:09	106:17	6.54
8.25	6-96	106:12	106:20	6.54
8.00	7-96	105:24	106:00	6.48
7.70	8-96	104:17	104:25	6.51
8.25	[illegible]	[illegible]	[illegible]	6.56

FNMA Issues

Rate	Mat.	Bid	Asked	Yld.
11.75	12-91	100:04	100:06	0.47
8.50	1-92	100:11	100:15	3.67
7.00	3-92	100:18	100:22	4.32
12.00	4-92	102:16	102:20	4.31
8.45	5-92	101:20	101:24	4.34
8.50	5-92	101:18	101:22	4.53
7.05	6-92	101:05	101:09	4.50
10.13	6-92	102:21	102:25	4.59
8.45	7-92	102:05	102:09	4.53
7.75	8-92	101:31	102:03	4.58
9.15	9-92	103:06	103:10	4.68
10.60	10-92	104:21	104:25	4.80
8.20	11-92	102:28	103:00	4.86
9.00	12-92	103:20	103:24	5.16
9.88	12-92	104:21	104:25	4.99
10.90	1-93	106:06	106:10	4.93
7.95	2-93	103:06	103:14	4.91
7.90	3-93	103:07	103:15	5.03
10.95	3-93	106:28	107:04	5.05
7.55	4-93	103:02	103:10	4.98
10.88	4-93	107:11	107:19	5.00
10.75	5-93	107:18	107:26	5.02
8.80	6-93	105:02	105:10	5.11
8.45	7-93	104:20	104:28	5.24
7.75	11-93	104:01	104:09	5.38
7.38	12-93	103:15	103:23	5.40
7.55	1-94	104:05	104:09	5.36
9.45	1-94	107:18	107:26	5.46
7.65	4-94	104:07	104:15	5.59
9.60	4-94	108:13	108:21	5.61
9.30	5-94	107:28	108:00	5.73
8.60	6-94	106:17	106:25	5.67
7.45	7-94	103:29	104:01	5.76
8.65	7-94*	102:15	102:23	7.48
8.55	8-94*	103:04	103:12	7.14
8.90	8-94	107:18	107:26	5.71
10.10	10-94	111:06	111:14	5.69
9.25	11-94	108:29	109:05	5.81
8.30	12-94*	103:12	103:20	6.95
9.00	1-95	108:20	108:28	5.83
11.95	1-95	116:21	117:01	5.86
8.90	2-95*	104:03	104:11	7.34
11.50	2-95	115:24	116:04	5.87
8.85	3-95	107:26	108:02	6.09
11.70	5-95	116:18	116:30	6.15
8.85	6-95*	105:22	105:30	6.92
11.15	6-95	115:13	115:25	6.10
10.50	9-95	113:29	114:09	6.19
8.40	11-95*	105:26	105:30	6.66
8.80	11-95	108:24	109:00	6.18
[illegible]	[illegible]	115:02	115:10	6.15
[illegible]	[illegible]	[illegible]	110:05	6.34
9.15	4-98	110:03	110:11	7.10
8.38	4-98*	105:13	105:17	7.27
8.15	5-98	105:12	105:16	7.07
8.20	8-98*	104:18	104:22	7.30
9.40	8-98	111:11	111:19	7.18
7.85	9-98	104:02	104:06	7.06
9.55	3-99	113:06	113:22	7.10
8.70	6-99	108:18	108:26	7.16
8.45	7-99	107:13	107:21	7.13
8.65	7-99*	106:02	106:10	7.54
8.55	8-99	107:17	107:25	7.22
9.00	10-99*	107:10	107:18	7.70
8.35	11-99	106:02	106:10	7.29
8.65	12-99*	106:04	106:16	7.55
9.30	2-00*	109:14	109:22	7.68
9.30	3-00*	108:10	108:18	8.25
9.05	4-00	110:05	110:13	7.36
9.80	5-00*	110:16	110:24	8.02
8.90	6-00	108:10	108:18	7.52
9.15	7-00*	108:12	108:20	8.11
9.20	9-00	110:00	110:08	7.58
9.15	10-00*	108:20	108:28	8.09
8.25	12-00	104:23	104:31	7.48
8.88	1-01*	107:07	107:15	8.04
8.50	2-01*	105:10	105:18	7.95
8.70	3-01*	105:28	106:08	7.74
8.63	4-01*	105:12	105:16	7.78
8.70	6-01*	106:12	106:16	7.72
8.88	7-01*	106:11	106:15	7.90
8.20	7-02*	100:23	101:07	8.03
8.20	9-02*	102:01	102:09	7.88
12.35	12-13*	111:05	111:21	10.94
12.65	3-14*	111:03	111:19	11.22
0.00	7-14	15:02	15:10	8.48
10.35	12-15	122:26	123:10	8.13
8.20	3-16	101:08	101:16	8.06
8.95	2-18	106:02	106:10	8.35
8.10	8-19	97:28	98:04	8.27
0.00	10-19	9:10	9:18	8.61
9.65	8-20*	108:00	108:08	8.90
9.50	11-20*	106:23	106:31	8.88

World Bank Bonds

Rate	Mat.	Bid	Asked	Yld.
15.13	12-91	100:10	100:14	0.75
5.38	4-92	100:01	100:05	4.84
14.75	6-92	104:20	104:24	4.85
13.63	9-92	106:08	106:12	4.74
10.90	3-93	106:15	106:19	5.48
10.38	5-93	107:03	107:07	5.13
5.88	9-93	100:10	100:14	[illegible]
6.50	3-94	101:06	[illegible]	[illegible]
6.38	10-94	[illegible]	[illegible]	[illegible]

Federal Farm Credit Bank

Rate	Mat.	Bid	Asked	Yld.
5.42	1-92	100:02	100:04	3.77
6.10	1-92	100:03	100:05	3.98
7.05	1-92	100:05	100:09	3.33
11.50	1-92	100:26	100:30	3.96
15.20	1-92	101:11	101:15	3.46
5.30	2-92	100:03	100:05	4.32
6.00	2-92	100:07	100:09	4.19
6.70	2-92	100:08	100:12	4.30
4.70	3-92	100:01	100:03	4.31
5.65	3-92	100:06	100:08	4.55
6.30	3-92	100:12	100:14	4.42
5.50	4-92	100:08	100:10	4.48
6.60	4-92	100:19	100:21	4.50
5.35	5-92	100:09	100:11	4.47
6.30	5-92	100:20	100:22	4.56
4.80	6-92	100:03	100:05	4.47
6.15	6-92	100:25	100:27	4.39
6.55	7-92	101:02	101:04	4.53
13.75	7-92	105:17	105:21	4.45
8.40	7-92	102:07	102:11	4.59
6.40	8-92	101:05	101:07	4.50
5.80	9-92	100:24	100:26	4.66
8.25	9-92	102:12	102:14	4.84
8.60	9-92	102:19	102:25	4.72
5.63	10-92	100:23	100:25	4.64
5.50	11-92	100:21	100:23	4.68
4.90	12-92	100:08	100:10	4.57
7.63	12-92	102:13	102:17	4.97
8.13	1-93	103:09	103:15	4.91
10.65	1-93	106:01	106:07	4.90
6.77	6-93	101:30	102:00	5.36
6.88	8-93	102:08	102:10	5.39
6.48	9-93	101:22	101:26	5.37
6.16	10-93	101:09	101:11	5.37
11.80	10-93	111:01	111:07	5.42
7.38	12-93	103:18	103:20	5.49
7.19	2-94	103:04	103:08	5.58
12.35	3-94	113:15	113:27	5.68
14.25	4-94	118:14	118:26	5.67
7.20	6-94*	101:12	101:14	6.56
7.45	7-94*	101:24	101:28	6.64
7.38	8-94*	102:02	102:04	6.49
6.90	9-94*	101:29	102:01	6.08
8.63	9-94	107:00	107:06	5.75
13.00	9-94	117:06	117:18	5.95
6.40	11-94*	100:30	101:02	7.86
11.45	12-94	114:19	114:27	5.96
8.30	1-95	106:27	107:03	5.78
7.70	3-96*	100:30	101:02	7.40
7.90	[illegible]	[illegible]	101:17	7.48
[illegible]	[illegible]	[illegible]	[illegible]	7.30

Student Loan Marketing

Rate	Mat.	Bid	Asked	Yld.
10.38	4-92	101:27	101:31	4.26
10.88	5-92	102:21	102:25	4.47
8.25	6-92	101:30	102:02	4.52
8.15	9-92	102:17	102:21	4.66
8.80	12-92	103:18	103:22	4.96
10.50	4-93	106:25	106:31	5.20
7.35	5-93	102:18	102:24	5.30
9.12	5-93*	102:06	102:10	7.41
8.20	5-93	104:05	104:13	5.02
6.87	6-93	102:06	102:10	5.30
8.50	7-93	104:22	104:26	5.30
12.00	12-93	112:09	112:13	5.46
11.88	12-93	112:03	112:07	5.46
7.38	1-94	103:20	103:28	5.40
9.38	2-94*	101:02	101:06	8.75
16.00	2-94	121:16	121:28	5.30
7.43	4-94	103:22	103:30	5.61
8.91	4-94*	102:01	102:05	7.90
7.35	5-94	103:18	103:22	5.72
7.30	5-94	103:13	103:17	5.74
9.38	5-94*	108:04	108:08	5.75
8.50	7-94	106:13	106:17	5.75
7.50	7-94	103:29	104:01	5.81
8.10	7-94	105:14	105:18	5.78
8.25	8-94*	102:11	102:15	7.21
8.30	9-94	105:23	105:27	5.99
7.54	10-94	104:17	104:25	5.70
0.00	11-94	83:25	83:31	6.10
8.91	3-95	108:09	108:13	6.02
7.63	3-95	104:16	104:24	6.00
9.07	3-95	106:16	106:20	6.79
8.85	4-95*	105:06	105:10	7.03
9.08	4-95*	105:20	105:24	7.11
9.13	5-95*	105:20	105:24	7.20
7.62	6-95*	103:06	103:10	6.55
8.63	8-95*	102:23	102:27	7.72
10.50	11-95	113:22	113:26	6.44
7.74	3-96*	102:16	102:24	6.98
7.75	12-96*	101:07	101:15	7.40
7.63	1-97*	100:30	101:10	7.31
9.50	9-97*	109:06	109:14	7.45
9.34	7-98*	107:25	108:05	7.74
9.78	1-99*	108:10	108:18	8.17
8.75	8-00*	104:26	105:02	7.93
9.80	9-00*	109:23	110:07	8.15
0.00	5-14	12:30	13:06	9.23
0.00	10-22	8:10	8:18	8.13

GNMA Mtge. Issues a-Bond

Rate	Mat.	Bid	Asked	Yld.
7.50	30Yr	96:26	97:02	8.13
[illegible]	30Yr	99:15	99:23	8.17
[illegible]	[illegible]	102:03	102:11	8.21

SOURCE: *The Wall Street Journal*, December 3, 1991. Reprinted by permission of *The Wall Street Journal*,

Agency Bonds

Exhibit 7.3 lists quotes from *The Wall Street Journal* for U.S. government agency bonds. Like the Treasury bond quotes, these figures give prices in order of maturity in points and 32nds of a point. Thus, the Federal National Mortgage Association (FNMA) 8.30 percent bond maturing in December 1994 (in the table, look for "8.30 12–94") is selling at an asked price of 103:20, or $1,036.25 [(103 × $10) + (20 × $0.3125)]. Investors can select the agency bond in the desired maturity range that provides the highest yield, found in the far right column.

Analysis of Longer-Term Bonds

Information from all sources reinforces the reasonable expectation that the U.S. government and its agencies enjoy an excellent credit relationship with investors, particularly institutional investors. Investing in this market, therefore, requires no detailed credit analysis of the security issuer, as would be necessary before investing in securities issued by corporations or other entities. The government bond buyer must, however, carefully analyze the direction of interest rates.

As mentioned earlier, if interest rates decline from present levels, the price of any given bond will increase from its present level, and the investment's rate of return will rise. The price rises because the interest rate on an outstanding bond remains at the level set at its issue, while new bonds pay lower current interest rates. This makes outstanding bonds more valuable than they were before rates fell, and their prices will rise. To realize the benefit of this rise in price, the investor must sell the bond and reap the capital gain benefit. This would require paying tax on the capital gain, of course, and the investor would have to reinvest the money in some other investment.

Beware of Rising Interest Rates The same features that provide this potential for return also give rise to the major risk of long-term government bonds: interest rate risk. Holders of long-term bonds can suffer temporary principal losses if interest rates rise, since higher interest rates force bond prices downward, as explained earlier. They also face an opportunity cost, since the money they have tied up in lower-rate bonds could be earning a higher rate of return if they could invest it in new bonds. Of course, they can hold the bonds to maturity and collect the entire principal they invested; they realize a loss only if they sell at a time when high interest rates have depressed bond prices.

An additional consideration concerns the time remaining until the bond's maturity. For the same rise in interest rates, a bond with fewer years remaining before repayment of its original principal value will decline in value less than one that has more years remaining until it matures. This is because the time until the bondholder realizes the bond's par value is shorter. A later section of this chapter deals with bond valuation; it will explore this relationship in detail.

Investors in long-term bonds cannot avoid interest rate risk. If you are concerned about fluctuations in the value of your bonds, you should probably stick to shorter maturities even at the price of some interest income. At the extreme, you could buy only Treasury bills to safeguard your capital, eliminating all concerns but the chore of reinvesting your money as bills mature. All bond investors must answer this basic question: Do I prefer stability of income or stability of price?

Tax-Exempt State and Municipal Bonds

States, municipalities, school districts, and road and park districts, with the consent of voters, can issue bonds that have the distinct advantage of paying interest that is exempt from federal income taxes. In addition, income from these **state and municipal bonds** is usually exempt from income taxes levied by the municipality that sells them. This feature makes state and municipal securities uniquely attractive to individuals and institutions in high tax brackets.

state and municipal bonds: Bonds issued by state, municipal, and local government units, interest payments on which are exempt from taxation by the federal government and by the state in which they are issued.

State and municipal bonds have some business risk, and they are exposed to interest rate risk and purchasing power risk, as are other bonds. After weighing the advantages against the disadvantages, however, investors have fueled strong growth in municipal securities. Well over $225 billion of state and municipal debt is outstanding, with annual additions amounting to over 10 percent of this amount.

This growth may slow down in the future as local opposition slows property tax increases and increases in government spending. The state and local government entities that issue these bonds face increasing pressure to spend taxpayers' money more frugally, avoiding projects that require long-term interest obligations. It is also more difficult for these government entities to find projects that meet IRS rules governing tax exemptions.

Individuals and commercial banks are the largest purchasers of bonds issued by states and municipalities. Together they provide approximately 80 percent of the funds these entities borrow, split about evenly between them. Insurance companies have supplied about 14 percent of these funds.

There are two basic types of state and municipal bonds: general obligation bonds and revenue bonds. These bonds are usually issued as **debenture contracts** in either straight maturities or serial maturities. **Straight maturities** mature in single lump sums. **Serial maturities** are partially paid off, or retired, every six months. When the bonds are issued, a schedule is published showing the proportions of interest charges and debt retirement in each semiannual payment.

debenture contract: A bond obligation that represents no claim to any specific assets of the issuer.

straight maturities: A bond issue in which all bonds mature at the same time in one lump sum.

serial maturities: A bond issue in which individual bonds are paid off at specified intervals, usually every six months.

General Obligation Bonds

General obligation bonds are supported by the full taxing authority of the issuing entity. They are guaranteed by the full faith and credit of a political unit that has the power to levy taxes. The base for the tax that supports the debt is usually the assessed value of real estate. Income taxes and sales taxes might also be pledged. The investment quality of such an issue depends on its legality and the ability of the issuing entity to generate sufficient funds to pay the interest and repay the principal at maturity. Obviously, this varies from community to community.

general obligation bonds: Municipal bonds supported by the full taxing authority of the issuer.

Legal counsel assesses the legality of a bond issue to make certain that political leaders have the right to issue a particular debt and that they have

EXHIBIT 7.4

Municipal Bond Yield Averages[a]

	SEPT.				AUG.	PAST 12 MONTHS		MONTHLY	
	27	20	13	6	30	HIGH	LOW	AUG.	JULY
20-Year Composite	6.63%	6.63%	6.60%	6.76%	6.76%	7.22%	6.85%	6.75%	7.01%
Aaa	6.43	6.49	6.47	6.63	6.63	7.05	6.68	6.62	6.82
Aa	6.57	6.55	6.51	6.68	6.68	7.16	6.81	6.65	6.89
A	6.66	6.64	6.62	6.77	6.77	7.26	6.86	6.76	7.12
Baa	6.86	6.83	6.81	6.97	6.97	7.43	7.02	6.95	7.18
10-Year State Bds									
Aaa	5.82	5.80	5.77	5.94	5.94	6.72	6.23	5.93	6.19
Aa	5.94	5.93	5.91	6.07	6.07	6.88	6.30	6.05	6.31
7-Day VMIGI[b]	5.10	5.13	4.90	4.65	4.70	6.40	5.41	4.49	4.02

[a] Municipal Bond Yield Averages are based on 10- and 20-year reoffering yields on selected general obligations.

[b] VMIGI averages are the mean of weekly rates determined and supplied to Moody's by various remarketing agents.

SOURCE: *Moody's Bond Survey*, September 30, 1991. Reprinted by permission.

the approval of citizens in the jurisdiction, who ultimately must repay the debt. The ability to pay interest and repay principal is a function of per-capita income and the amount of other debt outstanding. The income level of the taxpayers gives a guide to the issuer's capacity for repayment, along with the existing debt per capita, the relationship of debt to assessed valuation, and the issuer's past record. Many communities limit the amount of debt that can be issued. A common rule of thumb suggests that debt service (the amount of periodic interest payments) not exceed 25 percent of an issuer's annual budget. Obviously, a wealthy and growing community is in a better position to pay its debt than a mature community with a declining income or population. Many states' laws limit municipal debt to from 1 to 20 percent of the assessed value of property; a 7 percent limit is common.

Prices of general obligation bonds are not usually quoted in either local papers or *The Wall Street Journal*. State and municipal bonds are traded in the over-the-counter market through brokerage firms, many of which specialize in these securities. Major national brokerage firms provide both price information and advice. Standard & Poor's *Weekly Bond Outlook* and Moody's *Weekly Bond Survey* each provide a partial list of municipal bonds available to investors. Also, prices are listed in the **pink sheets**' quotations at brokerage offices.

pink sheets: Price quotation sheets in brokerage offices that give information about inactively traded bonds and over-the-counter stocks.

Exhibit 7.4 lists representative yields on municipal bonds. Since income from these bonds is exempt from federal taxes and from state taxes if paid to a resident of the state that issues the bonds, the yields generally are lower than yields on taxable bonds. From an investor's point of view, however, municipal bonds may well provide higher rates of return after deducting taxes from the income on the comparable taxable bonds. The relationship depends on the investor's tax bracket. Remember, though, that municipal bonds are riskier than taxable U.S. government obligations because they are not backed by the U.S. Treasury.

The market for municipal bonds is not as active as many other markets, so liquidity can be a problem. To preserve marketability, wise investors trade in units of 25 or more bonds. The price may become uncertain, or the wait for a transaction may become long, for trades below that amount.

Dealers trade municipal bonds based on the familiar bid–asked system. They buy bonds at the current bid price (which reflects the latest price offered, or bid, by buyers) and then resell them at the asked price (the latest price asked by owners of bonds who wish to sell). The dealers keep as profit the spread between the bid and asked prices. Suppose a bond paid 7 percent interest at a time when newly issued bonds were paying 8 percent. The price quotes for the 7 percent bond might be $850 bid and $875 asked for a small number of bonds. Clearly, this spread is larger than the spread for Treasury bonds discussed earlier; this reflects the slow market for municipal issues and the dealers' need to cover their costs and earn their profits despite fewer trades. Transactions that involve more bonds feature smaller spreads.

Revenue Bonds

revenue bonds: Bonds issued by a political subdivision, government unit, or public authority that fund payments solely out of revenues of the project.

Revenue bonds are debt securities issued by political subdivisions, government units, or public authorities that pay interest solely out of revenues from the project the bonds finance. Airport and highway construction bonds are excellent examples of this kind of security. A complete list would include a broad range of economic and business activities.

Municipalities favor revenue bonds because they do not increase the burden of interest payments on general revenues. This allows the municipality to issue them even when it has exhausted its capacity for general obligation debt. Users of a facility financed with revenue bonds pay fees tied to their use, and this income funds interest payments on the bonds. This enables communities to provide facilities at little or no cost to their general revenue funds.

The revenue bond investor must consider carefully whether revenues from a project will be sufficient to service the debt, including both interest payments and principal repayment. This requires that investors carefully analyze the project's business risk and cash flows, along with the integrity of the issuer, just as they would examine bonds issued by a private corporation. It may seem reasonable to expect government units to issue securities responsibly, but some municipalities have issued revenue bonds that turned out to be poor investments.

Price quotes for some of the more actively traded tax-exempt revenue bonds appear in *The Wall Street Journal*. Exhibit 7.5 shows a sample listing. A good example of an actively traded revenue bond is the Saint Petersburg,

EXHIBIT 7.5

Price Quotes on Tax-Exempt Revenue Bonds

TAX-EXEMPT BONDS

Representative prices for several active tax-exempt revenue and refunding bonds, based on institutional trades. Changes rounded to the nearest one-eighth. Yield is to maturity. n-New. Source: The Bond Buyer.

ISSUE	COUPON	MAT	PRICE	CHG	BID YLD
Ariz Transp Bd 91A	6.500	07-01-11	98	...	6.68
Burlington Kans.	7.000	06-01-31	101⅜	...	6.90
Calif Hsng Fin Agy	7.050	08-01-27	99¼	...	7.11
Calif Pub Wks Bd-n	6.500	09-01-19	96¾	+ ⅛	6.76
Charlte NC Part Conv	6.750	12-01-21	100¼	...	6.73
Chesapk Bay Br & Tun-n	6.375	07-01-22	95⅞	...	6.69
Colo Rvr Mun Wtr Tx9	6.625	01-01-21	98	...	6.78
E. Bay Mud Ca Ser 91	6.375	06-01-21	96¼	+ ⅛	6.67
Fla Bd Ed Pb Ed Cap-n	6.700	06-01-22	98¾	+ ⅛	6.80
Fla. Bd of Ed	6.750	06-01-21	99½	...	6.79
Fla. Dept Transp	7.125	07-01-18	101½	– ⅛	7.00
Hou Tx Wtr & Swr Ser91	6.375	12-01-17	95¼	+ ⅛	6.77
L.A. Dept Wtr & Pwr	6.625	10-01-31	98⅛	+ ⅛	6.76
LA Dept Wtr & Pwr	6.400	11-01-31	96¼	+ ¼	6.67
LA Tran Comm Calif-n	6.500	07-01-13	96¾	+ ⅛	6.79
LA Tran Comm Calif-n	6.500	07-01-15	97¾	– ⅛	6.69
Mass Wtr Res Ser 91A	6.875	12-01-11	98¾	...	7.00
Met Nashvl Aprt Ath-n	6.600	07-01-15	98⅝	+ ⅛	6.72
Metro Seattle Swr	6.875	01-01-31	99¼	+ ⅛	6.94
Mich Stat Fnd Ser 91D	6.875	12-01-21	100½	+ ⅛	6.84

ISSUE	COUPON	MAT	PRICE	CHG	BID YLD
NC Estrn Mun Pwr Agy	6.500	01-01-17	96⅛	...	6.82
NC Mun Pwr #1	6.500	01-01-10	98¾	+ ⅛	6.62
NE Ohio Reg Sewer 9	6.500	11-15-16	98½	...	6.62
NJ Hsing & Mtge Agcy	7.000	05-01-30	99⅞	...	7.01
NY MTA Trans 1987 SerV	7.000	07-01-12	97⅜	– ⅛	7.25
NY NJ Port Auth Rev	6.750	08-01-26	99½	– ⅛	6.79
NYS Local Govt	7.000	04-01-21	98⅛	– ⅛	7.15
NYS Med Cr Facil Fin	7.300	02-15-21	100	+ ⅛	7.30
NYS Muni Wtr Auth	7.000	06-15-15	98	...	7.17
NYS Power Auth	6.750	01-01-18	99¼	...	6.81
P.R. Elec Pwr Auth	7.000	07-01-21	100¼	...	6.98
Port Ath NY & NJ Rev-n	6.500	11-01-26	95¾	+ ¼	6.82
Portland Ore.	6.700	05-01-21	100⅛	– ⅛	6.69
RI Convtn Ctr Ser I	6.700	05-15-20	98¼	...	6.84
Royal Oak Hos Fn Au	6.750	01-01-20	97¾	+ ⅛	6.93
Sacramento City Fin	6.800	11-01-20	98⅛	...	6.95
St Pete FL Hlth Fac	7.000	12-01-15	100⅞	+ ⅛	6.93
Trib Brdg & Tun Auth	6.500	01-01-19	96⅛	+ ⅛	6.81
Triboro Br Tun NY	6.625	01-01-17	98⅜	– ⅛	6.76
WPPSS Refunding	6.875	07-01-17	98¾	+ ⅛	6.98

SOURCE: *The Wall Street Journal*, December 3, 1991. Reprinted by permission of *The Wall Street Journal*,

Florida, Health Facility bond maturing in 2015 listed toward the bottom of the right-hand column in Exhibit 7.5. This bond has a coupon rate of 7.0 percent and it sold for $1,008.875 on the day indicated by the table, found by multiplying the $100\frac{7}{8}$ percent of par in the price column by $10 per point of face value (100.875 × 10). The yield to maturity on the bond was 6.93 percent.

The Wall Street Journal list represents only a small sample of the municipal revenue bonds available in the market. Literally thousands of other revenue bonds are available through brokers. Information appears in brokerage pink sheets.

Municipal Bond Ratings

It is extremely difficult for the average investor to assess the creditworthiness of either general obligation bonds or revenue bonds issued by municipalities, even those issued by their own communities. To supply this critical but elusive information, a number of private bond **rating agencies** publish ratings of the creditworthiness of municipal and corporate bonds. The two largest and best-known rating agencies, Moody's and Standard & Poor's (S&P), provide **bond ratings** to individuals and institutions as part of a wide array of financial services and products. These agencies rate bond issues according to similar criteria from the highest-quality issues (designated AAA by S&P and Aaa by Moody's) down to bonds actually in default, that is, failing to make current interest payments (rated D by both agencies).

rating agency: A private corporation such as Standard & Poor's and Moody's that rates the creditworthiness of bonds.

bond rating: An indication published by rating agencies of the credit quality of a bond issue, from the highest quality (AAA) to the lowest (D) for bonds actually in default.

Exhibit 7.6 explains S&P's rating system. Bonds rated in the top four categories (AAA, AA, A, and BBB) are commonly called **investment grade bonds.** Under current bank regulations enforced by the Comptroller of the Currency, commercial banks cannot invest in bonds rated below investment grade. Bonds rated lower than BBB are called **junk bonds** by investors and the financial press. S&P defines bonds in this category (from Exhibit 7.6) as, "predominantly speculative with respect to capacity to pay interest and repay principal in accordance with the terms of the obligation."

investment grade bond: A bond rated in the four highest categories—AAA, AA, A, BBB.

junk bond: A bond rated lower than BBB that represents speculative investments.

Even rating agencies have sometimes found it difficult to rate municipal bonds accurately. When New York City was in difficult financial straits, the rating agencies did not begin to change their ratings on the city's securities until it was almost bankrupt, though in hindsight its expenditures were clearly rising more rapidly than its revenues. Unfortunately, information about such issues is scarce and comes to the marketplace slowly. This frustrates even professionals' efforts to determine a community's creditworthiness, so investors cannot rely solely on bond ratings as a guide to placing their money in municipal bonds. They must complete additional investigations for any bond issue they may want to buy, including studying the characteristics of the community issuing the bond.

After-Tax Yields

Historical yields on municipal bond issues appear in current issues of the *Federal Reserve Bulletin*. Over the past decade, yields on state and local government AAA-rated bonds have ranged from approximately 3 percent to almost 11 percent. In the early 1990s, tax-free municipal bonds earned approximately 7 percent. This would give an investor in the 33 percent tax bracket the same after-tax income as a bond paying 10.44 percent in fully taxable income. This figure, which represents the yield a fully taxable bond would have to pay to match the tax-free yield on a municipal bond, is called the **tax-equivalent yield** on the municipal issue. To calculate it, divide the tax-free interest rate by 1 minus the decimal equivalent of the investor's marginal tax rate.

tax-equivalent yield: The percentage yield required on a fully taxable bond to match the after-tax yield of a municipal bond, based on the tax bracket of the investor.

In effect, this calculation adjusts the yield on a tax-free bond for the tax savings it provides to allow comparison with bonds that pay taxable interest. An investor in the 33 percent tax bracket who earned 10.44 percent would

EXHIBIT 7.6

Standard & Poor's Corporate and Municipal Rating Definitions

Debt

A Standard & Poor's corporate or muncipal debt rating is a current assessment of the creditworthiness of an obligor with respect to a specific obligation. This assessment may take into consideration obligors such as guarantors, insurers, or lessees.

The debt rating is not a recommendation to purchase, sell, or hold a security, inasmuch as it does not comment as to market price or suitability for a particular investor.

The ratings are based on current information furnished by the issuer or obtained by Standard & Poor's from other sources it considers reliable. Standard & Poor's does not perform any audit in connection with any rating and may, on occasion, rely on unaudited financial information. The ratings may be changed, suspended, or withdrawn as a result of changes in, or unavailability of, such information, or for other circumstances.

The ratings are based, in varying degrees, on the following considerations:

I. Likelihood of default—capacity and willingness of the obligor as to the timely payment of interest and repayment of principal in accordance with the terms of the obligation;
II. Nature of and provisions of the obligation;
III. Protection afforded by, and relative position of, the obligation in the event of bankruptcy, reorganization, or other arrangement under the laws of bankruptcy and other laws affecting creditor's rights.

AAA

Debt rated 'AAA' has the highest rating assigned by Standard & Poor's. Capacity to pay interest and repay principal is extremely strong.

AA

Debt rated 'AA' has a very strong capacity to pay interest and repay principal and differs from the higher rated issues only in small degree.

A

Debt rated 'A' has a strong capacity to pay interest and repay principal although it is somewhat more susceptible to the adverse effects of changes in circumstances and economic conditions than debt in higher rated categories.

BBB

Debt rated 'BBB' is regarded as having an adequate capacity to pay interest and repay principal. Whereas it normally exhibits adequate protection parameters, adverse economic conditions or changing circumstances are more likely to lead to a weakened capacity to pay interest and repay principal for debt in this category than in higher rated categories.

BB, B, CCC, CC, C

Debit rated 'BB,' 'B,' 'CCC,' 'CC,' [or] 'C' is regarded, on balance, as predominantly speculative with respect to capacity to pay interest and repay principal in accordance with the terms of the obligation. 'BB' indicates the lowest degree of speculation and 'C' the highest degree of speculation. While such debt will likely have some quality and protective characteristics, these are outweighed by large uncertainties or major risk exposures to adverse conditions.

BB

Debt rated 'BB' has less near-term vulnerability to default than other speculative issues. However, it faces major ongoing uncertainties or exposure to adverse business, financial, or economic conditions which could lead to inadequate capacity to meet timely interest and principal payments. The 'BB' rating category is also used for debt subordinated to senior debt that is assigned an actual or implied 'BBB−' rating.

SOURCE: *Standard & Poor's Bond Guide*, August 1990. Reprinted by permission.

have to pay taxes equal to 33 percent of this yield, or 3.45 percent (0.33 × 10.44), leaving the remaining 67 percent (100 percent minus 33 percent) for an after-tax yield of 7 percent (0.67 × 10.44).

Exhibit 7.7 shows tax-equivalent yields for a variety of interest rates and marginal tax brackets. The investor's tax bracket makes a significant difference in tax-equivalent yields, so tax-free municipal securities generally hold the most appeal for investors in high brackets.

Municipal Bond Risks

Tax-exempt municipals carry risks similar to those of other bonds, including interest rate risk and purchasing power risk. In addition, revenue bonds are subject to the business risk of the various projects they finance, which can vary substantially. The attractiveness of municipal bonds depends on an

Standard & Poor's Corporate and Municipal Rating Definitions *(continued)*

B

Debt rated 'B' has a greater vulnerability to default but currently has the capacity to meet interest payments and principal repayments. Adverse business, financial, or economic conditions will likely impair capacity or willingness to pay interest and repay principal. The 'B' rating category is also used for debt subordinated to senior debt that is assigned an actual or implied 'BB' or 'BB−' rating.

CCC

Debt rated 'CCC' has a currently identifiable vulnerability to default, and is dependent upon favorable business, financial, and economic conditions to meet timely payment of interest and repayment of principal. In the event of adverse business, financial, or economic conditions, it is not likely to have the capacity to pay interest and repay principal. The 'CCC' rating category is also used for debt subordinated to senior debt that is assigned an actual or implied 'B' or 'B−' rating.

CC

The rating 'CC' is typically applied to debt subordinated to senior debt that is assigned an actual or implied 'CCC' rating.

C

The rating 'C' is typically applied to debt subordinated to senior debt which is assigned an actual or implied 'CCC−' debt rating. The 'C' rating may be used to cover a situation where a bankruptcy petition has been filed, but debt service payments are continued.

CI

The rating 'CI' is reserved for income bonds on which no interest is being paid.

D

Debt rated 'D' is in payment default. The 'D' rating category is used when interest payments or principal payments are not made on the date due even if the applicable grace period has not expired, unless S&P believes that such payments will be made during such grace period. The 'D' rating also will be used upon the filing of a bankruptcy petition if debt service payments are jeopardized.

Plus (+) or Minus (−)

The ratings from 'AA' to 'CCC' may be modified by the addition of a plus or minus sign to show relative standing within the major categories.

NR indicates that no public rating has been requested, that there is insufficient information on which to base a rating, or that S&P does not rate a particular type of obligation as a matter of policy.

Debt obligations of issuers outside the United States and its territories are rated on the same basis as domestic corporate and municipal issues. The ratings measure the creditworthiness of the obligor but do not take into account currency exchange and related uncertainties.

Bond Investment Quality Standards

Under present commercial bank regulations issued by the Comptroller of the Currency, bonds rated in the top four categories ('AAA,' 'AA,' A,' 'BBB,' commonly known as "Investment Grade" ratings) are generally regarded as eligible for bank investment. In addition, the Legal Investment Laws of various states may impose certain rating or other standards for obligations eligible for investment by savings banks, trust companies, insurance companies, and fiduciaries generally.

EXHIBIT **7.7**

Tax-Equivalent Yields on Municipal Securities

	MARGINAL TAX RATE		
TAX-EXEMPT YIELD	15 PERCENT	28 PERCENT	33 PERCENT
4.00%	4.71%	5.56%	5.97%
6.00	7.06	8.33	8.96
8.00	9.41	11.11	11.94
10.00	11.76	13.89	14.93
12.00	14.12	16.67	17.91
14.00	16.47	19.44	20.90
16.00	18.82	22.22	23.88

individual investor's tax bracket and the spread between tax-free interest rates and those on fully taxable bonds.

Most state and municipal bonds, however, offer stable income and quality investments. They appeal most to investors in higher tax brackets who are willing to carefully analyze the creditworthiness of the communities that issue them.

Term Structure of Interest Rates

Like all bonds, the prices of U.S. government and municipal bonds vary inversely with interest rates, climbing when rates fall and declining when rates rise. In addition, issues with different maturities react differently to a given change in interest rates. Understanding how changes in interest rates drive changes in bond values requires a knowledge of the **term structure of interest rates.** Total bond returns are measured in terms of **yields to maturity,** that is, the average annual compound rate of return earned by the bondholder over the time the bond remains outstanding. This includes interest earned and any capital gains (on a discount bond) or capital losses (on a premium bond). The time period over which the issuer will repay the debt is referred to as the **term to maturity** of the debt. The term structure of interest rates describes the relationship between the yield to maturity and the term to maturity of debt issues.

term structure of interest rates: The relationship between yield to maturity and term to maturity of debt obligations.

yield to maturity: Average annual compound rate of return earned over the life of a bond, including interest earned and any capital gain (on a discount bond) or loss (on a premium bond).

term to maturity: The time period over which an issuer repays debt.

The term structure of interest rates is often represented by a graph, called a **yield curve,** showing yield to maturity as a function of term to maturity. Since categories of debt securities have many different characteristics, they have many different types of yield curves. The yield curve for corporate bonds, for example, looks quite different from the yield curve for municipal bonds or U.S. government securities. Each category of debt has its own characteristic yield curve.

yield curve: A graph relating yield to maturity to term to maturity.

Exhibit 7.8 shows a typical yield curve for U.S. Treasury securities. This so-called *normal yield curve* shows long-term rates that are higher than short-term rates. Such a curve is also described as an upward-sloping, or a **positive yield curve.** This curve presents borrowers with the risk–return tradeoff described earlier: Long-term debt pays mroe interest than short-term debt, but it is riskier due to interest rate risk and purchasing power risk.

positive yield curve: A normal, or upward-sloping, yield curve that indicates higher rates on longer-term securities and lower rates on short-term securities.

Life is not normal all the time, however, and the yield curve does not always follow this pattern. Sometimes it slopes downward, giving a **negative yield curve,** which indicates that short-term rates are higher than long-term rates. This generally occurs during periods of very high interest rates. Prior to the 1970s, negative yield curves were fairly rare, but since then periods of highinflation coupled with high interest rates have made negative yield curves rather common.

negative yield curve: A downward-sloping yield curve that indicates lower rates on longer-term securities and higher rates on shorter-term securities.

Theorists have advanced a number of explanations for the term structure of interest rates. The two most commonly cited explanations are the liquidity

EXHIBIT 7.8

Representative Treasury Yield Curve

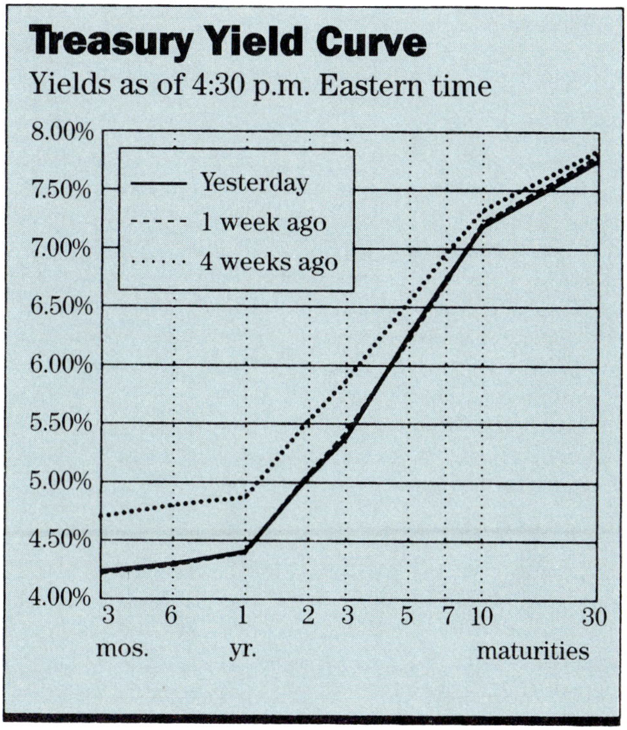

SOURCE: *The Wall Street Journal*, December 17, 1991. Reprinted by permission of *The Wall Street Journal*,

liquidity preference theory: An economic theory that the shape of the yield curve depends upon investors' and borrowers' preferences for liquidity.

preference theory and the expectations hypothesis. The **liquidity preference theory** holds that long-term interest rates should be higher than short-term interest rates due to the liquidity preferences of lenders and borrowers.

In an uncertain world, lenders normally prefer to lend short-term rather than long-term because they want the liquidity of short-term debt. Certainly the experience of home mortgage lenders during the 1980s underscored the dangers of long-term lending. Mortgage lenders could not escape commitments to long-term debt agreements with relatively low interest rates as market rates rose; they suffered losses as their cost of funds climbed, but their loan portfolios continued to provide relatively low rates of return. With no difference in yields, lenders would prefer short-term debt because it is

perspective on INTERNATIONAL INVESTMENTS

Investing in Foreign Government Debt Securities

Investors looking for long-term and short-term fixed-income securities might have done well to invest abroad in April 1992. In the global short-term debt market three-month Europound and Eurodeutschmark securities offered more than twice the rate of return that Eurodollar securities offered. In the global long-term debt market U.K. gilts offered one-third higher yields than ten-year U.S. T-notes. Such higher rates go a long way toward compensating the investor for any loss due to exchange rate risk.

International investments carry risks beyond just interest rate risk; they can also involve political risk. An investment in a country with an unstable government or monetary system, which describes many third-world countries, carries more risk than one in a stable country such as the United Kingdom or Germany. Unstable countries are those that suffer political and/or economic unrest, even extending to the possibility of government overthrow and default by the new regime. Investors might also be wary of otherwise stable governments undergoing restructuring, as in Canada where Quebec wants to secede. Although Canadian investments face no risk of default, the absence or presence of Quebec as part of Canada could affect the economic health of both the province and the nation. An unwary investor could lose either way through failure to read the situation correctly.

Another example would be the resurgent interest in pre-Castro Cuban bonds by optimists who hope that now a western-style democracy would make good on prerevolution government debts. This hope seems remote given the historic trends of new governments to start fresh, whatever their political alignments. Few people expect the Russian government to resurrect Tsarist bonds.

Caution is the key word when investing internationally, especially if returns are tied to unlikely or perilous events.

Global Short Rates versus Long Rates

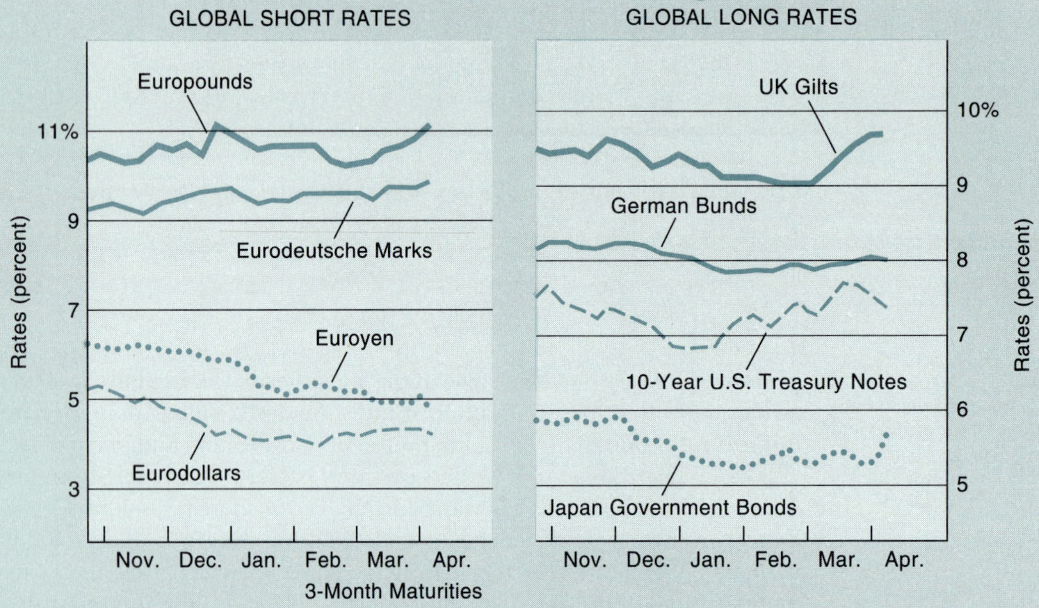

Charts adapted from *Barron's*, April 6, 1992, p. 54. Reprinted by permission of *Barron's*, © 1991 Dow Jones & Company, Inc. All rights reserved worldwide.

subject to less fluctuation in principal value as interest rates fluctuate. Investors who hold long-term bonds, on the other hand, suffer wide fluctuations in the principal value as interest rates fluctuate. Since long-term debt subjects lenders to more risk, they demand higher interest rates on long-term debt than on short-term debt. The additional interest charged on long-term debt is a premium for lack of liquidity.

On the other side of the transaction, borrowers normally prefer to avoid the risk that lenders may not be willing to renew their loans when they mature, or will renew them only at higher interest rates. Because of these risks, borrowers normally prefer to borrow long-term rather than short-term, and they are willing to pay higher interest rates for long-term debt than for short-term debt. The interaction of borrowers' and lenders' liquidity preferences normally results in an upward-sloping yield curve.

expectations hypothesis: An economic theory that the shape of the yield curve depends upon investors' expectations for future interest rates.

Because the yield curve is not always positive, however, other forces besides liquidity preference must be at work. The **expectations hypothesis** provides a convincing explanation of the effect of market participants' expectations for the future on the term structure of interest rates. Specifically, the expectations hypothesis states that capital market competition forces long-term rates to match the average annual compound rate of return that market participants expect to earn on short-term debt over the life of the long-term issue.

The yield to maturity on a ten-year bond, for example, should equal the yield investors expect to earn by continually reinvesting in one-year bonds over each of the next ten years. If they expect interest rates to rise over the next ten years, the current ten-year rate would be higher than the current one-year rate. This expectation would result in a normal, positive yield curve. In times of very high interest rates, investors expect short-term rates to decline in the future, so they anticipate reinvesting at lower and lower interest rates. Hence long-term rates would be lower than short-term rates and the yield curve would be negative. The expectations hypothesis is quite versatile. If investors anticipate stable future interest rates, the hypothesis projects a flat yield curve. The expectations hypothesis provides a convenient and intuitively appealing explanation for rising, falling, or flat yield curves.

The available empirical evidence indicates that both the liquidity preference theory and the expectations hypothesis have some validity. The term structure of interest rates seems to react to liquidity preferences and future expectations, as well as supply and demand conditions. The shape of the yield curve is the result of the interaction of all three forces, any one of which may dominate the others at any given time.

Bond Valuation

Bond valuation is a simple application of the time value of money concepts presented in Chapter 6. It requires discounting the cash flows at the appropriate discount rate. For bonds, we define the appropriate discount rate as the yield to maturity earned on newly issued bonds of the same term to maturity in the current market environment. The value of any bond is just the discounted present value of its expected future cash flows.

Coupon Bonds

coupon bond: A bond that makes periodic interest payments at a stated rate over its life.

A **coupon bond** generates two types of cash flows: the periodic interest payments and the repayment of the par value at maturity. Since almost all bonds pay interest semiannually, the discount rate used to value a bond is one-half the annual discount rate, and the number of discount periods will be twice the number of years to maturity. The value of such a bond, therefore, is the present value of the future interest payments plus the present value of the par value received at maturity.

The value of any bond may be found through present value tables like those we used in Chapter 6, through specially constructed bond valuation tables, or through any of the business-oriented handheld calculators. Using the notation introduced in Chapter 6, the equation for the value of a bond is as follows:

$$V = C\left[\frac{1 - 1/(1 + r/2)^{2n}}{r/2}\right] + P\left[\frac{1}{(1 + r/2)^{2n}}\right]$$

where

V = value of bond

C = semiannual coupon interest payments

r = annual discount rate, compounded semiannually

n = number of years to maturity

P = par value of bond received at maturity

The first term in the equation represents the present value of an annuity of n years' duration discounted semiannually at the rate of r/2. This is the present value of the semiannual interest payments. The second term in the equation represents the present value of the par value of the bond to be received n years (2n periods) from now.

Suppose the appropriate discount rate for Treasury bonds is 12 percent, compounded semiannually. What is the value of a seasoned Treasury bond with a $1,000 par value, an 8 percent coupon rate ($40 semiannual interest payments), and 20 years to maturity? Using the bond valuation equation, the value is:

$$V = \$40\left[\frac{1 - 1/(1 + 0.06)^{40}}{0.06}\right] + \$1{,}000\left[\frac{1}{(1 + 0.06)^{40}}\right]$$

$$= \$40(15.0463) + \$1{,}000(0.0972)$$

$$= \$601.85 + \$97.20 = \$699.05$$

A more common use of the bond valuation equation is to determine the yield to maturity on a bond that is available at a known price. This calculation uses the same bond valuation equation, but you treat V, C, n, and P as given and solve for r, the discount rate. In the previous example, the yield to maturity would be 12.36 percent, the effective rate of return on 12 percent compounded semiannually $[(1.06)^2 - 1]$.

To simplify the extremely difficult problem of solving for r directly using the bond valuation equation, financial service firms have published very extensive **bond yield tables.** Such tables are available at most banks, brokerage houses, and large public libraries. The rapid growth in the use of handheld business calculators has made such tables less necessary. Most calculators will solve bond yields with very short programs, and the business-oriented calculators have preprogrammed functions to find bond yields and solve other types of present value problems.

bond yield table: A numerical table that lists yields to maturity for various combinations of bond prices, coupon rates, and times to maturity.

Zero Coupon Bonds

Zero coupon bonds became popular in the early 1980s. These bonds make no periodic interest payments; instead, investors earn as interest the difference between their original, discounted purchase prices and their full par values at maturity. Investors find zero coupon bonds very attractive because they eliminate **reinvestment risk,** the risk that the investor could not reinvest income from a conventional coupon bond (or another asset) at the same rate that the current bond is earning. This risk is particularly important during periods of high interest rates. For example, an investor who bought a newly issued bond at par to yield 14 percent would not actually earn a 14 percent yield to maturity unless he or she could reinvest the future interest payments at 14 percent for the life of the bond. Since the zero coupon bond provides no cash interest payments to reinvest, it eliminates this risk.

zero coupon bond: A bond that makes no periodic interest payments, but instead is sold at a discount from par value and pays full par value at maturity.

reinvestment risk: The chance that an investor may be unable to reinvest the periodic interest payments from a bond at the same rate that the bond earns due to a drop in interest rates after the bond is purchased.

Zero coupon bonds offer another advantage to their issuers. Because the bond eliminates reinvestment risk, investors will accept lower rates of return on zero coupon bonds than they would accept on conventional bonds. This can lower the issuer's interest costs. The issuer's future repayment obligation is very large, however, relative to the cash proceeds of a zero coupon issue, so zero coupon bonds sometimes have **sinking fund** provisions. A sinking fund is a plan for repaying the bond principal over the life of the bond instead of in one lump sum at maturity. This normally is accomplished by redeeming a certain number of bonds each year for the life of the bond issue.

sinking fund: A plan for repaying the principal value of a bond issue over its life instead of in one lump sum at maturity.

Unfortunately, the Internal Revenue Service has taken the position that amortization of the discount on a zero coupon bond is taxable as if the bond were paying current interest. This means an investor must pay tax annually on the proportion of the increase in value of a zero that is attributable to holding it for the current year, even though he or she receives no cash flow from the bond until its maturity or sale. Hence zero coupon bonds are generally best-suited for nontaxable investors such as corporate pension funds,

tax-deferred plan: A retirement investment plan such as an IRA or Keogh retirement plan on which income taxes are deferred until funds are withdrawn from the plan.

individuals' IRA or Keogh plans, or other **tax-deferred plans.** Some municipalities have begun to issue tax-exempt zero coupon bonds that may be suitable for individuals.

Zero coupon bonds may be valued like any other financial asset. The present value of a zero coupon bond is simply the present value of its par value paid at maturity. For example, the present value of a ten-year, $1,000 par, 12 percent zero coupon bond is as follows:

$$V = \$1{,}000\left(\frac{1}{1.12^{10}}\right)$$

$$= \$1{,}000(0.3220) = \$322$$

stripped Treasury bond: A security equivalent to a zero coupon bond that is issued by the U.S. Treasury by separating individual interest payments from conventional Treasury bonds.

Stripped Treasury Bonds The U.S. Treasury offers investors the equivalent of zero coupon bonds in its **stripped Treasury bonds.** Under a program called STRIPS, the U.S. Treasury separates the interest and principal payments on a Treasury bond to establish an individual investment pool for each payment and one for the principal repayment. A 15-year, 9 percent Treasury bond would end up as a principal repayment pool due in 15 years and 30 interest pools of $45 per bond (one for each semiannual interest payment). An investor could buy a STRIP in the five-year pool through a financial institution and own the equivalent of a five-year zero coupon Treasury bond.

At a 9 percent discount rate, a 15-year stripped Treasury bond with a maturity value of $1,000 would have a present value of approximately $275. An investor who purchased the bond for $275 would receive $1,000 in 15 years, earning a 9 percent average annual compound rate of return.

As for corporate zeros, the investor must pay taxes on the annual increase in value of a stripped Treasury bond. The $275 stripped Treasury bond would increase to approximately $300 at the end of the first year, generating $25 of taxable interest. If the security is held in an IRA, Keogh, or other tax-deferred plan, the owner is not required to pay annual taxes on the income.

Financial institutions have offered a variety of stripped Treasury securities to their clients. Merrill Lynch, for example, sells TIGRs, while E. F. Hutton offers TBRs, and Salomon Brothers sells CATs. The advantage of the government zeros is their quality and compounding rate. Their weakness is the possibility of changes in market interest rates, and the possibility of a decline in market value if interest rates move higher before maturity. An investor should shop around to find the zero with the highest yield and the lowest transaction cost.

SUMMARY

The U.S. Treasury issues Treasury bills that mature over periods from 91 days to one year. The major advantages of investing in T-bills is their safety, liquidity, minimal price fluctuation in response to changes in interest rates, and exemption from state and local income taxes. Treasury bills are sold at a discount from maturity, or face, value of $10,000. The amount of the discount represents the interest the owners earn for holding the T-bill to maturity. The bond equivalent yield on a Treasury bill can be calculated to compare T-bill yields directly to other debt securities that pay interest semiannually.

Treasury notes and bonds and U.S. government agency notes and bonds sell at face value when issued and pay interest semiannually. In general, notes have original maturities of 1 to 10 years and bonds have maturities of 10 to 30 years. Notes and bonds of government agencies are not full faith and credit obligations of the U.S. government, but they are backed by the creditworthiness of the issuing agencies and are considered to be moral obligations of the U.S. government.

Interest payments on notes and bonds issued by states and municipalities are exempt from federal income taxes. These bonds are particularly attractive to individuals in high tax brackets. There are two basic types of municipal bonds: general obligation bonds and revenue bonds. Issuers pay interest on general obligation bonds from their general funds, and the bonds are backed by the issuers' full power to levy taxes. The investment quality of each issue depends on its legality and the ability of the issuing political unit to pay interest when due and to repay the principal at maturity.

Issuers pay interest on revenue bonds solely from user fees and other revenues earned by the project the bonds are issued to finance. Airport and highway construction bonds are good examples of this type of bond. The investment quality of such bonds depends on whether or not project revenues are sufficient to pay the interest and retire the principal.

The tax-equivalent yield on a municipal bond is the fully taxable yield a bondholder would have to earn to net the same after-tax rate of return as the municipal bond provides.

The term structure of interest rates describes the relationship between the terms to maturity on bonds and their yields to maturity. A graph showing this relationship is called a yield curve. The yield curve typically slopes upward, called a positive yield curve, although negative yield curves are common during periods of high interest rates. Two explanations have been advanced to explain the shape of the yield curve: liquidity preference theory and the expectations hypothesis. Both explanations have some validity.

Bond valuation is a simple application of the time value of money concepts learned in Chapter 6. The value of a bond is just the present value of all future interest payments plus the present value of the par value received at maturity.

Zero coupon bonds sell at a discount from par value and pay interest in the form of the difference between their purchase prices and the par values bondholders realize at maturity. These bonds have no coupons and pay no current interest. The U.S. Treasury offers investors the equivalent of zero coupon bonds in the form of stripped Treasury bonds.

INVESTMENT MANAGEMENT CONCEPTS

1. U.S. Treasury bills offer a safe, liquid investment opportunity that provides the worldwide standard for a risk-free investment.

2. U.S. Treasury notes and bondsx offer a long-term investment opportunity that is free from default risk and generally pays a higher interest rate than Treasury bills.

3. U.S. government agency notes and bonds pay higher interest than direct obligations of the U.S. Treasury and yet are extremely high-quality securities.

4. Investors in high tax brackets find state and municipal bonds to be very attractive investments if their tax-equivalent yields are higher than yields on Treasury and agency bonds.

5. Investing in municipal revenue bonds requires careful analysis of both the issuers and the projects the bonds finance. These bonds are backed only by the revenues earned from the projects they finance, and some have defaulted in the past.

6. Unless you become a real expert on municipal bond investing, you would be wise to limit your municipal bond investments to bonds in the top three rating categories.

REVIEW QUESTIONS

1. What are the main advantages of owning Treasury bills?
2. What are the disadvantages of owning Treasury bills?
3. What is the difference between a Treasury note and a Treasury bond?
4. What is meant by the statement that Treasury bills are sold on a discount basis?
5. What are U.S. government agency bonds?
6. Why do U.S. government agency bonds offer higher yields than U.S. Treasury bonds?
7. What is a tax-exempt municipal bond?
8. What is a municipal general obligation bond?
9. What is a municipal revenue bond?
10. Explain the S&P rating system for municipal bonds.
11. What is the tax-equivalent yield on a municipal bond?
12. What is the term structure of interest rates?
13. What is a yield curve?
14. What is the normal shape of a yield curve?
15. Explain the liquidity preference theory.
16. Explain the expectations hypothesis.

17. How can you determine the value of a bond?

18. What is a stripped Treasury bond?

SELF-CORRECTING PROBLEMS

1. You have $20,000 to invest. Because you expect interest rates to rise, you wish to confine your investments to one-year and five-year maturities. You therefore plan to invest $10,000 in one-year investments and $10,000 in securities that mature in five years. You want only securities backed by the full faith and credit of the United States. On the basis of information from the tables in this chapter, select investments that will offer you the highest yield.

2. Eric bought a five-year, $1,000 face value government bond to yield 7.75 percent to maturity. The coupon on the bond was 7.75 percent.

a. What yield will he earn annually over the life of the bond, assuming he holds it to maturity?

b. How much income, in dollars, will he receive annually?

c. How much will he receive at maturity?

d. What did he pay for the bond?

3. Sean bought a three-year government bond in 1992 to yield 7.5 percent to maturity. The coupon on the bond was 7.5 percent. One year later, the bond's current yield had risen to 8.0 percent. What was the price of the bond? What was Sean's return for the one-year period?

4. If your marginal income tax rateis 28 percent, what tax-equivalent yield would you earn on a municipal bond that paid 6.0 percent interest?

5. Suppose 20-year U.S. Treasury bonds are currently yielding 7.5 percent and 20-year general obligation bonds issued by your home state are yielding 6.2 percent. If your combined federal and state marginal income tax rate were 30 percent, which bond would provide a higher after-tax yield?

6. You are considering purchasing a seasoned 30-year Treasury bond with 15 years remaining to maturity and a coupon rate of 9.0 percent. Newly issued 30-year Treasury bonds have coupon rates of 7.5 percent. What is the price of the seasoned bond?

7. What is the price of a 20-year, $1,000 stripped Treasury bond if the appropriate discount rate is 8.0 percent?

8. If a 91-day, $10,000 Treasury bill is selling to yield 5.32 percent, what is the price of the bill?

Answers to Self-Correcting Problems

1. Invest $10,000 in the longest-term T-bill, which matures on November 19, 1992 (from Exhibit 7.1) at a yield of 4.64 percent. For the second $10,000, the $7\frac{1}{4}$ percent November 1996 Treasury bond offers a 6.41 percent yield.

2. a. 7.75 percent

b. 7.75 percent coupon rate times $1,000 equals $77.50

c. $1,000

d. $1,000 (The coupon rate equals the yield to maturity, so the bond must have been purchased at par.)

3. The $1,000 bond paid 7.5 percent, or $75 annual interest. Find the price that divides into $75 to yield 8.0 percent.

$$\$75/\text{Price} = 0.08$$

$$\text{Price} = \$75/0.08 = \$937.50$$

4. 6.0 percent/(1 − 0.28) = 8.33 percent

5. Tax-equivalent yield of municipal bond = 6.2 percent/(1 − 0.30) = 8.86 percent. The municipal bond provides the higher after-tax yield.

6.

$$V = \$45\left(\frac{1 - 1/(1.0375^{30})}{.0375}\right) + \$1{,}000\left(\frac{1}{1.0375^{30}}\right)$$

$$= \$45(17.8292) + \$1{,}000(0.3314)$$

$$= \$802.32 + 331.40 = \$1{,}133.72$$

7.

$$V = \$1{,}000\left(\frac{1}{1.08^{20}}\right)$$

$$= \$1{,}000(0.2145)$$

$$= \$214.50$$

8. $10,000 − (532 × 91 × $0.0027778) = $9,865.52

SELECTED READINGS

Berlin, Howard. *The Dow Jones-Irwin Guide to Buying and Selling Treasury Securities,* second ed. Homewood, Ill.: Dow Jones-Irwin, 1988.

Fabozzi, Frank J., and T. Dessa Fabozzi. *Bond Markets, Analysis, and Strategies.* Englewood Cliffs, N.J.: Prentice-Hall, 1989.

Feldstein, Sylvan G., and Frank J. Fabozzi. *The Dow Jones-Irwin Guide to Municipal Bonds.* Homewood, Ill.: Dow Jones-Irwin, 1987.

Lamb, Robert. *How to Invest in Municipal Bonds.* New York: Franklin Watts, 1984.

Mossavar-Rahmani, Sharmin. *Bond Index Funds.* Chicago: Probus Publishing, 1990.

New York Institute of Finance. *Fixed Income Investments: A Personal Seminar.* Englewood Cliffs, N.J.: Prentice-Hall, 1989.

Sherwood, Hugh C. *How Corporate and Municipal Debt Is Rated: An Inside Look at Standard and Poor's Rating System.* New York: John Wiley and Sons, 1976.

Stigum, Marcia, and Frank J. Fabozzi. *The Dow Jones-Irwin Guide to Bond and Money Market Investments.* Homewood, Ill.: Dow Jones-Irwin, 1987.

Thau, Annette. *The Bond Book; Everything Investors Need to Know about Munis, Treasuries, GNMAs, Funds, Zeros, Corporates, Money Markets, and More.* Chicago: Probus Publishing, 1991.

chapter 8

Corporate Bonds and Preferred Stock

Dr. and Mrs. Jim Wilson were going over their investment holdings with their family and business accountant, Mr. Ben Baldwin, of Baldwin and Associates, CPAs. Ben had been their accountant for nearly all of the 30 years that Dr. Wilson had practiced medicine in a small suburb outside of Chicago. Dr. Wilson, now in his early sixties, wanted to work out a plan for retirement. Fortunately, Dr. Wilson had built up a successful practice and had always been very conscientious about making monthly contributions to his retirement plan. Along with the proceeds of the sale of Dr. Wilson's practice to two younger associates, the Wilsons expected to have a portfolio of just over $1 million to invest for their "golden years."

Ben opened the meeting: "Doc, I know $1.2 million is a lot of money, but the actuarial tables say that you and Mrs. Wilson can plan on one of you living for another 20 years or more, so we need to make sure that the money will provide enough purchasing power out to at least the year 2010 and further, if necessary."

"I hadn't really thought of it that way," said Jim. "I was looking at the interest rate on long-term government bonds the other day. If I put all of my money in 30-year Treasury bonds at the current rate of 8.2 percent, I could earn about $98,000 in interest next year. That's sure a lot more money than I am going to spend in a year."

Ben started shaking his head as he always did when he was about to make a point. "But doc, you've got two problems. First, you've got to pay about $32,000 federal and state income tax on that money, so you really will only earn $66,000 after tax. That's still more than you spend in a year now that the house is paid off and the kids are out of college, so you're certainly in good shape financially if you want to retire."

"So what's the second problem?" asked Mrs. Wilson.

"The second problem," continued Ben, "is inflation. That $66,000 a year after tax may be a lot of money now, but 20 years from now, that $66,000 will have about the same purchasing power as $25,000 a year today—then you've got a real problem."

"I assume you have a solution?"

"Well," said Ben, "I've at least got a suggestion. Let's look into putting some of your assets into corporate debt securities to get a higher yield than government bonds. You can then reinvest some of that extra yield to earn more interest in the future."

"What about convertible bonds?" asked Mrs. Wilson. "I was watching 'Wall Street Week' on public television last Friday and the guest speaker was a bond analyst from one of the big firms in New York. He said something about buying bonds that pay high interest now and can be converted later into common stocks when the price of the stock goes up. He said you get the best of both worlds: high yields in the present and growth of capital in the future. What do you think about those?"

"Well, it sounds like a good idea to me. Let's set up a meeting with your investment adviser and your broker and see what we can do."

Introduction

Corporate bonds and preferred stock are the two primary classes of long-term fixed-income securities that corporations issue to finance their activities. Fixed-income securities are securities that pay fixed dollar amounts of interest or dividends at regular intervals. Corporations issue fixed-income securities in order to borrow large sums of money from individual and institutional investors through the securities markets. Investors purchase these securities in order to earn regular income to support living expenses or to reinvest for future capital growth. Additionally, as pointed out in the discussion of asset allocation in Chapter 6, recessions make bonds extremely attractive since interest rates normally decline during those economic conditions, causing prices of fixed-income securities to increase.

Of course, the investor in corporate fixed-income securities must accept more risk than U.S. Treasury securities would bring, since Treasuries are

default risk: The chance that a bond or preferred stock issuer will fail to make required interest or dividend payments on time, or that a bond issuer will not repay the principal amount when due.

backed by the full faith and credit of the U.S. government, which eliminates default risk. **Default risk** is the chance that a security issuer will fail to make required interest or dividend payments on time or to repay principal when due. Corporate securities give no guarantee that issuers will pay as promised, so they carry some risk of default. As discussed in Chapter 7, agency securities represent moral obligations of the U.S. government so they have only minimal default risk.

Corporate fixed-income securities may be more or less risky than municipal bonds. A bond issue of a AAA-rated corporation, for example, would be considered less risky than a BBB-rated municipal revenue bond. The difference arises from the characteristics of the issuers.

This chapter will examine corporate bonds and preferred stocks, including convertible bonds, bonds with warrants, and convertible preferred stock. In addition, it will present the techniques of preferred stock valuation, building on the discussion of bond valuation in Chapter 7.

Corporate Bonds

A corporate bond is a long-term, written promise to repay an amount a corporation borrows at the end of a set time, and to pay interest at a specified rate while the bond is outstanding. Buyers of a corporate bond issue essentially make loans to the issuing corporation. Since corporations usually need larger loans than individual investors could make, they divide their total debt requirements into increments, usually $1,000, and sell securities that represent individual increments to many investors. The $1,000 (or other increment) represents the **face value,** or par value, of a bond, that is, the principal amount of the debt that the issuer promises to repay at maturity. Besides repaying the principal at maturity (or when market conditions lead the firm to call the issue before maturity), the borrowing corporation promises to pay interest periodically, usually either quarterly or semiannually. In general, bonds that require investors to accept higher risk pay interest at higher rates.

face value: The principal amount that a bond issuer borrows and promises to repay at maturity.

Bond Indentures

bond indenture: The written agreement that states the terms and conditions of the lending agreement between a corporation that issues bonds and the trustee that represents the bondholders.

trustee's certificate: Identification of the bank or corporation that acts as trustee for bondholders to enforce the terms of a bond indenture.

The **bond indenture** is the written document that states the terms and conditions of the lending agreement between the issuer of the bonds and the trustee that represents the bondholders. The bond indenture specifies such features as the dollar amount of interest that will be paid annually, the coupon rate of interest (the annual dollar amount divided by the par value), the **trustee's certificate** (which identifies the bank or corporation that acts as trustee for all bondholders to enforce the terms of the indenture), any property pledged as security for the debt, and any agreements, restrictions, or remedies in case the company should default. If the issue gives bondholders any special rights, such as the right to convert the bonds to stock at some future time, the indenture states the terms exactly.

One of the first provisions of a bond indenture is a statement concerning the time of repayment of the principal, typically 20 years or longer after issue. The indenture also specifies any security pledged to ensure repayment of the debt. As explained shortly, some bond issues are retired proportionally over their lives.

callable bond: A bond that the issuer may recall for early redemption.

In contrast to Treasury bonds, most corporate issues are **callable bonds,** which means that the corporation has the right to repay the principal and retire the debt before maturity. This may be advantageous for the company if it has surplus funds, if it can issue new debt at a lower interest rate, or if it needs to clean up its capital structure in anticipation of new financing. The timing of a possible call can affect the yield investors will receive by reducing their holding periods. The **first call date** specifies the earliest time at which the issuer can call a bond.

first call date: The first date on which an issuer can call a bond issue.

A call provision can critically affect the return on a bond purchased at a premium, that is, at a price above par value, particularly when the call price is substantially below the market price. The previous two chapters explored the concept of yield to maturity in detail. To assess the yield potential of a callable bond, it is important to calculate its **yield to first call date,** as well. The yield to first call date calculation is just the yield to maturity calculation modified to reflect the assumption that the issuer will call the bond on its first call date at the call price specified in the indenture.

yield to first call date: The yield to maturity for a callable bond calculated on the assumption that the issuer will call the bond on the first call date.

Suppose you paid $1,020 for a 10 percent coupon bond that was callable at par any time after five years. You would calculate the yield to first call date based on a purchase price of $1,020, annual interest payments of $100 per year for five years, and repayment of the $1,000 par value after five years. This would give you a built-in capital loss of $20 over the five-year period since the issuer can call the bond at par value, reducing the yield to first call date below the 10 percent coupon rate to approximately 9.5 percent. Of course, the bond would be trading at a premium only if current market rates were less than the 10 percent coupon rate. Chapter 7 discussed this relationship in detail.

serial retirement: A systematic method for repayment of the principal for a bond issue over the life of the issue rather than in one lump sum at maturity.

Indentures for some bond issues provide for **serial retirement.** Instead of paying off the entire principal amount of an issue on the same maturity date, the issuer repays portions of the principal on specified dates over the life of the issue. A 20-year serial bond issue might be retired at the rate of one-fortieth of the principal every six months. An investor who purchases such a bond knows the exact dates on which the issuer will make repayments and can calculate a yield to maturity for each period.

Security Provisions and Types of Bonds

Investors divide bonds into classes depending upon the issuers' provisions for security of principal. Corporate debentures are full faith and credit obligations of the issuing corporations. The company says, in effect, "In exchange for your investment I promise to pay the claim when due. You have all my resources to support this pledge or bond."

subordinated debenture: A debenture that gives the holder a junior claim to interest payments and corporate assets as compared to the claim of a senior debenture.

Subordinated debentures are debentures with claims to corporate assets that are junior to those of an existing, or senior, bond issue. Holders of subordinated debentures are entitled to payment only after holders of the senior securities are paid. In the event of bankruptcy, owners of senior securities are repaid from the proceeds of liquidation of the issuer's assets before owners of junior securities are repaid.

mortgage bond: A bond issue that pledges specific real property as security for the debt.

Mortgage bonds pledge real property as specific security for the debt. Their claims to the pledged property are senior to those of debentures. Investors should check the terms of mortgage bond pledges carefully because corporations can issue first mortgage bonds and second, or junior, mortgage bonds. A first mortgage bond has a senior claim to the mortgaged asset, and owners of these bonds are fully repaid out of the proceeds from selling the assets before owners of junior mortgage bonds receive anything. Many mortgage bond issues have **after-acquired clauses,** which pledge all new property acquired after the bonds are issued as further security for the debt. This prevents dilution of the first mortgage bondholders' position and security.

after-acquired clause: A bond indenture provision that pledges all property acquired after issue of the bond as further security for the existing debt.

equipment trust certificate: A bond issue that pledges a specific piece of equipment, such as a railroad car, as collateral.

collateral trust bond: A bond issue that pledges specific personal property or another security as collateral.

Equipment trust certificates, which pledge specific pieces of equipment as collateral for debts, are quite common in the railroad industry to finance purchases of equipment or rolling stock (such as freight cars). Sometimes corporations issue **collateral trust bonds,** which pledge personal property, other bonds, or common stock as security for the debt.

receivers' certificate: A bond issued to raise money to continue business operations of a company that is under court protection during reorganization.

Sometimes a bond issue is guaranteed by another company or secured jointly by two or more companies. **Receivers' certificates,** in spite of their poor-sounding name, are prime securities sold by corporations in receivership (under protection of a bankruptcy court) to raise money to continue business operations. These securities have senior claims over those of existing debt.

Security of Interest Payments Before you buy a bond, it is important to assess the prospects that the issuer will make interest payments and repay principal as promised. Part of this assessment is a review of the bond's legal position if the company defaults, that is, fails to pay interest or principal on schedule. The most important question, however, concerns the firm's ability to pay interest as it comes due and its ability, over time, to generate a sufficient flow of cash to repay the debt.

sinking fund: A systematic repayment schedule that allows an issuer to pay off a bond over time.

Some issues set up **sinking funds** to set aside current income to retire debt. A sinking fund indenture provision may require the issuing corporation to make annual payments into an account that will accumulate sufficient funds to pay off the bonds at maturity. More commonly, sinking fund provisions set up systematic schedules on which the firm buys back its bonds in the open market or calls bonds for repayment. This increases the investor's assurance that the bonds will be paid off on schedule.

protective covenant: A bond indenture provision that requires an issuing corporation to take some specific action to protect the credit quality of a bond issue.

Additional Protection for Investors Bond indentures commonly include **protective covenants** that require the issuer to take certain actions to protect the credit standing of the bond issue. One common protective covenant, for example, prevents the issuer from issuing any new debt securities that are senior to the existing bond issue. This assures the buyers of the existing bond that they will maintain their relative seniority in the event of bankruptcy. Often bond indentures limit common stock dividends, stating that the corporation can pay no dividends if cash falls below a certain level. Sometimes mortgage bond indentures prevent the firm from borrowing more than 50 percent of the value of the property to protect the credit standing of the bond. The after-acquired clause, described earlier, is another common protective covenant.

The Investment Quality of Corporate Bonds

The quality of a corporate bond depends on the issuer's overall creditworthiness, including its past history, its current ability to make promised payments, any pledges of other assets as security, and a number of other factors. As noted in Chapter 7, Standard & Poor's and Moody's publish quality ratings for bond issues. They assign ratings of triple A (AAA on Standard & Poor's scale and Aaa on Moody's scale) to the best-quality debt obligations on which they have no question that the issuers will make timely interest and principal payments. From this high level, ratings range down to a low of C (Moody's) or D (S&P) for bonds actually in default.

Bonds in the top four rating categories are considered investment-grade securities: AAA, AA, A, and BBB on Standard & Poor's scale, or Aaa, Aa, A, and Baa on Moody's. Federal law prohibits commercial banks from investing in debt securities rated below investment grade. To be safe, unsophisticated bond investors (which includes just about all nonprofessionals) should follow the same rule as commercial banks and select bonds only from the top four rating categories.

Nearly all libraries and all brokerage offices have copies of Moody's and Standard & Poor's publications. The S&P *Bond Guide* ratings definitions appeared in the previous chapter. The comparable information for Moody's appears in Exhibit 8.1.

Yield and Investment Quality

Yields on bonds peaked in the early 1980s and declined in the late 1980s and early 1990s. Bond yields increase as quality declines and risk increases; a lower bond rating implies a higher yield. Except for AAA bonds, yields normally are higher on public utility issues than on bonds issued by industrial firms. Because these relationships change over time, you should re-examine current conditions before making any investment decisions. Exhibit 8.2, taken from Standard & Poor's *Bond Guide,* shows the range of yields on bonds in various rating categories along with the average yields of U.S. government and municipal bonds.

EXHIBIT 8.1

Moody's Bond Rating Definitions

MOODY'S BOND RATINGS

Purpose: The system of rating securities was originated by John Moody in 1909.

The purpose of Moody's Ratings is to provide the investors with a simple system of gradation by which the relative investment qualities of bonds may be noted.

Rating Symbols: Gradations of investment quality are indicated by rating symbols, each symbol representing a group in which the quality characteristics are broadly the same. There are nine symbols as shown below, from that used to designate least investment risk (i.e., highest investment quality) to that denoting greatest investment risk (i.e., lowest investment quality):

Aaa Aa A Baa Ba B Caa Ca C

Absence of Rating: Where no rating has been assigned or where a rating has been suspended or withdrawn, it may be for reasons unrelated to the quality of the issue.

Should no rating be assigned, the reason may be one of the following:

1. An application for rating was not received or accepted.
2. The issue or issuer belongs to a group of securities or companies that are not rated as a matter of policy.
3. There is a lack of essential data pertaining to the issue or issuer
4. The issue was privately placed, in which case the rating is not published in Moody's publications.

Suspension or withdrawal may occur if new and material circumstances arise, the effects of which preclude satisfactory analysis; if there is no longer available reasonable up-to-date data to permit a judgment to be formed; if a bond is called for redemption; or for other reasons.

Changes in Rating: The quality of most bonds is not fixed and steady over a period of time, but tends to undergo change. For this reason changes in ratings occur so as to reflect these variations in the intrinsic position of individual bonds.

A change in rating may thus occur at any time in the case of an individual issue. Such rating change should serve notice that Moody's observes some alteration in the investment risks of the bond or that the previous rating did not fully reflect the quality of the bond as now seen. While because of their very nature, changes are to be expected more frequently among bonds of lower ratings than among bonds of higher ratings, nevertheless the user of bond ratings should keep close and constant check on all ratings—both high and low ratings—thereby to be able to note promptly any signs of change in investment status which may occur.

Limitations to Uses of Ratings: Bonds carrying the same rating are not claimed to be of absolutely equal quality. In a broad sense they are alike in position, but since there are a limited number of rating classes used in grading thousands of bonds, the symbols cannot reflect the fine shadings of risks which actually exist. Therefore, it should be evident to the user of ratings that two bonds identically rated are unlikely to be precisely the same in investment quality.

As ratings are designed exclusively for the purpose of grading bonds according to their investment qualities, they should not be used alone as a basis for investment operations. For example, they have no value in forecasting the direction of future trends of market price. Market price movements in bonds are influenced not only by the quality of individual issues but also by changes in money rates and general economic trends, as well as by the length of maturity, etc. During its life even the best quality bond may have wide price movements, while its high investment status remains unchanged.

The matter of market price has no bearing whatsoever on the determination of ratings which are not to be construed as recommendations with respect to "attractiveness." The attractiveness of a given bond may depend on its yield, its maturity date or other factors for which the investor may search, as well as on its investment quality, the only characteristic to which the rating refers.

Since ratings involve judgments about the future, on the one hand, and since they are used by investors as a means of protection, on the other, the effort is made when assigning ratings to look at "worst" potentialities in the "visible" future, rather than solely at the past record and the status of the present. Therefore, investors using the rating should not expect to find in them reflection of statistical factors alone, since they are an appraisal of long term risks, including the recognition of many non-statistical factors.

Though ratings may be used by the banking authorities to classify bonds in their bank examination procedure, Moody's Ratings are not made with these bank regulations in view. Moody's Investors Service's own judgment as to desirability or non-desirability of a bond for bank investment purposes is not indicated by Moody's Ratings.

Moody's Ratings represent the mature opinion of Moody's Investors Service, Inc., as to the relative investment classification of bonds. As such, they should be used in conjunction with the description and statistics appearing in Moody's Manuals. Reference should be made to these statements for information regarding the issuer. Moody's Ratings are not commercial credit ratings. In no case is default or receivership to be inputed unless expressly so stated in the Manual.

KEY TO MOODY'S CORPORATE RATINGS

Aaa

Bonds which are rated **Aaa** are judged to be of the best quality. They carry the smallest degree of investment risk and are generally referred to as "gilt edge." Interest payments are protected by a large or by an exceptionally stable margin and principal is secure. While the various protective elements are likely to change, such changes as can be visualized are most unlikely to impair the fundamentally strong position of such issues.

Aa

Bonds which are rated **Aa** are judged to be of high quality by all standards. Together with the **Aaa** group they comprise what are generally known as high grade bonds. They are rated lower than the best bonds because margins of protection may not be as large as in **Aaa** securities or fluctuation of protective elements may be of greater amplitude or there may be other elements present which make the long term risks appear somewhat larger than in **Aaa** securities.

A

Bonds which are rated **A** possess many favorable investment attributes and are to be considered as upper medium grade obligations. Factors giving security to principal and interest are considered adequate but elements may be present which suggest a susceptibility to impairment sometime in the future.

Baa

Bonds which are rated **Baa** are considered as medium grade obligations, i.e., they are neither highly protected nor poorly secured. Interest payments and principal security appear adequate for the present but certain protective elements may be lacking or may be characteristically unrealiable over any great length of time. Such bonds lack outstanding investment characteristics and in fact have speculative characteristics as well.

Ba

Bonds which are rated **Ba** are judged to have speculative elements; their future cannot be considered as well assured. Often the protection of interest and principal payments may be very moderate and thereby not well safeguarded during other good and bad times over the future. Uncertainty of position characterizes bonds in this class.

B

Bonds which are rated **B** generally lack characteristics of the desirable investment. Assurance of interest and principal payments or of maintenance of other terms of the contract over any long period of time may be small.

Caa

Bonds which are rated **Caa** are of poor standing. Such issues may be in default or there may be present elements of danger with respect to principal or interest.

Ca

Bonds which are rated **Ca** represent obligations which are speculative in a high degree. Such issues are often in default or have other marked shortcomings.

C

Bonds which are rated **C** are the lowest rated class of bonds and issues so rated can be regarded as having extremely poor prospects of ever attaining any real investment standing.

Note: Moody's applies numerical modifiers, **1, 2** and **3** in each generic rating classification from **Aa** through **B** in its corporate bond rating system. The modifier **1** indicates that the security ranks in the higher end of its generic rating category; the modifier **2** indicates a mid-range ranking; and the modifier **3** indicates that the issue ranks in the lower end of its generic rating category

Moody's bond ratings, where specified, are applied to senior bank obligations with an original maturity in excess of one year. Obligations relying upon support mechanisms such as letters-of-credit are excluded unless explicitily rated. Obligations of a branch of a bank are considered to be domiciled in the country in which the branch is located. Unless noted as an exception, Moody's rating on a bank's ability to repay senior obligations extends only to branches located in countries which carry a Moody's sovereign rating. Such branch obligations are rated at the lower of the bank's rating or Moody's sovereign rating for the bank deposits for the country in which the branch is located. When the currency in which the obligation is denominated is not the same as the currency of the country in which the obligation is domiciled, Moody's ratings do not incorporate an opinion as to whether payment of the obligation will be affected by the actions of the government controlling the currency of denomination. In addition, risk associated with bilateral conflicts between an investor's home country and either the issuer's home country or the country where an issuer branch is located are not incorporated into Moody's ratings. Moody's makes no representation that rated bank obligations are exempt from registration under the U.S. Securities Act of 1933 or issued in conformity with any other applicable law or regulation. Nor does Moody's represent any specific bank obligation is legally enforceable or a valid senior obligation of a rated issuer.

SOURCE: *Bond Record*, Moody's Investors Service, January 1991. Reprinted by permission.

EXHIBIT 8.2

Standard & Poor's Bond Yield Index

Weekly Averages 1991	PUBLIC UTILITY AA	PUBLIC UTILITY A	PUBLIC UTILITY BBB	INDUSTRIAL AAA	INDUSTRIAL AA	INDUSTRIAL A	INDUSTRIAL BBB	INDUSTRIAL BB	INDUSTRIAL B	COMPOSITE AA	COMPOSITE A	COMPOSITE BBB	GOVERNMENT Long-Term	GOVERNMENT Inter-mediate	GOVERNMENT Short Term	Muni-cipals
November 27	8.97	9.18	9.29	8.46	8.78	9.31	9.60	11.50	14.67	8.87	9.24	9.45	7.93	7.02	5.73	6.68
November 20	8.99	9.13	9.23	8.41	8.72	9.25	9.54	11.44	14.71	8.85	9.19	9.39	7.89	7.00	5.80	6.66
November 13	8.97	9.10	9.20	8.38	8.69	9.22	9.52	11.34	14.65	8.83	9.16	9.36	7.89	7.08	5.94	6.60
November 6	9.01	9.15	9.26	8.44	8.77	9.28	9.58	11.49	14.70	8.89	9.22	9.42	7.98	7.08	5.69	6.61
Monthly Averages 1991–1990																
November	8.99	9.14	9.25	8.42	8.74	9.27	9.56	11.44	14.68	8.86	9.20	9.41	7.92	7.05	5.79	6.64
October	8.99	9.12	9.22	8.41	8.73	9.24	9.55	11.59	14.99	8.86	9.18	9.39	7.94	7.17	5.98	6.59
September	9.02	9.18	9.27	8.49	8.81	9.28	9.69	11.59	14.42	8.92	9.23	9.48	8.06	7.36	6.20	6.80
August	9.12	9.35	9.44	8.47	8.98	9.44	9.81	11.51	14.38	9.05	9.39	9.62	8.19	7.47	6.15	6.89
July	9.43	9.66	9.74	8.78	9.29	9.75	10.10	11.84	14.28	9.36	9.71	9.62	8.57	8.00	6.66	7.03
June	9.49	9.70	9.80	9.08	9.37	9.79	10.24	12.02	14.42	9.43	9.74	10.01	8.65	8.07	6.83	7.09
May	9.38	9.54	9.61	8.87	9.16	9.63	10.19	12.09	15.03	9.28	9.58	9.90	8.42	7.83	6.61	6.95
April	9.35	9.49	9.67	8.84	9.13	9.60	10.23	11.99	15.84	9.24	9.55	9.95	8.38	7.84	6.80	7.05
March	9.45	9.57	9.82	8.95	9.24	9.71	10.43	11.97	16.86	9.34	9.64	10.12	8.48	7.92	6.98	7.07
February	9.24	9.36	9.61	8.71	9.12	9.55	10.67	12.30	19.04	9.18	9.45	10.14	8.22	7.63	6.82	6.90
January	9.42	9.59	9.88	9.01	9.45	9.79	11.62	12.24	19.63	9.43	9.69	10.75	8.45	7.88	7.14	7.05
December	9.38	9.56	9.85	9.03	9.40	9.77	11.28	12.41	19.05	9.39	9.67	10.57	8.38	7.88	7.32	7.04
November	9.58	9.76	10.03	9.25	9.56	9.97	11.24	12.92	19.55	9.57	9.87	10.63	8.70	8.19	7.61	7.10
Annual Ranges																
1991 High	9.54	9.75	9.99	9.14	9.55	9.89	11.83	12.58	20.53	9.54	9.80	10.86	8.70	8.13	7.20	7.15
Low	8.96	9.09	9.16	8.34	8.68	9.16	9.52	10.80	14.11	8.82	9.12	9.35	7.88	7.00	5.69	6.52
1990 High	10.17	10.36	10.60	9.76	10.13	10.50	11.48	14.12	19.85	10.15	10.43	10.98	9.32	9.13	8.99	7.56
Low	9.09	9.39	9.68	8.78	9.06	9.55	10.06	11.94	13.80	9.07	9.47	9.87	8.22	7.75	7.22	6.99
1989 High	10.14	10.47	10.56	9.92	10.29	10.70	11.06	12.30	13.95	10.21	10.59	10.81	9.50	9.68	9.97	7.68
Low	8.98	9.28	9.55	8.62	8.91	9.45	9.90	11.20	11.93	8.95	9.36	9.69	7.97	7.71	7.61	6.87
1988 High	10.38	10.65	10.97	9.95	10.33	10.85	11.22	11.35	12.51	10.35	10.66	10.98	9.60	9.24	9.18	8.10
Low	9.27	9.52	9.93	9.05	9.41	9.89	10.44	10.96	11.89	9.34	9.71	10.24	8.44	7.99	7.15	7.41
1987 High	10.96	11.27	11.78	10.74	11.09	11.48	12.06	—	—	11.03	11.37	11.92	10.30	9.89	8.90	9.31
Low	8.59	8.89	9.13	8.37	8.89	8.83	9.52	—	—	8.76	8.88	9.36	7.57	6.90	6.26	6.53
1986 High	10.24	10.69	11.06	9.80	10.41	10.58	11.26	—	—	10.32	10.58	11.15	9.51	9.15	8.44	8.21
Low	8.76	9.05	9.36	8.50	9.18	8.99	9.81	—	—	8.98	9.19	9.61	7.23	6.98	6.27	6.73
1985 High	12.54	12.87	13.24	12.00	12.43	12.50	13.19	—	—	12.48	12.62	13.14	11.84	11.89	10.82	9.93
Low	10.01	10.49	10.93	9.50	10.13	10.20	11.13	—	—	10.07	10.34	11.03	9.24	8.86	8.11	8.41
1984 High	14.45	14.78	15.60	13.66	14.13	14.42	15.12	—	—	14.23	14.54	15.32	13.89	13.79	13.22	11.14
Low	11.94	12.31	12.80	11.40	11.73	12.06	12.78	—	—	11.84	12.18	12.79	11.25	11.30	10.19	9.48
1983 High	13.05	13.14	13.74	12.38	12.62	12.94	13.67	—	—	12.83	13.04	13.63	11.99	12.03	11.26	10.01
Low	10.85	11.10	11.49	10.51	10.72	11.07	11.68	—	—	10.78	11.08	11.58	10.18	9.83	9.21	8.72
1982 High	16.13	16.39	17.14	14.76	15.13	15.57	17.03	—	—	15.63	15.91	17.08	14.32	14.56	14.57	13.34
Low	11.39	11.78	12.68	10.55	10.96	11.75	13.28	—	—	11.18	11.80	13.17	10.18	9.91	9.57	9.16
1981 High	16.63	17.01	18.19	15.67	15.89	16.23	16.82	—	—	16.26	16.62	17.51	15.08	15.56	16.13	13.20
Low	13.05	13.19	14.35	12.03	12.27	12.77	13.20	—	—	12.66	12.98	13.77	11.52	12.10	12.37	9.47

† AAA public utility & composite bond yields discontinued January 1984.

SOURCE: *Bond Guide*, Standard & Poor's Corp., December 1991. Reprinted by permission.

leveraged buyout: A purchase of enough common stock to control a corporation financed with a large amount of debt, normally in the form of junk bonds.

The very high yields for BB- and B-rated bonds shown in Exhibit 8.2 reflect the collapse of the junk bond market in 1989 and 1990. Junk bonds range from the lowest rating categories up to just below investment grade. During the 1980s many groups recklessly issued unsecured junk bonds to finance **leveraged buyouts** to acquire the common stock and, therefore, control of public corporations. The bonds issued for these transactions were very risky, and they paid extraordinarily high interest rates. The economic recession and collapse of real estate values in the late 1980s, however, sank many of these issues into default, leaving investors with worthless paper, and junk bonds with a tarnished reputation. This forced yields on bonds rated below investment grade still higher. Exhibit 8.2 shows a 1991 yield for B-rated industrial bonds of 20.53 percent, compared to 9.14 percent for AAA-rated industrial bonds.

Price Quotes, Other Information, and Transaction Mechanics

Investors buy and sell corporate bonds through brokers, paying commissions that range from $25 for a single-bond transaction to $2.50 per bond for a transaction involving many bonds. A large broker may not charge a commission directly. Instead it may buy for or sell from its own inventory, earning a profit on the sale rather than a commission.

The Wall Street Journal and other publications list bond price quotations. Exhibit 8.3 shows a sample price quote for bonds listed on the New York Bond Exchange. Moving from left to right, the first column gives the name of the bond, its coupon interest rate, and the year the issue matures. The second column gives its current yield. The third column lists trading volume, that is, the number of bonds in the issue that changed hands on a given day. The last two columns give the bond's closing price in units of $10 and the price change from the previous day's closing price.

An example will show how to use these tables. In the first column of Exhibit 8.3, find an entry that reads "GMA 8s02." This is the listing for a bond issued by General Motors Acceptance Corporation, the finance subsidiary of General Motors Corporation. The notation "8s02" means that this bond has an 8.0 percent coupon rate and matures in the year 2002. The current yield on the bond is 8.3 percent, as shown in the next column, and 50 bonds were traded on the day of the quote. Multiplying the listed price of 96⅜ by the unit of $10 gives a dollar price for the bond of $963.75. (Corporate bonds are traded in eights.) Finally, the net change of ⅞ represents a price change of $8.75 from the previous day.

The Wall Street Journal publishes a daily feature called the Bond Market Data Bank that provides information on prices and yields for government and corporate bonds. A sample appears in Exhibit 8.4. A brief scan of this column offers a quick panorama of current conditions in the long-term debt markets

Investment Goals for Corporate Bonds

Corporate bonds are an attractive investment for institutional investors and individuals who desire current income, particularly when they can lock in high yields by buying long-term, noncallable bonds when interest rates are high. Corporate bonds involve risk, however, especially interest rate risk and default risk, depending upon the quality ratings. Bond returns may suffer from purchasing power risk, as well, if high inflation erodes the purchasing power of the fixed principal and interest payments. People in

EXHIBIT 8.3

Price Quotes on Corporate Bonds

NEW YORK EXCHANGE BONDS

Quotations as of 4 p.m. Eastern Time
Thursday, January 2, 1992

Volume $49,560,000

SALES SINCE JANUARY 1
(000 omitted)

1992	1991	1990
$49,560	$33,410	$32,625

	Domestic Thu.	Domestic Tue.	All Issues Thu.	All Issues Tue.
Issues traded	583	621	586	622
Advances	269	338	270	339
Declines	201	161	202	161
Unchanged	113	122	114	122
New highs	87	103	87	103
New lows	2	5	2	5

Dow Jones Bond Averages

–1991– High	–1991– Low	–1992– High	–1992– Low		–1992– Close	–1992– Chg.	–1992– %Yld	–1991– Close	–1991– Chg.
98.93	91.30	98.96	98.96	20 Bonds	98.96	+0.03	8.42	91.63	+0.06
100.81	93.44	100.67	100.67	10 Utilities	100.67	−0.04	8.45	93.73	+0.29
97.15	89.06	97.26	97.26	10 Industrials	97.26	+0.11	8.39	89.54	−0.17

Bonds	Cur Yld	Vol	Close	Net Chg.
CmwE 9⅛08	8.8	22	103⅞	+½
CmwE 11⅛10	10.3	1	107½	+½
ConrPer 6¾01	cv	253	88¼	+1¾
Consec 12¾97	12.0	110	106¼	+½
ConEd 4⅜92w r	4.5	9	98 1/16	+2 1/16
ConEd 9⅜00	9.1	15	103⅜	+⅝
ConEd 7.9s01	7.9	19	100	−¾
ConEd 8.4s03	8.3	5	101¾	...
ConEd 9⅛04	8.8	4	104	+1¼
CnNG 8⅛97	7.9	3	103	+2½
ConNG 7¼15	cv	27	102¼	+¾
CnPw 8⅛01	8.1	5	99¾	−⅛
CnPw 8⅝03	8.6	10	100½	...
CnPw 8⅝07	8.5	5	101¼	−¼
CtlOil 8⅞01	8.8	24	101	+1⅞
viCtlInf 9s06f	cv	15	6⅜	+⅛
Crane 7s93	7.0	5	100½	+½
Dana dc5⅞06	cv	10	74½	+½
DtaDsg 7s01	cv	4	42	...
DatGen 8⅜02	9.7	10	86¼	+⅜
DataGn 01	cv	26	107	−½
Datpnt 8⅞06	cv	58	46	−½
DaytP 8⅛01	8.2	5	99½	+½
Deere 8.45s	8.4	75	101	+1⅞
DetEd 6.4s98	6.8	2	94	...
DetEd 9.15s00	9.0	9	102	...
Disney zr05	...	2359	57	+¾
Dow 8⅞2000	8.7	33	102	...
Dow 8.92000	8.6	1	103⅞	...
Dow 8½s05	8.4	1	100¾	−1¼
duPnt 8.45s04	8.2	60	103¼	...
duPnt 8½06	8.2	15	103⅛	+⅞
duPnt dc6s01	6.5	10	92	+1¼
duPnt 8½16	8.3	24	102½	+1½
duPnt zr10	cv	6	25⅛	...
DukeP 7⅜01	7.4	23	99⅛	+⅛
DukeP 8⅜06	8.1	58	103¼	
DukeP 8⅛07	8.1	26	100⅜	−⅝
DuqL 8⅜07	8.4	10	99½	−1
EKod 8⅝16	8.5	206	101	+½
EKod zr11	...	246	29⅜	+½
EmbSuit 10½94	10.3	15	102	...
Ens 10s01	cv	38	102½	−¼
EnvSys 6¾11	cv	20	72	+1¾
Exxon 6s97	6.1	51	97¾	−⅝
Exxon 6½98	6.5	20	99¼	+¼
FMC 9½2000	9.5	13	100½	−½
viFairfd 13¼92	...	10	39	−½
FdMog 8⅜93	8.5	50	99	+2
FedN zr14s	...	20	15¾	−¼
Fldcst 6s12	cv	22	62⅜	−⅜
FleetF 11¼93	10.7	15	105	+1
Flemg 6½96	cv	5	98	+½
Flwr 8¼05	cv	36	109	−3
FrdC 8.7s99	8.7	10	100⅜	−¾
FrdC 7½93	7.4	10	101	+1
FrdC 8⅜01	8.4	175	99½	−¼
FrdC 8⅜02	8.4	75	99½	+⅝
FrdC 8½02	8.6	20	99⅜	...
FrpMCG zr11	...	20	27⅛	+⅝
FreptM 10⅞01	10.7	23	102	+¾
Frpt dc6.55s01	cv	1	92	+2
FreptM zr06	...	3	28⅞	+⅛
Fuqua 9½98	10.8	67	88	+1
Fuqua 9⅞97	10.5	6	94	−¼
GMA 7¾94	7.8	544	100	...
GMA 7¼95	7.3	42	99⅝	+¼
GMA 7.85s98	7.9	64	99	−1
GMA 8⅞99	8.8	100	100⅜	−⅝
GMA 8¾s00	8.7	26	100⅛	+⅛
GMA 8¾s01	8.8	39	99⅞	+½
GMA 8⅛96	8.1	43	100⅜	−¼
GMA 8s02	8.3	50	96⅜	−⅞
GMA 8s07	8.5	10	94	−1
GMA 8¼06	8.4	27	98¼	+1¼
GMA 8.65s08	8.8	210	98¾	...
GMA dc6s11	8.2	20	72¾	+⅝
GMA zr12	...	114	139⅛	+1⅛
GMA zr15	...	89	111	+2¼
GMA 10⅜95	10.1	112	102⅝	−⅛
GMA 8⅞96	8.7	320	102⅛	+⅝
GMA 8s96	8.0	110	100½	...
GMA 8¼16	8.9	92	92¾	+¼
GMA 8s93J	7.8	35	102	−⅛
GMA 8s94	7.8	85	103	−¼
GMA 7⅞97	7.9	106	99⅝	−⅜
GTE 10⅝95	10.2	50	104	−⅞
GdDyn 5¾11	...	40	83	...
GnDyn 9s16	9.1	30	99⅜	...
GnEl 7½96	7.3	160	102¼	...
GnEl 8½04	8.3	35	102½	−⅜
GMills 9⅜09	9.3	2	100½	−4 5/16
GM 8⅝s05	8.7	45	99	−¾
MGMUA 13s96f	...	329	61⅞	−⅛
MfrH 8⅛07	8.6	5	94½	+1⅛
MarO 8.5s06	8.5	25	99¾	+¾
MarO 9½94	9.0	182	105¼	+⅛
MarO 9¾99	9.3	1	104¾	−⅛
MarkIV 12⅜03	11.9	20	104	+¼
MarkIV 13⅜99	12.5	4	107¼	−¼
Marriott zr06	...	17	30	+½
Masco 5¼12	6.5	29	80½	+1½
Maxus 8½08	10.4	1	81½	−1½
McCro 7⅝97	24.6	10	31	−½
McDe 10s03	10.0	18	100¼	+¼
McDnl zr94	...	100	89⅜	−½
McDnl 9¾19	9.3	30	105⅛	−⅛
Mead 6¾12	cv	4	92½	+1¼
MichB 7¾11	7.8	5	98⅞	−⅛
MichB 7s12	7.5	5	93	+1
MichB 9.6s08	9.2	12	104 7/32	+3/16
MidlBk 11.35s93	12.7	154	89¼	−⅛
MMM 8.85s	8.6	1	102¼	...
MPac 4¼05	6.3	8	67⅜	+¼
MPac 5s45f	...	6	57½	+½
Mobil 8½01	8.3	59	102⅜	+⅜
Mobil 7⅛92	7.1	50	99 27/32	−17/32
Mobil 8⅝94	8.1	25	106⅞	−½
MobO 7⅜01	7.4	30	99⅝	−⅜
Monog 10s99	19.9	10	50⅜	−1⅞
Mons 9⅛00	8.9	10	103	+1⅛
MorKnd zr05	...	37	40	+¼
Motrla zr09	...	181	36	+¼
MtSTI 7⅜11	7.7	20	95⅜	+⅛
MtSTI 7¾13	8.0	74	97⅛	−⅜
MtSTI 9¾12	9.3	12	104⅜	−1⅜
MtSTI 9⅝15	9.2	53	105	...
MtSTI 8s17	8.1	45	98⅞	−⅜
MtStTI 9¼14	8.9	3	103⅝	−⅝
NJBTI 7¾13	7.8	3	98¾	...
NJBTI 8¾18	8.5	7	102⅞	−1⅛
Nabis 7¾s03	8.2	15	94⅛	−¼
viNtGyp zr04	...	343	4¼	...
NtEdu 6½11	cv	5	67	−¾
NMed zr04	...	40	42⅜	+1⅞
NavFin 11.95s95	11.6	25	103	+1
Navstr 9s04	9.6	80	94	+⅜
NYEG 9⅜05	8.9	12	104⅞	+1⅞
NYEG 8⅝07	8.7	1	99½	+⅛
NoPac 4s97st	4.6	23	87¼	+2¼
NwnBl 7⅞11	8.0	5	98¾	−¼
NwnBl 7½05	7.5	20	100	+2⅞
NwnBl 10s14	9.5	10	105¼	−½
NwnBl 8⅝12	8.5	10	102	...
NwnBl 9½16	9.1	20	104	...
Oakin 10½02	cv	4	95	−⅛
OcciP 10⅞96	10.3	35	105¼	−⅛
OcciP 11¾11	10.0	60	118	−⅛
OcciP 10¾98	9.9	8	108⅛	+1⅛
OcciP 9⅝99	8.9	265	108¾	+⅛
OcciP 10⅛01	9.0	2	112⅜	+¼
OhBIT 7½11	7.9	20	95¼	−½
OhBIT 7⅞13	8.0	14	98⅝	...
OhEd 8½06	8.4	30	101	...
OhEd 9½08	9.2	1	103⅝	−1¾
Omnicm 7s13	cv	15	129	+1¼
RapA 11s05f	...	1	¾	−⅛
RelGp 9⅞98	11.6	5	85	−2
RelGp 9⅞99	11.6	25	85	−¾
RelGp 14s96	14.4	12	97	+½
RelGp 11s96	13.6	15	81	−1
RelGp 14¼98t	15.0	10	94¾	+¼
viRepStl 8.9s95f	...	20	12¼	−¾
Revln 11¾95	11.7	40	100½	+½
RiteA zr06	cv	80	38½	−1
RocInt 8⅞99	8.4	2	106	−1⅞
Rohr 7s12	cv	65	78	+½
SallM zr22	...	20	8 19/32	...
SalmIn 8s97	8.0	125	100	+⅛
SalmnIn 8s96	8.0	115	100	−⅜
Seagrm zr06	...	6	51	+¾
Sears 7½99t	7.5	15	100	...
Sears 9½99	8.6	147	109⅞	+⅞
SensorE 01	cv	5	129	−6
Sequa 10½98	10.6	85	99	−1
SvceCp 6½11	cv	1	108½	−1
SvceCp 6½01	cv	51	104	+2
ShrLehm 10¾96	10.0	1	107½	−2
ShellO 8½00	8.3	46	102⅛	−⅛
ShellO 8¾05	8.5	36	103	+⅞
ShellO 8s07	7.9	20	101⅜	−⅝
SNET 8⅛08	8.1	25	100½	+⅛
Sonat zr05	...	14	36¼	−⅛
SoCG 8.85s95	8.7	5	101¼	+¼
StdCmcl 07	cv	1	115	+9½
StdPac 12¾99	12.8	33	100	...
StrlSft 8s01	cv	78	112½	−5½
StoneCn 13⅝95	13.3	362	102¾	+⅜
StoneCn 11½99	11.4	663	100¾	−¼
StoneCn 11⅞98	11.5	80	103¼	+½
Sunsh 9s94f	...	36	24⅛	−2⅞
Sunsh 9½94f	...	76	26	...
Sunsh 8s95f	...	5	26	...
Sunsh 8½95f	...	25	27	...
Sunsh 9½95f	...	46	27	−¼
Sunsh 10¾95f	...	29	28½	+½
SwstFrst 12⅛01	12.4	12	98	+6½
TCFox 10¼98	10.5	24	98	+1½
TCFox 13¼00	13.2	7	100¾	−¼
TVA 7s97	6.9	46	101	−¾
TVA 7.4s97	7.3	55	101¼	−1⅛
TVA 7.4s97r	7.3	17	101½	+⅛
TV 7¾s98C	7.6	20	102	...
TV 7¾98Cr	7.6	29	102	...
Teledy 10s04A	10.0	69	100½	−⅛
Teledy 10s04C	9.9	101	100⅞	...
TencCr 8⅜97	8.5	100	98¼	+¼
TencCr 9¾94	9.4	10	103⅝	−⅛
TencoCr 9s95	8.7	5	103	+1
TennGas 8⅜02	8.6	20	97⅞	+1⅜
TennGas dc6s11	8.7	58	69⅛	...
TennGas 10¼16	9.9	5	103¼	+⅝
TennGas 9⅜17	9.6	56	97½	−¾
Tenco 10s08	9.2	10	109	+7
Tesor dc12¾01	15.7	25	81	+2⅞
Texco 9s99D	8.6	10	105⅛	−1⅞
Texco 5¾97	6.0	48	95⅜	−⅝
Texco 8⅞05	8.6	10	102¾	...
Texco 8½06	8.4	11	101¼	...
TxInd 9s08	cv	56	90	+2¼
Textrn 9¼16	9.3	50	100	+2
Tidwtr 7s10	cv	55	79⅛	−⅜
Time 9⅞09	9.9	2	99¼	...
Time 8¾17	9.8	25	89⅜	−2
TolEd 9s00	8.9	20	101¼	−1½
TolEd 8s03	8.1	10	98½	+1⅞
TrailF 8½96	9.3	30	91	−2
TrvIr 8.7s95	8.6	5	101	−¼
TrvIr 7⅝97	7.6	175	100¼	...
TrvIr 8.32s15	cv	33	94½	−1
TucEP 8⅛01	9.2	21	88	+2½
TucEP 7.65s03	8.9	65	86	+½
TucEP 10½05	10.6	35	99	−1¾
UCCEL 7¼95	cv	5	88⅛	...
UGI 9s19x	9.2	15	98⅛	+⅝
UJer 7¾97	8.4	5	92	...
UNC 7½06	cv	1	74½	−½
viUSHo 13¼94f	...	20	48⅞	−⅜
US West zr11	...	525	26⅛	...
USAir 12⅞00	13.4	75	95¾	+1
USG na16s08	...	161	12¾	+⅛
USGy 7⅞04	16.5	10	53	...
USLICO 8s11	cv	4	88	...
USLICO 8½14	cv	15	94½	...
USX 4⅝96	4.9	31	93½	+¼
USX 7¾01	7.9	10	98½	...
USX 5¾01	cv	11	77¾	...
USX 9s92	9.0	5	100	...
USX 7s17	cv	74	93½	...
USX zr05	cv	142	34¼	−¾
UCarb 5.3s97	6.0	4	88¾	−½
UCarb 7½12	cv	120	84	+1
UCarb 9¾94	9.5	5	102⅜	−½
Unisys 13⅞92	14.8	777	94	−1¼
Unisys 10¾95	14.1	46	76½	+⅛
Unisys 8.2s96	11.8	10	69¾	+1¾
Unisy na15s97	...	5	82	+1
UnTel zr06	...	101	32⅜	+⅛
Utilicp 6⅝11	cv	25	121	+1
Valhi 12½98	12.5	75	100⅛	+⅜
WPI 10s01	10.3	29	97	+1¾
WarC 9⅛96	9.1	51	100	...
WarC 10⅞95	10.5	21	103¾	+¾
WasteM 01s	...	20	146½	+2½
WasteM zr12	...	23	36⅝	+⅜
Weingrt 8s09	cv	25	101½	+½
Wendys 7¼10	cv	5	91	...
Wendys 7s06	cv	50	101	...
WstCNA 7¼15	cv	8	53	+1¼
WstDig 9s14	cv	9	37½	+½
WstC 8⅜96	8.4	10	100	...
WstgE 9s09	cv	116	120	+¾
Wstvco 8⅛07	8.6	40	94	...
Weyh 5¼17	cv	5	76	−3½
Whirl zr11	...	60	30	−½
Witco 5½12	cv	70	91	+2½
WUTI 16s91f	...	4	26	+1
Xerox 6s95	cv	26	99⅛	−⅞
Xerox 8⅝99	8.5	10	102	...
viYngS 4½90f	...	5	105	−1
viYngtS 4½90r	...	12	105	−¼
viYngS 10½00f	...	13	139	−1
Zenith 6¼11	cv	78	47½	+¾

FOREIGN BONDS
Volume, $160,000

Bonds	Cur Yld	Vol	Close	Net Chg.
Asian zr92s	...	45	96¾	+11/32
Austla 13⅜07	12.5	16	107	...

EXPLANATORY NOTES
(For New York and American Bonds)

Yield is current yield.

cv-Convertible bond. cf-Certificates. dc-Deep discount. ec-European currency units. f-Dealt in flat. il-Italian lire. kd-Danish kroner. m-Matured bonds, negotiability impaired by maturity. na-No accrual. r-Registered. rp-Reduced principal. st-Stamped. t-Floating rate. wd-When distributed. ww-With warrants. x-Ex interest. xw-Without warrants. zr-Zero coupon.

vj-In bankruptcy or receivership or being reorganized under the Bankruptcy Act, or securities assumed by such companies.

SOURCE: *The Wall Street Journal*, January 3, 1992. Reprinted by permission of *The Wall Street Journal*,

EXHIBIT 8.4

The Wall Street Journal's Bond Market Data Bank

BOND MARKET DATA BANK 1/2/92

MAJOR INDEXES

HIGH	LOW (12 MOS)		CLOSE	NET CHG	% CHG	12-MO CHG	% CHG	FROM 12/31	% CHG
U.S. TREASURY SECURITIES (Lehman Brothers indexes)									
3554.97	3112.54	Intermediate	3550.40	− 4.57	− 0.13	+ 422.04	+ 13.49	− 4.57	− 0.13
4351.88	3612.40	Long-term	4323.72	− 28.16	− 0.65	+ 600.15	+ 16.12	− 28.16	− 0.65
1442.36	1283.22	Long-term (price)	1432.41	− 9.95	− 0.69	+ 91.35	+ 6.81	− 9.95	− 0.69
3736.97	3223.97	Composite	3726.75	− 10.22	− 0.27	+ 463.61	+ 14.21	− 10.22	− 0.27
U.S. CORPORATE DEBT ISSUES (Merrill Lynch)									
568.73	478.95	Corporate Master	567.23	− 1.50	− 0.26	+ 83.01	+ 17.14	− 1.50	− 0.26
424.52	363.43	1-10 Yr Maturities	423.86	− 0.66	− 0.16	+ 58.51	+ 16.01	− 0.66	− 0.16
425.49	351.49	10+ Yr Maturities	423.93	− 1.56	− 0.37	+ 66.16	+ 18.49	− 1.56	− 0.37
234.98	172.49	High Yield	234.98	+ 0.30	+ 0.13	+ 60.52	+ 34.69	+ 0.30	+ 0.13
413.97	346.64	Yankee Bonds	412.38	− 1.59	− 0.38	+ 61.77	+ 17.62	− 1.59	− 0.38
TAX-EXEMPT SECURITIES (Bond Buyer; Merrill Lynch: Dec. 31, 1986 = 100)									
96-16	90-22	Bond Buyer Municipal	96-16	unch		+ 4-25	+ 5.21	unch	
139.54	123.64	New 10-yr G.O. (AA)	139.54	+ 0.04	+ 0.03	+ 15.13	+ 12.16	+ 0.04	+ 0.03
144.49	126.80	New 20-yr G.O. (AA)	144.49	+ 0.05	+ 0.03	+ 15.79	+ 12.27	+ 0.05	+ 0.03
164.99	141.51	New 30-yr revenue (A)	164.99	+ 0.06	+ 0.04	+ 21.94	+ 15.34	+ 0.06	+ 0.04
MORTGAGE-BACKED SECURITIES (current coupon; Merrill Lynch: Dec. 31, 1986 = 100)									
172.60	142.87	Ginnie Mae (GNMA)	171.82	− 0.78	− 0.45	+ 26.61	+ 18.33	− 0.78	− 0.45
171.29	142.71	Fannie Mae (FNMA)	171.26	− 0.03	− 0.02	+ 26.27	+ 18.12	− 0.03	− 0.02
170.01	142.28	Freddie Mac (FHLMC)	169.98	− 0.03	− 0.02	+ 25.30	+ 17.49	− 0.03	− 0.02
CONVERTIBLE BONDS (Merrill Lynch: Dec. 31, 1986 = 100)									
149.59	121.66	Investment Grade	149.59	+ 0.46	+ 0.31	+ 26.77	+ 21.80	+ 0.46	+ 0.31
139.63	99.48	High Yield	139.63	+ 0.83	+ 0.60	+ 38.60	+ 38.21	+ 0.83	+ 0.60

CORPORATE BONDS

Quotes of representative taxable issues at mid-afternoon New York time, provided by First Boston/CSFB Ltd.

ISSUE (RATING: MOODY'S/S&P)	COUPON	MATURITY	PRICE	CHANGE	YIELD	CHANGE
FINANCIAL						
Citicorp (Baa3/BBB+)	9.000	04/15/99	92.939	0.135	10.401	− 0.027
Ford Credit Co (A2/A)	8.875	06/15/99	104.069	0.690	8.135	− 0.123
Ford Credit Co (A2/A)	9.300	03/15/95	106.368	− 0.187	7.038	0.062
GMAC (A1/A)	8.000	10/15/93	102.878	− 0.163	6.263	0.093
GMAC (A1/A)	8.250	08/01/96	102.717	− 0.299	7.535	0.077
Household Fin (A3/A+)	7.750	10/01/99	97.770	0.423	8.140	− 0.076
UTILITY						
Commonwlth Ed (A3/A−)	9.625	07/01/19	107.439	− 0.546	8.896	0.050
Pacific G&E (A1/A)	8.125	01/01/97	102.038	− 0.216	7.626	0.052
Sou Bell Tel (Aaa/AAA)	8.500	08/01/29	101.69[illegible]	− [illegible]	8.351	0.050
Sou Cal Ed (Aa2/AA)	9.375	02/15/17	106.82[illegible]	− 0.537	8.700	0.050
US West Commun (Aa3/AA−)	8.875	06/01/31	104.821	− 0.598	8.450	0.050
INDUSTRIAL						
Amoco (Aaa/AAA)	8.625	12/15/16	104.551	− 0.550	8.193	0.050
Capital Cities (A1/A+)	8.750	03/15/16	102.061	− 0.518	8.545	0.050
Du Pont & Co (Aa2/AA)	6.000	12/01/01	90.420	0.339	7.378	− 0.052
Exxon Shipping (Aaa/AAA)	Zero	09/01/12	19.024	− 0.155	8.194	0.042
East Kodak (A2/A−)	9.125	03/01/98	107.069	unch	7.661	unch
Mobil (Aa2/AA)	8.625	07/01/94	107.128	0.059	5.530	− 0.027
FOREIGN						
Hydro-Quebec (Aa3/AA−)	8.500	12/01/29	100.894	− 0.576	8.420	0.050
Int Bk Recon Dev (Aaa/AAA)	9.875	10/01/97	115.722	− 0.312	6.545	0.059
Sweden (Aa1/AAA)	8.125	11/01/96	104.612	− 0.227	6.980	0.054
Victoria Finance (Aa2/AA)	8.450	10/01/01	104.994	− 0.358	7.709	0.051

SOURCE: *The Wall Street Journal*, January 3, 1992. Reprinted by permission of *The Wall Street Journal*, high tax brackets may prefer municipal bonds to corporate bonds since the government will tax away much of the interest from corporate issues. Also, if market interest rates increase, investors will suffer dropping principal values of their bonds and capital losses if they cannot wait for better times to sell.

Some speculators seek profits by trading bonds. If you anticipate trends in the money markets correctly, you may purchase bonds cheaply when interest rates are high and sell them at high prices when yields fall. If you had purchased bonds in August 1984 and held them through March 1985, you might have earned a return of about 20 percent. Such a high return generally requires the perfect vision of hindsight, but this kind of pattern may well develop in future bond markets.

The "Bond Markets" and "Financing Business" columns in *The Wall Street Journal* help investors keep informed about conditions in the money and bond markets. In addition, these columns furnish general news about the national economy, the U.S. Treasury, the Federal Reserve System, and the current political environment. Moody's *Manuals* and Standard & Poor's *Bond Guide* provide ample financial information about specific bond issues. Other sections of *The Wall Street Journal* and Standard & Poor's *Trade and Security Statistics* provide additional factual data about bond yields and prices. You should become familiar with these sources of information.

Convertible Bonds and Bonds with Warrants

Special types of corporate bonds include convertible bonds, which allow bondholders to exchange their bonds for stated amounts of common stock, and bonds with **warrants,** which give holders rights to buy common stock directly from issuing corporations at specified prices for specified periods of time. These securities offer an opportunity to share in the growing earnings of a company or to continue to receive fixed income payments.

warrant: A certificate attached to a bond issue granting the right during a period of time to buy a specified number of shares of common stock directly from the issuing firm at a specified price.

The chance for profit participation offered by convertible bonds and warrants eliminates the major disadvantage of corporate bonds: their fixed interest payments in changeable times. These attractive features have their prices, though. Convertible bonds generally have lower ratings than nonconvertible bonds of the same company. Convertible bonds are usually rated Baa and pay interest at lower rates than nonconvertible Baa bonds. Bonds with warrants generally pay lower rates of interest than comparable conventional bonds. Investors who buy bonds with warrants or convertible bonds hope to trade some current yield for a chance to participate in the company's earnings growth through the increased value of its common stock.

Convertible Bonds

Convertible bond indentures state the terms under which bondholders can convert their bonds into set numbers of shares of common stock. The

conversion price: The common stock price at which the par value of a convertible bond may be exchanged for common stock.

conversion value: The value of a convertible bond in terms of shares of stock for which the holder can exchange it, found by multiplying the number of shares to which the bond converts by the current market price of the stock.

defensive–aggressive characteristic: The combination of debt and equity characteristics of a convertible bond that allows the investor to profit in a rising stock market while at the same time enjoying the safety of contractually mandated interest payments.

conversion price, or number of shares to which each bond converts, is determined by the company in terms either of a given number of shares or a price at which the par value of the bond can be exchanged. At a conversion price of $20, a $1,000 bond would convert into 50 shares.

The firm sets the conversion price above the market price for the stock when it issues the bonds. Suppose that the stock is trading for $18 per share when the firm sets a conversion price of $20. This gives a value for the bond in terms of stock, or a **conversion value,** of $900, or 50 shares times $18 market price per share. When the market price of stock increases in the future, the conversion value of the bond will also increase. If the price of stock were to increase to $25 per share, the conversion value of the bond would increase to $1,250 (50 shares times $25). Convertible bonds normally sell at premiums over their conversion values because they offer both the price appreciation potential of common stock and higher cash yields.

If the price of the stock falls, so will the conversion value and, therefore, the price of the convertible bond. Since the bond still pays interest, however, its price will move with the market prices of other bonds of comparable quality, even when the price of the stock falls substantially. An investment in convertible bonds increases in value when the market price of the stock increases, but it does not decline proportionally if the market price of the stock decreases. This gives the convertible bond a considerable advantage in its **defensive–aggressive characteristic.**

Excellent sources of information about convertible securities are found in the Kalb, Voorhis and Company's weekly *Convertible Factfinder* and *Convertible Bond Chart Book*, RHM Associates' *Convertible Survey*, and the convertible bond section of Standard & Poor's *Bond Guide*.

Bonds with Warrants

Firms sometimes package warrants to buy stock with either bonds or preferred stock. A warrant is an option to buy a certain number of shares of common stock directly from the issuing company at a set price for a limited number of years. A warrant attached to a bond gives the bondholder the chance to participate in the company's earnings growth without relinquishing the safety of the bond. If the common stock price increases, the holder can either sell the warrants, since their value follows the stock price, or exercise the warrants and buy the stock. The substantial risk in the stock market may keep the investor from profiting from the warrants, but he or she still owns the bond, whatever happens to the common stock.

Preferred Stock As an Investment

Investors refer to preferred and common stock of corporations as equities, or ownership securities. Equity securities represent capital invested in a corporation by its owners, as compared to debt securities, which

EXHIBIT 8.5

Corporate Balance Sheet Accounts

ASSETS	LIABILITIES
WHAT A COMPANY OWNS	WHAT A COMPANY OWES
Current assets	Current liabilities
Cash in banks and in securities	Accounts payable—charges for purchases of materials
Accounts receivable from customers	Loans from banks
Inventories for production	Long-term debt
Fixed assets	Long-term bonds
Buildings and land	Borrowed capital
Equipment to produce products	Net worth—what is provided by the owners
	Preferred stock
	Common stock
	Retained earnings

Assets = Liabilities plus net worth

represent capital corporations must repay to lenders. Owners of both preferred and common stock receive dividends as payment for use of their capital in the business, although preferred stock dividends normally are fixed and do not change with the changing fortunes of the firm. The ownership or equity position of preferred and common stockholders is reflected in both the balance sheet and the income statement of the corporation.

Exhibit 8.5 shows the relationship of preferred and common stock to the firm's other assets and liabilities. No numbers are provided since we want to focus on the relationships involved. The balance sheet lists preferred and common stock as parts of the net worth of the company. Both classes of stock give their owners claims against the assets of the company, but only after the suppliers of debt capital, both long-term and short-term, are satisfied. This means that owners accept more risk than lenders. However, some owners—the preferred stockholders—have a senior position in relation to the common stockholders, who have only residual claims, after all other claims are satisfied.

The income statement in Exhibit 8.6 shows that the firm pays dividends on preferred stock before common dividends and after corporate taxes. It pays interest on debt before taxes and before any dividends on any classes of stock.

Any earnings the firm retains and reinvests in the business increase the assets of the business and its net worth. This benefits common stockholders directly since they can claim all earnings after bondholders and preferred stockholders are paid. Retained earnings only indirectly improve the security

EXHIBIT 8.6

Corporate Income Statement Accounts

Sales or revenues
− Cost of goods (use of inventory sold)
= Gross profit
− Selling expenses
− General expenses
− Depreciation (use of fixed assets)
= Net profit
+ Other income (interest and dividends)
− Other expenses (interest expense—use of debt capital)
= Net income before federal income taxes
− Federal income taxes
= Net income available for owners
− Preferred dividends
= Net income available for common stockholders
− Common dividends
= Net income reinvested in business assets
(Increases retained earnings and assets)

of lenders and preferred stockholders, whose dividends do not rise with rising earnings, by improving the solvency of the business. These relationships should guide evaluation of preferred and common stock for investments. Common stock offers a potential for higher returns, but only at the cost of higher risk.

Preferred stock represents a part of the permanent ownership capital of a business. Unlike common stock, however, the dividend on preferred is usually fixed, making it more appealing to risk-averse investors. It gets the name *preferred* from the fact that its dividends must be paid before dividends on common stock can be paid, so it gives the owner a more secure return than does common stock.

Preferred stockholders also have preferred claims to assets over common stockholders if the company should fail and be liquidated or reorganized. In the event of bankruptcy, proceeds from liquidation of assets must first satisfy claims of secured creditors who held claims to specific assets through mortgage bonds or similar securities. Bondholders are paid next, and then preferred stockholders receive their share. Anything that remains is distributed to the common stockholders.

The amount of the dividend on preferred stock is usually stated as a dollar amount, or as a percentage of the par value of the stock, and paid quarterly. Unlike a bond, the par value of which is returned to the owner at maturity, the par value of a share of stock is simply an arbitrary value set to aid bookkeeping because stock has no fixed maturity date.

Most preferred stock carries a par value of $100. Thus an 8 percent, $100 par value share of preferred stock paying quarterly dividends would pay a dividend of $8 per year, at the rate of $2 per quarter.

Usual Features of Preferred Stock

cumulative dividend: A preferred stock dividend that accumulates if not paid on time and must be paid in full before any dividends may be paid on common stock.

arrearage: A cumulative preferred stock dividend that has not yet been paid.

nonparticipating preferred stock: Preferred stock that does not share in the increased earnings of a corporation, but instead generates a set dividend payment, whatever the company's fortunes.

Typically, preferred stock pays **cumulative dividends.** A firm faces no contractual obligation to pay dividends, even on preferred stock, that is comparable to the obligation to pay interest on bonds. If it fails to pay preferred dividends, however, they accumulate and it must pay the total accumulated sum before it can pay any common stock dividends. Unpaid, accumulated dividends are called **arrearages.**

Although holders of preferred stock enjoy preferential treatment with respect to assets and earnings, they usually have no authority to vote in ownership decisions. They may get the right to vote in some director elections if preferred dividends are in arrears.

Preferred stock has no maturity date, but management can normally call it as it can call bonds. Investors should review details of this provision carefully, since the company may call a high-yielding preferred issue in a time of low interest rates.

Most preferred issues are **nonparticipating preferred stock.** They do not participate in a company's earnings growth, but continue to earn the same dividends whether the company prospers or flounders. Dividends on participating preferred stock are structured to increase with increases in earnings.

Convertible Preferred Stock

Some preferred stock issues offer a convertibility feature, allowing owners to exchange their preferred shares for common stock at some predetermined ratio. Convertible preferred stock functions in essentially the same way as convertible bonds.

Most investors who buy convertible preferred stock want higher dividends than common stocks pay, but they want to participate in the increases in the firm's common stock price. Since the preferred stockholder can convert his or her shares into common stock at a fixed conversion rate, the price of the convertible will increase if the price of the common increases.

Investors can find information about convertible preferred stock in a variety of sources. Price information is available in *The Wall Street Journal*, but the listings of preferred stocks do not indicate which issues are convertible. Even if they did, the terms of conversion from preferred to common would remain a mystery. Instead, look to Standard & Poor's *Stock Guide* for information about convertible issues.

Preferred Stock Yields and Prices

If you wanted to invest in preferred stocks, where would you find information on which to base your trading decisions? You would want to know issues' prices, yields, quality ratings, and risk levels, all in the context of opportunities offered by other investments. First, you would need information about which firms have issued preferred stock, the current prices of these shares, the dividends they pay, and their current yields (found by dividing dividend by price). *The Wall Street Journal* stock listings, like the sample in Exhibit 8.7, can provide all this information.

To find a listing for a preferred stock issue, look down the third column, headed "Stock," for a listing with the designation "pf." This abbreviation indicates a preferred stock. In the third column of the sample in the exhibit, "BethSteel" indicates a preferred issue of Bethlehem Steel Corporation. The listing shows that this stock pays a dividend of $5.00, which gives a current yield of 10.4 percent. The two columns at the far left show that, over the previous 52 weeks, the stock ranged in price from a low of 37⅛ to a high of 50. The column headed "Vol 100s" reports that 3,800 shares of the Bethlehem Steel preferred traded during the previous day. Its high and low prices for the day were 48¼ and 43¾, and the stock closed at 48¼.

Preferred stocks are riskier investments than bonds because, unlike bond interest payments, firms have no contractual obligation to pay preferred stock dividends. Therefore, the familiar risk–return tradeoff would lead us to expect rates of return on preferred stock to exceed those on bonds, but this is not the case. Preferred stock generally provides lower rates of return than bonds due to the **intercorporate dividend credit,** a provision in the tax law that allows one corporation to avoid paying taxes on 70 percent of the cash dividends from the preferred stock of another corporation. Without this provision corporations would suffer double taxation of their earnings, since the corporation that issued the preferred would pay tax on its earnings, then the corporation that owned the stock would pay tax on the same earnings when distributed in the form of dividends.

intercorporate dividend credit: The provision in the tax law that allows a corporation to escape taxation on 85 percent of dividends from preferred stock of another corporation.

Bond interest, on the other hand, is deductible from taxable income for the issuer, but fully taxable for the bond owner. Thus a dollar of preferred dividends is worth much more to a corporation than a dollar of bond interest, so corporate investors are willing to accept much lower yields on preferred stock than on bonds. For this reason individual investors generally find preferred stocks attractive only if they are convertible or participating, or if other market forces push their yields above bond yields for a time.

Preferred Stock Ratings and Issuer Information

Both Moody's and Standard & Poor's rate preferred stock in much the same way that they rate bonds. No preferred issue can receive a D rating, though, because preferred stocks are equity securities, so failure to pay dividends

EXHIBIT 8.7

Price Quotes on Preferred Stock

Quotations as of 5 p.m. Eastern Time
Thursday, January 2, 1992

52 Weeks Hi	Lo	Stock	Sym	Div	Yld %	PE	Vol 100s	Hi	Lo	Close	Net Chg
		-A-A-A-									
16⅞	9¼	AAR	AIR	.48	3.6	18	722	13⅜	12⅞	13⅜	− ⅛
11⅝	10⅜	ACM Gvt Fd	ACG	1.26	11.2	...	938	11⅜	11⅛	11¼	...
9¾	8¾	ACM OppFd	AOF	1.01e	10.5	...	134	9⅝	9½	9⅝	...
11	9⅜	ACM SecFd	GSF	1.26	11.7	...	1050	10¾	10⅝	10¾	...
9½	8¼	ACM SpctrmFd	SI	1.01	11.2	...	426	9⅛	9	9	...
n 9⅛	7⅝	ACM MgdIncFd	AMF	1.01	11.1	...	169	9⅛	9	9⅛	+ ⅛
12⅞	11½	ACM MgdMultFd	MMF	1.35	10.6	...	185	12¾	12⅝	12¾	+ ⅛
21½	5	ADT adr	ADTA	.32e	4.4	2	164	7¼	7	7¼	+ ⅛
n 9½	5	ADT	ADT		...	...	1096	7⅜	7⅛	7⅜	+ ¼
24¾	14⅜	AL Labs A	BMD	.16	.7	26	341	24¼	23	23½	−1
1⅞	¾	AM Int	AM		...	...	415	15/16	⅞	15/16	...
12	4⅛	AM Int pf		1.50j	...	...	75	5	4⅞	5	...
11¾	9⅛	AMEV Sec	AMV	1.08	9.6	...	29	11⅜	11¼	11¼	− ⅛
71⅛	44¼	AMR	AMR		...	...	4053	70¼	68⅜	69½	−1
44¼	33⅛	ARCO Chm	RCM	2.50	6.3	20	81	39¾	39½	39⅝	− ⅛
2⅝	1	ARX	ARX		...	...	15	1⅝	1½	1½	...
56	41½	ASA	ASA	3.00	6.4	...	770	47¼	46¼	46¾	− ⅛
6½	**2⅛**	**ATT Cap yen wt**			...	...	**145**	**4½**	**4¼**	**4½**	+ ¼
69¾	39¼	AbbotLab	ABT	1.00	1.5	27	8941	67⅞	66	67¼	−1⅝
14⅝	9⅞	Abitibi g	ABY	.50	...	...	12	12½	12½	12½	...
6	3⅜	AcmeElec	ACE		...	...	43	4¾	4⅝	4¾	...
7½	4½	AcmeCleve	AMT	.40	5.5	...	234	7¼	7	7¼	...
40	22¾	Acuson	ACN		...	22	1691	32¼	30¾	32⅛	...
20¼	14¼	AdamsExp	ADX	1.63e	8.6	...	231	19	18⅞	19	...
9⅜	3⅞	AdobeRes	ADB		...	...	210	5⅜	5	5⅛	− ¼
20⅛	12⅞	AdobeRes pf			...	...	41	15¼	14½	14½	− ½
18	10¾	AdobeRes pf			...	...	64	12	11¾	12	− ¼
▲ 17¾	4	AdvMicro	AMD		...	...	11925	18	17⅜	17⅞	+ ⅜
43	18	AdvMicro pf		3.00	7.0	...	557	43	42¼	42⅞	+ ⅝
▲ **5⅛**	**2¼**	**Advest**	**ADV**		...	...	**926**	**5⅞**	**5**	**5¾**	+ ⅝
70⅜	54¾	Aegon	AEG	3.72r	5.3	7	2	70⅜	70¼	70⅜	+ ⅜
49⅛	31⅞	AetnaLife	AET	2.76	6.4	9	3037	43¾	42⅝	43¼	− ¾
10⅝	6⅝	AffilPub	AFP	.24	2.8	78	508	8⅝	8⅜	8⅝	...
n 23¾	21½	AgriMinl	AMC		...	...	469	23⅜	22⅞	22⅞	− ⅜
20⅞	12	Ahmanson	AHM	.88	5.2	10	3224	17⅝	16¾	17	− ⅜
26¼	24	Ahmanson pf		2.40	9.4	...	149	25⅞	25¼	25½	− ⅛
20	2⅞	Aileen	AEE		...	16	248	18½	18⅛	18⅜	− ¼
74⅛	51¼	AirProduct	APD	1.56	2.1	17	995	74⅛	72⅞	73⅞	...
30	16½	AirbornFrght	ABF	.30	1.2	18	912	24⅜	23⅞	24¼	...
24½	12⅛	Airgas	ARG		...	25	82	24	23⅜	23⅝	− ⅜
▼ **15½**	**9**	**Airlease**	**FLY**	**1.68**	**19.8**	**5**	**235**	**9½**	**8½**	**8½**	−1
26⅜	21	AlaPwr pf		2.06e	8.0	...	45	26⅜	25⅞	25⅞	+ ⅛
11	9⅜	AlaPwr pf		.87	8.3	...	25	10¾	10½	10½	− ¼
107	100	AlaPwr pf		9.44	9.1	...	z80	104	104	104	...
101	88¼	AlaPwr pf		8.16	8.2	...	z2700	100½	99½	99¾	−1¼
101½	87½	AlaPwr pf		8.28	8.3	...	z200	100¼	100¼	100¼	...
25⅜	17¼	AlaskaAir	ALK	.20	.9	...	1040	21¾	21⅝	21¾	...
20	**10**	**AlbanyInt**	**AIN**	**.35**	**2.1**	**60**	**496**	**16¾**	**15⅞**	**16¾**	+ ⅞
34¼	20½	AlbertoCl	ACV	.22	.7	27	195	31½	30¾	30¾	− ⅞
25½	16¾	AlbertoCl A	ACVA	.22	.9	21	649	25	24¼	24¾	− ⅜
51⅜	32⅝	Albertsons	ABS	.56	1.4	21	1593	38⅞	38	38¾	− ½
24	18	Alcan	AL	.60	3.0	26	2267	20⅛	19¾	20⅛	+ ⅛
35⅞	29	AlcoStd	ASN	.92	2.6	18	1148	35¼	34⅛	35¼	+1
27⅝	18	Alex&Alex	AAL	1.00	5.0	18	1018	20⅞	19¾	20	− ½
37½	19¾	Alexanders	ALX		...	...	26	24⅜	24	24⅜	+ ⅛
111	78⅝	AlleghanyCp	Y	1.86t	1.7	13	9	110	108	108½	−2½
29⅛	20¼	AllegLud	ALS	.88	3.1	20	711	28½	27½	28⅛	+ ½
46½	34⅞	AllegPwr	AYP	3.20	7.2	12	1133	44⅞	44⅜	44½	...
20⅛	8¾	AllenGp	ALN	.20b	1.0	15	716	19¾	19½	19¾	+ ⅛
24½	16½	AllenGp pf		1.75	7.7	...	64	22¾	22⅜	22¾	− ¾
25½	16¾	Allergan	AGN	.36	1.5	19	512	24¼	23⅜	24	− ½
34⅜	15¼	AllncCapMgt	AC	2.02e	6.3	17	342	33⅛	31¾	31⅞	−1¼
13⅜	9⅞	AllncGlblEnv	AEF	.18e	1.6	...	68	11⅝	11½	11½	− ⅛
29¼	13	AlliantTech	ATK		...	5	208	22⅛	21¼	21½	− ½
25	18¼	AlldIrishBk pf		2.97	12.6	...	264	23¾	23½	23⅝	...
22	17	AlldIrishBk	AIB	.99e	5.4	...	7	18¼	18¼	18¼	+ ¼
6¾	2¼	AlliedPdts	[illegible]				152	3¼	3⅛	3⅛	...
45	25⅞	[illegible]	[illegible]				[illegible]	[illegible]	40⅞	42	−1⅞

NYSE EXTENDED TRADING

January 2, 1992

	Total Volume	Market Value
First crossing session	75,600	b-$2,733,787
Second session (baskets)	3,871,203	$120,488,968

MOST ACTIVE ISSUES

(First session)

Issue	Sym.	a-Volume 100s	NYSE Close	Comp. Close
Archer-Daniel	ADM	45	31⅞	31⅞
Citicorp	CCI	45	10⅞	10⅞
Amoco Corp	AN	40	50½	50½
Westinghouse	WX	37	18¼	18¼
PepsiCo	PEP	33	33⅞	33⅞
Unisys Corp	UIS	32	4⅝	4⅝
Sears Roebuck	S	25	38⅝	38⅝
Chrysler Corp	C	25	12½	12½
AMR Corp	AMR	23	69½	69½
Hewlett-Pkrd	HWP	23	55⅞	55⅞

a-From 4:15 p.m. to 5:00 p.m. Eastern time, NYSE only. b-WSJ calculation, estimate.

52 Weeks Hi	Lo	Stock	Sym	Div	Yld %	PE	Vol 100s	Hi	Lo	Close	Net Chg
		-B-B-B-									
42⅝	33⅜	BCE Inc g	BCE	2.56	6.2	...	402	41⅜	41	41⅜	+ ⅛
16¼	7¾	BET	BEP	1.50e	10.2	13	168	14⅞	14⅜	14¾	+ ¼
29⅝	13¼	BJ Svc	BJS		...	8	787	15	14⅝	15	+ ⅜
9⅜	3⅛	BMC	BMC			10	42	7¾	7⅝	7¾	+ ⅛
32⅝	26⅝	BP Prudhoe	BPT	4.04e	14.1	7	526	28⅝	27⅞	28⅝	+ ½
30	22¾	BRE Prop	BRE	2.40	8.4	14	68	28½	28⅜	28½	+ ⅛
4⅜	1¾	BRT RltyTr	BRT		...	...	51	2¼	2⅛	2⅛	...
9	3¾	Bairnco	BZ	.20	2.8	15	206	7½	7⅛	7⅛	− ¼
18¼	14⅜	BakrFentrs	BKF	1.60e	9.3	...	144	17¾	17	17¼	− ⅜
31	**17⅞**	**BakrHughs**	**BHI**	**.46**	**2.3**	**17**	**10756**	**20⅜**	**19⅛**	**20⅜**	+1⅛
25	15⅝	BaldorElec	BEZ	.48	2.0	18	26	23⅝	23⅛	23⅝	+ ½
38¼	25⅝	Ball Cp	BLL	1.20	3.2	17	608	38¼	37¾	38	...
6½	1⅞	BallyMfg	BLY				3381	5¼	4⅞	5	− ¼
11⅜	3⅞	BaltimrBcp	BBB		...	...	244	5⅜	5¼	5⅜	+ ⅛
34¼	25¾	BaltimrGE	BGE	2.10	6.2	16	1589	34¼	33½	34⅛	− ⅛
4¾	**2⅜**	**BancFla**	**BFL**		...	...	**133**	**3⅛**	**2¾**	**3⅛**	+ ½
52¾	24⅞	BancOne	ONE	1.16	2.2	17	2621	52⅝	51¾	52	− ⅝
13/16	**7/32**	**BancTexas**	**BTX**		...	...	**289**	**7/16**	**⅜**	**7/16**	+ 1/32
25⅜	24½	BancoBilV pf			...	...	324	25⅜	25⅛	25⅜	+ ⅛
32¾	23⅜	BancoBilV	BBV	1.49e	5.4	6	276	28¼	27½	27¾	− ¼
24⅜	18	BancoCentrl	BCM	.97e	4.9	6	11	20	19⅞	19⅞	− ⅛
55⅞	38¾	BancoSantdr	STD	2.17e	5.1	7	5	42½	42½	42½	− ½
s 47¾	28¼	BcpHawaii	BOH	1.20	2.6	11	573	46	44¼	46	+1
120	81½	Bandag	BDG	1.20	1.0	21	139	119⅝	117⅝	118⅞	−1
18⅛	14¼	BangorHyd	BGR	1.32	7.3	12	54	18	17¾	18	+ ⅛
12⅞	3	BankBost	BKB			...	3805	12	11½	12	+ ½
33	11¼	BankBost pfA		3.37e	10.7	...	9	31½	31¼	31½	...
32	10¾	BankBost pfB		3.25e	10.6		24	30¾	30	30¾	+ ¾
36⅛	16½	BankNY	BK	1.52	4.8	25	1598	31⅜	30	31⅜	+ ½
44¾	23⅛	BankAmer	BAC	1.20	3.2	8	8514	37⅝	35⅜	37⅝	+1¾
46¾	33⅛	BankAmer pfA		3.28e	7.3	...	89	44⅞	43⅝	44¾	− ⅛
73⅜	55¼	BankAmer pfB		6.00	8.2	...	68	73⅜	73⅛	73⅜	
28⅛	25	BankAmer pfF		2.41	8.7	...	116	28	27⅝	27¾	− ¼
56	45½	BankAmer pfG		3.25	6.5	...	395	50¼	49	50¼	+ ½
68	39½	BankTrst	BT	2.80	4.4	9	1808	63⅝	62⅛	63⅝	− ⅛
n 10¾	6¾	BannerAero	BAR		...	9	18	7⅜	7¼	7¼	...
1⅛	5/16	BanyanMtgInv	VMG				240	⅝	9/16	9/16	...
27⅛	23	Barclays pr		2.78	10.6	...	215	26¼	26	26¼	...
27⅛	22½	Barclays prB		2.72	10.5	...	160	26	25¾	26	+ ⅛
27⅝	22¾	Barclays pfC		2.81	10.5	...	103	27⅛	26⅝	26⅞	+ ⅛
27¾	24¾	Barclays pfD		2.87	10.6	...	180	27¾	27⅛	27⅛	− ⅝
36	24	[illegible]					[illegible]	[illegible]	[illegible]	27½	− ½
52	26	Beneficial pf		4.50	8.7		z10	52	52	52	+ ½
▲ 18⅜	12¾	Benetton	BNG	.38e	2.1		22	18½	18¼	18¼	...
1½	**11/16**	**Benguet**	**BE**		...	...	**381**	**13/16**	**¾**	**13/16**	+ 1/16
9125	6550	BerkHathwy	BRK		...	27	z70	8950	8625	8725	−325
n 11	7⅜	BrkshreRlty	BRI	1.50	16.9		389	9	8½	8⅞	+ ¼
20¼	12¾	Berlitz	BTZ	.56	2.8	36	82	20⅛	19½	20⅛	+ ⅜
16½	10½	BerryPete	BRY	.60	5.3	17	142	11¼	11	11¼	+ ⅛
35⅜	5¼	BestBuy	BBY			17	819	16¾	15¾	15⅞	− ⅝
n 26⅜	15⅛	BetHldg	BTV		...	...	611	22⅛	21⅜	21⅞	...
18½	10¾	BethSteel	BS	.40	2.8		2834	14⅛	13⅞	14⅛	+ ⅛
50	37⅛	BethSteel pf		5.00	10.4		38	48¼	47¾	48¼	+ ⅞
25½	19⅜	BethSteel pfB		2.50	10.2	...	56	24⅝	24¼	24½	+ ⅛
12⅜	**6⅞**	**BeverlyEnt**	**BEV**		...	**32**	**4149**	**9⅜**	**8⅞**	**9⅜**	+ ½
19⅜	13⅛	BiocraftLabs	BCL	.10e	.6	...	118	17⅛	16⅜	17	+ ¾
n 13½	7½	BioWhit	BWI		...		184	8¾	8½	8⅝	...
23½	12½	BirmghamStl	BIR	.50	2.2	27	820	22⅞	21¾	22¾	+ ⅞
19⅝	8½	BlackDeck	BDK	.40	2.4	38	2028	17	16½	17	...
43	29⅛	BlackHills	BKH	1.76	4.3	17	111	41½	41	41¼	− ⅛
n 10¾	9⅞	Blackstn1998	BBT	.85	8.2		731	10½	10¼	10⅜	− ⅛
n 11⅜	10	BlackstnAdv	BAT	.98	8.7		141	11¼	11	11¼	...
▲ 10¾	8¾	BlackstnIncTr	BKT	1.00	9.3	...	2134	10⅞	10⅝	10¾	+ ⅛
n 10⅛	9½	BlackstnMuni	BMN	.05e	.5		715	9¾	9⅝	9¾	+ ⅛
n 15⅛	15	BlackstnNoAm	BNA				330	15⅛	15	15⅛	+ ⅛
10⅞	9⅞	BlackstnStrat	BGT	.98	9.1		551	10¾	10½	10¾	+ ⅛
10⅞	9⅞	BlackstnTgt	BTT	.95	8.7		767	10⅞	10¾	10⅞	...
s 38¼	19⅞	BlockHR	HRB		...	28	3080	36⅞	35⅝	36½	−1
s 15¼	7¾	BlockbstrE	BV		...	24	6033	12¼	11⅞	12¼	+ ¼
7¾	5½	BluChipValFd	BLU	.78e	10.1		246	7¾	7⅝	7¾	+ ⅛
53	41¼	Boeing	BA	1.00	2.1	11	10311	47¼	46⅝	47¼	− ½
29¼	**18⅜**	**BoiseCasc**	**BCC**	**.60**	**2.6**	...	**1648**	**23⅜**	**21⅛**	**23⅜**	+1⅛
9⅜	4¼	BoltBerNew	BBN	.06	1.2	19	398	5⅜	5	5⅛	− ¼
15	8⅜	BordChm un	BCP	1.98e	13.4	10	745	14¾	14⅛	14¾	+ ½
14¾	8⅛	BordChm	BCU	1.98e	14.0	10	210	14⅛	13¾	14⅛	+ ⅜
38¾	28¼	BordenInc	BN	1.14	3.5	14	6475	33⅜	32¾	32⅞	+ ¼
20⅞	16	BostCelts	BOS	2.25e	11.4	12	118	19⅞	19½	19¾	− ¼
24⅞	18¼	BostEdsn	BSE	1.64	6.7	13	532	24⅝	24⅜	24⅜	− ⅜
104½	89	BostEdsn pf		8.88	8.7		z570	103	102	102¼	− ¼
▲ 18⅛	14½	BostEdsn pf		1.46	8.1	...	13	18¼	18⅛	18⅛	+ ⅛
30⅜	18⅝	Bowater	BOW	1.20	5.5	14	1043	22⅛	21¼	22	− ⅛
18⅜	**6⅜**	**BrazilFd**	**BZF**		...	...	**1939**	**16**	**14⅝**	**15⅞**	+1⅛
44¾	24½	BriggsStrat	BGG	1.60	3.7	17	206	44	43	43½	− ⅝
s 38	13½	BrinkerInt	EAT			38	490	37⅜	36½	37⅜	− ⅛
89⅜	61⅛	BrisMyrsSqb	BMY	2.76	3.1	23	11171	88¼	86½	88¼	...
44⅜	24½	BritAir	BAB	2.03e	4.7		1088	43½	43⅛	43⅛	−1¼
51⅜	39	BritGas	BRG	3.06e	6.3	10	472	49½	48¾	48¾	+ ⅛
8⅜	1⅛	BritPetrol wt			...	...	1853	1½	1¼	1½	...
77½	61⅞	BritPetrol	BP	4.65e	7.1	16	2793	66⅜	65½	65¾	...
27¾	**11⅛**	**BritSteel**	**BST**	**1.95e**	**14.6**	**8**	**4406**	**13½**	**12⅝**	**13⅜**	+ ¾
74	51¼	BritTelcom	BTY	3.20e	5.1	10	1215	62¾	62½	62⅝	+ ⅛
23⅜	22⅞	BritTelcom pp			...	...	610	23¼	23¼	23¼	...
19⅞	**4⅝**	**BroadInc**	**BRO**	**.20**	**1.1**	**14**	**2016**	**19½**	**18⅛**	**18½**	−1¼
15½	12⅜	BroadInc pf			...		14	14⅝	14½	14⅝	− ¼
47½	29	BrokenHill	BHP	1.25e	3.0	14	8	41⅜	41	41⅜	+ ½
9⅝	4¾	BrookeGp	BGL	.56b	9.1		57	6⅜	6	6⅛	+ ¼
6¼	½	BrookeGp rt			...		2	5¾	5¾	5¾	− ⅛
31¼	27	BklynUnGas	BU	1.94	6.4	14	366	30⅜	30	30⅛	− ¼
33¾	27½	BklynUnGas pf		2.47	7.6		4	32⅞	32½	32½	− ¾
12⅝	6⅜	BrownShrp	BNS			...	50	9¼	9⅛	9¼	+ ⅛
85	67½	BrownFormn A	BF A	2.44	2.9	16	32	84½	84	84	− ¼
84½	64¾	BrownFormn B	BF B	2.44	2.9	16	532	83½	81½	83½	+1¼
6	4½	BrownFormn pf		.40	6.8		6	5⅞	5¾	5⅞	+ ⅛
28⅜	**21⅝**	**BrownGp**	**BG**	**1.60**	**6.0**	**20**	**431**	**26⅞**	**25⅜**	**26⅞**	+1½
30¾	16⅞	BrownFer	BFI	.68	3.2	15	5356	21¾	20⅞	21½	− ¼
16⅜	8	Brunswick	BC	.44	3.2	63	3694	14⅜	13¾	13⅞	
20	9½	BrushWell	BW	.20	1.5	18	156	13⅝	13⅜	13⅝	+ ¼
28¾	23⅝	BuckeyePtr	BPL	2.60	9.7	11	124	26⅞	26½	26¾	+ ⅛
16½	13	BunkerHill	BHL	1.64a	10.3	...	67	16	15¾	16	+ ¼
13¾	10¼	BurgerKgInv	BKP	1.56	13.3	14	33	11⅞	11¾	11¾	+ ⅛
21⅜	8½	BurlgtnCoat	BCF			13	179	18	17	18	+ ¼
41⅞	26¼	BurlgtnNthn	BNI	1.20	3.0		2614	40⅜	39⅝	40	− ½
9⅜	8	BurlgtnNthn pf		[illegible]	[illegible]		[illegible]	[illegible]	8⅝	8⅝	...
43¾	32⅞	BurlgtnR[illegible]									...

SOURCE: *The Wall Street Journal*, January 3, 1992. Reprinted by permission of *The Wall Street Journal*, © 1992 Dow Jones & Company, Inc. All right reserved worldwide

EXHIBIT 8.8

Moody's Preferred Stock Ratings

Moody's Rating Policy Review Board extended its rating services to include quality designations on preferred stock on October 1, 1973. The decision to rate preferred stock, which Moody's had done prior to 1935, was prompted by evidence of investor interest. Moody's believes that its rating of preferred stock is especially appropriate in view of the ever-increasing amount of these securities outstanding, and the fact that continuing inflation and its ramifications have resulted generally in the dilution of some of the protection afforded them as well as other fixed-income securities.

Because of the fundamental differences between preferred stocks and bonds, a variation of our familiar bond rating symbols is being used in the quality ranking of preferred stock. The symbols, presented below, are designed to avoid comparison with bond quality in absolute terms. It should always be borne in mind that preferred stock occupies a junior position to bonds within a particular capital structure and that these securities are rated within the universe of preferred stocks.

Note: Moody's applies numerical modifiers **1**, **2**, and **3** in each rating classification: the modifier **1** indicates that the security ranks in the higher end of its generic rating category; the modifier **2** indicates a mid-range ranking and the modifier **3** indicates that the issue ranks in the lower end of its generic rating category.

Preferred stock rating symbols and their definitions are as follows:

"aaa"

An issue which is rated "**aaa**" is considered to be a top-quality preferred stock. This rating indicates good asset protection and the least risk of dividend impairment within the universe of preferred stocks.

"aa"

An issue which is rated "**aa**" is a considered a high-grade preferred stock. This rating indicates that there is a reasonable assurance that earnings and asset protection will remain relatively well maintained in the foreseeable future.

"a"

An issue which is rated "**a**" is considered to be an upper-medium grade preferred stock. While risks are judged to be somewhat greater than in the "**aaa**" and "**aa**" classification, earnings and asset protection are, nevertheless, expected to be maintained at adequate levels.

"baa"

An issue which is rated "**baa**" is considered to be a medium-grade preferred stock, neither highly protected nor poorly secured. Earnings and asset protection appear adequate at present but may be questionable over any great length of time.

"ba"

An issue which is rated "**ba**" is considered to have speculative elements and its future cannot be considered well assured. Earnings and asset protection may be very moderate and not well safeguarded during adverse periods. Uncertainty of position characterizes preferred stocks in this class.

"b"

An issue which is rated "**b**" generally lacks the characteristics of a desirable investment. Assurance of dividend payments and maintenance of other terms of the issue over any long period of time may be small.

"caa"

An issue which is rated "**caa**" is likely to be in arrears on dividend payments. This rating designation does not purport to indicate the future status of payments.

"ca"

An issue which is rated "**ca**" is speculative in a high degree and is likely to be in arrears on dividends with little likelihood of eventual payments.

"c"

This is the lowest rated class of preferred or preference stock. Issues so rated can be regarded as having extremely poor prospects of ever attaining any real investment standing.

SOURCE: *Bond Record*, Moody's Investors Service, December 1991. Reprinted by permission.

does not constitute default. Ratings range from AAA down to C. Obviously no rating system or advisory service can guarantee perfect trading results, but the information in Moody's *Bond Record* or Standard & Poor's *Stock Guide* can support informed decision making about the rewards and risks of preferred stocks. Exhibit 8.8 lists Moody's preferred stock rating categories and the characteristics of issues in each category.

Moody's *Industrial*, *Transportation*, *Public Utility* and *Banking and Finance Manuals* can provide detailed information about preferred stocks and their issuers to help investors make sense of the newspaper price listings. Moody's manuals contain sufficient historical data to support careful analysis of companies and their operations to make certain that their preferred stocks are adequately secured by assets and earnings. Annual and quarterly reports of companies also provide data about the financial soundness of their preferred stocks.

Analysis of a Preferred Stock

The soundness of an investment in a preferred stock depends on three relationships: net asset value per preferred share, earnings per preferred share, and dividend coverage per preferred share. These figures indicate how much the investor can rely on the firm to pay the preferred dividend.

net asset value per preferred share: Total assets minus total liabilities of a corporation divided by the number of shares of preferred stock outstanding.

earnings per preferred share: Net income of a corporation before payment of preferred stock dividends divided by the number of shares of preferred stock outstanding.

dividend coverage per preferred share: Net income of a corporation before payment of preferred dividends divided by the total dollar amount of preferred dividends.

Net asset value per preferred share is found by subtracting total liabilities from total assets, as listed on the company's balance sheet, and then dividing the result by the number of shares of preferred stock. A higher net asset value per share, other things remaining equal, indicates a more secure investment.

Earnings per preferred share is net income before preferred dividends divided by the number of shares of preferred stock outstanding. The amount and stability of earnings per preferred share determine the resources from which the firm can pay preferred dividends.

Dividend coverage per preferred share is net income per share before subtracting preferred dividends divided by the dollar amount of preferred dividends per share. If net income covers the preferred dividend more times, the preferred stock investment is more secure.

Any analysis must focus on the trends of earnings per preferred share and dividend coverage in addition to the raw numbers. Increasing earnings per share and a stable or increasing dividend coverage ratio indicate a strong, secure investment. Remember, however, that the firm must pay creditors before it pays preferred stockholders if it should fail and liquidate its assets. Therefore, an increase in debt outstanding, other things remaining equal, reduces the security of the preferred stock.

Preferred Stock and Interest Rate Risk

Most investors buy preferred stock in pursuit of current income since most preferred issues pay higher current dividends than common stock. Since changes in interest rates affect the income available from competing investments, especially bonds, changing interest rates cause the relative attractiveness of preferred issues and, therefore, their prices to change. If interest rates rise, the market prices of preferred stock issues will tend to fall. If interest rates fall, the prices of preferred issues generally rise.

Investing in preferred stock can be risky. The issuing company may fail, leaving the stock worthless, or its board may decide to skip a dividend payment. Interest rates may rise, sending the preferred stock price down. Also, no one guarantees that individual investors will realize better yields from preferred stock than they could get from bonds.

Exhibit 8.9 shows the trend in yields on preferred stocks issued by public utility companies from 1977 through 1991, broken down by Moody's rating categories. The exhibit shows strong fluctuations in preferred stock dividend yields during this period, which implies similar fluctuation in prices, mostly due to changes in interest rates. Preferred stock dividends remained fairly secure through all this change, but prices and, therefore, yields can fluctuate quite a bit.

perspective on **ETHICS**

Junk Bonds and the Takeover Boom

The rise and fall of junk bonds in the 1980s provided one of the great financial dramas of the century. There were more takeovers—friendly or hostile acquisitions of corporations—during the 1980s than in any other 10-year period in history. Such mergers and acquisitions ("M&As" in Wall Street terminology) reached an unprecedented level during this so-called "deal decade." According to *Mergers and Acquisitions* magazine, the decade of the 1980s was a period of "the most prolific and sustained M&A wave in history," where dealmakers executed "31,105 transactions with an aggregate value of $1.34 trillion."

Much of the merger mania of this period was financed by junk bonds issued for the specific purpose of seeking out takeover targets. Debate about the impact and the ethics of the takeover explosion will likely continue throughout the end of the 1990s. Both sides offer reasonable arguments. At one extreme, the antitakeover side contends that hostile takeovers have had a negative impact on the economy and the country, as can be seen by the shutdown and downsizing of many acquired firms, with a concomitant loss of jobs. On the other side, the takeover advocates argue that they serve to shake up entrenched managements and force corporations to become more efficient—in order to pay off the huge debt financing incurred during the takeovers.

A survey reported in *Fortune* noted that of 173 chief executives interviewed, 69 percent said that, on balance, the wave of hostile takeovers has hurt the economy. Typical of their negative comments was the observation by Ryal Popps, Chief Executive Officer of Storage Technology: "It was raw foolishness. We bought the self-righteous and self-serving arguments that justified a raider strategy to pursue wealth."

Richard A. Bernstein, CEO of Western Publishing Company, noted: "To me, it was the worst disaster since the Great Depression. It became an evil game in and of itself, inhabited by people who added nothing to the economy."

On the other side of the argument are people like J. Tracy O'Rourke, CEO of Varian Associates, who told *Fortune*: "There were a bunch of ineffective, inefficient companies out there that trimmed down to better performance, and that was a decent outcome. No one would listen to the tighter-ship concept in the 1970s."

On balance, it seems that the majority who felt takeovers had a harmful effect on the economy are probably correct. Among the major negatives of takeover mania cited by CEOs are the trading of debt for equity by takeover targets, diversion of management attention from the long-term to the short-term, reduction of American competitiveness, job losses, and the destruction of some target companies. These disadvantages in aggregate seem to far outweigh the sense that many companies were forced to become more efficient in order to protect themselves from corporate raiders.

SOURCES: Martin Sikora, "The M&A Bonanza of the '80s," *Mergers and Acquisitions*, March/April, 1990, p. 5. Richard S. Teitelbaum, "LBOs Really Didn't Pay, Say the Chiefs," *Fortune*, August, 26, 1991, p. 73.

Preferred Stock Valuation

The calculation of the value of preferred stock builds on the time value of money and bond valuation concepts introduced in the previous two chapters, altered to reflect the perpetual nature of preferred stock investments. Preferred stock has no maturity date so it pays a constant stream of dividends forever, at least in theory. Thus the value of a share of preferred stock equals the present value of the dividend payment from the date of purchase to infinity.

EXHIBIT 8.9

Yields on Preferred Stocks

	JAN.	FEB.	MAR.	APR.	MAY	JUN.	JUL.	AUG.	SEP.	OCT.	NOV.	DEC.
aa-Rated Issues												
1977	8.36%	8.23%	8.21%	8.16%	8.14%	8.03%	7.91%	8.02%	7.95%	8.08%	8.15%	8.14%
1978	8.31	8.38	8.35	8.51	8.61	8.84	8.80	8.56	8.43	8.61	8.75	8.94
1979	9.05	9.11	9.10	9.14	9.19	9.03	8.98	9.07	9.60	10.62	10.66	10.86
1980	10.96	11.62	13.09	11.67	10.80	10.59	10.98	11.47	12.02	12.55	13.18	13.15
1981	13.13	13.42	13.35	13.61	13.71	13.75	13.88	14.18	14.68	15.12	13.75	14.97
1982	15.00	14.89	14.44	13.85	13.37	14.30	14.28	12.87	12.84	12.00	11.55	11.63
1983	11.36	11.21	11.17	11.06	11.09	11.34	11.73	11.73	11.70	11.77	11.80	12.18
1984	11.96	12.00	12.40	12.50	12.96	13.28	13.05	12.55	12.31	12.24	12.18	12.25
1985	11.72	11.39	11.62	11.24	10.66	10.25	10.38	10.41	10.60	10.58	10.05	10.00
1986	9.54	8.78	8.61	8.13	8.39	8.54	8.49	8.01	8.09	7.88	7.83	7.98
1987	7.78	7.85	7.82	7.99	8.90	8.66	8.73	8.90	9.40	9.67	9.19	9.35
1988	9.06	8.91	9.13	9.20	9.38	9.28	9.52	9.55	9.40	9.33	9.40	9.50
1989	9.33	9.42	9.54	9.49	9.33	8.93	8.80	8.82	8.91	8.78	8.80	8.88
1990	8.84	9.06	9.16	9.22	9.20	9.17	9.06	9.33	9.30	9.20	9.09	9.08
1991	8.97	8.73	8.87	8.75	8.70	8.77	8.70	8.57	8.39	8.38	8.31	—
a-Rated Issues												
1977	8.83	8.80	8.75	8.61	8.64	8.47	8.23	8.30	8.32	8.50	8.55	8.59
1978	8.70	8.74	8.79	8.88	9.07	9.39	9.33	8.97	8.82	9.07	9.27	9.65
1979	9.61	9.66	9.63	9.71	9.91	9.55	9.60	9.74	10.34	11.38	11.23	11.49
1980	11.79	12.92	14.74	12.22	11.69	10.97	11.49	12.15	12.92	13.55	13.97	14.01
1981	13.85	14.21	13.72	14.04	14.20	14.15	14.30	15.03	15.28	15.60	14.10	15.47
1982	15.55	15.36	14.81	14.35	13.89	14.69	14.65	13.40	13.49	12.48	12.13	12.20
1983	11.93	11.86	11.79	11.57	11.46	12.05	12.29	12.21	12.15	12.18	12.46	12.61
1984	12.56	12.59	13.12	13.47	14.04	14.22	13.86	13.37	13.13	12.89	12.57	12.97
1985	12.37	11.84	12.32	11.99	11.25	10.83	11.07	11.09	11.05	11.27	10.64	10.28
1986	10.05	9.11	9.05	8.67	9.04	9.32	9.20	8.55	8.76	8.37	8.54	8.64
1987	8.36	8.43	8.36	8.81	9.44	9.13	9.41	9.57	10.19	10.48	10.01	10.24
1988	9.62	9.44	9.69	9.87	10.05	9.89	10.52	10.04	9.89	9.81	9.91	10.06

Discounting out to infinity does not seem so unreasonable when two factors are considered. First, although we can expect no corporation to survive for an infinite number of years, some have existed for 50 or more years and seem likely to survive that long into the future. Second, the present value of a given sum changes in such tiny increments as it approaches infinity that the returns for the far distant future have little effect on today's value of an investment. Assuming a 12 percent discount rate, for example, the present value of $1 to be received 50 years from now is $0.003. At 60 years, the present value of $1 drops to $0.001, or one-tenth of a penny. We can safely disregard an amount this small and define economic infinity at a 12 percent discount rate as about 50 years.

Making the simplifying assumption that the issuer pays dividends annually, the value of a share of preferred stock is given by:

$$V = \frac{D}{(1+K)} + \frac{D}{(1+K)^2} + \frac{D}{(1+K)^3} + \cdots \frac{D}{(1+K)^\infty}$$

Yields on Preferred Stocks *(continued)*

	JAN.	FEB.	MAR.	APR.	MAY	JUN.	JUL.	AUG.	SEP.	OCT.	NOV.	DEC.
a-Rated Issues												
1989	9.89	10.08	10.13	9.99	9.86	9.37	9.37	9.32	9.43	9.26	9.25	9.30
1990	9.30	9.50	9.56	9.64	9.60	9.46	9.46	9.67	9.70	9.51	9.32	9.30
1991	9.23	8.98	9.07	8.93	8.85	8.89	8.87	8.65	8.59	8.54	8.43	—
baa-Rated Issues												
1977	9.01	8.98	9.01	9.00	9.04	8.92	8.63	8.72	8.87	8.98	8.96	9.03
1978	9.17	9.17	9.24	9.34	9.54	9.81	9.76	9.54	9.62	9.66	9.89	10.48
1979	10.42	10.37	10.33	10.43	10.82	10.49	10.33	10.49	10.97	11.94	12.18	12.75
1980	12.74	14.08	15.22	13.13	12.29	12.05	12.32	13.05	13.76	14.32	14.86	14.56
1981	14.45	14.82	14.57	15.12	15.34	15.02	15.47	15.85	16.01	16.16	14.74	15.83
1982	15.83	15.65	15.48	15.09	14.93	15.67	15.40	14.21	14.11	13.29	12.94	13.26
1983	12.76	12.66	12.51	12.34	12.07	12.47	12.81	12.73	12.72	12.64	12.91	13.34
1984	12.81	13.03	13.55	13.97	14.49	14.85	14.88	14.21	14.28	14.04	13.50	13.71
1985	12.99	12.87	12.98	12.58	12.26	11.97	11.74	12.38	12.52	12.40	11.27	11.09
1986	10.75	9.93	9.78	9.18	9.68	9.89	9.60	9.26	9.36	9.09	9.01	9.27
1987	8.76	8.88	8.90	9.38	10.07	9.75	9.71	9.93	10.47	10.69	10.19	10.45
1988	9.92	9.88	9.97	10.02	10.25	10.09	10.19	10.25	10.17	10.06	10.15	10.37
1989	10.14	10.27	10.38	10.24	10.13	9.73	9.59	9.58	9.73	9.39	9.30	9.38
1990	9.39	9.54	9.64	9.68	9.73	9.71	9.63	9.73	9.84	9.77	9.49	9.54
1991	9.42	9.10	9.20	9.12	9.08	9.19	9.10	8.91	8.82	8.68	8.64	—

Note: There is no aaa average because of the dearth of prime-quality preferred stocks. Yields are based on prices for the last Friday of each month.

Moody's ratings are subject to change. Because of the possible time lapse between Moody's assignment or change of a rating and your use of this publication, we suggest you verify the current rating of any security or issuer in which you are interested.

SOURCE: *Bond Record*, Moody's Investors Service, December 1991. Reprinted by permission.

where:

V = value of preferred stock
D = annual dividend payment
K = appropriate discount rate
∞ = infinity

Since the present value of each year's dividend gets smaller each year, as explained above, this equation represents an infinite series of decreasing numbers. Though it goes on forever, a mathematical technique gives the sum of such a series as:

$$V = \frac{D}{K}$$

This represents the annual dividend divided by the appropriate discount rate. The discount rate (K) used here is exactly comparable to the discount rate (r) used for bond valuation in Chapter 7. At a discount rate (K) of 12 percent, the value of a share of preferred stock that pays an $8 annual dividend is:

$$V = \frac{\$8.00}{0.12}$$

$$= \$66.67$$

SUMMARY

Corporate bond issuers accept contractual obligations to pay bond buyers fixed amounts of interest on fixed dates, usually quarterly or semiannually, and to repay principal at maturity. The bond indenture is the contract that states the terms and conditions of the debt arrangement between the corporation that issues the bonds and the trustee that represents the bondholders.

There are many different types of bonds, including debentures, subordinated debentures, mortgage bonds, equipment trust certificates, collateral trust bonds, and receivers' certificates. The types of bonds have varying degrees of creditworthiness and claims on the assets of the corporation in the event of default. Most bond indentures include protective covenants to strengthen the creditworthiness of the issues.

Two major bond rating organizations, Moody's and Standard & Poor's, evaluate the quality of bond issues and rate them from triple A, for the most secure issues of the strongest corporations, down to D, for issues actually in default.

Convertible bonds and bonds with warrants offer investors opportunities to share in the earnings growth of the issuing corporations. A convertible bond gives the bondholder the option during a specified number of years to convert the bond into a specified number of shares of common stock. A warrant attached to a bond gives the bondholder the right during a period of time to buy a stated number of shares of stock directly from the issuing firm at a specified price per share.

Preferred stock is part of the permanent ownership (equity) capital of a business. Two attributes make it appealing to some investors: fixed dividend payments and preferred status in dividend payments and liquidation over common stock. Most preferred stock dividends are cumulative and nonparticipating. Preferred stock also may be convertible. Because the intercorporate dividend credit normally keeps preferred yields below comparable bond yields, individual investors normally focus on convertible or participating preferred stock. Moody's and Standard & Poor's rate preferred stock issues' quality on a system ranging from triple-A down to C. Like bonds, shares of preferred stock are subject to interest rate risk.

Preferred stock valuation builds on the time value of money concepts introduced in Chapter 6 and the application of these concepts to bond valuation explained in Chapter 7. The value of a share of preferred stock is equal to the discounted present value of all future dividends. This requires summing an infinite series, which reduces through algebraic manipulation to equal the dividend in dollars divided by the discount rate.

INVESTMENT MANAGEMENT CONCEPTS

1. Fixed-income securities are valuable investments because they provide relatively high levels of cash income and their prices appreciate if interest rates decline.

2. Investors should carefully check the call provision in a bond indenture to avoid paying a premium price for a bond that might be called in the near future.

3. Investment grade bonds (those rated BBB and higher) offer better security for the investor's principal than lower-rated bonds.

4. *The Wall Street Journal* feature "Bond Market Data Bank" gives a quick survey of yields available in the bond market.

5. Convertible bonds give both aggressive and defensive benefits since they couple high income with the opportunity to convert to common stock if its price rises.

6. A nonconvertible and nonparticipating preferred stock issue is seldom a good investment for an individual because it offers a lower yield than bonds of comparable risk due to the intercorporate dividend credit.

REVIEW QUESTIONS

1. Are the highest-rated corporate bonds more or less risky than U.S. Treasury bonds? Why?

2. What is default risk?

3. How risky are corporate bonds as compared to municipal bonds?

4. What two promises does a corporation make to investors when it borrows money by issuing bonds?

5. What is a bond indenture?

6. What is the difference between yield to maturity and yield to first call date for a callable corporate bond?

7. What is the difference between a debenture and a mortgage bond?

8. What functions do protective covenants on corporate bonds serve?

9. How do ratings differ between investment grade bonds and junk bonds?

10. What is the meaning of a bond listing in *The Wall Street Journal* that reads "ABC 8.25s07"?

11. What is the difference between a convertible bond and a bond with warrants?

12. What is the primary advantage of investing in convertible bonds?

13. In what two ways does preferred stock have preference over common stock?

14. Although preferred stock is riskier than bonds, yields on preferred stocks are often lower than yields on comparable bonds. Why?

15. What three important statistics should investors check before buying preferred stock?

16. How can you calculate the value of preferred stock?

SELF-CORRECTING PROBLEMS

1. Suppose you bought a bond at a price of $1,020 that paid interest of $85 per year and was callable at a price of $1,010 one year after your purchase. Using the formula for computing the one-year return on investment introduced in Chapter 6, calculate the yield to first call date on the bond.

2. Suppose the bond in the previous problem was callable after 5 years at a price of $1,000. Use the same formula to calculate the approximate average annual yield to first call date over the 5-year period.

3. Suppose you bought a bond at a price of $985. The bond paid annual interest of $75 and matured in 7 years. What approximate annual return could you expect on the bond?

4. Belchfire Motor Works preferred stock currently trades at a price of $23.75 and pays an annual dividend of $1.85. What is the current yield on the preferred stock?

5. If the appropriate discount rate for preferred stock in Belchfire's risk class is 9.25 percent, what is the value of Belchfire preferred stock? Compared to its current market price, is Belchfire preferred a good buy?

Answers to Self-Correcting Problems

1. [($1,010 − $1,020) + $85]/$1,020 = $75/$1,020 = 7.35 percent.

2. Average annual capital loss = $20/5 = $4; Annual interest = $85; Average annual total return = $85 − $4 = $81; Average annual investment = ($1,020 + $1,010)/2 = $1,015; Average annual total return percentage = $81/$1,015 = 7.98 percent.

3. Average annual capital gain = $15/7 = $2.14; Annual interest = $75; Average annual total return = $75 + $2.14 = $77.14; Average annual investment = ($985 + $1,000)/2 = $992.50; Average annual total return percentage = $77.14/$992.50 = 7.77 percent.

4. $1.85/$23.75 = 7.79 percent.

5. $1.85/0.0925 = $20.00. Belchfire preferred is not a good buy since its current market price is higher than its value according to the valuation model.

SELECTED READINGS

Fabozzi, Frank J., ed. *The New High-Yield Debt Market: A Handbook for Portfolio Managers and Analysts.* New York: Harper Business, 1990.

Fabozzi, Frank J., and T. Dessa Fabozzi. *Bond Markets, Analysis, and Strategies.* Englewood Cliffs, N.J.: Prentice-Hall, 1989.

Fridson, Martin S. *High-Yield Bonds: Identifying Value and Assessing Risk of Speculative Grade Securities.* Chicago: Probus Publishing, 1989.

McGuire, Simon. *The Handbook of Convertibles.* Englewood Cliffs, N.J.: Prentice-Hall, 1991.

New York Institute of Finance. *Fixed-Income Investments: A Personal Seminar.* Englewood Cliffs, N.J.: Prentice-Hall, 1989.

Thau, Annette. *The Bond Book; Everything Investors Need to Know about Munis, Treasuries, GNMAs, Funds, Zeros, Corporates, Money Markets, and More.* Chicago: Probus Publishing, 1991.

chapter 9

Understanding Corporate Financial Statements

John Hall is a successful management and business consultant who has several clients. Rather than work for one employer and risk giving his life to the "company store," he chose to work for several businesses as a management consultant. He worked one day a week with each of three corporate clients, each of whom paid him $25,000 a year. The rest of the week he worked with several other clients on special projects and wrote articles for management and business journals. In addition, he was writing a book on improving the productivity of middle management. John was intelligent, experienced, hard working, and extremely successful in his profession.

His success brought him and his family a wide assortment of the best goodies the free enterprise system can provide. He and his wife had both enjoyed the lifelong benefits of a good education, and they made sure their children did, too. They owned several expensive cars, a beautiful house in the suburbs, and a vacation home on the lake. John's total net worth of over a million dollars was not a huge amount of money in today's world for a 50-year-old man, but it put him much closer to the top of the economic pile than to the bottom.

Despite his obvious success and business knowledge, John revealed a disturbing weakness in his understanding of finance in a chat after church one Sunday. After catching up on news of family and friends, John asked one of the authors to help him with a business problem. "My trouble is with my company's stock," he said. "Can you help me increase my stock account in my company?"

The request was vaguely worded, but John seemed to want to increase the value of his stock so that he and his company would prosper. "Just take care of your assets," the author responded. "As they increase in value, so will the value of your stock."

John was not satisfied. "No, you don't understand! I don't want to fool around with assets. I just want to increase my stock account." John did not realize that the stock in his company represented nothing more than ownership of company assets and the current and future earnings those assets would generate. The only way he could increase the value of his common stock was to increase the value of the company's assets and future earnings to induce other investors to pay more for the shares.

Despite enviable success in business, John Hall really did not understand the nature of common stock and the balance sheet. He had identified the correct goal for his business, though. Finance theorists believe that the main effort of management should be to increase the value of the firm's common stock. Assessing this value and targeting operations to increase it require a thorough understanding of the financial statements that report information about a firm's business.

Introduction

financial accounting: Accounting standards that govern preparation and presentation of corporate financial statements.

generally accepted accounting principles (GAAP): A set of conventions that have evolved over the years to govern financial accounting.

Preparation and presentation of corporate financial statements are governed by the standards of **financial accounting.** The objective of financial accounting is to present fairly the financial condition of the firm to current and potential stockholders or creditors, securities analysts, and other interested parties. An independent certified public accountant (CPA) must certify that an audit in line with generally accepted auditing standards has found the financial statements of a publicly traded corporation to fairly present the financial condition of the firm. The statements must present information in accordance with **generally accepted accounting principles (GAAP),** which are a set of objectives, conventions, and principles that have evolved through the years to govern the preparation and presentation of information in financial statements. If the statements do not conform to GAAP, the audit will so note.

GAAP rules actually leave corporations a good deal of latitude in applying them to account for particular transactions. However, all firms report on their operations and financial conditions by means of three types of financial reports: balance sheets, income statements, and statements of changes in financial position. We will examine each of these three reports in turn.

Balance Sheets

balance sheet: A statement of the financial condition of a company at a given time, listing all of its assets, liabilities, and owners' equity.

The **balance sheet** gives a sort of snapshot of the financial condition of the firm at a given time. The balance sheet is a stock statement, reporting the firm's stock of assets, liabilities, and equities at a particular moment in time. Exhibit 9.1 illustrates the balance sheets for Typical Manufacturing Company on December 31, 1992, and 1991.

The balance sheet has three major sections. It lists assets on the left-hand side (or at the top, in some cases), liabilities on the right-hand side (or below assets), and equity accounts below liabilities. The statement gets its name from the fact that the two sides must balance. The bottom line of one side, total assets, must equal the bottom line of the other, total liabilities and equity. The equity account is equal to the difference between total assets and total liabilities, which reflects the fact that the owners have claims to all assets that remain after the firm has satisfied its lenders' claims.

assets: Resources of the firm expressed in dollars; the dollar value of what a company owns.

liabilities: The dollar value of creditors' claims against a company's assets; the dollar amount that the firm owes parties other than its owners.

equity: The net worth of a company, equal to its total assets minus its total liabilities.

basic accounting equation: Assets = Liabilities + Equities.

The **assets** side of the balance sheet lists the total resources of the firm in dollars. It breaks assets down into such categories as cash, accounts receivable, inventories, plant and equipment, property used under capital leases, and other business resources. The liabilities and equity side of the balance sheet lists various claims against these assets. **Liabilities,** such as accounts payable, notes payable, obligations under capital leases, and long-term debts, represent claims of various creditors against the firm's assets. The excess of assets over creditors' claims represents the **equity,** or net worth, of the firm's owners.

Viewed overall, the balance sheet provides a detailed listing of accounts that sum to give the **basic accounting equation:**

$$\text{Assets} = \text{Liabilities} + \text{Equities}$$
$$\text{Total business resources} = \text{Creditors' claims} + \text{Owners' claims}$$

current asset: An asset that the firm will convert to cash within a year or one operating cycle, whichever is longer.

marketable security: A short-term investment of cash in highly liquid, low-risk security.

accounts receivable: Amounts customers owe a company for goods it has shipped or services it has rendered, but for which the customer has not yet paid.

Exhibit 9.1 shows the logical structure of the balance sheet. The first section of the assets side lists **current assets,** including cash and assets that would normally be converted into cash within a year or one operating cycle, whichever is longer. Such assets as marketable securities, accounts receivable, and inventories appear as current assets. **Marketable securities** represent short-term investments of cash in highly liquid, low-risk securities such as U.S. Treasury bills or prime commercial paper. Most firms report their marketable securities holdings at cost, listing their market value in footnotes.

Accounts receivable represent amounts customers owe the company, but have not yet paid, for goods it has shipped or services it has rendered. The accounts receivable figure on the balance sheet reflects a reduction as an allowance for bad debts, that is, an experience-based estimate of the total dollar amount of current receivables that the firm will never collect. Most firms report the dollar amount of the bad debt allowance in a footnote.

EXHIBIT 9.1

Typical Manufacturing Company
Balance Sheet

Assets	DECEMBER 31 1992	DECEMBER 31 1991	Liabilities and Equity	DECEMBER 31 1992	DECEMBER 31 1991
Cash	$ 315,000	$ 297,000	Accounts payable	$ 696,000	$ 874,000
Marketable securities	57,000	25,000	Notes payable	1,645,000	965,000
Accounts receivable	2,594,000	2,177,000	Accrued expenses payable	628,000	553,000
Inventories	2,257,000	1,986,000	Accrued taxes payable	340,000	308,000
Total current assets	$5,223,000	$4,485,000	Total current liabilities	$3,309,000	$2,700,000
Plant and equipment	3,621,000	3,231,000	Long-term debt	$1,695,000	$1,429,000
Other assets	526,000	609,000	Total liabilities	$5,004,000	$4,129,000
Total fixed assets	$4,147,000	$3,840,000	Stockholders' equity:		
Total assets	$9,370,000	$8,325,000	Preferred stock ($100 par, 6 percent)	425,000	597,000
			Common stock ($5 par value)	520,000	510,000
			Paid-in capital	420,000	405,000
			Retained earnings	3,001,000	2,684,000
			Total stockholders' equity	$4,336,000	$4,196,000
			Total liabilities and equity	$9,370,000	$8,325,000

Notice that the balance sheet lists current assets in order of liquidity. Cash comes first, and the least liquid current assets, inventories, come last in the current asset section. Most firms report inventories at cost or market value, whichever is lower. Footnotes generally give details of the company's inventory valuation method.

The bottom section of the asset side of the balance sheet lists the company's investment in **fixed assets** such as property, plant, and equipment. These assets are much less liquid than current assets and the company uses them over long periods of time. The generally accepted method of valuing fixed assets is to list them at their historical costs (the costs of acquiring them originally) less accumulated depreciation as of the date of the balance sheet. **Accumulated depreciation** represents the cumulative total dollar amount the firm has charged off against the historical cost of its current stock of fixed assets for depreciation. Footnotes give details about a company's depreciation policy.

fixed assets: Illiquid assets that a company will use over a long period of time, such as buildings and vehicles.

accumulated depreciation: The cumulative total of depreciation of company assets over time.

current liabilities: Debts the company must repay within one year or one operating cycle, whichever is longer.

The right-hand side of the balance sheet lists the firm's liability and equity accounts in a logical format similar to that for the asset information. First, it reports **current liabilities,** debts that will fall due within one year or one operating cycle. Current liabilities include such items as **accounts**

accounts payable: Money a firm owes its suppliers for goods or sevices for which it has not yet paid.

payable (money the firm owes its suppliers for goods or services it has purchased but not yet paid for), short-term notes payable, current payments on long-term debt, and various categories of accrued expenses. Accrued expenses represent expenses the firm has incurred but not yet paid in cash as of the balance sheet date, including such expenses as salaries and wages due to employees, interest due on loans, accrued utility expenses, and similar items.

short-term liquidity: The ability of a company to meet its short-term debt obligations as they come due.

net working capital: Current assets minus current liabilities.

One extremely important balance sheet relationship is that of current assets to current liabilities. Recall that current assets are assets that the firm expects to turn into cash within one year, and current liabilities are obligations that it expects to pay in cash within one year. The relationship between these amounts has an important effect on the **short-term liquidity** of the firm, or its ability to meet its current obligations as they fall due. The excess of current assets over current liabilities is the firm's **net working capital.** A common rule of thumb suggests that most firms' current assets should be approximately double their current liabilities.

spontaneous financing: Short-term liabilities, such as accounts payable, that grow spontaneously with growth in sales.

The reasoning behind this rule of thumb is rather simple. Working capital represents the funds a business firm needs to pay for normal operations. The firm needs cash to pay its obligations to suppliers and others as they fall due. To get this cash, it continually draws down its bank balances, collects its accounts receivable, and sells marketable securities it holds. It also incurs new short-term debts, or liabilities, as sales grow and it buys more supplies, inventories, and other current assets on open accounts, for which it does not pay for a period of time determined by suppliers' credit terms. Accounts payable thus rise as sales grow, providing a form of **spontaneous financing.** Given the lags between the conversion of inventories to receivables and then to cash, and given the necessity of paying current liabilities when due, normal prudence suggests that the firm should maintain a safe margin of current assets over current liabilities.

A second reason for maintaining a margin of safety arises from the nature of current assets. Marketable securities may fall in value from the time the firm buys them to store its excess cash and the time it needs the cash to pay current bills. Bad debt losses may erode the value of accounts receivable. Finally, inventories may suffer physical deterioration, or changing styles may make them unsalable at full price. A surplus of current assets over current liabilities will help the firm balance these potential declines in asset values against the fixed requirement to pay its debts in full when due. Experience indicates that a two-to-one margin is appropriate for many classes of firms. In summary:

Net working capital = Current assets − Current liabilities
Typical Manufacturing's Net working capital (1992)
= $5,223,000 − $3,309,000
= $1,914,000

long-term liabilities: Long-term debt with a payback period extending more than one year into the future.

After current liabilities, the liabilities and equity section of the balance sheet lists **long-term liabilities.** This category includes any long-term debt the firm owes to banks or other creditors and any obligations under capital leases. Detailed information about the characteristics of the firm's long-term debt appears in the footnotes to the balance sheet.

After it reports all liabilities, the balance sheet lists equity accounts, which represent the preferred and common stockholders' interests in the corporation. Remember from Chapter 8 that the par value of preferred stock is related to the amount of dividends the firm pays on the stock. The par value of common stock has no real, economic significance, however; it merely meets a bookkeeping need to show a definite value on the balance sheet. When a firm sells common stock, it must enter the sale on its books at an assigned or legal value, so the firm designates a par value. The dollar amount for which owners can sell the stock depends on the market's assessment of the value of the firm, not on the firm's bookkeeping requirements. Since most states prohibit public corporations from selling stock below its par value, most set rather low par values.

paid-in capital (paid-in surplus): Amounts a company receives when it issues common stock in excess of the par value of the stock.

The firm reports the difference between the amount it receives for stock it sells and the stock's par value as **paid-in capital** or **paid-in surplus.** Since the term *surplus* often has a misleading connotation, many financial statements replace it with the phrase "amount contributed in excess of par value." Typical Manufacturing's balance sheet for 1992 shows 104,000 shares of common stock outstanding (divide the $520,000 figure on the common stock line by the $5 par value per share), and that Typical sold these shares for a total of $940,000 ($520,000 par value plus $420,000 paid-in capital).

retained earnings: Net earnings over the life of the corporation that it has not paid out in dividends, but rather reinvested in company assets.

The final stockholders' equity account, **retained earnings,** represents earnings management has reinvested in the firm over the years instead of paying them out in dividends. Common stockholders own this proportion of the firm's value; it is part of their equity interest, which has built up over time.

It is important to notice the major difference between preferred and common stock. As explained in Chapter 8, the preferred stockholders have a prior claim to the $6 annual preferred dividend over common stockholders' claim to any dividends, and they would receive preference over common stockholders in distribution of asset values in the event of liquidation. In return for this preferred status, the preferred stock gives up any claim to earnings above $6 per share. These additional earnings belong to the common stockholders.

In return for this theoretical chance for unlimited gains, the common stockholders accept the risk of variable dividends and the risk of changing stock values in response to the changing fortunes of the company. If the firm has insufficient earnings remaining after it pays off all expenses and preferred stock dividends, the board of directors may vote not to pay common stock dividends. If the firm incurs a loss in a given year, the full amount of this loss is deducted from the retained earnings account and

perspective on **ETHICS**

Ethics and the Association for Investment Management and Research

The Association for Investment Management and Research (AIMR) is composed of two constituent organizations: the Institute of Chartered Financial Analysts (ICFA) in Charlottesville, Virginia, and the Financial Analysts Federation (FAF) in New York. The ICFA administers the study and examination program leading to the professional designation of Chartered Financial Analyst (CFA), a designation that has become an important credential for career advancement in the fields of investment analysis and portfolio management. One of the important missions of AIMR is to sponsor and enforce the *Code of Ethics* and *Standards of Professional Conduct*, which apply to all AIMR members. The *Code of Ethics* is a brief document that provides overall conduct guidance for financial analysts. The full code is as follows:

A financial analyst should conduct himself[a] with integrity and dignity and act in an ethical manner in his dealings with the public, clients, customers, employers, employees, and fellow analysts.

A financial analyst should conduct himself and encourage others to practice financial analysis in a professional and ethical manner that will reflect credit on himself and his profession.

A financial analyst should act with competence and should strive to maintain and improve his competence and that of others in the profession.

A financial analyst should use proper care and exercise independent professional judgment.

The *Standards of Professional Conduct* has eight major sections that expand on the general ethical requirements espoused in the *Code* and provide a detailed interpretation of the ethical and professional requirements of financial analysts who are members of AIMR. An abbreviated outline of the *Standards* follows:

I. Obligation to Inform Employer of Code and Standards

II. Compliance with Governing Laws and Regulations and the Code and Standards
   - A. Required Knowledge and Compliance
   - B. Prohibition Against Assisting Legal and Ethical Violations
   - C. Prohibition Against Use of Material Nonpublic Information
   - D. Responsibilities of Supervisors

III. Research Reports, Investment Recommendations and Actions
   - A. Reasonable Basis and Representations
   - B. Research Reports
   - C. Portfolio Investment Recommendations and Actions
   - D. Prohibition Against Plagiarism
   - E. Prohibition Against Misrepresentation of Services
   - F. Fair Dealing with Customers and Clients

IV. Priority of Transactions

V. Disclosure of Conflicts

VI. Compensation
   - A. Disclosure of Additional Compensation Arrangements
   - B. Disclosure of Referral Fees
   - C. Duty to Employer

VII. Relationships with Others
   - A. Preservation of Confidentiality
   - B. Maintenance of Independence and Objectivity
   - C. Fiduciary Duties

VIII. Use of Professional Designation

IX. Professional Misconduct

If you are interested in a career in investments or would like further information on the *Code* or *Standards*, you can contact the ICFA at P.O. Box 3668, Charlottesville, VA 22903.

[a] Masculine personal pronouns, used throughout the *Code* and *Standards* to simplify sentence structure, shall apply to all persons, regardless of sex.

common stockholders' equity decreases. Common stockholders' equity is sometimes referred to as the firm's *equity cushion*.

The presentation of owners' equity reflects the legal status of the business. Typical Manufacturing's balance sheet illustrates the most common form of organization, the corporation. Two other forms are the sole proprietorship, in which a single person owns all of the firm's assets and has complete responsibility for all of its liabilities, and the partnership, in which two or more people share these benefits and burdens. Balance sheets of sole proprietorships and partnerships generally have simpler equity sections. For a sole proprietorship, the equity section would consist of a statement of the owner's equity in the business. For a partnership, the equity section would show the partners' interest in the firm. Of course, a business organization the size of Typical would almost invariably be organized as a corporation because of the tax advantages and the limitations on owners' personal liability. Sole proprietorships and partnerships are normally smaller business firms or professional organizations such as law firms, CPA firms, and the like.

Book Value of Securities

net book value (net asset value): The value of a corporation's assets to which each class of security has a claim, based on the book values of assets.

Figures in the balance sheet allow investors to calculate the **net book value,** or **net asset value,** of a company's securities. (Recall that Chapter 8 discussed this figure for preferred stock as an important indicator of the security of dividend payments.) The net book value of a security represents the value of the corporation's assets to which each class of security has a claim. Stated another way, assuming that the firm could sell all its assets and pay off all its liabilities at their book values (the values at which they appear on the balance sheet), the net book value represents the dollar value of the remaining assets that would be available to pay off each class of security in order of its preference in liquidation, first bonds, then preferred stock, then common stock.

Perhaps the best way to understand net book value is by means of an example. Assuming that Typical's \$1,695,000 of long-term debt consists of 1,695 bonds with face values of \$1,000 each, the net asset value per bond is determined as follows:

$$\text{Net asset value of all bonds} = \text{Total assets} - \text{Current liabilities}$$
$$= \$9{,}370{,}000 - \$3{,}309{,}000 = \$6{,}061{,}000$$
$$\text{Net asset value per bond} = \$6{,}061{,}000/1{,}695 \text{ bonds} = \$3{,}576$$

Since bonds have first preference in liquidation, they have the highest degree of safety. Typical Manufacturing has \$3,576 of net assets (at book value) available to meet the \$1,000 claim of each bond.

Preferred stock is next in order of preference in liquidation. Typical had 4,250 shares of preferred outstanding at the end of 1992, found by dividing the \$425,000 total book value of the preferred stock by the \$100 per share par value. The net asset value per share of this preferred stock is computed as follows:

$$\text{Net asset value of all preferred stock} = \text{Total assets} - \text{Current liabilities} - \text{Long-term debt}$$
$$= \$9{,}370{,}000 - \$3{,}309{,}000 - \$1{,}695{,}000$$
$$= \$4{,}366{,}000$$
$$\text{Net asset value per preferred share} = \$4{,}366{,}000/4{,}250 \text{ shares} = \$1{,}027$$

Finally, the net book value per share of common stock is computed by determining the amount of money, based on book values, that the holder each of Typical's 104,000 shares of common stock would receive in the event of liquidation. Typical's net book value per share of common stock is \$37.89, computed as follows:

$$\text{Net book value of all common stock} = \text{Total assets} - \text{Current liabilities} - \text{Long-term debt} - \text{Preferred stock}$$
$$= \$9{,}370{,}000 - \$3{,}309{,}000 - \$1{,}695{,}000 - \$425{,}000 = \$3{,}941{,}000$$
$$\text{Book value per common share} = \$3{,}941{,}000/104{,}000 \text{ shares} = \$37.89$$

An alternative and equivalent procedure to calculate the net book value per share of common stock sums the common stock, paid-in capital, and retained earnings accounts from the balance sheet:

$$\text{Net book value of all common stock} = \text{Common stock} + \text{Paid-in capital} + \text{Retained earnings} = \$520{,}000 + \$420{,}000 + \$3{,}001{,}000 = \$3{,}941{,}000$$
$$\text{Book value per common share} = \$3{,}941{,}000/104{,}000 \text{ shares} = \$37.89$$

Both calculations must, of course, yield the same answer since common stockholders' equity is equal by definition to total assets less all liabilities and preferred stock.

Book value calculations, particularly for common stock, normally do not have a major effect on investment decisions. In most cases, investors make a reasonable "going concern" assumption that liquidation is not imminent, so the liquidation value of the company is not the most relevant influence on value of its securities. Also, remember that book value computations implicitly assume that the firm could sell all assets at book value; this may be true, or it may not. Finally, the market values of securities are determined by market forces that may be only marginally related to book values. The market values of bonds and preferred stock are determined mainly by the credit rating of the company and prevailing interest rates. For common stock, corporate earnings and the future economic outlook are the keys to market value.

Stock Splits and Stock Dividends

As corporations prosper over time, their earnings increase and the prices of their outstanding common stock also increase. Many managers feel that if the price of their company's stock rises above a certain level, it becomes too expensive for individual investors to purchase round lots. Opinions about the limits of the desirable price range vary between management groups, but most managers would probably agree that a price greater than $80 to $100 per share is rather high.

stock split: A corporate action to reduce the per-share price of its stock by issuing additional shares for every existing share to increase the number of shares outstanding without changing the value of stockholders' shares.

To reduce the price without reducing the value of existing shareholders' stock, management can arrange a **stock split.** A stock split distributes the value of a company among more shares, resulting in a smaller price per share. To keep the value of current stockholders' positions constant, the company gives them new shares in proportion to their holdings before the split. Firms commonly split their stock in a 2-for-1 ratio, but they can adjust this ratio upward or downward depending on the circumstances.

In a 2-for-1 split, each current stockholder receives one additional share of stock for each share he or she owns. Since all these investors have twice as many shares of stock after the split as they had before, each share represents half as valuable a claim to the firm's earnings. Therefore, the market price of the stock will normally decline to one-half of its price before the split.

stock dividend: Payment of a dividend in shares of stock rather than cash.

The effect of a **stock dividend** is similar to that of a stock split, except that the company issues a smaller number of shares, and the shares take the place of cash dividend payments. In a 5 percent stock dividend, for example, a firm gives all existing shareholders 5 shares of stock for every 100 shares they already own. This has the same impact on the stock price as a stock split, but the accounting adjustments to the balance sheet are slightly different.

On the company's balance sheet, a 2-for-1 stock split does not change the total book value of common stock, but this total is divided by twice as many shares to give a book value per share equal to half of the previous value. The per-share value of the company's assets and earnings fall, but the total value of the company remains the same. When a stock dividend is paid, the equity account is adjusted to show the issue of new shares used to pay the dividend. These shares are issued and paid at the existing par value, and, therefore, no adjustment to par is made.

The stock split benefits the firm, if at all, only to the extent that it makes the shares more marketable. Company earnings and dividends still must increase for the stock price to rise in the future. The company hopes that a lower market price will increase the attractiveness of company shares by making round lots more affordable for investors, and this may increase the stock price somewhat. Without an increase in earnings and dividends, however, the value of outstanding shares will not change.

Income Statement

income statement: A statement that shows the flow of revenues, costs, and expenses through a firm during an accounting period.

Exhibit 9.2 presents Typical Manufacturing Company's income statement. If the balance sheet is a snapshot or stock statement, then the income statement may be thought of as a moving picture of company operations, or a flow statement. The **income statement** presents the flow of revenues, costs, and expenses through the corporation in a given year. The relationship of the income statement to the balance sheet can be visualized as follows:

Stock of financial resources on December 31, 1991
↓
Flow of revenues and expenses during 1992
↓
Stock or financial resources on December 31, 1992

Balance sheet on December 31, 1991
↓
Income statement for 1992
↓
Balance sheet on December 31, 1992

This diagram conveniently expresses both the major difference and the key relationship between the balance sheet and the income statement. The balance sheet represents the financial position of the firm at a given instant, while the income statement portrays the results of operations for a period of time. The two balance sheets show the firm's stock of assets and liabilities at two points in time, while the income statement shows how the firm got from one point to the other.

The upper half of the income statement in Exhibit 9.2 shows Typical Manufacturing's annual sales revenue, its costs and expenses of various kinds, its net earnings before and after it paid taxes, and its earnings per share of common stock. The sales figure represents the firm's total sales revenue for the year, after adjustment for any returns or discounts it allowed. Cost of goods sold represents the cost of materials, direct factory labor, factory overhead, and other expenses that contributed directly to the production of the products Typical sold to generate its sales revenue. Depreciation represents the total dollar amount by which plant and equipment declined in value in the course of the year, while selling and administrative expenses represent all other categories of operating expenses.

Deducting total operating expenses from sales leaves operating profit, or the gross profit Typical earned from its normal operations. The other income account normally reports miscellaneous income from sources other

EXHIBIT 9.2

Typical Manufacturing Company
Income Statement

	FOR THE YEAR	
	1992	1991
Sales	$13,413,000	$11,575,000
Operating expenses		
Cost of goods sold	7,467,000	7,194,000
Depreciation	376,000	334,000
Selling and administrative expenses	4,575,000	3,092,000
Total operating expenses	$12,418,000	$10,620,000
Operating profit	995,000	955,000
Other income	186,000	184,000
Total income	$ 1,181,000	$ 1,139,000
Interest expense	(180,000)	(184,000)
Earnings before taxes	1,001,000	955,000
Provisions for income taxes	(382,000)	(371,000)
Net income	$ 619,000	$ 584,000
Common shares outstanding	104,000	102,000
Net earnings per share of common stock	$5.71	$5.38

Statement of Accumulated and Retained Earnings

	1992	1991
Retained earnings at January 1	$ 2,684,000	$ 2,390,000
Net income for year	619,000	584,000
Total	$ 3,303,000	$ 2,974,000
Less dividends paid on		
Preferred stock	25,500	35,000
Common stock	276,500	255,000
Retained earnings at December 31	$3,001,000	$2,684,000

than normal operations, such as interest on notes receivable the company held, capital gains and losses, and similar items. Next comes the interest expense account. This item is normally listed separately since it represents a financing expense, that is, an expense that resulted from management's decision about the proportions of debt versus equity to use to finance the company. This expense does not really arise from the normal operations of the company.

Deducting interest expense from total income yields the company's earnings before tax; deducting taxes it paid yields the well-known bottom line—net income for the year. Since the owners of the company are normally most concerned with earnings per share of common stock, the bottom line is expressed as net income per share. This requires deducting any preferred stock dividends paid from net income and dividing the remainder by the average number of shares of common stock outstanding during the year.

Preferred dividends are deducted from after-tax income because, unlike interest paid to bondholders, they are not tax-deductible expenses of doing business. Just like common stock, preferred stock is an ownership security, and any dividends paid are considered a distribution of profits to the legal owners of the company. Typical calculates its earnings per share as follows:

	1992	1991
Net income	$619,000	$584,000
Less: Preferred dividends	(25,500)	(35,000)
Earnings available to common stockholders	$593,500	$549,000
Common shares outstanding	104,000	102,000
Earnings per share of common stock	$5.71	$5.38

The bottom section of Exhibit 9.2, the statement of accumulated and retained earnings, illustrates a key relationship between the balance sheet and the income statement. Retained earnings for the year just ending must equal retained earnings at the end of the previous year (which is also the beginning of the current year), plus net income for the current year (or minus net loss), less any distributions of net income, usually dividends. Occasionally firms deduct losses, such as final settlement of litigation from prior years or unusual tax payments, from their retained earnings accounts. Typical Manufacturing illustrates the more typical case:

Retained earnings, prior year + Net income − Dividends
= Retained earnings, current year

$2,684,000 + $619,000 − $302,000 = $3,001,000

Statement of Changes in Financial Position

Recall the earlier definition of net working capital as current assets minus current liabilities, and the discussion of the importance of working capital. Firms have determined that this critical feature of business operations merits a separate financial statement to report changes in a company's working capital position over the course of a year. This is the purpose of the **statement of changes in financial position,** also commonly called a *sources and uses of funds statement,* or a *funds-flow statement.* The statement of changes in financial position for Typical Manufacturing appears in Exhibit 9.3.

statement of changes in financial position: A flow statement that shows the changes in a company's net working capital during an accounting period.

EXHIBIT 9.3

Typical Manufacturing Company
Statement of Changes in Financial Position

Sources of Funds			
From operations			
Net income	$619,000		
Depreciation	376,000		
Total from operations		$995,000	
Disposal of other assets		83,000	
Increase in long-term debt		266,000	
Sale of common stock		25,000	
Total sources of funds			$1,369,000
Applications of Funds			
Additions to plant and equipment			766,000
Refunding of preferred stock			172,000
Dividends on preferred stock			25,500
Dividends on common stock			276,500
Total applications of funds			$1,240,000
Net increase in working capital			$ 129,000
Analysis of Changes in Working Capital—1992			
Cash and marketable securities		$ 50,000	
Accounts receivable		417,000	
Inventories		271,000	
Accounts payable		178,000	
Notes payable		(680,000)	
Accrued expenses payable		(75,000)	
Accrued taxes payable		(32,000)	
Net increase in working capital		$ 129,000	

Laypersons can be misled by the relatively specialized meaning to accountants and financial analysts of the word *funds*. Common usage equates the term to cash, but in accounting and finance, it refers to net working capital, so a funds-flow statement reports changes in working capital over the course of an accounting period:

$$\text{Funds} = \text{Net working capital} = \text{Current assets} - \text{Current liabilities}$$

The purpose of the statement of changes in financial position is twofold. First, it shows where the firm acquired and spent funds during the year and the resulting change in its net working capital. Second, the statement shows the changes in the individual working capital accounts that resulted in the overall change in net working capital. Increases in current assets increase working capital, while increases in current liabilities decrease working capital. Conversely, decreases in current assets decrease net working capital, and decreases in current liabilities increase net working capital. Stated differently, to increase its net working capital, a firm can work either to increase its current assets or to decrease its current liabilities, or both.

As simple as this may seem, constructing a statement of changes in financial position is a relatively complex task that strains the skills of professional accountants. Interpreting the statement is reasonably straightforward, however, and it is critically important to the analysis of the total financial resources available to the company over the previous year and the distribution of those resources.

An investor could find the overall change in net working capital for Typical Manufacturing during calendar year 1992 as follows:

$$\text{Net working capital, end of 1991} = \$4{,}485{,}000 - \$2{,}700{,}000$$
$$= \$1{,}785{,}000$$
$$\text{Net working capital, end of 1992} = \$5{,}223{,}000 - \$3{,}309{,}000$$
$$= \$1{,}914{,}000$$
$$\text{Change in net working capital during 1992} = \$1{,}914{,}000 - \$1{,}785{,}000$$
$$= \$129{,}000$$

Focusing first on the bottom section of Exhibit 9.3, the analysis of changes in working capital in 1992, increases in all current asset accounts (cash, marketable securities, accounts receivable, and inventories) and a decrease in one current liability account (accounts payable) contributed to increases in the company's net working capital. These increases were partially offset by increases in the remaining current liability accounts (notes payable, accrued expenses payable, and accrued taxes payable). The net result yields the $129,000 increase:

Increases in Working Capital	
Current asset increases	$ 738,000
Current liability decreases	178,000
Total increases in net working capital	$ 916,000
Decreases in Working Capital	
Current liabilities increase	(787,000)
Net increase in net working capital	$ 129,000

The top section of Exhibit 9.3 shows the sources and applications of funds during the year that summed to the net working capital increase of $129,000. The sources section always begins with funds provided by operations during the year, including net income as reported on the income statement plus any noncash charges, such as depreciation. Since depreciation represents the declining values of past fixed asset investments, the depreciation deduction on the income statement does not represent a cash expense. The firm must add this amount to net income to find the total funds provided by operations.

To this total, the firm adds funds from various nonoperating sources such as sales of fixed assets, new long-term borrowing, stock sales, and similar items. Adding all these inflows to funds provided by operations represents the total funds available to the corporation during the year.

The applications section provides a fairly clear listing of corporate uses of funds during the year. Typical Manufacturing used funds to purchase new plant and equipment, to buy back some preferred stock, and to pay dividends. Total sources of funds minus total applications of funds must equal the previously determined figure of $129,000:

Funds from operations	$ 995,000
Funds from nonoperating sources	374,000
Total sources of funds	$ 1,369,000
Applications of funds	(1,240,000)
Net increase in working capital	129,000

Clearly, the statement of changes in financial position provides important information about the managers' use of the stockholders' resources. It also gives a useful picture of the flow of resources through the corporation, and its overall operations. With a secure understanding of the three types of financial statements, the discussion will now explain how to analyze them with the goal of improving investment decisions.

Financial Statement Analysis

financial statement analysis: The art of analyzing and interpreting data from financial statements.

Financial statement analysis includes a wide range of efforts to interpret the implications for company operations of the raw data in financial statements. Effective analysis of financial statements requires the establishment of a systematic, logical procedure that leads toward the goal of making informed decisions. An equity investor, a supplier of debt capital, or a corporate staff analyst all have the same final objective—to build a support structure for rational decision making.

The type of decision under consideration does have a strong influence on the focus of financial statement analysis, however. Stock investors, bank loan officers, and corporate financial staffers all analyze financial statements to support their decision making, but each focuses on different aspects of those statements. The bank loan officer may look for indications of short-term liquidity and the collateral value of liquid assets, while the stock investor will be more concerned with long-term profitability and capital structure. Financial staffers often search through financial statement data for clues about how to improve company operations and profitability. Each financial statement user seeks to develop a solid foundation of information on which to base a decision.

To reach this ultimate goal, intelligent analysts work toward two intermediate goals. They begin with an effort to understand the numbers and their meaningful relationships to develop a picture of the firm's current business. They then extend these relationships in light of the firm's likely economic environment to develop reasonable forecasts for the future. Virtually all decision making, financial or otherwise, is oriented toward the future. The primary use of the tools and techniques of financial statement analysis is to help interested parties make reasonable assessments of a firm's prospects based on analysis of its present and past financial condition together with the best available estimate of the future economic environment.

Financial statement analysis begins with careful scrutiny of reported financial statements, including in-depth consideration of the footnotes, and then proceeds with restatement of the available data to better meet the decision needs of the analyst. Some may wonder why analysts do not accept financial statements at face value. Why juggle such carefully compiled figures into other configurations?

Some rearrangement is generally necessary to understand what public data imply about company operations. This is part of the work of extracting sensible information from the raw data presented in the financial statements. Also, various parties make extremely important decisions involving large amounts of money on the basis of financial analysis, so they generally want to assure themselves that presented financial data truly reflect current conditions and future prospects. The pages that follow develop a framework for doing this.

Ratio Analysis

ratio analysis: Analysis of numerical relationships that reveal the key operating characteristics of a company.

Ratio analysis is a valuable tool of financial statement analysis that allows the analyst to view isolated data, which have little meaning on their own, in relation to other data. A given level of sales can look good or bad, for example, depending upon the amount of assets the firm used to generate those sales. Recasting raw data in the form of ratios, for example relating sales to assets used to generate them, gives the analyst a set of meaningful statistics that reveal the key financial characteristics of an organization.

Almost all analysts use ratios in two major ways. First, they compare ratios for an organization with industry standard ratios. A number of sources can provide information about industry standards, including trade associations and commercial services such as Dun & Bradstreet or Robert Morris Associates. If no information about standards for a given industry is readily available, or if the organization does not fall easily into a recognized industry category, the analyst may have to develop standards for comparison by calculating average ratios for the company's leading competitors. Whatever the source of the ratios, to develop a fair picture, the analysis must compare a company's ratios to standards for similar companies of approximately the same asset size.

Besides facilitating comparisons with industry standards, the second major role of ratio analysis is to reveal trends over time for a particular company. Tracking key ratios over a five- or ten-year period shows how the company has developed, and how it has reacted to varying economic conditions. In particular, ratio performance through previous economic recessions can give the analyst an idea of how well the company will hold up financially during future periods of economic adversity.

For both comparison with industry standards and discovering trends in individual companies, pictures often speak the loudest. Graphs can often portray the results of analysis better than long blocks of text ever could. A single graph that presents both the industry standard and the company trend for a given ratio often gives the best view of the information.

Analysts group key financial ratios into four major categories according to the aspects of the company's financial condition the individual ratios attempt to highlight. The four major categories are:

1. Profitability ratios. These bottom line ratios measure the company's earning power and profitability record.
2. Liquidity ratios: These ratios measure the company's ability to meet its short-term liabilities as they come due.
3. Operating efficiency ratios: These ratios measure how efficiently management employs corporate resources to earn a profit.
4. Capital structure (leverage) ratios: These ratios measure the company's use of debt financing.

A variety of ratios within each of these categories helps the analyst develop a complete picture of a company's current condition and likely future success. The following discussion will examine each category in turn, and explore major ratios within each group.

profitability ratios: Measures of a company's earning power and profitability.

Profitability Ratios Three commonly used **profitability ratios** are return on sales (ROS), return on investment (ROI), and return on equity (ROE). Return on sales is determined by dividing after-tax profits by net sales, where net sales represents the dollar volume of sales less any returns, allowances, and cash discounts.

$$(\text{ROS}) = \frac{\text{Earnings after taxes}}{\text{Net sales}}$$

The second profitability ratio, return on investment (ROI), relates after-tax earnings to the corporation's total asset base.

$$\text{ROI} = \frac{\text{Earnings after taxes}}{\text{Total assets}}$$

ROI is sometimes called *return on assets (ROA)* or *return on total assets (ROTA)*. All three expressions—ROI, ROA, and ROTA—have the same meaning.

The final profitability ratio, return on equity (ROE), relates after-tax earnings to stockholders' equity. Stockholders' equity normally excludes any intangible assets (for example, goodwill, trademarks, and so on) and is determined by deducting total liabilities and intangible assets from total assets.

$$\text{ROE} = \frac{\text{Earnings after taxes}}{\text{Stockholders' equity}}$$

Many analysts consider return on equity to be the most important of the profitability ratios. As a general guide, a return on equity of at least 15 percent is a reasonable objective to provide adequate dividends and fund expected future growth, but, like other standards, this varies among industries.

liquidity ratio: A measure of the ability of a company to meet its short-term debt obligations as they come due.

Liquidity Ratios The most popular **liquidity ratio** is the current ratio, which measures the relationship between current assets (mainly cash, marketable securities, accounts receivable, and inventories) and current liabilities (mainly accounts payable, current notes payable, and currently due portions of any long-term debt). One common rule of thumb maintains that this ratio should be at least 2-to-1, that is, current assets should equal at least twice current liabilities, for most business concerns.

$$\text{Current ratio} = \frac{\text{Current assets}}{\text{Current liabilities}}$$

Another common liquidity ratio, which is related to the current ratio, is the quick ratio, also called the *acid-test ratio*. This ratio measures the relationship between "quick" assets (those that the firm can quickly convert to cash) and current liabilities. It is computed as follows:

$$\text{Quick ratio} = \frac{\text{Cash} + \text{Marketable securities} + \text{Accounts receivable}}{\text{Current liabilities}}$$

As the formula indicates, the quick ratio essentially measures the relationship between current assets other than inventories and current liabilities. It excludes inventories because they lack the liquidity of the other assets, since it can take a considerable period of time to sell off the finished goods a firm holds in stock, and still longer to liquidate inventories of raw materials and goods in production but not yet completed. A rule of thumb maintains that this ratio should be at least 1-to-1.

Two final liquidity ratios, average collection period and inventory turnover, measure the speed with which the firm converts accounts receivable and inventories into more liquid forms of current assets. The average collection period measures how quickly it turns its receivables into cash:

$$\text{Average collection period} = \frac{\text{Accounts receivable}}{\text{Average daily sales}}$$

$$\text{Average daily sales} = \frac{\text{Net sales}}{\text{365 days}}$$

As a rule of thumb, the average collection period should not exceed the time allowed by the firm's credit policy by more than 10 to 15 days. If it sells on terms of net 30 (which means the net amount of an invoice is due 30 days after the sale), its average collection period should not exceed 40 or 45 days.

The analyst can express the inventory turnover ratio as an annual turnover rate or as the number of days' sales tied up in inventories. This ratio measures the speed with which the firm turns its inventories into sales (generating accounts receivable):

$$\text{Inventory turnover} = \frac{\text{Cost of goods sold}}{\text{Average inventory}}$$

$$\text{Days' sales in inventory} = \frac{\text{365 days}}{\text{Inventory turnover}}$$

operating efficiency ratios: Measures of the efficiency with which a company employs its resources.

Operating Efficiency Ratios **Operating efficiency ratios** measure the relationship between annual sales and investments in various classes of assets. The net sales-to-inventory ratio resembles the inventory turnover ratio, but it has one essential difference. The inventory turnover ratio estimates physical turnover rates since its numerator is cost of goods sold. The sales-to-inventory ratio replaces this numerator with net sales, which represents cost of goods sold plus the firm's gross profit margin. Thus, while the net sales-to-inventory ratio does not measure physical turnover, it does provide an important indicator of a firm's need for inventory stocks to support its sales. Other ratios in this category are self-explanatory. Net sales to total assets, or asset turnover, becomes useful later in a unified system of ratio analysis.

$$\text{Net sales to inventory} = \frac{\text{Net sales}}{\text{Inventory}}$$

$$\text{Net sales to working capital} = \frac{\text{Net sales}}{\text{Working capital}}$$

$$\text{Net sales to total assets} = \frac{\text{Net sales}}{\text{Total assets}}$$

$$\text{Net sales to fixed assets} = \frac{\text{Net sales}}{\text{Fixed assets}}$$

$$\text{Net sales to equity} = \frac{\text{Net sales}}{\text{Stockholders' equity}}$$

Capital Structure (Leverage) Ratios In general, the term *leverage* refers to the extent to which a firm employs debt capital to finance its operations. Firms that employ more debt are more highly leveraged. In general, high leveraging is riskier because a firm might not be able to meet its debt service payments (principal plus interest) if revenues decline. On the other hand, as will be seen shortly, high leveraging increases return on equity capital. **Leverage ratios** give the analyst quick indicators for this important variable. The debt ratio indicates the proportion of total debt in the firm's total capital base. The debt–equity ratio expresses the relationship between debt and common equity.

leverage ratio: A measure of the extent to which a company finances its operations with debt capital.

$$\text{Debt ratio} = \frac{\text{Total debt}}{\text{Total assets}}$$

$$\text{Debt–equity ratio} = \frac{\text{Long-term debt}}{\text{Stockholders' equity}}$$

A third key leverage ratio, the times-interest-earned ratio, measures the amount of income before interest and taxes the firm has to cover each dollar of interest expense. The ratio is computed with earnings before interest and taxes (EBIT) in the numerator and interest expense in the denominator:

$$\text{Times interest earned} = \frac{\text{Earnings before interest and taxes}}{\text{Interest expense}}$$

To compute EBIT, sum earnings after taxes plus interest expenses plus income-tax expenses from the income statement. For most corporations, a times-interest-earned ratio between 4.0 and 5.0 is considered quite strong. A ratio between 3.0 to 4.0 should indicate adequate protection against possible future adversity.

Interrelationships among Ratios The individual ratios in isolation can illuminate certain aspects of a company's operations, but the interrelationships among the ratios really fill in the picture. A firm's profitability, liquidity, operating efficiency, and leverage all affect one another, and no single indicator of performance can tell the whole story independent of other aspects.

Two formulations give particularly helpful perspectives on the interrelationships among ratios. The first, the DuPont system of analysis, relates return on investment to profit margin and asset turnover:

$$\text{ROI} = \text{Profit margin} \times \text{Asset turnover}$$

$$\frac{\text{Net income}}{\text{Total assets}} = \frac{\text{Net income}}{\text{Sales}} \times \frac{\text{Sales}}{\text{Total assets}}$$

ROI depends on the interaction of two important components, the firm's profit margin (net income/sales) and asset turnover (sales/total assets). As a shortcut, analysts say that ROI equals margin times turnover. This important relationship shows that ROI, an overall performance measure, derives from profitability (measured by profit margin) and operating efficiency (measured by asset turnover). Analysis of total return, therefore, requires consideration of more than one or the other measure of performance; both are essential.

As a tool to aid diagnosis of performance problems, this formula shows that an ROI deficiency may result from either an income statement problem (a low profit margin) or an asset management problem (a poor asset turnover). The case study later in this chapter will illustrate a practical application of this relationship.

A second formulation of a similar nature provides an interesting and useful insight into the relationships among return on investment, return on equity, and leverage:

$$\frac{\text{Net income}}{\text{Stockholders' equity}} = \frac{\text{Net income}}{\text{Total assets}} \times \frac{\text{Total assets}}{\text{Stockholders' equity}}$$

$$\text{ROE} = \text{ROI} \times \text{Equity multiplier}$$

The equity multiplier simply expresses the other side of the leverage relationship that the debt ratio expresses. It shows the proportion of equity in the total capital structure.

This equation shows the direct relationship between ROE, ROI, and leverage. Higher leverage (as measured by the equity multiplier) increases ROE relative to ROI. More debt allows a firm to generate higher returns from the assets it employs because the use of debt allows a firm to increase its assets without increasing equity.

Suppose two firms both have 9.0 percent ROIs. If Firm A has a ratio of total assets to stockholders' equity (an equity multiplier) of 2.0-to-1, while Firm B has an equity multiplier of 1.5-to-1, the ROE figures for the two firms will be:

$$\text{ROE}_A = 9 \text{ percent} \times 2.0 = 18.0 \text{ percent}$$

$$\text{ROE}_B = 9 \text{ percent} \times 1.5 = 13.5 \text{ percent}$$

This example shows that although the two firms generate equal operating profits (their ROIs are equal), Firm A provides a much higher return on equity, due solely to its financial structure. In return for this added ROE, the equity holders must accept the higher risk associated with added leverage, however.

This shows the limited benefits of generating a single set of ratios for a given company in a given year. Ratio analysis gives a much more complete picture when it compares performance indicators for a company in a single year to similar figures for the same company in other years and for other companies of approximately equal asset size in similar industries. The next section shows this need for benchmarks to aid comparison in another financial statement analysis technique, the common-size financial statement.

Common-Size Financial Statements

common-size income statement: An income statement that shows all accounts as percentages of net sales.

common-size balance sheet: A balance sheet that shows all asset accounts as percentages of total assets, and all liability and equity accounts as percentages of total liabilities and equity.

Common-size financial statements express all accounts as percentages of some key figure. The **common-size income statement** expresses all accounts as percentages of net sales. The **common-size balance sheet** expresses all asset accounts as percentages of total assets and all liability and equity accounts as percentages of total liabilities and equity.

These statements provide crucial supplements to the information revealed by the various ratios discussed earlier. Analysis of the common-size balance sheet focuses on the firm's internal structure and the allocation of its financial resources. On the asset side, the common-size statement portrays the proportions of the firm's total investments in financial resources committed to various types of assets. This is an especially effective display of the firm's distribution of resources between current and fixed assets and its distribution of current assets among various working capital categories, including cash, accounts receivable, and inventories. On the liabilities and equity side, the common-size balance sheet shows the percentage of its financing the firm receives from current liabilities, long-term debt, and equity capital. This gives a particularly interesting view of the relationship between long-term debt and equity and the split between short-term and long-term sources of financing.

The common-size income statement shows the proportions of each dollar of sales that the various cost and expense items absorb. Once again, however, remember that the relationships portrayed by common-size statements cannot be considered in isolation. They do not escape the need for comparison with year-to-year trends and industry standards.

Sequence of Analysis

Analysis of a firm's financial statements should follow a logical procedure designed to achieve the overall goal of gathering a body of complete and accurate information on which to base a decision, either about investing in the firm or about adjusting its operations. Depending upon the analyst's purposes and the nature of the firm, different analyses will emphasize different information, but regardless of the intent of the analysis, it should not ignore any aspect of the firm's operations. Instead, it must encompass in one logical framework the entire organization, including its profitability, liquidity, operating efficiency, and capital structure.

This effort should begin with a clear statement of the objectives of the analysis. This guides the analyst in developing a set of key questions he or she needs to answer to attain this objective. With this plan set out, the analyst prepares the data necessary to answer the questions raised earlier. This step normally involves the preparation of key ratios and common-size statements.

With the data in hand, the analyst can begin to study and interpret it to discover the firm's current and likely future strengths and weaknesses. It is generally best to begin with ratio analysis in order to develop an overall feel for potential problem areas, and then move on to the common-size financial statements. Preliminary questions and opinions developed during the analysis of the ratio data often provide valuable insights that may help focus the review of the common-size statements.

The analyst completes the investigation by forming conclusions from the data and answering the questions posed at the beginning of the process. This generally requires presenting specific recommendations, backed up by data, along with a brief summary of the major points developed previously. If others will review the analysis, it is common practice to begin a written report with a short summary of the conclusions developed in this final phase. This allows readers to grasp the main issues of the case and then selectively read more detailed areas according to their major interests.

Case Study

To illustrate the techniques of financial statement analysis, the end of the chapter will review the financial statements of Technosystems, Inc., a wholesale distributor of plumbing, heating, and air-conditioning equipment. Joseph A. Gilberti founded the company in 1987 with two business associates, Hugh Maguire and Carla Diamond. Technosystems sells most of its goods to contractors who work on commercial projects such as office buildings and warehouses. All three founders of the company, as well as its three sales representatives, are engineers.

Before he founded Technosystems, Gilberti worked as sales manager for Diamag Equipment Company, which was wholly owned by Maguire and Diamond, its president and vice president, respectively. Diamag had enjoyed impressive success specializing in the sale and leasing of heavy construction equipment. Through his contacts as sales manager for Diamag, Gilberti began to explore the possibility of setting up a new company. Although Maguire and Diamond had no interest in operating the new company, they agreed with Gilberti's assessment of its economic potential and decided to finance the venture. Gilberti soon resigned as sales manager for Diamag and became vice president and general manager of Technosystems.

Technosystems began operations with a $100,000 loan from Diamag, payable in ten annual installments of $10,000 plus 14 percent interest on the declining principal balance. The 10,000 shares of common stock the company issued upon incorporation were divided equally among the three founders, each of whom paid $0.10 per share, the par value of the stock. Exhibits 9.4 and 9.5 report Technosystems' current financial condition.

Key Financial Ratios Key financial ratios for Technosystems, along with comparable industry standards, are given in Exhibit 9.6. These data show that Technosystems suffers from a malady common to many small, rapidly growing firms in early stages of development—it is severely undercapitalized, that is, it uses an inordinately high level of debt. This is clear from its very high debt ratio, both in comparison with industry standards and on an absolute scale. Total debt accounts for almost 80 percent of total assets, compared with the industry standard of approximately 50 percent. The ratio of long-term debt to equity exceeds 1.3; normal prudence suggests keeping this from exceeding 1.0. On the other hand, the times-interest-earned ratio appears quite satisfactory, showing a major improvement in 1992 to 5.79 from a meager 2.74 in 1991 and a break-even level of 1.06 in 1990.

On the positive side, notice that all ratios improved substantially from 1990 to 1992. Further, Technosystems' heavy debt results directly from the owners' decision to finance the firm with an initial loan from Diamag. The long-term notes on the balance sheet thus represent debt owed to the majority stockholders, who are unlikely to put unreasonable pressure on their own firm should it have temporary trouble meeting its obligations.

Operating efficiency analysis yields mixed results. All ratios are well above the industry averages. This indicates either that operating efficiency is extremely high or that Technosystems is operating on a shoestring relative to other firms in the industry. The previous discussion of Technosystems' high leverage makes the shoestring hypothesis appear extremely likely, particularly with the sales-to-equity ratio of 20.4 versus the industry average of 4.5.

Technosystems' low current ratio indicates limited working capital, so the inordinately high ratio of sales to working capital (11.1 for Technosystems versus 5.2 for the industry) is not too surprising. This seems to reinforce the shoestring hypothesis, as do the ratios of sales to inventory, sales to fixed assets, and sales to total assets.

Analysis of Technosystems' liquidity position yields mixed results as well. The current ratio is approximately 30 percent below the industry average, but the three-year trend shows great improvement, and the quick ratio appears strong. The average collection period is well below the industry average, indicating that management is doing a good job of collecting accounts receivable. The days' sales-to-inventory figure also shows close attention to inventory control.

EXHIBIT 9.4

Technosystems, Inc.
Condensed Balance Sheets

Assets	1992	1991	1990
Cash	$ 40,400	$ 31,800	$ 60,300
Accounts receivable	114,300	200,200	126,400
Inventory	93,900	65,600	66,200
Prepaid expenses	5,000	1,800	500
Total current assets	$253,600	$299,400	$253,400
Fixed assets (net)	30,500	23,900	5,200
Total assets	$284,100	$323,300	$258,600

Liabilities and Equity	1992	1991	1990
Accounts payable	$ 94,200	$124,400	$111,100
Notes payable	24,800	45,400	11,600
Accrued expenses	900	4,200	3,700
Taxes payable	11,600	9,500	—
Deferred taxes	6,700	1,100	—
Total current liabilities	$138,200	$184,600	$126,400
Long-term notes	83,200	118,500	130,000
Total liabilities	$221,440	$303,100	$256,400
Stockholders' equity			
Capital stock	1,000	1,000	1,000
Retained earnings	61,700	19,200	1,200
Total equity	$ 62,700	$ 20,200	$ 2,200
Total liabilities and equity	$284,100	$323,300	$258,600

EXHIBIT 9.5

Technosystems, Inc.
Condensed Income Statements

	1992	1991	1990
Sales	$1,277,000	$1,159,000	$773,300
Cost of sales	952,700	900,500	627,000
Gross profit	$ 324,300	$ 258,500	$146,300
Interest income	800	200	1,000
Total income	$ 325,100	$ 258,700	$147,300
Sales salaries	96,200	90,300	42,200
Office salaries	63,300	46,900	28,200
Office equipment rental	28,200	29,800	25,500
General and administrative[a]	65,500	56,900	50,300
Total expenses	$ 253,200	223,900	$146,200
Income before tax	71,900	34,800	1,100
Income taxes	29,200	10,500	300
Net income	$ 42,700	$ 24,300	800
Earnings per share (10,000 shares)	$ 4.27	$ 2.43	$ 0.08

[a]Includes interest expense of $15,000 (1992), $20,000 (1991), and $17,000 (1990).

Profitability figures show thoroughly satisfactory results for both the overall trend and the absolute level of earnings. Return on sales exceeds the industry average by a good margin and shows a strong upward trend. Return on investment also seems to be increasing rapidly. The firm's extremely high return on equity is clearly a direct result of its high leverage and low equity.

We can trace Technosystems' improvement in ROI to its improvement in both return on sales and asset turnover. Recall that these two key ratios combine to produce return on investment, as follows:

$$\text{ROI} = \text{Profit margin} \times \text{Asset turnover}$$

$$\text{ROI}_{1992} = 3.34 \text{ percent} \times 4.5 = 15.03 \text{ percent}$$

$$\text{ROI}_{1991} = 2.10 \text{ percent} \times 3.6 = 7.56 \text{ percent}$$

To see how Technosystems' high level of debt financing produces its 68.1 percent return on equity capital, remember the mathematical relationship between return on investment, return on equity, and the equity multiplier:

EXHIBIT 9.6

Technosystems, Inc.
Key Financial Ratios

Profitability	1992	1991	1990	INDUSTRY AVERAGES
Return on sales (percent)	3.34	2.10	0.10	1.77
Return on investment (percent)	15.03	7.52	0.31	8.66
Return on equity (percent)	68.1	120.3	36.4	16.43
Liquidity				
Current ratio (times)	1.84	1.62	2.00	2.63
Quick ratio (times)	1.12	1.26	1.48	1.15
Average collection period (days)	33	63	60	45
Days' sales in inventory (days)	31	27	39	36
Operating Efficiency				
Sales/Inventory (times)	13.6	17.7	11.7	6.0
Sales/Working capital (times)	11.1	10.1	6.1	5.24
Sales/Total assets (times)	4.5	3.6	3.0	5.44
Sales/Equity (times)	20.4	57.4	351.5	4.50
Sales/Fixed assets (times)	41.9	48.5	148.7	2.56
Leverage				
Total debt/Total assets (percent)	77.9	93.8	99.1	49.5
Long-term debt/Equity (times)	1.32	5.86	55.09	1.16
Times interest earned	5.79	2.74	1.06	4.37

$$\begin{aligned}\text{ROE} &= \text{ROI} \times \text{Equity multiplier}\\ &= 15.03 \text{ percent} \times \frac{\$284{,}100}{\$62{,}700}\\ &= 15.03 \text{ percent} \times 4.53 = 68.1 \text{ percent}\end{aligned}$$

This equation clearly shows that Technosystems' lofty rate of return on equity is a direct result of its extremely high leverage.

Common-Size Analysis Analysis of the common-size financial statements of Technosystems reveals several interesting trends. The common-size balance sheet in Exhibit 9.7 shows that the proportion of total assets devoted to fixed assets increased markedly from 1990 to 1992. The reason for the

EXHIBIT 9.7

Technosystems, Inc.
Common-Size Balance Sheet

Assets	1992	1991	1990
Cash	14.2%	9.8%	23.3%
Accounts receivable	40.2	61.9	48.9
Inventory	33.1	20.3	25.6
Prepaid expenses	1.8	0.6	0.2
Total current assets	89.3%	92.6%	98.0%
Fixed assets (net)	10.7	7.4	2.0
Total assets	100.0%	100.0%	100.0%

Liabilities and Equity	1992	1991	1990
Accounts payable	33.2%	38.5%	42.9%
Notes payable	8.7	14.0	4.5
Accrued expenses	0.3	1.3	1.4
Taxes payable	4.1	2.9	—
Deferred taxes	2.4	0.3	—
Total current liabilities	48.6%	57.1%	48.9%
Long-term notes	29.3	36.7	50.3
Total liabilities	77.9	93.8	99.1
Stockholders' equity			
Capital stock	0.4	0.3	0.4
Retained earnings	21.7	5.9	0.5
Total equity	22.1%	6.2%	0.9%
Total liabilities and equity	100.0%	100.0%	100.0%

Note: Some totals may not add due to rounding off.

sharp downward movement of the long-term debt–equity ratio toward the industry average seen in Exhibit 9.6 becomes clear with a look at the increase in the retained-earnings account and hence total equity. Also, notice the steady decrease in long-term debt as a percentage of total capital over the three-year period.

Finally, the working capital accounts show a steady decrease in total current assets as a percentage of total assets. The other current asset or liability accounts show no other pattern, except for the relatively small dollar amounts involved in prepaid expenses, accrued expenses, taxes payable, and deferred taxes. No general conclusion is therefore apparent relative to Technosystems' management of its working capital accounts.

Technosystems' common-size income statement (Exhibit 9.8) shows a very encouraging pattern. The gross profit margin increased steadily over the three-year period, from 18.9 percent in 1990 to 25.4 percent in 1992. Similarly, the pretax and after-tax profit margins have shown steady improvement, from 0.14 percent to 5.6 percent, and from 0.1 percent to 3.3 percent, respectively. The only area that merits further investigation is the steadily increasing percentage of total expenses to sales, particularly the increase in office salaries. Normally, the total percentage of these expenses decreases as a firm grows and achieves some economies of scale, but the opposite has occurred here. In the absence of more detailed information,

EXHIBIT 9.8

Technosystems, Inc.
Common-Size Income Statement

	1992	1991	1990
Sales	100.0%	100.0%	100.0%
Cost of sales	74.6	77.7	81.1
Gross profit	25.4%	22.3%	18.9%
Interest income	0.1	0.0	0.1
Total income	25.5%	22.3%	19.0%
Sales salaries	7.5	7.8	5.5
Office salaries	5.0	4.0	3.6
Office equipment rental	2.2	2.6	3.3
General and administrative	5.1	4.9	6.5
Total expenses	19.8%	19.3%	18.9%
Income before taxes	5.6	3.0	0.14
Income taxes	2.3	0.9	0.04
Net income	3.3%	2.1%	0.1%

Note: Some totals may not add due to rounding off.

however, the existing data support no general conclusion about the cause of this increase.

Conclusions Overall, the trend in the financial condition of Technosystems appears very encouraging. Profitability is excellent and appears to be improving. The liquidity position is adequate and is also improving. However, these encouraging trends are counterbalanced by the firm's severe undercapitalization; it desperately needs an injection of additional equity capital to ensure its long-term survival. Additionally, Technosystems management must pay more attention to cost control.

A potential creditor would view the results of this analysis extremely unfavorably. Clearly, a loan to Technosystems, either short-term or long-term, is out of the question. The firm is already heavily in debt, and it offers little protection for any new injections of debt capital. Assuming that its future sales are reasonably well-assured, investment of some equity funds may be appropriate. The firm is growing very rapidly and has been quite profitable. Additional equity capital would relieve much of the burden on its capital structure. Although the investment would appear to have above-average risk, the potential rewards at this stage in the firm's development also seem to be exceptional. The firm may be suitable for investment by a venture capital company or a wealthy individual who is willing and able to assume the risks involved in a new and rapidly growing firm.

SUMMARY

The balance sheet provides a snapshot of the financial condition of a company as of a given date. It lists the company's assets, and liabilities, and the equity of its owners. By definition, assets must equal liabilities plus equity.

The income statement shows the flow of revenues and expenses through the company over the course of a year or other accounting period. The statement of changes in financial position shows the sources and uses of funds during the year and the resulting change in the firm's net working capital. It also shows the changes in the individual working capital accounts that produced the overall change in net working capital.

Financial statement analysis is the art of transforming financial statement data into information that can support informed decision making. Two commonly used tools of financial statement analysis are ratio analysis and common-size financial statements. Major areas of emphasis include profitability, liquidity, operating efficiency, and capital structure.

A logical sequence for the analysis effort begins with specifying one's objectives. The analyst then develops key ratios and common-size financial statements, and analyzes and interprets the information thus generated. Finally, the analyst develops a set of conclusions and recommendations, backed up by the data.

INVESTMENT MANAGEMENT CONCEPTS

1. Generally accepted accounting principles are a set of conventions that have evolved through the years to govern the preparation of financial statements.

2. The balance sheet is a stock statement showing the financial condition of a company on a specific date.

3. The income statement is a flow statement showing the flow of revenues and expenses through a company during a specific time period.

4. The statement of changes in financial position, another flow statement, shows the flow of working capital through a company during a given time period.

5. The major goals of financial statement analysis are to extract meaningful information from raw financial data, and to provide a basis for financial forecasting and informed decision making.

6. Key financial ratios include profitability ratios, liquidity ratios, operating efficiency ratios, and leverage ratios.

7. The interrelationships between return on investment, return on equity, sales-to-asset ratios, profit margins, and the assets-to-equity ratio provide key insights to understanding the financial operations of a company.

REVIEW QUESTIONS

1. What is the objective of financial accounting?
2. What are generally accepted accounting principles?
3. Why is a balance sheet said to be a stock statement?
4. What is the basic accounting equation that governs the balance sheet?
5. Why is an income statement said to be a flow statement?
6. What is the difference between the income statement and the statement of changes in financial position?
7. Why is working capital important?
8. What are the major objectives of financial statement analysis?
9. How do financial analysts use ratio analysis?
10. What are the most important profitability ratios?
11. How are ratios used to measure liquidity?
12. What do operating efficiency ratios tell you about a company's financial position?
13. What are leverage ratios?
14. Describe the relationship among ROI, profit margin, and asset turnover.
15. What is the basis for the assertion that ROE is a direct function of ROI and leverage?
16. What are common-size financial statements and what do they tell an analyst about the financial condition of a company?

SELF-CORRECTING PROBLEM

Based on the balance sheet and income statement for Typical Manufacturing Company in Exhibits 9.1 and 9.2, compute the company's key financial ratios as listed on the following worksheet. Develop a preliminary analysis of Typical's financial position based on the ratios.

	1992	1991
Profitability		
Return on sales (percent)	______	______
Return on investment (percent)	______	______
Return on equity (percent)	______	______
Liquidity		
Current ratio (times)	______	______
Quick ratio (times)	______	______
Average collection period	______	______
Days' sales in inventory (days)	______	______

	1992	1991
Operating Efficiency		
Sales/Inventory (times)	______	______
Sales/Working capital (times)	______	______
Sales/Total assets (times)	______	______
Sales/Equity (times)	______	______
Sales/Fixed assets (times)	______	______
Leverage		
Total debt/Total assets (percent)	______	______
Long-term debt/Equity (times)	______	______
Times interest earned (times)	______	______

Answer to Self-Correcting Problem

	1992	1991
Profitability		
Return on sales (percent)	4.61	5.05
Return on investment (percent)	6.61	7.02
Return on equity (percent)	14.18	13.92
Liquidity		
Current ratio (times)	1.59	1.66
Quick ratio (times)	0.90	0.93
Average collection period	71	69
Days' sales in inventory (days)	110	101
Operating Efficiency		
Sales/Inventory (times)	5.94	5.83
Sales/Working capital (times)	7.00	6.48
Sales/Total assets (times)	1.43	1.39
Sales/Equity (times)	3.07	2.76
Sales/Fixed assets (times)	3.23	3.01
Leverage		
Total debt/Total assets (percent)	53.40	49.60
Long-term debt/Equity (times)	0.39	0.34
Times interest earned (times)	6.56	6.19

Note: Calculation based on year-end balances and 365-day year.

Preliminary analysis: Profitability has deteriorated as measured by return on sales and return on investment (ROI). Return on equity (ROE) has improved slightly, but this is the result of an increase in leverage (the ratio of total debt to total assets increased from 49.6 percent to 53.4 percent). Recall from the chapter that:

$$\text{ROE} = \text{ROI} \times \text{Equity multiplier}$$

Thus,

$$\text{ROE}_{1992} = 6.61 \times \frac{\$9{,}370{,}000}{\$4{,}336{,}000} = 6.61 \times 2.15 = 14.2 \text{ percent}$$

$$\text{ROE}_{1991} = 7.02 \times \frac{\$8{,}325{,}000}{\$4{,}196{,}000} = 7.02 \times 1.98 = 13.9 \text{ percent}$$

Clearly, the increase in Typical's ROE resulted solely from additional indebtedness. Overall, then, aside from the leverage effect, profitability has decreased.

Liquidity has decreased marginally, but the change does not appear significant. Operating efficiency shows improvement on all counts as sales have increased more rapidly than assets. (Sales are up 15.9 percent; total assets are up 12.6 percent.)

All ratios show an increase in leverage. Indeed, the firm appears to be very highly leveraged, as shown by its debt ratio of 53.4 percent. We lack sufficient data to judge how seriously this leverage may threaten Typical's earnings stability, but judging on an absolute basis, Typical's leverage is fairly high.

SELECTED READINGS

Bernstein, Leopold A. *Financial Statement Analysis*, 4th ed. Homewood, Ill.: Richard D. Irwin, 1988.

Droms, William G. *Finance and Accounting for Nonfinancial Managers*, 3d ed. Reading, Mass.: Addison-Wesley, 1990.

Helfert, Erich A. *Techniques of Financial Analysis*, 6th ed. Homewood, Ill.: Richard D. Irwin, 1987.

chapter 10

Common Stock

Higher Returns and Higher Risks

Terry had worked hard for his success in the commercial leasing business. His firm did not have a pension plan, so, even though he was only in his early 30s, he had established an individual retirement account (IRA) to provide for his and his wife's retirement needs. He had invested the funds in this plan in a mixture of fixed-income securities, common stocks, and international mutual funds.

While reviewing these investments with an advisor, Terry's wife Ann said she was comfortable with the fixed-income securities in the portfolio, but she worried about the common stock investments. The advisor explained that over the 69-year period ending in 1989, the common stocks included in the Dow Jones Industrial Average posted an average annual return, considering returns from both dividends and capital growth, of 10.4 percent. This excellent long-term rate of return substantially exceeded the 3 percent inflation rate for the same period of time, and it was almost twice the return earned on long-term Aaa-rated corporate bonds.

Ann remained unconvinced, fearing that the undeniable risks of investing in common stocks could consume the couple's nest egg. The advisor suggested evaluating those risks and stock market returns for the 20-year period ending in 1990. If they had bought the stocks in the Dow Jones Industrial Average over that time, how many years would the couple have earned gains and how many years would have brought losses?

A review of this period would show that common stocks provided positive rates of return during 15 of these 20 years and lost money during the other five. On the average, stocks earned a total return of approximately 11 percent per year, but there were many ups and downs during individual years. During the worst year, 1974, stocks lost about 25 percent of their value, and during the best year, 1975, stocks went up over 35 percent. There were also three other years during the period when stocks provided total returns in excess of 30 percent—1980, 1985, and 1989. In summary, returns had been quite good during the 1970s and '80s, but they also had been quite volatile from year to year.

These results do not guarantee that a particular investor could match this record for every 20-year period, but it shows that Ann and Terry would probably not lose by investing in stocks with the quality of those in the DJIA. Ann felt reassured, but she remembered, "My uncle bought stock in a bank and lost more than half of his money. I don't want that to happen to us."

"A single stock can surely go sour," the advisor answered, "but if you diversify with quality investments over the long term, you will earn a much higher return than the inflation rate. In real terms you will be better off."

Introduction

Over long periods of time, investments in common stocks offer opportunities for greater profits and rates of return than those in long-term bonds or Treasury bills. Over the short term, however, the course of common stock investing has its dips and rises. Prices of Dow Jones Industrial Average stocks were rather flat during the 1970s: The average annual rate of return for the ten-year period from 1971 to 1980 was only 7.3 percent. The rate of return on the S&P 500 stocks from 1981 to 1990, however, was 14.8 percent. In early 1991 the U.S. economy was facing a domestic recession and war in the Middle East, and stock prices had tumbled almost 5 percent in 1990, causing many individual investors to lose interest in common stocks.

This attitude about the stock market is normal. Many people share Ann's fear of investing in common stock. Yet over the last 40 years the price trend for common stocks has clearly risen, and stock investors have prospered. To verify this, review the return data for the S&P 500 stocks in Exhibit 10.1. The data reveal higher variability for stock market returns compared to other investments, however, and therefore higher risk. This means that stock investors had to devote more work and care to the management of their investments to earn these good returns, but they built excellent hedges against inflation for themselves in the process.

EXHIBIT 10.1

Year-by-Year Total Returns, 1926–1990

	COMMON STOCKS	SMALL-COMPANY STOCKS	LONG-TERM CORPORATE BONDS	LONG-TERM GOVERNMENT BONDS	INTERMEDIATE-TERM GOVERNMENT BONDS	U.S. TREASURY BILLS	INFLATION
1926	11.62%	0.28%	7.37%	7.77%	5.38%	3.27%	−1.49%
1927	37.49	22.10	7.44	8.93	4.52	3.12	−2.08
1928	43.61	39.69	2.84	0.10	0.92	3.56	−0.97
1929	−8.42	−51.36	3.27	1.17	6.01	4.75	0.20
1930	−24.90	−38.15	7.98	4.66	6.72	2.41	−6.03
1931	−43.34	−49.75	−1.85	−5.31	−2.32	1.07	−9.52
1932	−8.19	−5.39	10.82	16.84	8.81	0.96	−10.30
1933	53.99	142.87	10.38	−0.07	1.83	0.30	0.51
1934	−1.44	24.22	13.84	10.03	9.00	0.16	2.03
1935	47.67	40.19	9.61	4.98	7.01	0.17	2.99
1936	33.92	64.80	6.74	7.52	3.06	0.18	1.21
1937	−35.03	−58.01	2.75	0.23	1.56	0.31	3.10
1938	31.12	32.80	6.13	5.53	6.23	−0.02	−2.78
1939	−0.41	0.35	3.97	5.94	4.52	0.02	−0.48
1940	−9.78	−5.16	3.39	6.09	2.96	0.00	0.96
1941	−11.59	−9.00	2.73	0.93	0.50	0.06	9.72
1942	20.34	44.51	2.60	3.22	1.94	0.27	9.29
1943	25.90	88.37	2.83	2.08	2.81	0.35	3.16
1944	19.75	53.72	4.73	2.81	1.80	0.33	2.11
1945	36.44	73.61	4.08	10.73	2.22	0.33	2.25
1946	−8.07	−11.63	1.72	−0.10	1.00	0.35	18.16
1947	5.71	0.92	−2.34	−2.62	0.91	0.50	9.01
1948	5.50	−2.11	4.14	3.40	1.85	0.81	2.71
1949	18.79	19.75	3.31	6.45	2.32	1.10	−1.80
1950	31.71	38.75	2.12	0.06	0.70	1.20	5.79
1951	24.02	7.80	−2.69	−3.93	0.36	1.49	5.87
1952	18.37	3.03	3.52	1.16	1.63	1.66	0.88
1953	−0.99	−6.49	3.41	3.64	3.23	1.82	0.62
1954	52.62	60.58	5.39	7.19	2.68	0.86	−0.50
1955	31.56	20.44	0.48	−1.29	−0.65	1.57	0.37
1956	6.56	4.28	−6.81	−5.59	−0.42	2.46	2.86
1957	−10.78	−14.57	8.71	7.46	7.84	3.14	3.02
1958	43.36	64.89	−2.22	−6.09	−1.29	1.54	1.76
1959	11.96	16.40	−0.97	−2.26	−0.39	2.95	1.50

Characteristics of Common Stock

stock certificate: A document that represents ownership interest in a corporation.

Common stock allows investors to own shares of corporations, which entitle them to shares of corporate profits and increase the rates of return on their invested funds. As evidence of this ownership, the investor receives a **stock certificate,** which is freely transferable to another owner. Brokers trade shares of stock on securities exchanges for the benefit of owners in exchange for commission payments, as explained in Chapter 5. Each share of common stock outstanding represents ownership of, or equity in, a small part of the net worth of the issuing company, represented on its balance sheet in the liabilities and equity section, as discussed in Chapter 9.

Year-by-Year Total Returns, 1926–1990 *(continued)*

	COMMON STOCKS	SMALL-COMPANY STOCKS	LONG-TERM CORPORATE BONDS	LONG-TERM GOVERNMENT BONDS	INTERMEDIATE-TERM GOVERNMENT BONDS	U.S. TREASURY BILLS	INFLATION
1960	0.47%	−3.29%	9.07%	13.78%	11.76%	2.66%	1.48%
1961	26.89	32.09	4.82	0.97	1.85	2.13	0.67
1962	−8.73	−11.90	7.95	6.89	5.56	2.73	1.22
1963	22.80	23.57	2.19	1.21	1.64	3.12	1.65
1964	16.48	23.52	4.77	3.51	4.04	3.54	1.19
1965	12.45	41.75	−0.46	0.71	1.02	3.93	1.92
1966	−10.06	−7.01	0.20	3.65	4.69	4.76	3.35
1967	23.98	83.57	−4.95	−9.18	1.01	4.21	3.04
1968	11.06	35.97	2.57	−0.26	4.54	5.21	4.72
1969	−8.50	−25.05	−8.09	−5.07	−0.74	6.58	6.11
1970	4.01	−17.43	18.37	12.11	16.86	6.52	5.49
1971	14.31	16.50	11.01	13.23	8.72	4.39	3.36
1972	18.98	4.43	7.26	5.69	5.16	3.84	3.41
1973	−14.66	−30.90	1.14	−1.11	4.61	6.93	8.80
1974	−26.47	−19.95	−3.06	4.35	5.69	8.00	12.20
1975	37.20	52.82	14.64	9.20	7.83	5.80	7.01
1976	23.84	57.38	18.65	16.75	12.87	5.08	4.81
1977	−7.18	25.38	1.71	−0.69	1.41	5.12	6.77
1978	6.56	23.46	−0.07	−1.18	3.49	7.18	9.03
1979	18.44	43.46	−4.18	−1.23	4.09	10.38	13.31
1980	32.42	39.88	−2.62	−3.95	3.91	11.24	12.40
1981	−4.91	13.88	−0.96	1.86	9.45	14.71	8.94
1982	21.41	28.01	43.79	40.36	29.10	10.54	3.87
1983	22.51	39.67	4.70	0.65	7.41	8.80	3.80
1984	6.27	−6.67	16.39	15.48	14.02	9.85	3.95
1985	32.16	24.66	30.90	30.97	20.33	7.72	3.77
1986	18.47	6.85	19.85	24.53	15.14	6.16	1.13
1987	5.23	−9.30	−0.27	−2.71	2.90	5.47	4.41
1988	16.81	22.87	10.70	9.67	6.10	6.35	4.42
1989	31.49	10.18	16.23	18.11	13.29	8.37	4.65
1990	−3.17	−21.56	6.78	6.18	9.73	7.81	6.11

SOURCE: *Stocks, Bonds, Bills, and Inflation, 1991 Yearbook* (Chicago: Ibbotson Associates, Capital Market Research Center, 1991). Annually updates work by Roger G. Ibbotson and Rex A. Sinquefield.

Preemptive Rights

preemptive right: The right of an existing stockholder to maintain a proportionate share in the ownership of the company in the event of a new stock issue.

Common shareholders' ownership positions give them shares of the assets and control of a company. This includes rights to pro rata amounts of earnings per share in the future. To protect the value of these rights, shareholders also have a **preemptive right,** which allows them to maintain their ownership proportions of a company by purchasing new shares on favorable terms in proportion to their current holdings whenever the company issues new shares of stock. This right protects shareholders from a reduction in the value of their holdings that would result if the company issued new shares, each with its own right to earnings per share and voting control, which would divide a stable pool of earnings among more shares, giving less to each share. The preemptive right is not granted in all states, which means that new owners may provide new capital and old owners have their ownership proportion dilated.

rights offering: A new issue of stock under the terms of shareholders' preemptive rights.

When a company sells new shares, in accordance with the preemptive right, the sale is called a **rights offering** in investment banking circles. With the help of an investment banker or underwriter, the company gives its current stockholders the right to buy a share (or fraction of a share) of stock for each share they hold at a subscription price that is below the current market price. Besides protecting the shareholders, this helps to guarantee a successful stock sale since many current shareholders seize the attractive opportunity to buy more shares at a lower-than-market price.

When the company announces its intention to sell stock with a rights offering, it automatically attaches a right to each outstanding share on the date of record of the new issue. This might give a stockholder the right to buy one new share for every ten shares he or she currently owned at a $5 discount from the market price. This right attached to each share would be worth $0.50 ($5 saved for every ten shares, or $0.50 per share). The rights expire, however, after a limited time, and owners may trade them in the marketplace. Because these rights have value, shareholders should either sell them or exercise them and buy stock before expiration.

A rights offering is an excellent opportunity to buy additional stock in the company at a lower price than a normal market purchase would require. In fact, an investor who did not currently own shares may find it beneficial to buy the rights in the marketplace, since brokers charge comparatively small commissions for such purchases, and then exercise the rights before they expire.

Voting Control

To control the corporation they own, stockholders have the right to elect directors and vote on corporate matters. They should protect their financial interests by exercising their power to vote at every opportunity. Corporations provide for shareholder voting by two methods—ordinary voting and cumulative voting.

ordinary voting: A procedure for voting common shares that allows one vote per share for each issue under consideration.

Ordinary Voting **Ordinary voting** gives shareholders one vote for each share they hold on each issue under consideration. In a director election, each share gives the owner one vote for each seat on the board of directors. Anyone who can control one more than half of the outstanding shares can elect all of the directors, potentially cutting a large block of shareholders out of any representation on the board.

cumulative voting: A procedure for voting common shares that allows a stockholder to cast all of his or her votes on one issue.

Cumulative Voting **Cumulative voting** can give a strong minority proportional representation. It allows the shareholder to vote his or her shares for each director, or to accumulate votes and cast them all for one director. In an election for seven directors, an investor who owned six of ten outstanding shares would have 42 votes. The owners of the other four shares would have 28 votes. Suppose the majority shareholder tried to elect all the directors by casting 6 votes for each candidate. The minority shareholders could cast 10, 9, and 9 votes for each of three candidates and thereby win three seats.

Because the majority shareholder lacks the votes to control all of the seats, he or she should concentrate votes in favor of the four most desirable directors. This gives the minority owners the power to elect three directors to represent their interests. In this way cumulative voting leaves the majority in control, but the minority shareholders still have some influence on the board.

Two Sources of Returns: Dividends and Capital Gains

Common stock provides its owner two kinds of sources of returns: dividends and capital gains. Corporations pay dividends (usually quarterly and in cash) as a way to distribute shares of company profits among the owners. Stock dividends are paid to shareholders as long as the firm's directors vote to declare dividends to common stockholders. As an alternative, the board may decide to retain the proportion of company earnings it would otherwise pay out as dividends and reinvest these funds in the business.

Common stock can provide a second type of income or returns in the form of capital gains when the stockholder sells shares that have appreciated in price since he or she bought them. If you sell shares of stock for a higher price than you paid to acquire them, you earn a capital gain; if you sell shares for a lower price than you paid, you suffer a capital loss. Note, however, that to realize a capital gain or loss, you have to sell your stock. If you hold the shares forever, you will receive only dividends per share.

cash flow: The sum of earnings plus depreciation and other noncash expenses.

Cash Flow per Share Dividend income depends upon cash flow per share. **Cash flow** is net income after taxes plus any expenses that did not require the expenditure of cash. Suppose a company buys 100 automobiles for use by executives, paying the dealer $1.5 million from its cash account. The corporation's cash balance diminishes by the full amount of the purchase, but it writes off only one-seventh of the price of the cars, one option that the IRS allows, as depreciation in each of the next seven years.

After allowing for the $100,000 scrap or residual value of the autos, the company deducts $200,000 each year for depreciation ($1,400,000 /7) from its gross earnings each year, though it spends no cash after the initial purchase. This depreciation figure is referred to as a *noncash expenditure*. An investor must add the amount of depreciation on the income statement back into net income to get the true cash flow of the company.

To get cash flow per share, you divide the cash flow by the number of shares of stock outstanding. This yields an important influence on management's decision about how much to pay in dividends to shareholders.

Common Stock Dividends

The previous discussion is a quick overview outlining common stock dividends. This critical topic requires more elaboration, however, because dividends are such an important part of share valuation.

Cash Dividends

Usually corporations pay dividends to stockholders quarterly in cash. Corporate directors set the amount of the cash dividend. Many corporations have paid regular dividends to their stockholders for 50 years or more. *The Wall Street Journal* reports the amount of the current dividend on any common stock along with the price of the stock.

Journal quotations stated that AT&T paid a dividend of $1.34 per share in early January 1991. This resulted in a current yield of 4.47 percent on the current price at the time of $30 per share. The performance over time of AT&T has earned its stock an A+ rating from Standard & Poor's in recognition of its characteristics as an excellent growth stock. A growth stock is one whose earnings and dividends have grown strongly in the past and are likely to continue to grow. Since AT&T pays a relatively low dividend, reinvesting much of its earnings in projects to sustain its growth, an investor would buy this stock primarily for growth of principal.

An investor to whom current income was more important than capital growth might buy another stock that had a history of paying large amounts in dividends, with less emphasis on an appreciating market price. Such an income stock provides an investor a stable source of funds to meet current living requirements. A retired person, for example, usually requires maximum income. A growth stock, on the other hand, provides limited current income, but offers the promise of capital appreciation. A person who planned to retire in 10 years, but who had adequate funds from other sources for current expenses, might do well to invest in growth stocks.

dividend payout ratio: The percentage of its earnings a corporation pays out in dividends.

Dividend Payout Ratio The **dividend payout ratio** is the percentage of a firm's earnings that it pays out as dividends. U.S. corporations, on average, pay out approximately 50 percent of their earnings in dividends to stockholders. Remember, however, that the dividend payout is not automatic. Often a company with substantial growth in earnings may pay out only a modest current dividend, retaining the rest of its earnings to finance expansion.

Assessing the investment merits of a common stock requires exploring the company's previous earnings history and then estimating its likely future earning potential. The future stream of earnings will determine the amount of the company's future dividends, and therefore its future stock price. The combination of expected dividends and expected price determines whether a common stock will become a successful investment.

Stock Dividends

Some companies, especially growth companies, pay dividends in the form of stock. Approximately 5 percent of companies listed on the New York Stock Exchange do this as a regular policy. The investor benefits from receiving stock rather than cash as a dividend since no income tax is due on stock dividends until the owner sells the stock, as long as the stock distributed is the same type as the stock on which the firm is paying the dividend. The stock the company distributes becomes part of the investor's asset base, and he or she must pay no federal income tax at distribution. This makes stock dividends extremely attractive to investors who are in high tax brackets.

Note, however, that stock received as a dividend could lose value if the issuing company's earnings were to weaken in the future. A policy of paying stock dividends does not automatically brand the issuer as a growth company. If the shares do not increase in value, the stock dividend becomes less attractive, as well. When considering stock dividends, investors must consider more than just their tax positions. They should look for a likelihood of future earnings growth that will keep both the dividend and the stock price growing.

Stock and Cash Dividends Some companies pay dividends in the form of combinations of stock and cash. Inflation is leading investors to favor higher cash dividends, however, since the value of an uncertain future payment with an uncertain rate of inflation is doubly difficult to estimate. If they could be more sure of their eventual returns, investors might prefer smaller cash dividends, and the lower tax bills that would accompany them, with company earnings being reinvested in future growth.

Often a company's decision to add a small cash dividend to a stock dividend reflects its state and local tax position. Some states tax stocks that pay no cash dividends at higher rates.

Property and Scrip Dividends

property dividend: A distribution of corporate assets instead of a cash dividend.

scrip dividend: A distribution of interest-bearing corporate IOUs instead of a cash dividend.

When a company declares a **property dividend,** it distributes company products or securities it owns to stockholders instead of cash dividends. Property dividends are rare.

In the past, companies that lacked cash to pay dividends would declare **scrip dividends** rather than not pay any dividends. In essence, they issued IOUs for which they would later exchange cash, paying interest on top of the amounts of the dividends. In a sense investors received interest-bearing dividends. This may suit investors quite well, provided they have confidence in the company's creditworthiness.

The terms of such a dividend have varied, making general evaluation difficult. Whenever an investor selects a common stock, he or she must

perspective on **INTERNATIONAL INVESTMENTS**

Common Stock As an Investment

Just as in any market, global markets, including U.S. securities, have winners and losers. The list of global winners and losers in the table indicates that U.S. securities held their own in the best performance category in the first quarter of 1992. Japan's securities were well-represented in the group of worst performers.

When investing in global markets, however, taxes become critical. Foreign stock investments can be taxed by each of two countries and in as many as three ways: transaction taxes, capital gains taxes, and income taxes on dividends. International convention requires the investor pay taxes in at least one country. Wary investors know that, regardless of how well an investment performs, its return can lose value rapidly to taxes.

Global Winners and Losers (in local currencies)

Best Performers

		PER SHR. PRICE 3/31/92	% CHG. OVER 12/31/91
Nobel Industrier	Sw Kr	18.50	180.3%
Unisys	US$	9.875	139.4
Wang Laboratories B	US$	5.75	100.0
Valmet	Fin Mrk	30.00	81.8
Oerlikon-Buehrle b'r	Swiss Fr	413.0	75.7
Norske Bank A free	Nor Kr	15.50	63.2
Midland Bank	£	3.49	62.3
Vard A	Nor Kr	80.00	60.0
Regal Hotels Int'l	HK$	1.26	59.5
Citicorp	US$	16.50	59.0
Oerlikon-Buehrle reg	Swiss Fr	143.0	58.9
Cerus	Fren Fr	146.30	58.7
Institut Merieux Int'l	Fren Fr	6,550.00	57.8
Bank Boston	US$	18.125	57.6
Mitel	Can$	1.55	56.6
Tucson Electric Power	US$	7.00	55.6
Chemical Banking	US$	32.75	54.1
DNL Norske Luft B	Nor Fr	128.50	53.9
Marieberg Tidn. A free	Sw Kr	123.00	53.8
Owens-Corning Fiberglas	US$	34.125	52.5

Worst Performers

		PER SHR. PRICE 3/31/92	% CHG. OVER 12/31/91
Greycoat	£	0.39	−65.5%
Koito Mfg	Yen	925.00	−63.0
Godo Shusei	Yen	1,070.00	−57.7
Lonrho	£	0.66	−57.7
Sceptre Resources	Can$	0.85	−50.0
Nissan Fire & Marine	Yen	1,500.00	−48.8
Hafnia Holding A	Den Kr	307.00	−48.6
Daito Woolen Spinning	Yen	969.00	−47.6
Ratners	£	0.15	−44.4
Shimura Koko	Yen	701.00	−44.4
Data General	US$	9.25	−43.9
Nippon Carbon	Yen	1,050.00	−43.2
Yasuda Trust	Yen	937.00	−42.9
Gota A	Sw Kr	20.00	−41.2
Kurabo Industries	Yen	481.00	−40.6
Hafnia Holding B	Den Kr	252.00	−38.5
Ferranti International	£	0.04	−38.5
Mitsui Taiyo Kobe Bank	Yen	1,110.00	−38.3
Jennings Group	A$	0.62	−38.0
Sanrio	Yen	1,200.00	−37.8

Based on 2,500 stocks in Morgan Stanley Capital International Perspective.

evaluate exactly what return the investment will pay and when. This requires careful examination of the amount, type, and timing of all dividends before buying common stock.

Declaration of Dividends

A corporation's board of directors periodically declares that the firm will pay dividends to stockholders of record. The directors publicly announce the amount of the dividend they will pay, when they will pay it, and to whom they will pay it. Three dates affect dividend declarations: the **dividend announcement date,** the **date of record,** on which the company determines who is entitled to the dividend, and the **dividend payment date,** on which it actually pays the dividend. The new owner of stock traded after the date of record will not receive the dividend; instead, the dividend will stay with the owner as of the date of record.

dividend announcement date: The date on which corporate directors announce a dividend.

date of record: The date on which a company identifies owners to whom it will pay an announced dividend.

dividend payment date: The date on which a company actually pays a dividend.

ex-dividend date: Four days prior to the date of record.

Part of any plan to sell stock involves checking when the next dividend is due. Selling the stock before the **ex-dividend** date entitles the buyer to the dividend. This boosts the share price by the present value of the dividend since the new owner receives this much additional return. In effect, the seller obtains the amount of the dividend he or she has earned by holding the stock for a period of time in advance as part of the purchase price.

Waiting until after the date of record to sell the stock entitles the seller to the dividend on top of the purchase price for the shares, which, of course, will fall by the amount of the dividend. Investors say the stock "goes ex-dividends" when a new owner is no longer entitled to the dividend, that is, four days prior to the date of record. Standard & Poor's *Stock Guide* can provide information about dates of record and dividend dates, as can brokers, investment advisers, or bank trust officers.

Capital Gains: The Second Component of Stock Returns

Price increases give rise to capital gains, the second, and frequently the most important, component of returns on common stocks. The stocks in the S&P 500 index earned an average annual rate of return of 14 percent for a recent ten-year period. The returns due solely to dividend payments averaged around 3.5 percent annually, leaving 10.5 percent of the annual rate of return that must have come from capital gains. Capital gains due to increasing stock prices accounted for 75 percent of total returns on common stocks! This should give the investor ample inspiration to investigate the prospects for future price changes of any stock he or she may think about buying.

Determinants of Future Prices

The primary influence on the future price of a stock is the amount of earnings and dividends expected in the future. Every market price is a function of the value the market gives to the earnings and dividends a security will provide. Investors value a particular stock's stream of earnings and dividends based on varying price–earnings ratios. Low interest rates and low inflation encourage investors to pay higher multiples of a given amount of earnings, as do high expected growth rates of earnings and dividends per share. Conversely, the expectation of higher interest rates and higher inflation or lower earnings and dividend growth reduces investors' enthusiasm, and they pay lower prices for a given amount of earnings and dividends.

A number of other variables have important effects on prices the market pays for earnings and dividends. A stronger dollar in international markets leads investors to pay more for U.S. common stocks. Future stock prices depend, as well, on the general confidence level of all U.S. citizens in the national economy.

Economic growth without inflation is the best environment for common stock prices. The expectations about government fiscal and monetary policy are also important. A deficit-free budget with an easy monetary policy would be an ideal combination, but not a likely one to occur given recent experience.

Stock prices also react to peace and war. The stock market likes a peaceful world environment. Major wars bring inflation and lower stock prices. Short, regional wars bring moments of market panic, but only short-term declines in stock prices.

As difficult as it is to estimate a company's future earnings and dividends, the real problem is estimating how the future market will value these earnings. Chapter 11 will cover this essential task of the market analyst and investor in greater depth.

The 1991 Return Scoreboard

The Wall Street Journal compared the returns of various assets for 1991 in the chart reproduced in Exhibit 10.2. The 30 stocks in the Dow Jones Industrial Average earned +24.53 percent, while the stocks in Standard & Poor's 500 index earned +30.51 percent. The stocks in the Wilshire 5000 earned even more, +34.20 percent. All three of these indicators had turned in negative numbers in 1990, but earned substantial positive returns in 1989. This gives some impression of the roller coaster path that stock prices can take.

The results for mutual funds show a similar pattern for the three-year period. The Lipper International Fund Index shows poor performance in 1990, sandwiched between strong years in 1989 and 1991. On the other hand, bonds outperformed stocks in 1990, but they compared poorly in 1989 and 1991.

At the beginning of each year *The Wall Street Journal* publishes a similar review for the previous year. Saving a copy of this information can give a useful, if rather broad impression of market activities in previous years.

A Proxy for Stock Performance: the Dow Jones Industrial Average

Chapter 5 reviewed the history of the Dow Jones market averages and explained their role as indicators of overall stock market movements. The Dow Jones Industrial Average can also contribute to an understanding of the generic characteristics of common stock and the opportunities and risks it brings for an investor. Exhibit 10.3 provides information for year-end 1990 about the 30 stocks that compose the DJIA's statistical sample.

The first column lists the names of the companies as they appear in the financial press. Most of the abbreviations are easy to interpret, although they do vary by source. American Telephone & Telegraph is listed as "AmT&T," for example. When in doubt about the name of the company, use its stock symbol for proper identification.

The second column provides the stock symbols of the companies, T for American Telephone & Telegraph. The stock symbol identifies price quotations from the New York Stock Exchange, the NASDAQ system, or other markets.

The third column, headed "Price EOY," gives individual stock prices as of the end of the year, obtained from the Value Line Investment Survey. The fourth column states the dollar amount of each stock's dividend per share. The fifth column translates this raw data into an important bit of information, the current **dividend yield**, which is the dollar amount of the dividend divided by the share price. All of the DJIA companies except Navistar paid cash dividends in 1990. Alcoa paid an extra dividend.

dividend yield: The return on a common stock investment due solely to the dividend, found by dividing dividends paid per share by the share price.

In 1990 the DJIA stocks provided an overall dividend yield of 3.82 percent based on the dividends paid on the average divided by the value of the index. The simple average of the dividend yields of the 30 companies was 4.11 percent. This figure is relatively low, based on past years' performance. Historically, the DJIA dividend has seldom fallen below 3 percent or risen much above 6 percent.

The sixth column reports the other component of stock returns, capital gains, giving the change in the price of each issue from the end of 1989 to the end of 1990. The value of the DJIA Index declined 4.34 percent in 1990, but individual results ranged from a 24.3 percent gain for Philip Morris to Goodyear's loss of 56.6 percent.

total return: The return a stockholder earns on an investment, including capital gains and dividends, as a percentage of the purchase price of the investment.

Adding dividend yields to capital gains or losses improves the results somewhat. The DJIA earned a **total return** for 1990 of −0.52 percent

EXHIBIT 10.2

Data From *The Wall Street Journal's* 1991 Scoreboard

INVESTMENTS—TOTAL RETURNS	1991[a]	1990	1989
Stocks[a]			
Dow Jones Industrial Average (30 stocks)	+24.53%[b]	−0.52%	+32.37%
Standard & Poor's 500 Stock Index	+30.51[b]	−3.18	+31.53
Wilshire 5000 Stock Index	+34.20[b]	−6.18	+29.17
Bonds[a]			
Shearson Lehman Long-Term Treasury Index	+17.17[b]	+6.30	+18.94
Shearson Lehman Long-Term AA-Rated Bond Index	+19.91[b]	+6.86	+15.59
Shearson Lehman Municipal Bond Index	+10.31[b]	+7.29	+10.79
Shearson Lehman Intermediate-Term Treasury Index	+13.68[b]	+9.45	+12.70
Shearson Lehman Mortgage-Backed Securities Index	+15.45[b]	+10.72	+15.35
Mutual Funds[a]			
Lipper Growth Fund Index	+35.75[b]	+4.98	+28.55
Lipper Growth and Income Fund Index	+27.10[b]	−5.54	+22.52
Lipper Balanced Fund Index	+26.41[b]	−0.60	+21.45
Lipper International Fund Index	+12.76[b]	−8.50	+24.20
Bank Instruments[a]			
(Bank Rate Monitor National Index)			
One-Year Certificate of Deposit	6.03	7.52	8.67
30-Month Certificate of Deposit	6.46	7.63	8.59
Money Market Deposit Account	5.24	5.86	6.46

(−4.34 percent index decline + 3.82 percent dividend yield). Goodyear led 18 losing stocks with a −47.1 percent rate of return. Philip Morris led the winners with +27.6 percent. Returns for 1990 shown in Exhibit 10.2 show this 0.52 percent return on the DJIA.

These data show that 1990 was not a good year for the stock market. Further, the unusually wide range of the returns for individual companies strongly suggests that an investor who did not own all of the stocks in the DJIA could well have suffered even worse results, since two-thirds of the DJIA stocks experienced negative rates of return.

Data From *The Wall Street Journal's* 1991 Scoreboard *(continued)*

INVESTMENTS—TOTAL RETURNS	1991[a]	1990	1989
Money Market Fund[a]			
Donoghue's 12-month yield on all taxable money funds	5.70%[b]	7.82%	8.87%
Precious Metals			
Platinum (50 oz. bar of bullion)	−19.47	−16.65	−5.67
Gold (100 oz. bar of bullion)	−9.71	−2.36	−1.83
Silver (1,000 oz. bar of bullion)	−7.93	−19.54	−13.63
Residential Real Estate			
Increase in average price of new single-family home	−1.1[b]	+2.4	+10.9
Collectibles			
Sotheby's Old Master Paintings Index	−10.0[b]	+15.0	+40.7
Rare coins, top investment grade (Coin World Trends survey)	−6.02[c]	−20.6	50.6

[a] Includes reinvestment of dividends or interest, if any

[b] Estimate

[c] As of Nov. 30

SOURCE: *The Wall Street Journal*, January 2, 1992. Adapted by permission of *The Wall Street Journal*, © 1992 Dow Jones & Company, Inc. All rights reserved worldwide.

Some Statistical Data about the DJIA

Estimated 1990 Earnings and Cash Flow per Share The data in Exhibit 10.4 for estimated 1990 earnings and cash flow per share indicate as wide a range of performance as the total return data discussed earlier. Price per share seems to bear a relationship to earnings per share, with higher earnings generating higher prices. Still, the wide disparity between earnings per share and cash flow per share is striking. Some advisers have suggested leaning toward stocks with high cash flows per share, other things being

EXHIBIT 10.3

End-of-Year 1990 Performance Data for DJIA Stocks

COMPANY	STOCK SYMBOL	PRICE EOY	DIVIDEND DOLLARS	YIELD PERCENT	PERCENT CHANGE	RETURN PERCENT
AliedSig	ALD	27	1.00	6.7%	−22.6%	−15.9%
Alcoa	AA	58	1.60	2.8	−23.2	−20.4
AmExp	AXP	21	0.92	4.5	−40.9	−36.4
AmT&T	T	30	1.32	4.4	−33.8	−29.4
BethStl	BS	15	.40	2.7	−20.3	−17.6
Boeing	BA	45	1.00	2.2	14.9	17.1
Chevron	CHV	73	3.10	4.3	7.2	11.5
CocaCola	KO	47	.80	1.7	20.4	22.1
DuPont	DD	37	1.68	4.5	−11.4	−6.9
EastKod	EK	42	2.00	4.8	1.2	6.0
Exxon	XON	52	2.68	5.2	3.5	8.7
GenElec	GE	57	2.04	3.6	11.4	−7.4
GenMotrs	GM	35	3.00	8.7	−18.6	−9.9
Goodyr	GT	19	1.80	9.5	−56.6	−47.1
IBM	IBM	113	4.84	4.3	20.1	24.4
IntPaper	INT	54	1.68	3.1	−5.3	−2.2
McDnlds	MCD	29	.34	1.2	−15.6	−14.4
Merck	MRK	90	2.24	2.5	16.0	18.5
MinnM&M	MMM	86	2.92	3.4	7.7	11.1
Navstar	NAV	2	—	—	−41.9	−41.9
PhilMorr	MO	52	1.72	3.3	24.3	27.6
Primrica	PA	23	.40	1.7	−19.7	−18.0
Prct&Gm	PG	87	2.00	2.3	23.3	25.6
SearsRoe	S	25	2.00	7.9	−33.4	−25.5
Texaco	TX	60	3.00	5.3	2.8	8.1
USX	X	30	1.40	4.6	−14.7	−10.1
UnCarb	UK	16	1.00	6.1	−29.6	−23.5
UnitTch	UTX	48	1.80	3.8	−11.8	−8.0
Wstnghs	WX	29	1.40	4.9	—	4.9
Wolwrth	Z	31	1.04	3.4	−5.1	−1.7

equal, because they feel cash flow is a more reliable measure of earning power; cash flows can be reinvested in income-producing assets. Looking at Exhibit 10.4, this would lead the investor to focus on Bethlehem Steel, DuPont, General Motors, Goodyear, Texaco, and USX. Again, individual companies' ratios varied quite widely in 1990, and generalization seems impossible.

Growth Rate of Earnings and Dividends The ten-year growth rate of earnings and dividends might help investors foresee something of the future,

EXHIBIT **10.4**

Earnings, Cash Flow, and Dividends per Share for DJIA Stocks, 1990

COMPANY NAME	EPS ESTIMATE	CASH FLOW	TEN-YEAR GROWTH IN EPS	TEN-YEAR GROWTH IN DPS	(TRAILING P/E APPROX.)	ESTIMATED BOOK VALUE/SHARE	MARKET TO BOOK
AliedSig	$ 3.25	$ 6.85	3.5%	3.5%	7.8	$24.60	1.1
Alcoa	6.45	14.40	5.5	6.0	7.7	62.35	0.9
AmExp	2.50	—	8.5	11.0	9.7	13.25	1.6
AmT&T	2.50	5.65	—	—	12.3	13.40	2.2
BethStl	.50	4.65	25.5	−23.0	11.5	22.50	0.7
Boeing	3.75	5.70	5.0	10.5	25.3	20.60	2.2
Chevron	5.00	12.90	—	7.0	15.0	41.40	1.8
CocaCola	2.05	2.40	11.0	7.5	24.1	4.75	9.8
DuPont	1.62	7.55	5.5	5.0	9.6	24.20	1.5
EastKod	4.00	8.30	3.0	5.5	16.0	22.50	1.9
Exxon	4.10	8.40	7.5	9.5	13.4	26.00	2.0
GenElec	4.85	6.75	10.5	9.5	11.0	24.75	2.3
GenMotrs	4.75	17.85	0.5	−1.0	9.3	62.00	0.6
Goodyr	4.70	7.00	9.0	3.0	10.0	34.70	0.5
IBM	10.15	19.95	6.0	4.5	11.1	71.40	1.6
IntPaper	6.50	12.45	5.5	2.5	6.6	52.30	1.0
McDnlds	2.20	3.40	15.5	24.0	12.6	11.20	2.6
Merck	4.50	5.15	15.5	16.0	17.7	10.45	8.6
MinnM&M	6.10	9.55	7.5	8.0	14.0	27.50	3.1
Navstar	0.00	0.25	−27.0	—	—	2.85	0.8
PhilMorr	3.85	5.25	19.0	23.0	13.4	12.45	4.2
Primrica	3.45	—	—	—	8.6	26.70	0.9
Prct&Gm	4.13	6.61	7.5	7.0	18.2	18.82	4.6
SearsRoe	3.80	6.25	4.5	5.0	8.3	41.30	0.6
Texaco	4.75	11.45	−2.5	—	14.1	31.50	1.9
USX	3.30	8.20	19.0	−3.5	10.3	22.85	1.3
UnCarb	2.40	7.00	5.5	2.5	5.8	18.00	0.9
UnitTch	5.70	11.50	7.0	4.5	8.0	37.25	1.3
Wstnghs	3.45	5.00	12.5	15.0	7.7	16.35	1.7
Wolwrth	2.80	4.55	7.0	8.0	9.7	17.95	1.7

at least in broad outlines. These data support two observations. Like other performance data, earnings and dividend growth rates of the DJIA stocks varied all over the map in 1990. Second, earnings growth rates seemed to have little relationship to dividend growth rates. This suggests that investors must focus on each company's policies and performance without trying to generalize results for a class of securities.

P/E Ratios Similar comments can be made about the variation of price–earnings ratios for DJIA stocks. This is usually calculated by dividing the current stock price by the year's earnings per share. P/E values for 1990, considering only companies with positive earnings, ranged from 5.8 for Union Carbide to 25.3 for Boeing. The overall P/E ratio for the DJIA stocks of 13.7 is, therefore, misleading. Each company has its own historic range of values which require individual attention without reference to any average. Some analysts have suggested that investors should look for companies with low P/E ratios. Such a decision rule would identify Allied Signal, Alcoa, American Express, DuPont, International Paper, Primerica, Sears, Union Carbide, United Technologies, Westinghouse, and Woolworth as attractive prospects, based on 1990 data.

Book Value and Market-to-Book Value Ratios Recall from Chapter 9 that book value is the dollar amount of the net worth of a company's common stock divided by the number of shares outstanding. Some investment analysts advise investors to avoid stocks whose market values far exceed their book values. This means steering clear of excessive ratios of market to book value, which are found by dividing current share price by book value per share.

This decision rule requires interpretation of the word *excessive*. This depends on market relationships between prices and book values and on standards established by the analyst. In his book *The Intelligent Investor*, Benjamin Graham suggests that an investor should pay no more than 1.25 times book value for a company's shares. Several DJIA companies met Graham's standard in 1990, including Allied Signal, Alcoa, Bethlehem Steel, General Motors, Goodyear, International Paper, Navistar, Primerica, Sears, USX, Union Carbide, and United Technologies. Stocks that are clearly overpriced by this yardstick are Coca Cola, Merck, 3M, Philip Morris, and Procter & Gamble. These issues have given excellent performance in the past few years, however, which suggests that no single rule can determine whether a particular security represents a good purchase or not. Still, the relationship between market price and book value should influence a common stock investment decision.

Measuring Expected Returns from Common Stock

If you can estimate the future dividends a stock will pay and the price at which it will trade, you can estimate the return you might receive from investing in that stock. Suppose the current stock price is $25, and that the previous relationship between price and earnings, together with a three-year earnings forecast, lead you to expect a stock price three years in the future of $34. (Chapter 11 will discuss methods to assess the value of a common stock in detail.) If the stock will likely pay an annual dividend in each of the next three years of $1 per share, what total return can you expect from your investment?

First, you calculate your annual capital gain. Adding this figure to your estimate of dividend income and dividing the total by the average investment gives your estimated total return. Ignoring commissions and income taxes, the capital gain on the stock for the three-year period is $9 ($34 value in Year 3 minus the $25 purchase price), so the average annual capital gain is $3. Add the annual dividend of $1 to the $3 average annual capital gain, and you have a total annual gain per year of $4 per share. To find your estimated rate of return, you must divide this gain by the amount of the investment necessary to obtain it.

To find the average annual investment for the period, you add $25 (the investment at the beginning of the period) to $34 (the investment at the end of the period) and divide this total, $59, by 2. Dividing the $4 average annual gain by the average annual investment worth $29.50 per share, you get a total return estimate of 13.6 percent. This is an excellent rate of return despite the risks of common stocks.

The investor's overriding goal is to maximize total annual return with the minimum possible risk. The investor must either estimate these variables himself or herself, or find others' estimates in reliable information sources. Some investment services can provide estimates of total annual return, but they do not make them readily available to all investors. Therefore, the investor should learn to make these estimates. While prone to errors, this effort toward self-reliance can free the investor from professional advisors, or at least give him or her a basis from which to evaluate their advice.

Expected Returns for DJIA Stocks, 1993–1995

To assess the value of investing in common stocks between 1993 and 1995, you can review the estimated annual returns for the entire market, taking the DJIA as the market's representative, as before. The second column in Exhibit 10.5 lists estimated rates of return from Value Line (a generally reliable source of such information) for each of the companies in the Dow Jones Industrial Average. Value Line found these rates of return by adding its high estimate of each return to its low estimate and dividing by 2.

Some of the returns seem impressive. Bethlehem Steel offers a tantalizing estimated return of 42 percent, and General Motors, Goodyear, and Navistar offer returns of 36.5, 37.5, and 38.0 percent, respectively. Only one stock on the list, Texaco, should have an unacceptable return of 8.5 percent. A cautious investor would probably reject a few other comparatively poor performers, as well, including Boeing, Chevron, Coca Cola, Exxon, and Union Carbide.

EXHIBIT **10.5**

Risk and Return-to-Risk Ratios for DJIA Stocks, 1990

COMPANY NAME	EXPECTED ANNUAL RETURN	ESTIMATED STANDARD DEVIATION	RETURN-TO-RISK RATIO
AliedSig	26.5%	9.5%	2.8
Alcoa	24.5	12.0	2.0
AmExp	22.5	13.0	1.7
AmT&T	18.5	9.0	2.1
BethStl	42.0	15.0	2.8
Boeing	12.5	9.5	1.3
Chevron	10.5	9.5	1.1
CocaCola	12.5	10.0	1.3
DuPont	17.5	11.0	1.6
EastKod	25.5	10.0	2.6
Exxon	10.5	8.0	1.3
GenElec	22.0	11.0	2.0
GenMotrs	36.5	10.0	3.7
Goodyr	37.5	11.5	3.3
IBM	18.0	9.0	2.0
IntPaper	24.0	13.0	1.8
McDnlds	21.5	10.0	2.2
Merck	25.0	10.0	2.5
MinnM&M	16.0	10.5	1.5
Navstar	38.0	12.0	3.2
PhilMorr	21.5	11.0	2.0
Primrica	24.0	13.0	1.8
Prct&Gm	13.5	9.5	1.4
SearsRoe	25.5	11.5	2.2
Texaco	8.5	7.0	1.2
USX	19.0	10.0	1.9
UnCarb	10.5	12.5	0.8
UnitTch	25.0	11.5	2.2
Wstnghs	26.5	12.0	2.2
Wolwrth	23.0	12.5	1.8

SOURCE: Value Line Publishing, Inc.

These estimates make the rest of the DJIA stocks seem like excellent investment prospects. Their returns beat inflation and outpace most other long-term investments. This picture is not complete, though, since it gives no impression of the risk an investor would have to accept to have a chance at these big returns.

Risk and the Common Stock

The strong variations in performance of DJIA stocks suggest that common stocks put the investor's capital at substantial risk. Other data support this conclusion. Over the 65-year period from 1926 through 1990, stocks included in Standard & Poor's 500 Composite Index averaged a return of 10.1 percent per year. Returns varied widely from year to year. For about two-thirds of these 65 years, the returns on S&P 500 stocks ranged between (approximately) −11 and +31 percent. In some years the return fell far short of its 10 percent average, and in others it beat this average by a healthy margin.

For many investors the thought that their securities' prices could drop 10 or even 20 percent in a single year is quite disconcerting. The chance that their securities could rise by that much or even more, however, keeps common stocks among the most popular investments.

Measuring Risk: Standard Deviation

As mentioned in Chapter 6, investors measure investment risk, or the variability of returns, with a statistic called *standard deviation*. Calculation of standard deviation is quite simple. First, find the average, or mean, of a series of returns, perhaps ten years' returns on a particular stock. Next, subtract the mean from each annual return, then square each annual difference. Sum these figures and divide by one less than the number of periods; then take the square root of this sum. This is the standard deviation of the series of returns.

Statistical theory holds that annual returns for two-thirds of the years in any period will fall within one standard deviation above or below the mean. Empirical results show that higher returns give higher standard deviations, or levels of risk, reaffirming the premise of the risk–return tradeoff.

Past experience leaves little doubt that an investor who wants a chance at the high returns in the stock market must face real risks. Intelligent choices of which risks to accept and which to avoid depend on past returns and their variations. Knowledge of the past does no good in itself, since future returns and variability determine the performance of current investments, but information about the past gives a solid foundation on which to build estimates of future returns and their variability. The quality of these estimates determines future success or failure.

Return-to-Risk Ratio

return-to-risk ratio: A measure of return per unit of risk, found by dividing expected return by standard deviation.

The fourth column in Exhibit 10.5 shows **return-to-risk ratios** for the DJIA stocks, found by dividing each stock's ten-year standard deviation of annual returns into Value Line's estimate of its return. A higher ratio indicates a more favorable tradeoff between return and risk. Maximizing this ratio gives the investor the best chance possible of enjoying a high return without losing too much to variations in price. This calculation of the reward-to-risk ratio is a simplification of a calculation known as the Sharpe Index. The Sharpe Index first subtracts the risk-free rate (measured by the 91-day Treasury-bill rate) from a security's total return, then divides the difference by the standard deviation of return. This ratio measures return in excess of the risk-free rate per unit standard deviation.

General Motors, for example, has a return-to-risk ratio of 3.7. The GM stockholder can expect to receive a 3.7 percent return for every 1 percent increment of risk. This stock looks like a good deal. On the other hand, Union Carbide provides only 0.8 percent return for each 1 percent of risk—a poor exchange. An investor should probably be willing to invest in a stock that could give 1 percent of return for every 1 percent of risk.

Using a return-to-risk ratio of 1.0 as the standard, the investor would avoid Union Carbide stock, especially since its rate of return is relatively low. DJIA stocks with relatively attractive risk-to-reward ratios include Allied Signal, Bethlehem Steel, Eastman Kodak, General Motors, Goodyear, McDonald's, Merck, Navistar, Sears, United Technologies, and Westinghouse.

The return-to-risk ratio gives investors no automatic answers to the complicated question of where to put their money. They must apply this principle as part of the overall investment decision process. First, they seek out the best companies in the best industries. From the list of companies that offer the highest expected returns, they select those companies with the highest return-to-risk ratios.

Appraising Risk: Standard & Poor's Stock Ratings

Professional information services provide help in determining the riskiness of common stock issues. Although their rating systems are imperfect, Standard & Poor's *Stock Guide* and similar publications rank stock performance with emphasis on stability and growth of earnings and dividends. A sample page from Standard & Poor's *Stock Guide* appears in Exhibit 10.6. An A-rated company has shown growth of earnings and dividends among the most stable in the stock market. A C-rated company has shown some of the least stable earnings and dividends. In between, various risk categories emphasize gradations in stability of earnings and dividends growth.

Although S&P ratings can be only approximate guides to value, they give the investor a general idea of the risk and profit potential of investing in a particular common stock. The stock ratings appear in the column headed "Com. Rank. & Pfd. Rating." Besides these ratings, the *Stock Guide* provides a wealth of information similar to that discussed in this chapter. Investors can find a great deal of support for their decisions in this source of information.

Advantages and Disadvantages of Common Stock Ownership

Most investors purchase common stock with the hope of obtaining higher returns than any other type of security can provide. Over long periods of time long-term bonds can never match the returns on stocks. Since stock returns have two components, dividend yields and capital gains, they can help the investor achieve both income and growth goals.

In addition, the tax laws improve the profitability of common stock as compared to other investments. Investors must pay taxes on capital gains only when they sell their securities and realize the gains. As explained earlier, capital gains account for the bulk of common stock returns. This delays the tax bill on the investor's investment returns and, in effect, allows him or her to leave money to compound untaxed.

Some disadvantages counterbalance these powerful advantages, though. Common stock ownership brings more risk of capital losses than some other investments. The stock investor must contend with substantial instability in prices and dividend yields. Also, most common stocks pay rather low levels of current dividends as compared to interest income from fixed-income securities, discouraging an investor whose primary need is current income from buying stocks.

Common stocks can have either advantages or disadvantages in times of inflation. Some common stocks have been very good hedges against inflation. Extremely rapid inflation like the double-digit percentage price increases experienced in the 1970s sends interest rates upward while stock prices fall.

Stock market prosperity reached record levels in the late 1950s, again in the early 1960s, and once again in the mid-1980s. The economy in each of these periods featured low interest rates and extremely stable prices. These conditions promoted corporate growth, so stock prices soared and investors made money. On the other hand, high inflation in 1973, 1974, and 1979 depressed common stock prices substantially.

In general, investors can expect rapid inflation, such as that caused by oil shortages in the 1970s, to erode stock prices. The best hope of general improvement in common stock prices comes from increasing corporate productivity and real output in the national economy, and from reducing inflation. Lower interest rates reduce yields on fixed-income securities, which increases demand and therefore prices for common stocks. Common stocks are generally preferable investments under stable world conditions, and over time they have tended to outperform long-term bonds and other types of securities.

Investment Climate Analysis and Common Stock Selection

The stock price listings in any newspaper graphically demonstrate that investors must choose among a bewildering array of companies and security issues. Fortunately, a method by which to make this choice emerges from an understanding of the sensitivity of stock prices to the performance of the national economy, industries within it, and individual companies within various industries.

EXHIBIT 10.6

Sample Page of Standard & Poor's *Stock Guide* with Common Stock Rank and Preferred Stock Rating

16 AME-AME Standard & Poor's Corporation

¶ S&P 500 # MidCap 400 • Options Index	Ticker Symbol	Name of Issue (Call Price of Pfd. Stocks)	Market	Com. Rank. & Pfd. Rating	Par Val.	Inst. Hold Cos	Inst. Hold Shs. (000)	Principal Business	Price Range 1971-90 High	1971-90 Low	1991 High	1991 Low	1992 High	1992 Low	Feb. Sales in 100s	February, 1992 Last Sale Or Bid High	Low	Last	%Div Yield	P-E Ratio
1	AHE	**Amer Hlth Prop**	NY,M,Ph	NR	1¢	108	6563	Real estate investment trust	24⅝	12	35⅝	22¾	37	27⅞	23486	36⅜	27⅞	29⅞	9.0	14
2	AHI	**Amer Healthcare Mgmt**	AS,M	C	1¢	21	4764	Health care facilities	12¼	1/16	4⅞	⅞	6	4	9585	5⅝	4¾	5	...	12
3	AMHC	**Amer Healthcorp**	OTC	NR	.001	24	1436	Oper diabetes treatm't ctrs	....	....	21¼	9¼	23½	17½	4165	23½	17½	19¼B	...	34
4	AHL	**Amer Heritage Life**	NY,M	A	1	28	661	Insur hdg co: life, accident	25½	3⅝	32¼	20	37⅝	30½	432	36¾	34¼	36	3.1	14
¶5•[1]	AHP	**Amer Home Products**	NY,B,C,M,P,Ph	A+	33⅓¢	911	195014	Drugs, food,household/ware	55⅛	10¾	86¼	46½	84¼	72½	120907	82¼	72½	79	3.3	18
6	Pr	**$2.00 cm Cv Pfd (60) vtg**	NY	NR	2½	2	4	pkgd medicine,med prod	483⅛	101	760	460¾	748¾	684	4	702½	684	711B	0.3	
7	AIFC	**Amer Indem/Fin'l**	OTC	B−	3.33	11	506	Property & casualty insur	25⅝	2¾	7¾	3¾	9¼	4¾	424	7½	6½	6⅝B	1.2	6
8	AIIÇ	**Amer Integrity**	OTC	C	1¢	16	1575	Supplemental accid,life ins	29⅜	1⅛	6⅜	2⅛	5	3⅞	5749	4⅞	4	4½B	...	d
¶9•[2]	AIG	**Amer Intl Group**	NY,B,M,P	A	2½	720	107275	Major int'l insur hldg co	89⅝	4⅛	102	72	98⅞	85½	56678	93¼	85½	87½	0.6	12
10	AIP	**Amer Israeli Paper Ord**	AS,B,M,Ph	NR	[53] .	1	3	Paper mfg fr imported pulp	34⅛	4	46½	29¼	49¼	40¾	95	49¼	45¾	46⅜B	0.7	14
11	AMZ	**Amer List**	AS,M	B+	1¢	23	642	Comput'zed H.S. student lists	24⅜	¼	27⅝	14¼	18¼	15	139	18¼	15¼	17⅝B	e...	18
12	AZE.A	**Amer Maize-Prod 'A'**[54]	AS,M	B	80¢	28	1768	Corn processing:tobacco prd	26⅝	3¾	23⅛	16¾	25¾	20¼	1177	25¾	22¼	24⅛	2.7	14
13	AZE.B	**Class B vtg**	AS,M	B	80¢	10	436		24⅞	3¾	22	17⅝	25½	20	84	25½	22½	25¼	2.5	14
14	AMSY	**Amer Mgmt Systems**	OTC	B+	1¢	48	4710	Computer sys mgmt/admin	19⅞	1 9/16	28½	16¼	25	19¼	4371	25	21¾	21¾B	...	19
15	AMI	**Amer Medical Hldgs**	AS,B,M,P	C	1¢	64	22944	U.S./int'l hospitals: services	37¼	11/16	13	4¼	11⅝	8⅞	18671	11⅝	9¾	10	...	..
16	AXT	**Amer Muni Term Trust**	NY,M,Ph	...[55]	1¢	1	10	Closed-end muni bond fund	....	....	10⅜	9⅝	10⅝	10	577	10½	10⅛	10⅜	6.3	..
17	BXT	**Amer Muni Term Trust II**	NY,M,Ph	...[55]	1¢	..	...	Closed-end muni bond fund	....	....	10⅜	9½	10¼	9¾	717	10⅛	9⅞	10	6.2	..
18	ANAT	**Amer Nat'l Insur**	OTC	A−	1	55	4512	Life insurance	50¾	5⅜	41¾	27	45	39	2324	43	39	40B	4.7	8
19	ANUC	**Amer Nuclear**	OTC	C	4¢	8	184	Uranium properties in Wyo	19⅛	⅜	3⅞	1¼	3	2	694	2⅝	2	2⅜B	...	d
20	AOG	**Amer Oil & Gas**	AS,M	B−	4¢	40	4576	Nat'l gas PL,well svc	11⅞	2⅛	13	6¼	12	10¾	1467	12	11	11¾	...	16
21	OIF	**Amer Opportunity Income**	NY,M	...[55]	1¢	6	110	Closed-end diversified inv co	10⅛	8¼	11	9⅜	11½	10⅜	3664	11¼	10¾	10⅞	e9.2	..
22	APFC	**Amer Pacific**	OTC,P	B−	10¢	30	1604	Chemical/real estate dvlp	89	½	18	8¼	41¼	16¾	21318	41¼	22½	40B	...	24
23•[3]	APCC	**Amer Power Conversion**	OTC	NR	1¢	98	9894	Mfr constant pwr supply prod	9¾	15/16	28¼	7⅛	38¼	25¼	43765	38¼	30½	35⅞B	...	52
24	APR	**Amer Precision Ind**	NY,M	B+	66⅔¢	18	1025	Ind'l process eq: electr comp	18	¼	15	6¼	8½	7⅝	2240	8½	7⅝	7⅝	2.6	15
#25•[4]	APS	**Amer President Cos**	NY,B,M	B−	1¢	108	13478	Major U.S. containership oper	51	10⅜	43⅜	15¾	43⅞	30¾	28994	35⅜	30¾	32⅝	1.8	9
26	ACP	**Amer R.E.Ptnrs**	NY,M	NR	No	24	204	Acquire,manage real estate	17½	7⅝	11½	7¾	10⅜	9⅜	1744	10⅜	9¾	10¼	19.5	9
27	ARB	**Amer Realty Tr SBI(New)**	NY,M	NR	1¢	11	485	Real estate investment	72⅜	¾	7⅜	5	6½	5¼	370	6½	5¼	6½	...	d
☆28	**AMRC**	**Amer Recreation Ctrs**	**OTC**	**B**	**No**	**13**	**556**	**Bowling centers:catalog prod**	**11⅝**	**¼**	**9¼**	**4¾**	**8¼**	**6½**	**4240**	**7½**	**6¾**	**7¼B**	**2.5**	**12**
29	ARI	**Amer Reliance Group**	AS,M	B	1¢	14	130	Property & casualty insur	16½	6¾	17	9⅞	18½	16⅛	365	18½	17⅛	18	2.7	7
30	RMC	**Amer Restaurant Ptnrs'A'**[60]	AS	NR	No	2	6	Pizza Hut franchise	11⅝	7⅝	10⅜	7⅞	9⅛	7⅞	217	8⅞	8¼	8⅞	13.5	7
31	ASB	**Amer Svgs Bank**	NY,M	NR	No	14	546	Savings bank, New York	25⅛	1	2⅛	1/32	1⅜	¼	6300	1	7/16	½	...	d
32	Pr A	**$2.0625 Cv Pfd**	NY,M	NR	No	1	28		25⅜	1¼	3¼	⅛	1⅞	¼	1938	1	7/16	7/16	472.0	..
33	ASE	**Amer Science & Engr**	AS,B	C	66⅔¢	15	559	X-ray prod:rsch&engr svc	13⅞	11/16	8⅝	3⅞	6⅞	4	1413	6⅞	5¾	6¼	...	d
34	AMS	**Amer Shared Hosp Sv**	AS	NR	No	7	174	Medical diagnostic imag'g eq	12⅛	1	5⅝	1¼	9⅝	4⅞	3648	9⅝	7	7⅞	...	d
35	ABG	**Amer Ship Bldg**	NY,M	C	1	18	784	Ship construction, repairs	17	1⅛	4½	1¼	3½	2⅛	3811	3½	2⅝	2¾	...	d
36•[5]	AMSWA	**Amer Software'A'**	OTC	B+	10¢	105	11571	Mkts IBM compatible softwr	18¼	2 3/16	17¼	9	19¾	14	24957	19¾	16⅞	18B	1.6	21
37	ASR	**Amer Southwest Mtge Inv**	AS,M,P,Ph	NR	1¢	15	634	Real estate investment trust	12⅛	2⅞	9	4⅝	7⅝	5¾	12748	7⅛	5¾	7⅛	20.8	6
38	RODS	**Amer Steel & Wire**	OTC	NR	20¢	12	729	Manufactures steel rod/wire	10⅜	1¼	2⅝	1⅜	2⅛	1¼	2508	2⅛	1⅜	1¾B	...	d
¶39•[6]	ASC	**Amer Stores**	NY,B,M,P,Ph	A−	1	276	55062	Operates supermkts,drug strs	43⅛	⅞	46¼	26	37	31	25467	37	32⅞	35⅜	2.0	9
40	ASP	**Amer Strategic Inc Portfolio**	NY	NR	1¢	..	...	Closed-end diversified inv co	....	....	15⅝	15	15⅞	15¼	1130	15¾	15¼	15¼	8.9	..
41	AMSC	**Amer Superconductor**	OTC	NR	1¢	7	931	Dvlp stg: R&D superconduct'g pd	....	....	21	12¾	28¼	18⅝	2536	28¼	21½	22¼B	...	d
42	AMK	**Amer Tech'l Ceramics**	AS,M	B−	1¢	4	211	Mfrs ceramic capacitors	10½	1	2	1⅛	2⅞	1½	1298	2⅞	1½	2⅝	...	d
¶43•[6]	T	**Amer Tel & Tel**	NY,B,C,M,P,Ph	A−	1	925	399194	Telecom svcs/business sys	47⅜	14⅞	40⅜	29	41⅜	36¾	342368	38¾	36¾	37⅛	3.6	93
44•[7]	ATCMA	**Amer TV/Commun'ns'A'**[66]	OTC	NR	1¢	..	...	Operates cable TV system	55¼	14½	55¼	29¾	59¾	54½	103431	59¾	56½	57⅞B	...	39
45	ATVC	**Amer Travellers**	OTC	B	1¢	53	5920	Life,accident,health,insur	20	1 15/16	20¾	10½	14	11	22942	14	11¼	13⅝B	...	11
46	AMGD	**Amer Vanguard**	OTC	NR	10¢	3	9	Mfr agric-chem/dstr ind'l eqp	10	⅜	9	4½	8	5	70	8	5½	7¼B	...	d
#47	AW	**Amer Waste Svcs'A'**	NY,M,Ph	NR	No	49	5480	Waste mgmt/disposal svcs	12¾	9½	14⅞	5⅞	7⅜	4¾	11561	6	5	5⅛	...	19

Uniform Footnote Explanations-See Page 1. Other: [1]ASE:Cycle 1. [2]CBOE:Cycle 2. [3]ASE,CBOE:Cycle 3. [4]P:Cycle 1. [5]Ph:Cycle 1. [6]CBOE:Cycle 1. [7]ASE,CBOE:Cycle 1. [51]Incl $0.4025 non-taxable,'91. [52]10 Mo Dec '87. [53]Ord par 10 shekel. [54]Ltd vtg. [55]Rated"AAf"by S&P. [56]©$0.1429,'92. [57]Incl cap gains:short $0.147,long $0.003,'91. [58]100% non-taxable,'91. [59]®$2.47,'91. [60]L.P. Income Pref Units. [61]Excl Cl'B'&Cl'C'Units. [62]19 Wk Dec,'87. [63]Accum on pfd. [64]4 Mo Dec,'87. [65]Special divd. [66]Time Warrner(82%)plan acq,$82.50 notes.
☆ See Directory of Company Investor Contacts on page 254.

SOURCE: Standard & Poor's, *Stock Guide*, March 1992, pp. 16 and 17. Reprinted by permission.

Examination of the National Economy

Choosing a common stock requires understanding conditions in the national economy and their implications for the performance of all stocks. Unfortunately, most people are not economic forecasters, and they must rely on often conflicting advice from experts. The theorists do agree, however, that certain factors can have predictable effects on the national economy and securities markets.

First, a strong dollar in international monetary markets generally promotes growth in common stock prices. A strong dollar commands greater amounts of foreign currencies per dollar.

Sample Page of Standard & Poor's *Stock Guide* with Common Stock Rank and Preferred Stock Rating *(continued)*

Common and Convertible Preferred Stocks — **AME-AME 17**

Splits ◆ Index	Cash Divs. Ea. Yr. Since	Dividends: Latest Payment Period $	Date	Ex. Div.	Total $ So Far 1992	Ind. Rate	Paid 1991	Financial Position Mil-$: Cash& Equiv.	Curr. Assets	Curr. Liab.	Balance Sheet Date
1	1987	Q0.67¼	2-28-92	2-10	0.67¼	2.69	[51]2.56½	Equity per shr $17.87			9-30-91
2◆	...	None Since Public			...	Nil	...	14.7	59.2	39.7	9-30-91
3	...	None Since Public			...	Nil	...	4.56	11.7	4.72	11-30-91
4◆	1964	M0.093	4-24-92	4-7	0.183	1.12	1.06	Equity per shr $21.28			9-30-91
5◆	1919	Q0.65	3-1-92	2-7	0.65	2.60	2.37½	1833	3987	1369	9-30-91
6	1966	Q0.50	4-1-92	3-5	1.00	2.00	2.00	Cv into 9 common			
7	1939	Q0.02	2-15-92	2-3	0.02	0.08	0.08	Equity per shr $13.14			9-30-91
8	...	None Since Public			...	Nil	...	Equity per shr $4.53			9-30-91
9◆	1969	Q0.12½	3-20-92	3-2	0.12½	0.50	0.47	Equity per shr $48.48			6-30-91
10	1986	t0.34	6-4-91	5-2	...	0.34	t0.34	3.21	94.5	65.2	12-31-90
11	1989	†1.00	7-8-91	6-4	...	Nil	†1.25	5.94	9.57	0.62	11-30-91
12	1929	Q0.16	3-25-92	3-5	0.16	0.64	0.64	54.5	192	45.6	9-30-91
13	1969	Q0.16	3-25-92	3-5	0.16	0.64	0.64	...	...	...	
14◆	...	None Since Public			...	Nil	...	29.1	95.8	41.3	9-30-91
15	...	0.18	5-3-89	4-11	...	Nil	...	39.2	279	451	11-30-91
16	1991	0.054	3-25-92	3-2	0.163	0.65	0.433	Net Asset Val $9.86			2-21-92
17	1991	0.052	3-25-92	3-2	0.155	0.62	0.103	Net Asset Val $9.59			2-21-92
18	1923	Q0.47	3-20-92	3-2	0.47	1.88	1.76	Equity per shr $60.63			12-31-90
19	...	None Paid			...	Nil	...	0.08	0.07	0.62	11-30-91
20	...	None Since Public			...	Nil	...	18.9	73.4	46.1	9-30-91
21	1989	0.083	3-25-92	3-2	[56]0.39	⊙1.00	†[57]1.229	Net Asset Val $10.11			2-21-92
22	...	1.60	8-15-74	7-25	...	Nil	...	12.0	41.3	28.0	12-31-91
23◆	...	None Since Public			...	Nil	...	5.03	40.2	9.30	9-30-91
24◆	1973	Q0.05	4-15-92	3-23	0.10	0.20	0.19	1.30	19.4	4.54	9-27-91
25	1985	Q0.15	2-29-92	2-10	0.15	0.60	0.60	104	468	347	9-20-91
26	1987	Q0.50	2-14-92	12-24	0.50	2.00	[58]2.00	Equity per shr $16.22			9-30-91
27◆	...	0.60	5-15-90	4-24	...	Nil	...	Equity per shr $29.84			9-30-91
28◆	**1968**	**Q0.04½**	**4-8-92**	**3-16**	**0.09**	**0.18**	**0.17**	**13.7**	**18.9**	**7.53**	**11-27-91**
29	1987	Q0.12	3-10-92	2-13	0.12	0.48	0.47	Equity per shr $20.91			9-30-91
30	1987	Q0.30	1-31-92	1-6	0.30	1.20	†[60]1.67½	0.24	1.44	3.51	9-30-91
31	...	0.20	3-2-90	2-12	...	[63]Nil	...	Book Value Neg			12-31-90
32	...	0.453	5-1-90	4-9	...	2.063	...	Cv into 0.9302 com,$26.875			
33	...	5%Stk	8-25-81	8-3	...	Nil	...	1.59	10.1	2.72	12-25-91
34	...	None Since Public			...	Nil	...	1.91	14.9	18.4	9-30-91
35	...	0.10	5-22-87	5-4	...	Nil	...	2.05	12.9	30.8	9-30-91
36◆	1986	Q0.07	3-24-92	3-4	0.07	0.28	0.26	59.8	90.2	22.6	10-31-91
37	1988	Q0.37	1-15-92	12-24	0.37	1.48	†1.48	Equity per shr $9.35			9-30-91
38	...	[65]3.25	6-29-90	7-2	...	Nil	...	1.59	58.8	26.8	12-31-91
39◆	1949	Q0.17½	1-7-92	12-20	0.17½	0.70	0.63	84.2	2296	1948	11-02-91
40	1992	0.11¼	3-25-92	3-2	0.22½	1.35	...	Net Asset Val $13.64			2-21-92
41	...	None Since Public			...	Nil	...	4.57	4.69	0.79	p9-30-91
42	...	None Since Public			...	Nil	...	4.29	14.3	2.04	12-31-91
43	1881	Q0.33	2-1-92	12-24	0.33	1.32	1.32	1273	23089	18903	9-30-91
44	...	None Since Public			...	Nil	...	Equity per shr $0.43			9-30-91
45◆	...	None Since Public			...	Nil	...	Equity per shr $9.29			9-30-91
46◆	...	0.05	12-1-89	11-9	...	Nil	...	0.15	8.10	9.96	9-30-91
47	...	None Since Public			...	Nil	...	12.6	34.1	16.6	9-30-91

Index	Capitalization: Lg Trm Debt Mil-$	Shs. 000 Pfd.	Com.	Earnings $ Per Shr. Years End	1987	1988	1989	1990	1991	Last 12 Mos.	Interim Earnings Period	$ per Shr. 1990	1991	Index
1	250	...	17074	Dc	‡[52]1.34	1.58	1.71	1.90	P2.09	2.09				1
2	233	...	26936	Dc	d3.94	*0.21	△d2.59	d0.98	P0.43	0.43				2
3	...	...	5459	Au	...	...	0.60	d0.56	□0.49	0.57	3 Mo Nov	0.09	0.17	3
4	...	...	5932	Dc	1.72	1.82	△1.94	2.20	P2.54	2.54				4
5	98.6	57	315893	Dc	2.86	3.19	3.54	3.92	P4.36	4.36				5
6	...	57	...	Dc	n/a	n/a	n/a	b12.16	...	...				6
7	1.49	...	1924	Dc	△d1.83	1.53	d3.12	d0.33	P1.08	1.08				7
8	...	...	6940	Dc	△0.45	□d1.48	0.84	*d2.46	...	d1.66	9 Mo Sep	△d0.27	0.53	8
9	★3060	2	p212338	Dc	5.07	5.92	6.63	6.92	P7.28	7.28				9
10	46.0	...	3805	Dc	1.96	1.53	1.82	2.98	...	3.25	9 Mo Sep	1.96	2.23	10
11	...	...	2762	Fb	0.67	0.76	1.45	1.16	...	1.01	9 Mo Nov	0.95	0.80	11
12	136	...	±6418	Dc	□±2.17	±0.22	±d0.43	±2.04	P±1.76	1.76				12
13	...	...	1742	Dc	□±2.17	±0.49	±d0.43	±2.04	P±1.76	1.76				13
14	10.9	1170	10076	Dc	0.73	0.71	0.56	1.04	P1.12	1.12				14
15	1650	...	76615	Au	□1.26	△□1.21	d0.18	d1.25	d0.38	0.05	3 Mo Nov	d0.41	□0.02	15
16	...	★1	8455	Dc	...	...	...	...	...	...				16
17	...	★1	★7010	Dc	...	...	...	...	...	...				17
18	14.3	...	26504	Dc	△3.17	3.33	3.59	3.96	P4.76	4.76				18
19	0.11	...	7687	My	d0.18	d0.38	d0.13	d0.02	d0.05	d0.05	6 Mo Nov	d0.03	d0.03	19
20	61.1	24	16227	Dc	d0.79	d1.36	d1.83	*0.15	P0.72	0.72				20
21	...	...	21049	Au	...	...	...	§9.13	§9.81	...				21
22	★98.3	...	6095	Sp	0.30	0.58	0.25	1.42	1.59	1.66	3 Mo Dec	0.37	0.44	22
23	3.04	...	21476	Dc	*0.06	0.15	0.28	0.43	P0.69	0.69				23
24	4.27	...	7164	Dc	0.22	0.49	0.62	0.46	P0.50	0.50				24
25	452	1500	14675	Dc	3.42	3.46	d0.04	d3.46	P□3.65	3.65				25
26	272	...	14091	Dc	1.76	□1.85	1.84	1.23	...	1.17	9 Mo Sep	1.11	1.05	26
27	94.0	...	2117	Dc	11.76	2.58	1.79	d7.73	...	d7.83	9 Mo Sep	d4.58	d4.68	27
28	**27.4**	...	**4920**	**My**	**0.16**	**△0.24**	**0.17**	**0.31**	**0.52**	**0.63**	**6 Mo Nov**	**0.13**	**0.24**	**28**
29	3.94	...	2553	Dc	2.14	△1.66	2.47	2.66	P[59]2.49	2.49				29
30	10.2	...	[61]802	Dc	‡[62]0.43	1.14	1.29	1.21	P1.22	1.22				30
31	699	2875	5995	Dc	*2.69	4.67	d0.49	d14.03	Pd27.35	d27.35				31
32	...	2875	...	Dc	...	b1.81	b0.99	bd0.36	...	...				32
33	...	...	3961	Mr	d0.36	*0.07	d0.56	d0.14	...	d0.32	9 Mo Dec	d0.03	d0.21	33
34	52.5	...	2752	Dc	0.42	△0.64	△d1.16	d1.30	...	d0.67	9 Mo Sep	d0.62	△0.01	34
35	27.6	...	6784	Sp	d1.48	d1.06	d1.03	d0.96	d0.74	d0.74				35
36	0.29	...	±22836	Ap	0.38	0.45	△0.64	0.82	0.75	0.87	9 Mo Jan△	0.52	0.64	36
37	3003	...	p16455	Dc	‡[64]0.57	1.60	0.40	0.84	P1.25	1.25				37
38	73.7	...	8494	Je	d1.67	1.49	0.86	□0.08	d0.48	d0.73	6 Mo Dec	0.03	d0.22	38
39	★2802	...	69252	Ja	2.09	1.27	1.72	2.64	E3.85	3.86	9 Mo Oct	1.40	▲2.62	39
40	...	...	★4507	Dc	...	...	...	...	...	...				40
41	...	p...	★4837	Mr	d0.48	d0.95	d1.00	d0.63	...	d0.56	6 Mo Sep	d0.33	d0.26	41
42	3.71	...	3956	Je	d0.15	△0.18	0.20	0.02	d0.21	d0.08	6 Mo Dec	d0.07	0.06	42
43	★9492	...	1306187	Dc	1.88	d1.55	2.50	p2.40	P0.40	0.40				43
44	619	...	±109109	Dc	±0.45	±0.65	±0.87	±1.10	P±1.47	1.47				44
45	1.69	...	10147	Dc	0.51	△0.45	0.87	1.32	...	1.24	9 Mo Sep	1.02	0.94	45
46	6.94	...	2281	Dc	0.69	△0.60	1.55	d0.37	...	d0.41	9 Mo Sep	d0.05	d0.09	46
47	22.1	...	±29518	Dc	...	...	±p0.15	±0.37	P±0.27	0.27				47

◆Stock Splits & Divs By Line Reference Index [2]No adj for reorg,'90. [4]3-for-2,'87:4-for-3,'90:To split 4-for-3,ex Mar 2. [5]2-for-1,'90. [9]5-for4,'90. [14]2-for-1,'87. [23]5-for-4,'89:3-for-1,'90:2-for-1,'91. [24]5-for-4,'88,'90. [27]1-for-2 REVERSE,'89:1-for-3 REVERSE,'90. [28]Adj for 3%,'87. [36]3-for-2,'87,'89,'90. [39]2-for-1,'91. [45]2-for-1,'90. [46]5-for-4,'88.

Second, under strong inflationary pressures, a balanced federal budget is a plus. The federal government's annual expenditures have regularly exceeded its receipts for some time, creating an annual budget deficit. Such a deficit spending policy can bolster stock market performance when national economic resources are employed below capacity and prices are stable.

As mentioned above, inflation threatens stock price growth. Stable growth in gross national product (GNP), on the other hand, promotes strength in the stock market. A real economic growth rate close to the long-term trend of 3 percent would suit common stock investors best.

Stable long-term and short-term interest rates reflected in a neutral monetary policy, one that is not either restrictive or expansionary, should encourage stock investors. Relatively low interest rates stimulate economic growth, which helps the equity market. Full employment is another sign of economic health.

In the same way that these forces promote growth in common stock prices, the opposite conditions restrict it. A weak dollar, a budget deficit under conditions of inflation, substantial inflation, a stringent monetary policy, and rising unemployment would be signs of weakness in the national economy.

Assessment of the economic environment begins with a review of the current status of each of these factors. Based on current conditions, the investor can project likely future conditions in the economy and the equity market with special attention to probable changes. This assessment should guide the decision whether to invest in equities at all, given the current and likely future environment, or to hold funds in less risky investments and wait for better times.

Industry Analysis

industry: A group of competing companies that produce similar products or services.

If the general economy favors equity investments, the security selection process begins with a search for strong **industries.** The best company will stumble if adverse trends in customer attitudes, raw materials supplies, or other important variables cripple its entire industry.

Comparing relative size and growth of the industry to the size and growth of the national economy reveals which industries offer the best chances for sustained growth. In the early 1980s the computer industry became a national leader, and it remains strong today. The drug and health care industry also offers excellent investment opportunities.

Identifying Leading Competitors in an Industry

After identifying an industry with bright prospects, the investor proceeds to examine individual companies, looking for the characteristics that might make their stocks successful investments. This analysis covers several aspects of company operations.

First, select companies that are competitive leaders within their industries. A competitive leader has achieved the size and dominant position that assures survival and prosperity in the future. Look for firms that are large enough to be strong, but not so large that they have exhausted their potential for growth.

subindustry: A group of companies that compete within a broader industry classification to produce a limited range of directly comparable products or services.

This does not imply that investors should confine their investments to the giants of an industry. A competitive leader in a particular **subindustry** may combine the size and strength of an excellent investment candidate with remarkable potential for expansion of its business. Look for a company that has led its rivals for a long time.

Estimate Future Earnings With a manageable group of likely candidates for investment identified, the investor must estimate their earnings over a future investment period. Professional analysts tend to limit their forecasts to three years because the uncertainty of the more distant future makes longer-term projections extremely unreliable. To anticipate future growth of earnings, the investor needs to know something about a company's past earnings. Essentially, he or she extends current trends into the future, adjusting them for foreseeable changes. It is important to update and revise this forecast quarterly.

operating efficiency: The amount of goods or services produced per unit of assets.

Search for Efficiency In addition to earnings growth, stock investors want to identify efficiency. **Operating efficiency** refers to the firm's ability to produce goods and services at reasonable prices. Other things being equal, the more the firm spends to produce a dollar of sales, the less efficient it is. Lower per-unit production costs indicate higher efficiency. The analyst can measure operating efficiency in terms of sales per employee or profits per employee, or possibly sales or profits per dollar of plant investment. Whatever the units on which the comparison is based, the estimate of how a company's efficiency compares to that of its competitors determines how well it will fare in the battle for earnings.

current financial position: The relationship of cash and current assets to current liabilities.

Current Finances A secure **current financial position** assures that a company can continue to operate through varying market conditions and survive temporary setbacks. The firm's liquidity position depends on the margin by which its current assets exceed its current liabilities, as Chapter 9 explained. Every firm needs adequate working capital to meet its operating expenses. Industry competitive leaders almost always have this characteristic, but the investor still should perform a separate analysis to verify this important relationship.

capital structure: The sum of long-term debt and equity of a company.

Capital Structure Careful examination of the company's **capital structure** assures that it has the resources to operate effectively and to fund expansion when opportunities arise. The capital structure is the sum of long-term debt and equity of a company. Chapter 9 reviewed ratios that measure this relationship.

debt–equity ratio: The ratio of total debt to stockholders' equity.

In general, a firm's **debt–equity ratio** should not exceed 1 to 1. This should assure adequate protection against the threat of a temporary earnings decline rendering the firm unable to make interest payments on excessive long-term debt, which could send a potentially profitable company into bankruptcy.

Excellent Management Competitive success requires aggressive, able, intelligent management. Any checklist for investment analysis must include consideration of management performance in the effort to bring together land, labor, and capital to produce a good or service at a profit for the shareowner. Much of this analysis reflects back to the evaluation of the efficiency of the firm's operations.

Return, Risk, and the Return-to-Risk Ratio Finally, the investor must derive an estimate of the returns he or she expects to earn from the investment. As shown previously, the relative attractiveness of a stock's current price depends on its expected dividends and future price.

Assume a stock is selling at $50 a share and paying $1 per share annually in dividends. This gives an annual dividend yield of 2 percent. To be an attractive investment candidate, this stock's price would have to combine this dividend yield with capital growth at a rate of 12 to 16 percent per year. The current price of $50 must increase in three years to the range of $70 to $75 a share. If this seems likely, the investor should invest in the stock, but not otherwise. Recall that Value Line can provide return estimates to confirm or suggest alterations in investors' opinions.

Return means little, however, outside the context of risk. To assess the risk associated with a particular stock, calculate the standard deviation of its returns for the previous ten years. Based on this estimate of risk, calculate the stock's return-to-risk ratio.

Taken together, this information can support decisions that follow a number of different rules. The investor can:

Select companies with the highest expected returns

Select companies with the lowest expected risk

Select companies with the highest return-to-risk ratios

This discussion is designed only to highlight some general factors that should influence selection of common stocks for investment. Investors can supplement the procedure presented here with ratio analysis, as discussed in Chapter 9, or by reference to other investment books. Depending upon the individual company's situation, the influence of individual factors discussed here will vary. The list includes competitive position, operating efficiency, future profitability, financial condition, capital structure, management, future earnings, and expected returns and risks. Each of these factors affects the decision whether or not a stock's rate of return adequately compensates the investor for assuming its risks. Without such an analysis financial decisions are mere guesswork.

Final Questions about the Analysis The overall goal of all of this analysis is to compare the stream of income the investor expects to receive with an investment's current price. To prevent mistakes and be sure of making the right decision, the analysis culminates with answers to the following questions:

1. Are the sales figures realistic?
2. Are the earnings figures realistic?
3. Are the dividend estimates realistic?
4. Is the price estimate realistic?
5. Will the stock, based on a comparison of its current price with its future price, future earnings, and future dividends, provide an adequate rate of return?

In summary, analysis of a stock investment begins with examination of the national economy, then proceeds to identify the industries and companies that seem to offer the best prospects. The return from the company's stock, its risk, and its return-to-risk ratio then lead the investor to make sound investment decisions. Investing without completing this kind of rigorous analysis amounts to operating in the dark.

SUMMARY

Common stockholders own shares of the assets and future earnings of a company. Each owner has a right to maintain his or her proportional share of ownership by exercising the preemptive right.

The equity portion of the balance sheet reports the value of stockholders' stake in the firm in terms of the number of shares outstanding and their book value. The book value per share is found by dividing total stockholders' equity by the number of shares outstanding. If the company has issued preferred stock, its value must be subtracted from the net worth before calculating the book value per share of common stock. Stockholders' equity is determined by subtracting all liabilities from assets. Assets grow by increasing in value and by reinvesting business profits.

The investor receives dividends and capital gains as a benefit of ownership. Since future earnings are uncertain, so are the income and capital due to owners of common shares. Preferred shares, which are also ownership shares, usually pay fixed dividends and have fixed or limited claims on the assets of the company equal to the preferred's par value.

Share owners have voting rights to elect the firm's directors and vote on corporate matters. Indeed, all owners should vote on every matter for which they have responsibility.

The stockholder earns an uncertain return composed of dividends and capital gains. Annual dividends plus annual capital gains per share divided by the price at which the owner purchased the stock gives the annual rate of return on the stock. Over the years, common stock has been more profitable and more risky than other security investments including long-term bonds and Treasury bills. Common stock returns have outpaced the rate of inflation. The major advantage of common stock investment is the higher return. The major disadvantage is the higher risk.

Investors should conduct a complete analysis of a company before making an investment commitment. This includes analysis of the national economy to evaluate the future environment for investing and identification of strong industries within the economy. Investors select companies in which to invest that are competitive leaders, efficient, strong financially, well-managed, and among the leaders in rate of return.

Investors should select companies that have high expected returns and attractive return-to-risk ratios. Good analysis plus good return-to-risk ratios should provide the investor with good investments. Several examples were found among DJIA companies.

INVESTMENT MANAGEMENT CONCEPTS

1. Invest only in industries with good growth potential.
2. Invest in dominant companies in those industries.
3. Invest in companies with good management, sound finances, and predictable futures.
4. Buy stock that offers a high return based on estimates.
5. Buy stocks with favorable return-to-risk ratios.
6. Diversify to reduce risk and maximize return-to-risk ratio.
7. Make changes annually based on return-to-risk analysis.

REVIEW QUESTIONS

1. What is common stock?
2. Do the earnings of common stock vary?
3. Do dividends on common stock vary?
4. What is a stock certificate?
5. What is a preemptive right?
6. What is a rights offering?
7. What is the difference between ordinary voting and cumulative voting?
8. Explain the current yield on common stock.
9. What is a capital gain on a share of stock? A capital loss?
10. What is cash flow per share?
11. What is the dividend payout ratio?
12. What is a stock dividend?
13. What is a property dividend?
14. What are the two components of total return?
15. How is total return measured?
16. How do you estimate future return?
17. What are the components of future return?
18. How is future price estimated?
19. What is the DJIA?
20. What EPS growth rate has the DJIA posted?
21. What DPS growth rate has the DJIA posted?
22. What has been the average P/E ratio for the DJIA?
23. What is book value?

24. What is the significance of the market-to-book value ratio?

25. What have been the average return and variability of past returns of the DJIA?

26. How is risk measured on common stock?

27. What is the return-to-risk ratio and how is it calculated?

28. Explain Standard & Poor's stock ratings.

29. What are the advantages of common stock ownership?

30. What are the disadvantages of common stock ownership?

31. Why is it important to understand where the national economy is going before investing?

32. In what type of industries should investors invest?

33. List the attributes of a strong company for investment.

34. How can an investor use expected return and risk to make investment decisions?

SELF-CORRECTING PROBLEMS

1. An investor purchased IBM stock for $101 per share. The company pays a dividend of $4.84 per share. What is the current yield on the stock?

2. AT&T paid a dividend of $1.32 in 1991. You bought the stock for $38. What was your dividend yield?

3. The investor who purchased IBM shares at $101 found the price at $107 at the end of the year. What was the capital gain on each share? What was the capital gain return?

4. The price of AT&T had risen to $40 six months after you purchased it at $38. What annual rate of return did this capital gain give you (ignore dividends)?

5. If the price of IBM had risen by the same amount in Problem 3 over a year, what annual return would you have earned (include dividends)?

6. You purchased AT&T at $38 and held it six months, after which its price had risen to $40. What annual rate of return did you earn for the six-month period (include dividends)?

7. A stock posted the following annual percentage returns for the past 10 years: 15, 12, −5, 11, 15, 22, −5, 7, 15, and 10 percent. What was the average return? How risky was the stock?

8. A stock paid no dividends. The first year it rose to $56 from a purchase price of $50. The second year it rose to $61. What was the average capital gain for the two-year period?

Answers to Self-Correcting Problems

1. Divide $4.84 by $101 to find the current yield of 4.79 percent.

2. $1.32/$38 = 3.5 percent (rounded).

3. The gain was \$6 per share (\$107 − \$101 = \$6). The rate of return was 5.94 percent (\$6/\$101 = 0.0594).

4. \$40 − \$38 = \$2; \$2/\$38 = 0.0526 × 2 = 10.52 percent.

5. The total return is 10.73 percent, found by adding the rate of return on the capital gain to the rate of return on the dividend (5.94 percent + 4.79 percent = 10.73 percent). The formula is:

$$\frac{P_1 - P_0 + D_1}{P_0} = \frac{\$107 - \$101 + \$4.84}{\$101} = \frac{\$10.84}{\$101} = 0.1073 = 10.73 \text{ percent}$$

6. (\$40 − \$38 + \$0.66)/\$38 = \$2.66/\$38 = 0.07 = 7.00 percent × 2 = 14 percent.

7. The average return is found by adding the annual return and dividing by 10.

$$15 + 12 - 5 + 11 + 15 + 22 - 5 + 7 + 15 + 10 = 97$$
$$97/10 = 9.7 \text{ percent}$$

To estimate risk, calculate standard deviation:

$$(x_i - x)^2$$
$$(15 - 9.7)^2 = 5.3^2 = 28.09$$
$$(12 - 9.7)^2 = 2.3^2 = 5.29$$
$$(-5 - 9.7)^2 = -14.7^2 = 216.09$$
$$(11 - 9.7)^2 = -3^2 = 9.00$$
$$(15 - 9.7)^2 = -5.3^2 = 28.09$$
$$(22 - 9.7)^2 = -12.3^2 = 151.29$$
$$(-5 - 9.7)^2 = -14.7^2 = 216.09$$
$$(7 - 9.7)^2 = -2.7^2 = 7.29$$
$$(15 - 9.7)^2 = 5.3^2 = 28.09$$
$$(10 - 9.7)^2 = 0.3^2 = 0.09$$
$$\Sigma(x_i - x)^2 = 689.41$$

$$\text{Standard deviation} = \sqrt{\frac{(x_i - x)^2}{(N - 1)}} = \sqrt{\frac{689.41}{9}} = 8.75 \text{ percent}$$

8. $$\left(\frac{\$56 - \$50}{\$50} + \frac{\$61 - \$56}{\$56}\right)/2 = (\$6/\$50 + \$5/\$56)/2$$
$$= (12 + 8.9)/2 = 0.1045 = 10.45 \text{ percent.}$$

SELECTED READINGS

Amling, Frederick. *Investments: An Introduction to Analysis and Management*, 6th ed. Englewood Cliffs, N.J.: Prentice-Hall, 1989, Chapter 6.

Brealy, Richard A. *An Introduction to Risk and Return from Common Stocks.* Cambridge, Mass.: MIT Press, 1983.

Cohen, Jerome B. et al. *Investment Analysis and Portfolio Management.* Homewood, Ill.: Richard D. Irwin, 1987.

Cottle, Sidney et al. *Graham and Dodd's Security Analysis*, 5th ed. New York: McGraw-Hill, 1988.

Fama, Eugene F. "The Behavior of Stock Market Prices." *Journal of Business*, January 1965, pp. 34–105.

Ibbotson, Roger G. and Rex A. and Sinquefield. *Stocks, Bonds, Bills, and Inflation: The Past and the Future.* Charlottesville, Va.: Financial Analysts Research Foundation, 1982.

New York Institute of Finance. *Asset Plays: Profiting from Undervalued Stock.* Englewood Cliffs, N.J.: Prentice-Hall, 1988.

Reilly, Frank K. *Investment Analysis and Portfolio Management.* Fort Worth, Tex.: Dryden Press, 1989.

Ritchie, John. *Fundamental Analysis.* Chicago: Probus Publishing, 1989.

Stein, Lawrence M. *Value Investing: New Strategies for Stock Market Success.* New York: John Wiley & Sons, 1988.

Williams, John B. *The Theory of Investment Value.* Cambridge, Mass.: Harvard University Press, 1988.

chapter 11

Valuation of Common Stock

One of the authors' former investment professors, a brilliant scholar and a great teacher, did not talk much about common stock valuation models in class. The professor seemed to ignore common stock prices much of the time. Instead, he focused mostly on the quality of the company, its products, and the future growth of its sales and earnings. He seldom asked his students to estimate the rate of return on a common stock, nor did he ask them to calculate risk. In a sense, he advocated buying stock based on faith in the company and its managers, directly contradicting the opinion of many people that stock price information should drive everything the investor does. The professor's method yielded good results more often than it led to mistakes, though. Investors who used it learned to look for good companies and to be content with small dividends, while waiting for growing earnings to provide handsome capital gains.

When making an actual investment, however, the professor carefully estimated a stock's value based on the expected future performance of the company. A good example of his method came up during a discussion of an investment in 3M (Minnesota Mining & Manufacturing). The professor's careful investigation revealed 3M to be a well-managed company that had grown from a manufacturer of a few quality products to a diversified leader in so many different product categories that professional analysts have difficulty classifying the company, let alone appraising it—despite their sophisticated valuation equations.

The professor decided to place an order to buy 500 shares of 3M. Rather than buying the stock at its market price of about $39, which represented the best idea a market full of clever people could form about its correct price, he entered a limit order to buy at $36.50. Within a month 3M shares had fallen to that level, and he purchased the 500 shares for $2.50 less per share than he would otherwise have paid, saving himself $1,250.

The professor's broker wondered what sort of secret formula he had used to set his purchase price, but no secret was involved. The professor simply estimated 3M's future earnings per share, the future dividends per share those earnings would support, and the future price the market would pay for those dividends. He then found the present value of his estimate of the stock's future price at a discount rate that would provide a generous rate of return on the investment. That present value became his purchase price for the stock, and the market came to agree with his assessment within a short time.

Introduction

valuation: Estimating the value of and returns from an investment.

This chapter explains how to apply the stock valuation method summarized in the story above. Common stock **valuation,** that is, the process of estimating the values of and returns on common stocks, presents a much tougher challenge than finding a value for a savings account, money market account, or Treasury security. An investor must buy a common stock without knowing exactly how much it will pay in annual dividends in the future. No source of information can state exactly the company's future earnings per share. Investors can only estimate these critical variables and the future price they will lead the market to set for the shares.

Bonds, T-bills, and savings instruments like CDs and money market accounts all provide relatively certain streams of income over their times to maturity, coupled with easily predictable principal values. Exhibit 11.1 summarizes the features of these assets. If you own a $1,000, 6 percent savings account, you can confidently expect that the account will be worth $1,060 at the end of a year, assuming it pays interest annually. Daily compounding would raise this figure to approximately $1,063 for an annual yield of 6.3 percent. Still, you know these terms and the rate of return they will produce in advance with certainty.

Investors in these fixed-income assets face only one threat to their realization of promised income and principal payments—the risk that issuers will default on their obligations. As long as they minimize default risk by selecting high-quality securities, fixed-income investors can be relatively sure they will receive the returns they expect. Of course, rising interest

EXHIBIT 11.1

Debt Assets' Principal and Interest Characteristics

	PRINCIPAL	INTEREST
Savings account	Fixed	Fixed
Treasury bill (90 days)	Semifixed	Fixed
Money market fund	Semifixed	Semifixed
CD	Semifixed	Fixed
Long-term government bond	Variable	Fixed

rates can reduce the market values of these kinds of investments, but the investor can still receive periodic interest payments of set amounts and the full par values of the investments when they mature, regardless of market conditions.

To escape default risk entirely, you could buy a Treasury bill. The return on a T-bill would be fixed as the difference between the purchase price and the maturity value as long as you held it to maturity, usually only 90 days after purchase. While you held the T-bill, its market price would vary to reflect changes in money market yields, but if you held it to maturity, you would certainly receive the $10,000 the government owed you.

Both the T-bill and a short-term certificate of deposit (CD) illustrate another risk in fixed-income investing, reinvestment rate risk. These instruments make fixed principal and interest payments, but only for short periods, after which you have to resume your search for the best available rate of interest. If rates have fallen, you have to satisfy yourself with a smaller return on your money; this is the price of liquidity. Still, you can easily determine the values of these securities since they provide set interest payments and certain repayment of principal at maturity.

The interest rates on money market deposit accounts and money market mutual funds vary slightly with market rates over the short-term, and sometimes substantially over longer periods, but the changes occur in small increments, and you can easily and accurately predict their effects on investment returns. To avoid these variations and assure yourself of a set amount of interest income over a longer period of time, you could buy long-term bonds issued by creditworthy corporations or units of government. These virtually guarantee return of invested principal at maturity, though their market prices can drop if market yields to maturity rise.

Despite the risks of market prices declining in reaction to rising interest rates or of receiving lower returns on funds invested in maturing securities if market rates move downward, setting values on these kinds of securities involves simple present value calculations. Income streams and principal values are known with relative certainty.

perspective on **ETHICS**

Insider Trading

In normal business usage, the term *insider* generally refers to corporate officers, directors, and persons who hold more than 10 percent of the common stock of a corporation. One would logically expect insiders would own stock in their respective corporations and that they obviously would trade these securities. In fact, stockholders should demand insiders own stock in their corporations so that the insiders' financial interests will be tied into the corporations' financial interests. Although many people seem to get the opposite impression from media accounts, there is certainly nothing per se improper about insider trading. What *is* improper, however, is illegal insider trading.

Illegal insider trading generally refers to trading based on material, nonpublic information available only to insiders. In plain English, if only the corporate officers and directors know of important information that would have a significant effect on the value of a company's securities, it is illegal for them to buy or sell the securities before this information is disclosed to the public. This prohibition has been expanded over the years to extend also to *tipees* (those who knowingly receive material, nonpublic information—tips—from insiders) and others, such as accountants, bankers, and lawyers, who have access to inside information.

The initial prohibition against illegal insider trading was specified in rule 10b-5 of the Securities Exchange Act of 1934. In recent years the powers of the SEC to investigate and prosecute insider abuses have been strengthened by the Insider Trading Sanctions Act of 1984 and the Insider Trading and Securities Fraud Act of 1988. Prior to the 1980s, allegations of insider trading typically were settled in civil proceedings resulting in a consent decree and what is known as *disgorgement of profits*. In a consent decree, the person (or firm) accused of illegal insider trading essentially signs a decree that neither confirms nor denies illegality in the specific case, but agrees to pay a fine equal to the estimated profits from the alleged insider transaction. During the 1980s, however, the SEC began referring insider trading cases to the Justice Department for criminal prosecution and also began seeking triple damages in civil proceedings.

Widely publicized cases involving prominent investment bankers such as Michael Milken, Ivan Boesky, Martin Siegel, and others have increased the general public's as well as investment professionals' awareness of this issue. Although some have argued that illegal insider trading is a victimless crime, the unethical as well as illegal nature of insider trading is explained clearly in an SEC letter proposing the Insider Trading Sanctions Act of 1984:[a]

> Capital formation and our nation's economic growth and stability depend on investor confidence in the fairness and integrity of our capital markets.
>
> Insider trading threatens these markets. By abusing the trust and confidence reposed in them by shareholders, employers or clients, insider traders may reap huge profits in essentially risk-free transactions. Insiders—corporate officials, investment bankers, lawyers, accountants, financial printers, among others—often learn of profit or loss forecasts, imminent tender offers, mineral strikes, oil discoveries, lucrative contracts and product failures before such information is available to the investment public . . .
>
> If such information is material, insiders can earn substantial profits by engaging in securities transactions before that information becomes generally known in the marketplace. The abuse of informational advantages that other investors cannot hope to overcome through diligence or zeal is unfair and inconsistent with the investing public's legitimate expectation of honest and fair securities markets where all participants play by the same rules.

[a]Letter from the SEC to the Speaker of the House, September 27, 1992; quoted in Patricia A. O'Hara and G. Robert Blakey, "Legal Aspects of Insider Trading," *Ethics and the Investment Industry*, Oliver F. Williams, Frank K. Reilly, and John W. Houck, eds. (Savage, Md.: Rowman and Littlefield Publishers, 1989), p. 101.

Estimating Common Stock Returns

Now think of the problem associated with common stock. No corporation guarantees the amount of any future dividend, or even that it will pay a dividend at all. You certainly receive no promise that you will receive a fixed value for your investment at any time in the future. You can be sure that the future price will depend on the value other investors place on the company's future earnings, but you do not know exactly the amount of those earnings or what the market will be willing to pay for them.

future earnings, dividends, and prices per share: The estimate of earnings, dividends, and prices per share at some future time, usually three years from the current date.

Stock investors must estimate **future earnings, dividends, and prices per share.** Their only certainty in this effort is the knowledge that the future share price will be a function of the firm's future earnings per share times a market-determined price–earnings ratio. Most professional investors try to calculate these data three to five years into the future. They try to project future return on investment based on the current purchase price per share, likely future dividends, and future price. The authors use a three- to five-year time period because it seems realistic in light of rapid world economic changes.

They complete the arduous task of stock valuation as part of the decision about whether or not to invest in the stock. They base their final decisions on their estimates of its annual total return for the period and its risk, that is, the standard deviation of its past rates of return.

An Illustration of the Complexity of Valuation

In 1979 McDonald's Corporation stock sold at an average price per share of $4.50. During that year the company earned $0.47 per share and paid a dividend of $0.05125 per share. McDonald's P/E ratio averaged 9.57. Investors who bought this stock at $4.50 per share received a current dividend yield of 1.14 percent (found by dividing dividend per share by market price). This may have seemed disappointing when T-bills were yielding 10 percent and long-term government bonds were yielding 8.75 percent at the time.

Why did investors buy McDonald's stock when it was yielding only 1 percent? The answer is quite simple. They expected company earnings to rise to $0.55 per share in 1980, a 17 percent increase. Dividends were expected to increase to $0.07375 per share for a 44 percent increase.

Short-Term Estimates of Expected Price and Return

Based on these earnings and dividend estimates, what market price did investors expect for McDonald's stock in 1980? Multiplying the company's estimated earnings of $0.55 a share by its historic P/E ratio of 9.57 gives a market price of $5.25 per share. Those who bought the shares received a dividend yield of 1.6 percent on their purchase price of $4.50. In addition, they earned capital gains of \$0.76 per share, or 16.9 percent. They enjoyed total percentage returns of 18.5 percent (1.6 percent + 16.9 percent), a far better rate of return than T-bills or long-term bonds paid. McDonald's stock turned in superior investment performance.

Unfortunately, investors could not rely on this kind of hindsight. They faced the possibility that they would buy the stock at \$4.50 and watch it drop to \$3.875 per share. (Since price quotes list fractions, the McDonald's price would have been quoted at 4½ and it could have dropped to 3⅞.) During 1980, the stock sold as low as 3⅝. Part of the excellent return on McDonald's stock was simply compensation for investors' willingness to take this risk.

Long-Term Estimates of Value and Return

Few investors hold stock for only a single year. To understand how they evaluate prospects over a longer term, consider McDonald's subsequent performance. Investors expected its 1979 earnings of \$0.47 per share to double in the following five years to \$0.94 per share; they expected dividends to triple to \$0.15 per share. Assuming the 1979 average P/E ratio of 9.5 continued into 1984, they would have estimated a price per share of \$8.93 in 1984 (1984 earnings of 0.94 times 9.5 P/E ratio).

These estimates give a projected annual dividend yield per share of about 2.0 percent and an annual percentage capital gain of approximately 19.8 percent. To verify this, consider that the estimated price of \$8.93 in 1984 minus the \$4.50 purchase price gives a capital gain of \$4.43; divide this total capital gain by 5 to find the annual capital gain, \$0.89. Divide the annual capital gain by the purchase price, \$4.50, to get the average annual yield from the capital gain, 19.8 percent. Adding this figure to the annual dividend yield of 2.0 percent gives an estimated rate of return of 21.8 percent. Of course, as we learned in Chapter 6, this calculation yields an approximate return, but it is accurate enough for illustrative purposes.

Based on this analysis, McDonald's stock appeared to be an excellent investment in 1979. In fact, the company's actual earnings, dividends, and price exceeded these expectations and its stock generated an even higher rate of return than this analysis suggests!

This discussion may suggest that valuation is simple. All you need to do is multiply company earnings per share by some reasonable growth factor to estimate future earnings, and multiply this estimate by the current price–earnings ratio to estimate the future price per share. Multiplying the future earnings by the current dividend payout ratio could give an estimate of future dividends. Dividing both the dividend estimate and the share price estimate by the average share price over the previous year should give estimates for the two components of the stock's return, and summing them could give a final estimate of the rate of return on the investment. If this rate seemed satisfactory, you could buy the stock. Unfortunately, real life is never as simple as this kind of quick example may make it seem.

EXHIBIT 11.2

McDonald's Financial Information, 1979–1984

Per-Share Data ($)	1984	1983	1982	1981	1980	1979
Tangible book value	4.60	4.03	3.51	3.17	2.64	2.17
Earnings	0.98	0.85	0.74	0.65	0.55	0.47
Dividends	0.1687	0.1437	0.1175	0.0937	0.0737	0.0512
Payout ratio	17%	17%	16%	14%	13%	11%
Price High	12.50	11.12	9.75	7.25	5.25	5.12
Low	9.12	8.12	5.75	4.75	3.62	3.87
P/E ratio	13–9	13–10	13–8	11–7	9–7	11–8

SOURCE: Standard & Poor's *Stock Reports.*

Exhibits 11.2 and 11.3 report financial information for McDonald's for the period 1979 to 1984. Purchasing the stock at $4.50 in 1979 would have given poor returns in each of the next three years, during which the average annual price rose only slightly above the beginning price. In any one of those years a reasonable investor might have given up and sold the stock, missing out on the later surge that gave an annual average return of 22 percent for the period.

The sad fact is that stocks often fail to perform as well as expected because company growth fails to meet estimates. Only toward the end of the period 1979 to 1984 did the the national economy show strong recovery from a recession caused by high interest rates and inflation. This kind of overall growth makes for higher-than-usual returns.

This exercise in hindsight should teach you not to expect perfection from a valuation procedure. This does not imply that you should ignore the results of such an effort, though. Seek to estimate future earnings per share, stock price, and P/E ratio over a period of three to five years. Based on these figures, estimate the return you expect, and then have the confidence to hold the investment for the period of your plan unless major changes occur in your future estimates. If you bail out early, you probably will not achieve the results you expect.

Applying the Valuation Procedure

Now test your abilities to value a common stock. It is now the end of 1984 and McDonald's stock trades for $12. The company earned $0.98 per share in 1984, and it pays a dividend of $0.17 per share. Dividing the

EXHIBIT 11.3

Price and Earnings Charts for McDonald's, 1979–1984

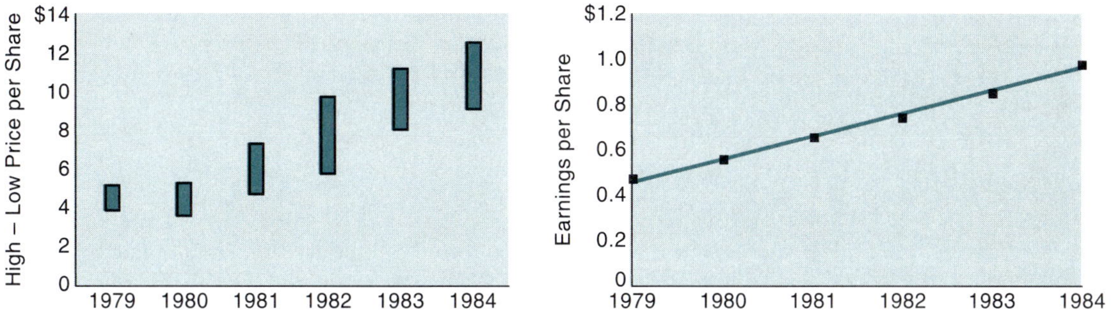

market price of the stock by the company's earnings per share gives a P/E ratio of 12. (A ratio calculated in this way is usually referred to as a "12-month trailing price–earnings ratio.")

Your latest information about McDonald's indicates that its earnings per share (EPS) grew 15 percent in the previous year, and dividends grew 17 percent, approximately. These figures were well below the company's five-year average growth rates for earnings and dividends per share. Using this information, what earnings and dividends would you expect in 1989? What price would you expect?

Estimating Earnings per Share

Look at EPS first. McDonald's EPS have grown at 15 percent annually. The future value of \$1 compounded at 15 percent for five years is \$2.01. This means that every dollar you leave to compound at a 15 percent annual rate will grow to \$2.01 in five years (found by 1.15^5). Multiply the company's current EPS of \$0.98 by this future value factor to estimate the amount to which current EPS will grow by 1989, \$1.97.

Compute a dividend estimate the same way. Compounding \$1 at 17 percent gives \$2.19 after five years. Multiply McDonald's 1984 dividends of \$0.17 by 2.19 to estimate its 1989 dividend, \$0.37. The estimated EPS of \$1.97 times the 12-month trailing P/E ratio of 12 gives an estimated price of \$23.64.

Estimating Rate of Return

What annual rate of return would these estimates give you for the five-year period? First, estimate dividends per share for the period. Add the beginning and ending dividends and divide by 2 [($0.17 + $0.33)/2] to find the average dividend, $0.25. Find the annual price gain for the period, $2.33, by dividing the difference between the ending and beginning prices by the number of years [($23.64 − $12.00)/5]. This gives an average annual dollar return for the five-year period of $2.58 ($0.25 annual dividend plus $2.33 annual capital gain). The average annual investment over the period is 17.82 [(12.00 + 23.64)/2]. Based on the $17.82 average price, you would get an expected total annual rate of return of approximately 14.5 percent.

The Investment Decision

Now that you have set a value on McDonald's stock, do you want to buy it? If you owned it, would you continue to hold it? You should answer both questions with definite nods of "Yes." The estimated rate of return is quite adequate—it is well above historic rates of return for the S&P 500 Index and compares favorably with past returns on McD.

Would you buy more of the stock if you already held some? You should probably buy more, depending upon what other stocks you owned and on how it compared to other stocks you might consider buying.

Updating the Analysis

Exhibits 11.4 and 11.5 provide the information with which to update your 1984 decision. On January 2, 1990, McDonald's sold at a price per share of 34⅞. In our valuation model, the price of 34⅞ represents the value of McD at the end of 1989. This exceeds your estimate by more than 50 percent. McDonald's turned out to be a successful investment, indeed!

Was it so successful that you should sell and take your profits? After all, the earnings and dividend growth rate are slowing down. To make this decision, you must make a valuation estimate for the next five years.

A statement in an S&P Stock Report suggested the McDonald's EPS would grow at 12.8 percent during 1990 and subsequent years, and that the dividend growth rate would remain flat. Over the longer term, the 12.8 percent EPS growth rate seems attainable through 1995. Dividends per share should continue to increase at a 12 percent rate. Earnings per share were $1.95 in 1989, and dividends were $0.2725 per share. Estimate 1994 EPS by multiplying the compound EPS growth factor of 1.826 (1.128^5) by the 1989 EPS of $1.95. Your estimate of 1994 EPS is $3.56.

Find the P/E ratio to use in estimating the future price by dividing the 12-month estimated EPS of $1.95 into the current price of 34⅞, for a value of 17.9. The 1994 EPS estimate times this P/E ratio gives a 1994 share price estimate of $63.72 ($3.56 × 17.9 = $63.72).

Your compound dividend growth factor for 12 percent over five years is 1.762 (1.12^5), giving an annual dividend estimate of $0.48 for 1994. The average dividend for the period becomes $0.376 [($0.48 + $0.2725)/2].

EXHIBIT 11.4

McDonald's Financial Information, 1985–1989

Per-Share Data ($)	1989	1988	1987	1986	1985
Tangible book value	8.40	8.25	7.03	5.84	5.25
Earnings	1.95	1.72	1.45	1.24	1.11
Dividends	0.2725	0.2725	0.2425	0.215	0.1912
Payout ratio	17%	16%	17%	17%	18%
Price High	33.00	25.50	30.62	25.62	18.25
Low	24	20.37	15.75	16.25	11.37
P/E ratio	12–7	15–12	21–11	21–13	16–10

SOURCE: Standard & Poor's *Stock Reports*.

EXHIBIT 11.5

Price and Earnings Charts for McDonald's, 1985–1989

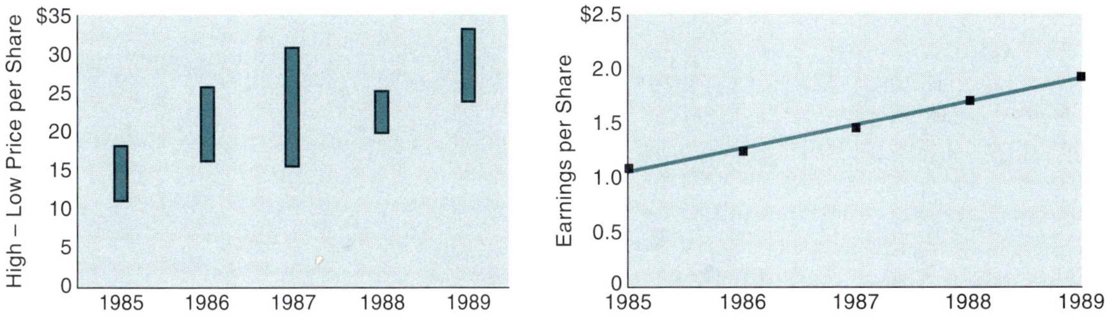

The total capital gain for the stock over the five-year period is $63.72 minus $34.875, or $28.845. Divide by 5 to find the annual capital gain of $5.769. Add the average annual dividend, $0.376, to this figure to find the total average annual dollar return per share, $6.145. Divide this dollar return by the average investment of $49.30 [(34.875 + 63.72)/2] to calculate your annual rate of return estimate of 11.7 percent.

This falls short of the 14.2 percent you enjoyed during the late 1980s, but it is still an excellent rate of return. You would probably buy McDonald's stock if you did not own any, hold any you did own, or buy more if your portfolio could use more consumer-oriented stocks.

The Problem with Estimates

There is only one problem with this estimate. It uses a P/E multiple that is at the top of McDonald's customary range. To be a bit more conservative, you might use an average P/E ratio for 1989 of around 14.5 [(17 + 12)/2]. This gives a revised price estimate for 1994 of 14.5 times $3.56, or $51.62. The revised total capital gain is found by subtracting the initial price of $34.875 from the new end-of-period price of $51.62, which leaves $16.745. Dividing by 5 gives an annual capital gain of $3.349. Add the $0.376 estimated average dividend for a total annual return of $3.725, and divide this by the average investment of $49.30 to find the revised estimate of your annual rate of return, 7.6 percent.

This does not inspire the same optimism as previous estimates. It is an adequate return, but the risks of common stock ownership might lead you to pass up an opportunity to buy at a price of approximately $35. If your portfolio could benefit from more of the stock, you might watch for an opportunity to buy it at around $30 per share. This might be possible if negative news were to depress the market temporarily.

The thought process of stock valuation is clearly based on estimates. To summarize the estimation process, remember that you can easily find the current price for a share of stock. In addition, you must estimate:

1. Dividends per share over the period under consideration
2. Earnings per share over the period
3. Stock price at the end of the period (found by multiplying earnings per share by an estimated price–earnings ratio for the period)
4. Expected annual rate of return over the period

These estimates give a good picture of the attractiveness of an investment.

The Basic Valuation Model

The stock valuation process outlined so far is routine enough that we can express it in a mathematical equation, or model. Such a model processes known information to yield an estimate of an unknown variable. Solving the stock valuation equation gives an estimate of the expected rate of return from an investment. Based on this estimate, the investor can make an intelligent decision about whether to buy, hold, or sell common stock. The valuation equation may seem complicated, but focusing on one variable at a time makes it easy to use.

The following basic valuation model simply restates the steps taken above to set a value on McDonald's stock in equation form:

$$P_c = \frac{D_0(1 + g_d)^1}{(1 + r)^1} + \frac{D_0(1 + g_d)^2}{(1 + r)^2} + \frac{D_0(1 + g_d)^3}{(1 + r)^3} + \frac{E_0(1 + g_e)^3(P_3/E_3)}{(1 + r)^3}$$

Most analysts work with three years' estimated data because this length of time is short enough to allow reasonably accurate predictions and long enough to cover various market cycles so temporary disruptions will not bias the results too badly. Many investors intend to hold stock they buy for more than three years. They can evaluate such a long-term investment by making a new three-year estimate each year, annually extending the projections another year into the future. In our example we used a five-year horizon.

The valuation model projects a future share price, dividend yield, and rate of return based on a firm's current earnings, dividends, and share price and the rates of growth of earnings and dividends. The variables in the model represent these familiar values:

P_c: Valuation model variable that represents the current price of a share of stock.

D_0: Valuation model variable that represents dividends per share in the base year.

E_0: Valuation model variable that represents earnings per share in the base year.

g_d: Valuation model variable that represents an estimate of the growth rate of dividends per share over a future three-year period.

g_e: Valuation model variable that represents an estimate of the growth rate of earnings per share for a future three-year period.

P_3/E_3: Valuation model variable that represents an estimate of the price–earnings ratio after three years.

$\mathbf{P_c}$ is the current price of a share of the stock.

$\mathbf{D_0}$ is the stock's most recent annual dividend per share.

$\mathbf{E_0}$ is the firm's most recent annual earnings per share.

Estimating Future Dividends

The model gets its estimate of the future dividend by multiplying the base-year dividend (D_0) by 1 plus the annual growth rate of dividends for the period (g_d). This growth rate is an experience-based estimate of the change in the firm's dividend payment investors can expect over the next three years. Dividends can grow at a constant rate, or the rate can vary. Unless some insight into the firm's business leads them to expect variations, investors normally assume a constant growth rate for simplicity.

Estimating Future Earnings

In addition to dividends, company earnings affect the price of a stock. This means the valuation model must include an estimate of earnings per share, which it supplies by multiplying current EPS by 1 plus an estimated earnings growth rate (g_e). As in the McDonald's example, earnings can grow at a rate different from dividends. This calculation has a critical effect on the estimate of the future share price. As for dividends, most investors assume a constant growth rate for earnings per share, but they watch for signs that the rate may change.

Estimating the Future P/E Ratio

As in the McDonald's example, the estimated future share price comes from multiplying the future earnings per share by the future price–earnings ratio, which reflects how much investors will be willing to pay for a given amount of EPS. A small change in the P/E ratio, $\mathbf{P_3/E_3}$ in the model, can have a powerful influence on the stock price, even if company earnings remain constant, so the analyst must estimate this variable carefully.

Inflation and high interest rates push P/E ratios downward. Investors are willing to pay less for a given amount of future earnings because they expect inflation to erode the value of those earnings. Deflation and low interest rates push P/E ratios upward. The analyst must adjust any estimate of a future price–earnings ratio for likely changes in inflation and changes in interest rates.

Solve for r

r: Valuation model variable that represents the discount rate that forces equality between the present value of the future dividends and share price and the current share price, which gives an estimate of the annual rate of return on a stock.

The goal of all this estimating is to provide values to plug into the valuation model to find an estimate of the future rate of return on the stock. To complete this process, substitute estimates of P_3/E_3, g_d, and g_e into the valuation equation and solve by trial and error for **r**, the estimate of the compound annual rate of return for the period, or the internal rate of return. A comparison between this estimated rate of return and the rates of return on other available investment opportunities determines whether or not the investor should buy the stock.

The Fine Art of Estimation

Analysts have developed two basic techniques for developing the many critical estimates they require for stock valuation. The primary, trend-based technique makes the questionable assumption that the variables will continue to move at the same rates at which they have moved in the past. The analyst reviews the growth rates of dividends per share and earnings per share for the previous ten years to develop average growth rates. Similarly, the ten-year average P/E ratio becomes the estimate for the end-of-period P/E ratio. This picks up market trends, ignoring market cycles. This method is called **trend analysis,** since it extends ten-year trends by taking average values.

trend analysis: A technique for estimating valuation model variables that uses ten-year averages for the growth rates of earnings and dividends per share and the P/E ratio.

This second estimation method assumes that the current P/E ratio more closely represents the probable future value. Like the trend method, it averages ten-year growth rates of earnings and dividends per share as estimates for the following three to five years. This method of combining trends in earnings and dividend growth with a current P/E ratio is called **trend-current analysis.**

trend-current analysis: A technique for estimating valuation model variables that combines ten-year average growth rates of earnings and dividends per share with a current P/E ratio.

ABE—Analysts' Best Estimate A third, composite method bases valuation estimates on professional analysts' opinions of the growth rates of dividends and earnings per share as well as the future P/E ratio. Rather than being an estimation technique in its own right, this **analysts' best estimate (ABE)** method really relies on others' applications of the previously discussed techniques. Thorough review of reports from Standard & Poor's, Value Line, *Barron's* and other publications, and similar sources of information

analysts' best estimate (ABE): A technique for estimating future growth rates of earnings and dividends per share and P/E ratios by relying on published opinions of investment professionals.

can provide a consensus of the thinking of investment professionals. Alternatively, a confident investor might base these estimates on his or her own opinion of the probable values of these variables over the following three years. The information to form this opinion might come from the same sources as information about professional analysts' opinions, and from public statements of company officials, the company's quarterly or annual reports, or other sources.

Historical Market Valuation: S&P 500

The earlier example of stock valuation dealt with an individual common stock—McDonald's. The basic valuation model can also give a value for the market as a whole by substituting estimates of the variables for all the companies in a market index like the S&P 500. The following valuation analysis shows how an analyst might have evaluated market conditions in 1981, a time of great uncertainty. Inflation was out of control and the Federal Reserve Board had forced interest rates to all-time highs to put on the brakes and stop the inflationary cycle. What did investors at the time foresee?

Trend Analysis

Using the trend technique, an investor would have reasoned that the previous ten years' earnings growth rates, dividend growth rates, and P/E ratios would continue over the next three years. The S&P 500 Index was at 125 at the end of 1980 (note that closing price at the end of 1980 equals the opening price in 1981). In 1980 the S&P 500 stocks had earned $14.79 per share and paid $6.55 dividends per share. To apply the valuation model, substitute 125 for P_c, $14.79 for E_0, and $6.55 for D_0. For the ten-year period ending in 1980, earnings of the S&P 500 companies grew at an average annual rate of 10.85 percent, dividends grew at an average annual rate of 9.2 percent, and the ten-year average price–earnings ratio was 11 ($g_{e,10}$ = 10.85 percent; $g_{d,10}$ = 9.20 percent; P/E_{10} = 11). Substituting these estimates into the valuation equation gives the following:

$$\$125 = \frac{\$6.55(1.092)}{(1 + r)} + \frac{\$6.55(1.092)^2}{(1 + r)^2} + \frac{\$6.55(1.092)^3}{(1 + r)^3} + \frac{\$14.79(1.1085)^3 11}{(1 + r)^3}$$

$$= \frac{\$7.15}{(1 + r)} + \frac{\$7.81}{(1 + r)^2} + \frac{\$8.53}{(1 + r)^3} + \frac{\$221.60}{(1 + r)^3}$$

$$= \frac{\$7.15}{(1 + r)} + \frac{\$7.81}{(1 + r)^2} + \frac{\$8.53 + \$221.60}{(1 + r)^3}$$

$$= \frac{\$7.15}{(1 + r)} + \frac{\$7.81}{(1 + r)^2} + \frac{\$230.13}{(1 + r)^3}$$

With the equation resolved to this point, the analyst must solve for r by trial and error. Starting with r = 24 percent provides a present value of 131.55, which is above the current value of 125. To bring the model's answer in line with the current value, the denominator must increase. Try 26 percent:

$$\$125 = \frac{\$7.15}{(1 + 0.26)} + \frac{\$7.81}{(1 + 0.26)^2} + \frac{\$230.13}{(1 + 0.26)^3}$$

$$= \frac{\$7.15}{1.26} + \frac{\$7.81}{1.5876} + \frac{\$230.13}{2.0004}$$

$$= \$5.6746 + \$4.9194 + \$115.0420$$

$$= \$125.64$$

The answer, 125.64, is still higher than 125, so the discount rate in the denominator must increase again. Raising it to 26.1 gives a present value of 125.36. After several small increases, it becomes apparent that a rate of 26.18 percent makes the model's value equal the known value 125.

Trend analysis indicates that the investor would earn a return of 26.18 percent for the three-year holding period from the end of 1981 through the end of 1984. Comparing this return with those from other investments would establish whether or not it were satisfactory. A return of around 26 percent would please most investors quite well.

Trend-Current Analysis

Trend-current analysis uses the ten-year growth rates of earnings and dividends per share as the estimate for the future three-year holding period, but it uses the current P/E ratio. The analyst would substitute most of the same values into the equation. The only change is to adjust the P_3/E_3 estimate from 11 to 8, the index's current P/E ratio.

The new valuation model becomes:

$$\$125 = \frac{\$6.55(1.092)}{(1 + r)} + \frac{\$6.55(1.092)^2}{(1 + r)^2} + \frac{\$6.55(1.092)^3}{(1 + r)^3} + \frac{\$14.79(1.1085)^3 8}{(1 + r)^3}$$

$$= \frac{\$7.15}{(1 + r)} + \frac{\$7.81}{(1 + r)^2} + \frac{\$8.53 + (\$20.145)8}{(1 + r)^3}$$

$$= \frac{\$7.15}{(1 + r)} + \frac{\$7.81}{(1 + r)^2} + \frac{\$8.53 + \$161.16}{(1 + r)^3}$$

$$= \frac{\$7.15}{(1 + r)} + \frac{\$7.81}{(1 + r)^2} + \frac{\$169.69}{(1 + r)^3}$$

$$= \$126.82 \text{ at } r = 14\%$$

$$= \$123.78 \text{ at } r = 15\%$$

Again, solving for r by trial and error gives a value between 14 and 15 percent. (It might be a good learning exercise for the reader to verify this calculation.) This suggests that the stock market offered returns comparable to those the investor might have earned with less risk on long-term bonds at the time. This would have dampened an investor's enthusiasm to rush into the market with the S&P 500 index at 125, despite the attractive return projected by trend analysis.

These estimates would have guided the opinion of an informed analyst about likely market conditions in the early 1980s, including overall company earnings, dividends, and P/E ratios. As in the earlier company analysis, the analyst would have formed his or her best estimates of the growth rates of earnings and dividends over the forecast period. EPS at the beginning of the period times the estimated earnings growth rate would give earnings at the end of the period; multiplying future earnings by the P/E ratio expected in the third year results in a price estimate. In this way, the analyst plugs estimates of variables' values into the valuation equation to obtain the expected annual return for the period.

In December 1981 one analyst expected the total earnings of the S&P 500 companies to increase 10 percent annually from 1981 to 1984. That would drive earnings per share upward to \$18.15 in 1982 from the estimated \$16.50 per share in 1981. This analyst estimated that earnings would reach \$19.97 and \$21.96 in 1983 and 1984, and that dividends would increase 9 percent per year over the forecast period from the 1981 level of \$7.14. The analyst expected a P/E ratio of 11 in 1984. Based on these estimates, the valuation model gives:

$$\begin{aligned}
\$125 &= \frac{\$6.55(1.09)}{(1 + r)} + \frac{\$6.55(1.09)^2}{(1 + r)^2} + \frac{\$6.55(1.09)^3}{(1 + r)^3} + \frac{\$16.50(1 + 0.12)^3 11}{(1 + r)^3} \\
&= \frac{\$7.14}{(1 + r)} + \frac{\$7.78}{(1 + r)^2} + \frac{\$8.48}{(1 + r)^3} + \frac{\$23.18(11)}{(1 + r)^3} \\
&= \frac{\$7.14}{(1 + r)} + \frac{\$7.78}{(1 + r)^2} + \frac{\$8.48 + \$255}{(1 + r)^3} \\
&= \frac{\$7.14}{(1 + r)} + \frac{\$7.78}{(1 + r)^2} + \frac{\$263.48}{(1 + r)^3}
\end{aligned}$$

Trial and error gives a value for return (r) of 31.6 percent. Based on this analyst's best estimate, the S&P 500 should rise from its level of 125 far enough to provide the investor with a 31.6 percent rate of return over the following three years. This would be an excellent return compared to long-term bonds, given the risks involved.

Different methods have given distinctly different estimates of the rate of return on the S&P 500 during the early 1980s. Which, if any, was correct? What did the S&P actually earn between the end of 1981 and the end of 1984? The average rate of return was 16.8 percent, substantially below the trend analysis and analyst's best estimate projections, and slightly above the trend-current analysis figure. Still, during that time the market would have provided an investor with satisfactory returns and a climate suited to successful investment.

Another Valuation Method: Dividend Discount Model

dividend discount model: A stock valuation model that calculates expected future rate of return as dividend yield plus the growth rate of dividends.

The valuation model just described has its roots in an earlier and somewhat simpler valuation model known as the **dividend discount model.** The dividend discount model for common stocks is actually a simple extension of the valuation model presented for preferred stocks in Chapter 8. The major difference between the dividend discount model for common stocks and the dividend discount model already presented for preferred stocks is that common stock dividends are not constant over time as are preferred stock dividends. Additionally, common stock dividends do not have the payment preference guarantees of preferred stock.

The dividend discount model proceeds from the realization that, from a potential investor's perspective, expected returns on common stocks come in two forms: dividends received over an investor's stock holding period and the price expected to be received when the stock is sold. The nature of these cash flows presents two major concerns from a valuation standpoint. First, for most corporations, earnings and dividends per share are expected to increase over time. Hence, expected future dividends will not be a constant annual amount as is the case with preferred stock dividends and bond interest. It is therefore not possible to use annuity formulas for common stock valuation because calculating the present value of an annuity requires that cash flows be a constant annual amount.

The second major concern stems from the uncertainty surrounding the expected future dividend payments and expected future stock price. Common stock dividends are never guaranteed, and the price of the stock is subject to even more uncertainty than the amount of the dividend payments. As most people who read the papers know, stock prices do fluctuate. The price at which a share of stock will be selling in the future will be dependent primarily on the earning power of the corporation at that time and on the general state of the stock market and the national economy. Uncertainty is normally handled in the valuation process by assigning a higher capitalization rate to common stocks than to bonds or preferred stocks.

A number of valuation models have been developed that attempt to deal with the special valuation problems posed by common stocks. Most of the models are based on the premise that common stock values are a function of expected future cash flows from dividends and the expected future value of the stock. One widely accepted model was developed by Professor Myron Gordon.[1] The Gordon model views the value of a share of common stock as ultimately dependent on the dividend-paying capacity of the corporation.

A simple intuitive explanation of the model begins with the observation that the present value of a share of stock (P_0) is equal to the present value of the next year's dividend (D_1) plus the present value of the stock's price at the end of the next year (P_1). However, the price of the stock at the end of year 1 is equal to the present value of the dividend to be received in year 2 (D_2) plus the present value of the price at the end of year 2 (P_2). P_2 is in turn equal to the present value of D_3 plus the present value of P_3. The argument continues that the price at the end of any year is always equal to the present value of the following year's dividend and price. As the price is pushed further and further out to economic infinity, the present value of the terminal price (the price in the final year) becomes zero for valuation purposes.

Obviously no individual investor expects to hold a stock to infinity. However, from the point of view of the value of a stock in the capital market, the time horizons of any particular investor are irrelevant. What is relevant is the fact that the value of any financial asset is equal to the present value of future cash flows. Since the stock will theoretically exist forever, and as a practical matter may well exist until economic infinity, the only cash flows that will be received from a share of common stock are the dividends. Hence, the present value of a share of common stock is equal to the present value of future expected dividends from now until infinity.

As is true for preferred stocks, the value of common stock thus is the sum of an infinite series of dividends. Unlike preferred stock, the dividends are not constant. Two simplifying assumptions, both of which may be relaxed in applying the model, must be made in order to sum the infinite series. Mathematically the growth rate of dividends must be constant and less than the capitalization rate in order to apply the rule for the sum of an infinite series. Applying this rule results in the following formulation for the value of a share of common stock:

$$P_0 = \frac{D_1}{K - g}$$

where

P_0 = present value of a share of common stock

D_1 = expected dividend in year 1

K = appropriate capitalization rate

g = expected future growth rate of dividends

A simple example will illustrate the application of the model. Suppose that XYZ common stock is expected to pay a dividend of $2.16 in the coming year and that this dividend is expected to increase at an average annual rate of 8 percent per year for the foreseeable future. Suppose further that the appropriate capitalization rate for stocks in XYZ's risk category is 20 percent.

What is the present value of XYZ's common stock? Applying the Gordon model yields the following result:

$$P_0 = \frac{\$2.16}{0.20 - 0.08}$$

$$= \frac{\$2.16}{0.12}$$

$$= \$18.00$$

If the expected future growth rate is not constant, then the model must be modified. In this case each future year's expected dividend must be discounted separately out to the year for which it is estimated that dividend growth will "settle down" to some constant rate. The value of the stock at the end of the last year of irregular growth can then be determined using the Gordon model. The present value of the stock price plus the present value of the dividends received during the irregular growth period will equal the present value of the stock.

If the growth rate exceeds the capitalization rate, a similar procedure is followed. Simple logic dictates that a corporation cannot be expected to grow indefinitely at a rate substantially in excess of the average growth rate of the national economy. If it did, it would eventually have to acquire all other corporations. For a corporation temporarily experiencing supernormal growth, the value of the dividends received during that period must be discounted separately. The value of the stock at the end of the supernormal growth period can then be determined using the Gordon model. The present value of the stock is then the present value of the dividends received during the supernormal growth period plus the present value of the stock price at the end of the same period.

Finally, what of the case of the stock that pays no dividends? There are many such stocks selling for positive prices in the market. Capitalizing dividends obviously presents a problem. The solution to this problem is to estimate when in the future the company will be able to start paying dividends. The value of the stock at that time can then be determined using the Gordon model. This value is then discounted back to the present to determine the present value of the stock.

Exhibit 11.6 illustrates the application of the Gordon model to three cases: the no-growth stock, the normal growth stock, and the supernormal growth stock. The resulting stock values show why high-growth companies typically sell at higher multiples of earnings (price/earnings, or P/E ratios) than do lower-growth stocks: Growing dividends impart more value to the stock price. The example also shows why high-growth stocks normally have much lower dividend yields than low-growth stocks. The value of the growth potential of a high-growth stock drives up the price of the stock and, thus, drives down the dividend payment as a percentage of the stock price.

EXHIBIT 11.6

Application of the Gordon Model

Assumptions: The following assumptions apply to all cases:
(a) Earnings per share = \$4.00
(b) Dividends per share = \$2.00
(c) Appropriate capitalization rate = 18%

Case 1: no growth (g = 0%)

$$P_0 = \frac{D_1}{K - g} = \frac{\$2.00}{0.18 - 0} = \$11.11$$

Case 2: normal growth (g = 9%)

$$P_0 = \frac{D_1}{K - g} = \frac{(\$2.00)(1.09)}{0.18 - 0.09} = \frac{\$2.18}{0.09} = \$24.22$$

Case 3: supernormal growth (g = 25% for three years, 9% thereafter)

$$D_1 = (\$2.00)(1.25) = \$2.50$$

$$D_2 = (\$2.00)(1.25)^2 = \$3.13$$

$$D_3 = (\$2.00)(1.25)^3 = \$3.91$$

$$P_3 = \frac{D_4}{K - g} = \frac{(\$3.91)(1.09)}{0.18 - 0.09} = \$47.35$$

Note: P_3 is the value of the stock at the *end* of year 3.

$$P_0 = \frac{D_1}{(1 + K)} + \frac{D_2}{(1 + K)^2} + \frac{D_3}{(1 + K)^3} + \frac{P_3}{(1 + K)^3}$$

$$= \frac{\$2.50}{1.18} + \frac{\$3.13}{1.18^2} + \frac{\$3.91}{1.18^3} + \frac{\$47.35}{1.18^3}$$

$$= \$2.12 + \$2.25 + \$2.38 + \$28.82 = \$35.57$$

SUMMARY:	P_0	P/E RATIO	DIVIDEND YIELD
No growth	\$11.11	2.8	18.0%
Normal growth	\$24.22	6.1	8.3
Supernormal growth	\$35.57	8.9	5.6

Intrinsic Values and Market Values

As noted, there is a wide variety of common stock valuation models, and different investors may use different models and different sets of assumptions. The value of a share of stock as determined by a valuation model is called its *intrinsic value*. If everyone used the same model and the same set of assumptions, then all market participants would value the stock at the same price, and the market price would equal the intrinsic value. When the market price equals the intrinsic value, the stock price is said to be *in equilibrium*. Changes in market capitalization rates used by investors or changes in the growth outlook for the stock would cause the intrinsic value and the market price to fluctuate.

The traditional approach to security analysis is for an analyst to compare his or her intrinsic value estimate to the current market price of a stock. If the market price is less than the intrinsic value, then the stock is said to be *undervalued* and should be purchased. If the stock is currently priced above its intrinsic value, then it is said to be *overvalued* and should be sold (or, for the aggressive investor, sold short). If the stock is priced at its intrinsic value, then it is in equilibrium and may be held or purchased. The dividend discount model also can be used to estimate expected future return:

$$r = \frac{D_0}{P_c} + g_d$$

where:

r = estimated rate of return

D_0 = base year, or current year, dividend

P_c = current stock price per share

g_d = esimated growth rate of dividends

Would this model give a more accurate estimate of the return on the stocks in the S&P 500 index after 1980? To answer this question, insert the following values into the model:

P_c = \$125

d_0 = \$6.55

g_d = 9.2 percent

Substituting these values into the equation provides the following return estimate:

$$r = \frac{\$6.55}{\$125} + 0.092$$

$$= 0.0524 + 0.092$$

$$= 0.1444$$

$$= 14.44 \text{ percent}$$

An investor could have expected a compound return of 14.44 percent over the three years following 1980, a rate that is lower than that estimated by the first valuation model, but still high enough to influence a positive decision. Also, the dividend discount model's estimate came rather close to the rate of return the S&P 500 index actually posted.

Revisiting McDonald's Stock Value

Applying the valuation models to McDonald's common stock beginning in 1989 will show how to set a value on an individual stock issue, and also give another view on this particular stock to supplement the anlysis completed earlier. The pertinent data are as follows:

P_c: \$33

E_0: \$1.95

D_0: \$0.28

P/E_c: 17

P/E_{10}: 13

Ten-year average g_e: 15 percent

Most likely g_e: 11 percent

Ten-year average g_d: 16 percent

Most likely g_d: 6 percent

The growth rates of earnings per share and dividends have declined, so the ten-year average growth rates would probably overstate future results. To get the most accurate estimates possible, the analysis will use the most likely growth rates.

Ten-Year Trend Analysis

Substituting McDonald's data into the trend analysis and solving for r gives us:

$$\begin{aligned}
\$33 &= \frac{\$0.28(1.06)}{(1+r)} + \frac{\$0.28(1.06)^2}{(1+r)^2} + \frac{\$0.28(1.06)^3}{(1+r)^3} + \frac{\$1.95(1.11)^3 13}{(1+r)^3} \\
&= \frac{\$0.30}{(1+r)} + \frac{\$0.315}{(1+r)^2} + \frac{\$0.33}{(1+r)^3} + \frac{\$34.67}{(1+r)^3} \\
&= \frac{\$0.30}{1.02} + \frac{\$0.315}{(1.02)^2} + \frac{\$0.33}{(1.02)^3} + \frac{\$34.67}{(1.02)^3} \\
&= \$0.294 + \$0.303 + \$0.311 + \$32.71 \\
&= \$33.62
\end{aligned}$$

Solving for r, a 2 percent discount rate provided a high present value of \$33.62 per share, indicating a need to increase the discount rate. Trying 2.5 percent gives:

$$\$33 = \frac{\$0.30}{1.025} + \frac{\$0.315}{1.025^2} + \frac{\$0.33}{1.025^3} + \frac{\$34.67}{1.025^3}$$

$$= \frac{\$0.30}{1.025} + \frac{\$0.315}{1.0506} + \frac{\$0.33}{1.0769} + \frac{\$34.67}{1.0769}$$

$$= \$0.293 + \$0.300 + \$0.306 + \$32.194$$

$$= \$33.09$$

This suggests that McDonald's stock purchased for \$33 per share would earn only about a 2.5 percent annual rate of return, a rate that most investors would find unacceptable.

Ten-Year, Trend-Current Analysis

The trend-current version of the valuation model (that is, changing the P/E ratio to 17) using the same growth rates would give the following results:

$$\$33 = \frac{\$0.30}{(1 + r)} + \frac{\$0.315}{(1 + r)^2} + \frac{\$0.33}{(1 + r)^3} + \frac{\$1.95(1.11)^3 17}{(1 + r)^3}$$

$$= \frac{\$0.30}{(1 + r)} + \frac{\$0.315}{(1 + r)^2} + \frac{\$0.33}{(1 + r)^3} + \frac{\$45.34}{(1 + r)^3}$$

McDonald's annual capital gain, using a current P/E ratio of 17, would equal \$4 per year for about a 13 percent return. Adding this to the likely 1 percent dividend yield suggests a discount rate of 14 percent as a first approximation of the estimated rate of return. This valuation model looks like this:

$$\$33 = \frac{\$0.30}{1.14} + \frac{\$0.315}{1.14^2} + \frac{\$0.33}{1.14^3} + \frac{\$45.34}{1.14^3}$$

$$= \$0.263 + \$0.242 + \$0.223 + \$30.594$$

$$= \$31.32$$

The 14 percent discount rate is too high. A 12 percent rate gives:

$$\$33 = \frac{\$0.30}{1.12} + \frac{\$0.315}{1.12^2} + \frac{\$0.33 + \$45.34}{1.12^3}$$

$$= \$0.268 + \$0.251 + \$32.507$$

$$= \$33.026$$

The present value of the McDonald's stock discounted at 12 percent is only a few cents over \$33. This suggests that an investor could expect a rate of return of 12 percent, an attractive return for this type of stock.

Dividend Discount Model

The dividend discount model gives a different return estimate for McDonald's stock:

$$r = \frac{D_0}{P_c} + g_d$$

$$= \frac{0.31}{33} + 0.06$$

$$= 0.0094 + 0.06$$

$$= 0.0694$$

$$= 6.94 \text{ percent}$$

The dividend discount model would lead an investor to expect a rate of return of 6.94 percent, based upon a revised estimate for dividend growth. Few people would purchase McDonald's stock expecting such a poor return.

Deriving a Price from a Required Rate of Return

If its current price of $33 seems too high, at what price would an investor want to buy McDonald's? Considering the risks involved with common stock investment, a rate reaching 15 percent would be very attractive.

Trend Analysis to Set a Desirable Price Trend analysis estimated a revenue stream from McDonald's stock of $0.30 plus $0.315 plus $35.00 in the three years of the forecast period. The present value of this stream at 15 percent is:

$$\$33 = \frac{\$0.30}{1.15} + \frac{\$0.315}{1.15^2} + \frac{\$35.00}{1.15^3}$$

$$= \$0.261 + \$0.238 + \$23.01$$

$$= \$25.51$$

This suggests the stock would become a good buy if it were to fall to 25½.

Trend-Current Analysis to Set a Desirable Price The previous trend-current analysis projected a revenue stream from McDonald's stock of $0.30 plus $0.315 plus $45.67. The present value of this stream at 15 percent is:

$$P_c = \frac{\$0.30}{1.15} + \frac{\$0.315}{1.15^2} + \frac{\$45.67}{1.15^3}$$

$$= \$0.261 + \$0.238 + \$30.03$$

$$= \$30.53$$

This would lead an investor to willingly pay 30½ for the stock. This price is based on estimates that might or might not turn out to be correct. Therefore, the investor must monitor and reassess all the estimated data to make certain they reflect emerging information as closely as possible.

Conclusion on McDonald's Value

McDonald's is an excellent company, but its stock does not offer a really satisfactory rate of return at its current price of $33. An investor might wish to buy the stock if its price should fall, though. This analysis suggests that McDonald's would be a good investment at between $25.50 and $30.50.

Book Value and Stock Valuation

Many analysts' appraisals take book value as one indicator of relative stock value. In particular, they review the ratio of market price to book value, also called the *market-to-book value ratio* as discussed in Chapters 9 and 10, to assess how well the market has valued the stock.

Many investors carefully avoid paying excessive prices relative to book values. They would consider a stock selling at 5 or more times its book value to be overpriced and they would avoid it. They would find a stock selling at its book value, that is, one with a market-to-book value ratio of 1.0, to be extremely attractive.

Interrelationships of such statistics can become complicated and difficult to interpret. Decision rules vary with individual situations. Historical analysis suggests, however, that the market-to-book value ratio for the S&P 500 has been around 1.50 most of the time.

While a high market-to-book value ratio may be a good indicator of overpricing by the market, a low ratio certainly does not guarantee investment success. If management cannot use company assets effectively, a company can remain unprofitable despite a high book value.

As mentioned in Chapter 10, one author has suggested avoiding any stock with a market-to-book value ratio in excess of 1.25. This kind of arbitrary standard can mislead inexperienced investors. Many people found great success applying this standard in the 1930s, but it no longer made sense when the market-to-book value ratio for the S&P 500 companies reached above 2.6 in the 1990s. The judgment of investors and market conditions had changed. Investors were willing to pay more for a dollar of earnings and tended to ignore book value.

In addition, recall that companies calculate the book values of assets based on their original cost less depreciation, and other accounting conventions affect the final figures, as well. Further, different companies calculate some of their asset values differently, making comparison difficult. Finally, the stated value of the company's stock of assets might not reflect their current market values.

Like other variables, investors must evaluate market-to-book value ratios relative to prevailing conditions and long-term trends. Time marches on and familiar ratios and other relationships change. The investor who fails to watch for these changes may well be left behind.

The real trick in book value analysis is to detect hidden value in a company's stock of assets. When the market discovers this value, it might push the price of the company's stock upward to reflect the new information.

Adjusted Book Value—A Search for Hidden Value

adjusted book value: The book value of a company adjusted to reflect any hidden value.

This discussion should not deter investors from evaluating the assets of a firm and its character to learn if its balance sheet accurately reports the value of its assets or if the firm has hidden assets. An **adjusted book value** that reflected any hidden value could give an investor a profitable inside track in the race to discover the next market winner.

As one example of this kind of adjustment, consider a paper company that carried timberland on its books at $1 an acre when the land had a market value of $500 an acre. An adjustment of this type would raise the book value of the company and could foreshadow a later market move for the company's stock.

Another type of adjustment seeks to evaluate intangible assets, which generally do not appear on a company's balance sheet. A company might have hidden value in a competitive advantage built through an especially effective organization structure, a superior franchising system, or valuable patents or copyrights. What is the value of the names *Coke* and *Big Mac*? A firm might have developed a particularly low-cost production system that allows it to underprice competitors and rapidly expand its market share.

Many features of a company's operations that affect its future earnings and, therefore, its stock price do not appear on its balance sheet. Finding these hidden values might change an investor's perception and require an adjustment in a stock issue's book value.

McDonald's Book Value

McDonald's estimated book value in 1989 was approximately $9.25 a share. At its share price of $33, this gave it a market-to-book value ratio of 3.57, clearly above the ratio for the market at the time of about 2.5, and more than double the market's historical ratio of 1.50. This high ratio told the investor that the market was paying a high price for the assets of McDonald's, which should have suggested that caution was appropriate.

Hidden Value in McDonald's? A close look at McDonald's operations would have calmed these fears somewhat. McDonald's was the dominant force in its industry, and its franchise fees and valuable real estate holdings, which may have been undervalued on its balance sheet, give it strong protection against inflation. The company was expanding globally, which could have given it profitable opportunities for new growth. Further, the company enjoyed a reputation among consumers as a quality enterprise. Perhaps in part because of these factors, McDonald's had tended to sell at a high market-to-book value ratio over the recent past.

At first glance, McDonald's market-to-book value ratio appeared dangerously high. More thorough investigation suggests that hidden assets may well bring the real ratio down to more normal levels.

Risk and Common Stock Valuation

The discussion of stock valuation has not yet mentioned the critical factor of risk. Statistical theorists have developed two ways to measure risk quantitatively. Chapter 6 introduced a rather general one, the standard deviation of past returns. A second measure, beta, reflects the risk of common stock specifically; it indicates the variations of movements in a stock's price from movements in the overall market, as represented by the S&P 500 index.

The standard deviation of past returns measures the risk of any investment. Assume the following returns on a stock investment for each of the past five years:

YEAR	RATE OF RETURN
1	12%
2	15
3	8
4	10
5	20
Average	13

To find the standard deviation of the stock's return, subtract the average value from each year's return, square the result, sum the squares, divide by the number of years minus one, and take the square root of this result. For the investment described above, this process gives:

YEAR	ANNUAL RATE OF RETURN	AVERAGE RATE OF RETURN	DIFFERENCE	DIFFERENCE SQUARED
1	12%	13%	−1	1
2	15	13	2	4
3	8	13	−5	25
4	10	13	−3	9
5	20	13	7	49
Total	65			88/4 = 22.0

Average rate of return = 65/5 = 13 percent

$\sqrt{22.0} = 4.69$

The standard deviation of the return on this investment is 4.69 percent. How much risk does this represent? A larger standard deviation of past returns indicates greater risk. For a stock, a standard deviation less than its average return indicates relatively low risk. Since the stock's rate of return exceeded 5 percent, the standard deviation calculated above reflects low risk. A standard deviation equal to the average rate of return indicates a low level of risk, and a standard deviation substantially higher than twice the average rate of return suggests excessive risk.

Comparison with the S&P 500 Comparison with the standard deviation of the market gives a more exact impression of the relative level of risk represented by the standard deviation calculated for a single stock. Assume that the S&P 500 posted the following rates of return in each of the past five years:

YEAR	ANNUAL RATE OF RETURN	AVERAGE RATE OF RETURN	DIFFERENCE	DIFFERENCE SQUARED
1	10%	10%	0	0
2	13	10	3	9
3	−3	10	−13	169
4	12	10	2	4
5	18	10	8	64
Total	50			246/4 = 61.5
Average rate of return = 50/5 = 10 percent				$\sqrt{61.5}$ = 7.84

The S&P 500 had a standard deviation of 7.84 percent, higher than that of the stock. This shows that the stock had a lower degree of risk than the overall market. Since it generated a higher rate of return than the market, it seems more attractive than the market.

Return-to-Risk Ratio Chapter 10 introduced a ratio to capture the relationship of risk and return on a stock, the return-to-risk ratio. Recall that this ratio indicates the amount of return a stock will provide per unit of risk the investor must accept. Calculate the return-to-risk ratio by dividing the average annual rate of return by the standard deviation for both the stock and the market:

	AVERAGE RETURN	STANDARD DEVIATION	AVERAGE RETURN-TO-RISK RATIO
Stock	13%	4.69%	2.77
S&P 500	10	7.84	1.28

The stock clearly had a better return-to-risk ratio than the S&P 500 index, so it was a more attractive investment prospect than the average for the market.

beta: An indicator of variations in a stock's returns from the returns of the overall market found by regression of the stock's returns against those for a market index.

Beta

A second measure of risk on a stock, **beta,** measures the variability of the rate of return on the stock in relation to the variability of the market, represented by the S&P 500 index. This is to say, beta indicates how closely the returns on a stock track those on the market.

If a graph line shows the relationship between the returns on the stock and those on the overall market, beta is the slope of this line. Assume returns for a stock and the S&P 500 for each of five years as follows:

YEAR	RATE OF RETURN S&P 500	RATE OF RETURN STOCK
1	10%	12%
2	13	15
3	−3	8
4	12	10
5	18	20

Exhibit 11.7 plots these data in a graph.

The next step is to fit a line to the data. The slope of the line, $\Delta y/\Delta x$ is read 4/8 or 0.5, gives the value of beta in the equation:

$$R_5 = \alpha + \beta X_{S\&P\ 500} + E$$

Alpha, the Y intercept, is 8, and E (error about the regression line) is about 1. This gives a risk equation for the stock of $8 + 0.5X_{S\&P\ 500} + 1$. This beta of 0.5 means the stock is only half as risky as the market. The positive alpha is beneficial for the stock at all levels of market return. The higher the E, the less reliable is the expected relation between the stock and the market. A regression equation with alpha and E both equal to zero and a beta equal 1.0 would indicate a return that exactly follows the market return.

Data for Beta Value Line reports betas for all the stocks it follows. As an alternative, an investor can calculate it by fitting a regression line between the return on the S&P 500 index on the X axis and the return of the stock on the Y axis.

The investor must calculate standard deviations based on past annual return data, which Value Line can provide. Most analysts average the high and low prices to find the capital gain or loss for each year. They add the annual dividend to the capital gain or loss to get the annual dollar return. Finally, they divide annual total dollar return by the average price to find a rate of return estimate.

McDonald's Risk

S&P's *Stock Report* gives McDonald's beta as 1.05. This suggests that the stock has about the same risk as the market index. This beta of 1.05, is quite close to the S&P beta of 1.0.

EXHIBIT 11.7

Regression Line of a Stock's Annual Returns to Those of the S&P 500

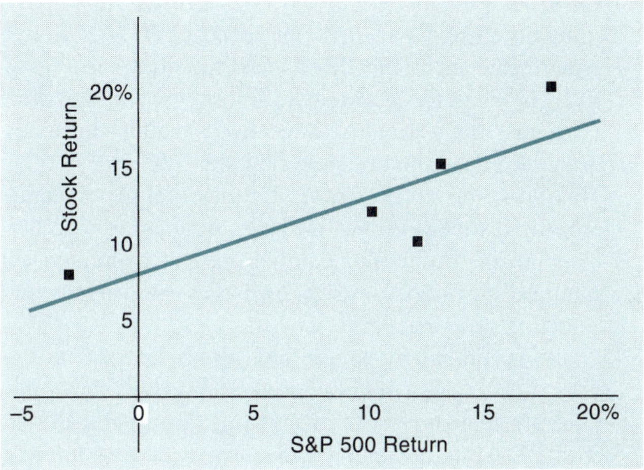

SUMMARY

Valuation of common stock is much more difficult than valuation of fixed-income securities because stock issuers guarantee no fixed expected yield or rate of return. The stock analyst must, therefore, estimate future earnings per share, dividends, and share price.

The returns on common stock over time have been both higher and more variable than the returns on bonds and other fixed-income securities. The variability of past returns is a measure of risk. Under normal conditions, common stock has more risk than fixed-income securities.

Investors must estimate the expected returns and risk for a common stock before making investment commitments. In order to estimate the expected rate of return, the investor must estimate the future share price and dividends. The expected returns on a stock have two components: the expected dividends and the expected capital gain. The capital gain comes from subtracting the initial price from the expected future price, which is a function of expected earnings per share times an appropriate price–earnings ratio. The expected rate of return is found by solving the valuation model for the discount rate that gives these estimated returns a present value that matches the current share price.

The valuation formula for determining the rate of return is:

$$P_c = \frac{D_0(1 + g_d)^1}{(1 + r)^1} + \frac{D_0(1 + g_d)^2}{(1 + r)^2} + \frac{D_0(1 + g_d)^3}{(1 + r)^3} + \frac{E_0(1 + g_e)^3(P_3/E_3)}{(1 + r)^3}$$

P_c is the current price; D_0 is the initial dividend per share; E_0 is the company's initial earnings per share; g_d is the three-year expected dividend growth rate; g_e is the three-year expected earnings per share growth rate; P_3/E_3 is the price–earnings ratio expected in the third year.

Once the estimates have been made, the analyst simply substitutes them into the valuation equation and solves for r, the internal rate of return. This equation gives a rate of return value for comparison with those for other investment opportunities to determine whether an investment seems likely to be profitable. Comparing the estimated rate of return with the standard deviation, a risk measure, indicates whether the investment's return is proportional to its risk.

It is difficult to know how much to trust any estimate. The investor does not know whether projected values for important variables truly measure realistic future expectations until after the end of the period under study. Despite this uncertainty, investors have found good proxies for return estimates in ten-year average growth rates of earnings and dividends, and either ten-year average or current P/E ratios.

Successful valuation requires the best estimates of earnings, dividends, and P/E ratios available. Investors can learn to make their own estimates from forecasts of sales or revenues, but this requires a great deal of skill and effort. As a substitute, several familiar sources of information can provide estimates of earnings, including brokerage firm research reports, Value Line publications, and Standard & Poor's publications like its *Stock Reports*. From whatever source they come, careful estimates of return and risk are an important part of every investment decision process.

The dividend discount model gives investors an alternative, or supplemental, model by which to appraise a security's estimated rate of return. The equation is $r = D_1/P + g$. In this equation, r is the expected return, D_1 is the dividend in year 1, P is the current price and g is the expected growth rate of dividends. As with the more complex valuation model, the result is only as good as the estimates.

In the appraisal or performance analysis of securities, the investor should estimate the potential that hidden values will support stronger-than-expected future growth of earnings. Company assets that will support future stock values can give important market advantages to the analyst who discovers them. Unneeded company assets can also generate profits if the company liquidates or redeploys them. Adjusting book value for the effects of hidden value is not an easy task, but it has potential for future rewards.

In the final analysis, successfully estimating return and risk are the two vital components of prosperous investing.

INVESTMENT MANAGEMENT CONCEPTS

1. Over long periods of time common stocks have been more profitable investments than fixed-income securities.

2. Valuation models like the one presented in this chapter help even novice investors to estimate future returns accurately.

3. The dividend discount model gives another useful technique for appraising the value of a stock.

4. It is important to generate earnings growth estimates or obtain them from the most reliable sources possible.

5. Return and risk estimates support investors' decisions on individual investments and portfolio combinations. The entire process allows the investor to maximize returns and minimize risks.

REVIEW QUESTIONS

1. Are common stocks generally more profitable than bonds or money market funds?
2. Are returns on common stocks easy to estimate?
3. What is the difference between the current dividend return and the total return earned on a common stock?
4. What is the difference between dividend yield and total return?
5. What is a valuation model?
6. Describe the valuation model presented in this chapter.
7. What does r represent in the equation?
8. Why is the growth of earnings per share so important in the valuation model?
9. Where can the investor obtain estimates of earnings growth?
10. How important is dividend growth per share to the valuation model?
11. How do investors determine future dividends and their growth rate?
12. How important is the estimate of the P/E ratio in the valuation equation?
13. What influence does a high rate of inflation have on the P/E ratio?
14. What influence does a low rate of inflation have on the P/E ratio?
15. Do high interest rates have any effect on market P/E ratios?
16. What effect do book value and hidden asset values have on the valuation of a share of common stock?
17. What is risk and how important is it to the investment decision?
18. What is the return-to-risk ratio?
19. How much influence should the return-to-risk ratio have on decisions?

SELF-CORRECTING PROBLEMS

1. The current price of a stock is $30 and it pays an annual dividend of $1.00. What is the current yield? Is this a satisfactory rate?

2. Dividends per share on the stock described in Problem 1 are expected to increase 12 percent per year in each of the next three years. This matches the average rate for the previous ten years. What is the expected dividend at the end of the third year?

3. The price of a stock is $30 and the company's earnings per share are $3.00. What is the P/E ratio? If the ten-year average P/E ratio is 12, is the current P/E ratio satisfactory?

4. The earnings per share of the company in Problem 3 are expected to grow 6 percent annually, which is approximately equal to the ten-year annual average. What earnings per share can investors expect for the company at the end of the next three years?

5. Based on the growth rate of earnings per share and the current P/E ratio of the same company, what price per share should investors expect for the stock at the end of the third year?

6. Based on expected earnings per share growth, dividends per share growth, and the current P/E ratio of the same company, what annual rate of return should investors expect over the next three years? Does this rate of return seem attractive?

7. In Problem 6, substitute the ten-year average P/E ratio for the current P/E ratio and calculate the rate of return. What happened to the rate of return? Does the new rate of return estimate make the stock appear attractive?

8. Apply the dividend discount model to the information in Problem 7 and calculate the estimated rate of return. Is this higher or lower than the rates of return calculated in Problems 6 and 7? Based on the dividend discount model, does the stock seem to be an attractive investment?

9. The standard deviation of the last ten years' annual returns on the stock from Problems 6 and 7 is 12. Comparing the ratio of return and risk in Problem 7, is this an attractive investment?

10. Calculate the return-to-risk ratio under the conditions in Problem 8 using the standard deviation given in Problem 9. Based on this return-to-risk ratio, is the stock a good investment?

Answers to Self-Correcting Problems

1. $1.00/$30 = 3.33 percent, a low rate of return. It is satisfactory only if the stock will also provide high expected capital gains through price appreciation.

2. $1.00(1 + 0.12)(1 + 0.12)(1 + 0.12) = $1.00(1.4049) = $1.4049 = $1.40.

3. $30/$3 = 10, a low P/E ratio relative to the ten-year average, but still satisfactory.

4. $3.00(1.06)(1.06)(1.06) = $3(1.1910) = $3.573 = $3.57.

5. \$3.57(10) = \$35.70.

6. \$30 = [\$1(1.12)]/[1 + r] + [\$1(1.12)(1.12)]/$(1 + r)^2$ + [\$1(1.12)(1.12)(1.12)]/$(1 + r)^3$ + [\$3(1.19)(10)]/$(1 + r)^3$ = \$1.12/(1 + r) + \$1.25/$(1 + r)^2$ + \$1.40/$(1 + r)^3$ + \$35.70/$(1 + r)^3$). Through trial and error we substitute values for r until the present value of the income stream on the right is equal to the price on the left.

Starting with 8 percent revealed a need to increase the discount rate. At 10 percent the equation was \$30 = (\$1.12/1.10) + (\$1.25/1.21) + (\$1.40/1.33) + (\$35.70/1.33) = \$29.95. This comes close to equality, indicating that the estimated return is approximately 10 percent, which is above the historic average of 9 percent for all stocks but still low for current expected returns on common stocks over the past decade, when even U.S. government bonds yielded 8 percent.

7. Starting where Problem 6 left off, change the price to reflect the ten-year average P/E ratio of 12. This increases the expected future price to \$3.57(12) = \$42.84. The rest of the equation remains the same. The dividend stream is \$1.02 + \$1.03 + \$1.05 = \$3.10. The present value of the expected future price is \$42.84/1.33 = \$32.21. The present value of price and dividend stream is \$32.21 + \$3.10 = \$35.21. This indicates that the discount rate from Problem 6 no longer reduces the future income stream to \$30, the current price per share for the stock. To find the new projected rate of return, raise the discount rate to 16 percent. \$30 = (\$1.12/1.16) + (\$1.25/1.345) + (\$1.40/1.561) + (\$42.84/1.561) = \$30.24. This indicates that the new expected rate of return is slightly over 16 percent, so the stock would be an attractive investment.

8. The dividend discount model is $r = D_1/P_0 + g$. In the problem, r = (1.12/30) + 12 percent = 3.7 + 12 percent = 15.7 percent, which makes this seem to be an attractive investment.

9. The return-to-risk ratio calculation is: 19 percent/12 = 1.33. This is an attractive return-to-risk ratio.

10. This return-to-risk calculation is: 15.73 percent/12 = 1.31, indicating an attractive investment.

SELECTED READINGS

Cottle, Sidney, et al. *Graham and Dodd's Security Analysis*, 5th ed. New York: McGraw-Hill, 1988.

New York Institute of Finance. *Asset Plays: Profiting from Undervalued Stock*. Englewood Cliffs, N.J.: Prentice-Hall, 1988.

Ritchie, John. Fundamental Analysis. Chicago: Probus Publishing, 1989.

Stein, Lawrence M. *Value Investing: New Strategies for Stock Market Success*. New York: John Wiley & Sons, 1988.

Williams, John B. *The Theory of Investment Value*. Cambridge, Mass.: Harvard University Press, 1938.

IV

Alternative Investment Opportunities

CHAPTER 12

Investment in Real Assets

CHAPTER 13

Option Strategies and Financial Futures

CHAPTER 14

Closed-End Investment Companies and Mutual Funds

CHAPTER 15

Life Insurance As an Investment Asset

chapter 12

Investment in Real Assets

In 1965 a finance professor traveled to Europe for a three-month study of capital budgeting procedures in business firms there. He took his family to combine some pleasure with his business. While visiting Zurich, the professor's wife purchased a Bucherer clock, scraping together $75 from a limited budget.

Although $75 may not seem like much money today, at the time a popular travel guide promised tourists they could travel in Europe for $5 per day, and the professor's family of five covered food and housing expenses for $30 per day. The clock was an expensive purchase, but it became a family heirloom. Its owners report that it has kept excellent time for more than 25 years and has never needed repair.

In spring of 1990 the professor and his wife returned to Switzerland. The modern edition of the same travel guide they had used in the 1960s had increased its estimate of the cost of touring Europe to $40 per day, and the couple's actual daily expenses approached $200 per day without transportation. This gives a crude but impressive index of inflation.

In an upscale jewelry store the couple saw, prominently displayed, a Bucherer clock similar to the one they had purchased 25 years before. The professor was amazed to learn that the price of this clock in American dollars was almost $1,500. His wife was pleased to learn that her investment had paid off so handsomely, but she added, "We should have bought five of them."

Certainly that would have been a good idea in retrospect, assuming they could have financed the purchase somehow, but how could they have known that the value of their clock would increase 20 fold over a 25-year period? Few people buy household assets like furniture and decorations for their investment values; in fact, most such purchases lose value over time due to wear and tear, changes in fashion, or other causes.

With a little forethought, however, one could meet the need for furniture with an antique Windsor chair instead of a vinyl-covered recliner and still own a valuable asset long after the recliner would have made the final journey to the landfill. One acquaintance owns such a chair that cost $10 in 1972 and was worth over $300 in 1990. Instead of a department store seascape, one could hang a signed John Stobart print over the fireplace. An acquaintance purchased such an artwork for $250 in 1976, and it had a market value before commission costs of $2,000 in 1990. Even after paying a 25 percent commission to sell the print, it would net a rate of return between 13 and 14 percent, an excellent compound growth rate.

Rare, good-quality assets like these generally increase in price, though such purchases involve considerable risk, and careful shopping is crucial. Often these kinds of real assets cost more initially than routine, depreciating goods, but they can add to your net worth instead of detracting from it, and at the same time enrich your enjoyment of daily life.

Introduction

Until the boom in prices of **commodities** in 1980, most Americans had not invested in assets such as gold, silver, coins, antiques, and artwork. In many other countries across the globe, however, individuals routinely hold wealth in the form of gold coins, silver, or jewels. Historically, the closest Americans have come to this practice is collecting coins, stamps, or antiques.

commodity: Any useful thing people buy or sell in commerce.

In fact, from 1933 until 1975 federal law prohibited Americans from owning gold. Since the mid-1970s Americans have become increasingly interested in owning investment-quality gold coins, gold bullion, and other precious metals. Since 1986 the U.S. Treasury has sold gold coins in various denominations, and some conservative financial institutions have even arranged to purchase gold for their clients. Inflation seemed to awaken investor interest in real assets as protection against rising prices, since these assets' prices often increase at least as rapidly as the prices of other goods.

EXHIBIT 12.1

Average Prices of New Houses, 1980–1990

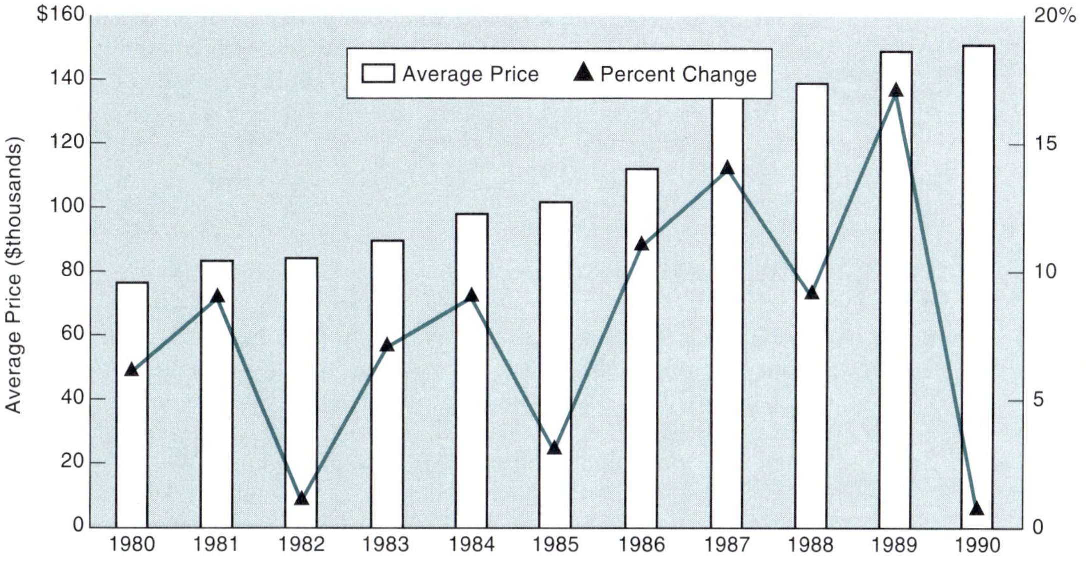

There is one exception to Americans' characteristic disinterest in real assets: real estate. Favorable tax treatment and steadily rising housing prices have made home ownership a profitable and popular investment. Exhibit 12.1 illustrates the increase in new housing prices during the 1980s. Instability in the real estate market and changes to tax laws in 1990 may add some uncertainty to this trend, but real estate remains an important option for real asset investment.

To satisfy the demand for home ownership, many types of financial institutions have made mortgage loans in the past. Typically savings and loan associations, commercial banks, mortgage companies, and life insurance companies have made mortgage loans. Threats to asset values due to high inflation induced some financial institutions to purchase real estate directly as an investment, or to arrange deals to share in the profits from commercial real estate sales they helped to finance. The rising value of its real estate holdings and extra income from profit participation protect the financial institution from inflation and help it keep borrowers' mortgage rates reasonable. The explosion in real estate prices may have ended, but past price trends have alerted investors to possible solutions of the problems of inflation and to profitable opportunities created by the substantial leverage that is typical of real estate investing.

To be sure, a long-run solution for inflation requires a coordination of constraints on monetary growth, federal government spending, importation of energy, and expectations for wage and price increases. In addition, the economy will need more investment of private capital, more saving, and greater worker productivity. Until society achieves utopia, which is not likely to occur very soon, investors will need protection from inflation. Real assets can help them protect the purchasing power of their investment dollars and keep their net worths growing. This chapter will examine the investment characteristics of these real assets, including real estate, precious metals, collectibles like coins and stamps, jewels, artwork, and antiques.

Global Importance of Nonfinancial Assets

R. C. Ibbotson, L. B. Siegel, and K. S. Love, in their study "The World Wealth: Market Values and Returns," point out the extent of world investable wealth.[1] They indicate that in 1984, world investable wealth approached $14 trillion. Of this total, 5.5 percent took the form of U.S. and foreign cash; the value of business, farm, and consumer real estate represented 35.6 percent; U.S. bonds and stocks accounted for 18.8 percent; foreign bonds, stocks, and cash accounted for 26.7 percent; and monetary metals represented 5.7 percent, and other assets 7.7 percent.

Studying returns on worldwide nonsecurity investments gives important insight into ways of life, rather than just suggesting another investment option. Consumers spend more when their financial assets increase in price. As a corollary, individuals will spend more as the total value of their nonfinancial assets increase, as well, including their real estate. In fact, as individuals enjoy increasing wealth from all assets, they should be willing and able to accept the risks of security investments. A careful look at the returns and risks of all assets investors hold can broaden understanding of the risks security investors assume.

Real Estate: A Real Inflation Hedge

Real estate prices in most areas of the United States have risen substantially in response to the growing demand for housing. In Hawaii, California, and Washington, D.C., housing prices have increased at annual rates in excess of 15 percent per year. In Georgetown, a fashionable and expensive area of Washington, an investor could easily buy a house for $100,000 and sell it six months later for $125,000.

The speculative fever in housing was so bad in Los Angeles in 1979 that builders had to allot their houses among clamoring buyers by lottery.

The lucky winners could buy the houses and either move in or immediately resell them at significant profits and get in line for the next auction.

The Washington, D.C., market surged due to renovation of houses on Capitol Hill, close to the Congress, and in other areas of the city. An investor could easily pay $100,000 for a house, spend $30,000 on renovations, and then rent the house for $6,000 a year or sell it for $150,000, for a gain of $20,000 in a year. Prices peaked in Washington from 1988 to 1989, however, and slowed or even declined in the early 1990s. Prices will likely show renewed growth after this slowdown. Based on the trend shown in Exhibit 12.1, an annual future price increase of 5 percent for the overall real estate market seems realistic.

Determinants of Success in Real Estate Investing

Chapter 3 discussed some aspects of real estate ownership in the context of home ownership as an important beginning to the investor's lifelong progress toward financial independence. This chapter deals, instead, with real estate purchased as investments, such as rental properties, small shopping centers, and the like. Of course, real estate investors must deal with many of the same considerations as home owners, so some of the material covered in the two chapters may overlap.

The profitability of a real estate investment depends on several factors that are unique to this market. Failure to understand how these forces influence market prices makes investment success unlikely.

Location A property's location determines much about its potential of maintaining or increasing its value. Choosing a property in which to invest requires thorough study of trends in real estate prices in a given area with special attention toward the magnitude of price changes as well as the stability of prices. This often requires quite a bit of work, but the effort will pay large returns in the form of price appreciation, or at least with regard to avoiding losses.

Houses in one neighborhood, for example, increased in value an average of 8 percent annually over a five-year period, from $50,000 to $73,500. In another section of the same city, slightly more expensive houses increased, on average, from $60,000 to $96,700, a 10 percent annual growth rate. Clearly, the more expensive neighborhood was more desirable financially than the first area. The future seldom exactly repeats the past, but such a trend analysis will reveal clues to the better areas for investment. Also, as houses in these two neighborhoods were rising in value, owners were abandoning houses in other neighborhoods, sending average prices there plummeting. Neighborhood trends can forewarn an investor of this kind of activity and help prevent a financial disaster.

Price analysis reinforces the old joke among real estate agents that the three most important factors in selecting real estate are: (1) location, (2) location, and (3) location. Only through careful neighborhood price analysis can the investor make this critical decision intelligently. This means buying a well-constructed house on an attractive lot that satisfies all the requirements, both physical and aesthetic, that a potential buyer might have. The investor should look for a house that is close to public transportation, stores, schools, and recreational facilities. The neighborhood should be quiet, properly zoned, adequately protected by police and fire departments, and a pleasant place to live. The criteria for commercial real estate differ from those for residential real estate, but the analysis must be at least as thorough.

Most large American cities have suffered serious declines in their central areas, unless they have made massive efforts at redevelopment. Where these efforts have been made, central neighborhood values have tended to increase. Baltimore, Boston, and New York show how effectively this kind of turnaround can halt a downward trend. Astute investors can find opportunities for investment in these areas, especially where strong back-to-the-city movements are flourishing. However, renewed development might lead to excesses as it has in Portland, Maine, and the northeastern United States. As the cost of energy increases and public transportation improves, the interest in city living should intensify.

To resolve any doubts about the value of a neighborhood, lot, or house, consultation with a knowledgeable real estate agent, a reputable developer, or a mortgage banker could give valuable insight. All of these professionals watch trends in property values in their areas closely.

Buy at a Fair Price To preserve the opportunity for future capital gains, a real estate investor must buy a property at a fair, affordable price. The fairness of any real estate price depends on the selling prices of comparable properties. A real estate salesperson can supply a list of these so-called **comparables** in a given neighborhood and advise a potential buyer about the price per square foot of a commercial property.

comparable: A property in the same area and with similar features used to judge the market value of a piece of real estate.

Armed with a comparable list, the buyer can make a serious analysis to determine how realistically a seller has priced a property. The seller has established the asking price in the same way, setting what he or she thinks is a fair price.

For example, assume that six slightly different but comparable houses in the same neighborhood sold, respectively, for $54,500, $53,500, $56,000, $55,000, $57,500 and $53,000, within the past six months. An investor likes another house in the same neighborhood that sold for $55,000 six months ago and that the owner now wants to sell for $61,000 because of improvements made to the house.

The investor begins the negotiation by making a written purchase offer through a real estate agent. In a tight market with a limited supply of houses for sale, wisdom might suggest offering close to the asking price. If the house has been on the market for a few months, or if a number of other sellers are offering similar houses, the investor might offer only $59,000.

Eventually, by exchanging offers and counteroffers, buyer and seller agree on the price and the other terms of the deal.

Understand the Contract for Purchase When they reach agreement, the parties sign a legal contract that states the purchase price, provides for the borrower to make a good-faith deposit (usually 10 percent of the price), and transfers title to the buyer. A "clean" contract for the example described above might indicate offer and acceptance of $61,000 to purchase the house with a deposit of $6,100 and a statement that the balance will be paid when title passes to the new owner in 60 days.

An "unclean" contract might be contingent upon some future event. Some contracts require that the seller paint the house inside and out, that the offer be subject to the mortgage lender's approval, and similar conditions. A seller may agree to such conditions in the purchase contract in a slow market with scarce buyers and a large group of competing sellers. In a tight market, if the investor wants the house, he or she should keep the contract as simple and clean as possible.

Understand the Credit Statement Along with a signed contract and deposit money, many sellers require buyers to provide credit sheets that detail their financial positions, including assets, liabilities, and income. This information tells the seller whether the purchaser has the financial ability to qualify for a mortgage and complete the transaction. This is particularly important when the seller must accept a note from the buyer as part of the price of the house.

Analyzing the Investment

Before signing the contract, however, the buyer must carefully evaluate the deal to assure himself or herself that it will be a good investment. This requires estimating the future growth of income and expenses, rents, property taxes, insurance, management costs, and maintenance. Thorough investigation might reveal that property taxes on the property have increased 8 percent per year, rents have increased 10 percent every two years, maintenance expenses have increased 7 percent per year, and insurance costs have increased 5 percent per year. The insurance premium might rise 10 percent over three years because the policy must cover the cost of the property, which could rise at a 12 percent annual rate. In addition, mortgage interest, taxes, and depreciation expenses are all important components of rate of return estimates.

Mortgage lenders are generally willing to loan 75 percent of the value of an investment property, commonly for terms of 25 years. The interest rates on commerical loans usually exceed those on loans for owner-occupied houses.

Suppose current money market conditions dictate a rate of 11 percent. With a purchase price of $57,000, the mortgage would total $42,750, so the buyer would have to make a down payment of $14,250 (the remaining 25 percent). The buyer would have to make monthly mortgage payments, including principal and interest, of $419 over the 25-year life of the mortgage. The IRS requires investors to calculate depreciation on houses by the straight-line method, that is, deducting an equal amount each year over the depreciable life of the building, usually 20 or 25 years. Note that the depreciation deduction calculation must exclude the value of the land, perhaps $10,000 in this case, leaving a value for the building of $47,000.

Closing Costs

closing costs: Fees associated with transfer of title to a piece of real estate.

When planning for the cash needs of a real estate purchase, an investor must think about **closing costs** in addition to the down payment and the monthly mortgage payments. Both seller and buyer pay closing costs at the settlement meeting, or closing, for the transaction. These costs cover fees for services associated with the transfer of title to a property, including a survey, document preparation, registration of the transaction with local government authorities, and similar details.

This list of individual charges can sum to a significant amount. For example, Exhibit 12.2 lists the approximate closing costs for a $57,000 house with a mortgage of $42,750 in Montgomery County, Maryland. Including prorated real estate taxes, the closing costs represent more than 10 percent of the total cash required at settlement. The pie chart in Exhibit 12.3 breaks down the sample closing costs in Exhibit 12.2 as percentages of the total.

The buyer can deduct some of the fees and taxes he or she pays at closing from taxable income. Certainly real estate taxes are deductible, as are state and county transfer taxes, revenue stamps, settlement fees, and possibly title insurance.

Estimating Income and Expenses

To begin estimating the financial effects of a real estate transaction, assume that the investor's income places him or her in the 28 percent tax bracket, and that all settlement costs are deductible as business expenses. (This may not be true in a particular transaction; the advice of a tax expert could prevent unpleasant discussions with the IRS.) These assumptions give total after-tax closing costs of 72 percent of $1,686.50, or $1,214.28. The buyer's initial cash investment increases by this after-tax total.

Assume further that the investor has to pay $1,000 for points, which are essentially prepayment of additional interest to induce a mortgage lender to make a loan at a given interest rate. Points are deductible, so this after-tax cost comes to $720. Adding the after-tax totals for points and closing costs to the down payment gives the investor's total cash expense at the settlement.

EXHIBIT 12.2

Sample Closing Costs

Recording fees	$ 12.00
Municipal transfer tax (1 percent)	570.00
Tax certificate	6.00
Survey	100.00
Plat	2.50
Notary fees	5.00
Title examination	132.50
Settlement fee	57.00
Preparation of papers, note, and deed of trust	65.00
Title insurance	166.50
Subtotal	$1,116.50
Real estate taxes prorated from June 30 to January 1 (settlement date)	570.00
Total taxes and closing costs	$1,686.50

EXHIBIT 12.3

Sample Closing Costs As Portions of Total

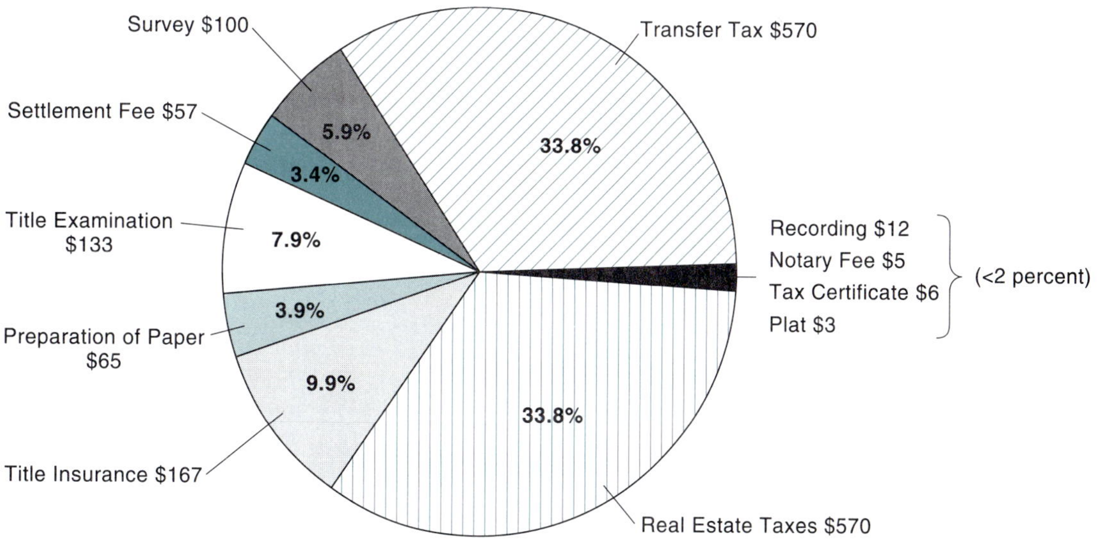

EXHIBIT 12.4

Income and Expense Estimates for Investment Property

	YEAR				
	1	2	3	4	5
Gross rental income	$ 5,400	$ 5,400	$ 5,940	$ 5,940	$ 6,600
Management fee	540	540	594	594	594
Net rental income	$ 4,860	$ 4,860	$ 5,346	$ 5,346	$ 6,006
Expenses					
Taxes	$ 800	$ 864	$ 933	$ 1,008	$ 1,088
Insurance	200	210	221	232	243
Maintenance	750	802	859	919	983
Interest	4,686	4,646	4,602	4,552	4,515
Depreciation	5,540	5,003	4,517	4,077	3,681
Total tax-deductible expenses	$11,976	$11,525	$11,132	$10,788	$10,510
Operating loss before taxes	−$ 7,116	−$ 6,665	−$ 5,786	−$ 5,442	−$ 4,570
Operating loss after taxes	−5,124	−4,799	−4,164	−3,918	−3,290
Tax savings deductible against ordinary income	$ 1,992	$ 1,866	$ 1,620	$ 1,524	$ 1,280

Exhibit 12.4 details projected income and operating expenses for renting the property after the investor buys it. Note that the investment yields operating losses, from $7,116 in the first year down to $4,570 in the fifth year. Careful review of the data reveals that the bulk of these losses result from deductions for depreciation, a noncash charge. Though the investor need not cover the losses in cash each year, he or she can reduce taxable income by the amount of the losses and generate higher cash flows from the property (within limits imposed by the 1986 Tax Act).

Exhibit 12.5 recaps income and expense projections adjusted to reflect actual cash flows. It shows a net projected cash loss after taxes of $74 the first year, and losses of $178, $65, $317, and $122 in years two through five, respectively.

net worth: The total remaining after subtracting liabilities from assets, which represents the proportion of an asset's value the owner can claim.

Exhibit 12.6 shows the **net worth** of the owner's investment in the property at the end of each of five years, assuming its value increases. The net worth of the owner's investment is simply the difference between the value of the property and the amount of the outstanding mortgage. This represents the owner's equity in the property.

If the investor were to sell the property at the end of five years for $100,454 less a 6 percent sales commission, he or she would receive net proceeds from the sale of $94,427. The depreciated value of the house (calculated by the straight line method over 20 years) would be $47,000 minus 25 percent or $11,750, that is, $35,250. Adding the value of the land,

EXHIBIT 12.5

Cash Income and Expenses for Investment Property after Tax Effect

	YEAR				
	1	2	3	4	5
Cash income	$4,860	$4,860	$5,346	$5,346	$5,940
Cash expenses					
Taxes	800	864	933	1,008	1,088
Insurance	200	210	221	232	243
Maintenance	750	802	859	919	983
Principal repayments plus interest	5,028	5,028	5,028	5,028	5,028
Cash losses	($1,918)	($2,044)	($1,685)	($1,841)	($1,402)
Annual tax savings	1,972	1,866	1,620	1,524	1,280
Net cash gains (losses)	($ 74)	($ 178)	($ 65)	($ 317)	($ 122)

EXHIBIT 12.6

Property Value and Net Worth Projections for Investment Property

BASE YEAR	1	2	3	4	5	6
Property value	$57,000	$63,840	$71,502	$80,081	$89,691	$100,454
Mortgage value	42,750	42,408	42,026	41,600	41,124	40,613
Net worth	$14,250	$21,432	$29,475	$38,481	$48,567	$ 59,841

$10,000, to the depreciated value of the house would give an adjusted cost basis for the property of $45,250. Subtracting the owner's cost of $45,250 from the purchase price of $94,427 leaves a capital gain of $49,177. The investor would pay income tax on this gain at a maximum rate of 28 percent, for a total of $13,770.

After taxes, the sale of the property would give the owner $80,657. Paying off the mortgage of $40,613 would leave $40,044 in the hands of the investor. To find the total cost of the investment, add the initial investment of $16,184 to the annual cash losses: $74 in the first year and $178, $65, $317, and $122 in each of the next four years.

Estimating the Rate of Return

To estimate the rate of return from this investment, the investor must discount the revenue streams back to the original value, based on the present value factors from the table in Chapter 6. As in the valuation model for a stock, the rate of return on the investment equals the discount rate that forces equality between the proceeds of the investment at the end of five years and the present value of its total cost over five years. Exhibit 12.7 shows the method of calculation and the final result.

The present value of the investment at the end of five years discounted at 20 percent is slightly lower than the present value of the original investment. Adjusting the discount rate downward finally gives equality between returns and the present value of costs at a rate between 19.5 and 19.9 percent. This is an attractive after-tax rate of return.

Beating the Tax Collector

No investor can avoid paying taxes on income from a real estate venture forever. It is possible, however, to postpone the tax deadline for a long time. The central technique in this effort allows the investor to benefit from increases in a property's value without having to sell it. As the property increases in value, the investor can increase the amount of the mortgage against it by refinancing as long as he or she can find a lending institution willing to make a mortgage loan.

Suppose the value of the property from the previous example were to increase to $80,081 at the end of three years. Mortgage lenders will generally lend 75 percent of a property's value, so this property has a **mortgage value** of approximately $60,000. By increasing the mortgage to $60,000 (from $42,026, the amount outstanding after three years' payments), the investor could realize $17,974 of the total capital gain on the property, which would cover the initial cash investment on another house.

mortgage value: The amount a lender will lend, usually 75 percent of the value of a property for a commercial loan.

This windfall has its cost, though. The investor assumes increasing indebtedness and the higher monthly payments that go with it. In addition, the new mortgage may charge a higher rate of interest, which reduces the investor's advantage. The investor must have rental income or income from other sources to cover the increased borrowing costs.

Some lending institutions might refuse to increase the mortgage on a property, particularly when money is tight. Lending policies of financial institutions do change, sometimes focusing on owner-occupants and excluding investors. On the other hand, with some effort, a real estate investor who intends to reinvest borrowed funds in a profitable venture should manage to find a lender.

Opportunities to borrow increasing amounts of money against rising property values could finance additional real estate investments and generate substantial profits through a form of pyramiding. This assumes that rising prices boost the investor's equity in each house by enough to meet the initial cash requirements to buy another house every three years. The schedule in Exhibit 12.8 begins with a purchase of one house. In three years the investor buys a second house with cash obtained by increasing the mortgage on the first house.

The investor now owns two houses. Assuming that prices continue to increase, the conservative investor can buy another house in the sixth year

EXHIBIT 12.7

Present Value of Cash Flows and Rate of Return on Real Estate

	ACTUAL INVESTMENTS (1)	PRESENT VALUE FACTOR AT 20 PERCENT (2)	PRESENT VALUE AT 20 PERCENT (1) × (2) = (3)
Initial investment—Year 0	$16,184	—	$16,184.00
Annual deficit			
Year 1	$ 74	0.833	$ 61.44
Year 2	178	0.694	123.53
Year 3	65	0.579	37.64
Year 4	317	0.482	152.79
Year 5	122	0.402	49.04
Total present value of investment at 20 percent			$16,608.44
Present value of $40,044 in year 5 = $40,044 × 0.402			$16,097.00

EXHIBIT 12.8

Real Estate Investment/Pyramid

YEARS 0	3	6	9
First house	First house	First house	First house
	Second house	Second house	Second house
		Third house	Third house
			Fourth house

with funds from larger mortgages on both houses. An extremely aggressive investor could buy two houses in year 6, maximizing the mortgages on each of the first two houses, and then four more houses in year 9, maximizing the mortgages on the four he or she owned at the time; the example will assume a more prudent strategy of buying one house every three years.

As long as real estate prices rise and mortgage lenders remain agreeable, the investor must contend with only one obstacle: finding income from rents and other sources to make rising payments on larger mortgages. A successful investor could parlay a house worth $100,000 with a mortgage of $80,000 and equity of $20,000 into houses worth $569,000 with a total mortgage balance of $455,000 and equity of $114,000. That seems like a nice return from an initial investment of about $20,000. The investor cannot claim all of this gain since he or she has not paid taxes on the total. Still, this **real estate investment pyramid** seems to offer the potential for substantial gains.

real estate investment pyramid: Refinancing mortgages on currently owne
tain f
real estate.

What Can Go Wrong? Building a pyramid of real estate can yield exciting profits. Further, the assumptions that underlie the technique seem reasonable, since property values have appreciated more strongly than the example suggests and debt remains a high but not excessive percentage of value. Still, three things could go wrong: A recession could disrupt the upward price trend; the flow of mortgage money could dry up; or poor income and expense estimates could reduce cash flows so far that the investor could have trouble making debt payments.

Falling Real Estate Prices The American economy runs in cycles. In general, every three of four years an economic slowdown disrupts business and results in losses to real estate investors, businesses, and workers who become unemployed. This happened in 1969, in 1974 through 1975, and in 1981 through 1982. In the early 1980s, unemployment rose above 9.8 percent; the inflation rate was in the 12 percent range; and mortgage interest rates increased to as high as 17.5 percent. Over several quarters the economy posted negative growth and corporate profits declined. Another slowdown began in 1990 with a full-blown recession occurring in early 1991, and recovery starting in late 1991.

Few investors manage to profit during recessions, but all should prepare strategies for coping with them since they seem virtually inevitable. In the recession of the mid-1970s, financial institutions lost billions of dollars borrowing cheap short-term funds and investing them in mortgages earning rates of interest that seemed high at the time. Later, however, they had to renew their short-term loans at rates that approached 20 percent, while their assets, the mortgages, earned them less than 17 percent. In 1990 many Washington, D.C., real estate developers collapsed into bankruptcy as property values fell in a weak market.

Individual investors have suffered recession-induced losses, as well. In particular, some tried to cash in on the booming real estate market by buying shares in **real estate investment trusts (REITs)**, companies that sell shares of portfolios of real estate investments they hold. Some people borrowed heavily to buy REIT shares, thus increasing their leverage and, they hoped, the amount of profit these investments would generate. As property values fell, however, the REIT shares declined in price and investors' budding fortunes became costly debts, dragging their finances downward. The recessions of the mid-1970s, early 1980s, and early 1990s provide many vivid examples of what can go wrong in the real estate market.

real estate investment trust (REIT): A company that obtains funds by selling shares to investors, and that invests these funds in real estate and mortgages.

Poor Estimates Since investors base all of their investment decisions on estimates, incorrect estimates can turn apparently valuable real estate investments into financial disasters. A recession, or a host of other causes, could force the market value of a property downward, or keep it from rising as rapidly as expected. An uninsured mud slide, a flood, or a neighborhood blight created by intrusion of some undesirable business or government operation could decimate a property, or at least its market value.

For example, county government officials decided to place a landfill near an affluent area of Potomac, Maryland. The residents blocked the move in court by arguing that a landfill attracts birds that would menace air navigation in the commercial and general aviation routes over the area; instead, the county authorities planned a sewage treatment plant for the site.

Estimates might fail to state correctly either income or expenses. Rents may not increase as expected because of a glut of rental units in a market with weak demand. High tenant turnover, one of the major risks of owning rental property, may leave the investor with no income from vacant commercial or residential properties. One unfortunate investor owned four single-family rental properties. During one year all four properties sat vacant for four consecutive months, and the investor had to pay all four mortgages from ordinary income. Failure to pay could lead to mortgage foreclosure. Any real estate investor must establish an adequate reserve fund to cope with such unexpected contingencies.

Expenses could also exceed original expectations. Real estate taxes could rise more than anticipated. Maintenance expenses might be high, particularly if tenant turnover is a problem. Insurance costs increase with inflation and could reduce profits. One or all of these expense increases might result in lower profits and unfavorable investment returns.

Real estate tax increases pose a particularly serious threat as county governments try to fund more activities with declining contributions from state and federal governments. In Biddeford Pool, Maine, not far from Walker's Point, where former President Bush vacationed, assessed values of ocean-front property have increased dramatically. One house built 10 years ago for $140,000 was reappraised at $500,000, boosting taxes on the property almost 50 percent.

Real estate investment offers relatively high rates of return, but it involves substantial risks, as well. An incautious investor lured by high profits could find himself or herself mired in losses. This applies as much to commercial real estate as to residential ventures.

Investment in Land or Farms

One investor bought a farm in northern Maine several years ago. Besides serving as a new home, it provided a form of protection against inflation through likely increases in value in the future. The farm also served as a vacation retreat and a profitable hobby, and it allowed the owner to consider unusual investment opportunities like raising exotic deer for food.

Many investors favor raw land for its scarcity and historic increases in value. In spite of a deep recession in the mid-1970s, farm land grew in value, but this trend reversed during the 1980s, and further weakness seems likely in the 1990s. The choice of the right piece of land in the right location at the right time is critical. In addition, the carrying costs of ownership, including taxes and interest on loans, can become substantial burdens. Since empty land seldom generates income to offset these costs, investors should keep carrying costs on any land purchases to a minimum.

Selection Process

path of development: The areas toward which real estate development is tending.

Several well-known principles guide investment in land. First, it is wise to buy land well ahead of the **path of development** where sequences of development projects define clear trends. This principle implies two dangers: The investor might buy too far ahead of development so carrying costs eat up the profit by the time development reaches the parcel to raise its value, or the path may change so development never reaches the parcel.

Another principle of land investment suggests that investors look for land that will be developed as soon as possible to maximize the return on the investment. In contradiction to this principle, however, land investors must be patient. In order to ensure satisfactory rewards for their patience, they must make certain that they can afford all payments on the property, including taxes, interest, insurance, and development costs.

The adequacy of financing can determine the success of a land investment. Often, an owner will accept 29 percent of a parcel's purchase price as a down payment, extending a mortgage for 71 percent to be paid over several years. (This follows current IRS rules.) This benefits the owner by stretching capital gains, and the taxes due on them, over several tax years. Each time the borrower makes a payment on the mortgage, the seller effectively sells a proportional part of the property and recognizes a proportional part of the capital gain. While the seller avoids paying tax on the entire gain in a single year, the investor has a built-in financing arrangement.

Land generally changes hands in large units. In large metropolitan areas, 200-acre tracts of land close to the city may sell for as high as $10,000 per acre, or $2 million for the tract. Smaller tracts located closer to the city center may sell for $18,000 an acre to residential developers. A small tract of land well beyond ordinary commuting distances might sell for less.

Land Partnerships

One of the big obstacles to land investment is the requirement for large amounts of cash and the right financing. Unless the investor can pay cash for a purchase, it might be difficult to play the game. This forces the smaller investor into other avenues, like buying developed lots and holding them for resale. This can require long holding periods, since such lots often carry inflated prices.

Land syndicates or partnerships provide another way to make small investments in land. Before entering into a syndicate arrangement, make certain it is legitimate, with no suspicion of fraud, and economically sound. Steer clear of any deal in which the principal partners have shady or unknown past histories.

Match the Loan Term to the Holding Period

It seems like a great idea to borrow at low short-term rates and renew every 180 days rather than accepting a long-term obligation at a higher rate. In periods of high and rising interest rates, however, the cost of short-term borrowing will increase. If the lender will even consider renewing the loan, it will charge high rates that will consume eventual profits and inflate carrying costs. Therefore, arrange financing that keeps costs and income in balance, which implies a need for long-term financing.

For Small Players in a Big Game: REITs

The previous discussion of the threat of falling real estate prices mentioned real estate investment trusts (REITs). Though they bring some of the risks of direct real estate investments, they dilute these risks through diversification. The REIT obtains a pool of funds by selling shares to investors and invests these funds in real estate and mortgages, borrowing heavily to maximize leverage. Investors then participate in the gains (or losses) on the REIT's portfolio.

Though shares in an REIT involve less risk than a direct real estate investment, since they invest in a range of properties, adequate diversification still requires buying into more than one company. Analyze the shares of an REIT like any other security. As mentioned earlier, several REITs failed in the mid-1970s because borrowing money to make long-term mortgages cost more than the mortgages earned. An investor who needs an inflation hedge should avoid ventures that invest only in mortgages.

Returns on REITs

Exhibit 12.9 lists returns on various kinds of REITs between 1980 and 1990. Altogether, these returns averaged 9.6 percent. This fell a little short of the returns on the S&P 500 index for about the same level of risk. Exhibit 12.10 illustrates the trends in REIT returns in graph form.

The equity REITs underperformed the S&P 500 index earning a return of 11.9 percent with risk (measured by standard deviation) of 13 percent.

EXHIBIT 12.9

Return and Risk for Various Types of REITs, 1980–1990

	ALL	EQUITY	MORTGAGE	HYBRID
1980	24.43	17.16	13.74	39.33
1981	8.8	7.49	6.51	11.64
1982	26.58	17.04	42.38	27.6
1983	25.32	31.88	15.24	30.38
1984	13.1	16.25	8.45	15.28
1985	5.33	20.35	−8.71	5.95
1986	18.78	18.51	18.02	21.52
1987	−10.68	−3.51	−15.81	−17.01
1988	12.03	14.39	9.42	10.12
1989	−0.51	8.23	−12.10	−9.15
1990	−17.99	−17.24	−16.43	−26.20
Average	9.563	11.868	5.519	9.951
Standard deviation	12.814	12.970	17.542	17.951

SOURCE: National Association of Real Estate Investment Trusts, Washington, D.C., 1991.

EXHIBIT 12.10

Annual Returns for Selected REITs, 1980–1990

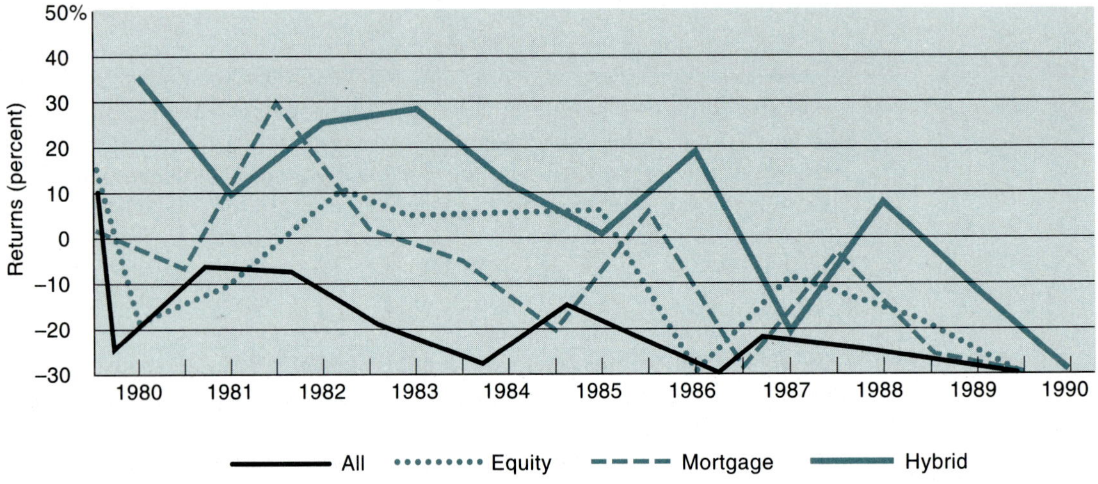

The S&P 500 earned a higher return during the period. Mortgage REITs had the lowest returns of the REITs despite their high risk. An equity REIT would have given the investor a fair return-to-risk performance, but underperformed the stock market for the decade of the 1980s.

Golden Investments

Gold, that soft, lustrous, yellow metal, has served many purposes at different times in history. Primitive people have hoarded it as a sole source of wealth; artists have valued it as a medium for their self-expression; it has lured adventurers, changed hands in mundane transactions, and formed the foundation for the world's entire monetary system. Today it serves as a valuable commodity in its own right, a private store of value, a hedge against inflation, and a substitute for a depreciating paper currency. Human love for gold seems so universal that the more gold people produce, the more of it they demand.

For investors, the main benefit of gold and other precious metals comes from their tendency to increase in value rapidly during inflationary times. Especially in an uncertain economy, investors have bought precious metals to pursue this goal, and to avoid the taxes that real estate would involve. Of course, an investor must pay tax on the capital gain if he or she sells a real asset, or any asset, at a profit. Besides protection from overall losses on their holdings, investors also appreciate the chance for a quick run up in prices (although, of course, they rather dislike sharp drops in prices like those in 1988 through 1990).

The primary reason for owning precious metals sometimes changes from investment to speculation. As the rate of inflation rises, speculators anticipate more demand for gold and rush to buy it, forcing its price upward. In this way, the price of gold rose to a new high in 1980, only to drop dramatically in 1981. Exhibit 12.11 demonstrates the variability of the return on gold and the risk involved in its ownership.

After Congress returned Americans' legal right to own gold at the end of 1974, its price declined steadily to a low point of $116.50 per ounce. It then began a dramatic rise in 1978, finally peaking at over $860 per ounce in 1980 in a speculative flurry not seen for many years. By the middle of 1980, the price had declined to $600 per ounce, and it dropped further in 1982 to trade below $400. Thus, investors could have made substantial profits in gold or, alternatively, tremendous losses, depending on when they made their purchases. Investors can check their local newspapers or *The Wall Street Journal* for the latest gold price. Exhibit 12.12 illustrates the roller coaster ride gold prices have taken.

gold bullion: Uncoined ingots, sticks, or bars of gold.

As in the past, depending on when a speculator purchased gold during recent years, he or she could have made good money or lost a fortune. The rate of return on **gold bullion** between 1980 and 1989 was −2.4 percent,

EXHIBIT **12.11**

Annual Rates of Return for Gold and Silver, 1980–1990

	GOLD PRICE (DOLLARS PER OUNCE)	GOLD RETURN	SILVER PRICE (DOLLARS PER OUNCE)	SILVER RETURN
1980	$601.0		$16.4	
1981	400.4	−33.378%	8.2	−50.000%
1982	445.8	11.339	10.8	31.707
1983	380.5	−14.648	2.8	−18.519
1984	308.3	−18.975	6.4	−27.273
1985	326.9	6.033	5.5	−9.375
1986	329.2	19.058	5.8	−8.621
1987	481.5	23.715	6.7	26.415
1988	416.4	−13.520	6.1	−8.955
1989	412.8	−0.865	5.6	−8.197
1990	383.8	−7.037	4.0	−28.036
Average	394.56	−2.828%	6.77	−10.085%
Standard deviation	48.36	17.124	1.87	23.170

EXHIBIT **12.12**

Annual Prices and Rates of Return for Gold, 1980–1990

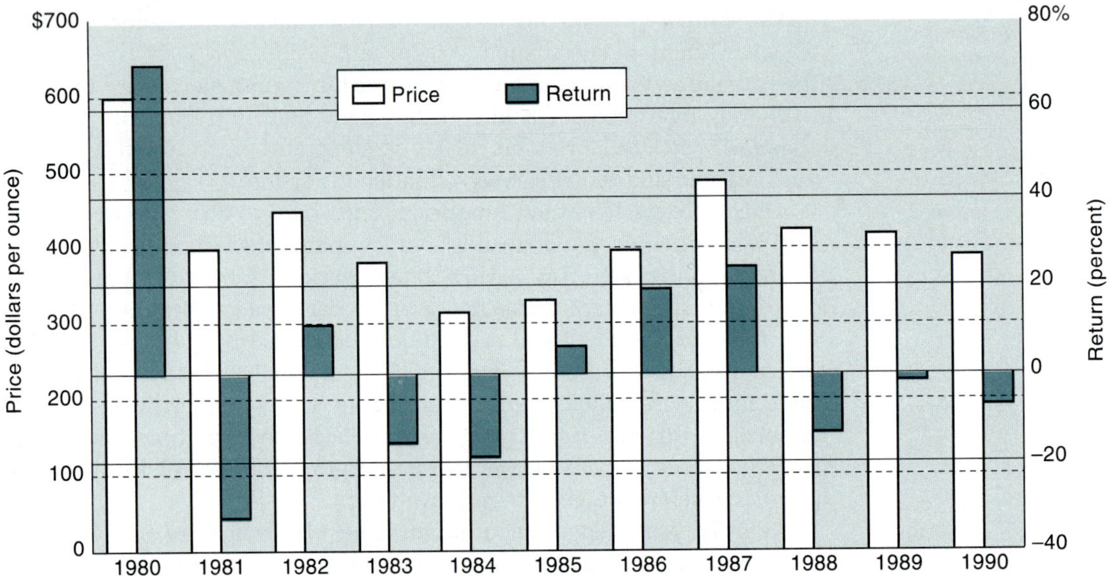

and it was highly variable. Someone who bought gold between 1980 and 1984 and held it to 1990 would have had substantial losses in most years. Someone who bought at the beginning of 1984 would have earned a good profit by holding it until 1990, but he or she would have lost out by selling at the end of 1986.

An investor, as opposed to a speculator, would buy gold for only one reason: to guard against expected inflation. If prices were to rise generally, that investor would make money, but he or she would have to tolerate considerable risk and volatility. The rate of return on gold tends to move in the opposite direction of the rate of return on common stocks. That is, low common stock returns generally accompany high returns on gold. This means that gold gives an investor good protection when inflation drives stock prices down. Combining a little bit of gold in a portfolio of common stocks can prevent dramatic losses in the stock market from eroding the investor's total net worth too badly.

Institutional investors have shown ever stronger interests in real assets that will protect their clients from losing purchasing power to inflation. Some institutional investors are prohibited by law from owning these **unproductive assets** that produce no current income. Most that have the option have considered investing in gold and silver, but few have accepted the risk of large swings in prices due to both ebbs and surges in supply and demand.

unproductive asset: An asset that produces no income.

These risks are real, but the returns may correspond to the risks. The returns on precious metals generally exceed the returns on common stocks during periods of high inflation. The following paragraphs will examine a few ways in which investors may share in the growing value of gold.

Vehicles for Investing in Gold

Investors can own gold in the form of jewelry, coins, bullion, and common stock in gold mining companies.

Gold Jewelry Many people own gold jewelry, including necklaces, bracelets, rings, chains, earrings, watches, medallions, and even art objects. Unfortunately, these people receive the poorest return on their gold of any type of gold investor. The value of jewelry has two basic components: the purity of the gold and the artistic value of the design. The purity of gold is measured in karats; 24-karat gold is the purest and most expensive. The pliability of pure gold requires jewelers to mix it with other metals to increase its strength. This reduces the gold's karat weight, and its value. Jewelers commonly sell 12-, 14-, and 18-karat objects. Since an investor wants to know the value of pure gold in a piece of jewelry by weight, he or she must assess the pure gold equivalent.

The second component of the value of jewelry comes from the artistic merit of its design. This is difficult to evaluate and usually requires expert opinion. Certainly, investors should obtain an expert opinion and appraisal before a major expenditure for gold jewelry.

The price of gold jewelry followed the dramatic increase in the price of gold and has declined equally as dramatically. Comparing the price of a gold necklace verifies this. A gold necklace purchased for $125 in 1976 was worth over $460 in 1983 but under $200 in 1993. This rate of decline is unlikely to continue in the future at the same rate, but fluctuations may result in net losses over some periods.

Still, many owners feel gratification from using and enjoying such an asset, while it retains some lasting value and contributes to their net worths. Ordinarily, jewelry represents an inefficient way of investing in gold, yet it continues to be a store of value; over a long period of time, a piece of jewelry could prove to be a satisfactory investment.

Gold Coins One way for an investor to derive both pleasure and profit from gold is to purchase jewelry items made from gold coins and bars. Both gold coins and five-gram wafers of pure gold can be purchased as pendants with gold chains. Five-gram wafers can make attractive cufflinks that will increase and decrease in value with the price of gold. Of course, such items are beautiful and interesting to wear. Jewelers make attractive bracelets and pendants from $20, $10, and $5 gold pieces, but the coins might lose value in the transformation, and they wear from exposure.

The United States Treasury has created another way to own gold, introducing the $20, legal tender, gold American Eagle in 1986. Each coin weighs one ounce. **Proof sets,** uncirculated specimens, of the coin sold for $550 in 1986, but in 1990 they had fallen in value to less than $400. Still, the coins held the interest of foreign and domestic dealers and collectors.

proof set: A set of uncirculated, newly minted coins.

Before the Treasury's new coin, investors could own gold only by buying coins from numismatic dealers. One of the most popular coins over time among collectors and investors has been the South African **Krugerrand,** which contains 1.00 Troy ounce of gold that is 916.66/1,000 fine. Investors buy the coin for its gold content rather than its value as a collector's item. Investors may also buy a two-rand South African coin that has about one-fourth the gold content of the Krugerrand. The ban on the importation of Krugerrands into the United States as a result of racial discrimination in South Africa has diminished interest in these coins. Unfortunately, this has hurt small, individual investors who own a few coins. The American Eagle and the Maple Leaf, a similar coin issued by the Canadian government, have taken the market from the Krugerrand.

Krugerrand: A gold coin minted by the South African government.

Collectors have held the old U.S. Double Eagle $20 coin. Each coin contains 0.9675 Troy ounces of gold that is 900/1,000 fine. The circulated coins make fine pieces of jewelry or beautiful collector's items. In 1974 a coin of this type sold for $90. In 1990 such a coin in reasonable condition sold for over $600. U.S. gold coins in $5 and $10 denominations give investors two more easy ways to own gold. Each coin varies in price, depending upon its quality and gold content. An investor who contemplates a major purchase should seek expert advice.

These coins listed on the next page are also considered appropriate forms in which to purchase gold.

COIN	FINENESS	WEIGHT (OZ.)
Mexican 50 peso	900/1,000	1.2056
Austrian 1 ducat	986.66/1,000	0.1109
Austrian 4 ducat	986.66/1,000	0.4438
Austrian 100 corona	900/1,000	0.9802
Hungarian 100 korona	900/1,000	0.9802
English old sovereign	916.66/1,000	0.2354

Gold Bars Before December 31, 1974, federal law prohibited American citizens from owning, buying, or selling gold bullion. The change in the law beginning in 1975 offered Americans the first opportunity since the United States abandoned the gold standard in 1933, 41 years before, to own gold. Between 1933 and 1975, individuals could own gold only in the form of coins, jewelry, and art objects. Since then, gold bars or bullion have given Americans the cheapest and most direct way to own gold.

Before 1975, the federal government owned the only gold in the country outside narrow limits, and for a period gold served as a monetary base and reserve for U.S. currency. While it maintained these restrictions, the government fixed the price of gold. Under regulation, the price moved from $20.66 an ounce before 1934 to $42.22 in 1974. The free market price of gold rose to $175 an ounce during this time.

Swiss banks sell gold bars in denominations from 5 grams to 10 ounces. U.S. dealers also sell gold bars. One dealer sells its own 999/1,000 fine gold bars in 1.5 ounces or 10 ounces. Each bar is numbered and sealed in a clear plastic package. This dealer's repurchase agreement on the back of each package reads:

> Should [we] repurchase this bar, we will do so at the prevailing spot price of gold. We will charge the customer no assaying or refining costs provided that the packaging or the security paper within is not disturbed, altered, or damaged in any way.

This provides the dealer's customers with a simple, inexpensive, and safe way of buying gold bars.

gold mining share: A share of common stock in a gold mining company.

Gold Mining Shares **Gold mining shares** give individual investors another way to participate in the potential profit of owning gold. An investor who buys a share in a gold mining company buys a portion of that company's profits rather than any of the gold it produces. Obviously, however, if gold prices rise, the value of the company's output and, therefore, the company's stock will also rise. In addition to volatility due to the price of gold, the investor must look for probable effects of the financial and competitive positions of the company before making an investment.

gold mutual fund: A mutual fund that invests in gold mining stocks.

If an investor wants to avoid the risk of one gold mining company losing value, he or she can invest in a **gold mutual fund** to achieve better diversification. Exhibit 12.13 reports the average return investors earned on U.S. Gold Shares, one such mutual fund, during the 1980s. The average

EXHIBIT 12.13

U.S. Gold Shares Return, 1980–1990

	NAV/SHARE	DIVIDENDS	CAPITAL GAIN	TOTAL RETURN
1980	8.3	$0.59	0.00	
1981	5.21	0.88	0.00	−26.627%
1982	8.11	0.44	0.00	64.107
1983	7.85	0.39	0.00	1.480
1984	5.22	0.32	0.00	−29.299
1985	3.6	0.27	0.06	−24.957
1986	4.63	0.35	0.06	40.000
1987	5.53	0.54	0.00	31.102
1988	3.34	0.82	0.00	−35.684
1989	5.31	0.17	0.00	64.072
1990	3.35	0.07	0.08	−34.087
Average	5.216	0.36	0.02	5.027
Standard deviation	1.543	0.21	0.03	38.920

SOURCE: Wiesenburger Mutual Funds Investment Report, 1990.

return of 5.03 percent, with a standard deviation of 38.92, indicates a higher return than gold itself provided, but also a higher risk. This left U.S. Gold Shares with a higher return-to-risk ratio than gold. These relationships made U.S. Gold shares a more attractive investment than gold from 1980 to 1990.

Silver and Platinum

Like gold, silver has performed well during periods of high inflation over the years. Anyone who owns silver coins, flatware, tea services, or jewelry enjoyed both value increases that have rivaled inflation and the use of beautiful items. Unfortunately silver's investment performance suffered in the 1980s (see Exhibit 12.14).

Cash prices of silver appear with other commodity prices in the financial press, including *The Wall Street Journal.* The price of silver was $5.34 on December 9, 1986, and about $4.00 in 1990. A purchase of silver would have been a poor investment for this period.

Vehicles for Investing in Silver

Investors can buy silver in many of the same forms as gold. The price of silver bullion increased steadily from 1976 to a peak in 1980. From 1980 to

EXHIBIT 12.14

Annual Rates of Return for Silver, 1980–1990

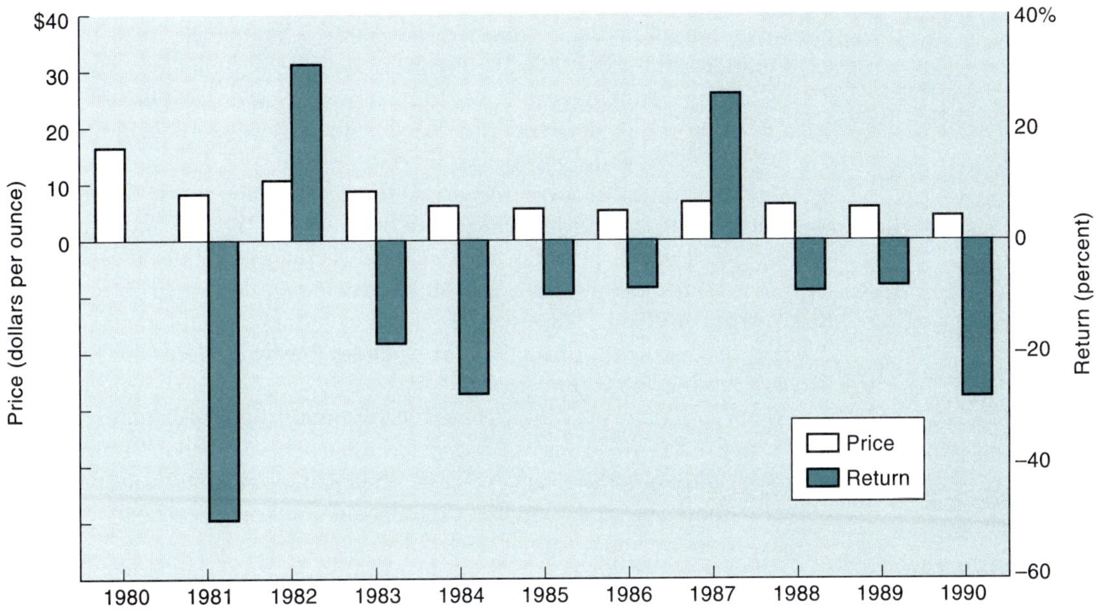

the end of 1989, the price of silver declined unevenly. Exhibit 12.14 shows how the price of and return on silver varied during the 1980s. The average return for the period was unsatisfactory at −10 percent.

Sterling Silver Objects It is almost impossible to keep up with the price changes in all silver objects, but a few examples can give an investor a notion of trends over the past 30 years. One four-place International Sterling pattern cost $34 a setting in 1950. In 1989 the same pattern sold for over $300. A sterling tea service purchased for $600 in 1960 had a retail price of $3,000 in 1986, but half that in 1990. Besides contributing to an investor's net worth, sterling silver flatware provides daily enjoyment through its use. This is certainly an excellent combination, but price variations and low current prices suggest high risk.

Colonial families had an interesting attitude toward silverware. A wealthy family in colonial Deerfield, Massachusetts, for example, would have several silver mugs, one perhaps made by Paul Revere (which would be priceless today). A poor family might have only one mug or dish, but it represented a major part of the family assets. Following this example, an investor need not buy 12 place settings of silver to enjoy both utility and profit. A collection can begin with the purchase of a single spoon.

Silver Coins Many coin collectors hoard silver dollars such as the Eisenhower dollar and other silver coins. In addition, a new silver coin, the silver American Eagle, reached the market October 26, 1986. It has a legal tender value of $1.00 and contains one ounce of 0.999 fine silver, but it sells for a premium over its silver bullion price. Some states do not charge sales taxes on trades of silver American Eagles. There is no guarantee that the price of these coins will rise in the future.

Before issuing the silver American Eagle in 1986, the U.S. Treasury had not minted coins from silver since 1964, when the metal's value rose to a level that made the coins more valuable as pieces of silver than as U.S. currency. Many people then sold any silver coins they held in a market that peaked in 1980. This rush of supply set the stage for the following decline, but at least through 1981 refiners busily melted down coins, flatware, and jewelry to make into silver bars.

Since so many coins disappeared at this time, they became extremely scarce and current owners of bags of these coins can obtain a premium price. In addition, they can exchange their coins for 0.999 fine bars and wafers without paying tax on any capital gains they may realize.

Investors can buy bags of these silver coins from dealers. A 55-pound bag of 90 percent silver coins issued before 1964 contains 712 ounces of silver with a market value of $3,987 at a market price of $5.60 per ounce. The coins' total face value of $1,000 per bag effectively protects the owner from price declines below this level. Investors can also purchase 760-ounce bags of 40 percent silver dollars (for 295 ounces of silver per bag). The coins in these bags also have total face values of $1,000.

Bars of Silver The standard 1,000-ounce silver bar represents the global trading unit. A smaller trading unit, the 100-ounce silver bar, has also become popular. The two bars generally sell at different per-ounce prices; an investor must pay a premium of $0.50 per ounce for the smaller bar. The price of silver bars also varies from market to market and from dealer to dealer.

Silver Futures Commodities traders handle futures contracts for silver. Dealers quote prices of these **silver futures** in cents per 5,000 Troy ounces. A futures contract is a commitment to buy or sell a commodity at some future specified time and place. Traders establish the market price of such a contract in the open market on a futures exchange.

silver future: A contract for future delivery of silver at a specified price, time, and place.

Only a small percentage of futures trading actually leads to a delivery of a commodity because a contract may change hands or be liquidated before the delivery date. Participants comprise commercial hedgers who use futures to minimize price risks inherent in their marketing operations, and speculators who seek profits through price changes. Futures traders buy contracts on margin, making partial payments and borrowing the difference.

Suppose the price of silver for delivery three months from now is 556.0 cents per Troy ounce, based upon a 5,000-ounce contract. The buyer would accept the obligation for the total cost of the contract of $27,800 through the Commodity Exchange (CMX) in New York. He or she would make this purchase expecting the cash price in three months to exceed $5.56 per ounce. If it did, the price of the futures contract would rise, and the owner could sell it for a gain. If the price did not rise, the owner would lose and allow the contract to expire or sell it at a loss before expiration.

Although few do so, the owner can exercise the contractual option to buy the silver and take delivery. He or she must then store, insure, and protect the silver, all of which increase the cost of the investment. In an inflationary environment, however, silver should increase in price. The owner could, therefore, hold the silver as an inflation hedge and to counterbalance possible losses on common stock investments.

Platinum

Another precious metal, platinum, has value both in the form of jewelry and as a raw material for industrial products. Industrial demand for platinum soared in 1986 for its use in making electrical contacts and sparking points since the metal resists high temperatures and damage from electrical arcs. Production of jewelry, dental products, and alloys also consumes a large amount of platinum.

U.S. mines produce only a small amount of platinum. Production began in the South American countries of Colombia and Brazil, and other operations in South Africa and the Canadian province of Ontario also supply the metal. Russia has become a dominant producer. With such a small range of suppliers, platinum production remains limited and its price is high and volatile. On December 9, 1986, the market price of platinum hovered around $447.00 per ounce. At that time, futures contracts for October 1987 delivery of platinum implied an expected price of $487.10, reflecting a consensus that the price of the metal would rise because of higher demand and lower supply. Instead, the price fell to $387 by mid-1992.

Investors can purchase platinum in many of the same forms as gold and silver. Some governments have even minted platinum coins. The **Noble**, a one-ounce coin of 0.9995 fine platinum from the PABJOY Mint on the Isle of Man, entered circulation in Europe in 1983. The coin sells at a 4 to 7 percent premium over the metal's bullion price. The Swiss government has minted a one-ounce, 0.999 fine platinum coin called Shooting in Switzerland. Uncirculated, the coin is worth $750 with a bullion value of $480.

Noble: A platinum coin minted on the Isle of Man.

Other Real Assets

Collecting Coins and Stamps

An investor can turn the often interesting and educational hobby of coin collecting into a profitable medium for investment. A dean of a leading U.S. school of business once said that he knew of no other hobby that allowed him to keep the money he spent and still have a chance of beating inflation. Coin collecting differs from investing in precious metals by buying coins, since collectors prize a rare or beautiful design where the metal investor sees only a thin chunk of valuable material.

Each individual coin has its own value depending upon a number of factors, so no one can generalize about marketwide price movements. Popular denominations of coins have only monetary value. Many old coins, like the Eisenhower dollar, have high silver contents so they have value both as quantities of silver and as collector's items. Early in 1980 silver dimes sold for over $1.50 each, quarters brought $3.75, half-dollars were worth $7.50, and Kennedy half-dollars minted between 1965 and 1969 sold for $2.50 each. In 1992, a Kennedy half-dollar sold for $1.10. High-quality individual specimens may sell for higher prices. A 1909 SVDB penny sold for $45 in 1969 and $300 in 1990. A 1955 Double Die penny sold for $100 in 1969 and $350 in 1992. Certainly, these coins could have made profitable investments, besides their value as rare artifacts.

Rare stamps have increased in value in similar amounts. A 5¢ 1925 Norse American sold for $2.25 in 1969 and $30 in 1992. This shows how a pleasurable pastime can double as an affordable avenue for investment. A higher-priced stamp, the 1892 $5 Black Columbian, sold for $235 in 1969, and one in mint condition sold for $3,500 in 1992. This stamp would certainly have been a good investment.

Collectible assets vary widely in value, so any collector must study the subject area carefully to earn profits from the money invested in the hobby. Professional advice can give invaluable pointers to help you set out in the right direction. In any case, a smart investor will limit the amount of his or her net worth invested in these kinds of assets, since collector's items tend to be risky investments.

Assets that Sparkle

Most people like diamonds. They make dazzling beauty out of ordinary light, and they have provided a good hedge against inflation in the past, or they had until 1982, when prices declined sharply.

Diamonds purchased through retail jewelers might lack real investment potential, since jewelers' markups on diamonds can exceed 100 percent. Still, the investor can expect a top-quality gem to increase in value over a ten-year period, and he or she can maximize the return on this investment by keeping costs down through wholesale purchases in the gem markets of New York, London, and Amsterdam.

This requires the ability to cover the large units of investment the market commonly expects. A one-half–carat diamond might range in price from $500 to $2,000, and a one-carat stone might range from $2,500 to $7,500, depending on quality. Jewel traders measure stones in carats and points, where each carat represents 100 points. Bigger stones are more valuable per carat of weight.

As a general rule, the highest-quality stones have generated the highest investment profits over time. Since an investor might buy only one diamond in a lifetime, he or she may benefit the most from buying the biggest, highest-quality stone the individual can afford at the lowest possible price. A wholesale purchase of a high-quality diamond engagement ring can provide emotional satisfaction while increasing in monetary value.

DF: A quality grade for a colorless, D, flawless, F, diamond that is the standard for the industry.

Usually, investors look for finished gemstones weighing one carat or more. The value of a particular stone depends on its color and flaw characteristics. A rating of *F* designates a flawless stone and *D* designates a colorless stone. A rating of **DF** indicates a diamond of the best possible quality. Such a stone weighing one carat would have sold for $6,700 in 1976, $63,000 in March 1980, $14,000 in 1986, $20,000 in 1988, and $18,000 in 1992. This kind of variability should discourage the faint-hearted investor. Exhibit 12.15 illustrates changes in the annual rate of return investments in diamonds have provided.

More Beautiful Assets: Paintings and Antiques

Almost any piece of art or an antique that is scarce, attractive, and useful will probably increase in value. Two examples indicate the monetary gains these assets can generate. A painting by Andrew Wyeth, a successful, living artist from New England, sold for $5,500 in 1969; the same painting sold for $16,000 in 1978. This indicates a high unit of investment, but the gains can be substantial. A small collection of prints by John Stobart, a successful painter of marine scenes, has risen in value from total purchase prices of approximately $3,500 (paid between 1976 and 1986) to a retail value of $11,000 in 1992.

Antiques offer investors a chance for almost boundless returns, but they require a great deal of study. As the vignette at the beginning of the chapter suggested, investors can even make money from objects that they use daily. An antique O.G. clock, for example, might have cost $20 in 1955. Today, prices range from $250 to $350. Such a clock would keep good time, require winding only every eight days, and decorate the owner's home. Timeless aesthetic values and rising monetary values seem to make antiques appealing to most people.

EXHIBIT 12.15

Compound Annual Rates of Return on Diamonds

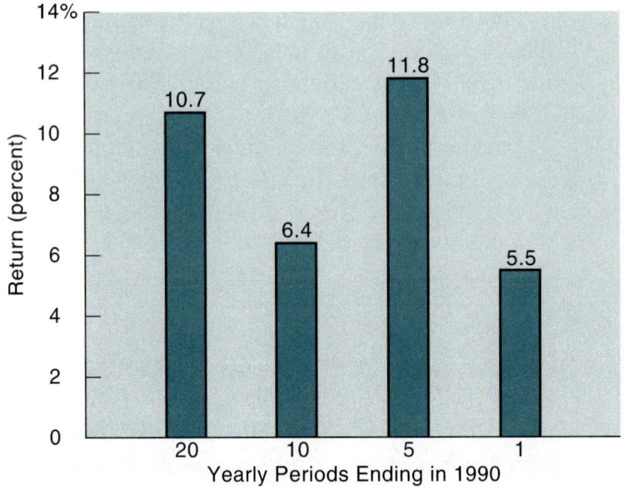

SOURCE: Salomon Brothers, with permission.

Sotheby's Art Index: Index of the market for transactions involving art objects through Sotheby Auctioneers.

Sotheby's Index *Barron's* created **Sotheby's Art Index** in November 1981 to track the overall markets for art and antiques. Exhibit 12.16 indicates how prices of various classes of assets within these categories have behaved. An investor who purchased assets at prices implied by Sotheby's Index would have earned an average return of 14.4 percent for the period 1975 through 1991. Exhibit 12.16 also shows what happened between 1986 and 1991. The aggregate index increased from 403 in 1986 to 787 in 1991 for a 95.3 percent increase. The years 1989 through 1991 showed a loss in the index.

Comparative Rates of Return on Real Assets

What rates of return would an investor earn from investments in real assets such as real estate, precious metals, coins, stamps, artwork, and antiques? In addition, how much risk would an investor have to accept to have a chance at those returns?

Morgan Stanley & Co., Inc.: A large, world-known New York investment banking firm.

Morgan Stanley & Co., Inc. provides some answers to these questions. From 1945 to 1991, an inflationary period, investors enjoyed appreciation on assets such as farmland, housing, commercial real estate, and art (see Exhibit 12.17). Stocks did far better, while gold and silver did not fare well. T-bills, bonds, and commercial paper also did not perform well.

EXHIBIT 12.16

Sotheby's Art Index

CATEGORY	1975	1976	1977	1978	1979	1980	1981	1982	1983	1984	1985	1986	1987	1988	1989	1990	1991
Old master paintings	100	105	131	173	224	255	201	205	239	278	289	303	373	469	754	865	728
19th century European paintings	100	99	118	160	215	225	179	184	201	230	249	279	323	421	575	634	625
Impressionist art	100	107	114	133	175	206	248	267	307	356	380	490	723	1,255	1,845	1,471	913
Modern paintings	100	105	108	132	178	204	249	245	282	336	364	512	757	1,138	1,684	1,600	1,018
Contemporary art	100	105	127	159	197	239	285	342	392	444	497	551	609	856	1,627	1,456	1,165
American paintings	100	129	171	255	315	350	450	450	556	589	667	698	871	958	1,371	1,174	1,142
Continental ceramics	100	121	154	213	261	336	293	266	284	284	284	290	331	467	505	572	796
Chinese ceramics	100	159	181	241	353	462	445	436	459	486	486	526	581	815	875	997	1,003
English silver	100	89	95	124	165	205	175	189	219	261	306	343	381	388	420	453	439
Continental silver	100	89	92	113	146	179	140	139	156	175	181	201	220	296	367	395	436
American furniture	100	109	120	134	150	172	209	213	239	289	330	404	459	484	510	510	516
French and continental furniture	100	104	121	148	197	232	228	234	257	272	273	299	319	409	500	564	648
English furniture	100	125	156	195	244	256	279	267	328	382	419	517	634	822	822	867	924
Aggregate	100	111	128	164	217	253	249	252	286	324	344	403	512	737	1,038	983	787

What Is the Sotheby's Art Index?

Sotheby's Art Index tracks price trends in different sectors of the art market. It does not predict prices nor indicate what a particular piece is worth, but it does provide, easily and clearly, historic perspective on where prices are at the moment.

It is a formal index that has been created using methods which follow closely others in common use, such as the main stock market and consumer price indices.

What Types of Works of Art Does Sotheby's Index Cover?

The works of art which have been selected for inclusion in each sector are good quality, from the middle range of the market. Examples of the highest priced items have been deliberately excluded because the infrequency with which they come up for sale at auction makes them unrepresentative of the overall market. Likewise, material at the lower end has also been excluded, since it is not predominantly of interest to serious collectors.

(continued)

EXHIBIT 12.16

Sotheby's Art Index *(continued)*

What Types of Works of Art Does Sotheby's Index Cover? *(continued)*

The items included in each sector have been selected from property sold by all the major auction houses around the world. The works chosen specifically have not been confined to items sold by Sotheby's; the aim has been to create the widest and most representative portfolios possible.

Each sector of the Index is constantly reviewed and updated when any event takes place which has a bearing on that particular market. Such occasions include major sales by any of the major auction houses, as well as important exhibitions, or the publication of scholarly works.

How Does the Index Operate?

In the same way as the consumer price index measures price variations by monitoring the changing value of a fixed basket of goods representative of typical family expenditure, Southeby's Art Index also uses the basket method to measure changes in the art market.

This exercise was carried out for each sector of the Index. The experts were free to choose however many items were necessary to achieve a balanced portfolio; no ceiling was imposed. On average between 30 and 40 works were selected for each sector of the Index. Whenever a particular sector is updated (usually between two and three times a year) the value of each constituent item is re-assessed by the expert in the light of prevailing market conditions. Factors taken into account on an ongoing basis include the underlying structure of the art market, namely supply and demand, who is consigning property and why, and any changes in the nature of buyers (new private collectors, etc.). In addition, whenever possible underlying reasons for the outcome of a sale are considered, especially where these relate to events outside the art market, such as the influence of exchange rate movements or leading economic indicators.

The total of the basket is then calculated and the ratio of this figure to the corresponding total in the base year (1975) is then expressed as an index.

Although art market prices are not determined by the same precise forces which regulate, say, stock market prices, nevertheless, Sotheby's Art Index is the only formal measure of art market prices available.

Notes Relating to the Art Index:

1. In each case, the figures are shown in absolute terms, without making any allowances for inflation.
2. All figures are expressed in terms of the U.S. dollar.
3. The basis for the series is September 1975 = 100.
4. Up to and including 1980, the figures were calculated yearly only, in September of each year. From 1981, the figures quoted are calculated in December of each year.
5. The Aggregate Index is a weighted figure.

 Sotheby's Art Index reflects subjective analyses and opinions of Sotheby's art experts, based on auction sales and other information deemed relevant. Nothing in Sotheby's Index is intended as investment advice or as a prediction or guarantee of future performance or otherwise.

EXHIBIT 12.17

Annual Rates of Return to 1991

	MODERN TIMES (1945–1991)		LAST TEN YEARS		LAST FIVE YEARS		1991
	ANNUALIZED RETURN	STANDARD DEVIATION	ANNUALIZED RETURN	STANDARD DEVIATION	ANNUALIZED RETURN	STANDARD DEVIATION	ANNUAL RETURN
Nominal U.S. GNP	7.4%	3.5%	6.4%	2.1%	5.9%	1.7%	2.9%
S&P 500	11.8	16.6	17.6	11.5	15.4	13.7	30.6
Small stocks	13.3	26.0	12.0	20.7	6.9	23.4	44.6
Emerging growth stocks	14.9	29.2	12.3	18.5	12.8	22.8	52.3
T-bills	4.9	3.3	7.7	1.7	6.7	1.1	5.6
Inflation	4.5	3.9	3.9	1.2	4.6	1.1	3.2
U.S. government bonds	4.8	9.8	15.6	12.8	9.8	8.1	19.3
Intermediate-term bonds	5.8	6.3	13.1	7.2	9.4	4.6	15.5
Corporate bonds	5.4	9.9	16.3	12.3	10.4	7.1	19.9
Commercial paper	5.7	3.6	8.5	1.8	7.6	1.1	6.1
U.S. farm land	10.0	7.5	3.3	5.9	8.9	1.8	7.5
Residential housing	7.4	4.0	4.2	1.4	4.5	1.3	4.6
Commercial real estate	7.5	5.2	6.9	4.6	3.4	3.5	−2.3
Venture capital	18.0	35.8	15.8	29.2	2.3	33.2	N.A.
Gold	5.1	26.2	−1.3	14.7	−2.1	13.5	−10.3
Silver	4.4	56.8	−7.3	18.3	−6.4	15.5	−7.8
Art	8.5	15.0	12.4	16.6	16.4	22.1	−19.9
EAFE	N.A.	N.A.	18.0	24.1	8.7	17.9	12.1
Japanese stocks	17.4	28.9	18.9	21.3	6.5	28.2	8.9
Foreign bonds	N.A.	N.A.	14.2	15.0	12.5	13.9	17.9
Emerging market equities	18.5	N.A.	12.3	27.8	18.5	32.5	13.2

SOURCE: *Morgan Stanley Research*. This memorandum is based on information available to the public. No representation is made that it is accurate or complete. This memorandum is not an offer to buy or sell or a solicitation of an offer to buy or sell the securities mentioned. Morgan Stanley & Co. Inc. and others associated with it may have positions in and effect transactions in securities of companies mentioned and may also perform or seek to perform investment banking services for those companies.

In the 1990s, reawakened inflationary forces could return commodities and collectibles to a privileged place in investors' portfolios, but the risks are high. If prices remain stable, investors should stay focused on stocks.

SUMMARY

Real estate paid substantial profits to investors during the inflationary 1970s and mid-1980s but declined in the late 1980s. In the 1990s and beyond it might lose some of the attraction it has had in the past, especially since changes in tax laws have restricted its value as a tax shelter. Limited and selective investment in real estate, however, may present favorable opportunities. In areas where demand remains high, such as the market for shoreline property, real estate might remain attractive.

One major advantage of real estate comes from the investor's ability to borrow large amounts of money to finance the purchase since real estate makes good collateral for loans. In the real estate market an investor can acquire extremely valuable assets for relatively small amounts of cash. The depressed prices of real estate in 1991 suggested relatively good investment opportunities. The real estate investor must plan carefully to make sure that income from property rents and other sources will cover debt payments.

Other real assets, including gold, silver, diamonds, and antiques, represent potentially profitable investments. Gold has paid modest returns over long periods of time, but it lost some of its luster in the late 1980s. It also is a high-risk investment. Silver and diamonds turned in similar performance. Shares in gold mutual funds can be more profitable than gold over the long term.

The individual investor should not buy real assets simply as additions to a portfolio. All of the assets reviewed in this chapter have their own characteristics and present unique opportunities for investment. Changing market conditions make blanket recommendations impossible. Instead, an individual investor must look carefully at expected returns and risks at a particular time rather than assuming past returns imply similar future returns. Some real asset investments generally seem attractive, and some seem unattractive based on expected future returns and risks.

Many real asset investment alternatives represent limited proportions of an overall investment portfolio. In particular, those acquired in the course of a hobby can augment or protect returns from the more substantial parts of the portfolio. Collecting coins, stamps, or baseball cards can be profitable, but wise collectors do not mortgage their houses to buy these assets. Over long periods of time, common stock is your best investment.

INVESTMENT MANAGEMENT CONCEPTS

1. When purchasing any asset, look for an opportunity to increase your wealth.

2. Always consider the long-term value of an asset, and its contribution to your net worth.

3. Purchase real assets as protection from the ravages of inflation.

4. Base investment decisions on your total wealth, measured in both real and financial assets.

REVIEW QUESTIONS

1. What is the most important influence on the success of any investment in real estate?

2. Shoud everyone invest in real estate beyond the purchase of a primary residence?

3. List the advantages and disadvantages of investing in real estate.

4. What price changes do you expect for residential real estate in the future?

5. In some areas of the country, an investment in land or a farm makes sense. What benefits can such investments provide? What drawbacks do they have?

6. Describe the profitability and riskiness of REITs.

7. Under what conditions should investors consider buying shares in REITs?

8. What rate of return would you have earned if you had bought an ounce of gold in 1980 and held it to 1990? How much risk would you have accepted?

9. If you had bought the ounce of gold in 1985 and held it to 1990, what return would you have earned?

10. What conclusions can you draw about the investment characteristics of gold from your answers to Questions 8 and 9?

11. Assume that you bought an ounce of silver in 1985 and held it until 1990. What average return would you have earned on the investment? Was it a good investment? Was it risky?

12. What average return would you have earned if you had bought U.S. Gold Shares in 1980 and held them to 1990? Was this a risky investment?

13. Which investment would you have preferred, gold or U.S. Gold Shares?

14. Assume that you bought a diamond in 1985. Would it have been your best friend (or at least one of your most profitable friends) since then?

15. Based on Sotheby's Art Index, if you had purchased a piece of American furniture in 1985 and held it to 1990, would you have made a profitable investment? Would you have accepted much risk? Would your answers change if you had bought the furniture in 1975?

16. Assume you bought English furniture in 1985. Would you have enjoyed better investment performance than someone who bought American furniture at the same time?

17. Based on the data in Exhibit 12.17, which investment performed the best over the last five years?

18. Based on the data in Exhibit 12.17, which performed the best over the last ten years?

19. Based on the data in Exhibit 12.17, how well did stocks and bonds perform over the last ten years? Which was better?

20. List the three investments from Exhibit 12.17 that gave the highest and most consistent return for each period.

SELF-CORRECTING PROBLEMS

1. A college freshman wonders if buying a condominiun would be a better financial option than renting a dorm room. This person intends to rent rooms to two people at the same rate the college charges for dorm rooms. By adding the equivalent of dorm rent to the renters' contributions, the freshman can break even on the out-of-pocket costs, including mortgage payments and taxes. The freshman intends to put $10,000 down and take out a $90,000 mortgage on the $100,000 condo. At the end of four years, it should sell for $110,000 after real estate commissions and closing costs. Ignoring taxes, would this be a good deal?

2. You buy an ounce of gold for $360 and estimate that you will sell it for $450 an ounce in five years. What annual average rate of return will you earn? Is this a good investment?

3. You buy Keystone Precious Metals Holding, a Boston mutual fund, at $15.50 at the end of 1991 expecting the price to rise to $20.00 per share by the end of 1995. The company pays a dividend of $0.30 per year. What rate of return do you expect to earn? Is this a good deal?

4. The current price of silver is $4.50 an ounce. You think it will increase in price to $5.00 at the end of three years. Is this an attractive investment? Estimate its rate of return.

5. In Question 4, change the expected price in three years to $6.00. Does this change your answer about the attractiveness of the investment? Be sure to calculate the rate of return.

6. You are thinking of getting engaged. With your future mate, you must decide between investing in a one-carat, medium-grade stone for $2,500 or a top-quality stone for $5,000. The medium-grade stone should increase in value $200 a year for ten years, and the top-quality stone should increase $450 per year. Both stones are beautiful; only a professional can tell one from the other. Which would be the better investment? To answer this question, estimate the price of each after ten years and the rate of return that each would earn based on these estimates.

7. After the wedding, your mate wants to buy an English antique rocker for $300. If you use the data in Sotheby's Art Index, what value would you expect for the rocker at the end of ten years based on the annual growth rate for the past ten years?

"What privilege or rights does the call option on the stock give you? Well, for the $340 it costs you to buy the option, you have the right to buy 100 shares of Wal-Mart at a price of $35 per share for 90 days, at which time the option expires. If the market price of Wal-Mart increases to $43 per share by the end of the 90 days, you could exercise your option—buy the 100 shares at $35 and sell them in the market at $43. Your profit on the trade would be $4.60 per share, or $460, before selling commissions. Profit is calculated at $35 to buy the shares, $3 for the option and $.40 per share for the brokerage commissions, for a total cost of 100 shares of $3,840 ([$35 + $3 + $.40] × 100). You sell the shares for $4,300 less brokerage commissions of about $80, and you end up with a net profit of $380 ($4,300 − $80 − $3,840). This gives you a return of over 100 percent for the period on your investment.

"Alternatively, you can sell your Wal-Mart call option contract just before expiration. The price of the option will rise with the price of the stock. If the price of the call option rises to $800, you will receive approximately $760 from its sale after deducting commissions, and your profit will be $420—the difference between the base price of $340 for the option and the sale price of $760 after commission. Because it would be more profitable to just sell the option in this case, you would not buy the stock but would simply resell the option.

"So, you see, understanding options can be profitable. Of course, the price of the stock might fall over the 90-day period in which case you will lose your entire investment. What do you think of the call option concept?" I asked.

"Sounds good to me," Mike said. "I'd like to learn more about options before I go into the market with real money." Alice responded by saying, "I think they might be useful, but I wouldn't want to lose money." Betsy said she, too, would like to know more about options; it worked out well on the Chanel dress.

Whether or not we choose to use stock options we should at least know about them. They are an important tool used in financial markets.

Introduction

Investors and speculators trade millions of stock option contracts each day on the Chicago Board Option Exchange (CBOE), the American Stock Exchange, the Philadelphia Exchange, and the Pacific Exchange. A

stock option: Contract for the exchange of the right to buy or sell 100 shares of stock for a fixed price during a fixed period of time.

stock option is a right, but not an obligation, to buy or sell a certain amount of stock at a fixed price for a short period of time. Although traders can exchange stock options in the over-the-counter market that are not listed on these exchanges, the discussion in this chapter focuses on the listed options market, which includes most of the opportunities available to the individual investor.

Conservative investors use stock options to protect against losing portfolio gains or to soften losses due to adverse market moves. Speculators buy and sell options in an effort to profit from changes in prices of the options themselves. A closer look at the characteristics and performance of options will reveal many more benefits that they can provide.

Option Basics

Call Options

call option: The right, but not the obligation, to buy 100 shares of stock from the option writer for a fixed price during a fixed period of time.

Option agreements generally follow the form created for a call option contract. A single **call option** contract gives its owner the right, but not the obligation, to buy 100 shares of stock at a fixed price for a fixed period of time in exchange for a fixed price. An option seller receives the price paid and agrees to take the other side of the transaction, accepting the obligation to sell 100 shares of the stock at the same fixed price for the same fixed period of time. The owner buys the contract from an option seller through a stockbroker who earns a commission for this service. The price the buyer pays the seller (called the *writer*) of the option is called a *premium*.

expiration date: The end of the period during which an owner can exercise an option, always the first Saturday after the third Friday in the month of expiration.

Suppose you wanted to buy a call option on 100 shares of McDonald's stock in early August 1990. The stock closed at 30¼ on Friday, August 3, 1990. On that day a single call option to buy McDonald's stock at $30 per share on or before September 21, 1990, closed at $1. (Like all options, this one would have its **expiration date** on the third Friday of the month; a trader would call it a "September call.")

strike price (exercise price): The price per share at which an option allows its owner to buy or sell stock.

On August 3, 1990, you would have paid a premium of $100 plus the minimum brokerage commission, $24, for a call option to buy 100 shares of McDonald's at $30 per share for 52 days. The price at which the option owner can buy the stock is the option's **strike price** or **exercise price.** Different option contracts carry strike prices that vary in $5 increments. Through the Chicago Board Options Exchange, you could have bought McDonald's options with several strike prices that would expire in the following August, September, or December.

The premium and, therefore, the profit and loss potential on the McDonald's call option would depend on the difference between its strike price and the market price of the stock. If you paid $1 per share for the option and the market price of the stock rose to $31, you would just break even. Turning this logic around, the call option to buy the $31 stock for $30 would be worth $1 per share.

EXHIBIT 13.1

AT&T Option Prices

OPTION & NY CLOSE	STRIKE PRICE	CALLS–LAST AUG.	CALLS–LAST SEPT.	CALLS–LAST OCT.	PUTS–LAST AUG.	PUTS–LAST SEPT.	PUTS–LAST OCT.
AT&T 37	35	2	$2\frac{1}{8}$	$3\frac{1}{8}$	$\frac{3}{8}$	$\frac{1}{2}$	$\frac{7}{8}$
37	40	$\frac{1}{8}$	$\frac{3}{8}$	$\frac{5}{8}$	$3\frac{3}{4}$	r	$3\frac{7}{8}$
37	45	r	s	$\frac{1}{8}$	r	s	r

r = not traded

s = no option

SOURCE: *The Wall Street Journal*, July 31, 1990, p. C11.

The Wall Street Journal publishes price quotations for options grouped by the securities exchanges on which they trade. A sample quote for AT&T call options appears in Exhibit 13.1. The quotes show that AT&T common stock had a price of 37 at the end of July 1990. The August call option with a strike price of 35 carried a premium of 2, indicating the option seller's willingness to accept the obligation to sell 100 shares of AT&T common stock within 21 days at a price of $35 per share in exchange for $200 ($2 per share) in premium income. The brokerage commission would run about $40 for this option transaction.

Exhibit 13.2 shows the profit and loss possibilities for the option transaction without brokerage commissions. If the stock price were to decline to 35 by the expiration date, the option would expire worthless, and the buyer would lose $200. If the price were to stay at 37, the buyer would break even. If the price were to rise to 41, the buyer would earn $400 on the $200 investment.

Exhibit 13.1 showed other AT&T options with strike prices of 40 and 45. As the strike price of the option increases, the premium decreases because the stock price has to rise much farther before a buyer would make a profit. Also notice that the call option with the strike price of 45 did not trade (indicated by the designation *r*), and the quote listed no September call option with a strike price of $45. The strike prices increase in $5 increments, following a stock exchange rule.

The $2 premium for the call option with the $35 strike price suggests that the market expected the price for AT&T stock to rise in August to 37. The premiums for the September and October options indicate expected prices of about $37 and $38, respectively, during those months. The premiums reflect buyers' decisions about how much to pay for call options based on the difference between the options' strike prices and the buyers' expectations for the market prices of the underlying stocks.

In fact, a buyer would agree to the transaction only if he or she expected a stock price that would exceed the option's strike price plus its premium.

EXHIBIT 13.2

Buying an AT&T Call

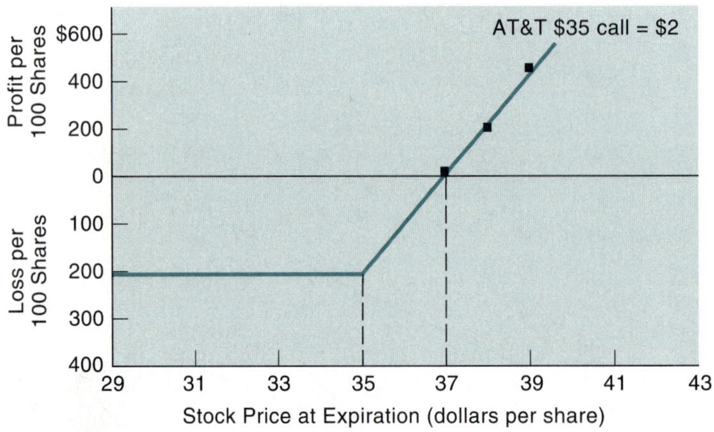

Of course, buyers would eagerly bid for options with strike prices and premiums far below a reasonable market price on the stock, which would guarantee fat profits. This bidding would drive the premium upward until it just equaled the difference between the option's strike price and the stock's expected market price.

If the stock performed as was expected, the buyer's reason for buying would determine whether he or she would exercise the option. If the market price reached 37, the buyer could either exercise the call option contract and buy the stock or simply sell the option contract for $200. Many investors also buy options as hedges to protect against adverse price moves in other trades. Someone who had sold stock short might have bought the call to guard against the stock's price rising unexpectedly sharply, forcing him or her to repurchase shares at a much higher cost than the proceeds received from selling the shares initially. This short seller would only exercise the option if the stock's price surged substantially. If the market came to expect a lower stock price, no rational buyer would exercise an option to buy stock at a strike price above the market price. Even if the stock price climbed to 41, a buyer could sell the option for a nice profit rather than exercising it and acquiring 100 shares at a good price.

A later section of the chapter will discuss in detail the factors that influence the price of a call option. For now, remember that the premium depends primarily on the relationship between the option's strike price and the market price of the underlying stock. The length of time over which the buyer can exercise the option also affects this value, as do interest rates and the characteristic price volatility of the stock.

Put Options

put option: The right, but not the obligation, to sell 100 shares of stock to the option writer at a fixed price for a fixed period of time.

In addition to call options, Exhibit 13.1 quoted premiums for AT&T put options. A **put option** gives the buyer the right to sell 100 shares of common stock at a fixed strike price for a fixed period of time in exchange for a premium. The exhibit quotes a premium for the AT&T August put with a strike price of 35 as 3/8; the September and August puts had premiums of 1/2 and 7/8. The higher premiums for the put options with strike prices of $40 and $45 reflect the value of the right to sell a stock for more than its current price of $37.

The buyer of a put option expects the price of the underlying stock to decline over the option period. The buyer of an AT&T August put with a 35 strike price (called an August 35 put) would pay a premium of 3/8 per share for the right to sell 100 shares of AT&T at a price of $35. The total premium would cost $37.50 ($0.375 per share times 100 shares). This would give the put buyer the right to sell 100 shares of AT&T to the option writer for $3,500. Deducting the option premium from the strike price shows the potential profit or loss on the transaction. Ignoring commissions, the put buyer would break even on this transaction only if he or she could buy 100 shares of stock to pass along to the option writer for $3,462.50 or 34 5/8 a share. Stated another way, the buyer would pay 3/8 for the August put only if he or she expected the stock price to decline below 34 5/8 by the time the option expired in the third week of August.

Actually, the put investor would not have to deliver the stock to earn a profit. Any drop in the stock price would increase the price of the put option, as shown in Exhibit 13.3. Without considering commissions, the stock needs to drop only 3/8 of a point to increase the value of the put enough to cover its cost. If AT&T dropped to 32 before the option expired, the price of the put option would increase to $3 per share to provide a total profit of $262.50. If the price of AT&T were to rise instead, the put option would expire worthless, and the buyer would lose the entire cost of the premium and the commission. Thus, buying options is a risky speculation that can result in a 100 percent loss.

Rather than speculating on stock prices in this way, many investors buy put options to protect against drops in the prices of stocks they own. If they fear a decline in a stock's price, for a relatively small premium they can guarantee themselves the opportunity to sell at a good price, or they can sell the put at a profit to offset the loss on the stock. A later section will explore strategies for using puts in detail.

Combining a Call and Put Option

straddle: The combination of a call and a put at the same strike price.

Various combinations of put and call options create many interesting profit opportunities through straddle and spread techniques. A **straddle** combines

EXHIBIT 13.3

Buying a Put

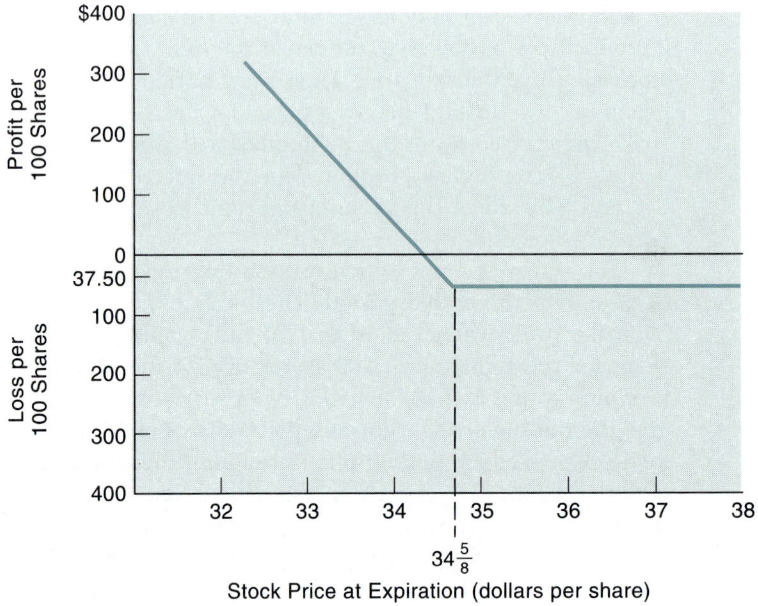

spread: The combination of options at different strike prices.

a put and a call, both at the same strike price. In a **spread,** the investor combines options at different strike prices.

To see how a straddle might work, return to Exhibit 13.1, which quotes AT&T common stock at $37 per share on July 31, 1990. Suppose AT&T intended to announce its earnings for the previous quarter, which would send AT&T stock significantly higher if the earnings exceeded expectations, or lower if earnings fell short of expectations. To take advantage of this investment opportunity, an investor might buy the AT&T August 35 call option for a premium of 2 and the AT&T August put option for a premium of 3/8. This combination of options would limit the investor's potential loss to the sum of the premiums paid ($3/8 \times 100 + 2 \times 100 = \$237.50$). Exhibit 13.4 illustrates the potential returns from this tactic.

If AT&T common stock were to sell below 32⅝ or above 37⅜, the investor would profit; these are the breakeven prices. If AT&T stock closed at 32⅝, the investor could sell the put option for 2⅜, which would cover the cost of the entire premium on both options. If the stock closed at 37⅜, the call option could be sold for 2⅜, covering the cost of the premiums on both options. If AT&T common stock failed to leave the range between

EXHIBIT 13.4

Buying a Put and a Call (Straddle)

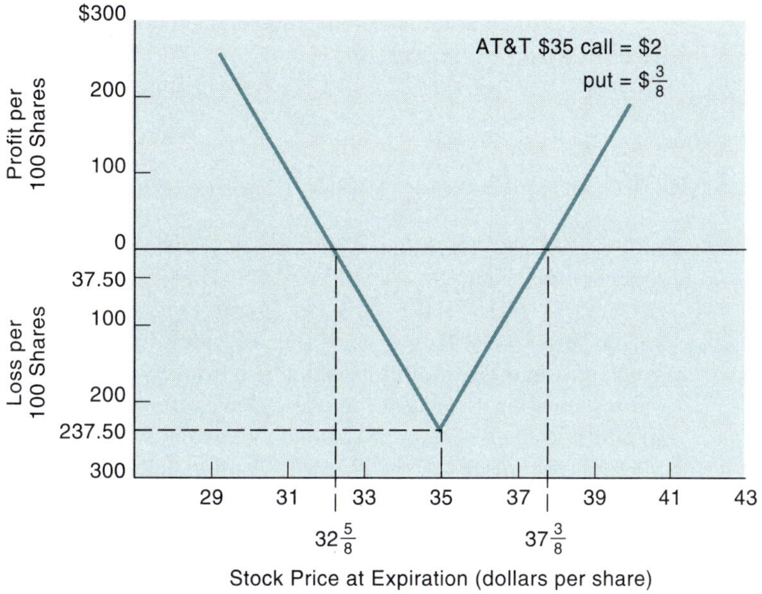

32⅝ and 37⅜, the investor would lose money on the straddle. The amount would depend on where in this range the stock price ended up, but in no case could this loss exceed the total of the option premiums.

The straddle would earn the investor a profit if the stock price moved in either direction farther than the breakeven prices. If AT&T stock were to close at 40, for example, the investor would sell the 35 call option for $5 per share (the $40 common stock price minus the $35 exercise price). The gain of $500 minus the premiums on the options of $237.50 gives a profit of $262.50, a fine return of 110.5 percent on such a small investment over such a short time. Converting this to an annualized rate of return gives a shocking figure of 1,326 percent! Actually, commissions would reduce the gain to approximately $262.50 minus $48.00, or $214.50. The net return for the one-month investment would equal 90.3 percent, which gives a net annual rate of return of 1,084 percent. Before you rush to call your broker, remember that these are hypothetical gains and that you run the risk of a 100 percent loss. Investors seldom manage to generate such amazing returns.

These brief examples merely illustrate the characteristics of put and call options. An option contract gives the investor the right, but no obligation, either to buy, for a call, or to sell, for a put, 100 shares of stock at a fixed price for a fixed time period. The purchaser of a put believes that the underlying common stock will decline in price; the purchaser of a call believes that the price of the stock will rise. Of course, neither receives any guarantees.

The option market uses rather specialized terminology. This terminology is summarized in Exhibit 13.5.

Markets for Options

As was mentioned previously, several securities exchanges list options, including the New York Stock Exchange, the American Stock Exchange (AMEX), the Chicago Board Options Exchange (CBOE), the Pacific Stock Exchange, and the Philadelphia Stock Exchange. These exchanges handle trading in call and put options in much the same way as other securities. Over 300 companies have options listed on these exchanges. In addition to the major exchanges, investors trade a significant number of put and call options in the over-the-counter market. Option contracts listed on the CBOE and other exchanges offer many advantages, among them low transaction costs, liquidity through an organized secondary market, and several standardized features including:

1. Strike prices, which increase in increments of $5
2. Standardized expiration dates, which occur on the Saturday following the third Friday of the designated month
3. Methods of adjusting strike prices for stock dividends, revenue splits, stock splits, rights, and warrants, but not for cash dividends
4. Standardized contract amounts, each of which represents 100 shares of common stock

Option Values

Intrinsic Value and Time Value

intrinsic value: The value of an option created by the difference between the price of the underlying stock and the option's strike price.

time value: The amount of a premium remaining after subtracting intrinsic value.

The premium measures the value of an option. This value has two essential components, intrinsic value and time value. **Intrinsic value** of a call equals the difference between the price of the underlying stock and the option's strike price, with a minimum of zero. **Time value,** measured by the amount of the premium remaining after subtracting the intrinsic value, reflects the possibility that the price of the underlying stock will change in a way that increases the intrinsic value before the option expires. Assume, for example, that a stock sells for $100 per share. A call for that stock with a $90 strike price expires in one month and has a premium of $12. This option has an

EXHIBIT 13.5

option: Contract for the exchange of the right to buy or sell 100 shares of stock at a fixed but no-obligation price for a fixed period of time.

call option: Right, but no obligation, to buy 100 shares of stock from the option writer for a fixed price during a fixed period of time.

put option: Right, but no obligation, to sell 100 shares of stock to the option writer for a fixed price during a fixed period of time.

strike price (exercise price): Price per share at which an option allows its owner to buy or sell stock.

premium: Price per share of an option contract which, multiplied by 100 shares, gives the cost of the option investment. The premium is quoted as a price per share for the option.

option buyer: Person or institution that purchases the option contract.

expiration date: End of the period during which an owner can exercise an option, always the first Saturday after third Friday in the month of expiration.

option writer: Person or institution that sells the option contract.

option seller: Another term for the option writer.

covered option writer: Writer who owns the stock that underlies the option.

naked option writer: Writer who does not own the stock that underlies the option.

straddle: Combination of a call and a put at the same strike price.

spread: Combination of call and put options at different strike prices.

SOURCE: Frederick Amling, *Investments: An Introduction to Analysis and Management, 6th ed., (Englewood Cliffs, N.J.: Prenctice-Hall, 1989), p. 702.*

intrinsic value of $10 ($100 minus $90) and a time value of $2 ($12 minus $10).

Even if an option has no intrinsic value, it may have some time value. Assume that a second call option contract on the $100 stock has a strike price of $105 and a premium of $3.50. The call option's intrinsic value is zero (the greater of zero or $100 minus $105). The premium still reflects a time value of $3.50, however, because the market recognizes a possibility that the stock's market price may rise above the option's strike price before the expiration date.

The intrinsic value of a put is the mirror image of a call because the put is an option to sell. The put's intrinsic value is the strike price minus the stock price. A $105 put, for example, on a $100 stock has an intrinsic value of $5 ($105 − $100). Time value is calculated the same way. In this case, if the put premium is $7, the time premium is $2 ($7 − $5).

American option: A contract that allows the owner to exercise the option at any time before the expiration date.

European and American Options

European option: A contract that allows the owner to exercise the option only on the expiration date.

The terms under which owners can exercise options affect those options' values. The previous examples all considered **American options** which allow their owners to exercise them at any time before they expire. The owners of **European options** can exercise them only on their expiration dates. Generally speaking, American options tend to have higher values since the

perspective on **ETHICS**

Suitability Standards for Risky Investments

When brokers or investment advisors recommend options, futures, or other risky investments for their clients, they have an ethical and legal responsibility to consider whether or not such investments are suitable for their clients. As noted in the discussion of the securities arbitration process in Chapter 5, investing the client's money in high-risk investments when such investment is not suitable to the client's financial and personal circumstances has resulted in a number of successful lawsuits against brokers and advisors.

Of course, options are not necessarily risky in all cases. Selling a covered call or buying a protective put against stock already owned, for example, is a fairly low-risk options strategy and could well be appropriate for the most risk-averse client. On the other hand, it would be difficult to see buying a naked call or a put for the purpose of speculating on the future direction of the market as anything but a high-risk transaction suitable only for speculators who are willing to risk a 100 percent loss if the market does not go their direction.

The most important factors to be considered in determining suitability for options trading include the client's age, investment objectives, risk tolerance, investment sophistication, investment time horizon, and financial status. Most of the options-related lawsuits alleging lack of prudence have been speculative options transactions undertaken on behalf of financially unsophisticated investors who could not afford to lose the money lost when the transactions went badly.

As a general rule, investors who depend on their securities portfolios for income to support themselves should not engage in options trading other than for hedging purposes via covered calls and protective puts. Covered calls in particular can be very appropriate for risk-averse, income-oriented investors. Selling a covered call provides two benefits to such an investor. First, since the call is sold, additional portfolio income is generated. Second, if the price of the stock drops, the proceeds of the call sale offset some or all of the loss in the stock, thereby reducing portfolio volatility. In this sense, covered calls provide a double benefit to income-oriented investors. The price of this benefit, of course, is that if the price of the stock rises dramatically, the investor either will have the stock called away or will have to buy back the call at a loss.

Investors with short investment time horizons and investors whose financial status cannot allow for a large loss also are well advised to avoid speculative transactions in the options markets. When considering whether or not to engage in options speculating, it is probably a good idea to consider the age-old advice given to card players and horse players everywhere: Don't bet the rent money!

right to exercise the option prior to expiration prevents the possibility that the stock price could change to make the option valuable only to retrace its path and leave the option worthless on its expiration date.

at the money: An option with a strike price equal to the stock's market price.

in the money: An option with a strike price that gives the contract a positive intrinsic value at the stock's current market price.

Options in, at, and out of the Money

Option traders have developed three terms to describe the relationship between an option's value and the price of the underlying stock. If a call option's strike price equals the stock's market price, the call option is **at the money.** If the same option's strike price is below the stock's market price, the call is **in the money.** Finally, if this option's strike price exceeds the stock's market price, the call is **out of the money.**

out of the money: An option with a strike price that gives the contract a negative intrinsic value at the stock's current market price.

The relationships exactly reverse themselves for put options. A put is in the money if its strike price exceeds the stock price. If the put strike price is less than the stock price, the put is out of the money. As for a call, the put is at the money if its strike price equals the stock price.

Setting the Premium

To value an option at expiration, simply compare its exercise price to the price of the underlying common stock. Prior to expiration, however, valuation becomes much more complex. Several factors affect the level of an option premium.

1. Price of underlying stock, S
2. Strike price, E
3. Time until option expiration, t
4. Return variability of the underlying stock, σ
5. Market interest rates, i
6. Cash dividend on the underlying stock, d

Though they act in unison, to simplify the discussion, the following paragraphs will consider each factor in isolation.

Underlying Stock Price, *S*, and Strike Price, *E*

As mentioned briefly above, the difference between the option's strike price and the market price of the underlying stock affects the amount of the option premium. Call option premiums fall to their lowest levels when the option reaches the month of expiration still well out of the money, with a strike price well above the underlying stock price. At expiration, in-the-money options (call options with strike prices below underlying stock prices or puts with strike prices higher than underlying stock prices) sell at premiums approximately equal to their intrinsic values. Premiums for at-the-money options always exceed those for out-of-the-money options and always fall short of those for in-the-money options. This seems intuitively obvious since an option that is in the money has a higher intrinsic value at expiration than an option that is at or out of the money, so it should command a higher price.

Applying these criteria to the AT&T call options in Exhibit 13.1, the August 35 call is in the money, and it does indeed have a higher premium than the other August call options whose strike prices of $40 and $45 place them out of the money. The August 35 put, on the other hand, is out of the money, but the August 40 and 45 puts are in the money, and they have higher premiums.

Time to Expiration, *t*

An option with a longer time remaining before expiration gives a higher probability of a change in the stock's market price that will increase the value of the option, that is, a higher time value, all other factors remaining equal. This implies a higher option premium. As the time before expiration grows shorter, the probability of a favorable move in the stock price diminishes and so do the option's time value and premium.

Return Variability of the Underlying Stock, σ

A higher variability of return on a stock implies a greater probability that its price will either increase or decrease. Stock investors come to regard this price volatility, measured as in previous chapters by the standard deviation of past returns, as an enemy. Since an option buyer cannot lose more than the option premium, however, and the upside potential is substantially larger, option buyers seek out high price volatility, and they willingly pay higher option premiums to get it.

Interest Rates, *i*

Higher interest rates also cause larger option premiums. This seems basically logical, since interest rates affect the returns on competing investments so the returns on all investments must react to them. For example, a $100 savings account that earns 6 percent interest will be worth $106 at the end of the year. At 8 percent it would be worth $108. Option premiums respond to interest rates in a similar manner.

Dividends on the Underlying Stock, *d*

A higher cash dividend on the underlying stock tends to reduce the premium for an option. Because cash dividends add value to the underlying stock and the option buyer does not have a claim on that dividend, dividends on the stock reduce the value of the call option.

The Sum of the Parts: Option Premium Valuation

The factors that influence the option premium affect the decision whether or not to buy or sell (write) an option contract. As for other investments, this decision hinges on a comparison between the estimated value of the option and its market price, that is, its premium. How do investors determine a fair premium for an option?

In general, the efficient market keeps the price in equilibrium at a fair value from the competing perspectives of both the purchaser and the writer. The call writer will agree to sell the option, and the call buyer will agree to buy for a premium that compensates the writer for the risk he or she takes, while still giving the buyer an adequate return based on the estimated future prices of the stock and the option. If the premium rises above this normal level, other option writers will quickly enter the market while some discouraged buyers will leave, so the increase in supply and the reduction in demand will drive the premium back downward. If the premium falls below the normal level, the lower price will attract more enthusiastic buyers as some sellers abandon the market, so the increase in demand and the drop in supply will force the price back up to its normal level. In a perfectly efficient market, the effort at valuation would pay no excess returns, since the market price would always exactly equal the correct value.

Option writers' and buyers' opinions on value differ, however, so both parties generally try to determine the value of an option and then compare this value to the option premium. Even when the market is in equilibrium, each party can get a good deal. Sophisticated option traders use complex mathematical valuation models to determine the expected fair market value of the options they trade.

Expected Returns: Option versus Stock

The purchaser must determine the average return from an option based upon an estimate of the future price of the underlying stock. In one method, he or she can establish an array of possible future common stock prices along with estimated probabilities of their occurrence. Each price will generate a particular return for the option, and the option buyer then averages these returns, weighted by the estimated probabilities that they will occur. The decision whether or not to purchase the option depends on this **probability weighted average return** as compared to the level of risk.

probability weighted average return: The estimate of the average rate of return on an investment using probability estimates as weights.

Exhibit 13.6 generates a probability weighted average return using values from Exhibit 13.1 for AT&T stock and options. The stock has a market price of $37. The option returns reflect a call option with a strike price of $35, a premium of $2, and 90 days remaining to expiration. The call option is in the money since its strike price is below the current market price of the underlying stock.

The return estimates hinge on the probability estimates for the common stock prices on the option's expiration date. With estimates of stock prices completed, the calculation of the weighted average expected returns presents few difficulties. Based on estimated stock prices weighted by probability estimates, the common stock has a weighted average expected return of 8.1 percent over the 90 days before the option expires. This gives the call a weighted average expected return of 165 percent over the same time period. These calculations portray the call as an extremely attractive profit opportunity. If the investor were confident of the stock price and probability estimates, he or she would probably buy the option.

Never forget, however, that the probability weighted average return calculations depend entirely on estimates of stock price and probabilities. Differences in individual investors' expectations could lead to markedly

EXHIBIT 13.6

Probability Weighted Average Return on Stock

CURRENT PRICE	EXPECTED STOCK PRICE 90 DAYS HENCE	PROBABILITY	RETURN PERCENT	WEIGHTED RETURN PERCENT
$37	$30	0.10	−18.9%	−1.89%
37	35	0.20	−5.4	−1.08
37	40	0.40	8.1	3.24
37	45	0.20	21.6	4.32
37	50	0.10	35.1	3.51
Weighted average rate				8.10%

Strike price = $35

Probability Weighted Average Return on Call

COST OF CALL	GAIN OR LOSS AT EXPIRATION	90-DAY RATE OF RETURN PERCENT	PROBABILITY	
$200	−$200	−100%	0.10	−10
200	−200	−100	0.20	−20
200	300	+150	0.40	+60
200	800	+400	0.20	+80
200	1,300	+650	0.10	+65

Weighted average rate 175%

different probability weighted average expected returns. Each individual will base investment decisions on his or her own expectations.

Option Strategies

Options help investors achieve a variety of goals, including speculation, hedging, and generating additional revenue from an otherwise stable portfolio. Within these objectives, investors employ several option trading strategies.

Speculation

Someone may have thought that AT&T looked overpriced in July 1990 at $37 per share. To take advantage of the expected price change when the market corrected its perceived mistake, this person could have purchased an August put option that would have given him or her the right to sell 100 shares of AT&T for $40 any time before the option expired. For this right the put option purchaser would have paid a premium of 3¾ points, which would have resulted in a total outlay of $375. On August 21, AT&T common stock closed at $33 per share, boosting the price of the put option to $7. This speculator could have sold the option for $700, realizing a profit of $325 before commissions, earning an excellent return of 86.7 percent for an investment of only three weeks.

This looks great, but suppose that when the put option expired, AT&T common stock had closed at a price of $42. The speculator clearly would not benefit by exercising the option and selling 100 shares of AT&T common stock at a price $2 below the market price. Instead, the speculator would allow the option to expire worthless and sacrifice the premium he or she paid for the put. In this case, the speculator suffers a 100 percent loss.

Hedging

In addition to high-risk, high-return speculation, options can help an investor reduce risk. Consider an investor who purchased IBM stock some time ago that has increased in value significantly since then, generating large paper profits. If this stockholder feared that IBM might decline in price, he or she could buy an IBM put option to protect those profits. The put would increase in value if the price of IBM declined, which would offset the decline in the value of the stock. Should IBM stock defy this investor's expectations and continue to increase in price, the put option would simply expire worthless and the investor would lose only the premium on the option.

Hedging gives an investor a form of insurance. The investor pays a fixed amount to protect against losses from potentially large stock price declines. A later subsection will explore specific techniques to accomplish this popular goal.

Generating Additional Income

Suppose an IBM stockholder owns 100 shares, and the price has risen to $102 per share. The investor bought the stock as a long-term commitment, however, and does not want to liquidate it to take his or her profits. This investor could increase the income from the IBM stock by writing a call option with a strike price of $105 and an expiration date three months into the future. A speculator would take the other side of the transaction, purchasing the call for a premium of perhaps $1.50 per share ($150 contract premium). If IBM common stock were to fall below $102 during the three months, the option would expire worthless and the stockholder would have earned the $1.50 per share premium, increasing the income from holding the stock. The option buyer, of course, would have lost the full amount of this premium.

If the price of the stock were to increase above $105, however, the option holder would exercise the option and call the stock away from the option writer. The stockholder would effectively have sold the IBM stock for $103.50 per share ($102 plus the $1.50 premium).

Successful trading in call and put options, whatever its goal, depends on the ability to estimate the future price of the underlying stock. Stockholders may use call and put options as hedges to protect the values of their portfolios. They may also sell call options to generate extra income if conditions favor it. Speculators seek to profit from expected movements in the prices of underlying stocks, because options can generate larger returns for the same change in stock price than buying the stock directly. Common strategies for using stock options include the following:

1. Writing a call against a stock the writer owns—writing a covered call
2. Buying a call
3. Writing a call against a stock the writer does not own—writing a naked call
4. Writing a put
5. Buying a put
6. Buying a protective put

Writing a Covered Call

covered call: Selling a call option on stock the option writer owns.

An investor may write a **covered call** to increase the income and overall return the stock provides, while at the same time reducing the volatility of that return. The investor achieves this by selling a call option on common stock he or she owns. As mentioned above, the premium the stockholder receives for selling the call option will effectively increase the income from the stock and also provide a cushion against losses if the stock price declines.

To see how this also reduces the volatility of returns, assume that an investor owns 100 shares of stock with a current market price of $132¾ per share. Fearing that this represents too high a price and that the market will soon adjust the price downward, the stockholder sells a $135 call option to expire in three months, earning a premium of $5⅞ per share, or $587.50. If the price declines as expected, or fails to appreciate to the option's strike price, the call option will expire without being exercised. This will leave the stockholder with the stock, plus the option premium, which will offset the drop in the stock price and therefore reduce the variability of returns on the stock.

Suppose, however, that the price of the stock increases above $135. The option buyer will call the stock at a price of $135, giving the stockholder a gain of $2¼ per share on the stock ($135 − $132¾) plus the $5⅞ per share option premium. This limits the stockholder's net gain to $8⅛ regardless of how high the stock moves, so he or she would hesitate to write a covered call if the price seemed likely to rise by more than 8⅛.

Essentially, the covered call writer trades the chance for gains above a certain level on stock he or she owns for additional income plus a cushion against potential losses. The price of the stock must decrease by more than the option premium for the combined stock and option position to show a loss. The stockholder enjoys the maximum possible gain when the common stock closes at $135, so he or she has both the option premium and an increase in the stock price. A stock price above $135 would give the stockholder no additional return because it would lead the option buyer to call the stock away. This reflects the risk–return tradeoff that characterizes efficient markets, since the stockholder can reduce risk only by sacrificing some potential return.

Buying a Call

Assume that over a period of time the price of IBM drops to 105, and an investor believes that it will increase again over the next three months. In order to take advantage of this expected price increase without tying up substantial capital in IBM shares, the investor could purchase a three-month call option on the stock with a strike price of $110 for a premium of $2. This position would generate a profit if the price of IBM stock were to rise above $112 (strike price plus premium) before the option expired. If IBM's stock price were to remain under $110 during the next three months, the call buyer would let the option expire without exercising it, or perhaps sell it before expiration at a loss. Either way, the investor could lose no more than the $200 he or she paid for the option, though, and any rise above $112 per share would bring substantial profits for this limited investment. If the price at expiration were above $110 but below $112, the option could be sold for a small loss.

This strategy requires special attention to the timing of stock price movements. The underlying stock must increase in price above the exercise price by more than the amount of the option premium, and this price increase must come by the time the option expires. Careful purchases of call options on undervalued stocks can, however, earn significant profits while limiting risk to the amount of the premium paid for the option.

Writing a Naked Call

naked call: Writing a call option on a stock the option writer does not own.

Besides writing covered calls, the investor can write call options on stock he or she does not own, called **naked calls.** The investor would do this hoping to receive a premium for an option that would expire worthless. Suppose GM common stock was selling for $74 per share and a three-month GM $80 call option carried a premium of $3. The writer of the naked call would collect this $3 per share premium ($300 per option contract) and hope that GM stock remained below $80.

He or she would break even if GM traded at $83 when the option expired. The call buyer would require delivery of 100 shares at a price of

EXHIBIT 13.7

Writing a Naked Call

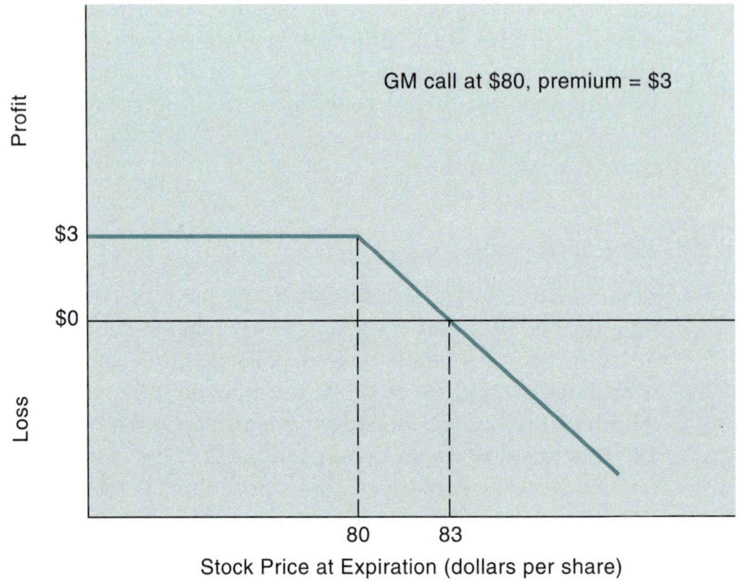

$80, but the option writer would have to purchase the shares in the open market for a price of $83. The $3 loss from the stock transaction exactly offsets the $3 premium he or she received for the call options. (See Exhibit 13.7.)

Recognize, however, that this strategy brings unlimited potential for loss. If GM stock were to rise to 90, the naked call writer would lose $10 per share on the stock bought to deliver according to the terms of the option contract. This, or an even larger potential loss, could make the $3 per share premium look rather meager. On the other hand, if the price of GM were to close below $83 when the option expired, the naked call writer would realize a profit; if GM stock were to fail to reach the option's strike price, this profit would equal the entire option premium. Though the profit cannot exceed the original option premium, it requires the option writer to invest no cash of his or her own other than to meet the exchange's margin requirement. In practice, rather than actually buying the stock in the market and delivering it, a naked call seller would simply buy back his or her call in the options market to "close out" the position prior to expiration.

EXHIBIT 13.8

Writing a Put Option

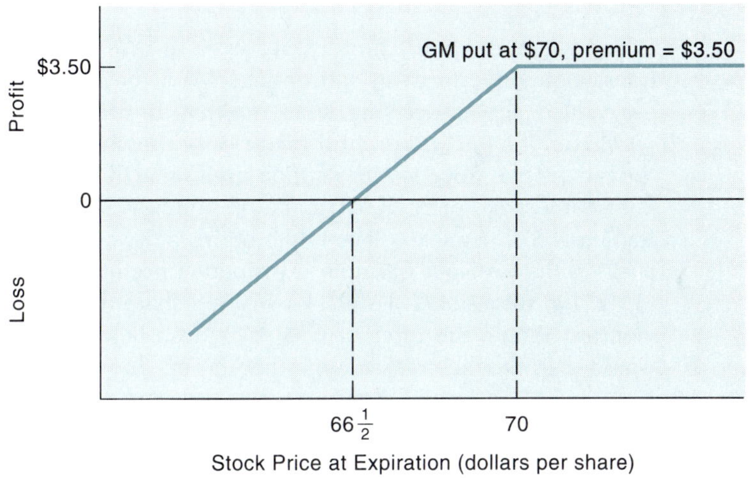

Writing a Put

In a similar strategy, an investor can generate profits by writing put options. Suppose GM stock had fallen to $70 per share, and GM $70 puts with three months until expiration were trading for a premium of $3.50. An investor could write a put and immediately receive the $3.50 per share premium in exchange for assuming the obligation to buy GM stock at $70 per share. If the stock were to rise in price, the put writer would keep the premium and not have to buy any stock since the put buyer could get more for GM shares in the open market than exercising the option contract would bring.

In fact, GM would have to trade at $66.50 per share at expiration of the option for the put writer to break even, as Exhibit 13.8 illustrates. This breakeven price simply reflects the option's strike price less the amount of the premium the option writer receives. If GM stock were to remain above $66.50 when the option expired, the writer of the put would gain, and he or she would keep the entire premium if the stock price remained above the option's strike price. Should the stock price fall, however, the put writer would still have to buy GM at $70, and the option premium would not offset the difference between this purchase price and the market value of the shares at a market price below $66.50 per share.

The put writer can earn no more from this strategy than the amount of the option premium, though he or she need not invest any cash (other than meeting margin requirements) to earn this return. This strategy involves significant risks, however, because a large drop in the stock's price can bring significant losses.

Buying a Put

Every put writer must find a put buyer to take the opposite side of the transaction. Investors buy put options when they feel that the market has overvalued the underlying stock so that it will decline in price. The purchaser of a put will profit if the price of the underlying stock falls below the put's strike price less the option premium. Recall the three-month GM put with a strike price of $70 and a premium of $3.50 when GM stock was trading at $70 per share. The buyer of this put would pay the writer (whose position the previous example explained) a premium of $3.50 for the right to sell 100 shares of GM stock for $70 per share during the following three months. Should the price of GM stock drop below $66.50, the put buyer would gain on the transaction, since he or she could sell GM shares for $70, giving a net gain after subtracting the premium paid for the put. As with most option transactions, however, the put buyer would not actually buy the stock and then exercise the put option. The buyer would simply make his or her profit by selling the put before the end of the expiration day. Doing this minimizes commission costs.

Should the price of GM stock close above this breakeven level when the option expired, the put buyer would realize a net loss. If the stock were to remain at $70 per share or even increase, the put option buyer would lose 100 percent of the premium paid, or $3.50 per share. The put writer's profits would exactly offset the losses of the put buyer.

Buying a Protective Put

Investors use put option contracts to hedge a stock position. Assume that an investor believes McDonald's current price of $30 makes it an attractive investment prospect. Some uncertainty remains, however, about the stock's growth potential in a highly competitive market. The investor can reduce the risk of buying McDonald's stock at its current $30 market price by simultaneously purchasing a three-month put with a strike price of $30 for a premium of $4.

If McDonald's stock were to rise to $34 by the time the option expired, the investor's net profit from the stock and option positions would equal zero because the loss of the $4 put option premium would offset the gain on the stock. Sacrificing this potential gain brings some very real protection, though. If the price of McDonald's stock were to fall to $26 or lower, the put would allow the investor to deliver the stock for $30 protecting him or her from the drop in the stock's value, at the price of the option premium. Buying a put option on a stock the investor already owns is known as a **protective put.** (See Exhibit 13.9.)

protective put: A put option owned in conjunction with underlying stock.

EXHIBIT 13.9

Hedging with a Put Option (Protective Put)

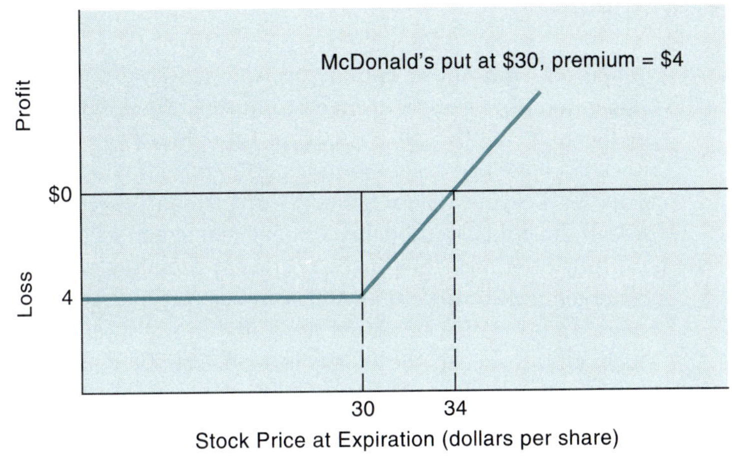

Summary Comments about Option Strategies

Careful buying and selling of options can give an investor a powerful boost toward his or her goals. Market innovators have developed many more option techniques than this chapter can discuss, so it has pursued the goal of illustrating selected possibilities rather than covering the entire range of potential strategies.

Option traders work toward three general goals: speculating on changes in the premiums on options, hedging positions in underlying stocks, or generating additional income from those positions. Speculators enjoy the opportunity to increase leverage, since option premiums often change by much larger percentages than the prices of underlying stocks. By combining a put and a call to form a straddle or spread, the investor can even play both sides of the market, hedging against or generating profits from either a surge or a decline in an underlying stock outside a certain range.

Buying either call or put options can limit losses to the amount of the option premium. In order to be profitable, however, the investor must correctly predict the direction, timing, and amount of price change for the underlying stock. Writing naked call or put options can be very risky; profits are limited to the premium, while losses can be many times this amount. Any speculation or hedging strategy should stress careful valuation of options, since incorrect value estimates reduce the chance that the strategy will provide the desired results.

Stock Index Options

In addition to options on common stock, investors trade puts and calls based on a variety of market indexes. Since 1983, when options based on the S&P 500 began trading on the Chicago Board Options Exchange, investors have had access to index options with which to speculate on short-term market movements, hedge investment positions, and improve the overall flexibility of their investment management programs.

Index options allow investors and speculators to buy or sell interests in a market index without owning the underlying stocks that make up the index. Index option investors normally do not intend to trade the common stocks that make up the index; instead, exercising an index option entitles the owner to a cash settlement with the party on the opposite side of the option contract. This should not seem especially surprising, since investors can evaluate and trade common stock options with no intention of ever exercising them to take or dispose of positions in the underlying stocks. Traders of both common stock options and index options focus on changes in the values of the options in reaction to movements in the values of the securities or market indexes that underlie the options.

index option: An option underlaid by a stock index, the exercise of which results only in a cash settlement rather than a trade of securities.

Stated formally, an **index option** is a call or put option on the performance of a market index, based on the prices of the common stocks that make up the index. No ownership shares change hands between buyer and seller. Major market indexes currently trading include the S&P 100, New York Stock Exchange, Composite Index, American Stock Exchange, Major Market Index, Value Line Composite Index, and the National OTC Index.

The S&P 500 option contract for example, reflects the value of the 500 stocks in the S&P 500 Composite Index. On April 11, 1990, when the S&P 500 closed at 342, the CBOE offered a June call option with a strike price of 345 at a premium of 9⅞. To buy 100 shares of the index (if that were possible), an investor would pay $34,200 ($342 times 100 shares). The investor could buy the call option instead for $987.50 ($9.875 times 100 shares) plus transaction costs. The call would have allowed the owner to participate in the change in value of 100 shares of the S&P 500 from a beginning price of 345 until June 1990. An investor might buy this option expecting the index to rise to 354⅞ (the beginning index plus the option premium) or higher by date of expiration.

When an owner exercises a common stock option, he or she receives the right to buy or sell stock. At settlement of an index option the owner receives cash equal to the difference between the premium on the option as of the exercise date and the original premium he or she paid to purchase the option. For example, if the owner of the S&P 500 call option mentioned above were to exercise it when its premium had risen to 12⅞, he or she would receive $300 less any transaction costs.

Investment Characteristics

Details of timing and exercise terms of index options vary between individual contracts, but they all share some general characteristics. Contracts state strike prices in five-point increments, and the exchanges introduce new contracts as changes in the index values pass or fall back from existing strike prices. Following the notation for common stock options, the exchanges quote contracts' premiums in points that reflect 100 shares in contract value. As mentioned, traders settle index option contracts in cash only, rather than by trading any ownership shares or other securities.

Contracts carry different expiration dates. AMEX index option contracts expire monthly with three-month maximum durations. Options on the NYSE Composite expire monthly with three-month (quarterly) durations, as do the S&P 500 contracts traded on the CBOE. Options on the Pacific Stock Exchange expire monthly with four-month maximum durations.

Index Option Strategies

Index put and call options serve exactly the same purposes as common stock options. An investor who expects the index to decline may sell an index call option. An investor who expects the index to rise may buy a call option. Stockholders can hedge with index options just as they can with stock options, after accounting for probable differences between the performance of a stock and that of the market index. Investors can evaluate the prices of index options by the same technique outlined above for common stock options.

Program Trades and Index Options

Stockholders who try to hedge stock positions must consider performance variations between the stock and the index. A unique, and widely publicized, trading technique called *program trading*, allows investors to construct an index **arbitrage** position that attempts to capitalize on this variation. Earlier discussion of hedging explained how investors trade options hoping to offset changes in the values of stocks by changes in the values of the options. This helps reduce the risk of a stock investment to try to approximate the risk-free rate of return.

arbitrage: The simultaneous purchase and sale of the same commodity in different markets in order to profit from price discrepancies between the markets.

If an investor could establish a position that paid a risk-free return in excess of the market risk-free rate of interest, investors would bid up prices to eliminate the excess. Despite this efficient-market assumption, arbitrageurs have created elaborate program trading techniques to try to identify and exploit inefficiencies by trading index options when their values vary from those of the stocks in the indexes. In this way, program trading systems seek to establish risk-free positions that pay returns higher than the market risk-free rate of interest.

Arbitrageurs see such opportunities when the price of an index option violates its normal relationship with stock prices. If the option seems undervalued, arbitrageurs sell the underlying stocks and purchase option contracts; if it seems overvalued, they buy the stocks and sell options.

Investors also may try to construct risk-free positions similar to arbitrage by combining options, futures contracts, and cash investments. The synthetic positions constructed in this way may offer attractive risk-free rates of return that function in the same way as more traditional positions.

In their search to profit from market inefficiencies, program trading systems and other types of arbitrage tend to improve the efficiency of pricing in the financial markets. Should prices deviate significantly from theoretically correct levels, speculators will pounce on these profit opportunities, and their actions will push prices back toward correct levels.

This benign impression of arbitrage activities changed somewhat after the market decline of October 19, 1987 (Black Monday), when many analysts blamed program trading for casting the entire market into free-fall. In response, the SEC and securities exchanges have placed limitations on program traders' access to the markets. In fact, some institutional investors will no longer trade with brokers who use the technique.

Financial Futures Contracts

The discussion of program trading and index arbitrage mentioned futures contracts on stock market indexes, and previous chapters have briefly mentioned other types of futures contracts in which parties commit themselves to transactions for later settlement under specified terms. Futures on stock market indexes and other **financial futures contracts** represent agreements among buyers and sellers for the future delivery of financial instruments such as long-term government bonds at specified prices on specified future dates. Investors contract to buy financial instruments in this way, just as they buy commodities such as corn for later delivery.

financial futures contract: Contract for the future delivery of a financial instrument at a currently specified price.

To understand the investment potential of a financial futures contract, begin by contrasting it to a normal government-bond purchase. If you decided to buy $100,000 worth of five-year Treasury bonds, you would call your broker and place the order. If you had placed such an order on September 14, 1990, the broker would have quoted a price of 100-16 for government bonds with an interest rate of 8.625 percent that would mature in October 1995. You would have paid a price of $100\frac{16}{32}$ or 100.5. Recall that bond quotes state prices as percentages of the bonds' par values, so you would have written a check for $1,005 for each $1,000 par-value bond, giving you a yield to maturity of 8.50 percent. The broker's bill for the transaction would have totaled $100,500 plus commissions, and for the next five years you would have received $8,625 in annual income from those bonds.

You may not have had $100,000 or so available to invest in Treasury bonds when you wanted to make the purchase, but suppose you expected to have enough money in 90 days. How could you make certain that you could earn the current interest rate and yield without buying bonds immediately? With a small margin deposit, you could buy a financial futures contract that would give you the right to buy $100,000 of five-year government bonds after three months at a fixed price with a fixed rate of interest and yield to maturity.

In mid-September 1990, price quotations in *The Wall Street Journal* reported a price of $97,315 for a three-month futures contract for the purchase of $100,000 worth of five-year government bonds with an 8 percent coupon and a yield to maturity of approximately 8.54 percent. You could have bought this $97,315 contract for a deposit of $2,000 plus commissions, locking in a higher current return than a direct investment in the bonds would have provided. This feature would be particularly valuable if you expected a drop in interest rates over the following 90 days. When you had the money to invest in December, you could have exercised the contract and taken title to government bonds.

Exhibit 13.10 gives an idea of prices for various futures contracts. Contracts traded on the Chicago Board of Trade carry units of $100,000, and prices are quoted in thirty-seconds of a point. The first contract for Treasury bonds listed beside June prices indicates settlement price of a futures contract for June delivery of 8 percent Treasury bonds as 100.03. This translates into a price of $100,093.75 for $100,000 worth of bonds, which gives a yield to maturity of 7.991 percent. The quote also indicates substantial trading volume and open interest (that is, currently outstanding contracts).

Purchasing the June futures contract on February 13, 1992, would have allowed an investor to lock in a 7.991 percent yield on a position he or she would take at the end of June 1992. The prospect for falling interest rates at the time made price increases in outstanding bonds likely, and this would have reduced the yields on these investments below yields to maturity that were available at the beginning of the year. The futures contract would have allowed the investor to guarantee the more attractive yield without investing the cash necessary to buy Treasury bonds.

Few individual investors' portfolios become complex enough to involve financial futures, but they can give opportunities for speculating on or hedging risk from interest rate changes.

SUMMARY

Investors can use put and call options to both add profits and reduce losses from stock holdings. A call option gives the buyer the right, but not the obligation, to buy 100 shares of stock at a fixed strike price for a fixed time

EXHIBIT 13.10

Financial Futures Prices Quotes

INTEREST RATE

TREASURY BONDS (CBT)–$100,000; pts. 32nds of 100%

	Open	High	Low	Settle	Chg	Yield Settle	Yield Chg	Open Interest
June	100-03	100-07	99-29	100-03	+ 2	7.991	– .006	284,705
Sept	98-31	99-03	98-25	98-31	+ 2	8.105	– .006	36,197
Dec	97-26	98-00	97-23	97-28	+ 2	8.218	– .007	8,694
Mr93	96-30	97-00	96-29	96-29	+ 2	8.320	– .007	1,397
June	96-02	96-02	96-00	96-00	+ 2	8.417	– .007	796
Sp93	....	....	....	95-05	+ 2	8.508	– .007	216
Sp94	....	....	....	92-17	+ 1	8.800	– .004	100

Est vol 160,000; vol Fri 494,460; op int 332,225, –2,182.

TREASURY BONDS (MCE)–$50,000; pts. 32nds of 100%

	Open	High	Low	Settle	Chg	Yield Settle	Yield Chg	Open Interest
June	99-31	100-07	99-30	100-03	+ 1	7.991	– .003	11,622
Sept	98-26	99-03	98-26	98-31	+ 1	8.105	– .003	735

Est vol 2,880; vol Fri 6,083; open int 12,368, +239.

T–BONDS (LIFFE) U.S. $100,000; pts of 100%

	Open	High	Low	Settle	Chg	Lifetime High	Lifetime Low	Open Interest
June	99-26	100-05	99-25	100-05	+ 1-02	100-09	96-30	4,241

Est vol 1,867; vol Fri 1,104; open int 4,241, n.a..

GERMAN GOV'T. BOND (LIFFE)
250,000 marks; $ per mark (.01)

	Open	High	Low	Settle	Chg	Lifetime High	Lifetime Low	Open Interest
June	n.a.	n.a.	n.a.	n.a.	n.a.	89.15	85.45	103,300
Sept	87.39	87.52	87.35	87.47	+ .07	89.46	86.99	21,452

Est vol 44,457; vol Fri 42,874; open int 124,752, n.a..

TREASURY NOTES (CBT)–$100,000; pts. 32nds of 100%

	Open	High	Low	Settle	Chg	Yield Settle	Yield Chg	Open Interest
June	103-03	103-08	103-00	103-02	....	7.558	....	100,399
Sept	101-28	102-02	101-27	101-29	....	7.723	.....	4,526

Est vol 16,000; vol Fri 52,862; open int 104,973, +3,516.

5 YR TREAS NOTES (CBT)–$100,000; pts. 32nds of 100%

	Open	High	Low	Settle	Chg	Yield Settle	Yield Chg	Open Interest
June	04-225	104-31	04-225	104-28	+ 3.5	6.833	– .025	131,630
Sept	03-215	03-265	03-215	03-235	+ 3.5	7.100	– .025	6,035

Est vol 11,111; vol Fri 42,400; open int 137,666, +3,211.

2 YR TREAS NOTES (CBT)–$200,000, pts. 32nds of 100%

	Open	High	Low	Settle	Chg	Yield Settle	Yield Chg	Open Interest
June	04-122	04-155	04-122	04-147	+ 2½	5.611	– .041	16,603
Sept	103-20	103-21	103-20	03-207	+ 2½	6.036	– .041	534

Est vol 400; vol Fri 1,129; open int 17,137, +153.

30-DAY INTEREST RATE (CBT)-$5 million; pts. of 100%

	Open	High	Low	Settle	Chg	Yield Settle	Yield Chg	Open Interest
May	96.27	96.28	96.27	96.27	....	3.73	....	2,063
June	96.31	96.32	96.31	96.31	+ .01	3.69	– .01	2,431
July	96.29	96.29	96.29	96.29	+ .01	3.71	– .01	986
Aug	96.25	96.25	96.25	96.25	+ .02	3.75	– .02	708
Sept	96.17	96.17	96.17	96.17	+ .01	3.83	– .01	717
Oct	96.10	96.10	96.10	96.10	+ .03	3.90	– .03	502
Nov	95.92	96.92	96.92	95.92	+ .01	4.08	– .01	543

Est vol 651; vol Fri 872; open int 8,037, –52.

TREASURY BILLS (IMM)–$1 mil.; pts. of 100%

	Open	High	Low	Settle	Chg	Discount Settle	Discount Chg	Open Interest
June	96.33	96.35	96.33	96.34	+ .02	3.66	– .02	29,534
Sept	96.08	96.11	96.07	96.10	+ .03	3.90	– .03	12,975
Dec	95.60	95.60	95.59	95.60	+ .01	4.40	– .01	5,032
Mr93	95.36	95.36	95.35	95.36	+ .01	4.64	– .01	1,140

Est vol 3,537; vol Fri 7,081; open int 48,681, +1,298.

LIBOR-1 MO. (IMM)–$3,000,000; points of 100%

	Open	High	Low	Settle	Chg	Discount Settle	Discount Chg	Open Interest
May	96.12	96.13	96.11	96.12	+ .01	3.88	– .01	10,241
June	96.08	96.10	96.08	96.09	+ .02	3.91	– .02	9,475
July	96.04	96.06	96.03	96.05	+ .02	3.95	– .02	3,174
Aug	95.96	95.97	95.93	95.93	+ .01	4.07	– .01	531
Sep	95.84	95.85	95.82	95.82	+ .01	4.18	– .01	482
Oct	95.75	95.75	95.72	95.75	+ .03	4.25	– .03	198

Est vol 2,062; vol Fri 3,761; open int 24,102, +952.

MUNI BOND INDEX (CBT)-$1,000; times Bond Buyer MBI

	Open	High	Low	Settle	Chg	High	Low	Open Interest
June	95-02	95-10	95-02	95-08	+ 5	97-02	92-14	9,766
Sept	94-09	94-10	94-08	94-10	+ 5	95-10	92-08	118

Est vol 1,000; vol Fri 3,161; open int 9,886, –291.
The index: Close 95-22; Yield 6.72.

EURODOLLAR (IMM)–$1 million; pts of 100%

	Open	High	Low	Settle	Chg	Yield Settle	Yield Chg	Open Interest
June	95.99	96.02	95.98	96.00	+ .02	4.00	– .02	263,236
Sept	95.68	95.70	95.66	95.68	+ .01	4.32	– .01	276,885
Dec	95.00	95.02	94.99	95.01	+ .01	4.99	– .01	224,407
Mr93	94.79	94.83	94.79	94.81	+ .01	5.19	– .01	150,461
June	94.26	94.31	94.26	94.30	+ .03	5.70	– .03	101,772
Sept	93.79	93.84	93.79	93.83	+ .04	6.17	– .04	73,200
Dec	93.22	93.28	93.22	93.27	+ .04	6.73	– .04	65,044
Mr94	93.09	93.15	93.09	93.14	+ .04	6.86	– .04	48,664
June	92.82	92.87	92.81	92.86	+ .04	7.14	– .04	32,058
Sept	92.55	92.61	92.55	92.60	+ .05	7.40	– .05	27,764
Dec	92.14	92.22	92.14	92.20	+ .06	7.80	– .06	25,605
Mr95	92.09	92.16	92.09	92.16	+ .07	7.84	– .07	20,972
June	91.89	91.97	91.89	91.96	+ .07	8.04	– .07	15,271
Sept	91.75	91.83	91.75	91.82	+ .07	8.18	– .07	12,861
Dec	91.52	91.59	91.52	91.59	+ .07	8.41	– .07	17,079
Mr96	91.54	91.62	91.54	91.62	+ .07	8.38	– .07	8,822

Est vol 128,678; vol Fri 425,086; open int 1,364,091, +31,367.

EURODOLLAR (LIFFE)–$1 million; pts of 100%

SOURCE: *The Wall Street Journal*, February 14, 1992, p. C12. Reprinted by permission of *The Wall Street Journal*, © 1992, Dow Jones & Company, Inc. All rights reserved worldwide.

period in exchange for payment of a premium plus brokerage commissions. The writer of the call receives the premium in exchange for accepting the obligation to buy the stock at the same fixed price for the same period of time. A put option buyer pays a premium in exchange for the right to sell 100 shares of the underlying stock at a fixed price for a fixed period of time, and the put writer accepts this premium along with the obligation to buy 100 shares under the same terms. Owners of European options can exercise them only on their expiration dates. Owners of American options can exercise them any time before they expire. Options expire on the Saturday after the third Friday of the month.

Buying a put and a call at the same strike price is a straddle. An option combination at different prices is a spread. Spreads and straddles allow investors to take positions on both sides of the market, profiting from or protecting against any market move outside a well-defined trading range.

Investors trade options on stock exchanges, and price quotes appear in *The Wall Street Journal* and other major newspapers. All option contracts share several standard features, including strike prices (in $5 units), expiration dates, and contract amounts (in 100-share units). Investors close out most option positions with offsetting transactions rather than by exercising the options.

Options give extreme flexibility, supporting both speculation and hedging strategies and allowing stockholders to generate additional income from their shares.

The intrinsic value of an option is the greater of zero or the difference between the price of the underlying stock and the option's strike price. An option is in the money when the difference between its strike price and the market price of the stock give it some positive intrinsic value. An at-the-money option has a strike price equal to the stock's market price. If the difference between the strike price and the stock's market price gives the option no intrinsic value, it is out of the money.

Call premiums increase with any change in several variables, including increasing differences between strike prices and stocks' market prices, longer times before expiration, more volatile stock prices, higher risk-free interest rates, and lower dividends. The investor must estimate the value of an option and, therefore, the appropriate premium, based on the expected return on the underlying stock.

Writing a covered call can generate additional income to offset an expected loss on a stock that seems likely to fall in price over the life of option, but this strategy limits potential returns from price increases on a stock. Buying a call can give access to shares at an attractive price, or provide large increases in the value of the option itself, if the price of the stock rises. Writing a naked call can generate fat profits if the stock's price falls and the option expires unexercised, since the call writer receives the premium without investing any cash. If the stock's price rises, however, the call writer must buy the stock high and sell it low, generating a potentially unlimited loss.

The investor may buy a put if the price of the common stock is expected to fall. Writing a put brings the potential for high rates of return if the stock's price rises, but if the stock's price falls, the put writer may have to buy shares for more than their market price.

Several characteristics of options limit their use. First, the cost of hedging with options reduces stockholders' returns, but judicious hedging reduces portfolio risk and increases risk-adjusted returns. Also, option valuation relies entirely on uncertain estimates. Profitable speculation with options requires the investor to correctly predict the direction and timing of changes in a stock's price, which taxes the abilities of even the best market analysts.

Investors trade calls and puts on stock market indexes, as well. Such options are settled in cash rather than via a securities trade. A one-point move in the index premium causes the option contract's value to change by $100. Index options expire on schedules similar to those of stock options.

Program traders attempt to profit from market inefficiencies that create temporary distortions of price relationships between stocks' index options and the underlying stocks. Some market analysts say this practice disrupts the capital markets. Others think the profit-oriented search for market inefficiencies improves the overall efficiency of the market.

Financial futures contracts allow investors to alter the timing of their purchases and sales of financial assets. Sometimes these investments can bring large returns on positions that require only small margin deposits.

INVESTMENT MANAGEMENT CONCEPTS

Options can increase the flexibility of an investment management strategy, but most individual investors should trade them to hedge against market risk or to generate modest additional income. Speculation with options brings too many risks for most investors. The guidelines below should help keep options within their proper role:

1. Use options to enhance investment returns from long-term, buy-and-hold positions within well-diversified portfolios.
2. Write covered call options to generate additional income and offset losses from overvalued stocks.
3. Consider buying call options on high-quality stocks that appear to be underpriced to fix the price relationship until sufficient funds for a stock purchase become available.
4. Consider buying put options to offset expected losses if a stock you own seems likely to fall in price.
5. Avoid the excessive risk of writing naked calls and puts.
6. Expect no free lunch in using options. Hedging with options can reduce risk, but the additional cost will reduce overall returns.

REVIEW QUESTIONS

1. What is an option?
2. What right does a call option confer?
3. What right does a put option confer?
4. What is an option premium?

5. How does an option's strike price affect its value?
6. What does an option's expiration date indicate?
7. Where are options traded?
8. What function does an option writer perform?
9. How might a stockholder use a covered call strategy?
10. What is a naked call?
11. How does a spread strategy work?
12. How does a straddle work?
13. How do exchanges set strike prices?
14. When do options expire?
15. How do most investors close out option contracts?
16. How can speculators use options?
17. How can hedging with options benefit an investor?
18. How can an option generate additional income for a stock portfolio?
19. What is the primary difference between American and European options?
20. What six factors affect the amount of an option premium?
21. How do investors estimate the expected return on a stock?
22. How do they estimate the expected return on an option?
23. Explain at least five ways in which options can serve investors.
24. What outcomes can a call option purchaser expect?
25. Why might someone write a naked call?
26. What does the writer of a put option expect?
27. What does the purchaser of a put option expect?
28. What is an index option?

SELF-CORRECTING PROBLEMS

To find answers to the self-correcting problems below, refer to the quotations in the table, which come from the Friday, January 3, 1992 edition of *The Wall Street Journal*. The market price for the S&P 500 Index on this date was 417.26. Like all the table data, this price reflects market activity on January 2, 1992.

1. a. If you purchased a March call on McDonald's stock with a strike price of 30, what total premium would you pay?

   b. What price does this imply for McDonald's stock in March, ignoring commissions?

   c. Is the March option in or out of the money?

Options

Chicago Board

OPTION & NY CLOSE	STRIKE PRICE	CALLS–LAST JAN.	CALLS–LAST FEB.	CALLS–LAST MAR.	PUTS–LAST JAN.	PUTS–LAST FEB.	PUTS–LAST MAR.
MCD	30	r	s	9 7/8	r	s	r
39 1/4	35	4 1/4	r	5	r	s	r
39 1/4	40	5/8	1 3/8	1 5/8	r	3/8	3/8
DIS	95	19 7/8	s	r	r	s	3/4
115 7/8	100	14	r	r	3/16	3/4	1 3/8
11 7/8	105	11 1/4	10 5/8	12 1/2	1/4	1	2 1/4
115 7/8	110	6 7/8	7 1/8	10	11/16	2 1/4	4 1/8
115 7/8	115	3 1/8	5 1/4	7	2 1/8	4 1/4	5 1/2
115 7/8	120	1	2 7/8	4 1/2	6 1/2	r	r
115 7/8	125	1/8	1 3/8	2 5/8	r	r	r
115 7/8	130	1/16	s	1 7/8	r	s	r

r = not traded; s = no option

S&P 100 Index–$100 times index

	STRIKE PRICE	CALLS–LAST JAN.	CALLS–LAST FEB.	CALLS–LAST MAR.	PUTS–LAST JAN.	PUTS–LAST FEB.	PUTS–LAST MAR.
	330	....	....	54 1/4	1/8	5/8	1 1/2
	335	49 5/8	....	....	3/16	7/8	1 13/16
	340	....	....	....	5/16	1 1/16	2
	345	39 5/8	....	....	5/16	1 5/16	2 1/2
	350	33 3/4	36	....	3/8	1 1/2	2 7/8
	355	34	30 1/2	....	7/16	1 7/8	3 1/2
	360	29 1/2	31	28 3/4	1/2	2 1/4	4 1/2
	365	24 1/8	22	....	3/4	3 3/8	5 1/2
	370	19 1/2	18 1/2	20 3/8	1 1/8	3 7/8	6
	375	15 1/8	17 3/4	17 1/2	1 3/4	4 3/4	7 1/2
	380	11	14 1/2	15	2 5/8	6 3/8	9
	385	7 1/4	10	11 1/2	3 7/8	7 7/8	11
	390	4 1/2	8 1/4	9 1/4	6 1/2	12	15
	395	2 11/16	5 3/4	6 1/2	13 1/4	....	....
	400	1 1/2	3 3/4	5	16 1/8	18	....
	405	13/16	2 3/8	3 3/4	22 5/8	....	....

Total call volume 108,872 Total call open interest 335,926
Total put volume 132,847 Total put open interest 447,655
The index: High 387.05; Low 381.46; Close 387.00, +1.44

2. a. If you purchased a March call on McDonald's stock with a strike price of 35, what total premium would you pay?
   b. What price does this imply for McDonald's stock in March?
   c. Is the option in or out of the money?

Options *(continued)*

Chicago Board

OPTION & NY CLOSE	STRIKE PRICE	CALLS–LAST			PUTS–LAST		
		JAN.	FEB.	MAR.	JAN.	FEB.	MAR.
S&P 500 Index–$100 times index							
	325	....	....	88	....	....	$\frac{7}{16}$
	350	....	....	$64\frac{3}{4}$	....	....	$1\frac{1}{4}$
	355	....	....	....	$\frac{1}{8}$	$\frac{3}{4}$	....
	360	....	....	....	$\frac{1}{8}$	....	$1\frac{5}{8}$
	365	....	....	....	$\frac{1}{4}$	....	$1\frac{7}{8}$
	370	$43\frac{5}{8}$	....	....	$\frac{5}{16}$	$1\frac{3}{8}$	$2\frac{1}{4}$
	375	39	....	....	$\frac{7}{16}$	....	$2\frac{7}{8}$
	380	$40\frac{1}{4}$	$34\frac{1}{2}$	37	$\frac{7}{16}$	$2\frac{1}{8}$	$3\frac{1}{8}$
	385	30	....	$33\frac{3}{8}$	$\frac{11}{16}$	$2\frac{3}{16}$	$3\frac{3}{4}$
	390	$25\frac{3}{8}$	....	$29\frac{1}{4}$	$\frac{1}{2}$	$3\frac{1}{8}$	$4\frac{3}{4}$
	395	21	....	25	$\frac{15}{16}$	$3\frac{1}{8}$	$5\frac{3}{8}$
	400	21	$20\frac{7}{8}$	21	$1\frac{1}{16}$	4	$6\frac{1}{4}$
	405	14	$15\frac{1}{2}$	$18\frac{1}{8}$	$2\frac{1}{2}$	$5\frac{1}{2}$	$8\frac{3}{4}$
	410	$11\frac{3}{4}$	$15\frac{3}{4}$	$15\frac{5}{8}$	$2\frac{3}{4}$	$6\frac{1}{8}$	$10\frac{1}{8}$
	415	$8\frac{5}{8}$	$9\frac{1}{2}$	12	$4\frac{5}{8}$	8	$11\frac{3}{4}$
	420	$5\frac{3}{8}$	8	10	$5\frac{7}{8}$	$9\frac{7}{8}$	$12\frac{5}{8}$
	425	2	6	7	$8\frac{1}{2}$	....	14
	430	$1\frac{5}{16}$	$4\frac{5}{8}$	6	$18\frac{1}{2}$	....	....
	435	$\frac{5}{8}$	$2\frac{5}{8}$	$4\frac{3}{8}$	....	....	....
	440	....	....	$27\frac{1}{8}$	....	....	$28\frac{3}{8}$
	450	....	....	$1\frac{5}{16}$	....	....	....

Total call volume 17,296 Total call open interest 314,779
Total put volume 29,737 Total put open interest 411,306
The index: High 417.27; Low 411.04; Close 417.26, +0.17

SOURCE: *The Wall Street Journal*, January 3, 1992. Reprinted by permission of *The Wall Street Journal*,

3. a. If you purchased a March call on McDonald's stock at a strike price of 40, what total premium would you pay?
   b. What price does this imply for McDonald's stock in March?
   c. Is the option in or out of the money?

4. Which of these McDonald's options seems the most attractive? Why?

5. The table lists a January call on Disney stock with a strike price of 115 for a premium of $3\frac{1}{8}$ and one with a strike price of 120 for a premium of 1. Which seems the better deal?

6. a. If you purchased a March Disney put at $5\frac{1}{2}$, how much would you pay in premiums, ignoring commissions?

   b. The strike price for the March put is 115, with a premium of $5\frac{1}{2}$. What effective purchase price do these figures imply?

7. a. You can buy a March call on the S&P 500 with a strike price of 370 for a premium of $20\frac{3}{8}$. The March 375 call has a premium of $17\frac{1}{2}$. Which is cheaper?

   b. What total premium would you pay for the March 370 call?

   c. What is the total value of stock purchased for the March 370 call?

8. a. The S&P 500 closed at 417.26 on January 2, 1992. The March 420 put had a premium of $12\frac{5}{8}$. What level would the S&P 500 have to reach for a buyer to break even on this option?

   b. What level would the S&P 500 have to reach for a buyer to make a profit?

9. In Problem 8 above, if the S&P 500 declined 10 percent from its January 2 close, what total profit would a buyer earn on the March 420 put?

10. How much would the buyer of the March 420 put lose if the S&P 500 rose to 470 by the end of March?

Answers to Self-Correcting Problems

1. a. 100 shares $\times$ $9\frac{7}{8}$ = \$987.50

   b. $39\frac{7}{8} = 30 + 9\frac{7}{8}$

   c. Out of the money

2. a. 100 shares $\times$ 5 = \$500

   b. $40 = 35 + 5$

   c. Out of the money

3. a. 100 shares $\times$ $1\frac{5}{8}$ = \$162.50

   b. $41\frac{5}{8} = 40 + 1\frac{5}{8}$

   c. Out of the money

4. The March option at a premium of $9\frac{7}{8}$ and a strike price of 30 is best. It gives the lowest total price for the McDonald's stock.

5. Both options are out of the money. The call at a strike price of 115 would be better since it would give a price per share for the stock of $118\frac{1}{8}$, compared to a price of 121 for an option with the strike price of 120.

6. a. $5\frac{1}{2} \times 100$ = \$550

   b. \$115 $-$ $5\frac{1}{2}$ = \$109.50

7. a. The price with the March 370 call is 390⅜. The price with the March 375 call is 392½. The March 370 call gives the cheaper alternative.

   b. 20⅜ × 100 = $2,037.50

   c. 100 × 390⅜ = $39,037.50

8. a. 420 − 12⅝ = 407⅜. The index would have to decline to 407⅜ for the option buyer to break even, ignoring commissions.

   b. The index would have to drop below 407⅜ to make the option buyer a profit.

9. The net price of the March put was 420 − 12⅝ = 407⅜. The S&P 500 declined from 417.26 to 417.26 − 41.73 = 375.53. The purchase profit equaled 407.375 − 375.53 = 31.845. The total profit was 31.845 × 100 = $3,184.50.

10. The loss on the March 420 put was 12⅝ × 100 = $1,262.50.

SELECTED READINGS

Bernstein, Jake. *How the Futures Markets Work.* Englewood Cliffs, N.J.: Prentice-Hall, 1989.

Bookstaber, Richard M. *Option Pricing and Investment Strategies,* 3d ed. Chicago: Probus Publishing, 1991.

Gastineau, Gary. *The Stock Options Manual,* 2d ed. New York: McGraw-Hill, 1979.

Gross, Leroy. *The Conservative Investor's Guide to Trading Options.* Englewood Cliffs, N.J.: Prentice-Hall, 1989.

Hull, John. *Options, Futures, and Other Derivative Securities.* Englewood Cliffs, N.J.: Prentice-Hall, 1989.

Kolb, Robert W. *Understanding Futures Markets.* Glenview, Ill.: Scott, Foresman, 1988.

Mesler, Donald T. *Stock Index Options.* Chicago: Probus Publishing, 1985.

New York Institute of Finance. *Futures: A Personal Seminar.* Englewood Cliffs, N.J.: Prentice-Hall, 1989.

Siegel, Daniel R., and Diane F. Siegel. *Futures Markets.* Fort Worth, Tex.: Dryden Press, 1990.

Walker, Joseph A. *How the Options Markets Work.* Englewood Cliffs, N.J.: Prentice-Hall, 1991.

chapter 14

Closed-End Investment Companies and Mutual Funds

In 1981 Carla Gilberti graduated from college and began her first job as a computer programmer for an insurance company located in a suburb of San Francisco. Carla knew little about investing, but college work in math had acquainted her with the amazing potential of compound interest. Carla decided that, whatever course her life might take, she would always work toward financial independence. She knew that this would require her to develop a habit of thrift, and the best time to begin was early in life.

At her starting salary of $23,000 per year, Carla figured that she should try to save about $100 per month. This represented about 5 percent of her monthly income, a savings goal commonly suggested by financial planning experts.

Once she had settled on a goal, Carla faced the next problem of where to invest her money. Fortunately, reports in such magazines as *Barron's*, *U.S. News and World Report*, *Money*, and *Business Week* had made her aware of the benefits of mutual funds. After reviewing several of these reports, Carla selected a conservative stock fund and began making monthly deposits of $100. Every year when her pay increased, she increased the amount of her monthly deposit to keep it roughly equal to 5 percent of her monthly income.

In early 1988 Carla got married, and the family grew with the birth of a child in 1991, two weeks after Carla's 32nd birthday. At that time, Carla and her husband decided that she should leave the work force for five years to raise their child and perhaps have a second one. Because she would not earn any income during this time, Carla thought this would be a good time to reconsider her investments.

The growth of her capital amazed her. The stock fund had matched the robust performance of the overall stock market from 1982 to 1991, raising her balance close to $30,000. Since Carla's salary had grown to approximately $37,000 per year, her 5 percent monthly deposits had grown to $150, and she had deposited a total of $15,000 over the previous ten years. The rest of her account balance, about $15,000, had come from reinvesting the annual returns on her investment.

Carla determined that her account had grown at an average rate of approximately 12 percent per year. If it continued to grow at this rate, her balance would reach slightly more than $50,000 over the next five years, even if she made no new deposits. Carla felt rich for the first time in her life, all from a commitment to a modest savings plan.

Introduction

investment company: A company that invests funds raised from selling stock in the securities of other companies.

Often investors feel that they lack the expertise to analyze and select individual issues of stocks and bonds. Instead of taking on the responsibility of selecting individual securities, many people rely on expert portfolio managers by investing in **investment companies,** which invest funds deposited by their shareholders in the securities of other companies. An investment company purchases existing common stock, bonds, short-term debt instruments, or other securities for the benefit of investors who buy shares in the investment company.

Individual investment companies fall into three categories: closed-end investment companies (publicly traded funds), unit investment trusts, and open-end investment companies (mutual funds). Investors trade shares in closed-end investment companies just like those in other companies, on major stock exchanges through brokers. Stock brokers sell shares in unit investment trusts, but these shares generate very limited secondary market trading volume. Investors can purchase shares in open-end investment companies, also known as mutual funds, either directly from the funds or through brokers.

This chapter will describe these three types of investment companies in detail. The discussion of mutual funds will examine information sources, advantages of mutual fund investing, the types of mutual funds, families of mutual funds, investment strategies, government regulation, and the special tax status and dividend payment procedures of mutual funds.

Closed-End Investment Companies

closed-end investment company: An investment company that issues no new shares after its initial stock issue; shares trade in securities markets.

Closed-end investment companies sell stock to the general public and invest the proceeds of these sales to benefit their stockholders. Unlike other publicly owned companies, however, closed-end investment companies invest their funds in securities of other companies rather than plant and equipment or other assets to produce products or services for sale to customers. Shares in these closed-end investment companies trade on the various stock exchanges just like shares of industrial companies. Investors pay normal brokerage commissions for their trades. No one can buy or sell shares in a closed-end investment company directly from the company any more than one can buy or sell stock in General Motors by writing to GM.

The stock market determines the value of a share in a closed-end investment company in the same way it sets the value of any other stock. Investors value these shares based on company performance. For an industrial company they measure performance by earnings per share, return on assets, and other familiar concepts; for a closed-end investment company, they measure performance by evaluating changes in the value of its portfolio of securities brought about by price changes and reinvestment of dividends and interests.

Some closed-end investment companies use leverage to increase returns. They add borrowed money to money contributed by the owners, and purchase securities with the total. A simple illustration will show how leverage can benefit an investment company. Assume that a closed-end investment company sells $1 million of common stock to various investors. The company's managers invest the $1 million stockholders pay for their shares in the securities of other corporations, so the balance sheet of the investment company shows assets of $1 million worth of common stock and stockholders' equity of $1 million.

The investment company managers then decide to issue $500,000 worth of long-term bonds and invest the proceeds of the debt issue in more securities. The bondholders receive only their interest payments and eventual principal repayment. Any profits the investment company earns on securities purchased with the borrowed money in excess of the interest payments will belong to the common stockholders.

Suppose that the investment company buys $500,000 worth of common stock with the proceeds of the bond issue, and the value of this stock increases to $700,000. The value of the investment company's stock increases, in turn, by the portion of the $200,000 gain that remains after paying interest on the bonds. This is a form of asset leverage, and the gain it generates goes to the shareholders of the closed-end investment company.

Unfortunately, the value of the assets the company buys with the borrowed money could decline. The common stockholders of the closed-end investment company would suffer this loss. Like any investor, the closed-end investment company makes no guarantee that the shares it purchases will actually increase in value. However, successful use of leverage can benefit the owners of the company.

Net Asset Value (NAV)

The price the fund is worth

net asset value (NAV): The per-share value of an investment company's total portfolio.

total dollar value ÷ # of shares

The market prices of closed-end investment company shares depend on the net asset value of the company's portfolio. **Net asset value** is simply the total dollar value of securities in the company's portfolio divided by the number of shares of stock the company has issued to its stockholders. For example, suppose the ABC Fund has 10 million shares outstanding, and it owns a diversified portfolio of common stocks with a total market value of $158.7 million. The net asset value of ABC Fund is $15.87 ($158,700,000 divided by 10,000,000 shares). This means that each share of the fund represents ownership of $15.87 of the fund's assets.

Logic suggests that the market price of stock in the fund should match the fund's net asset value. ABC Fund should sell for $15.87 per share. However, this logic does not hold up in the market. Nearly every closed-end fund trades at a premium or a discount to its net asset value. A fund that sells at a premium has a market price that exceeds its net asset value; a fund that sells at a discount has a market price below its net asset value.

No one really knows for sure why shares in closed-end investment companies trade at discounts or premiums, but the supply of and demand for shares in the company play major roles. Heavy demand and short supply drive the price of a fund upward, perhaps above its net asset value. To see why demand may become so heavy, consider the Korea Fund. American investors cannot easily buy shares directly in Korean companies due to restrictions that country's government places on sales of Korean companies to foreign investors. The Korea Fund navigates through these restrictions to invest in Korean companies, so it offers a convenient way for Americans to invest in one of the world's most dynamic economies. The strong growth prospects of Korean companies coupled with the restricted supply of their stock fuels strong demand for shares in the Korea Fund. Since supply of these shares cannot exceed the shares already outstanding, this demand has boosted the fund's market price. In contrast, the Italy Fund has not generated the same enthusiastic demand in the United States, and it generally sells at a discount from its net asset value.

Exhibit 14.1 reproduces price quotations for closed-end investment companies from *The Wall Street Journal*. The list divides the funds into four broad classes: diversified common stock funds, bond funds, flexible portfolio funds, and specialized equity and convertible funds. The Korea Fund and the Italy Fund appear with the specialized equity and convertible funds. The quotations report the net asset value of each closed-end investment company, the current market price of its stock, and the percentage premium or discount. This exhibit shows that most funds trade at discounts from their net asset values.

EXHIBIT 14.1

Price Quotations for Closed-End Investment Companies

PUBLICLY TRADED FUNDS

Friday, February 7, 1992

Following is a weekly listing of unaudited net asset values of publicly traded investment fund shares, reported by the companies as of Friday's close. Also shown is the closing listed market price of each fund's shares, with the percentage of difference.

Fund Name	Stock Exch.	N.A. Value	Stock Price	% Diff.
Diversified Common Stock Funds				
Adams Express	NYSE	20.31	19	− 6.45
Allmon Trust	NYSE	10.48	9 3/4	− 6.97
Blue Chip Value	NYSE	8.16	7 5/8	− 6.56
Clemente Global Gro	NYSE	b11.17	9 1/2	− 14.95
Gemini II Capital	NYSE	17.05	13	− 23.75
Gemini II Income	NYSE	9.27	13 1/2	+ 45.63
General Amer Invest	NYSE	29.21	28 1/8	− 3.71
Liberty All-Star Eqty	NYSE	11.12	10 7/8	− 2.20
Niagara Share Corp.	NYSE	15.24	14 3/8	− 5.68
Quest For Value Cap	NYSE	24.40	18 3/8	− 24.69
Quest For Value Inco	NYSE	11.50	13 1/4	+ 15.22
Royce Value Trust	NYSE	11.95	11 1/8	− 6.90
Salomon Fd	NYSE	15.48	13 7/8	− 10.37
Source Capital	NYSE	42.81	44 7/8	+ 4.82
Tri-Continental Corp.	NYSE	28.26	27 1/4	− 3.57
Worldwide Value	NYSE	16.03	13 1/8	− 18.12
Zweig Fund	NYSE	12.00	13 5/8	+ 13.54
Closed End Bond Funds				
CIM High Yield Secs	AMEX	7.42	7 1/2	+ 1.08
Franklin Multi Inc Tr	NYSE	b10.01	9 1/2	− 5.09
Franklin Prin Mat Tr	NYSE	b8.23	8 1/4	+ 0.24
Franklin Universal Tr	NYSE	b8.20	7 7/8	− 3.96
Municipal High Inco	NYSE	9.47	9 1/2	+ 0.32
Muni Yield Fd	NYSE	14.47	15 3/8	+ 6.25
Strat Global Inc Fd	NYSE	14.04	15 1/8	+ 7.73
Zenix Income Fund	NYSE	6.34	6 1/2	+ 2.52
Flexible Portfolio Funds				
America's All Seasn	OTC	6.05	4 13/16	− 20.45
European Warrant Fd	NYSE	7.75	6 7/8	− 11.29
Zweig Total Return Fd	NYSE	a9.49	10 5/8	+ 11.96
Specialized Equity and Convertible Funds				
Alliance Global Env Fd	NYSE	14.16	12	− 15.25
American Capital Conv	NYSE	22.17	19 3/4	− 10.92
Argentina Fd	NYSE	11.65	13 3/8	+ 14.81
ASA Ltd	NYSE	bc23.32	29 1/8	+ 24.89
Asia Pacific	NYSE	13.52	14 1/2	+ 7.25
Austria Fund	NYSE	10.30	9 1/8	− 11.41
Bancroft Convertible	AMEX	22.32	19 3/8	− 13.19
Bergstrom Capital	AMEX	100.45	116 1/2	+ 15.98
BGR Precious Metals	TOR	be8.31	7 3/4	− 6.74
Brazil	NYSE	b16.02	15 3/8	− 4.03
CNV Holdings Capital	NYSE	11.80	7 1/2	− 36.44
CNV Holdings Income	NYSE	9.46	12 1/4	+ 29.49
Castle Convertible	AMEX	24.32	21 3/8	− 12.11
Central Securities	AMEX	12.23	10	− 18.23
Chile Fund	NYSE	31.84	26 7/8	− 15.59
Couns Tandem Secs	NYSE	15.72	13 7/8	− 11.74
Duff&Phelps Utils Inc.	NYSE	9.08	10	+ 10.13
Ellsw Conv Gr&Inc	AMEX	a9.01	7 5/8	− 15.37
Emerging Ger Fd	NYSE	9.33	7 7/8	− 15.59
Emerging Mexico Fd	NYSE	b21.25	18 1/2	− 12.94
Engex	AMEX	12.60	10 1/4	− 18.65
Europe Fund	NYSE	12.88	11 3/4	− 8.77
1stAustralia	AMEX	10.12	9	− 11.07
First Financial Fund	NYSE	10.07	9	− 10.63
First Iberian	AMEX	9.44	8	− 15.25
First Philippine Fund	NYSE	12.37	9 5/8	− 22.19
France Growth Fund	NYSE	11.19	9	− 19.57
Future Germany Fund	NYSE	15.26	12 7/8	− 15.63
Gabelli Equity Trust	NYSE	11.01	11 1/8	+ 1.04
Germany Fund	NYSE	11.49	11 3/4	+ 2.26
Global Health Sciences Fd	NYSE	13.97	15 1/8	+ 8.27
Growth Fund Spain	NYSE	12.15	10 3/8	− 14.61
GT Greater Europe Fd	NYSE	11.22	9 1/2	− 15.33
H&Q Healthcare Inv	NYSE	23.29	25 5/8	+ 10.03
Hampton Utils Tr Cap	AMEX	b14.02	12 7/8	− 8.17
Hampton Utils Tr Pref	AMEX	b49.71	54 1/2	+ 9.64
India Growth Fund	NYSE	f18.77	15 5/8	− 16.76
Indonesia Fund	NYSE	8.41	10 7/8	+ 29.31
Inefficient Market Fund	AMEX	11.91	10 3/8	− 12.89
Irish Investment Fd	NYSE	10.02	7 3/4	− 22.65
Italy Fund	NYSE	11.50	10	− 13.04
Jakarta Growth Fd	NYSE	6.77	7 7/8	+ 16.32
Japan OTC Equity Fund	NYSE	10.40	10 3/8	− 0.24
Jundt Growth Fd	NYSE	15.51	14 5/8	− 5.71
Korea Fund	NYSE	12.27	14 1/8	+ 15.12
Latin America Equity Fd	NYSE	17.39	16 1/2	− 5.12
Latin America Inv Fd	NYSE	29.40	29	− 1.36
Malaysia Fund	NYSE	15.07	13 3/8	− 11.25
Mexico Equity Inc Fd	NYSE	b16.43	13 3/4	− 16.31
Mexico Fund	NYSE	b28.67	24	− 16.29
Morgan Grenf SmCap	NYSE	13.39	12 7/8	− 3.85
Morgan Stan Em Mks Fd	NYSE	15.49	15 5/8	+ 0.87
New Germany Fund	NYSE	13.41	11 1/4	− 16.11
Pacific Eur Growth Fd	NYSE	10.63	9 1/2	− 10.63
Patriot Prem Div Fd	NYSE	9.69	9 5/8	− 0.67
Patriot Prem Div Fd II	NYSE	11.60	11 1/8	− 4.09
Patriot Select Div Trust	NYSE	15.60	17 1/8	+ 9.78
Petrol & Resources	NYSE	27.28	26 3/4	− 1.94
Pilgrim Regional	NYSE	10.88	10 5/8	− 2.34
Portugal Fund	NYSE	10.43	10 1/4	− 1.73
Preferred Income Fd	NYSE	17.06	17 3/4	+ 4.04
Putnam Dividend Inco	NYSE	11.16	11 3/4	+ 5.29
RI Estate Sec Inco Fd	AMEX	7.76	7 3/4	− 0.13
ROC Taiwan Fund	NYSE	10.60	12 7/8	+ 21.46
Scudder New Asia	NYSE	16.18	15 1/8	− 6.52
Scudder New Europe	NYSE	10.35	9 1/8	− 11.84
SE Savings Inst Fd	OTC	b9.84	8 5/8	− 12.35
Singapore Fd	NYSE	b12.22	11	− 9.98
Spain Fund	NYSE	12.29	11 3/4	− 4.39
Swiss Helvetia Fd	NYSE	14.28	12 3/4	− 10.71
TCW Convertible Secs	NYSE	8.32	9	+ 8.17
Templeton Em Mkts	NYSE	b18.40	22 1/2	+ 22.28
Templeton Global Util	AMEX	12.61	12 1/2	− 0.87
Thai Capital Fund	NYSE	9.49	8 3/4	− 7.80
Thai Fund	NYSE	15.97	17 1/2	+ 9.58
Turkish Inv Fund	NYSE	7.61	7 7/8	+ 3.48
United Kingdom Fund	NYSE	10.53	8 3/4	− 16.90
Z-Seven	OTC	16.73	20 1/2	+ 22.53

a-Ex-dividend. b-As of Thursday's close. c-Translated at Commercial Rand exchange rate. e-In Canadian Dollars. f-As of Wednesday's close.

Source: Investment Company Institute, Washington, DC.

SOURCE: *The Wall Street Journal*, February 10, 1992, p. C18. Reprinted by permission of the Wall Street Journal,

Unit Investment Trusts

unit investment trust: An investment company that holds debt securities in trust to maturity, paying out income to trust certificate holders as it receives interest payments and refunding principal values at maturity.

unmanaged fund: A unit investment trust or other fund that acquires securities and holds them, rarely or never trading them.

Larger brokerage firms have established increasingly popular special-purpose investment companies called **unit investment trusts** in recent years. Brokers sell shares in these investment companies in units of $1,000.

Most unit investment trusts are **unmanaged funds,** which means that the trusts buy portfolios of securities, usually focusing on a particular type of fixed-income security, and hold them to maturity. A unit investment trust rarely trades securities after its establishment. It distributes income on trust assets among share owners. When its securities mature, the unit investment trust refunds the principal amounts investors originally paid for their shares. Minimal trading keeps the costs of portfolio management low. Brokers sell shares of unit investment trusts, generally for commissions of 3 to 4 percent.

A simple example of one type of unit trust will show how these investments work. One large brokerage firm offers a unit investment trust that invests in certificates of deposit issued by foreign banks. These certificates usually carry large denominations of $1 million or more and pay fairly high interest rates. The brokerage firm sells unit investment trust certificates in units of $1,000 to many individual investors and invests the proceeds of this sale in a portfolio of large, foreign certificates of deposit. When the certificates mature, usually in a year or two, the brokerage repays the owner of each certificate $1,000 plus interest. By forming a unit investment trust, the brokerage firm can pool many small investments to finance large investments in bank certificates.

Brokerages have established many different types of unit investment trusts. A particular fund might invest in municipal bonds, special types of government agency certificates, foreign bank certificates, corporate bonds, and so forth. An investor can find out what sorts of unit investment trusts the market offers by checking with a broker.

Mutual Funds

mutual fund: An investment company that constantly sells and redeems shares at their net asset value; also called an **open-end investment company.**

Open-end investment companies, better known as **mutual funds,** hold more assets than the other two classes of investment companies. A mutual fund operates in a simple manner. It pools individual investors' money and buys securities such as stocks, bonds, and Treasury bills. Owners of shares in a mutual fund own shares in the fund's investment portfolio. Mutual funds appeal to people who have too little investment cash to achieve sufficient diversification and to investors who doubt their own ability to select winning individual securities. Mutual funds allow such investors to participate in the performance of a widely diversified portfolio of securities selected by professionals.

The name *open-end* investment company reflects the fact that a mutual fund continually sells and redeems shares at their net asset value. (As for closed-end investment companies, NAV equals the per-share value of the fund's portfolio.) As investors buy shares, the fund simply invests their money and divides the total by the new, higher number of shares outstanding. When investors redeem shares, the fund exchanges them for cash in the amount of its net asset value times the number of shares redeemed and divides the new, smaller total assets by the proportionally smaller number of shares outstanding.

Most mutual funds are organized as corporations. An investor in the mutual fund has the legal status of a stockholder in the corporation. Shareholders vote for the directors on the fund's board and on other major issues that affect fund operations. A few mutual funds are organized as trusts rather than corporations, but they function in much the same way as corporate mutual funds. A very small number of special-purpose mutual funds are organized as partnerships.

Since mutual funds sell and redeem all shares at net asset value, the investor cares little whether sales outpace redemptions or vice versa. These transactions simply increase or decrease the overall size of the fund without affecting its value per share, or net asset value, since a reduction in the value of the fund due to a share redemption implies a proportional reduction in the number of shares outstanding, so the transaction does not affect the value of an individual share.

The market values of the fund's securities do change every day, however, so its net asset value also changes daily. In some cases, a large cash outflow resulting from net redemptions can affect overall fund performance because limitations on the pool of available funds can disrupt the timing of investments. These cases are relatively rare, however.

A mutual fund's managers calculate its net asset value per share at the close of each business day by dividing its total assets by the total number of shares outstanding. They then account for each day's transactions at that day's net asset value per share. Suppose, for example, that the XYZ Fund processed your check for $1,000 worth of its shares on Thursday. If the fund had 1,275,000 shares outstanding at the close of business Thursday and its portfolio had a value of $17,357,000 at that time, its net asset value per share would be $13.61 ($17,357,000 divided by 1,275,000). Your $1,000 would, therefore, buy you exactly 73.475 shares. (Mutual funds typically compute the number of shares an investor owns to three decimal places.) Similarly, anyone redeeming $1,000 worth of the XYZ Fund on Thursday would own exactly 73.475 fewer shares. These computations assume that neither investor pays any commissions, a point to which we shall return.

A mutual fund investor does not care whether the net asset value of the fund is high or low. He or she buys a given dollar amount, not a particular number of shares. A large number of low-priced shares worth $1,000 are exactly as valuable as a small number of high-priced shares worth $1,000. Instead, the investor focuses on the change in net asset value after he or she acquires the shares. If the value of the fund's portfolio rises, then the net asset value of each share also rises. If the value of the portfolio drops, so does the net asset value of each share.

Transaction Costs for Mutual Funds

no-load fund: A mutual fund that sells shares directly to investors at net asset value, bypassing brokers to avoid the cost of commissions.

load fund: A mutual fund sold through a broker at net asset value plus a load, or commission charge.

Transactions in mutual fund shares can cost anywhere from zero to 8.5 percent of the value of the shares. **No-load funds** sell shares directly to investors and charge no commissions. An investor in a **load fund** purchases shares through a broker or dealer, which requires paying a commission, or *load,* to cover the broker's costs and profit. The National Association of Security Dealers establishes the maximum commission a load fund can charge. Load funds usually charge lower percentage commission on larger dollar transactions.

No-load funds may be purchased directly from their sponsors at net asset value. A simple example will demonstrate the difference between a load and a no-load fund. Suppose you have $1,000 to invest and you want to buy a mutual fund. You are comparing two funds, both of which have a net asset value per share of $10. One fund is a no-load fund, and the other is a load fund charging a commission of 8.5 percent.

If you buy one of these funds, what will you get for your $1,000? If you buy the no-load fund, you will get 100 shares of the mutual fund worth $10 per share. If you buy the load fund, however, the 8.5 percent commission will be deducted from your $1,000 before any shares are purchased. Thus, your $1,000 will buy $915 worth of shares after deducting the commission. You will therefore receive 91.5 shares worth $10 each if you buy the load fund.

low-load fund: A mutual fund that charges a front-end load less than the maximum allowed by the NASD of 8.5 percent.

front-end load: A commission charged on the initial sale of mutual fund shares.

redemption fee (back-end load): A commission charge to redeem fund shares held for less than a specified minimum time period.

12b-1 fee: A fee assessed by a mutual fund to pay for the fund's sales and marketing expenses.

In addition to this traditional type of load, many funds charge loads calculated in other ways. **Low-load funds,** for example, charge lower initial loads (called **front-end loads**) as a sort of compromise between load funds and no-load funds. Funds also may add on **redemption fees** (also called **back-end loads**), if investors redeem shares they have not held for specified minimum periods of time. For example, a typical low-load fund might assess a 2 to 4.5 percent front-end load plus a 4 percent redemption fee for any shares redeemed within one year of purchase. This kind of redemption fee normally declines as the investor holds shares for longer periods of time. In the second year, for example, the fee might decline to 3 percent, then to 2 percent in the third year, 1 percent in the fourth year, and zero after four years. Funds have adopted this system because rapid turnover of funds reduces their efficiency and increases their expenses. The redemption fee represents an attempt to collect these costs from shareholders who sell shares after short periods of time.

A low-load or no-load fund may also assess a **12b-1 fee,** which is a fee assessed against the entire asset base of the fund to cover its sales and marketing expenses. A 12b-1 fee sometimes is simply an alternate fee structure to allow for payment of commission to salespersons. A low-load or no-load fund that pays commissions to salespeople may cover this cost by assessing a 12b-1 fee in the range of 1 to 2 percent of assets. A no-load fund that does not pay commissions may assess a much lower 12b-1 fee in the range of 0.25 to 0.5 percent of assets to help defray marketing expenses.

Why do some funds charge loads? Load funds incur costs of marketing themselves actively through securities salespeople, including stockbrokers, insurance agents, and even door-to-door salespeople. Like all workers, these salespeople require compensation for the time and effort they spend selling mutual funds. No-load funds, on the other hand, do not employ commission salespeople. These funds attract investors by advertising in the financial press and they sell shares directly by mail. They are normally not available through salespeople or stockbrokers.

One exception to this rule is money market funds, that is, mutual funds that hold portfolios of short-term debt securities. None of the large money market funds charge loads, though many of them are available through brokers. In fact, the brokerage firm of Merrill Lynch, Pierce, Fenner and Smith sponsors the country's largest money market fund, and investors can purchase shares without paying a commission through any Merrill Lynch office.

Obviously, the lack of access to salespeople for a no-load fund means that investors have to do their own research about these funds. Commission salespeople eagerly explain the advantages and disadvantages of load funds, but they have little interest in others. This is the reason load funds pay commissions. Salespeople earn their commissions as compensation for guiding investors through the mutual fund maze. Investors who are willing to do a little research about no-load funds can save this cost.

Salespeople often imply that load funds offer better performance and higher rates of return than no-load funds, but no convincing evidence supports this claim. The commission on a load fund does not imply that it is a superior product. It implies only that the fund gives a less valuable asset than a no-load fund in return for a given amount of money; the difference represents the cost of compensating salespersons. If the fund is held for a long period of time, the impact of a front-end load decreases. Most investors should do their own research to find no-load funds that meet their investment objectives. They can then put the money they would have spent on loads to work earning returns.

management fee: A fee assessed by all mutual funds as a percent of total assets to compensate investment managers.

Management Fees Both load funds and no-load funds charge **management fees** to compensate fund managers for their professional services researching and selecting security issues. Expenses also are incurred for such administrative functions as recordkeeping, mailing statements, office management, and so forth. Most funds charge annual management fees in the range of 0.5 to 0.75 percent of the fund's assets. When choosing among various funds, compare their total expense ratios. The wide selection of available funds probably offers an acceptable replacement for a fund that has extremely high expenses.

Sources of Information about Mutual Funds

Researching mutual funds is reasonably easy. Two widely available publications can help any investor become knowledgable about mutual funds: Wiesenberger Financial Services' *Investment Companies*, published by Warren, Gorham, and Lamont of New York, and Standard & Poor's *Investment Survey of Investment Funds*. Most large public and university libraries offer copies of these publications. Careful reading of the reports in these publications should help an investor develop a list of funds that would meet his or her needs. He or she can then request that a fund's manager send a **prospectus** for more detailed research. The prospectus is a document that provides complete information about a fund (or another security issue) and makes an official offer to sell shares. After reading the prospectus, the investor can choose the fund that best meets his or her investment goals.

prospectus: Document that makes an official offer to sell mutual fund shares or another security and provides complete information upon which to base a purchase decision.

Another important information source provides a different perspective on mutual funds. In late August or early September each year *Forbes* magazine publishes an annual performance survey of nearly all American mutual funds. This survey rates each fund with a grade of A through F for performance in rising markets, and another grade for performance in declining markets. Anyone who plans to buy shares in any kind of mutual fund should spend time at the library reviewing *Forbes*'s most recent ranking of its performance. Other major business and financial magazines, including *Barron's*, *Money*, *Business Week*, and *U.S. News and World Report*, also publish quarterly or annual mutual fund reports. Many of these publicly available sources obtain their data from Lipper Analytical Services in New York. The Lipper service has long been considered the premier source of mutual fund data for investors.

Exhibit 14.2 lists the honor roll from *Forbes*'s annual mutual fund survey, one example of publicly available data about mutual funds. Besides an A to F grade, the honor roll also gives the name of the fund's manager, the length of time that manager has handled the fund, the fund's average annual compound return on investment since 1980, the growth of a hypothetical $10,000 investment over the same period of time, the fund's status as a load or no-load fund, and a number of other performance characteristics. Full reports published in the magazine detail this information for virtually all publicly available mutual funds.

Advantages of Investing in Mutual Funds

As mentioned briefly earlier, mutual funds provide two major advantages as compared to individual investors' efforts to buy securities directly. First, mutual funds sell shares in broadly diversified portfolios of securities. An individual investor with $50,000 to $100,000 to invest would find it difficult to buy an adequate number of round lots of investment-grade stocks, perhaps 15 to 20 security issues, to obtain significant diversification. (Recall that a round lot is a block of 100 shares of stock; an odd lot is a block smaller

EXHIBIT 14.2

Forbes Mutual Fund Honor Roll

FUND SURVEY

This list of the best-performing stock funds is not a mere ranking of straight-line performance. To make the honor roll a fund must demonstrate consistency of results and strength in bear markets.

The honor roll

By Steve Kichen

THE SIMPLEST WAY to rate funds is by percentage gains over some past period. That's what most mutual fund surveys do. Simple, sure, but more than a little deceptive. The implication is that if a fund was up 15% a year in the past, it's likely to do 15% a year in the future. That implication is wrong. It's a little like saying that the most likely winner of the 1991 World Series will be the Cincinnati Reds, since they won last year. That catchphrase of fund prospectuses, "Past performance is no guarantee of future results," is an understatement. Past performance is only a weak indicator of future results. You can usually bet that this year's hot performer will be next year's laggard.

What, then, should you look for in judging a fund's performance if not a raw percentage? Our honor roll looks at three other factors: consistency, risk and continuity.

Consistency is built into the grades we award stock funds. We divide the measurement period into three market cycles so we can evaluate a fund separately in bull and bear markets. Stock funds are rated in the table beginning on page 211 for performance over as few as two market cycles, but the honor roll is limited to funds that have been around for the full three. The grading formula calls for something more than a simple average of returns over the three ups or the three downs. Unusually strong (or weak) performance in any given period is scaled back (or up), because it is unlikely to be repeated. Gold funds in the late 1970s, technology funds in 1982-83 and, recently, health care funds—all have had winning streaks. In our rating system those streaks count for less than they would in any system that measures straight-line performance over

Fund/distributor	Performance UP markets	Performance DOWN markets	Lead manager (years)	Average annual total return[1]	Hypothetical investment results[2]
Bergstrom Capital/closed-end	A	A	Erik E Bergstrom (15)	19.2%	$51,258
Dodge & Cox Stock Fund/Dodge & Cox	A	B	Multiple managers (10)[7]	15.1	34,457
Fidelity Destiny Portfolio I/Fidelity Distributors	A+	B	George Vanderheiden (11)	18.3	36,841
Franklin Growth Fund/Franklin Distributors	B	B	Jerry Palmieri (26)	14.7	37,320
Fundamental Investors/American Funds Group	A	B	Multiple managers (7)[7]	15.6	33,154
Guardian Park Ave Fund/Guardian Investor Services	A	B	Charles Albers (19)	15.7	31,809
IAI Regional Fund/IAI Funds	A	B	Julian P Carlin (11)	16.0	35,024
Investment Co of America/American Funds Group	B	B	Multiple managers (8)[7]	15.9	32,526
Lindner Fund/Lindner Management	D	A+	Robert A Lange, Eric E Ryback (10)	16.8	37,458
Mutual Benefit Fund/Mutual Benefit Financial Service Co	A	B	Multiple managers (7)[7]	15.9	34,367
New England Growth Fund/TNE Fund Group	A	B	G Kenneth Heebner (15)	18.0	41,307
Nicholas Fund/Nicholas Co	B	A	Albert O Nicholas (22)	16.2	39,780
Phoenix Growth Fund/Phoenix Equity Planning	A	A	Robert Chesek (11)	18.3	42,236
T Rowe Price International Stock Fund/T Rowe Price Associates	B[9]	B[9]	Martin G Wade (11)	20.4[10]	33,503[10]
Scudder International Fund/Scudder Investor Services	C[9]	B[9]	Nicholas Bratt (7)	20.4[10]	32,208[10]
Selected American Shares/Kemper Securities Group	C	A	Donald A Yacktman (8)	15.5	34,334
Shearson Appreciation Fund[11]/Shearson Lehman Brothers	B	B	Harold L Williamson Jr, Harry D Cohen (9)[7]	15.0	36,152
Source Capital/closed-end	D	A+	George Michaelis (13)	15.6	32,037
United Income Fund/Waddell & Reed	A	A	Russell E Thompson (12)	17.7	36,247
Washington Mutual Investors/American Funds Group	B	A	Multiple managers (8)[7]	16.9	36,424

[1]From 11/30/80 through 6/30/91, before deducting loads and taxes. [2]Value on 6/30/91 of $10,000 invested 11/30/80, after load and taxes, for hypothetical upper-income investor. Assumptions: Investor has $100,000 of gross income in constant 1984 dollars, deductions equal to 20% of income—15% after 1986—and four exemptions. Loads applied at 6/30/91 rate. [3]Average of price/earnings ratios for stocks in portfolio as of 3/31/91, weighted by size of holding. Source: CDA Investment Technologies. [4]Lesser of security sales or purchases, divided by average net assets. [5]Most funds have lower minimum requirements for IRAs and automatic savings plans. [6]Closed-end funds have no loads, but hypothetical results column assumes a 1% brokerage fee to buy shares. [7]Average tenure of managers, with ten years maximum credit for each. [8]Operates as a contractual plan, requiring monthly investment, with a decreasing load for larger investment

SOURCE: Forbes, September 2, 1991. Reprinted by permission of *Forbes* magazine.

Forbes Mutual Fund Honor Roll *(continued)*

five or ten years. Further reinforcing that consistency requirement, we exclude sector funds, which can do well by dumb luck—if their sector is hot.

To sum up: We don't dish up raw numbers. We mix in a substantial element of judgment.

Next, we rate risk. The honor roll is limited to funds that earn B or better in bear markets. There is no minimum for up-market grades. Lindner Fund, for example, gets an up-market D but a down-market A+. Why so much focus on bear market performance? It's a way of excluding funds that did well in the 1980s not so much from skillful stock picking as from taking aggressive or leveraged positions. Remember that the 10½-year measurement period has been a freakishly good one, in which the S&P 500 returned an average 14.2% a year. The emphasis on bear market grades makes up for the fact that the 1990s are likely to bring longer or more severe bear markets than we experienced in the recent past.

Finally, we rank funds on continuity. We limit the honor roll to funds whose managers have served in that position for at least seven years. Last year that rule forced us to drop Fidelity Magellan, which had been on eight previous honor rolls. Morris Smith has done a fine job at Magellan since taking over from Peter Lynch last year. Over the 12 months ended June 30 Magellan had a total return of 9.7%—better than the 6% return for the average stock fund in this survey. But this snapshot doesn't tell us how well Smith could guide the fund in a bear market. It doesn't give him a chance to prove any consistency of performance. In contrast, the Mutual Benefit Fund qualifies by dint of the long-tenured talent on its stock picking committee—never mind that its insurance company sponsor has been seized by New Jersey regulators.

A lot of funds have been around for three full market cycles, do better than the pack in bear markets and have had the same management for at least seven years. Out of this group we select the 20 best in long-term performance. Those results, labeled "Hypothetical investment results" below, measure what a $10,000 investment would have turned into over the three market cycles, after deductions for taxes and sales load. One more requirement: The fund must be open to new customers. That rules out the Vanguard Windsor Fund, CGM Capital Development Fund and two Mutual Series funds.

Getting on the Forbes honor roll is tough. The rules are demanding. Stock funds that don't meet these criteria, and fixed-income funds in various categories, still have a shot at the Best Buy rankings, where low cost counts heavily in the score. See pages 162, 164, 174, 198, 204, 292 and 293.

Net assets ($mil)	Maximum load	Annual expenses per $100	Weighted average P/E[3]	% of assets in cash	Portfolio turnover[4]	Minimum initial investment[5]	Fund (consecutive years on honor roll)
$89	NA[6]	$0.99	25	8%	10%	NA	Bergstrom Capital (8)
239	none	0.65	15	4	7	$2,500	Dodge & Cox Stock Fund (2)
2,024	NA[8]	0.44	17	0	71	NA	Fidelity Destiny Portfolio I (9)
275	4.00%	0.73	18	27	6	100	Franklin Growth Fund (3)
965	5.75	*0.70*	20	16	12	250	Fundamental Investors
259	4.50	0.67	15	8	47	1,000	Guardian Park Ave Fund (4)
325	none	*1.01*	22	23	169	5,000	IAI Regional Fund (3)
7,643	5.75	*0.55*	17	19	11	250	Investment Co of America (2)
783	none	0.83	16	13	13	2,000	Lindner Fund (3)
42	4.75	1.01	14	16	6	250	Mutual Benefit Fund (3)
734	6.50	*1.23*	27	0	185	1,000	New England Growth Fund (7)
1,715	none	0.81	16	9	22	500	Nicholas Fund (10)
977	4.75	*1.08*	23	22	275	500	Phoenix Growth Fund (3)
1,291	none	1.12	17	9	47	2,500	T Rowe Price International Stock (2)
899	none	1.17	22	9	70	1,000	Scudder International Fund
557	none	*1.10*	19	10	48	1,000	Selected American Shares (3)
1,410	5.00	0.84	18	11	30	500	Shearson Appreciation Fund (6)
304	NA[6]	0.97	17	20	43	NA	Source Capital (3)
1,894	8.50	0.67	16	4	31	500	United Income Fund (3)
6,792	5.75	*0.77*	16	4	11	250	Washington Mutual Investors (2)

contracts. Hypothetical investment result assumes a single investment of $10,000 on 11/30/80, with a simulated load of 12.4%. This load reflects both sales and account maintenance charges. [9]Grades for foreign funds depend on long-term performance against other foreign funds. [10]Average annual total return covers period from 9/30/82 to 6/30/91, the time span used to measure the performance of foreign stock funds. Hypothetical return is measured over the same period as domestic stock funds. [11]Formerly SLH Appreciation Fund. *Expense ratio is in italics if the fund has a shareholder-paid 12b-1 plan exceeding 0.1% (hidden load) pending or in force.* NA: Not available or not applicable.

than 100 shares.) This would mean buying odd lots of many stock issues, and the small trades necessary to establish and maintain these positions would run up substantial brokerage commission charges.

Diversification is essential to spread the risk of common stock investment among a reasonable number of stocks and reduce the chance that a loss on a single issue will hobble the entire portfolio. Diversifying beyond stocks into bonds and money market instruments presents an even more difficult challenge. Mutual funds automatically spread the investor's risk among a number of securities by selling shares in broadly diversified portfolios. Also, the large trades made by huge portfolios like mutual funds involve very small percentage commission rates as compared to the rates individuals pay.

The second major advantage of mutual funds comes from access to professional management at a relatively low cost. Total expenses, including management fees, generally run in the neighborhood of 1 percent of the dollar value of a fund's assets. This seems very reasonable considering that it covers salaries, research expenses, overhead, and other costs incurred by the fund. Along with professional management, mutual funds keep valuable records for investors, and most mutual funds will automatically reinvest dividends without charge, removing the responsibility of finding a new place to put periodic income payments.

Types of Mutual Funds

Mutual funds manage their portfolios to pursue a range of well-defined investment goals, from nondiversified, highly aggressive common stock funds to ultraconservative money market funds. Whatever objective an investor wants to achieve, some mutual fund has almost certainly targeted itself to serve that person's needs. Exhibit 14.3, taken from *Barron's* weekly summary of mutual fund performance, gives a good idea of the different categories of funds available and the dollar amount of money invested in funds from each category. The exhibit shows that investors own over $1.3 trillion worth of mutual funds of all types, with the largest amount of capital, approximately $450 billion, invested in money market funds. The next few pages describe the major categories of mutual funds.

Maximum Capital Gain Funds

maximum capital gain fund (aggressive growth fund): A stock fund managed with the sole investment objective of maximizing capital gains with no consideration for dividend income.

Most people think of mutual funds as growth-oriented funds that invest primarily in common stocks. This is only one category of funds, and it includes two subcategories differentiated by their stated investment objectives: maximum capital gain funds and growth funds. The two types of funds differ in degree of aggressiveness rather than in kind.

Maximum capital gain funds, as the name implies, dedicate their portfolios to a single objective: achieving maximum capital gains. These

perspective on **INTERNATIONAL INVESTMENTS**

Specialty Funds Simplify Investing in Japan

Experts say that mutual funds offer the best access to the Japanese stock market for the individual investor. Despite the plummeting Nikkei average, some mutual funds that hold only Japanese stocks have maintained growth rates twice the average for international stock funds. DFA Grp.: Japan Small Company, for example, has achieved 70 percent growth over the last five years despite the declining Nikkei. Compare that to the 30 percent growth of the average international fund.

Buying into Japanese mutual funds also brings advantages over buying Japanese stocks directly. Only nine Japanese ADRs trade on the New York Stock Exchange. Each of the nine would cost roughly $420 for a round lot, but investing only $1,000 in a Japan-only fund would give shares in roughly 50 Japanese stocks.

The guidance and expertise provided by the fund manager can give an especially important advantage in a mutual fund. Instead of trying to keep up with the Japanese market himself or herself, the investor can rely on a fund manager to provide expert knowledge and full-time attention to investments.

Various mutual funds invest in Japanese stocks, although only four U.S.-based funds invest solely in Japan. Another 22 funds hold securities issued throughout Asia, including Japan, and many international funds hold Japanese stocks as small percentages of their overall portfolios.

	TOTAL RETURN[a]		
FUND	FIRST QUARTER	ONE YEAR	FIVE YEARS
T. Rowe Price Intl.: Japan	−8.1%	new	new
GT Global Japan	−16.9%	−27.1%	+64.6%
Japan Fund	−15.2%	−19.3%	+19.8%
DFA Grp.: Japan Small Co.	−18.4%	−23.4%	+70.1%
Avg. intl. stock fund	−2.5%	+1.5%	+29.4%
Nikkei average[b]	−15.8%	−26.2%	−10.3%

[a] Includes dividends reinvested.
[b] Actual changes for periods shown. Figures are not total returns.
SOURCE: USA TODAY, April 6, 1992, p. 43.

funds explicitly reject any consideration of dividend income in their investment policies. As a general rule, such funds' prices show extreme volatility as compared to the stock market in general.

The maximum capital gain funds, also commonly called **aggressive growth funds,** invest primarily in common stocks of growth companies that pay low dividends (or no dividends at all). Like the funds that buy them, these stocks' prices are fairly volatile compared to the overall market.

Besides investing in aggressive stocks, such funds may also follow aggressive trading strategies calling for much more portfolio turnover than normal. (**Portfolio turnover** represents the percentage of the fund's assets it sells and reinvests in a year.) High turnover increases transaction costs, and thus increases a fund's total expenses compared to those of a fund with low turnover.

portfolio turnover: The percentage of a mutual fund's asset base that it sells and reinvests in a year.

EXHIBIT 14.3

Summary Transaction Data for Mutual Funds

MUTUAL FUND MONTHLY INDICATORS

Data for December: (Mil. $)	Latest Month	Preceding Month	Year Ago Month
Total Sales	28,184.1	r22,677.9	14,544.8
Aggressive Growth	2,504.2	r1,612.3	948.1
Growth	3,881.2	r2,654.0	2,016.5
Growth/Income	4,343.1	3,364.4	2,791.8
Precious Metals	99.2	97.4	81.7
International	769.0	616.9	534.6
Global-Equity	495.7	195.4	229.1
Income-Equity	832.3	638.8	619.7
Option/Income	15.1	24.3	9.1
Flexible Port	375.0	196.6	163.5
Balanced	779.9	482.8	501.1
Income-Mixed	1,539.1	r1,602.9	595.3
Income-Bond	1,257.0	1,039.7	545.8
Government	3,847.5	r3,480.7	1,140.5
GNMA (Ginnie Mae)	1,354.7	r1,137.3	531.1
Global-Bond	1,358.3	r1,341.2	884.8
Corporate Bond	502.2	r465.7	289.9

(Mil. $)	Latest Month	Preceding Month	Year Ago Month
High Yield Bond	604.7	536.6	334.3
Long-Term Municipals	2,024.9	r1,734.0	1,318.4
Single State Municipals	1,600.9	r1,456.9	1,009.4
Purchases of Common	23,631.0	r21,036.4	12,774.9
Sales of Common Stocks	18,039.3	r18,710.6	9,782.0
Other Purchases	45,096.1	r53,052.0	37,639.2
Other Sales	37,211.9	r43,681.2	32,801.3
Cash & S/T Holdings	60,986.7	r59,688.8	48,638.3
Liquid Asset Ratio	8.4%	9.3%	11.5%
Total Assets	1,346,594.7	r1,313,635.7	1,066,891.8
Money Market-Taxable	449,697.8	r468,560.1	414,733.3
Money Market-Exempts	89,895.8	r92,277.9	83,641.6
Stock Funds	366,186.3	328,871.7	245,788.2
Bond & Income Funds	440,814.8	r423,926.0	322,728.7
Redemptions	13,307.1	r10,847.5	8,544.6

SOURCE: *Barron's*, February 10, 1992, p. 110. Reprinted by permission of Barron's, © 1992, Dow Jones & Company, Inc. All rights reserved worldwide.

Investors can earn impressive returns from maximum capital gain funds if they can accept the kind of market and business risk exposure that these funds bring. Maximum capital gain funds have earned their shareholders superior long-run average rates of return compared to the average rates of return on less aggressive funds. This reinforces the familiar idea that risk always accompanies return in the securities markets.

Growth Funds

growth fund: A stock fund with capital gains as the major investment objective, giving income only minor attention.

Growth funds also pursue capital gains, but they follow somewhat less aggressive strategies in this effort than maximum capital gain funds. However, the line between the two types of funds is anything but clear. A growth fund's prospectus generally states that the fund pursues long-term growth of capital as its major objective, giving income only minor attention. Still, most growth funds do provide modest dividend yields.

Some growth funds also identify stability of capital as a major investment objective. Such a fund generally invests part of its portfolio in defensive common stocks, preferred stocks, bonds, and short-term debt instruments. This diversification takes them a step away from growth stocks toward securities with more stable prices.

emerging growth fund: A special type of growth fund that invests in companies in their early growth stages to pursue maximum capital gains at the cost of very volatile share prices.

Emerging Growth Funds **Emerging growth funds,** a special category of growth funds, have enjoyed increasing popularity during the last few years. These funds seek out relatively young, small companies that compete in new or rapidly growing industries. This search leads emerging growth funds to invest in over-the-counter stocks, restricted stocks, or stocks with limited marketability. At present, many emerging growth fund portfolios feature strong concentrations of high-technology companies. Several new funds that invest in emerging companies outside the U.S. also have begun trading recently as have funds that invest in companies located in the emerging economies of less-developed countries.

Most emerging growth funds pursue maximum capital gains as their primary investment objective. Investors should expect highly volatile prices for shares in these funds, with returns that outperform rising markets and underperform falling markets. Investing in these funds requires patience and rather steady nerves.

Growth and Income Funds

growth and income fund: A growth fund with larger emphasis on income from dividends.

Moving past the growth funds toward the conservative end of the mutual fund continuum, the investor next encounters **growth and income funds.** Growth and income funds generally look for higher dividend yields than growth funds, but they still focus primarily on the objective of capital growth. They pursue dividend income as a secondary, but important goal of investment policy.

Specialty Funds

specialty fund: A growth or maximum capital gain fund that focuses on some specialized investment objective, philosophy, or medium, such as precious metals or international equities.

Specialty funds manage their portfolios to achieve some specialized investment objective, philosophy, or medium. Such a fund may invest solely in one industry, focus exclusively or primarily on stock options or another type of security, tie all investments to a single type of product like natural resources or precious metals, or limit investments to securities from a certain nation or from non-U.S. companies. In following their narrow or unconventional investment policies, specialty funds usually hope to achieve maximum capital gains.

International Funds

international fund: A mutual fund that invests its securities in companies incorporated outside of the United States.

The term **international fund,** when used by U.S. fund managers, refers to a fund that invests its assets in companies outside of the United States. These funds may be either equity funds or income funds. In either case, the primary distinction of the funds is their investment outside of the United

perspective on **INTERNATIONAL INVESTMENTS**

Mexico Fund

Some mutual funds invest in one country exclusively. The Value Line synopsis below profiles one such fund, the Mexico Fund, which offers investors an opportunity to participate in a resurgence of growth south of the border. In early 1992 it offered the prospect of a 20 percent average annual total return over the next three to five years.

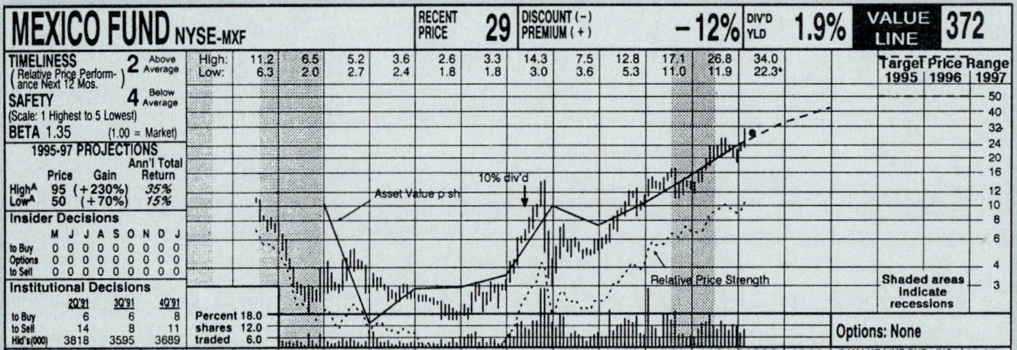

	1976	1977	1978	1979	1980	1981	F1982	F1983	1984	1985	1986	1987	1988	1989	1990	1991	G1992	1993	© VALUE LINE PUB., INC.	95-97
							10.17	1.72	2.89	2.95	3.53	9.84	7.37	10.26	15.38	24.07	*33.75*	*42.00*	Asset Val p sh (yr-end)	*60.30*
							.65	.24	.18	.25	.27	.27	.18	.62	.53	.34	*.55*	*.65*	Earnings per sh B	*1.25*
							--	--	--	--	--	--	--	--	--	--	*1.25*	*Nil*	Cap'l Gains Decl'd per sh	*Nil*
							--	.65	.24	.19	.25	.31	.15	.45	.56	.36	*.55*	*.65*	Inc Div'ds Decl'd per sh C	*1.25*
							--	d6.81	d1.54	d.95	d.32	5.54	2.52	5.02	9.43	17.33			Unrealized Apprec./sh	
							11.01	11.01	22.00	22.00	22.00	19.93	19.72	19.72	19.72	19.72	*26.30*	*26.30*	Common Shs Outst'g D	*26.30*
							NMF	49%	+54%	12%	31%	42%	11%	30%	11%	14%	*Bold figures are Value Line estimates*		Discount from NAV	*+10%*
							--	21.6%	6.7%	7.3%	11.3%	8.4%	4.8%	7.6%	4.8%	2.4%			Avg Ann'l Div'd Yield	*1.7%*

SOURCE: *Value Line*, March 27, 1992, p. 372. Copyright © 1992 by Value Line Publishing, Inc.; used by permission.

One source of this optimism comes from the possible completion of the North American Free Trade Agreement (NAFTA). This agreement would permit trade between Mexico, Canada, and the United States free of tariffs or excise taxes. The three North American countries would operate in much the same way as the European Community, but with greater outside trade than the EC.

American and Mexican firms alike support NAFTA, although agreements on some details have come slowly. Mexican companies would benefit from the open market for their goods, and they hope to see stronger growth in industries, as well. Free trade with Mexico would also offer opportunities for many small and medium-sized U.S. companies to exploit both relatively cheap sources of materials and labor and new markets for U.S. goods.

Larger U.S. companies such as General Motors also hope to profit by NAFTA. GM has decided to maintain an otherwise unprofitable Arlington, Texas, assembly plant, hoping that its proximity to the Mexican border will help the ailing car maker to utilize cheap Mexican parts. Increased business for Mexican auto part manufacturers could benefit Mexico Fund investors.

States, thus offering an opportunity for shareholders to diversify their holdings beyond what is available solely in the United States market.

Global Funds

global fund: A mutual fund that invests on a worldwide basis.

Global funds invest from a truly worldwide perspective and seek out securities in all world markets, including the United States. As is the case with other funds, these funds may be either equity or income funds. Because they invest across the world securities market, many investors feel that global funds offer the ultimate in diversification. As of early 1993, the United States securities market constituted just under 40 percent of the world securities market. Accordingly, one would normally expect a global fund to have a substantial stake in U.S. securities.

Income Funds

income fund: A mutual fund with the primary investment objective of earning high current income payments.

An investor who wants primarily to generate high levels of current income may find **income funds** attractive. Income funds invest primarily to earn the highest possible current yields. These funds build portfolios of widely varying compositions, and shareholders in such funds must read their prospectuses carefully to find one with a strategy that matches the investor's goals.

fixed-income fund: An income fund that invests primarily in bonds and preferred stocks.

equity-income fund: An income fund that invests primarily in common stocks with high dividend yields.

A typical income fund holds a mix of common stocks that pay high dividends, preferred stocks, and bonds. Some income funds invest in a single type of security. **Fixed-income funds** invest primarily in bonds and preferred stocks. **Equity-income funds** invest primarily in common stocks (equity securities). The familiar money market funds also fall into the income fund class of mutual funds.

Fixed-income funds generally offer the highest current yields on invested capital, but their prices also react most strongly to changes in interest rates. An income-oriented investor should diversify among fixed-income funds, equity-income funds, and money market funds.

Equity-income funds offer some attractive features compared to fixed-income funds and money market funds. These funds pay substantial dividend income and still offer the potential for capital growth through increases in share values over time. Also, dividends tend to grow along with share values as stocks in the portfolio increase their dividend payments.

Many people have become familiar with money market funds since they benefited from a tremendous surge in popularity when interest rates on short-term debt instruments rose sharply in the late 1970s and early 1980s. As noted earlier, money market funds hold over $400 billion in assets, more than funds in any other category. Recall from earlier chapters that money market funds invest in short-term debt instruments such as Treasury bills, bank certificates of deposit, bank and corporate commercial paper, and bankers' acceptances.

Like other funds, money market funds follow different investment strategies and some take more risks than others. The least risky funds invest solely in U.S. government securities and maintain very short average maturities. (The average maturity is the average time it takes for instruments owned by the fund to mature. Money market funds typically maintain average maturities of 30 to 60 days.) More risky funds may invest solely in corporate securities and maintain relatively long average maturities. Still, virtually all money market funds keep their risk levels relatively low; they represent very safe investment options.

Investors have found money market funds particularly attractive during periods of high inflation and volatile interest rates. These funds offer stable principal values and yields that keep pace with inflation. They offer no long-term growth potential, however. Shareholders can offset this lack of growth by reinvesting part of their income from dividends in new shares. This will keep the principal value of a fund account growing over time.

Balanced Funds

balanced fund: A mutual fund that invests in both stocks and bonds to balance the goals of capital gains and income.

Balanced funds attempt to combine the best features of both income and growth funds. Balanced funds are fairly rare; there are only about 25 balanced funds available, including both load and no-load funds. A typical balanced fund invests 25 to 50 percent of its assets in senior securities such as preferred stocks and bonds, investing the remainder of the portfolio in growth-oriented common stocks. Balanced funds pursue stable net asset values, solid dividend yields, and modest growth.

Municipal Bond Funds

municipal bond fund: A mutual fund that invests in municipal bonds to keep its dividend payments exempt from federal income tax.

An investor in a high tax bracket may favor **municipal bond funds.** Investors pay no federal income tax on interest they earn from the municipal bonds they hold. Individual investors also do not pay income tax on income from municipal securities issued by the state in which the shareholder lives.

Open-end municipal bond mutual funds have been available only since passage of the Tax Reform Act of 1976. Prior to that act, the tax law did not allow mutual funds to pass tax-free income through to individuals.

Just like the comparison between a municipal bond and a taxable bond, investors must compare the tax-equivalent yield on a municipal bond fund with the yield on a taxable fixed-income fund. Recall from Chapter 7 that the tax-equivalent yield is the yield a fully taxable investment would have to provide in order to yield the same after-tax return as a municipal security investment. The calculation requires simply dividing the municipal (tax-free) yield by 1 minus the investor's tax rate.

Suppose, for example, that an investor in a 28 percent federal tax bracket expects to earn 8 percent on a municipal bond fund. Dividing 8 percent by $(1 - 0.28)$ results in a tax-equivalent yield of 11.11 percent. If that investor earned fully taxable interest at an 11.11 percent rate, he or she would have 8 percent left after paying 28 percent of this income in taxes. A tax-free investment of $10,000 for one year at 8 percent would earn $800 in interest. To earn the same amount of interest from a taxable fixed-income fund, the investor would have to place the $10,000 in a fund that paid 11.11 percent interest, earning $1,111 in interest and paying $311 in taxes, leaving $800 after taxes. Assuming each fund holds bonds of comparable quality, the investor should buy shares in the fund that he or she expects to provide the highest after-tax yield.

Mutual Fund Families

mutual fund family: A group of mutual funds with varying investment objectives offered by a single sponsoring organization.

A single mutual fund corporation may offer a range of different funds, called a **mutual fund family,** that cover a broad spectrum of investment objectives. A large family may include one or more money market funds, several stock funds, a few fixed-income funds, a tax-free fund, and perhaps a specialty fund or two. Two of the largest no-load mutual fund families, the Vanguard and Fidelity groups, together offer a total of well over 100 funds.

Similarity of fund names within family groups sometimes complicates the process of locating the price listing for a particular fund. Most newspapers list family members alphabetically under the heading of the family to which they belong. The Explorer Fund, for example, appears under the Vanguard family name, and the Puritan Fund appears under the Fidelity family name.

Disciplined Mutual Fund Investment

Three principles combine to form a strategy of disciplined mutual fund investing: diversification, dollar cost averaging, and performance monitoring. If you follow these three principles, you should achieve highly satisfactory long-run investment results from mutual funds.

Diversification

As noted earlier, any successful investment plan must satisfy the demand for diversification. Everyone has heard the warning "Don't put all of your eggs in one basket"; this effectively sums up the critical investment principle of diversification. Every investor, no matter what his or her goals, should spread investment capital among asset categories and among securities within each asset category. Mutual funds find one of their chief strengths from their diversification among different issues of securities. All stock funds hold diversified portfolios of stocks, and all bond funds hold diversified portfolios of bonds. Some funds, such as the balanced funds, even diversify among types of securities.

A mutual fund investor can diversify among different classes of securities, or among different investment strategies, by buying shares in a number of funds that pursue different goals through investing in securities within a particular class. Even if you want to invest 80 percent of your assets in common stock funds, for example, you may still wish to select two or three funds that approach common stock investing in different ways.

The PASS scoring system introduced in Chapter 6 can help you establish a rough guideline for the percentage of your portfolio you should invest in each type of security. Based on your own independent research, you can then develop a list of funds that meet your goals and have investment philosophies compatible with your own attitudes and risk–return preferences.

After obtaining and studying the prospectuses of your investment candidates, you can make a final selection of the funds in which to invest. You can then begin your investment program, guided by the principle of dollar cost averaging.

Dollar Cost Averaging

dollar cost averaging: A technique investing a fixed dollar amount in mutual fund shares at fixed intervals, usually monthly or quarterly.

Dollar cost averaging is a simple but powerful technique that has served successful investors for many years. Dollar cost averaging involves buying a fixed dollar amount of mutual funds at regular intervals, usually monthly or quarterly. When market prices have fallen, this fixed amount buys more shares; when the market has risen, it buys fewer shares.

Dollar cost averaging eliminates the danger of committing too much capital in an overpriced market, leaving the investor with too many shares bought at a fund's highest price. The technique averages out the cost of the shares accumulated over time and removes the need to time the market, trying to buy at the lowest price and sell at the highest. As discussed in Chapter 1, few, if any, people can reliably time the market, so dollar cost averaging gives a prudent, long-term approach to avoid buying everything at the wrong time by abandoning the effort to buy everything at the right time. Spending a fixed dollar amount to buy more in a down market and less in an up market effectively diversifies an investment program across market cycles, leading to the most successful long-term results.

Selecting funds with good track records and investment strategies compatible with the investor's needs inspires the courage to keep making regular fund purchases in a declining market. This strains the confidence of any investor, who watches the value of purchases begin to drop immediately after acquisition. This requires a firm conviction that sound funds will rebound and provide good returns, and this conviction comes from careful selection of funds.

An initial deposit to establish an investment program generally requires quite a bit more money than normal monthly or quarterly purchases since nearly all funds require some minimum initial investment, usually $500 to $1,000. Buying initial shares in several funds, as this chapter recommends, can require substantial cash outlays. Subsequent, regular contributions to each fund can be more reasonable, however, since most funds impose rather low minimum purchase requirements for additions to an open account, often in the neighborhood of $50 to $100. Regularly adding increments of this amount to the account will produce the best long-term investment performance.

Performance Monitoring

performance monitoring: Technique tracking the risk-return performance of mutual fund investments and replacing funds that perform unsatisfactorily.

Performance monitoring is the final, critical principle of successful mutual fund investing. After establishing a portfolio of mutual funds, the investor must routinely monitor its performance. If one or more of the funds fail to perform satisfactorily, the investor should replace it with a new fund that meets his or her objectives.

One judges performance as satisfactory or unsatisfactory relative to the performance of other, comparable investments. A fund becomes a candidate for a sale if it provides below-average returns compared to returns from other funds with similar investment objectives, or compared to returns of broad market averages such as the Dow Jones Industrial Average or the Standard & Poor's 500. Investing money should not involve emotional attachment to a fund. If a fund does not perform as expected, or as well as its competitors, terminate your investment in it.

The time period over which to judge performance is a critical factor. Even a good fund can post poor results for a month, quarter, or year. As a general rule, no one should abandon an investment in a fund with a good past performance record and a suitable investment approach based on less than six months' to one year's performance. If the fund falters and fails to improve over this period of time, look for a better opportunity.

This advice contradicts that of some popular investment publications, which hold that some sort of market timing system should drive short-term movements of capital among funds. Some publications even advise investors on how to fool a fund into selling shares to them before they receive prospectuses, claiming some advantage from taking a quick position in a fund without information on which to base the trading decision. This advice is poorly founded.

Several well-designed research studies have shown that successful market timing requires at least 70 percent predictive accuracy. Only the most gifted (and/or lucky) professionals can achieve this kind of accuracy, if anyone can. For individual investors who cannot devote 50 or 60 hours a week to following the market, market timing is most likely to lead to wasted time and inferior results.

To follow daily price changes for mutual funds, check the listings in *The Wall Street Journal* or any other major daily newspaper. *Barron's* provides a useful weekly report of general mutual fund performance along with comparative data for the S&P 500 and the Dow Jones Industrial Averages. A sample of this Weekly Summary Report appears in Exhibit 14.4.

A number of well-established services can also provide help in following fund performance over longer terms. Resources at a public or university library can give current monthly performance data. Of these sources, the

EXHIBIT 14.4

Weekly Mutual Fund Performance Data

LIPPER MUTUAL FUND PERFORMANCE AVERAGES

Weekly Summary Report

February 6, 1992

Cumulative Performances With Dividends Reinvested

NAV Mil. $	No. Funds		10/11/90-2/06/92	7/12/90-2/06/92	1/07/91-2/06/92	12/31/91-2/06/92	1/30/92-2/06/92
General Equity Funds							
28,487.0	134	Capital Appreciation	+ 61.12%	+ 24.61%	+ 30.57%	+ 3.92%	+ 1.93%
107,569.0	298	Growth Funds	+ 56.84%	+ 22.86%	+ 26.39%	+ 2.36%	+ 1.52%
19,728.3	117	Small Company Growth	+ 88.23%	+ 36.00%	+ 44.22%	+ 7.60%	+ 2.85%
107,766.8	251	Growth and Income	+ 45.13%	+ 19.50%	+ 20.37%	+ 1.27%	+ 1.00%
29,258.9	74	Equity Income	+ 39.23%	+ 18.46%	+ 18.99%	+ 0.60%	+ 0.69%
292,810.0	874	Gen. Equity Funds Avg.	+ 56.70%	+ 23.45%	+ 26.87%	+ 2.84%	+ 1.54%
Other Equity Funds							
5,893.7	11	Health/Biotechnology	+ 110.99%	+ 76.94%	+ 56.95%	+ 2.68%	+ 1.63%
1,807.1	21	Natural Resources	+ 2.28%	− 5.54%	+ 0.75%	+ 0.14%	+ 0.39%
248.6	6	Environmental	+ 30.89%	− 3.97%	+ 7.04%	+ 8.72%	+ 1.67%
2,309.3	21	Science & Technol.	+ 93.11%	+ 32.68%	+ 35.62%	+ 8.70%	+ 2.80%
1,781.3	29	Specialty/Misc.	+ 54.62%	+ 19.24%	+ 26.42%	+ 4.18%	+ 1.44%
10,409.9	27	Utility Funds	+ 27.38%	+ 20.84%	+ 15.08%	− 3.18%	− 0.56%
480.6	11	Financial Services	+ 97.68%	+ 46.50%	+ 48.37%	+ 5.14%	+ 1.46%
196.2	6	Real Estate	+ 49.57%	+ 20.30%	+ 28.86%	+ 6.32%	+ 1.29%
1,341.7	6	Option Income	+ 36.16%	+ 15.62%	+ 14.13%	+ 2.11%	+ 0.75%
17,238.4	55	Global Funds	+ 25.55%	+ 3.80%	+ 13.34%	+ 2.10%	+ 1.87%
13,154.4	93	International Funds	+ 13.70%	− 3.50%	+ 7.27%	+ 1.86%	+ 1.75%
3,530.7	28	European Region Fds	+ 6.57%	− 8.60%	+ 2.30%	+ 2.17%	+ 2.26%
1,836.5	21	Pacific Region Funds	+ 11.43%	− 7.88%	+ 6.36%	+ 0.68%	+ 2.08%
2,748.2	36	Gold Oriented Funds	− 4.12%	− 9.48%	+ 5.40%	+ 1.72%	+ 1.84%
355,786.6	1245	All Equity Funds Avg.	+ 48.72%	+ 18.80%	+ 23.21%	+ 2.66%	+ 1.55%
Other Funds							
6,702.6	62	Flexible Portfolio	+ 36.99%	+ 20.85%	+ 18.61%	+ 1.21%	+ 1.07%
1,595.3	16	Global Flex Port.	+ 20.88%	+ 10.98%	+ 10.63%	+ 1.08%	+ 1.30%
19,400.8	67	Balanced Funds	+ 37.43%	+ 21.94%	+ 18.81%	+ 0.29%	+ 0.89%
863.5	7	Balanced Target	+ 40.37%	+ 24.25%	+ 18.43%	− 1.46%	+ 0.97%
2,244.6	28	Conv. Securities	+ 42.81%	+ 21.46%	+ 25.47%	+ 3.72%	+ 1.35%
5,880.7	15	Income Funds	+ 30.88%	+ 21.50%	+ 18.28%	+ 0.18%	+ 0.42%
29,113.6	91	World Income Funds	+ 11.79%	+ 19.53%	+ 6.33%	− 0.74%	+ 0.71%
214,747.7	641	Fixed Income Funds	+ 22.95%	+ 20.70%	+ 15.30%	− 0.23%	+ 0.73%
636,335.4	2172	Total Long-Term Funds					
		Long-Term Average	N/A	N/A	N/A	N/A	N/A
		Long-Term Median	N/A	N/A	N/A	N/A	N/A
		Funds with % Change	N/A	N/A	N/A	N/A	N/A
Lipper Indexes							
Current Value							
365.83	30	Capital Apprec Index	+ 61.22%	+ 27.93%	+ 32.53%	+ 3.21%	+ 2.13%
632.59	30	Growth Fund Index	+ 54.40%	+ 21.74%	+ 24.30%	+ 1.36%	+ 1.49%
367.12	30	Small Co Growth Index	+ 81.96%	+ 33.06%	+ 42.94%	+ 6.66%	+ 2.58%
924.38	30	Growth & Income Index	+ 42.23%	+ 18.42%	+ 19.41%	+ 1.51%	+ 1.05%
596.76	30	Equity Income Index	+ 38.36%	+ 20.47%	+ 19.63%	+ 0.47%	+ 0.79%
257.29	10	Sci & Tech Index	+ 86.98%	+ 30.04%	+ 36.00%	+ 6.56%	+ 2.80%
323.04	30	Global Fund Index	+ 21.54%	+ 1.31%	+ 12.64%	+ 1.89%	+ 1.85%
358.04	30	International Index	+ 13.28%	− 3.12%	+ 8.62%	+ 2.01%	+ 1.78%
145.20	10	Gold Fund Index	+ 2.46%	− 3.70%	+ 11.81%	+ 3.19%	+ 2.00%
722.85	30	Balanced Fund Index	+ 37.95%	+ 21.66%	18.81%	+ 0.39%	+ 0.87%
156.28	10	Conv Secur Index	+ 38.47%	+ 20.04%	+ 21.87%	+ 3.95%	+ 1.32%

Securities Market Indexes

Current Value						
U.S. Equities						
3.255/59	Dow Jones Ind. Avg. xd	+ 37.65	+ 9.62	+ 15.83	+ 2.74	+ 0.33
413.02	S&P 500 xd	+ 40.06	+ 13.24	+ 16.07	− 0.78	+ 0.53
492.61	S&P 400 xd	+ 42.02	+ 13.67	+ 17.18	− 0.02	+ 0.82
228.96	NYSE Composite xd	+ 41.16	+ 14.87	+ 17.57	− 0.21	+ 0.70
416.25	ASE Index	+ 41.72	+ 14.91	+ 24.38	+ 5.37	+ 1.30
210.26	Russell 2000 Index xd	+ 75.19	+ 24.10	+ 39.17	+ 10.72	+ 2.63
International Equities						
1,436.26	DAX Index	+ 17.70	− 12.27	+ 17.05	+ 6.54	+ 0.01
2,243.70	FT S-E 100 Index	+ 20.56	+ 6.91	+ 12.95	+ 1.65	− 0.65
2,410.44	Nikkei 225 Average xd	− 2.13	− 32.14	− 8.30	− 3.82	+ 2.54

xd-Price only index. Calculated without reinvestment of dividends. The Nikkei index value is divided by 10 due to space limitation.

SOURCE: *Barron's*, February 10, 1992, p. 110. Reprinted by permission of Barron's, best-known include Wiesenberger's *Current Performance and Dividend Record*, Standard & Poor's *Stock Guide* (in the back sections), and Lipper's *Mutual Fund Performance Analysis*. Wiesenberger also publishes *Investment Companies*, an extremely comprehensive annual review of investment company data. Most large libraries have copies, but this book is sold mainly to professional investment advisers, and it is not as easy to find as some other publications.

Daily price quotations for mutual funds in *The Wall Street Journal* and most other newspapers list two prices for each fund, its net asset value (NAV) and its offer price. In the price quotes, NAV indicates the price at which current shareholders can redeem shares. The offer price, equal to the fund's net asset value plus any load or other commission, gives the price at which investors can buy shares from the fund. For no-load funds *N.L.* appears in the offer price column, indicating that they charge no commissions. This gives a convenient means of identifying no-load funds.

Exhibit 14.5 reproduces a sample of mutual fund price quotations from *The Wall Street Journal*. As mentioned, these tables list funds alphabetically grouped under the name of the fund family. They list free-standing funds that operate independently of any family alphabetically by name. In addition to NAV and offer price, the daily listings also show price changes from the previous day.

The Seligman Group quotes show how the listings look for a family of load funds. The listing shows an NAV and offer price for each of the 26 funds listed under the Seligman Group heading. The Seligman Growth Fund had an NAV of $6.07 and an offer price of $6.37 at the close of business the day before the quote appeared in the newspaper. The difference between these two figures, $0.30, represents the commission cost of buying a share of this fund. The commission on this fully loaded fund equals 4.7 percent of the fund's offering price ($0.30/$6.37 = 4.7 percent). Note that the commission cost is 9.3 percent of the net asset value ($0.30/$6.07 = 5.0 percent). This example clearly demonstrates the substantial expense of buying shares in a fully loaded fund.

The quotes for funds in the Vanguard Group, one of the largest mutual fund families, give a good example of listings for a no-load fund family. Among the 47 funds under the Vanguard heading, find the listing for the Windsor Fund toward the bottom of the list. (Windsor is abbreviated "Wndsr.") The Windsor Fund's NAV was $12.30 and the quote shows "N.L." for its offering price, indicating a no-load fund.

To begin assessing the performance of mutual funds, consider Exhibit 14.6, which lists returns on selected no-load funds. These well-known, highly regarded funds have all achieved respectable past performance. Of course, past performance guarantees nothing about future performance, so review the data only as an illustration of the returns investors have enjoyed from some successful funds. To manage an actual portfolio of mutual funds, you would need to monitor performance statistics on a current basis.

EXHIBIT 14.5

Mutual Fund Price Quotations

	NAV	Offer Price	NAV Chg.
Tax Ex	8.71	9.14	...
TF Hi	8.65	9.08	...
TFHY t	13.96	13.96	+.01
TFIns t	14.71	14.71	−.01
USGv p	13.77	14.46	+.02
Util p	8.87	9.41	−.05
Vista p	7.39	7.84	−.02
Voyag p	10.19	10.81	−.08
Quest For Value:			
Fund	10.95	11.59	−.64
GIEq	12.38	13.10	...
NatITE	10.45	10.97	...
SmCap	15.38	16.28	−.03
USGov	11.75	12.34	+.02
RBB Fund:			
EqGth p	11.83	12.42	−.09
GvtSec p	10.28	10.79	+.01
HiYBd p	10.32	10.83	+.01
RIT Bal	1.55	1.55	−.01
RIT Inco	1.37	1.37	...
RSI Trust:			
ActBd p	22.58	NL	...
Core p	29.10	NL	−.13
EmGr p	27.85	NL	−.11
IntBd p	22.54	NL	+.01
STIF p	17.07	NL	...
Value p	22.84	NL	−.20
Rainbw	6.08	NL	−.07
RanGovt	9.72	10.02	...
RanGvII	10.02	10.02	...
ReaGr	13.31	13.97	−.03
Regis Fund:			
C&B Bal	12.23	NL	−.03
C&B Eq	12.93	NL	−.06
DSI Dv	10.65	NL	+.01
DSI LM	10.34	NL	+.01
ICMSC	14.07	NL	+.02
SirSEq	15.71	NL	−.13
SterBI	10.53	NL	−.01
RchTng	15.70	NL	−.07
Rey BC	15.46	NL	−.13
Rightime Group:			
BlueC p	29.30	30.76	−.19
RT fp	35.56	NL	−.03
GvSc p	12.79	13.43	...
Grth p	25.97	27.27	−.21
MidCap p	27.09	28.44	−.13
SocAw p	27.50	28.87	−.20
RobSEG p	19.21	NL	−.11
Rochester Fds:			
Convt p	9.71	10.04	−.03
RoMu p	16.84	17.54	...
LtdNY p	3.07	3.13	...
TxMgd p	9.57	10.46	−.07
Rodney Square:			
DivIn p	13.02	13.49	+.02
Gwth p	16.31	16.99	−.11
IntlEq p	11.17	11.64	+.01
Rushmore Group:			
AGas	9.51	NL	−.02
Nova	9.96	NL	−.08
SMP Id	16.89	NL	−.13
OTC Id	15.32	NL	−.09
USGLg	10.28	NL	−.01
US Gov	10.32	NL	+.01
MD TF	10.32	NL	...
VA TF	10.53	NL	+.01
SBK Select:			
USIncT	10.58	10.58	...
ValEqI	12.07	12.57	−.05
ValEqT	12.07	12.07	−.05
SBSF Cv	10.98	10.98	+.02
SBSF Gr	15.21	15.21	−.02
SEI Funds:			
Bond p	10.52	NL	...
BdIdx p	9.98	NL	+.01
CapGr	12.67	NL	...
GNMA p	10.05	[illegible]	
LtVBd p	[illegible]		
ShtGv [illegible]			
[illegible]			
NYTax	11.04	NL	...
OHTax	12.58	NL	+.01
PA Tax	12.90	NL	...
QualG	14.95	NL	−.09
ST Bond	12.16	NL	+.01
ST Glbl	12.05	NL	+.02
TxFHi	11.54	NL	+.01
TxFr93	10.72	NL	...
TxFr96	11.24	NL	...
Zr1995	12.38	NL	+.02
Zr2000	13.30	NL	−.01
Seafirst IRA:			
AstA f	12.81	NL	...
BICh f	15.52	NL	...
Bond f	10.86	NL	...
Security Funds:			
Action	10.02	....	−.02
Bond p	7.57	7.95	+.01
Equty	5.92	6.28	−.02
Invest	7.31	7.76	−.01
Ultra	8.08	8.57	...
Selected Funds:			
AmSh p	18.08	NL	−.10
SplSh p	21.28	NL	+.04
USGov	9.47	NL	−.02
Seligman Group:			
CapFd	17.14	17.99	−.12
ColoTx	7.20	7.56	...
CmStk	12.92	13.56	−.04
Comun	13.05	13.70	−.02
FLTax	7.40	7.77	...
GATxE	7.64	8.02	...
Growth	6.07	6.37	−.02
Inco	13.10	13.75	...
LaTx	8.19	8.60	...
MassTx	7.86	8.25	...
MdTx	7.94	8.34	...
MichTx	8.42	8.84	...
MinnTx	7.77	8.16	...
MO Tx	7.68	8.06	...
NatlTx	7.91	8.30	...
NJTE p	7.50	7.87	...
NY Tax	7.88	8.27	...
OhioTx	8.07	8.47	...
OrTE	7.48	7.85	...
PaTE p	7.79	8.18	...
CaTax	6.49	6.80	...
CaTxQ	6.67	6.98	...
SCTE	7.79	8.18	...
GvGtd p	7.15	7.51	...
HYdB p	6.17	6.48	...
MtgSc p	6.72	7.06	−.01
Sentinel Group:			
Balan	14.38	15.72	−.02
Bond	6.50	6.86	+.01
Com S	28.35	30.98	−.13
GvSecs	10.11	10.67	+.02
Grwth	17.42	18.39	+.01
TF Inc	12.80	13.51	...
Sentry	14.69	NL	−.08
Sequoia	52.66	NL	−.25
Shearson Funds:			
Advsr p	25.02	26.48	−.10
AgrGr	22.96	24.17	−.26
Aprec	10.18	10.72	−.03
ATG	9.06	9.54	−.03
ATIn	104.82	104.82	−1.70
AZ Mu	9.79	10.31	...
CalMu	15.84	16.67	−.02
FdVal	6.75	7.11	...
GlbOp	26.17	27.55	+.03
HiYld	13.31	14.01	+.01
MgdG	12.67	13.34	+.01
MMun	15.66	16.48	...
MAMu	12.39	13.04	...
NJMu	12.54	13.20	−.01
NYMu	16.63	17.51	...
1990s p	11.22	11.81	−.18
[illegible]	13.82	14.55	−.04
[illegible]	10.97	NL	
SAM SC	11.09	NL	−.03
SAM Val	14.00	NL	−.04
SCMBF	10.25	10.73	+.01
SpPtStk	36.02	36.02	−.30
Stagecoach Funds:			
AstAl	17.20	18.01	−.03
CpStk	30.00	....	−.19
GNMA	11.30	11.83	...
GthInc	12.93	13.54	−.07
USGovt	14.85	15.55	+.01
StarbGv	10.34	NL	...
State Bond Grp:			
Com St	9.00	9.45	−.07
Divers	9.38	9.85	−.06
Progrs	13.88	14.57	−.06
TaxEx	10.68	11.18	+.01
USGv p	5.19	5.46	−.02
St FarmFds:			
Balan	29.73	29.73	+.01
Gwth	22.05	22.05	−.05
Interm	10.53	10.53	+.01
Muni	8.22	8.22	...
StStreet Resh:			
Exc	197.46	197.46	−1.45
Gth	108.39	108.39	−.80
Inv	17.91	18.75	−.12
Steadman Funds:			
Am Ind	1.58	NL	...
Assoc	.73	NL	...
Invest	1.58	NL	...
Ocean	3.09	NL	+.03
Stein Roe Fds:			
Cap Op	25.22	NL	−.18
GvtInc	10.32	NL	−.01
HYMu	11.69	NL	−.01
Income	9.42	NL	−.01
IntBd	8.90	NL	+.01
IntMu	10.92	NL	−.01
MgdM	8.94	NL	...
PrimE	13.46	NL	−.05
Specl	20.68	NL	−.12
Stock	24.27	NL	−.14
TotRet	26.76	NL	−.07
Strategic Funds:			
Gold	2.04	2.23	+.01
Invst	1.83	2.00	−.01
Silvr	2.73	2.98	−.08
StratDv	27.57	NL	−.03
Strat Gth	20.31	NL	−.03
Strong Funds:			
Advtg	9.96	NL	...
CmStk	13.79	14.07	−.02
Discov	18.09	18.46	−.08
GovSc	10.59	NL	−.02
Inco	9.39	NL	+.01
Invst	19.50	19.70	−.03
MunBd	9.72	NL	...
Oppty	21.83	22.28	−.04
ST Bd	10.11	NL	+.01
Total	20.78	20.99	−.11
SunAmerica Fds:			
AgGth p	15.28	16.21	−.10
BalAs t	16.53	16.53	+.02
CapAp t	13.47	13.47	+.02
CvSec p	9.93	10.43	...
EmGr t	17.80	17.80	−.05
GlbIn t	9.69	9.69	...
Grwth p	15.07	15.99	−.10
HiInc t	7.81	7.81	−.02
HiYld p	9.30	9.76	−.02
Home t	10.78	10.78	+.01
IncPl t	7.49	7.49	−.01
Stripe p	12.37	12.99	...
TotRt p	14.62	15.51	−.04
GvIn p	10.01	10.51	+.01
USGv t	8.95	8.95	...
TNE F[illegible]			
InvQ fp	9.17	9.63	−.01
TFBd A	10.16	10.67	...
TrnsamericaSpcl:			
BlChp t	11.35	11.35	−.01
EmGA p	22.49	23.61	−.14
EmGB t	22.38	22.38	−.14
GvInc t	9.83	9.83	−.01
GrInB t	12.33	12.33	−.06
HYTF t	9.39	9.39	+.01
HiYld t	7.50	7.50	+.01
NatRs t	12.39	12.39	−.03
Trinity:			
Bond p	10.61	10.61	+.01
Equity p	12.89	12.89	−.07
ST Bd p	10.24	10.24	+.01
TCU Gv	10.02	10.02	...
20th Century:			
BalInv	16.27	NL	−.12
Gift	14.84	NL	−.18
Grwth	25.51	NL	−.22
HerInv	9.45	NL	+.01
IntlEq	5.92	NL	+.07
LTBnd	98.03	NL	+.29
Select	40.62	NL	−.38
TxEIn	101.92	NL	+.02
TxELT	102.78	NL	−.04
Ultra	17.89	NL	−.22
USGv	95.30	NL	+.21
Vista	12.67	NL	−.14
USAA Group:			
AgvGt	23.73	NL	−.12
Balan	11.75	NL	−.01
CA Bd	10.31	NL	...
Cornst	19.32	NL	−.02
GNMA	10.31	NL	−.02
Gold	6.66	NL	−.03
Grwth	17.37	NL	−.05
IncStk	13.34	NL	−.02
Inco	12.25	NL	−.02
Intl	12.30	NL	+.08
NYBd	10.99	NL	−.01
TxEH	13.64	NL	...
TxElt	12.35	NL	...
TxESh	10.50	NL	...
VA Bd	10.65	NL	...
USF&G Funds:			
AxeB p	9.81	10.41	−.02
AxeCr p	10.76	11.42	+.02
AxeGr p	7.65	8.12	−.06
AxeInc p	5.15	5.41	+.01
ChnFI p	10.42	10.94	+.03
ChnGI p	13.26	14.07	−.09
EurE p	10.54	11.18	+.13
EurG p	10.69	11.34	+.10
OTC S p	18.53	19.66	+.06
UST Master:			
Equity	16.59	17.37	−.09
Intl	8.90	9.32	+.04
IntTE	9.00	9.42	...
LT TE	9.31	9.75	+.01
MgdIn	9.32	9.76	...
NY TE	8.32	8.71	...
Unified Mgmnt:			
Gwth	14.58	15.27	+.04
Inco	11.40	11.94	−.04
Indian	9.07	9.50	...
Mutl	18.14	18.99	−.09
Union Inv:			
Balan	11.25	NL	−.01
GrEq	12.94	NL	−.02
IntBd	10.53	NL	+.01
VIMom	11.76	NL	−.05
United Funds:			
Accm	7.40	8.09	−.04
Bond	6.17	6.74	+.01
Con Inc	18.88	20.63	−.11
GldGv	6.81	7.44	−.05
GvtSc	5.11	5.34	...
HiIncII	3.89	4.25	−.01
[illegible]	8.62	9.42	[illegible]
Vanguard Group:			
AssetA	13.14	NL	−.05
BdMkt	9.82	NL	...
Convrt	11.05	NL	−.03
EqInc	12.29	NL	−.05
Explr	43.07	NL	−.11
Morg	12.40	NL	−.04
Prmcp	16.09	NL	−.10
V Pref	9.12	NL	...
Quant	16.22	NL	−.09
STAR	12.45	NL	−.01
TC Int	28.03	NL	+.10
TCUsa	27.89	NL	−.08
GNMA	10.32	NL	...
HYCorp	7.29	NL	+.01
IGCorp	8.68	NL	+.01
STCorp	10.90	NL	+.01
STFed	10.33	NL	+.01
ST Tr	10.15	NL	+.01
IT Tr	10.23	NL	...
LT Tr	10.15	NL	−.01
Idx 500	38.86	NL	−.24
IdxExt	16.69	NL	−.05
IdxEur	10.17	NL	+.07
IdxPac	9.02	NL	+.01
IdxInst	39.45	NL	−.25
SmCap	13.50	NL	−.02
MuHY	10.41	NL	...
MuInt	12.51	NL	...
MunLd	10.54	NL	...
MuLg	10.60	NL	...
MInLg	11.92	NL	...
MuSht	15.61	NL	...
Cal Ins	10.56	NL	+.02
NJIns	10.85	NL	−.01
NYIns	10.16	NL	...
OhioIn	10.70	NL	...
PennIn	10.58	NL	...
VSPE r	12.89	NL	+.09
VSPG r	9.34	NL	−.05
VSPH r	36.07	NL	−.20
VSPS r	20.40	NL	−.07
VSPT r	17.77	NL	−.02
WellsI	17.60	NL	−.03
Welltn	18.63	NL	−.07
Wndsr	12.30	NL	+.02
Wnds II	15.09	NL	−.04
WldInt	10.40	NL	+.05
WldUS	14.88	NL	−.12
Venture Advisers:			
IncPl	4.70	4.93	+.01
Muni t	9.35	9.35	+.01
NY Ven	10.26	10.77	−.03
RPFB t	6.74	6.74	−.01
RPFE t	27.25	27.25	−.04
Vista Funds:			
CapGr	26.09	27.32	−.09
GvInc	11.55	12.09	+.01
GrInc	26.98	28.25	−.10
NY TF	10.93	11.45	+.01
TF Inc	11.17	11.70	+.01
Volumet	15.62	NL	−.05
Voyageur Fds:			
AZIns	10.33	10.84	+.01
CO TF	10.23	10.65	+.01
GrSt fp	24.13	25.60	−.16
MNIns f	10.00	10.50	...
MNInt f	10.66	10.96	...
MNTF f	12.00	12.60	...
US Gv f	10.43	10.95	...
WallSt	7.70	8.02	−.04
Warburg Pincus:			
CapAp	13.04	NL	−.06
EGth	19.81	NL	−.12
FixInc	9.74	NL	+.01
GblFxd	10.86	NL	+.08
IntEqu	13.72	NL	+.09
IntGvt	[illegible]		
NY[illegible]			

SOURCE: *The Wall Street Journal*, February 10, 1992, p. C20. Reprinted by permission of The Wall Street Journal,

EXHIBIT **14.6**

Performance Statistics for Selected No-Load Mutual Funds

	1991	1990	1989	1988	1987	1987–1991
S&P 500 index	30.5%	−3.1%	31.7%	16.6%	5.3%	15.4%
Growth Funds						
Janus Fund	42.8	−0.7	46.3	16.6	3.9	20.2
20th Century Growth	69.0	−3.9	43.1	2.7	13.0	21.9
20th Century Select	31.5	−0.4	39.5	5.6	5.6	15.3
Growth and Income Funds						
Fidelity Fund	24.1	−5.0	28.7	17.9	3.3	13.1
Mutual Beacon	17.5	−8.2	17.4	28.9	12.7	13.0
Scudder Growth and Income	28.1	−2.3	26.4	11.9	3.5	12.9
Vanguard 500 Portfolio	30.1	−3.3	31.4	16.2	4.7	15.0
Windsor[a]	28.4	−15.5	15.0	28.7	1.2	10.2
Windsor II	28.4	−10.0	27.7	24.7	−2.1	12.5
Equity Income Funds						
Fidelity Puritan[b]	24.4	−6.2	19.6	18.8	−1.9	10.2
Rowe Price Equity Income	25.2	−6.7	13.6	27.7	3.7	11.9
Vanguard Equity Income	25.2	−11.9	26.5	—	—	—
International Funds						
Rowe Price International	15.8	−8.9	18.1	17.9	7.9	9.6
Scudder International	11.8	−8.9	27.0	18.8	0.9	9.2
Vanguard World International	4.7	−12.0	24.8	11.6	12.7	7.7
Balanced Funds						
Wellesley Income Fund	21.4	3.8	20.8	13.5	−1.9	11.1
Wellington Fund	23.5	−2.8	21.5	16.1	2.3	11.6
Fixed-Income Funds						
Fidelity Government Securities	15.9	9.4	12.6	6.4	1.1	9.0
Fidelity Intermediate Bond	14.5	7.5	11.8	7.1	2.1	8.5
Vanguard Fixed GNMA	16.8	10.3	14.8	8.8	2.2	10.5
Vanguard Fixed Invest Grade	20.9	6.2	15.2	9.7	0.2	10.2
Vanguard Fixed Short-Term	13.1	9.2	11.5	7.0	4.4	9.0
Vanguard Preferred Stock	20.9	6.4	18.7	7.9	−7.7	8.7

(continued)

EXHIBIT 14.6

Performance Statistics for Selected No-Load Mutual Funds *(continued)*

	1991	1990	1989	1988	1987	1987–1991
Municipal Bond Funds						
Fidelity High Yield	10.2	8.5	11.4	12.0	−3.7	7.5
Fidelity Limited Term	11.2	7.0	7.8	8.2	1.1	7.0
Vanguard High Yield	14.7	5.9	11.1	13.8	−1.6	8.6
Vanguard Insured Long-Term	12.5	7.0	10.6	12.8	0.1	8.5
Vanguard Intermediate	12.2	7.2	10.0	10.0	1.6	8.1
Vanguard Long-Term	13.5	6.8	11.5	12.2	−1.1	8.4
Vanguard Short-Term	7.2	6.6	7.0	5.6	4.1	6.1
Precious Metals Funds						
Lexington Gold	−6.2	−20.8	24.9	−15.0	46.3	2.9
Vanguard Specialty—Gold	4.3	−19.9	30.4	−14.2	38.7	5.3

[a] Fund is currently closed to new investors.

[b] Fund has a low load.

Data compilations have been obtained from sources believed to be reliable and, although carefully verified, cannot be guaranteed. Past performance results are not necessarily indicative of future performance. This list should in no way be construed as a list of recommended funds for any investor; it is merely a representative list of funds in various categories that have successful past performance records. Any investor interested in any fund on this list should carefully read the fund's prospectus before investing.

SOURCE: "The No-Load Fund Advisor," P.O. Box 283, Hastings-on-Hudson, NY 10706.

Mutual Fund Regulation

Federal law regulates few business entities more strictly than mutual funds. Federal statutes control their operations, as do most state securities laws (commonly called "blue sky laws"). Of course, no regulation can assure you of buying a fund that will make money or that will suit your investment objectives. The regulations do assure (among other things) that mutual funds fully and fairly disclose all the relevant facts necessary for an investment decision. The Securities and Exchange Commission (SEC) enforces various antifraud provisions of federal law, and it closely regulates the activities of mutual fund managers and advisers to ensure that they serve the interests of their shareholders.

Four major federal statutes regulate mutual funds' operations: the Securities Act of 1933, the Securities Exchange Act of 1934, the Investment Advisers Act of 1940, and the Investment Company Act of 1940, as amended by the Investment Company Amendments Act of 1970. Congress enacted these laws in response to widespread abuses and fraudulent business practices of a number of investment companies during the 1920s and 1930s. This federal protection restored investor confidence in the investment company industry.

The Securities Act of 1933 requires that mutual funds (and other issuers of securities) provide the SEC with full information about securities they offer to the public. A mutual fund must provide potential investors with a current prospectus that completely discloses the fund's investment policies, managers, and investment activities. The 1933 act also limits the advertising activities of funds.

The Securities Exchange Act of 1934 regulates the business and sales activities of mutual fund salespeople, and subjects their conduct to various antifraud provisions. The Investment Advisers Act of 1940 regulates the business practices of mutual fund investment advisers.

The Investment Company Act of 1940 and the Investment Company Amendments Act of 1970 impose the most important and detailed federal regulation of mutual funds. These laws define acceptable structures and policies for mutual funds and standards for conduct of their directors, managers, advisers, and sales representatives. Detailed provisions in the act seek to prevent conflicts of interest, protect the integrity of fund assets, and mandate financial and accounting practices.

One practical effect of mutual fund regulation requires that an investor deal with at least three separate organizations in his or her dealings with a fund. The first organization, the fund itself, refers to the investment company that sponsors the fund, that is, the corporation or trust in which the shareholder owns shares and whose board of directors or trustees the shareholder votes to elect. The fund sponsor manages the business activities of the fund and answers to its shareholders through the board of directors.

mutual fund investment adviser: An organization, separate from the corporation that offers a mutual fund, that manages the fund's investments.

As one of its most important responsibilities, the fund's board selects the **mutual fund investment adviser.** In essence, the fund hires the investment adviser, a separate organization, to manage the fund's investment portfolio. For its management services, the fund pays the adviser a fee based on a percentage of the fund's assets.

Most investment advisers are organized as either corporations or partnerships. They remain independent of the fund itself, at least theoretically. Some funds do, in fact, hire independent organizations as advisers; the funds and advisers have arm's-length relationships. The members of the boards of directors of most funds' investment advisers also serve on the funds' boards of directors, however, so that the same people exert significant control over both organizations in the vast majority of cases. This dilutes independence and leaves little likelihood that a fund will fire an adviser for poor investment performance. If the fund's returns fail to measure up, this structure may put the investor at a disadvantage. On the other hand, the fund board is also strongly influenced by the independent directors of the fund board.

mutual fund custodian: A bank or other organization, independent of the fund corporation and investment adviser, that holds a fund's investment securities in safekeeping.

Besides the fund and the investment adviser, the mutual fund investor must deal with the **mutual fund custodian.** This organization is always independent of both the fund and the adviser. The custodian, usually a bank or trust company, maintains physical possession of the securities the fund purchases, and acts as the transfer agent for fund shares. The custodian may also distribute the fund's shares.

The regulatory structure of the mutual fund industry ensures investor access to the information that must guide informed investment decisions. The independence of the custodian guarantees that investors' funds will remain in safekeeping outside the direct control of the fund or its investment adviser. In addition, close regulation ensures equitable conduct of the sales and other business activities of the fund. Unfortunately, no regulation can ensure that the value of shares in a fund will never fall or that mutual fund shareholders will never make poor investment decisions. To adapt a famous expression, eternal vigilance is the price of financial freedom.

Dividend Payment and Tax Status

regulated investment company: An investment company that passes at least 90 percent of all income from dividends, interest, and realized capital gains through to stockholders.

Federal tax law requires that **regulated investment companies** pass through to their stockholders at least 90 percent of all income from dividends, interest, and realized capital gains. Mutual funds that meet this requirement do not have to pay taxes on any income they pass through to shareholders, so virtually all mutual funds make sure they meet the standard, and elect to be treated as regulated investment companies. The IRS considers these mutual fund corporations to be conduits for returns on investments owned by fund shareholders, and it taxes only the individual shareholders on profits from fund investments.

Common stock mutual funds typically pay dividend income once or twice a year and pay income from capital gains annually. Fixed-income funds typically pay dividends monthly or quarterly. Money market funds declare dividends daily and pay them monthly. Regardless of how often a fund pays dividends, the payment reduces the net asset value of the fund by the amount of the dividend.

A mutual fund investor can elect to receive dividend payments or to have them reinvested automatically in his or her account. Those who elect automatic reinvestment, however, remain liable for taxes on this income. Most people prefer reinvestment, but they must plan to pay their tax bills on dividends, either by redeeming some shares at tax time or by diverting income from some other source.

The taxes on mutual fund dividends can have a major impact on investment planning for a large lump-sum purchase. Suppose, for example, that you wanted to invest $10,000 in mutual fund shares in December. The fund has a net asset value per share of $10, and it plans to pay a combined income and capital gain dividend of $1 per share.

Your $10,000 would buy you 1,000 shares, and you would collect a dividend of $1,000, part of which would be taxed as ordinary income and part as capital gains, leaving you a value of $9,000 for your original 1,000 shares. If your tax bracket dictated $300 in tax on the $1,000 in dividends, this payment would reduce the overall value of your investment to $9,700, the total of the mutual fund shares and the balance of the dividend after deducting the tax.

Suppose, however, that you were to postpone your purchase until after the fund paid its dividend. The dividend would reduce the fund's net asset value to $9 per share ($10 less the $1 dividend), and your $10,000 would buy 1,111.111 shares. By missing the dividend, you would give up $1,000 of immediate income, but you would also postpone any tax liability until after the next dividend payment date, and the value of your mutual fund shares would remain at $10,000.

Unless you hold the mutual fund shares in a nontaxable account such as a Keogh plan or an IRA, you must plan for the tax consequences of your mutual fund investments. Since income from IRAs and Keogh plans is tax-exempt, investments in these plans raise no tax timing problems.

Tax Treatment of Capital Gains and Losses

Besides taxes on dividends, mutual fund investors must also understand the treatment of short-term versus long-term capital gains and losses. A sale of shares in a mutual fund normally generates either a capital gain (if the shares rose in value above their cost) or a capital loss (if the shares fell in value below their cost). When a fund sells a security for a gain and declares a capital gain dividend, its shareholders also face capital gains tax on this income.

The IRS considers any gain or loss on shares sold more than six months after their purchase to be a long-term gain or loss for tax purposes. A gain or loss on shares held for less than six months is a short-term gain or loss. The Tax Reform Act of 1986 requires the same tax treatment for capital gains as for ordinary income.

The investor owes tax on the net capital gain after deducting capital losses. If total capital losses exceed total capital gains, the investor can deduct the net capital loss from taxable income, up to a maximum of $3,000 in any one year. The investor can carry losses in excess of $3,000 forward and deduct them from income in future years.

The tax treatment of capital gains and losses can affect a decision to switch funds, that is, to sell shares in one fund and replace them with shares in another fund. If the sale generates a capital gain, the investor must plan to pay tax on the gain. Suppose, however, that the investor has unrealized tax losses on another mutual fund investment, that is, the price of the fund has declined below the price the investor paid, but he or she still owns the losing shares so the loss remains unrealized.

tax swap: Strategy of selling a fund to realize a capital loss which can offset a capital gain or ordinary income and reduce taxes, then replacing it with a similar fund.

This investor may consider a year-end **tax swap.** The investor can sell the mutual fund that has fallen in price to realize the capital loss and then immediately reinvest the proceeds of the sale in a similar (but not the same) fund. In this way, the investor has mutual fund shares with the same value as before the sale, but he or she effectively recovers part of the loss in the form of tax benefits.

Suppose, for example, that a mutual fund investment has fallen in value by $3,000. If you sell that fund and replace it with a similar fund, you will incur a $3,000 capital loss that you can deduct from your taxable income. If your income placed you in the 28 percent tax bracket, you would have to pay $840 less in taxes than you otherwise would have owed, which would cut your actual loss to $2,160. Since you replaced your shares in the losing fund with shares in a similar fund, you would have the same amount of capital invested. If you also invest the tax savings, your portfolio will actually increase in value.

wash sale rule: An IRS rule that disallows a tax deduction for a capital loss if a tax swapper replaces a sold investment with the same or substantially the same investment within 30 days before or after the sale.

Tax swappers must pay careful attention to the IRS **wash sale rule,** which states that a taxpayer may not deduct a capital loss if he or she, or his or her spouse, replaces the sold investment with the same or substantially the same investment within 30 days either before or after the tax swap sale. The IRS will disallow a tax deduction for a capital loss on the grounds that it came from a wash sale if a mutual fund investor purchases shares in the same fund he or she sold within 30 days on either side of the date of sale. The investor must either reinvest in a different fund or wait 31 days to reinvest in the same fund.

This raises the question why you would want to repurchase shares in such a poorly performing fund, but remember that the loss in value could result from a general drop in the market. If you believe that the fund remains a sound investment, you may well want to maintain that position. If so, the law will allow you to park the money in a money market fund for the obligatory 31 days, after which you can repurchase your shares and deduct the capital loss. If the fund's performance seems unlikely to turn around, you can simply reinvest in a different fund.

SUMMARY

Investment companies fall into one of three classes: closed-end investment companies (publicly traded funds), unit investment trusts, and open-end investment companies (mutual funds). Closed-end investment companies issue stock to the public and then invest the proceeds of the stock issue in portfolios of securities. Shares in closed-end funds trade on the various stock exchanges just like shares in industrial companies. This means their values react to supply and demand, so closed-end investment company shares may sell at discounts or premiums to their net asset values.

Many large brokerage firms sponsor unit investment trusts. These unmanaged funds almost always invest in debt securities, which they hold until maturity and seldom trade. They pay out income earned on their investments to trust certificate holders as they earn it and then distribute the principal amount upon maturity.

Mutual funds, or open-end investment companies, hold the bulk of assets owned by investment companies. The term *open-end* reflects the fact that they constantly sell and redeem shares at their net asset values. The net asset value of a mutual fund changes daily as the total value of the securities in its portfolio changes. Investors purchase shares in a no-load fund directly from its sponsor, which charges no commissions on purchases or sales, selling and redeeming shares at their net asset value.

A load fund charges commissions, selling shares at an offering price that exceeds the fund's net asset value. The difference between the net asset value and the offering price represents the commission, or load, the fund pays to brokerage firms that sell its shares. This load may reach 8.5 percent of the offering price. Low-load funds charge less than the maximum commission. Funds may also assess redemption fees (back-end loads) or 12b-1 fees to cover sales and marketing expenses. Both load and no-load funds also charge management fees to compensate fund managers.

Mutual funds allow investors to achieve two important goals that they would find difficult on their own: Through their fund shares, investors own parts of broadly diversified portfolios of securities, and they receive the benefit of the experience and talent of professional investment managers at low cost. Individual mutual funds pursue a wide variety of investment objectives and practice a range of techniques, so an individual investor should have no trouble finding a fund that suits his or her goals and tastes. Classifying funds by their objectives, the most common types include maximum capital gain funds, growth funds, emerging growth funds, growth and income funds, specialty funds, global funds, international funds, income funds, balanced funds, municipal bond funds, and money market funds. A single organization may sponsor many different kinds of funds that together make up a mutual fund family.

Three principles should guide investors' use of mutual funds: diversification, dollar cost averaging, and performance monitoring. Besides enjoying the diversification offered by participation in a mutual fund portfolio, an investor should buy shares in a number of different mutual funds to diversify among different classes of securities and investment strategies. Dollar cost averaging dictates that an investor should buy fixed dollar amounts of mutual fund shares at regular intervals, usually monthly or quarterly. Investors must monitor the performance of their mutual fund investments and replace those funds that have failed to perform as expected.

Federal and state laws regulate mutual funds' operations more closely than those of most business entities. Four major federal statutes regulate mutual funds: the Securities Act of 1933, the Securities Exchange Act of 1934, the Investment Advisors Act of 1940, and the Investment Company Act of 1940 (as amended in 1970).

Virtually all mutual funds elect to be treated as regulated investment companies under federal tax law. This allows the fund to avoid paying taxes on income from dividends, interest, or capital gains as long as it passes 90 percent of all of this income through to fund shareholders. Shareholders then pay taxes on the income and capital gains, regardless of whether they take the gains in cash or reinvest them. Shareholders pay capital gains tax on any capital gains dividends the fund pays, as well as on any capital gains they realize by selling shares. Any capital losses on shares offset capital gains and/or ordinary income, provided investors observe the rules that govern tax swaps.

INVESTMENT MANAGEMENT CONCEPTS

1. Closed-end investment companies trade on securities exchanges and invest their shareholders' assets in the securities of other companies.

2. Closed-end shares usually trade at a discount, but may move to a premium when optimism is high or supply of a particular type of fund is tight.

3. Unit investment trusts normally hold unmanaged portfolios of debt securities, since the trust managers hold the securities until they mature rather than actively trading them in search of profits.

4. Load mutual funds charge commissions when investors purchase shares; no-load funds charge no front-end commissions. Funds may also assess redemption fees or 12b-1 fees as an alternate method of paying commissions to salespersons. Investors must read prospectuses carefully in order to understand all charges and expenses.

5. Investors gain two major advantages from investing in investment companies: broad diversification and professional management at a reasonable cost.

6. With such a broad variety of mutual fund types available, just about any investor can find a collection of funds that will meet his or her investment needs.

7. A mutual fund investor should invest in a diversified list of funds that meet his or her goals and use dollar cost averaging to build a portfolio of funds.

8. Mutual fund investors should carefully review the investment performance of mutual funds they own at least monthly.

9. Investors must pay taxes on dividends mutual funds pay them in the year they receive the dividends, whether they take cash or reinvest this money.

10. Year-end tax swaps allow investors to sell losing investments, take capital loss deductions, and then reinvest the proceeds of the sales in other assets.

REVIEW QUESTIONS

1. What is the difference between a closed-end investment company and an open-end investment company?

2. How do closed-end investment companies use leverage?

3. What is the net asset value of an investment company?

4. Do closed-end funds normally trade at discounts or premiums to their net asset values?

5. What is a unit investment trust?

6. What is the difference between a no-load and a load mutual fund?

7. What are redemption fees and 12b-1 fees?

8. What is a low-load fund?

9. What is a management fee?

10. Describe three sources of information on mutual funds.

11. What are the two major advantages of investing in mutual funds and closed-end investment companies?

12. Briefly describe the eleven different categories of mutual funds described in the chapter.

13. What is a mutual fund family?

14. How does dollar cost averaging work?

15. Where can an investor obtain current performance data to monitor the formance of mutual funds?

16. What are blue sky laws?

17. What four major federal statutes regulate mutual fund operations?

18. Describe the tax treatment of regulated investment companies.

19. If you elect to reinvest all of your dividends in a fund, when must you pay tax on these dividend payments?

20. What is year-end tax swapping?

21. How does the wash sale rule apply to tax swapping?

SELF-CORRECTING PROBLEMS

1. Dr. Melvin Vogel retired recently from the staff of a large urban hospital. In addition to income from his hospital pension plan and Social Security, Dr. Vogel can meet his needs in retirement from approximately $750,000 he has invested over the years in bank CDs. Dr. Vogel has become dissatisfied, however, with the relatively low returns on his CDs, and he wants some potential for capital growth. He has decided to invest in a group of conservative mutual funds, with 40 percent of his money in stock funds and 60 percent in bond funds. Design a conservative portfolio for Dr. Vogel, using at least five of the funds listed in Exhibit 14.6.

2. Nicholas Carosi and his wife, both in their early 40s, both work to support themselves and their three teenaged children. Through careful saving, they have accumulated approximately $100,000 that they would like to invest for long-term growth to help keep them comfortable in retirement in about 25 years. Their long time horizon allows them to tolerate the risk of investing at least 80 percent of their portfolio in stocks and the remaining 20 percent in bonds. Design a portfolio for the Carosis.

Answers to Self-Correcting Problems

1. To avoid the risk of putting all of his money into the stock or bond market at a bad time, Dr. Vogel should invest approximately $75,000 per month over the next ten months in the following funds:

Stock Funds	
20th Century Growth	$100,000
Vanguard 500 Portfolio	100,000
Scudder International	100,000
Bond Funds	
Vanguard Fixed GNMA	100,000
Fidelity Government Securities	100,000
Vanguard Limited Term Municipal	100,000
Fidelity Limited Term Municipal	150,000
Total	$750,000

2.

Stock Funds	
Janus Fund	$ 20,000
20th Century Growth	20,000
Vanguard 500 Fund	20,000
Rowe Price International	20,000
Bond Funds	
Vanguard Intermediate Municipal	10,000
Fidelity High Yield Municipal	10,000
Total	$100,000

SELECTED READINGS

American Association of Individual Investors. *The Individual Investor's Guide to No-Load Mutual Funds,* 10th ed. Chicago: Probus Publishing, 1991.

Andersen, Carl E., and James B. Ross. *Modern Mutual Fund Families and Variable Life.* Homewood, Ill.: Dow Jones-Irwin, 1988.

Cappiello, Frank. *The Complete Guide to Closed-End Funds: Finding Value in Today's Stock Market,* 3d ed. Chicago: Probus Publishing, 1991.

Dorf, Richard C. *The Mutual Fund Portfolio Planner: A Guide for Selecting the Best Funds for You in Today's Market.* Chicago: Probus Publishing, 1988.

Droms, William G. *The Dow Jones-Irwin Mutual Fund Yearbook, 1985.* Homewood, Ill.: Dow Jones-Irwin, 1985.

Haslem, John A. *The Investor's Guide to Mutual Funds.* Englewood Cliffs, N.J.: Prentice-Hall, 1988.

Investment Companies. New York: Wiesenberger Financial Services, 1990.

chapter 15

Life Insurance As an Investment Asset

David and Audrey Walker are a typical two-income couple with small children. They have a 10-year-old son, who is currently in fourth grade, and daughter, age 13, in the eighth grade. Audrey works full-time as a legal assistant in a large downtown law firm, where her job occasionally requires overtime and even Saturday or Sunday work two or three times a year. David is the branch manager of the local bank in the suburbs where the Walkers live. Fortunately the bank is close to where the children go to school, so David is available for those inevitable emergencies that arise when one of the children is ill or when school closes early. At this point in their lives, David and Audrey have come to the conclusion that increasing financial commitments such as their home mortgage and child-rearing expenses make it absolutely necessary that they both continue to work full-time. They also realize that they need to be prepared for the financial consequences if both of them are not available to produce income for the family. They are both adequately covered by disability income insurance at work, but feel that their life insurance coverages are much too low to replace the lost income of a deceased spouse. Therefore, they are looking hard at what products are available from the life insurance industry.

At the same time they reviewed their insurance, the Walkers also began to worry about their long-run investment planning.

The authors express their particular thanks to Ben G. Baldwin, CLU, ChFC, CFP, of Baldwin Financial Systems, and Andrew E. Gross, CLU, ChFC, CFP, of Dennis M. Gurtz and Associates for their careful review of this chapter and for their many beneficial suggestions.

Audrey felt that life insurance served an important purpose in addition to income replacement of a deceased spouse. It also offered protection of the surviving spouse's existing net worth because savings and investments would not have to be spent to replace lost income. David suggested that if they were going to get involved with paying regular insurance premiums, they should look into using their life insurance as a systematic investment program as well as income replacement. Both David and Audrey were persuaded by some articles they had read concerning the many new kinds of life insurance policies that offer investment opportunities. After learning more about these policies, they decided to buy one policy for Audrey that accumulated cash values in a common stock account, and one policy for David that accumulated cash values in a bond account. They did not put a lot of money into either policy, but they did purchase enough insurance to cover their potential financial needs and to help them accumulate some investment capital over a long period of time by making systematic payments into their policies.

Introduction

Most American families own some type of life insurance. Life insurance has always served as an important financial asset, protecting dependents from financial hardship caused by the premature death of a family breadwinner. During the last ten years, however, a whole range of new life insurance products have emerged to propel yesterday's financial safety net into a new status as a competitive investment medium. New tax laws and the proliferation of investment-oriented life insurance products such as universal life, variable life, variable-universal life, and single-premium life have added many new options, but also much new complication, to the life insurance decision.

This chapter will provide guidelines to determine how much life insurance an individual needs. It will also discuss ways to meet that need at a reasonable cost, explaining the various types of life insurance policies now available and their use as investment vehicles. The proper type and amount of life insurance can minimize overall financial expenditures, protect loved ones from the threat of financial hardship, and increase net worth.

Life Insurance Goals

The primary purpose of life insurance is to provide a sum of tax-free money should the insured person die. This money may help surviving dependents replace income that person would have provided to support those dependents, and it may also cover expected estate taxes or replace income a business might lose due to the death of a key employee. Most people's need for life insurance depends primarily on whether other people depend on them for support.

Traditionally, life insurance has replaced the income of a family's primary wage earner. It also commonly replaces the lost services of a spouse who is not employed outside of the home, helping to meet the major expenses of child care, cooking, cleaning, and so forth, which could become a serious burden for a surviving widow or widower who had relied upon these services. Insurance becomes doubly important for couples like David and Audrey who both work to support the family.

A young, single person with no dependents probably needs little, if any, life insurance, unless some personal situation, such as likely estate taxes on personal assets, creates a special need. At the other end of the age spectrum, an older, retired person who has accumulated substantial assets over the years probably would not require a large amount of life insurance to replace income. The desire to plan to pay estate taxes can, however, become more important for such a person.

premium payment: The amount of money the owner of an insurance policy pays the insurance company to keep the policy in force.

A life insurance salesperson may suggest that a young person buy life insurance early solely to take advantage of lower premium payments insurers charge young people. (The **premium payment** is the amount of money a policy owner pays the insurance company to keep a policy in force.) This generally is not a valid argument. Although insurers do charge lower premiums to cover young people, the insurance will require premium payments for longer periods of time, assuming normal life expectancies. Though a young person pays a smaller average annual premium, he or she will probably pay about the same total amount as would a person who waited until the need for life insurance actually arose.

Some advisers encourage people who have no need to protect dependents to buy investment-oriented life insurance as a means of forced savings. Life insurance gives poor results as a savings medium alone. Anyone can find a number of better ways to save. Those who actually need life insurance can use their policies to promote savings or investment goals, but life insurance should never be purchased solely as a savings or investment medium.

In addition to life insurance, individuals also must plan for coverage by medical and dental insurance, disability insurance, liability insurance, homeowner's insurance, auto insurance, and perhaps other types of insurance. Allocating appropriate portions of one's budget among insurance purchases requires careful planning, with the overall goal of providing an adequate amount of all types of insurance at a reasonable cost.

Determining how much life insurance an individual needs can require extensive analysis, or the answer can seem obvious. Someone may need no life insurance at all if he or she supports no dependents and has sufficient net worth to cover funeral expenses, estate taxes, and other final expenses. Someone who plans to pay funeral expenses from life insurance proceeds may need only a small policy. If, however, other people depend on a person's income for support, the answer gets a bit complicated. A detailed needs analysis will resolve this question, or a very simple shortcut technique may suffice.

Multiples of Salary

The shortcut technique determines the amount of life insurance a person requires by reference to a simple rule of thumb. As a rough approximation, financial planning experts estimate that family members can maintain their standard of living following the death of a breadwinner if their annual income does not fall below approximately 75 percent of their income before the death. They would likely suffer a major reduction in their standard of living if their income declined to less than 60 percent of what they earned prior to the death. This gives a rough guideline that someone who supports dependents should maintain an insurance policy in the amount necessary to replace 60 to 75 percent of his or her income.

This simple rule gets more complicated when the person must estimate the lump sum necessary to replace the missing income. To keep the decision simple, he or she could set some spending rule, assuming, for example, that the family will spend 8 percent of the insurance policy's principal amount each year. This expectation seems reasonable in light of the extensive data on rates of return available to long-term investors presented in Chapter 6.

Exhibit 15.1 shows one way to solve this problem using the 8 percent annual spending rule. Suppose, for example, that a person supported a family on an income of $60,000. This person should buy insurance to replace annual income between $36,000 (60 percent of $60,000) and $45,000 (75 percent). To do this, the policy should pay between $450,000 (since 8 percent of $450,000 equals $36,000) and $562,500 (since 8 percent of $562,500 equals $45,000).

Exhibit 15.1 assumes that the family would rely on the insurance policy to meet all of its income needs. In reality, a surviving family would probably benefit from some combination of Social Security income, private pension income, other payments from the deceased person's employer, and income on personal savings. The planner could, therefore, interpret the amounts in Exhibit 15.1 as maximum limits, adjusting the final policy amount downward for the impact of other benefits.

Considerable guesswork underlies these figures. Developing a reliable estimate of a particular family's need for life insurance requires completing a thorough needs analysis that takes all of the specific characteristics of the situation into account.

Needs Analysis for Insurance Planning

For someone who does not want to invest the time required for a thorough needs analysis, the multiples-of-salary rule certainly gives a better

EXHIBIT 15.1

Life Insurance Income Replacement Chart

CURRENT ANNUAL EARNINGS BEFORE TAXES	ANNUAL INCOME REPLACED		FACE AMOUNT OF LIFE INSURANCE WITH 8 PERCENT SPENDING LIMIT	
	75 PERCENT	60 PERCENT	75 PERCENT	60 PERCENT
$ 20,000	$ 15,000	$ 12,000	$ 187,500	$ 150,000
40,000	30,000	24,000	375,000	300,000
60,000	45,000	36,000	562,500	450,000
80,000	60,000	48,000	750,000	600,000
100,000	75,000	60,000	937,500	750,000
120,000	90,000	72,000	1,125,000	900,000
140,000	105,000	84,000	1,312,500	1,050,000
160,000	120,000	96,000	1,500,000	1,200,000
180,000	135,000	108,000	1,687,500	1,350,000
200,000	150,000	120,000	1,875,000	1,500,000

idea of needs than no planning at all. Unfortunately, this shortcut does not always lead to an appropriate life insurance plan because most families have some special requirements or circumstances that make them different from the typical family of four that most insurance rules of thumb assume. A truly effective life insurance plan requires detailed needs analysis to ensure that it will meet specific financial needs.

A needs analysis attempts to identify all the financial obligations that life insurance proceeds would have to meet to effectively replace a person's income. This analysis reviews the entire range of financial goals and needs. To illustrate this technique, the following pages will explain a needs analysis for Andy and Annette, a married couple with two children.

Andy is 35 years old and currently earns $40,000 per year. Annette is 33 years old; she currently devotes full time to raising their children, six-year-old Arthur and two-year-old Anne. Andy and Annette owe $75,000 on the mortgage against the family's home. They have approximately $15,000 in liquid savings and investments, and consumer debt totaling $6,000, most of it concentrated in an automobile loan. Andy owns a $125,000 life insurance policy purchased through his employer.

Exhibit 15.1 suggests that Andy should carry $300,000 to $375,000 worth of life insurance. Before he commits a large portion of the family budget to life insurance premiums, Andy wants to verify or adjust this figure through a careful needs analysis, as summarized in Exhibit 15.2.

Step One: Family Income Needs

The family's first and largest need, should Andy die, would be to provide a lifetime income for Annette and the children. The second-largest need

EXHIBIT 15.2

Summary of Life Insurance Needs Analysis for Andy

1. Present value of family income needs	
a. $24,000 per year for 57 years[a]	
($24,000) (26.8)	$643,200
b. Less Social Security survivors' benefits for 16 years	
($9,600) (16)	(153,600)
c. Less Annette's earnings for 20 years	
($12,000) (20)	(240,000)
d. Less Annette's Social Security retirement benefits, age 65–90	
($4,800) (25)	(120,000)
Net family income needs	$129,600
2. Debt liquidation	
Consumer debt	6,000
Home mortgage	75,000
3. Final expenses and estate tax	20,000
4. Emergency fund	10,000
5. College fund	70,000
6. Total needs	$310,600
Less current savings and investment	(15,000)
Total insurance needs	$295,600

[a]Assumes a 3 percent rate of return after inflation.

for which they must plan is paying the home mortgage—they want to have enough insurance money either to pay off the mortgage or to set up a separate investment fund that would generate income to pay mortgage payments. The choice between these two alternatives would depend upon current interest rates when the need arose. If Annette could invest the money at a higher interest rate than the interest rate on the mortgage, she should set up the investment fund. If the mortgage rate were to exceed the rate an investment would pay, then she should simply pay off the mortgage. For planning purposes, Andy and Annette resolve this uncertainty by assuming they will pay off the mortgage with the insurance proceeds. Annette would decide which option to take if and when the need arose.

Assuming there will be no mortgage payments to make, Andy and Annette have agreed that she and the children could maintain their current standard of living on 60 percent of the family's current gross income, or $24,000 per year (60 percent of $40,000). To ensure that Annette can count on this amount of income over her entire lifetime, the needs analysis assumes that she will live to age 90, so she will require $24,000 per year for as long as 57 years.

EXHIBIT 15.3

Abbreviated Annuity Table

	RATE OF RETURN ON INVESTMENT			
YEARS	3 PERCENT	6 PERCENT	8 PERCENT	10 PERCENT
10	8.5%	7.4%	6.7%	6.1%
15	11.9	9.7	8.6	7.6
20	14.9	11.5	9.8	8.5
25	17.4	12.8	10.7	9.1
30	19.6	13.8	11.3	9.4
35	21.4	14.4	11.6	9.6
40	23.1	15.0	11.9	9.8
45	24.4	15.4	12.1	9.8
50	25.7	15.8	12.2	9.9
55	26.4	16.0	12.3	9.9
57	26.8	16.1	12.3	9.9
60 (or more)	27.7	16.2	12.4	10.0

Two factors complicate the calculation of the lump sum required to provide $24,000 per year for the next 57 years. The family would need the total of $24,000 times 57 years, or $1,368,000, only if they could not invest the proceeds of the insurance policy over the 57 years so it would produce no rate of return at all. Annette would obviously invest the amount of any insurance proceeds that she did not need immediately. The actual lump sum the family needs equals the amount of money which, when invested at an assumed rate of return, would be sufficient to provide $24,000 per year for 57 years. When Annette withdrew $24,000 each year, however, she would take part of the principal and part of the interest earned on the principal so she would exhaust the total of the principal and interest at the end of 57 years.

Annuity tables like the abbreviated version in Exhibit 15.3 can help solve this problem and determine the amount of money the family would need to provide an annual income for a certain number of years. The exhibit shows the number of dollars they must invest at a given rate of return in order to provide one dollar per year of income for a given number of years. Recall from Chapter 6 that this number is called an **annuity factor.** The exhibit lists an annuity factor for 30 years at 6 percent of 13.8. This means that $13.80 invested at a 6 percent rate of return would provide $1 per year for the next 30 years. Over the course of the 30 years, the owner would withdraw a total of $30 from the original $13.80 investment: $13.80 principal and $16.20 in interest earned during the 30 years. To state this another way, $13.80 is the present value of $1 per year for 30 years at 6 percent.

annuity factor: The number of dollars one must invest at a given rate of return to provide $1 in annual income for a given number of years.

Inflation also complicates the effort to provide $24,000 per year for 57 years. The $24,000 per year will maintain Annette and the children's current standard of living for a while, but over time inflation would seriously erode the purchasing power of this money, that is, the amount of goods and services it would buy. During the 1980s, the purchasing power of the dollar declined by about one-half. In 1990, a person needed about $2 to buy what $1 would buy ten years earlier.

The family should plan to provide the same purchasing power each year that $24,000 currently has, and this would require a larger lump sum than simply providing the set amount of money annually. In the language of life insurance planning, the family needs the **purchasing power equivalent** of $24,000 per year for 57 years. The purchasing power equivalent is the amount of future dollars needed to buy the same quantity of goods and services at future (normally higher) prices that a given sum in current dollars can buy. To determine the lump sum required to produce the purchasing power equivalent, return to the annuity table in Exhibit 15.3.

purchasing power equivalent: The amount of future dollars needed to buy a quantity of goods and services that a current dollar will buy.

Results of this calculation will vary widely, depending on the rate of return selected. At a rate of return of 10 percent, $9.90 of investment capital will provide $1.00 per year for 57 years. On the other hand, at a rate of return of 3 percent, it will take $26.80 in investment capital to provide the same stream of income. Since this choice has such a strong effect on the results of the analysis, the family must estimate the rate of return at which they can expect to invest the life insurance proceeds with great care.

Andy and Annette want to provide the equivalent of $24,000 in annual purchasing power. To adjust for inflation, they should select their rate of return as the difference between the actual rate of return they expect to earn and the expected rate of inflation. This will provide enough investment capital to generate income with a constant amount of purchasing power.

Andy and Annette think that conservative investment of the life insurance proceeds should produce a 9 percent long-run rate of return. They also expect a 6 percent long-run inflation rate. Therefore they will assume a real rate of return of 3 percent to determine the amount of investment capital they will need to provide $24,000 in purchasing power per year over 57 years. In effect, they assume that Annette could invest the proceeds of Andy's insurance to produce a rate of return that exceeds the rate of inflation by 3 percent. They multiply the 3 percent annuity factor, 26.8, by 24,000 to arrive at a required lump sum of $643,200. This lump sum is about 45 percent of the sum they would require if the investment capital earned no real rate of return at all.

Long-term planning like that necessary for life insurance requires some difficult estimates. The sample estimates of 9 percent return on investment and 6 percent inflation represent long-term trends rather than cyclical highs or lows. Historical evidence supports the estimate of a 3 percent real rate of return as a reasonable planning bench mark.

Impact of Social Security Fortunately Andy and Annette need not rely on life insurance alone to provide the entire $643,200 lump sum the family needs. Annette would provide part of the family's income by returning to work if Andy should die. Social Security benefits payable to surviving spouses and dependent children would also contribute. In fact, such benefits would provide nearly $300,000 over Annette's lifetime.

This amount would consist of three benefit payments, one to the surviving spouse and a separate payment for each child. Each child's benefit would continue until he or she reached age 16. The surviving spouse's benefit continues until the youngest child reaches 18 years of age. The amount Social Security would pay would depend on how long and how much the deceased spouse paid into the Social Security system. Upon request at a local Social Security office, the agency will determine the amount due to a person's survivors at the time of the request.

Social Security does not pay benefits automatically, however; survivors must file claims with the Social Security Administration. Heads of households should make certain that their survivors understand the need to file claims to receive their benefits.

The Social Security system provides death, disability, and retirement benefits that are exempt from income tax up to certain income levels. These payments can sum to quite substantial amounts. Details of eligibility rules and exact determination of the amounts due to individuals require consultation with Social Security experts. The Social Security Administration explains some of these details in publications it offers through its local offices. A list appears at the end of this chapter. To obtain the address of a local office, look in the telephone directory under Social Security Administration or inquire at any post office.

You can obtain a report of earnings credited to the account under your Social Security number by phoning your local Social Security Administration office to request a short questionnaire. After you provide the necessary information to the Social Security Administration, it will return an accurate computerized Personal Earnings and Benefit Estimate Statement. Exhibit 15.4 provides an example of lists the approximate monthly Social Security benefits payable to survivors of covered workers.

On the basis of the time over which Andy and Annette have paid Social Security payments and the amount they have paid (through paycheck deductions under the heading "FICA"), Annette could expect to receive approximately $9,600 per year for the next 16 years. The amount of these payments would begin to decline after 12 more years, when the couple's older child, Arthur, would reach 18 years old and his benefits would terminate. Still, they should base their insurance needs analysis on the $9,600 approximation since forecasting further into the future would involve extreme uncertainty.

After 14 years, the younger child, Anne, would reach age 16, and Annette's surviving-spouse Social Security benefit would end. After 2 more

EXHIBIT 15.4

Approximate Monthly Social Security Survivors' Benefits

WORKER'S AGE	WORKER'S FAMILY	DECEASED WORKER'S EARNINGS IN YEAR BEFORE DEATH $10,000	$15,000	$20,000	$25,000	$30,000	$35,000	$43,800 OR MORE
25	Spouse and one child[a]	$668	$ 864	$1,060	$1,226	$1,318	$1,410	$1,572
	Spouse and two children[b]	717	1,073	1,263	1,432	1,539	1,646	1,834
	One child only	334	432	530	613	659	705	786
	Spouse at age 60	318	412	505	584	628	672	749
35	Spouse and one child	662	856	1,048	1,220	1,310	1,400	1,516
	Spouse and two children	706	1,046	1,252	1,424	1,529	1,635	1,769
	One child only	331	428	524	610	655	700	758
	Spouse at age 60	316	408	500	581	624	667	722
45	Spouse and one child	662	854	1,046	1,216	1,286	1,332	1,384
	Spouse and two children	705	1,054	1,251	1,420	1,502	1,555	1,616
	One child only	331	427	523	608	643	666	692
	Spouse at age 60	315	407	499	579	613	635	660
55	Spouse and one child	660	866	1,046	1,194	1,242	1,272	1,306
	Spouse and two children	703	1,067	1,250	1,395	1,451	1,485	1,524
	One child only	330	433	523	597	621	636	653
	Spouse at age 60	315	412	498	569	592	606	622
65	Spouse and one child	638	824	1,012	1,152	1,194	1,224	1,256
	Spouse and two children	682	1,021	1,206	1,345	1,395	1,429	1,468
	One child only	319	412	506	576	597	612	628
	Spouse at age 60	304	393	482	549	570	583	599

[a]Amounts shown also equal benefits paid to two children if no parent survives, or if surviving parent has substantial earnings.

[b]Maximum family benefit.

Note: The accuracy of these estimates depends on the pattern of the worker's earnings in prior years.

SOURCE: "Social Security: How It Works for You," U.S. Department of Health and Human Services.

widow's blackout period: The period of time after children reach age 16, when Social Security surviving spouse benefits end, and retirement age, when retirement benefits begin.

years, Anne would reach age 18 and her benefit payments would stop as well. Annette would become eligible for Social Security benefits again when she reached retirement age under the retirement provisions of that program. The period between the time she would lose surviving spouse benefits and the time she would become eligible for retirement benefits is often called the **widow's blackout period.** During this time Social Security pays no benefits to a surviving spouse.

Annette's Social Security retirement benefits would also reduce the family's need for insurance since they would provide additional income in her later years. Annette expects to return to work in about 12 years, when

Anne reaches the age of 14. At that time Annette will be 45 years old. She expects to work until age 65 and then retire. The Social Security payments she will make over this time should entitle her to retirement benefits of approximately $4,800 per year for the remainder of her life.

Therefore, to determine the family's life insurance needs, they must subtract the total of surviving spouse and retirement benefits from their original estimate of the lump sum ($643,200) they would need to supply income if Andy should die. They need not adjust the Social Security benefits for purchasing power changes because these payments automatically increase to keep pace with inflation under current law.

Finally, the family must deduct the total amount of Annette's expected earnings when she goes back to work at age 45 from their total income needs. Annette expects to earn the equivalent of $12,000 per year in current purchasing power upon returning to work. She anticipates receiving annual salary increases to keep pace with inflation. This annual income would total to $240,000 over the 20 years she expects to work.

Deducting Social Security benefits and Annette's income from the original $643,200 needs estimate gives the amount of life insurance necessary to meet the family's need for income if Andy should die prematurely. Based on the figures in Exhibit 15.2, Andy and Annette finally determine that Andy's policy would have to provide $129,600 for this purpose.

Step Two: Debt Liquidation

After providing sufficient income, Andy and Annette's life insurance plan proceeds to the next major goal: establishing a fund to either liquidate the family's indebtedness or to make required future debt payments. Almost every plan should assume liquidating small amounts of consumer debt, since high interest rates on such debt would almost certainly exceed rates of return on investments that could provide income to make payments. The decision whether or not to pay off a home mortgage, as noted previously, depends upon relative interest rates at the time. For planning purposes, Andy and Annette assume that she would pay off the mortgage in full, but she could change her mind if interest rates at the time made the alternative more profitable.

The total the family would need to liquidate debt seems like a large amount of money, but their total income covers payments quite reasonably. Their few small charge accounts and automobile loan give a total consumer indebtedness of $6,000. Adding the $75,000 home mortgage debt brings the total required for debt liquidation to $81,000.

Step Three: Final Expenses and Estate Taxes

Andy and Annette have budgeted a total of $20,000 for funeral arrangements, administrative expenses to distribute his estate, and estate taxes. Current tax law excludes a certain amount of an estate from taxation. To reach a level that would exceed this exclusion and require an allowance for estate tax, Andy's estate would have to grow substantially in the future.

Step Four: Emergency Fund

Andy and Annette want to ensure that the family would have an adequate fund of liquid assets available to meet unexpected emergencies. As a general rule, most people should keep three to six months' net income in such a fund. Andy has allocated $10,000 for this purpose.

Step Five: College Fund

Andy and Annette hope to send both of their children to four-year colleges. Based on current college costs, they have planned to spend about $35,000 for each child, or a total of $70,000. The actual costs may total more or less than this amount depending upon a number of factors, such as whether the children attend private or public colleges, receive scholarship assistance, or work part-time and during summers while they attend college. By the time the children attend college, college costs will have risen. However, the family could invest the total education allowance to earn a rate of return that would match inflation, so the $70,000 fund should provide adequate purchasing power to send the children to college if they attend a public college or receive scholarship assistance at a private college.

Step Six: Total Insurance Needs

As the sixth and final step in the needs analysis, Andy and Annette total the needs they outlined in Steps one through five and deduct any current savings and investments with which they could meet these needs. Their total needs add up to $310,600. They currently have $15,000 in savings and investments, so they need $295,600 in life insurance. Since Andy's employer provides a policy for $125,000, he should purchase additional insurance in the amount of approximately $170,000.

In addition to this insurance on Andy, the family also needs insurance on Annette. If Annette were to die before the children were old enough to care for themselves, Andy would have to purchase child-care services for the children. Also the time pressures of his job would leave very little time to devote to housekeeping, so he would have to hire a full-time housekeeper to look after himself and the children. Obviously, a full-time housekeeper cannot replace a wife and mother, but the housekeeper could at least provide some of the services required to keep the house running.

Three factors most critically affect the determination of the cost of child care and housekeeping services. First, the reduction in the family's expenditures if Annette should die would cover part of the cost of a housekeeper. Second, as the children grow up, they will require progressively less supervision. Third, statistics indicate that most widowers remarry within five years. The decreasing need for child care and the likelihood of Andy remarrying suggest that the family would probably require child care, and perhaps housekeeping, for a relatively short period of time. Based on these considerations, Andy and Annette agree that a $100,000 policy would ensure that the family would have the services it would need in the event of Annette's premature death.

Now that Andy and Annette have carefully determined the amount of insurance they need, they must perform one additional important task. They must decide what type of policy, and which company's policy, to buy.

The Right Kind of Insurance

Life insurance policies have a wide variety of terms and provisions. The heavy sales orientation and strong competition in the insurance industry induce major insurance companies to offer whatever options, combinations, and variations customers want. To simplify the choice among the many types of policies, keep in mind that all insurance protection takes one of two basic forms: **term insurance** (policies that provide only death benefits and do not build any cash values) and **cash-value insurance** (policies that provide death benefits while they build cash values). A clear understanding of the distinction between these two types of insurance will eliminate most of the confusion about buying life insurance.

term insurance: Insurance that provides only death benefits and does not build cash values.

cash-value insurance: Insurance that provides death benefits and builds cash values.

Term Insurance

Term insurance, the easiest type of insurance policy to understand, generally provides the most economical life insurance protection. In a term policy the insurance company agrees to pay a stipulated sum, the **face value** of the policy, to a person named by the policyholder if he or she should die. The policy specifies the person (or persons) the policyholder names to receive this face value as **beneficiaries.** A term policy remains in force for a fixed number of years, the policy's term, after which the policyholder must renew it by paying a new premium to keep the insurance in force. Because the policyholder will be older when the policy comes up for renewal, the renewal premium will be higher than the old premium.

face value: The amount of death benefit a life insurance policy provides.

beneficiary: The person named to receive the face value of a life insurance policy at the death of the insured person.

Insurance professionals generally regard term insurance as a temporary solution to insurance needs, such as providing life insurance protection for a parent until children reach maturity. Unlike cash value insurance, term policies remain in force only for fixed terms rather than over the policyholder's lifetime, although modern policies typically offer a renewal option.

The fixed term and increasing renewal rates give term insurance serious disadvantages. It has one major advantage that makes it attractive to young families: Term insurance offers the largest dollar value of coverage for the lowest cost. Most young, growing families require large amounts of coverage, but they face great pressure on their budgets. Term insurance often represents the only affordable means of providing adequate life insurance for such people.

Term policies generally take four major forms: straight term, renewable term, convertible term, and decreasing term.

Straight Term

straight term insurance: A life insurance policy that provides only a death benefit, and only for a fixed period of time.

A **straight term insurance** policy provides insurance coverage for a fixed number of years, usually 1, 5, 10, 15, or 20 years, or until age 65. These policies usually charge fixed annual premiums over their terms. If the policy expires before the policyholder dies, it has no value. If the policyholder wanted continued insurance coverage, he or she would have to buy a new policy, which would require passing a new physical examination. This creates a risk that the policyholder could no longer obtain a new policy or that he or she could obtain one only at a much higher premium. This risk prevents most people from buying straight term insurance.

Renewable Term

renewable term insurance: A term policy that allows the policyholder to renew at the end of the term without a new medical examination or proof of insurability.

Renewable term insurance gives the policyholder the option of renewing the policy at the end of the term without passing a new medical examination. The premium rises at renewal because the probability that the policyholder will die within the term of the policy increases with age.

A typical policy might remain in force for five years at a fixed premium, and give the policyholder the right to renew it every five years up to some maximum age, usually age 65 or 70. The premium would increase at each renewal, becoming quite expensive in later years, say at age 55 or 60. Renewable term policies can specify other terms, perhaps 10 or 15 years, to keep the premium level for a longer period of time; these have become very popular in recent years. Also, term policies that allow renewal until very late in life, even up to age 95 or 100, are becoming more popular. Nearly all currently issued renewable term policies are also convertible.

Convertible Term

convertible term insurance: A term policy that allows the policyholder to convert it to a cash-value policy with the same face value as the original policy, but a varying term.

Convertible term insurance allows the policyholder to convert the policy to cash value insurance with the same face value as the original policy, regardless of any subsequent health or occupation change. Few term insurance policies sold today lack the option to convert to cash value insurance. In addition, policies rarely separate features of convertibility and renewability; most offer both.

Decreasing Term

decreasing term insurance: A term policy with a level premium and a declining face value.

Decreasing term insurance features a level premium over its life, but the face value declines, increasing the cost per unit of coverage. These policies offer a popular way to pay off a home mortgage in the event of premature death by setting the face value of the policy to decrease at the same rate as the homeowner repays the principal amount of the home mortgage. Such "homeowners insurance" policies offered by mortgage lenders often waive the usual requirement for a physical exam, and many lenders will simply add the premium to the mortgage payment. Although convenient, these policies often are very expensive compared to other types of term policies. The policyholder pays for the convenience.

Cost of Term Insurance

The cost of term insurance, in fact all life insurance, varies widely among companies. Term provides some very useful bench mark costs, however, since it represents the pure cost of insuring someone's life, without the cost of building up any cash value or other features. Exhibit 15.5 shows representative costs for two types of term insurance, as provided by Baldwin Financial Systems, a personal financial planning firm located in Northbrook, Illinois. Column 1 shows the cost of a 3-year nonconvertible, nonrenewable, nonparticipating (no dividends are paid by the company to the policyholder) policy with a face value of $100,000 issued to a male nonsmoker; this represents the pure cost of term insurance without any extra features.

The annual cost per $1,000 of insurance for a nonrenewable and nonconvertible policy increases from $0.58 at age 35 to $10.76 at age 65. In addition to the cost per $1,000 of coverage, a policyholder also would have to pay an annual policy fee of $50 per year. Comparable costs for a female nonsmoker would be slightly lower than those in the table since women live longer than men on average.

Column 2 lists rates for a nonparticipating policy that offers renewal and convertibility features. Most people under most circumstances should prefer this policy. Costs for this policy increase from $1.26 per $1,000 at age 35 up to $16.33 per $1,000 at age 65. A renewable, convertible term insurance policy with a face value of $100,000 would cost a 35-year-old male $126 plus an annual policy fee of $30, for a total cost per year of $156. A 65-year-old male would pay $1,663 for the same amount of coverage, vividly illustrating the main disadvantage of term insurance: the sharp increases in the premium payment as the policyholder's remaining life expectancy decreases. Someone who anticipates a permanent need for insurance may prefer the fixed premium of a cash value insurance policy.

EXHIBIT 15.5

Illustrative Costs of Term Insurance

Face Amount $100,000 Plus, Male Nonsmoker Rates, Costs per $1,000 per Year

Column 1: Limited 3-year term insurance, nonconvertible, nonrenewable, nonparticipating; add $50 per year policy fee

Column 2: Yearly renewable, convertible term, nonparticipating; add $30 per-year policy fee

AGE	COLUMN 1	COLUMN 2	AGE	COLUMN 1	COLUMN 2
35	$0.58	$1.26	51	$2.54	$ 3.68
36	0.59	1.27	52	2.84	3.90
37	0.60	1.28	53	3.15	4.12
38	0.61	1.30	54	3.45	4.34
39	0.63	1.35	55	3.74	4.67
40	0.65	1.42	56	4.23	5.29
41	0.79	1.51	57	4.70	5.95
42	0.93	1.63	58	5.18	6.69
43	1.05	1.78	59	5.65	7.44
44	1.19	1.96	60	6.16	9.55
45	1.32	2.17	61	7.06	10.37
46	1.51	2.42	62	7.98	11.37
47	1.69	2.69	63	8.91	12.59
48	1.88	2.96	64	9.83	14.35
49	2.06	3.21	65	10.76	16.33
50	2.25	3.46			

SOURCE: Baldwin Financial Systems, Northbrook, Illinois.

Cash-Value Insurance

Cash-value life insurance begins with the pure protection of term insurance, then adds other features, most importantly the chance to accumulate a sum of cash over the life of the policy. Specific policy features determine how quickly the cash value builds up and also the size of the premium.

Depending on the structure of the policy, the accumulated cash value may make up part of the death benefit the policy pays to the beneficiary if the policyholder dies, or it may pay the cash value in addition to the face value. Whole life and its variations, universal life, variable life, and universal-variable life, have become the most popular array of cash-value policies available today.

whole life insurance: A life insurance policy that remains in effect at a constant premium over the entire lifetime of the insured, or for some specified number of years.

Whole Life Insurance

Whole life insurance (also called *straight* or *ordinary life*) continues in effect over the entire lifetime of the policyholder, so insurance professionals think of it as permanent insurance. The premium remains the same throughout the insured's lifetime, or for some stipulated number of years. The premium on whole life insurance exceeds the amount necessary to provide insurance coverage alone; the excess builds up a cash value that belongs to the policyholder. Because it accumulates cash value, many people claim that whole life insurance has living benefits as well as death benefits. If the policyholder dies before the policy matures, the beneficiary collects the face value of the policy. If the policyholder lives until the policy matures, he or she can exchange it for its cash value (**surrender** the policy, in insurance terminology).

surrender: The exchange of a cash-value policy for its full or partial cash value.

If the policyholder needs access to the cash in the policy, he or she can terminate the policy at any time and receive its value in cash. If the policyholder wants to keep the policy in force and still have use of its cash value, then he or she can borrow the cash value from the insurance company without submitting to a credit check, repaying the loan at his or her convenience, or perhaps never repaying the loan. If the policyholder dies prematurely, the insurance company simply deducts the accumulated interest and principal of the loan from the policy's death benefit and pays the difference to the beneficiary. As another alternative, the policyholder can exchange the policy for another, smaller policy with fully paid premiums, or for a term insurance policy that will continue in effect for a specified period of time.

In effect, whole life insurance combines life insurance benefits with a forced savings plan. A whole life policy may pay a lower rate of interest on the savings component than the rate of return that alternative investments would earn. To further complicate the insurance decision, calculation of the exact rate of return on the savings component of a life insurance policy is rather difficult, and the results may still remain subject to some dispute.

Although these drawbacks have led many people to view whole life as a poor investment, newer whole life policies often pay market-competitive interest rates and merit consideration as reasonable savings or investment options. Additionally, the interest rates on the savings components of some newer policies change in response to short-term market interest rates. Such a policy may compare favorably to short-term bond funds or money market funds.

Whole life gets its primary advantage from the fact that it remains in force over the entire life of the policyholder for a level, guaranteed premium payment. Many buyers of whole life insurance also like its forced savings aspect, since they feel a stronger compulsion to pay insurance premiums and keep the policy in force than to make regular deposits in a savings program. Although its savings component may (or may not) pay an inferior interest rate compared to some other alternatives, a whole life policy does enforce savings discipline, which many people lack.

Whole life also brings a tax advantage because interest earned on the cash value of the policy is exempt from current taxation. Even if a policyholder surrenders part or all of the policy and withdraws cash values, tax law generally treats the withdrawal as a return of premium payments to the policyholder, so this money, including accumulated interest, creates no tax liability as long as the cash value withdrawn does not exceed the cumulative amount of premiums paid. Beneficiaries also owe no income taxes on proceeds of any life insurance policy that result from the death of the policyholder (unless the policy is legally owned by the beneficiary), although this may generate an estate tax liability, depending upon the size of the deceased person's estate.

The 1986 Tax Reform Act made taxation of life insurance cash values and death benefits extremely complex. Although the general rules noted here hold in most cases, the complete details of these tax laws fall far outside the scope of this book. Any individual who considers investing large sums of money in a life insurance policy, or who receives cash values or death benefits from an insurance policy, should consult a competent tax expert.

The primary disadvantage of whole life insurance comes from the size of its premium payment. This amount can far exceed the premium payment on a term insurance policy with the same face value. To build cash value, a whole life policy generally requires much larger premium payments than a policy that provides only death benefits.

Modified Whole Life

modified whole life: A whole life policy with lower premium payments in early years and higher payments in later years.

Like term insurance, whole life insurance has many variations and combinations. One variation, **modified whole life,** charges lower premium payments in the early years of the policy, usually the first five or ten years, and then higher premiums later to make up the difference. This type of policy combines the lower premiums during the early years that term insurance buyers enjoy with the benefit of permanent insurance that attracts whole life buyers. In effect, modified whole life begins as a term policy to keep costs low initially, and then the savings component grows gradually until the policy becomes normal whole life insurance in the later years. This appeals primarily to young families that expect their incomes to increase over the years.

Limited Payment Life

limited payment life: A whole life policy that requires premium payments only for a fixed term.

Another whole life variation, **limited payment life,** requires premium payments for a fixed term, usually 20 years (called *20 pay life*) or to age 65 (*paid up to age* 65), rather than over an entire lifetime. Even though premium payments stop at some point, the insurance remains in force permanently. Since the policy spreads the same cost over fewer payments, each payment must be larger. This relatively high investment requirement gives limited payment life its primary disadvantage. Most young families would find limited payment life a very poor choice because the premium payments would strain their budgets too much.

Single-Premium Life

single-premium life: A whole life policy with payment of the entire premium in one lump sum.

Single-premium life, an extreme form of limited payment life, is a whole life insurance policy that requires a single, large payment. The insurance company pays an investment return on the one-time cash contribution. Since cash-value earnings on whole life policies escape current income taxes, the industry has marketed this policy primarily as a tax-advantaged investment that also happens to offer some insurance. This caught the attention of Congress, which has imposed some special tax rules on single-premium life policies.

A policyholder must pay income tax on loans and withdrawals from such a policy to the extent of policy earnings. Also, a policyholder must pay a 10 percent penalty for any loan or withdrawal made prior to age 59½. The same penalty applies to premature withdrawals from an IRA account. This new tax treatment, enacted in 1988, has diminished the attractiveness of single-premium life policies for most people.

Universal Life Insurance

universal life insurance: A cash-value life insurance policy that allows flexible premium payments and pays market-competitive interest rates on the cash value.

Universal life insurance is a form of cash-value life insurance that pays a market-competitive interest rate on the cash-value. The interest rate normally changes annually to follow market interest rates. After its introduction in 1979, universal life grew explosively in popularity, with over 1.5 million policies with a total face value of nearly $250 billion sold in the first five years. By the late 1980s, universal life accounted for over one-quarter of the dollar value of new life insurance sold.

Universal life offers flexible premium plans that allow the policyholder to vary the amount or timing of premium payments. Also, the policyholder can change the amount of the death benefit from time to time. As long as premium payments exceed the cost of insurance, cash values accumulate, to be invested in short-term, fixed-income securities, so they earn a current market rate of return. As with other cash value policies, the policyholder owes no current income tax on interest earned on the cash value portion of the policy. He or she can withdraw all or part of the cash value of the policy, also without owing income tax as long as the amount of the withdrawal remains below the total of the premium payments. Universal life gives the same access to cash value through loans that whole life gives.

Certain technical rules limit the exemption from income taxes of death proceeds from universal life policies. The tax law limits the amount of the premium that the policyholder may invest to build cash values. Violation of these limits can cost tax benefits. Be sure to check the tax status of a universal life policy with the agent and a competent tax professional before you buy it.

Variable Life Insurance

variable life insurance: A cash-value life insurance policy with set premiums that allows investment of cash value in a variety of stock, bond, and money market mutual funds.

Introduced in the United States in 1977, **variable life insurance** resembles universal life, but with two major differences. First, the policyholder can invest cash values in a variety of stock, bond, and money market mutual funds instead of in the insurance company's fixed-income portfolio. Second, variable life does not offer the flexible premium schedules of universal life. Instead, it fixes premium payments over the life of the policy, much like traditional whole life policies. Variable life has failed to achieve the popularity of universal life; total universal life coverage in force exceeds that for variable life by approximately ten times.

Variable-Universal Life

variable-universal life: A cash-value life insurance policy that allows investment of cash value in a variety of stock, bond, and money market mutual funds, along with flexible premium payments.

As its name implies, **variable-universal life** combines features of universal life and variable life policies. First introduced in 1985, variable-universal life insurance is the newest of the so-called *inflation-era policies.* Variable-universal life allows flexible premium payments, a flexible face value, and a selection of funds in which to invest cash values.

Selection of universal life and variable-universal life policies requires careful consideration. Some of these policies charge very high commission rates for agents and/or excessive first-year expense deductions. In addition, mutual fund purchases through a variable-univeral life policy could involve commission charges. Finally, if the funds selected for investment of cash values fail to perform well, the cash values will not earn the high returns for which the policyholder hoped. These last two disadvantages may account for much of the relatively low sales of variable-universal life policies as compared to universal life policies.

A variable-universal life insurance policy offers one unique advantage: its prospectus, which details its expenses and the investment strategies and track records of the managers of the various funds available for investing cash values. These policies also offer an important element of protection that others do not. Since the cash values build up in separate accounts, just like a mutual fund, rather than in the general accounts of the insurance company that issues the policy, the cash values remain outside the reach of the insurance company's general creditors, which could save the policyholder from disaster if the insurance company should get into financial difficulty. If the insurance company goes bankrupt, a policyholder's money in the separate accounts belongs to him or her, not to the company's creditors.

Life Insurance Annuity Products

Life insurance companies also offer other investment vehicles. A **life insurance annuity** is a contract issued by an insurance company that promises to pay a specified sum of money for a specified number of years

life insurance annuity: A contract in which an insurance company promises to make a specified stream of payments for a specified number of years to a specified individual.

annuitant: A person who receives life insurance annuity payments.

to a specified individual. The person who receives the annuity payment is called the **annuitant.**

Annuitants commonly purchase annuities with lump sums to provide retirement income. For example, a 65-year-old man could deposit $100,000 into an insurance annuity, which would pay him a guaranteed lifetime income of approximately $1,000 per month at rates that prevailed in the early 1990s. Although the most common use of annuities involves exchanging lump sums for guaranteed lifetime incomes, insurance companies sell many different types of annuities to meet many different investment objectives.

Immediate Annuities

immediate annuity: An annuity funded by a one-time payment with payments beginning immediately.

deferred annuity: A contract that accumulates payments made over time which the insurance company invests for the policyholder to fund annuity payments that begin at some later date.

fixed immediate annuity: An annuity that provides a fixed dollar payment over a fixed number of years.

variable immediate annuity: An annuity with payments that vary depending upon the investment performance of the assets in which the deposits are invested.

Life insurance annuities fall into two major categories, immediate annuities and deferred annuities. The previous paragraph described an **immediate annuity,** a one-time payment that funds future annuity payments for life or for a fixed period of time. Insurance professionals generally refer to immediate annuities as payout vehicles. A **deferred annuity,** on the other hand, is an accumulation vehicle; it accumulates payments that the insurance company invests for the policyholder. The policyholder can make payments into the deferred annuity at regular or irregular intervals or even all at once in a lump sum. Immediate annuities begin making payments immediately, whereas deferred annuities accumulate capital from which they make periodic or lump sum payments at some time in the future.

Both classes of annuities include both fixed and variable annuities. A **fixed immediate annuity** provides a fixed dollar payment over a fixed period of time, perhaps the life of the annuitant or over some number of years, as the annuitant chooses. The payout terms of these policies can vary in many ways. A married couple, for example, could specify that the insurer pay the fixed dollar amount over their joint life spans (i.e., until both spouses died), or for life, but with a fixed number of years guaranteed. A life-with-20-years-guaranteed contract, for example, specifies a fixed payment over the life of the annuitant, but if the annuitant dies before receiving 20 years' payments, the insurer would pay the balance of the remaining payments to a designated beneficiary.

A **variable immediate annuity** contract allows the amount of the annuity payments to vary with the investment performance of the assets in which the annuity deposits are invested. Variable annuity contracts typically invest in common stocks or some combination of common stocks, bonds, and cash equivalents. This contract specifies higher future payments from the annuity in relation to increases in the capital values and dividend and interest payments of the investments underlying the contract. This overcomes the problem caused by the declining purchasing power of the fixed annuity payments as inflation compounds over the life of the annuity. These contracts typically guarantee some minimum payment. A variable annuity brings the rather obvious risk that negative investment returns on the underlying securities can cause the annuity payments to decrease.

Deferred Annuities

single-premium deferred annuity: A deferred annuity purchased with a single payment.

flexible-premium deferred annuity: A deferred annuity that allows additional future payments after the first payment.

accumulation unit: A share in the underlying investment portfolio of an annuity contract, somewhat like shares in a mutual fund.

Deferred annuities help investors accumulate cash values. **Single-premium deferred annuities** pay regular payments of a specified amount for a specified period of time beginning at some future date in exchange for a single, lump sum payment. **Flexible-premium deferred annuities** allow the policyholder to make additional future payments into the policy after the initial deposit. These payments accumulate a balance over time to fund a stream of future annuity payments. The deferred annuities convert to immediate annuities when they begin making either guaranteed or variable annuity payments in the future, so, like immediate annuities, deferred annuities may be either fixed or variable.

The policyholder can choose among a selection of stock and bond portfolios in which to invest cash contributions. Payments into the policy purchase shares, called **accumulation units,** in these investment portfolios in much the same way that investors purchase mutual fund shares.

Potential for growth and tax advantages may make a deferred annuity contract attractive, even to a policyholder who does not intend to convert it to a lifetime income in the future. The annuitant must pay income tax on the earnings in an annuity policy only when he or she withdraws the money, at which time the earnings generate a tax liability as ordinary income. This tax break has a downside, however: The policyholder must pay a 10 percent tax penalty on any withdrawals made before age 59½ just as he or she would with an IRA investment.

This penalty may not apply under certain circumstances, however. The IRS waives the penalty if the policyholder converts the deferred annuity contract to an immediate annuity contract that makes payments over the life of the annuitant or the joint lives of annuitant and spouse. Thus, converting a lump sum accumulated in a deferred annuity into a lifetime income eliminates the 10 percent penalty. This same benefit applies to IRA accounts: An IRA account owner who converts the account into an immediate annuity prior to age 59½ need not pay the normal 10 percent penalty.

Special Types of Insurance Policies

ordinary insurance: A life insurance policy sold directly to an individual by an insurance agent.

Up to this point, the discussion considered only what insurance professionals call **ordinary insurance,** that is, policies sold directly to individuals by insurance agents. Exhibit 15.6 summarizes the most common types of ordinary insurance. In addition to ordinary insurance, two other major varieties of insurance are commonly available. The first of these, group life insurance, represents a very rapidly growing segment of the term life insurance market.

EXHIBIT 15.6

Summary of Ordinary Life Insurance Policies

1. Term insurance
   a. Straight term
   b. Renewable term
   c. Convertible term
   d. Decreasing term

2. Cash-value insurance
   a. Whole life
   b. Modified whole life
   c. Limited payment life
   d. Single-premium life
   e. Universal life
   f. Variable life
   g. Variable-universal life

Group Life Insurance

group life insurance: A life insurance contract an agent sells to a group of individuals, such as all employees of a company or all members of a union.

In contrast to ordinary life insurance, insurers sell **group life insurance** to groups of individuals such as employees of a given organization, members of a professional association, or members of some similar, identifiable group. The group negotiates an insurance contract with an insurer, then its members have the option of purchasing insurance through the group plan. The insurance company issues one master policy to cover the entire group. Each group member who purchases the insurance receives a certificate verifying coverage.

Insurance companies can keep administrative costs for group policies low, so they can offer correspondingly low premium rates to group members, usually significantly lower than the cost of comparable ordinary insurance policies. This gives a group term life policy one of its two major advantages. Although one cannot assume that every group life insurance policy will provide the lowest possible cost, in general, these types of policies generally provide cost-effective coverage.

The second major advantage of group life insurance comes from its elimination of the requirement for physical examinations. This can be a major advantage for someone whose health might cause an insurance company to raise the rates on a policy above the standard rate it would charge a normally healthy individual.

Credit Life Insurance

credit life insurance: Generally high-cost life insurance sold as part of a debt contract.

Borrowers should almost always avoid the second special type of life insurance policy, **credit life insurance,** due to its high cost. Lenders often sell credit life insurance as part of a debt contract, for example, on an automobile loan. This insurance works in much the same way as decreasing term insurance; if the borrower dies before paying off the loan, the credit life insurance retires the debt.

Current consumer protection laws prohibit a lender from requiring a borrower to buy credit life insurance as a condition for granting a loan. If a borrower wants to provide insurance proceeds to pay off a loan separate from normal needs analysis, he or she can almost always buy an ordinary term policy, or increase the face value of an existing policy, for less than the cost of a credit life insurance policy. Credit life does offer one advantage, however, since a borrower with poor health may manage to obtain insurance although insurers would refuse ordinary insurance.

Cost Comparisons

Life insurance policies vary widely in cost depending upon the types of policies and the companies that offer them. Even after allowing for wide cost variations, different features make direct cost comparisons for different policies quite difficult. A 30-year-old man, for example, might expect a premium payment on a five-year renewable term policy to equal about one-third of the premium payment on a whole life policy. This man could obtain about $300,000 worth of term insurance for the same premium payment as a $100,000 whole life policy would require. However, part of the whole life premium builds cash values, which complicates any comparison of the costs of the two policies. However, these factors certainly do not make meaningful cost comparisons impossible. This section of the chapter will examine the most common methods for comparing costs.

Any comparison reveals a major initial premium advantage for term insurance. As the policyholder ages, however, the premium required to renew term insurance becomes quite high. Someone who successfully builds a sufficient net worth by retirement age to provide for survivors may no longer require life insurance coverage. For this reason, many insurance experts advise individuals to buy cash-value insurance only if they anticipate a permanent need for insurance. Such a permanent need might arise from expected taxes on a large estate or to meet a desire to make a major charitable contribution.

Term Insurance versus Cash-Value Insurance

Considering both costs and benefits, which is better, term or cash-value insurance? Opinion is divided. One popular approach to insurance planning counsels, "Buy term and invest the rest." This concept takes advantage of the lower premium on term insurance, assuming that the policyholder will invest the difference between the term and whole life premiums to earn a rate of return higher than the whole life cash-value would earn.

Whether or not the policyholder benefits from the buy-term-and-invest-the-rest strategy over the long run depends on his or her investment results as compared to those available from an insurance contract. Another flaw in this strategy may arise from its assumption that the policyholder will faithfully invest the premium difference and steadfastly resist the temptation to spend the money on something else. The threat of a failure to resist temptation may give cash-value life insurance its strongest advantage.

The policyholder must contribute to a policy's cash-value component as a condition of keeping the life insurance in force. This practically compels saving, and the motivation gains even more force if a universal or whole life policy can provide a market-competitive rate of return. As alternatives, variable or variable-universal life insurance bring the additional opportunity to invest cash values in equity securities that may provide higher returns than interest-bearing securities would.

A cash-value policy softens the potential threat of having to save when an emergency absolutely prevents it by allowing the policyholder to borrow cash values without having to give up the policy. This option gives the policy attractive flexibility.

These arguments complicate resolution of the dispute over term versus cash-value insurance. The decision reduces, at least partially, to a matter of personal preference. This assumes, of course, that a family can afford to make the choice. Most young families simply cannot afford to buy enough cash-value insurance to meet their needs, so term insurance may give them their only practical option. On the other hand, policies that offer market-competitive rates of return can induce a family to consider a cash-value life insurance policy as an important part of their savings and investment programs, combined with insurance protection.

Comparing Costs among Companies

Someone who shops for insurance absolutely must compare costs among companies. Unfortunately, varying methods of quoting prices can confuse such cost comparisons. Also, the company that offers the best value on term insurance may not compete in whole life. One constant guides all cost comparisons: Policy costs will vary extremely widely from company to company.

To begin to compare costs of several policies, separate participating policies from nonparticipating policies. Participating policies rebate part of their premiums in the form of annual dividends. Nonparticipating policies do not rebate any dividends. This may make the participating policy appear to have a higher cost before subtracting dividends. In addition, potential policyholders must allow for wide variations in dividend scales and total accumulations of cash values from a given amount of premiums.

However difficult the process, the informed consumer must compare costs. Fortunately, the insurance industry provides cost comparison indexes that can allow direct comparisons among similar policies issued by various companies. Consumers commonly refer to two comparison indexes: the net payment cost comparison index and the surrender cost comparison index.

Interest-Adjusted Cost Method

Both indexes use the interest-adjusted cost method to calculate values based on the time value of money. Recall that this concept grows from the idea that one can invest a dollar in hand today at some rate of interest to make it grow to much more than a dollar over time. In fact, at an interest rate of 8 percent, $1.00 to be received after ten years has a present value of only $0.46; this means that, at 8 percent interest, $0.46 will grow to $1.00 in ten years.

interest-adjusted cost comparison index: An index number that combines premium payments, dividends, and cash-value buildup into a single number to simplify cost comparisons among similar policies.

Interest-adjusted cost comparison indexes combine a policy's premium payments, dividends, and accumulated cash value into a single index number to show the net cost per $1,000 of life insurance coverage. A lower index number indicates a policy with lower projected costs. The index number calculation assumes that the policyholder could earn some rate of return, usually 5 percent, on money currently in hand. Using this assumed rate of return, the cost comparison index takes into account the time value of money and adjusts for differences in the timing of dividend payments and cash value accumulations. Policy A, for example, may offer a higher cash value after 10 years than Policy B, but Policy B may offer a higher cash value at the end of 20 years.

net payment cost comparison index: An index number of the average yearly net cost per $1,000 of insurance coverage, taking into account premium payments, dividends, and the time value of money.

Net Payment Cost Comparison Index The **net payment cost comparison index** measures a policy's average yearly net cost per $1,000 of insurance protection based on premium payments, dividends, and the time value of money. More specifically, this index shows the net difference between premium payments to the company and dividend payments to the policyholder, adjusted for the time value of money. This time value of money adjustment becomes critical because nearly all participating policies pay increasing dividends over time. Since dividends vary from year to year, the index calculation must assume some number of years. Companies usually calculate indexes for 10 years and 20 years. For a nonparticipating policy, the net payment cost comparison index is based on the annual premium payment, since nonparticipating policies pay no dividends. A policy with a lower net payment index should offer the best value per premium dollar by providing insurance at the lowest yearly net payment.

Keep in mind, however, that insurers do not guarantee dividends, and actual payments have varied greatly in recent years. No one can know for sure that a particular policy offers the best value until after the period under study has passed and cost calculations can use all the actual numbers. Although the net payment cost comparison index provides an excellent guide for comparison, it cannot predict the future flawlessly.

surrender cost comparison index: An index number of the average yearly net cost per $1,000 of insurance coverage, taking into account premium payments, dividends, cash surrender value, and the time value of money.

Surrender Cost Comparison Index The **surrender cost comparison index** extends the net payment cost comparison index to include cash surrender values in its estimate of costs. It reflects the average yearly net cost per $1,000 of insurance protection, based on premium payments, dividends, cash values, and the time value of money. It is most useful for comparing policies that build substantial cash values. In calculating this index, the analyst assumes a policyholder will surrender the policy at the end of 10 or 20 years in exchange for its cash value. A lower index value indicates a better return for premiums paid upon cashing in the policy. Since term policies have no cash surrender value, their surrender cost indexes will match their net payment cost indexes.

Equivalent Level Annual Dividend

equivalent level annual dividend: The annual amount of a level dividend that would provide the same total present value as a stream of increasing annual dividends.

A third measure of life insurance value, the **equivalent level annual dividend,** shows the part dividends play in determining the net cost of a participating policy. The time value of money makes dividend dollars received early in a policy's term more valuable than dividend dollars paid after 5, 10, or 20 years. Since most policies pay increasing dividends over time, this can affect their costs. Variations in the timing of dividend payments suggest a need for some means of comparing future value to present value.

The equivalent level annual dividend shows the level of annual dividend that equates to a stream of increasing dividends. Taking the time value of money into account, the equivalent level annual dividend converts an increasing dividend stream into a constant dividend stream. Adding this level annual value to the net payment cost comparison index gives the total cost of a participating policy before deducting dividends.

Cost Comparison Summary

What final results do these cost comparison indexes imply? The indexes represent a kind of average yearly cost per $1,000 of life insurance protection over 10 or 20 years. A lower index number indicates a better life insurance buy than a similar policy with a higher index number. This requires comparisons between policies that have the same features and conditions (i.e., identical policyholder ages, face values, and other features). More common features among policies allow more reliable cost comparisons. Remember also that a low cost comparison index for one policy does not guarantee similarly low indexes for other policies issued by the same company. In particular, a company that offers low-cost term insurance may not offer low-cost whole life insurance, or vice versa.

The ledger sheet in Exhibit 15.7 gives cost data for a $200,000 whole life policy issued to a 50-year-old man. Since life insurance costs vary widely

EXHIBIT 15.7

Illustrative Ledger Sheet for $200,000 Whole Life Policy

Equitable Life Assurance Society of the United States
Standard Ledger Statement
Whole Life 50

Male nonsmoker age 50 — Face amount: $200,000
Dividends applied to paid-in cash for 40 years — Annual premium: $4,474

END OF YEAR	AGE	GROSS BASE PREMIUM	ANNUAL YEAR-END DIVIDEND	NET PREMIUM	CUMULATIVE NET OUTLAY	GUARANTEED CASH VALUE	TOTAL CASH VALUE	GUARANTEED CASH BENEFIT
1	51	$4,474	$ 0	$4,474	$ 4,747	$ 0	$ 0	$200,000
2	52	4,474	100	4,474	8,948	0	100	200,000
3	53	4,474	212	4,374	13,322	8,600	8,812	200,000
4	54	4,474	554	4,262	17,584	12,800	13,354	200,000
5	55	4,474	1,030	3,920	21,504	17,400	18,430	200,000
6	56	4,474	1,432	3,444	24,948	22,000	23,432	200,000
7	57	4,474	1,764	3,042	27,990	26,600	28,364	200,000
8	58	4,474	2,004	2,710	30,700	31,400	33,404	200,000
9	59	4,474	2,220	2,470	33,170	36,200	38,420	200,000
10	60	4,474	2,434	2,254	35,424	41,200	43,634	200,000
11	61	4,474	3,122	2,040	37,464	46,000	49,122	200,000
12	62	4,474	3,374	1,352	38,816	50,600	54,480	200,000
13	63	4,474	3,636	1,100	39,916	55,400	59,867	200,000
14	64	4,474	3,914	838	40,754	60,200	65,318	200,000
15	65	4,474	4,204	560	41,314	64,800	70,624	200,000
16	66	4,474	4,498	270	41,584	69,600	76,186	200,000
17	67	4,474	4,798	−24	41,560	74,400	81,802	200,000
18	68	4,474	5,102	−324	41,236	79,000	87,262	200,000
19	69	4,474	5,398	−628	40,608	83,800	92,969	200,000
20	70	4,474	5,694	−924	39,684	88,400	98,514	200,000
21	71	4,474	6,474	−1,220	38,464	93,000	104,124	200,000
22	72	4,474	6,804	−2,000	36,464	97,600	109,284	200,000
23	73	4,474	7,146	−2,330	34,134	102,200	114,346	200,000
24	74	4,474	7,496	−2,672	31,462	106,600	119,096	200,000
25	75	4,474	7,836	−3,022	28,440	111,000	123,836	200,000

26	76	4,474	8,158	−3,362	25,078	115,200	128,358	200,000
27	77	4,474	8,444	−3,684	21,394	119,200	132,644	200,000
28	78	4,474	8,686	−3,970	17,424	123,000	136,686	200,000
29	79	4,474	8,886	−4,212	13,212	127,000	140,886	200,000
30	80	4,474	9,060	−4,412	8,800	130,600	144,660	200,000
31	81	4,474	9,238	−4,586	4,214	134,400	148,638	200,000
32	82	4,474	9,426	−4,764	−549	138,000	152,426	200,000
33	83	4,474	9,644	−4,952	−5,501	141,400	156,044	200,000
34	84	4,474	9,890	−5,170	−10,671	144,800	159,690	200,000
35	85	4,474	10,142	−5,416	−16,087	147,800	162,942	200,000
36	86	4,474	10,380	−5,668	−21,755	150,800	166,180	200,000
37	87	4,474	10,594	−5,906	−27,661	153,600	169,194	200,000
38	88	4,474	10,778	−6,120	−33,781	156,400	172,178	200,000
39	89	4,474	10,932	−6,304	−40,085	159,000	174,932	200,000
40	90	4,474	11,066	−6,458	−46,543	161,600	177,666	200,000

	INITIAL PREMIUM				
BENEFITS INCLUDED	ANNUAL	SEMIANNUAL	QUARTERLY	REGULAR MONTHLY	SPECIAL MONTHLY
Base policy	$4,474	$2,304	$1,163	$389	$388

Supplemental Footnotes

Dividends, or any figures depending upon them, are illustrations based on the Equitable's 1987 dividend scale applicable to currently issued policies, which reflect interest earnings on policies issued since January 1, 1987. The dividends are neither guaranteed nor estimates. Future dividends will depend on experience.

Policy value columns which are not specifically referred to as guaranteed include nonguaranteed elements (i.e., dividends) in whole or in part.

This illustration assumes no loans are made.

5 PERCENT INTEREST-ADJUSTED INDEXES	10 YEARS	20 YEARS
Net payment	17.35	11.55
Surrender cost	1.75	−1.82

This illustration is not to be considered as policy cost as interest is not taken into account. Policy cash values and death benefits are shown as end-of-year values.

SOURCE: Baldwin Financial Systems, Northbrook, Illinois.

from company to company and from policy to policy, these figures may or may not represent the best comparable insurance buy available at the time. The intelligent purchaser of life insurance must plan purchases and research a potential company and policy very carefully. Life insurance is a long-term financial commitment that requires the most careful possible evaluation. Shopping wisely will pay benefits for many years into the future.

Common Life Insurance Policy Provisions

The process of buying insurance includes the chore of reading the policy carefully. Much of the information in the following brief summary of popular policy provisions comes from an Institute of Life Insurance publication, *Plain Talk about Your Life Insurance Policy*. This publication provides an excellent reference to explain the often confusing language in a life insurance policy.

Additional Benefits

rider: A clause added to an insurance contract to provide additional benefits.

waiver of premium benefit: A rider that waives the requirement for premium payments if accident or illness prevents the policyholder from working.

accidental death benefit (double-indemnity clause): A rider that pays double the face value of a life insurance policy in the event of an accidental death.

A life insurance policy normally provides a number of benefits in addition to its death benefits. Policy additions known as **riders** detail these optional provisions. One common feature, the **waiver of premium benefit,** states that the company will pay premium payments on the policy if illness or accident prevents a policyholder from working. This benefit normally goes into effect six months after total disability.

Another common additional benefit is the **accidental death benefit,** also called a **double-indemnity clause.** This benefit pays additional sums to a beneficiary in excess of the policy's face value if the policyholder dies as a result of an accident. The name *double indemnity* comes from the fact that most such benefits specify a total payment of double the face value of the policy in the event of accidental death.

These additional benefits add to the cost of the basic policy. The waiver of premium benefit has obvious value, and most insurance buyers should purchase it as a general rule. The accidental death benefit has questionable value. Beneficiaries should need no more insurance solely because of the manner of a policyholder's death. Many people buy this coverage because its low cost makes it seem an attractive gamble with destiny, but it makes little economic sense.

Nonforfeiture Rights

Insurers normally allow policyholders at least 30 days to make up missed payments without penalty, though the exact length of this grace period varies from company to company. If the insurer receives no payment by the end of the grace period, the policy is said to lapse. However, a cash value policy would still have value because of its nonforfeiture rights. Term insurance policies normally have no nonforfeiture rights.

nonforfeiture right: The right in an insurance policy that the policyholder retains even if the policy lapses.

Nonforfeiture rights include certain rights and values the policyholder retains even if the policy lapses. A policyholder who allows the policy to lapse will suffer unnecessary losses if he or she fails to exercise these nonforfeiture rights. Policies give four major nonforfeiture rights.

reinstatement right: The right to reinstate a lapsed policy by showing good health and paying missed premiums plus interest.

The **reinstatement right** allows a policyholder who remains in reasonably good health after the policy lapses to put the policy back in effect, that is, reinstate it, by paying the past-due premiums, with interest. Most insurance companies allow reinstatement of a policy up to five years after it lapses.

surrender value: The cash value available by surrendering a life insurance policy to the insurance company.

A second important nonforfeiture right comes from the **surrender value** of the policy. If a policy lapses and the policyholder chooses not to reinstate it, he or she can surrender it and obtain its cash value. A table in every cash value policy lists its cash value per $1,000 of face value at its anniversary date. Of course, one need not let a policy lapse in order to surrender it and collect its cash value. Policyholders always have the option of borrowing the cash value of the policy at a rate of interest specified in the contract, or simply cash surrendering the policy.

extended term value: The length of a fully paid term policy for which a policyholder can exchange a cash-value life insurance policy.

The third important nonforfeiture right comes from the policy's **extended term value.** If a policy lapses, rather than take its surrender value, the policyholder can exchange the cash value of the policy (less any outstanding loans) to buy a fully paid term insurance policy with the same face value that offers protection for a limited term. A table in the contract specifies the length of the term. For example, a typical $10,000 whole life policy that lapsed after 10 years of payments would allow an exchange of its cash value for $10,000 worth of term insurance valid for about 20 years. In most cases, if the policyholder does not specify another option when the policy lapses, the insurer automatically gives the extended term option.

reduced paid-up value: The amount of lifelong insurance for which a policyholder can exchange a policy's cash value without paying additional premiums.

A final important nonforfeiture right is a policy's **reduced paid-up value.** This figure states the amount of life insurance a policy's cash value will buy to remain in force for the remainder of the policyholder's life without payment of any additional premiums. If a typical $25,000 whole life policy lapses after 10 years, the cash value will buy about $8,500 in paid-up insurance. This insurance coverage remains in force for the rest of the policyholder's life without any premium payments required. The contract specifies the exact amount of any reduced paid-up insurance.

Settlement Options

settlement option: The choice of how to distribute the proceeds of an insurance policy to the beneficiary.

lump sum option: The payment of death benefits in one lump sum.

When an insured dies, most policies offer one of four basic **settlement options,** or choices of how the insurer should pay proceeds of an insurance policy to its beneficiary. These options can play an important role in retirement and estate planning. The policyholder can choose the means of settlement or leave it up to the beneficiary. The most common option, the **lump sum option,** pays the face value of the policy, less any outstanding loans, in one lump sum to the beneficiary. Unless the policyholder elects some other option, most policies automatically pay lump sums to beneficiaries.

income-for-life option: The payment of death benefits in the form of a lifetime income.

Under one alternative, the **income-for-life option,** the insurance company pays a lifetime income to the beneficiary. The amount of the income payments depends on the beneficiary's age and the amount of the proceeds from the policy. The policy should provide for a minimum guaranteed payment period, for example, ten years. If the beneficiary dies before this period ends, the insurer must make a lump sum payment to a person designated by the beneficiary. A table in the policy provides payment details.

specified period option: The payment of death benefits in the form of a specified income for a specified period of time.

interest-only option: payment of interest generated by investment of death benefits with no invasion of principal.

The **specified period option** provides regular payments of a chosen amount for as long as the policy's face value, plus interest on the undistributed balance, lasts. Finally, the **interest-only option** leaves the policy proceeds with the insurance company, which makes regular interest payments to the beneficiary. This option can create a family fund for emergencies, college expenses, or other future needs. The family can collect the income and leave the principal intact. Individual insurance companies offer many different alternatives and combinations of standard settlement options.

Other Policy Features

contingent beneficiary: The person who receives life insurance death benefits if the primary beneficiary dies before the policyholder.

In addition to nonforfeiture rights and settlement options, a number of additional policy features affect the value of a life insurance policy. Understanding these policy rights determines how much the policyholder benefits from owning the policy. Unless he or she assigns these rights, (that is, signs a statement transferring these rights to someone else), the policyholder controls all aspects of the policy. These rights include the rights to change the beneficiary, to state the frequency of premium payments, to borrow against the policy, to specify how the insurer will pay death benefits, and to choose how to apply dividends.

incontestability clause: The policy clause that denies the company the right to contest any nonfraudulent misstatement in a policy application after two years.

One right allows naming a **contingent beneficiary,** that is, a person who will receive the death benefit if the primary beneficiary should die before the policyholder. Two or more beneficiaries can split the death benefit.

suicide clause: The policy clause that makes the company liable only to repay the premium payments if the policyholder takes his or her own life within two years of purchasing the policy.

age clause: The policy clause that allows the company to pay the death proceeds due for the correct age if the application misstates the age of the applicant.

A number of other clauses protect either the policyholder or the insurer. An **incontestability clause** provides that after a policy has been in force for a stated period of time, usually two years, the company loses the right to challenge some statements made in the application. If the applicant inadvertently makes a nonfraudulent misstatement that does not materially affect the insurer's decision to issue insurance, the insurer loses the right to deny benefits after two years. A **suicide clause** states that if a policyholder dies by suicide within two years of buying the policy, the company will simply return the premium payments to the beneficiary. After two years the company must pay the full death benefit even if the policyholder takes his or her own life. Finally, an **age clause** says that misstatement of the policyholder's age in the application allows the company to calculate the death benefit based on the correct age.

automatic premium loan: The authorization for the company to borrow against the cash value of a life insurance policy to pay missed premiums.

dividend option: The option to take dividends in cash, apply them to reduce premiums, reinvest them in the policy, or spend them to buy more insurance.

The policy includes two more interesting details. The first, the **automatic premium loan,** allows the company to borrow against the cash value of a policy to pay any missed premiums. The **dividend option** allows the policyholder to take dividends in cash, apply them to reduce premiums, leave them with the company in an interest-bearing account, or buy more insurance with them.

This chapter will conclude by returning to the case of Andy and Annette and detailing their completed insurance plan. They need to take the final step of selecting an appropriate policy or policies to protect the family against the financial impact of the parents' premature deaths.

Andy and Annette's Insurance Plan

Andy and Annette's family situation indicated a requirement of approximately $295,000 in total insurance protection for Andy and a $100,000 policy for Annette. Group term insurance from Andy's employer already provides $125,000 of his total, so he needs to purchase an additional $170,000 in life insurance protection. His group term insurance costs $200 per year for $125,000 of coverage.

Because of his relatively high tax bracket, Andy likes the savings features of whole life and the permanency of this insurance. However, $170,000 in whole life costs too much. Andy decides to settle for $70,000 in five-year renewable, convertible term insurance with an initial annual premium of $110, and a $100,000 universal life policy. The universal life policy offers flexible premium terms depending on how quickly Andy wants to build cash value. Andy decides that he can afford to contribute $600 per year to this policy, so he meets his total insurance need of $295,000 at a total annual premium of $910.

To provide for Annette's insurance requirements, she settles on a five-year renewable, convertible term policy in the amount of $100,000. The nonparticipating policy costs $120 per year.

SUMMARY

The primary purpose of life insurance is to replace income lost because of the premature death of a person who others depend on for financial support. A careful needs analysis should reveal an accurate estimate of the amount of life insurance a family requires. The needs analysis should consider family income needs, Social Security benefits, debt liquidation requirements, final expenses and estate taxes, an emergency fund for the family, and a college fund for the children, if required. An adequate life insurance plan should allow for replacing the services of a spouse who works full-time as a homemaker.

The wide variety of available insurance policies can confuse the selection decision. Reduced to their bare essentials, most policies fall into one of two basic categories: term or cash-value life insurance. Cash-value policies accumulate cash balances over time by combining built-in savings features with insurance protection. Term policies build no cash values, but offer maximum death benefits for the lowest premium. Most young and growing families find term insurance the only financially feasible means of protection.

Policies differ in their premium rates, dividend payment policies, and cash-value provisions and also in the timing of these dollar streams. This makes comparing policy costs extremely difficult. The insurance industry offers two cost comparison indexes to simplify comparison shopping: the net payment cost comparison index and the surrender cost comparison index. In a comparison of similar policies issued by different companies, the lowest index indicates the best insurance value. The equivalent level annual dividend index eases comparisons of different dividend payment streams.

A potential policyholder must read life insurance policies to understand their provisions for a number of important benefits and rights. He or she should pay particular attention to the waiver of premium benefit, nonforfeiture rights, and settlement options.

INVESTMENT MANAGEMENT CONCEPTS

1. The amount of life insurance needed depends mainly on how much financial support the insured provides for other people.

2. A spouse who does not work outside of the home generally should carry life insurance to cover the cost of replacing his or her services.

3. The easiest way to estimate the need for life insurance coverage takes some multiple of the person's annual salary. A married person with dependent children should usually carry six to eight times annual income.

4. A careful needs analysis that calculates the present value of future financial obligations is the best way to estimate life insurance requirements.

5. A term insurance policy should offer both renewability and convertibility.

6. Many contemporary cash-value insurance policies with a wide variety of provisions offer market-competitive investment returns, effectively integrating insurance with an investment program.

7. Careful cost comparisons should guide the search for life insurance of any type; one company may charge two to three times as much as another company charges for the same coverage.

REVIEW QUESTIONS

1. What primary purpose does life insurance serve?

2. Discuss the pros and cons of using life insurance as a means of forced savings.

3. Discuss the advantages and disadvantages of life insurance planning based on multiples of salary.

4. Discuss the advantages and disadvantages of life insurance planning based on needs analysis.

5. Describe the procedure to determine the amount of money required to provide a lifetime income for a family whose primary income earner dies.

6. What is the major difference between term insurance and cash-value insurance?

7. State the differences among straight term, renewable term, convertible term, and decreasing term insurance.

8. Describe the following types of cash-value policies: whole life, modified whole life, limited payment life, universal life, variable life, and variable-universal life.

9. How does group life insurance work? What major advantage does it have over almost all other types of policies?

10. Explain the net payment cost comparison index and the surrender cost comparison index. How can these indexes help insurance buyers?

11. How do the waiver of premium and accidental death benefits improve an insurance policy?

12. Name and describe the four major nonforfeiture rights that accompany most cash-value insurance policies.

13. Name and describe the four basic life insurance settlement options.

SELF-CORRECTING PROBLEM

Tim is 34 years old and Julie is 32. They have a four-year-old daughter, Heather, and a two-year-old son, Paul. Tim earns $25,000 per year as a social worker. Julie earns $15,000 per year working part-time as a legal secretary. They owe a mortgage balance of $85,000 on their home in a suburb of San Francisco. They have a total of $1,500 in savings and about $4,500 in consumer debt.

If Tim were to die prematurely, Julie would receive about $600 a month in Social Security survivors' benefits. She would continue to work part-time, still earning $15,000 per year, until Paul reached age 18. After that she would go to work full-time at a salary of $26,000 per year. When she retired at age 65, Julie would receive total monthly retirement benefits of $800 from Social Security and payments from her employer's private pension plan.

At present, the family's only insurance is a $20,000 group term policy on Tim's life. Design an insurance plan for the family, clearly specifying the amount of insurance they need as well as the types of insurance policies they should buy.

Answer to Self-Correcting Problem

Tim and Julie could arrive at a rough estimate of their insurance needs through the multiples-of-salary approach. Six to eight times Tim's salary suggests they should buy life insurance with a death benefit of \$150,000 to \$200,000. For Julie, this standard suggests insurance coverage in the range of \$90,000 to \$120,000. Since this simple calculation has been shown to give a general guide for many families, it provides a useful bench mark.

A complete needs analysis involves a number of assumptions and estimates of distant future conditions and values. Recognizing the inexact nature of this process, analysts normally round off projections of coverage needs to give a figure to compare to the multiples-of-salary benchmark. Therefore, the needs analysis for Tim and Julie can make several simplifying assumptions. Even if assumptions differ slightly, different analysts usually develop remarkably similar answers.

As a first simplification, combine the amount of life insurance Tim and Julie need together and then split this coverage 60 percent to Tim and 40 percent to Julie, since Tim has the higher income. The upper ends of the multiples-of-salary estimates (\$200,000 for Tim and \$120,000 for Julie) give the same proportions.

Because both Tim and Julie are employed, plan to replace the lost income of either party, at least until the youngest child would enter college (or the work force) at age 18. Plan for college separately, assuming that the children will go to college and that the family will meet this need through a separate fund. A conservative assumption would replace at least 75 percent of the higher income ($0.75 \times \$25{,}000 = \$18{,}750$), less Social Security benefits, for a period of 16 years. If money would grow at a real rate of 3 percent (that is, the rate of return would exceed the inflation rate by 3 percent), the family would need a fund equal to the present value of a 16-year annuity in the amount of \$18,750 per year at a 3 percent discount rate. Rounded off, this sum is approximately \$295,000.

Next, plan for a fund of \$100,000 (in today's dollars) for the education expenses of both children. The family would need the money beginning in 14 years (when Heather reached age 18). Taking the same real rate of return, 3 percent, as the plan used above, we must find the present value of \$100,000 to be received 14 years from now at a discount rate of 3 percent. To be conservative, round this amount, \$66,000, up to \$75,000. Note that if inflation were to average 4 percent per year for the next 14 years and the money earned 3 percent above the inflation rate, this \$75,000 would grow to a sum of \$193,390, which would provide a bit more purchasing power than \$100,000 would currently provide.

Finally, experience shows that surviving spouses often like to pay off their home mortgages out of insurance proceeds. Plan for \$85,000 to pay off the mortgage, and for \$15,000 to pay off the existing consumer installment debt, less current savings of \$3,000 and to provide a fund for emergencies and funeral expenses. In total, then, Tim and Julie need \$470,000 in life insurance coverage ($\$295{,}000 + \$75{,}000 + \$85{,}000 + \$15{,}000$). Divide this total to insure Tim for \$300,000 and Julie for \$170,000.

Applying a sort of reasonableness test to these figures, if Julie were to die, Tim would receive \$170,000 from her life insurance. He could use this money to set up the college fund for the children, pay off the mortgage plus the consumer installment debt, and pay funeral expenses. With no home mortgage payment or eventual college expenses to meet, Tim's income would support himself and the children. On the other hand, if Tim were to die, Julie could use roughly \$170,000 to meet the same expenses and invest the remaining \$130,000 to supplement her income.

portfolio: A collection of securities chosen for their contributions to achievement of overall investment goals.

portfolio management: The process of selection and continuous management of a collection of securities to meet an investor's needs.

A review of basic terms will prepare for more detailed discussion. A group of securities that work together to meet an investor's objectives is referred to as a **portfolio.** Actually, the term could apply to any collection of securities owned by an investor, but rigorous evaluation and careful selection can create a beneficial synergy between portfolio elements.

Portfolio management is the process of selection and continuous management of securities to meet the investor's objectives. Portfolio management focuses on matching the investor's attitudes toward return and risk with the return and risk characteristics of securities. Complete, accurate records allow the portfolio manager to measure investment performance of the portfolio and to gauge progress toward meeting objectives. From time to time the manager must review the composition of the portfolio to reassess its fit with investment goals.

Portfolio management includes several activities. In the first, and perhaps the most important, the manager must formulate investment objectives and construct a plan to meet them. Second, selecting individual securities depends on refining the plan to develop appropriate criteria for choosing among available alternatives. Finally, the manager must supervise the portfolio he or she has constructed to assure that securities perform as expected, which should cause steady progress toward meeting portfolio objectives.

This chapter will describe and explain each phase of the portfolio management process. It begins with a discussion of Modern Portfolio Theory and its implications for the effort to build an investment portfolio based on return and risk expectations. Following this, the chapter reviews management techniques for controlling the performance of various kinds of portfolios. To apply portfolio theory, the manager must establish appropriate risk and return guidelines and find investment alternatives that satisfy these guidelines.

Modern Portfolio Theory (MPT)

As discussed in Chapter 6, Modern Portfolio Theory (MPT) assumes an efficient stock market with cheap, abundant information about the market itself and individual stocks on which to base assessments of prices. An efficient market quickly and accurately reflects new information in the new prices it establishes. Since no one can predict the flow of information, stock prices also defy prediction. Stock prices at one moment remain independent of stock prices in any other moment.

Also, since the market immediately reflects the effects of all information, no one can do much better, on average, than the market. Investors tend to earn the same return as the overall market provides, and those with securities in similar risk classes tend to earn similar rates of return.

The assumption that investors cannot beat the market implies that they should diversify their portfolios so as to earn the return the market provides for portfolios with a given level of risk. In addition, the inability to predict future prices suggests that investors should implement buy-and-hold policies.

The primary portfolio management decision concerns the risk level the investor is willing to accept. If the investor can accept the market risk, the portfolio should focus on common stocks that will provide the return and risk of the market portfolio, usually represented by some index such as the DJIA or the S&P 500. An investor who can accept more risk will invest in securities that have higher rates of return as compensation for higher risk. If the investor wishes to avoid the level of risk common in the stock market, he or she will focus on risk-free assets such as U.S. Treasury bills.

Most portfolio managers measure risk by the statistical beta of the investment portfolio, which reflects variations in portfolio performance from the performance of the market. Using the S&P 500 to represent the market, the portfolio of 500 stocks tracked for that index will have a beta of 1.0 by definition. Some managers measure risk in terms of the standard deviation of past portfolio returns.

MPT advocates investing with a long-term time horizon. This maximizes overall portfolio returns, since the effort to trade in response to short-term effects might lead to buying high and selling low, which would lead, in turn, to poor performance. Long-term investors refuse to panic as the market rises and falls, remaining confident that it will provide expected returns over time.

Assumptions of Modern Portfolio Theory

Like any theory, Modern Portfolio Theory relies on assumptions. The first of ten assumptions, as discussed above, is that the stock market is efficient. This implies that all investors have complete knowledge.

The second assumption is that investors are risk averse. They would prefer, other things remaining equal, to avoid losses and variability of prices and returns.

This suggests the third assumption: that an investor will require a higher return to accept higher risk. A market full of investors willing to make this tradeoff ensures that a higher return must always accompany higher risk. No investor can find an investment that offers a higher rate of return without similarly higher risk.

The fourth assumption combines the second and third into a statement that investors attempt to maximize returns and minimize risk. Therefore, they evaluate alternative investments' characteristics and choose those that provide the highest return-to-risk ratios.

The fifth assumption turns the third assumption around. It states that an investor who wants to reduce risk must accept smaller returns.

The sixth assumption of MPT limits investment choices to those that create efficient portfolios. This derives from the Nobel-prize-winning work of Harry M. Markowitz.

The seventh assumption states that managers calculate portfolio returns and risks for a single time period to maintain comparability.

The eighth assumption is that investors can hold small percentages of all investments. The ninth assumption is that all decisions depend on risk and expected return.

The tenth assumption is that the manager can evalutate the return and risk behavior of all securities. This means that, by changing the weights of securities in a portfolio, one can observe the effects on expected return, risk, and the return-to-risk ratio.

These ten assumptions seem reasonable, and they have underlied much of the discussion throughout the book. Still, developing a rational method of portfolio management requires stating them explicitly and evaluating their effects on trading decisions. The pivotal assumption of an efficient market has generated the most controversy.

Efficient Market Hypothesis (EMH)

The efficient market hypothesis forms part of the foundation of Modern Portfolio Theory. Studies have tested it at three levels of significance: the weak form, semistrong form, and strong form of the efficient market hypothesis.

weak form of the efficient market hypothesis: The hypothesis that current market prices fully reflect all information contained in past price movements so this information can give no indication of future returns.

Weak Form The **weak form of the efficient market hypothesis** states that current market prices fully reflect the effects of all information contained in past price movements. This means that information about past prices and events can give no help in the search for a stock that will provide exceptional future performance. All investors know everything past prices can tell them about a stock, and its current price reflects their assessment of its correct value. Eugene F. Fama found that future stock prices are completely independent of past prices.[3] Because of this independence, future prices describe a random distribution around past prices.

This has led to the random walk hypothesis, which states that a future price may diverge in any direction from the immediately previous price, so past prices tell the analyst nothing about the next price change. The independence of past and future stock prices gives substantial empirical support for the weak-form efficient market hypothesis and the random walk hypothesis.

semistrong form of the efficient market hypothesis: The weak form strengthened to state that current prices reflect all publicly available information, not just past price information.

Semistrong Form The **semistrong form of the efficient market hypothesis** states that current market prices reflect all publicly available information—not just past price information. This would mean that no one could earn abnormal returns (returns in excess of risk-adjusted market returns) by trading in reaction to publicly available information.

Studies suggest, however, that investors become aware of information at different times. Short periods elapse between announcement and full dissemination, during which some sharp investors can enjoy excess returns by trading on the basis of the information. An efficient market does not require, however, that every investor know everything. As professional traders and money managers react to new announcements, their trades close price gaps almost instantly, so only very few can benefit from this advantage, and even they cannot expect the first access to every announcement. In practice, even sharp investors find it extremely difficult to outperform the market consistently.

Further, questions remain about the assumption that investors can predict how a piece of information will affect a stock price. This requires analyzing an announcement in relation to the market's expectations, which may seem obscure. An investor who learns that a company's earnings will exceed its managers' expectations might suffer disappointment if the market had estimated the earnings correctly, so the stock price already reflected that information.

strong form of the efficient market hypothesis: The semistrong form strengthened to state that current prices reflect all information, both public and private.

Strong Form The **strong form of the efficient market hypothesis** suggests that stock prices reflect absolutely all information, both public and private. This would preclude even insiders from earning excess returns on the basis of their knowledge.

Most investors reject the strong form of the EMH. Empirical evidence suggests that insiders can make excess returns, and that market inefficiencies can allow abnormal returns when analysts correctly anticipate improvements in earnings, when small firms earn higher return-to-risk ratios than large firms, and when stocks earn poorer returns on Mondays than on the other days of the week. This empirical evidence tends to invalidate the strong form of the EMH.

Markowitz Diversification and Portfolio Theory

Markowitz diversification: A portfolio management technique based on identifying the efficient set of portfolios based on securities' returns, standard deviations, and coefficients of correlation to every other security.

Professor Harry Markowitz set out the basis for Modern Portfolio Theory in his 1952 article "Portfolio Selection."[4] **Markowitz diversification** allots available capital among several stocks to create an efficient portfolio based on three variables: expected return, expected standard deviation of return, and each security's coefficient of correlation with every other security in the portfolio. With these data as input, a computer model can calculate the expected return and risk of the portfolio, which together indicate which portfolio combinations make efficient portfolios. Recall from Chapter 6 that an efficient portfolio is the one with the highest return at any given level of risk, as measured by standard deviation.

The standard deviation of the portfolio equals the square root of its variance. The portfolio variance equation develops an overall figure from the variance and covariance of each individual security. The variance of a two-security portfolio can be found by:

$$\sigma_p^2 = W_1^2\sigma_1^2 + W_2^2\sigma_2^2 + 2W_1 W_2 R_{12}\sigma_1\sigma_2$$

Portfolio variance equals σ_p^2. The term that represents covariance is:

$$2W_1 W_2 R_{12}\sigma_1\sigma_2$$

EXHIBIT 16.1

Efficient Frontier

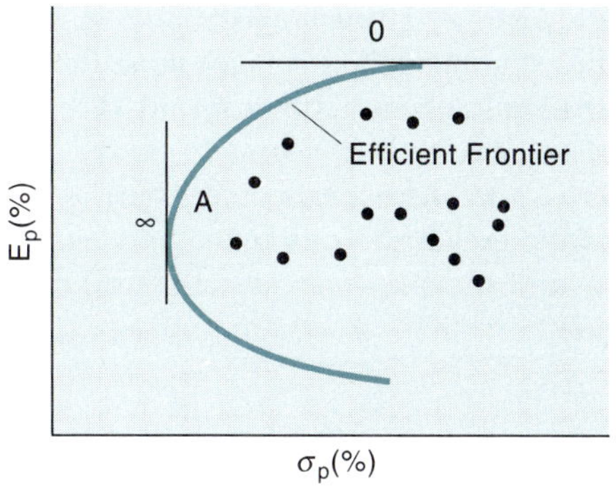

where W_1 and W_2 give the weights of securities 1 and 2 in the portfolio, that is, the percentages of total capital allotted to the individual securities. R_{12} gives the coefficient of correlation of security 1 to security 2, and $\sigma_1\ \sigma_2$ is the standard deviation of security 1 multiplied by the standard deviation of security 2.

The first term of the portfolio variance equation is the variance of security 1 multiplied by that security's weight in the portfolio squared ($W_1^2\ \sigma_1^2$). The second term in the equation is the product of the variance of security 2 (σ_2^2) and its portfolio weight squared (W_2^2).

Quadratic programming is required to solve the Markowitz portfolio selection model. The basic purpose of quadratic programming is to find the combination of securities that minimizes the portfolio's risk, as measured by portfolio standard deviation (σ_p), at every return level. Generally, the quadratic program identifies all portfolio combinations that have the lowest risk for each level of expected return, or all combinations that have the highest return for each level of expected risk, as shown in Exhibit 16.1.

The combination that gives the highest return is indicated by the point at which the efficient frontier has a slope of zero. The point at which the slope of the efficient frontier becomes infinite indicates the portfolio combination with the smallest risk. To find the slope of the efficient frontier at a given point, take the slope of the tangent to the curve at that point.

For every point A at which the efficient frontier has a slope between zero and infinity, the portfolio manager can find a specific return (E_p) and risk (σ_p) through the quadratic program. The objective function maximizes E_p at every level of σ_p and indicates the efficient portfolio that gives the highest return-to-risk ratio. To demonstrate the principles of quadratic programming, consider the combination of two securities to create a portfolio.

Portfolio Theory for a Two-Security Portfolio

Before deciding optimal allocations of portfolio capital among the two securities, the portfolio manager must first select those securities. Suppose he or she could choose only from the three securities listed in Exhibit 16.2.

Bristol Myers (BM) seems to be the best single security in this group since it has the highest expected return-to-risk ratio. Recall that the return-to-risk ratio equals the difference between the expected total return on the security and the risk-free rate of return divided by the security's standard deviation,

$$(E_r - r_f)/\sigma_r$$

Now the portfolio manager must select a second security, and then decide in what proportion to combine it with the first to create a portfolio. Pfizer (PI) has much lower risk than Johnson & Johnson (J&J) and a much higher return. The correct choice is obvious.

A portfolio invested 50 percent each in BM and PI would have an average return of 22.4 percent. To verify this, enter values from Exhibit 16.2 into the portfolio return equation:

$$r_p = w_i r_i + w_j r_j$$

where r_p equals the expected return of the portfolio, w_i and r_i give the portfolio weight and return of security i, and w_j and r_j give the portfolio weight and return of security j.

Since this portfolio includes equal proportions of both securities, both w_i and w_j equal 0.5. Taking return data from Exhibit 16.2, the equation becomes:

$$r_p = 0.5(21.6) + 0.5(23.1) = 22.4 \text{ percent}$$

In effect, a portfolio's return equals the weighted average of the returns on the individual securities.

Combining the securities, however, generally reduces the portfolio standard deviation below the weighted average of the individual securities' standard deviations. The amount of this reduction depends on the coefficient of correlation (R_{ij}) between the securities, which measures the degree to which changes in the return on one security mirror changes in the return on another.

An R_{ij} of 1.0 would imply that securities i and j move exactly in tandem, that is, their returns are perfectly positively correlated. An R_{ij} of -1.0 would imply that a change in one security's return would exactly offset a change in the other, called *perfect negative correlation*. The standard

EXHIBIT 16.2

Returns, Standard Deviations, and Return-to-Risk Ratios of Selected Securities*

	EXPECTED RETURN	STANDARD DEVIATION	RETURN-TO-RISK RATIO
Bristol Myers (BM)	21.6%	10.8	1.54
Pfizer, Inc. (PI)	23.1	12.5	1.45
Johnson & Johnson (J&J)	5.4	27.6	0.01
Risk-free rate	5.0		

*The objective of diversification is to maximize the return-to-risk ratio.

deviation of the portfolio would equal the weighted average of the standard deviations of the individual securities only when the securities showed perfect positive correlation.

The equation representing the standard deviation of the portfolio is:

$$\sigma_p = \sqrt{W_i^2\sigma_j^2 + W_j^2\sigma_j^2 + 2W_iW_jR_{ij}\sigma_i\sigma_j}$$

where σ_p is the standard deviation of the portfolio. As in the portfolio return equation, w_i and w_j represent the weights of stocks i and j, and σ_i and σ_j represent the standard deviations of the securities' expected returns. R_{ij} gives the coefficient of correlation between the returns on security i and security j. Finally, $\sigma_i\,\sigma_j$ is the covariance between security i and j.

Return to the example portfolio of Bristol Myers and Pfizer. Suppose these stocks' returns have a coefficient of correlation of 1.0. Plugging the return and risk data from Exhibit 16.2 into the equation would yield:

$$\begin{aligned}\sigma_p &= \sqrt{(0.5)^2(10.8)^2 + (0.5)^2(12.5)^2 + 2(0.5)(0.5)(1.0)(10.8)(12.5)}\\ &= \sqrt{0.25(116.6) + 0.25(156.3) + 67.5}\\ &= \sqrt{29.2 + 39.1 + 67.5}\\ &= \sqrt{135.8}\\ &= 11.7\end{aligned}$$

To go with the previously calculated expected return of 22.4 percent, an equally weighted portfolio made up of these stocks would have a standard deviation of 11.7 percent. Since the example supposes that the stocks' returns exhibit perfect positive correlation, the portfolio standard deviation equals the weighted average of the standard deviations of the individual securities:

$$0.5(10.8) + 0.5(12.5) = 5.4 + 6.3 = 11.7 \text{ percent}$$

The portfolio return-to-risk ratio would equal approximately 1.50 [(22.4 − 5.0)/11.7], which lies between the return-to-risk ratios of the component stocks. Since return is proportional to risk, investors would be indifferent to any combination of BM and PI, so they would base their allocation decision on their attitudes toward risk.

Suppose, however, that the returns on the stocks showed no correlation, that is, they had a coefficient of correlation of 0.0. This would imply that the return on BM would change completely independently of changes in the return on PI. Maintaining the assumption of equal proportions of the two securities, the portfolio risk calculation becomes:

$$\begin{aligned}\sigma_p &= \sqrt{(0.5)^2(10.8)^2 + (0.5)^2(12.5)^2 + 2(0.5)(0.5)(0)(10.8)(12.5)} \\ &= \sqrt{0.25(116.6) + 0.25(156.3)} \\ &= \sqrt{29.2 + 39.1} \\ &= \sqrt{68.3} \\ &= 8.3\end{aligned}$$

Note that the only change from the previous equation is the new correlation coefficient.

The drop in σ_p from 11.7 to 8.3 percent would result in a jump in the return-to-risk ratio to 2.10. While the expected return remains the same, diversification reduces risk, so the portfolio with zero correlation between the securities offers a better deal than the portfolio with a correlation coefficient of 1.0.

To extend this logic, assume that the returns on BM and PI are perfectly negatively correlated. Changing the correlation coefficient to −1.0 would give a portfolio standard deviation of 0.9 percent. This would boost the return-to-risk ratio to 19.33, making this the clear favorite among the three different alternatives.

Exhibit 16.3 illustrates the relationships between risk and return based on correlation coefficients of 1.0, 0.0, and −1.0. This defines the set of efficient portfolios including the two example stocks, BM and PI; that is, this exhibit shows the efficient frontier defined by combinations of these stocks. The investor would obviously benefit more from diversification among securities whose returns were negatively correlated, but achieving this ideal in practice can present many obstacles since most securities do well in a rising market and lose value in a declining market. The portfolio manager can, however, look for securities with the lowest possible positive correlations to maximize the benefits of diversification.

Even if negative correlation were common, finding the lowest possible risk would still require adjusting the balance between the two securities in the portfolio. Assuming two stocks have returns with perfect negative correlation, the portfolio manager must find the weights of the two stocks that yield the lowest portfolio risk. Trial and error could provide the answer,

EXHIBIT 16.3

Return and Risk Combinations of Pfizer and Bristol Myers Under Different Correlation Assumptions

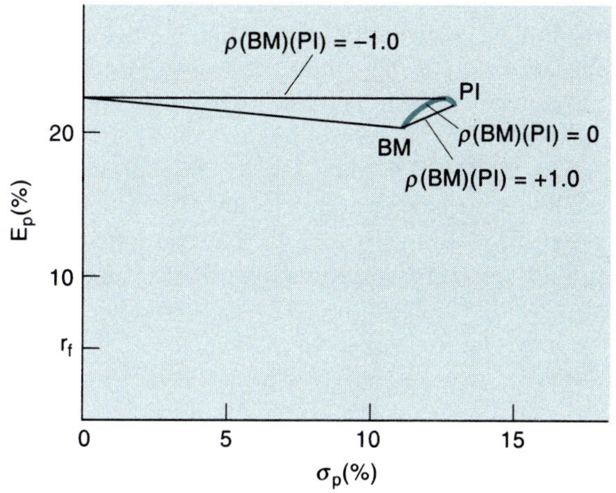

but there is an easier way that involves standard optimization calculus. The mathematics of this technique exceed the scope of this book, but the procedure would give optimal weights of 53.7 percent of BM and 46.3 percent of PI.

Calculating the Coefficient of Correlation

Modern portfolio theory does not allow real-world portfolio managers to guess at correlation coefficients. They must calculate these crucial values using the following equation:

$$R_{ij} = \sigma_{ij}/\sigma_i\sigma_j$$

where σ_i is the standard deviation of security i, σ_j is the standard deviation of security j, and σ_{ij} is the covariance between security i and security j.

The following equation gives covariance:

$$\sigma_{ij} = \sum_{t=1}^{n} P_t([r_{it} - E(r_i)][r_{jt} - E(r_j)])$$

P_t is the probability that a given return will occur. The term r_{it} gives the actual return on investment i at time t, while $E(r_i)$ gives the *expected* average return on investment i. In the same way, r_{jt} gives the actual return on investment j at time t, and $E(r_j)$ gives the *expected* average return on investment j.

Exhibit 16.4 charts the efficient frontier, representing the characteristics of the portfolio possibilities presented by combinations of BM and PI, assuming a coefficient of correlation between them of 0.5. Point PI indicates allocation of 100 percent to PI, and point BM represents an allocation of 100 percent to BM. The lowest risk portfolio (BM, PI) is an allocation of 64 percent to BM and 36 percent to PI. The investor would avoid the curve between (BM, PI) and BM because portfolios in this area would yield smaller returns with approximately the same risk as the portfolios along the curve from (BM, PI) to T to PI. The efficient frontier between (BM, PI) and PI encompasses the range of combinations of PI and BM that can provide the highest returns for a given level of risk. Stated another way, the efficient portfolio set indicates all of the portfolios that make two securities work equally hard for the investor. The optimal combination of BM and PI lies at the point of tangency (T) between curve (BM, PI) and the CML (capital market line).

Whatever securities one considers, Modern Portfolio Theory assumes that the market always makes another option available: investing in risk-free assets. From the data in Exhibit 16.2, this would provide a return of 5 percent with zero risk. In Exhibit 16.4, this would place the portfolio somewhere on the line between point r_f and the point of tangency with the efficient frontier, the curve between T and PI. This expands the portfolio manager's investment options to include those represented by the line r_f–TI–T. A particular investor's optimal selection from this set of possibilities will depend upon his or her attitude toward risk and return.

By now no doubt should remain that optimal diversification requires complicated analysis. The portfolio manager must calculate the expected return and standard deviation for each security in a portfolio and estimate the correlation between each pair of securities. This would take a substantial amount of time even for a two-stock portfolio; think about the magnitude of the statistical problem a portfolio of 30 securities would present!

This discussion has suggested three principles to guide this effort. First, look for efficient securities to include in the portfolio, that is, identify those that offer the highest expected return with the lowest expected risk. Second, in order to reduce risk, seek securities whose returns show negative or low positive correlations with each other. This will give the portfolio the highest possible return with the lowest possible risk. Third, after choosing securities, adjust their weights in the portfolio based on their contributions to the return and risk of the portfolio. Minimizing both individual stocks' standard deviations and the coefficients of correlation between them will reveal the combination with the minimum overall standard deviation. In this way, the portfolio manager can keep risk as low as possible for every level of return which will maximize the return-to-risk ratio.

EXHIBIT 16.4

Efficient Portfolio Set for BM and PI with R = 0.5

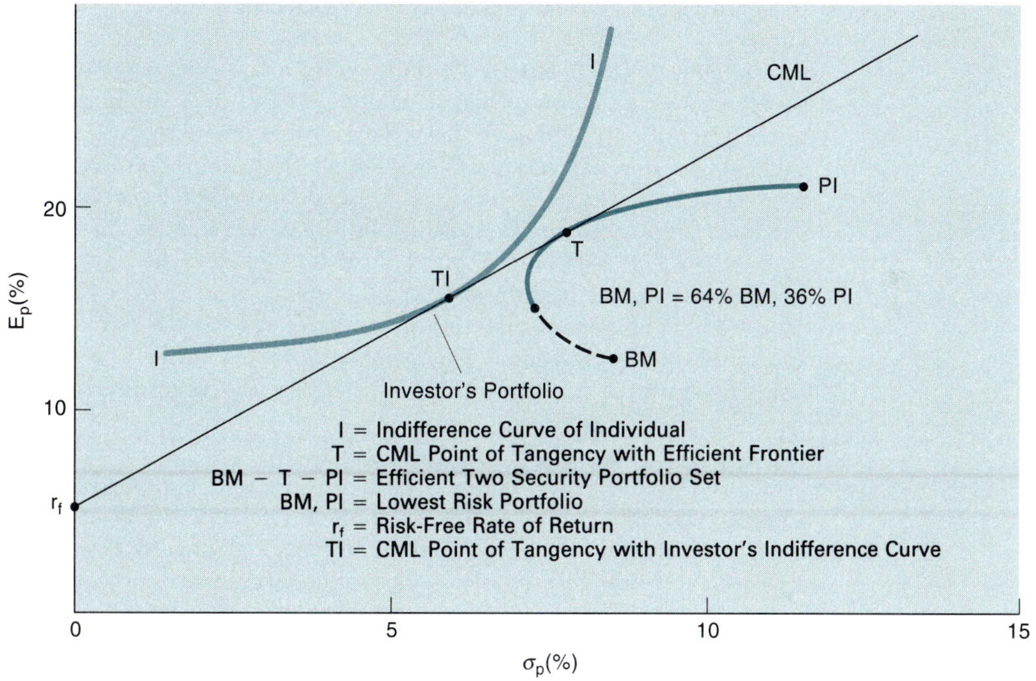

Placing a Portfolio on the Efficient Frontier

After defining a set of efficient portfolios, the portfolio manager must choose one. To do this, he or she compares the available portfolios with his or her indifference curve.

capital market line: The line from the y-intercept, which represents the return on the risk-free portfolio, tangent to the efficient frontier that establishes available portfolio choices.

This process begins with the **capital market line (CML),** r_fTZ in Exhibit 16.4, which represents all possible combinations of portfolio T and risk-free securities from point r_f to T and the borrowing portfolio beyond point T. Adding risk-free securities can reduce risk more than it reduces return so it can increase the return-to-risk ratio and overall portfolio performance. This can make a combination of risky and risk-free securities, such as the portfolios on the capital market line, more attractive than a portfolio limited to the common stocks on the efficient frontier. Theoretically, the investor could also borrow money at the risk-free rate (r_f), invest in portfolio T, and move upward and to the right along the capital market line.

Indifference Curve The positions portfolio managers choose on the capital market line depend on their attitudes toward risk and return. To extend the use of the diagram in Exhibit 16.4, they can illustrate these attitudes by drawing **indifference curves** like curve I. This curve represents the tradeoffs between risk and return that a particular investor would willingly make. Investors with different needs and goals will have different indifference curves.

indifference curve: The MPT graph line indicating investors' preference toward return and risk.

Actually, curve I represents only one of a set of such curves that an investor might draw; his or her range of needs and goals would give rise to a whole set of curves moving upward and to the left of curve I, because a rational investor will always be willing to trade more return for more risk. Modern Portfolio Theory suggests that the investor should hold the combination of securities that will fall on the capital market line where his or her highest indifference curve just touches it. The investor with indifference curve I would want to hold portfolio TI in Exhibit 16.4. Other investors might want higher returns or lower risk levels, but they could obtain efficient combinations only on the capital market line, so they, too, would look for the point at which their indifference curves just touched it.

Implications for Investment Practice

Optimal portfolios are those with the minimum possible risk levels for given returns. This solves the problem of diversifying among risky assets without the need to resort to naive diversification (holding equal amounts of each security), which would reduce portfolio performance below optimum levels. This leaves the portfolio manager to decide how to balance risky and riskless assets, though.

Markowitz diversification techniques assume accurate estimates of expected return and risk. This can present difficulties when the analyst bases these estimates on historical data, which often give poor indications about the future. In particular, a historic coefficient of correlation may not accurately reflect future relationships. This is only one of the values that change for individual securities and groups of securities over time.

Putting these techniques into practice can involve many other obstacles. Generating a reasonably large set of efficient portfolios requires a sophisticated computer program. Investor attitudes can become the largest obstacles, though. Markowitz suggests buying securities with negative correlations to achieve the best results. This means combining rising stocks with falling stocks to smooth overall portfolio changes. In a generally rising market, however, few investors want to buy stocks they expect to show low or declining rates of return; instead, they hope to profit from the upward volatility of their portfolio.

In spite of these weaknesses, the concepts Professor Markowitz pioneered give excellent portfolio management principles. For example, one academic study indicates that portfolio management based on the Markowitz principles can improve portfolio return by 2 percent over the return of the market. One can improve even this strong performance by creating a portfolio from stocks that have return-to-risk ratios of 1.00 or higher. In summary, Markowitz diversification involves three principles:

1. A security's individual risk (measured by standard deviation) and its correlation with other portfolio securities determine its weight in a portfolio.
2. A small amount of diversification can substantially reduce risk.
3. The investor's decision focuses on accurate estimates of expected return, expected risk, and the relationship of the return on one security to that on another.

Modern Portfolio Theory with Beta Analysis

Traditionally, applying the Markowitz diversification principles has required a complex computer model to calculate the coefficient of correlation for each pair of securities. Sharpe has argued that one can reduce the resources devoted to this work by relating the annual returns on each stock to returns on the market, as represented by the S&P 500, in a process called **beta analysis.**[5] He completed regression analysis to determine the risk characteristics of each security. Based on individual risk characteristics, he then combined stocks into a portfolio with acceptable overall risk and return characteristics.

beta analysis: Assessing the value of a portfolio combination by the relationship between the return on a stock or a portfolio of stocks and that of some market index, usually the S&P 500.

To measure a security's risk relative to the market, one uses the regression equation:

$$Y = \alpha + \beta X + \epsilon$$

In this equation, Y is the dependent variable and X is the independent variable. The constant α gives the y-intercept, while β represents the slope of the regression line measured in terms of $\Delta y/\Delta x$. Finally, ϵ is the error factor. This term reflects the vertical distance between the regression line and the data points; it should average to zero over the entire portfolio sample. The regression line in Exhibit 16.5 illustrates these variables and their relationships.

Regression analysis of an individual security plots its returns (R_s) over a period of time against the returns on the market (R_m) for the same period, with the S&P 500 serving as a proxy for the market. For example, point 3 in Exhibit 16.5 represents this relationship in year 3 when the market returned approximately 5 percent and the stock returned 5.5 percent. A relatively sophisticated hand calculator or a small computer can simplify the process of fitting a trend line to the data using the least squares method.

The regression line graphically represents the relationship between the annual returns on the security and those on the market. Exhibit 16.5 shows points for ten annual values. In practice, analysts often plot 60 points to reflect five years of monthly data. Generally, more frequent observations

EXHIBIT 16.5

Security Return Compared to Market Return

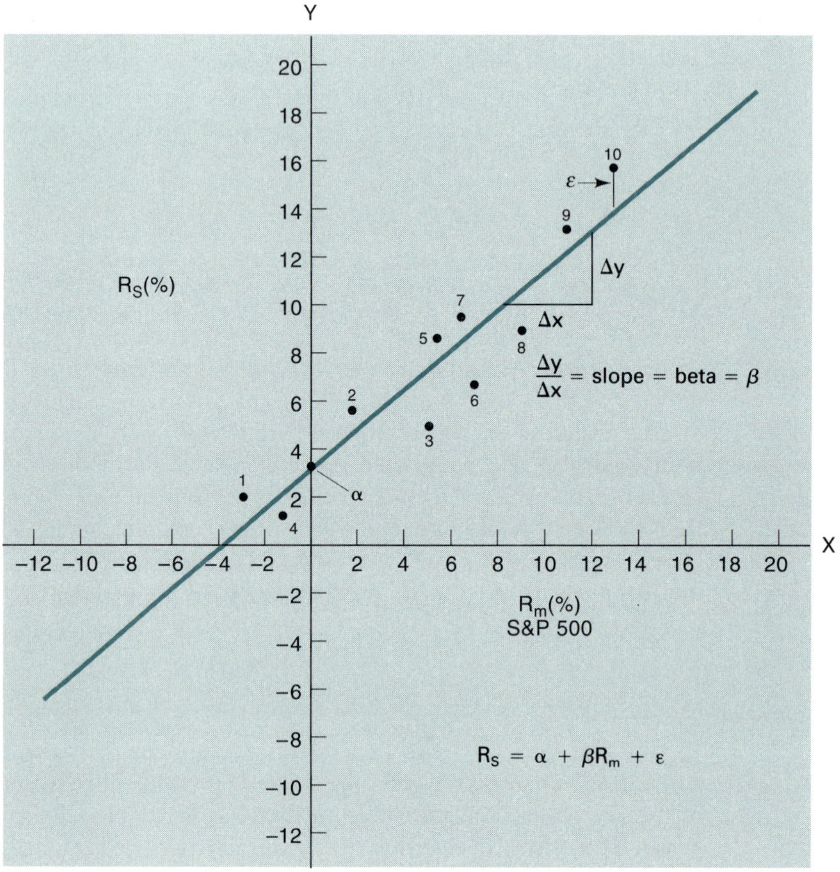

establish more reliable relationships, and several statisticians have suggested that 100 data points are necessary to identify reliable statistical relationships.

To use the regression equation set out above, the analyst must find correct α and β values for the security in question. The security in Exhibit 16.5 has a y-intercept, α, of 3.5 percent and a slope, β, of 0.89. Visual estimation gives a value for ϵ of approximately 1.0. These values give the regression equation:

$$R_s = 3.5 + 0.89R_m \pm 1.0$$

What does this equation tell the analyst about the stock's performance relative to the market? The beta term represents the stock's systematic risk relative to the market, that is, the degree to which it follows changes in the overall market. The α term, together with the error factor (ϵ), represent the stock's unsystematic risk. A β higher than the market beta, which is 1.00 by definition, indicates a stock that is riskier than the market; a β lower than 1.00 indicates a stock that is less risky than the market. A positive value for α indicates a stock that has outperformed the market; a negative value indicates a stock that has failed to keep pace with the performance of the market. The stock in Exhibit 16.5 is less risky than the market since its β is less than 1.0. The positive value for α implies that the stock outperformed the market, and the relatively small error factor does not affect the analysis significantly.

From the exhibit, the analyst could predict this stock's behavior if the market return (R_m) were 12 percent. Substituting this estimate into the regression equation gives the following result:

$$\begin{aligned} R_s &= 3.5 + 0.89(12) \pm 1.0 \\ &= 3.5 + 10.68 \pm 1.0 \\ &= 14.18 \pm 1.0 \end{aligned}$$

When the market earns 12 percent, the stock should return an average of 14.18 percent, with a range of 13.18 to 15.18 percent. Since the stock has less systematic risk than the market, implying a lower return, the analyst must attribute its favorable relationship with the market to positive, unsystematic forces.

Suppose, however, that the analyst expects the market to turn downward and earn a return of −3.6 percent, as the S&P 500 did in 1981. What return would the stock earn in this bear market? Substituting into the regression equation gives:

$$\begin{aligned} R_s &= 3.5 + 0.89(-3.6) \pm 1.0 \\ &= 3.5 - 3.2 \pm 1.0 \\ &= 0.3 \pm 1.0 \end{aligned}$$

Despite the weak market, the security should earn a positive average return, again outperforming the market. Note, however, that the error term indicates the possibility of a modest negative return of −0.7 percent.

Exhibit 16.6 summarizes the relationships of the terms in the regression equation which govern the analyst's interpretation of the relationship between the market index and the stock. In a rising market the portfolio manager should favor stocks with positive values for α, β values higher than 1.0, and ϵ values of zero. This would give the portfolio the maximum opportunity to benefit from the expected surge in stock prices. In a falling market the portfolio manager should seek stocks with positive values for α, β values *below* 1.0, and zero ϵ values to prevent the portfolio from following

EXHIBIT 16.6

Guidelines for Beta Analysis

VARIABLE	RELATIONSHIP WITH MARKET	INTERPRETATION
α (alpha)	Positive	Better
	Zero	Same
	Negative	Worse
β (beta)	Greater than 1.0	More risky
	Equal to 1.0	Same
	Less than 1.0	Less risky
ϵ (epsilon)	Greater than 0.0	Worse
	Zero	Same

the market all the way to its trough. Finally, to match the performance of the market exactly, a portfolio manager should look for α values of zero, β values of 1.0, and ϵ values of zero.

In practice, portfolio managers focus on β, which varies among stocks. Most stocks have low α and ϵ values, so a portfolio manager may find more profitable uses for time spent seaching for high-α stocks.

Capital Asset Pricing Model (CAPM)

While a little analysis based on past performance data can yield a stock's regression equation, this can give little predictive value because individual α, β, and ϵ values can change. In particular, many stocks' betas are unstable and tend to differ in rising and falling markets. One cannot avoid this risk simply by selecting individual stocks, but careful diversification can reduce it when changes in one stock offset changes in another.

Many academic studies have shown that groups of stocks tend to show more stability in their betas and other regression relationships than individual securities. The **Capital Asset Pricing Model (CAPM)** suggests that investors can diversify to reduce the portfolio's overall ϵ and α values to zero, eliminating the unsystematic risk entirely. This leaves systematic risk, or beta. A sufficient number of stocks can combine to give a portfolio beta of 1.00, matching the characteristics of the market, which, by definition, has a beta of 1.0 and α and ϵ values of zero. This requires holding shares in 25 to 35 different stock issues.

Capital Asset Pricing Model (CAPM): The method of estimating portfolio return based on beta analysis and estimates of market returns.

An investor may be willing to assume more risk than the market offers in pursuit of higher returns. This person could build a portfolio of stocks with higher betas. The dots in Exhibit 16.7 illustrate the positions along

EXHIBIT **16.7**

Capital Market Line

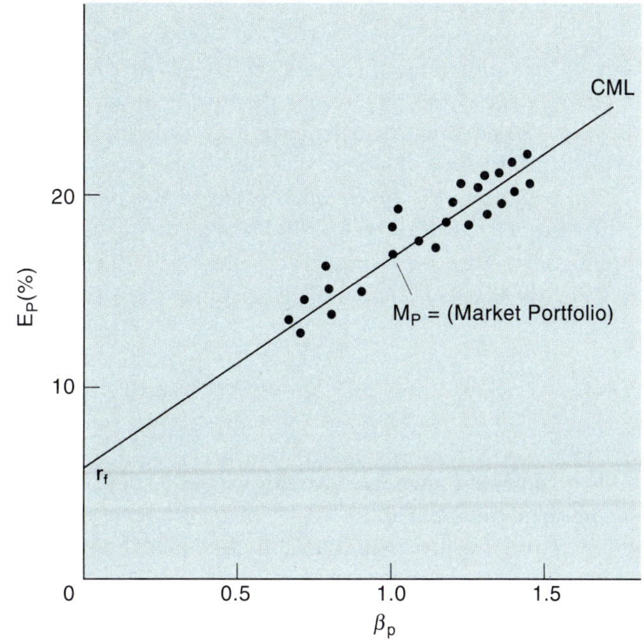

the capital market line of various portfolios as a function of their betas. Since portfolio betas show greater stability than betas of individual stocks, these values allow the portfolio manager to predict future portfolio returns with more confidence than predictions of future returns on an individual stock would inspire. Point M_p on the capital market line represents the portfolio of the overall market for risky securities; in this example M_p has a beta of 1.0 and a return of 17 percent. To match the performance of the market, the portfolio manager could aim for this spot. To build a riskier portfolio, he or she would find a position along the CML to the right of point M_p.

The portfolio manager could build a portfolio with less risk than the market in two ways: by buying stocks that would place the portfolio to the left of point M_p, or by investing in the market portfolio (M_p) and adjusting for risk by adding a certain percentage of risk-free assets at point r_f. The second option may seem easier since he or she could find risk-free assets at any Treasury auction, but low-risk stocks are more rare. Of course, reducing risk in this way would also reduce the portfolio return. The equation below specifies the relationship between market return and portfolio return in such a situation:

$$E_p = r_f + \beta_p(E_m - r_f)$$

E_p is the expected return on the portfolio, r_f is the risk-free rate of return, β_p is the portfolio beta, and E_m is the expected return of the market.

To understand the practical effects of these techniques, consider an example. Assume that the analyst expected a market return of 15 percent when the portfolio beta equaled 1.2, and risk-free assets were returning 11 percent. Assume, further, that he or she had completed normal diversification to reduce the unsystematic risk of the portfolio to zero. To determine the expected return of a portfolio of common stocks with no risk-free assets, substitute the appropriate variables into the regression equation below, which is adapted from the one given in the previous section:

$$\begin{aligned} E_p &= \alpha + \beta_p E_m \pm \epsilon \\ &= 0 + 1.2(0.15) \pm 0 \\ &= 18 \text{ percent} \end{aligned}$$

This portfolio manager would expect a return of 18 percent from this common stock portfolio.

The beta of 1.2 indicates higher risk than the market portfolio would provide. Another investor may want a lower-risk portfolio that matches the market levels of risk and rate of return. He or she could accomplish these goals by including risk-free assets in the portfolio in proportions indicated by the equation:

$$E_p = E_m = (W_{rf})\, r_f + (W_S)\, \beta_p\, (E_m)$$

where W_{rf} is the weight of risk-free assets in the portfolio and W_S is the weight of stocks in the portfolio. Together, these weights sum to 1.0, since each represents a portion of the total capital invested in the portfolio. Therefore W_S equals $1.0 - W_{rf}$. This allows one to alter the regression equation for the all-stock portfolio to find the appropriate weight for risk-free assets:

$$\begin{aligned} 0.15 &= (W_{rf})0.11 + (1 - W_{rf})0.18 \\ 0.15 &= 0.11W_{rf} + 0.18 - 0.18W_{rf} \\ -0.03 &= -0.07W_{rf} \\ 0.429 &= W_{rf} \end{aligned}$$

The investor would devote 42.9 percent of the portfolio to risk-free assets and the remainder, 57.1 percent, to risky stocks. This portfolio would then match the risk and return performance of the market portfolio.

perspective on **ETHICS**

Ethical and Legal Responsibilities of Investment Fiduciaries[a]

In common usage, a fiduciary generally is defined as someone acting in a position of trust on behalf of or for the benefit of a third party. Investment managers and trustees who serve in a fiduciary capacity would include such individuals as pension and endowment fund managers, trust fund managers, individuals who serve as members of pension and endowment fund advisory committees, bank trust officers, and anyone who manages investment funds on behalf of another person or organization. The legal and ethical responsibilities of fiduciaries are governed by a variety of federal and state laws and legal precedents from past court cases (known as common law or case law).

One of the most important federal statutes governing fiduciary responsibilities is the Employee Retirement Income Security Act of 1974 (ERISA), which governs the conduct of pension fund fiduciaries. Although ERISA technically applies only to pension fiduciaries, the language is important to other classes of fiduciaries as well, for two reasons. First is simply that the absolute dollar magnitude of the assets held in U.S. pension funds, estimated at approximately $2 trillion, is a good indicator that most professional investment managers have some exposure to managing pension funds. Second, ERISA is in many ways a codification of the common law and trust law governing fiduciary responsibilities that had evolved through 1974—the year ERISA became law. Thus, in a very practical sense, ERISA lays out the legal expectations for fiduciary conduct of pension fiduciaries, as well as codifies the standards established in trust law and the common law applicable to other classes of fiduciaries.

In addition to the common law and ERISA statute, there are a number of other important sources of fiduciary guidance. Historically, chief among them has been the late Professor Austin Wakeman Scott's *The Law of Trusts* and the American Law Institute's 1959 Restatement (Second) of Trusts, for which Professor Scott served as reporter. Other leading statutory and regulatory sources of guidance in addition to ERISA include the Investment Advisors Act of 1940, Uniform Management of Institutional Funds Act of 1972 (UMIFA), which applies to charitable organizations, and the regulations under Section 4944 of the Internal Revenue Code, which apply to private foundations.

In general, the law views the fiduciary responsibilities of an investment manager or trustee as consisting of two parts: reasonable care and loyalty.[b] The "prudent man rule" normally is cited as the standard of reasonable care. Under ERISA, the standard of prudence is raised to what is now known as the "prudent expert standard," imposing on investment managers the duty to exercise "the care, skill, prudence and diligence under the circumstances then prevailing that the prudent man acting in a like capacity and familiar with such matters would use in the conduct of an enterprise of a like character with like aims."[c] The duty of loyalty requires that managers and trustees act in a manner that puts their clients' interests above their own and that they act solely for the benefit of the clients. These standards will be explained in more detail in Chapter 17.

[a]This passage is based on William G. Droms, "Fiduciary Responsibilities of Investment Managers and Trustees," *Financial Analysts Journal*, July–August 1992, pp. 58–64.

[b]James L. Walters, "An Overview of Fiduciary Law," *The Investment Managers Handbook*, Sumner Levine, ed. (Homewood, Ill.: Dow Jones-Irwin, 1980), p. 575.

[c]ERISA, Section 404(a)(1)(B).

CAPM Decision Rules

Beta analysis and the CAPM seem attractive to many portfolio managers who accept the following assumptions:

1. Prices on various stock issues change independently of one another, and their past behavior gives no help in forecasting future prices.
2. Inability to predict stock prices defeats virtually all efforts to beat the market. Since the efficient market reflects all relevant information in each current stock price, the average investor cannot hope to outperform the market.
3. Transaction costs of frequent trading will wipe out any additional gains from trading, giving an advantage to buy-and-hold tactics.
4. Proper diversification can build a portfolio with a stable beta out of stocks with unstable individual betas. This allows a portfolio manager to consistently earn the return of the market. Alternatively, adjusting the beta above or below 1.0 can change the portfolio risk and return levels to better match specific investment goals. A portfolio of 35 to 50 security issues can provide this kind of diversification.
5. Besides stabilizing the portfolio beta, careful diversification can reduce unsystematic risk (α and ϵ) to zero, leaving only the systematic risk of the market (β).

In essence, practitioners of CAPM believe they cannot beat the market, so they join it.

Limits of CAPM

In building portfolios to match the returns of the market, CAPM theorists must surrender the hope of ever outperforming it. CAPM theory assumes that no one can earn any extra return from efforts to identify and select superior investments. Extensive empirical research suggests that about half of all professional investors outperform the market and half do not do as well as the market. Some evidence does suggest, however, that superior research will lead to superior investment results.

Richard Roll suggests that the S&P 500 does not really reflect the market for all stocks.[6] Therefore, even if an investor's portfolio matches the performance of the S&P 500, it could still fail to earn the return of the "real" market.

Edward Miller sees no sense in buying stocks without regard to price levels.[7] Miller thinks that emotional investors and speculators tend to bid prices up too high relative to future dividends and earnings. When investors perceive a stock to be attractive, they bid up its price, perhaps beyond the level that allows a fair return on the investment. Miller discusses the sad case of the last optimistic investor who typically buys at the top of the market and realizes a loss when prices subsequently fall. Conversely, the last pessimistic seller will hold a stock until it reaches rock bottom until hope for a rebound gives way to disappointment and disillusionment, and the investor sells the security just before its price begins to appreciate again. The cases of these unfortunate souls conflict with the assumptions of Modern Portfolio Theory that the stock market maintains an equilibrium, and that investors have homogeneous expectations about stocks.

Finally, Modern Portfolio Theory and its beta analysis techniques ignore the possibility of improving investment results through timely buying and selling. In fact, although it strains the limits of analysis, a successful effort to time the market can improve investment performance substantially.

Portfolio Management Using Modern Portfolio Theory and CAPM

Modern Portfolio Theory finds practical application in two ways: by guiding research efforts and by inspiring the creation of index funds and other market-matching portfolios.

Investment Research Large brokerage houses provide their investment clients with extensive research based on Modern Portfolio Theory. They have developed a large selection of reports and other publications that explain the theory to institutional investors in much the same way this chapter explains the subject.

For example, Kidder Peabody provides its clients with lists of securities that report expected returns based on regression analysis. If such a list suggests a 19 percent expected return for a stock when the market return is 17 percent, the investor can assume that the stock has a beta of approximately 1.1 (when α equals zero). This means the stock is 10 percent riskier than the market index. Though the entire investment industry shows the influence of MPT, only about 10 percent of the industry uses these methods exclusively.

index fund: A no-load mutual fund that invests in the same sample of stocks in the same proportions as a market index.

Index Funds Index funds owe their very existence to MPT concepts. An **index fund** is a no-load mutual fund that invests in all the stocks of a particular market index, often the S&P 500, weighting its holding of a particular stock in the same percentage that that particular stock represents of the total value of the index.

Suppose an index fund seeks to match the performance of a two-stock market index. Stock A sells at a price of \$50 per share and the company has 100 shares outstanding. Stock B sells at \$70 and 200 shares are outstanding. The total market value of the companies is:

$$\$50(100) + \$70(200) = \$5{,}000 + \$14{,}000 = \$19{,}000$$

Stock A represents 26.3 percent of the value of the index (\$5,000/\$19,000), and stock B represents 73.7 percent of this value (\$14,000/\$19,000). The index fund would invest 73.7 percent of its capital in stock B and 26.3

percent in stock A, so its performance would exactly match that of the index. As new investors bought shares in the fund, its manager would invest this new money in the two stocks in the same proportions to keep their weights in the fund equal to their weights in the index. This would keep the fund's rate of return and risk levels in line with those of the market.

Global Funds Global funds have emerged to follow the same procedures, basing their strategies on the World Index. Approximately 40 percent of the stocks in the World Index are American. Of the remainder, 20 percent come from Japan and 16 percent from Europe, including Britain. Stocks from Australia and other countries make up the balance.

Following Modern Portfolio Theory, global funds identify the efficient set of portfolios. An efficient portfolio consisting of one security will begin by selecting the stock with the highest return-to-risk ratio of all the securities available. Adding another security in an appropriate proportion will reduce risk, giving another efficient portfolio of two securities. This process continues until the entire efficient frontier is established.

The global fund's manager, like other MPT investors, then decides between risk-free assets and risky assets on the capital market line. He or she draws this line between the y-intercept, which reflects the return on the risk-free asset, to run tangent to the efficient frontier. The investor selects risk-free assets, risky assets, or some combination, depending on his or her attitude toward risk.

Investment Policy and Goals

investment policy: A statement of an investor's goals and objectives based upon return and risk expectations.

Whether guided by Modern Portfolio Theory or some other set of techniques, each investor must establish an **investment policy** to state goals his or her investments should achieve, and attitudes toward risk and expected return. An investor may say, "To accept 3 percent risk, I require at least a 7 percent return when the risk-free rate of return is 4 percent." This would assure the investor of a return-to-risk ratio of at least 1.0 [(7 − 4)/3 = 1]. To accept an opportunity to make an investment with a 14 percent standard deviation (the risk level of the S&P 500 during the 1980s), this investor would require a return of 18 percent, assuming the risk-free rate remained at 4 percent.

Modern Portfolio Theory reflects these investor decisions about risk and return in a carefully drawn set of indifference curves. In practice, an investor does not draw any indifference curves. Instead, he or she evaluates available investment alternatives based on expected return and risk and then chooses assets in which to invest. One person might place 100 percent of available funds in common stocks. Based upon past results, this investor could expect price appreciation of about 13 percent (including a dividend yield of about 4 percent) with a risk level of 14 percent. Notice that the previous discussion has followed the practice of MPT, lumping dividend and interest income together with price appreciation in order to consider total return.

Another person might require more current income from his or her investments. This might lead the income investor to allocate his or her capital to purchase 9 percent bonds with a standard deviation of 7 percent. An investor with $500,000 could produce only $20,000 of current income from common stocks based on a 4 percent dividend yield. The same amount invested in 9 percent bonds would provide $45,000 of income.

Besides supplying enough income to meet current needs, however, this investor may be concerned with the effect of inflation on his or her current income. Therefore, rather than investing 100 percent of the available capital in bonds, he or she might buy bonds with 70 percent and spend the remaining 30 percent on common stock. The $350,000 worth of 9 percent bonds would produce $31,500. The $150,000 worth of stocks would generate annual dividend payments of $6,000. This sums to $37,500 in total income rather than the $45,000 that a portfolio of bonds alone would generate. However, the value of the common stock would increase by $13,500 in a year (9 percent of $150,000), which would more than offset the reduction in current income, while increasing that capital available to provide income in the future.

Besides the income investor, another investor might resist the idea of sinking everything into common stock. Anyone who remembers the market collapse of 1987 and subsequent minor stumbles might well abhor the thought of putting all of his or her money at risk. Such an investor might put 70 percent in common stock and 30 percent in risk-free assets. If conditions remained the same as in the previous examples, he or she would earn an expected return of 13 percent from stocks and 4 percent from risk-free assets. This would give a total return on common stock of 13 percent times $350,000, or $45,500, of which $14,000 would come from dividends (4 percent times $350,000) and the balance from price appreciation. The risk-free assets would pay 4 percent of $150,000, or $6,000, raising the total current income from the portfolio to $20,000. The total return on the portfolio of $51,500 would represent a 10.3 percent return with a risk level of 10 percent or less since the low correlation between common stock and risk-free money market investments reduces covariance and risk.

Exhibit 16.8 lists some popular recipes for different portfolios geared toward specific return and risk goals. Notice that changing investment goals from income toward aggressive growth increases both the expected return and the standard deviation, the measure of risk, while the dividend declines. The exhibit data reflect conditions and market expectations in early 1992.

Exhibit 16.8 illustrates that no one portfolio mix can suit all investors. Instead, different solutions give investors a range of possible outcomes designed to achieve varying goals. A portfolio manager must construct a portfolio that responds to the individual needs, return objectives, and risk tolerances of the portfolio's owner.

EXHIBIT 16.8

Recipes for Different Portfolio Objectives with Return (r), Standard Deviation (σ_r), and Dividends (D) or Interest (I)

Income Investor	r	σ_r	D OR I
Four parts income common stocks with some growth	12.0%	13.0	6.0
Five parts bonds with short to medium maturities	7.0	7.0	7.0
One part cash	5.0	0.0	5.0
Overall portfolio	8.8	5.7	6.4
Growth and Income Investor			
Four parts growth stocks	15.0	16.0	2.0
Two parts income stocks	12.0	13.0	6.0
Two parts bonds	7.0	7.0	7.0
Two parts cash	5.0	0.0	5.0
Overall portfolio	10.8	10.4	4.4
Growth Investor			
Eight parts growth stock	15.0	16.0	2.0
Two parts cash	5.0	0.0	5.0
Overall portfolio	13.0	12.8	2.6
Aggressive Growth Investor			
Four parts risky growth stocks	18.0	19.0	1.0
Five parts growth stocks	15.0	16.0	2.0
One part cash	5.0	0.0	5.0
Overall portfolio	15.2	15.6	2.0
Tax-Exempt Investor			
Two parts growth stocks	15.0	16.0	2.0
Two parts long-term, tax-exempt bonds	6.0	5.0	6.0
Four parts medium-term, tax-exempt bonds	5.0	4.0	5.0
One part short-term, tax-exempt bonds	3.0	3.0	3.0
One part cash	5.0	0.0	5.0
Overall portfolio	7.0	6.1	4.4

Investor Objectives and Portfolio Management

investment objectives: Security of principal, growth of capital, current income, marketability, liquidity, and favorable tax treatment.

Planning, selection, and supervision of a securities portfolio depend upon its **investment objectives.** Individual investors develop specific objectives in a number of variables, but most of them generally agree on a few universal rules and objectives.

Security of Principal One critical objective of all investment is to maintain the security of the principal. This gives rise to a general aversion to risk and an overriding effort to maintain the principal value of the securities in a portfolio. In fact, this implies an effort to increase the value of these securities over time to compensate for the decline in purchasing power of invested dollars as a result of inflation. Therefore, maintaining principal requires an increasing value for a portfolio. As hard as most people must work to accumulate a reasonable sum for investment, their primary goal generally focuses on protecting this nest egg.

Growth in the size of an individual's investment fund frequently stimulates a change in attitude toward risk. An investor who begins a retirement fund with $2,000 annual investments may have little fear of loss while the balance remains small. After a time, however, the shocked investor will discover that the account has grown to hold assets with a substantial value. This realization may lead to a quick sell off of all common stocks in favor of a safe money market fund. Fear of loss can overcome more rational goals and lead to poor portfolio management decisions. Therefore, as the value of a portfolio grows to impressive proportions, outside counsel becomes more and more essential to provide impartial, professional guidance.

Growth of Capital Nearly all investors must emphasize growth over time. Some investors orient their portfolios strongly toward growth of principal, sacrificing the chance to generate income. Even those who want maximum current income, however, must achieve some growth in capital value to protect the source of future income. High tax brackets favor investing for capital growth since taxes will consume a portion of any current income. In addition, people in high tax brackets often have income in excess of their current needs.

Investors whose main goal is growth of capital require a different type of security than those who seek income first. They focus on growth of total principal value rather than growth of the income this principal could provide. In addition to stimulating growth in net worth, this can postpone taxes until the investor sells the stock or other asset and realizes a capital gain. Such investors generally look for common stocks with high total expected returns, and they prefer companies that retain earnings to finance future growth over those that pay out earnings in dividends.

Current Income Most investors like to receive some income from their investments, even though these small payments can support little additional consumption. Some people, however, identify the highest possible level of stable income as an essential investment goal, giving secondary importance to growth in principal value over time. This system of priorities may emerge from a need for current income to maintain one's livelihood. A retired person living on a modest pension and Social Security payments might well slant an investment portfolio toward providing as much current income as is possible.

To generate high levels of current income, an investor should purchase high-dividend common stocks to provide both income and growth. Over time, increases in dividends will improve the income the portfolio generates. Even growth-oriented investors may pursue some current income goals to defray investing expenses, or they may reinvest dividends to provide a major source of increases in future portfolio values. Many income-oriented investors combine fixed-income securities such as corporate bonds with income-oriented common stocks in order to maximize the stability and growth of income.

Marketability and Liquidity Marketability, the ability to sell a security easily and quickly, influences all investors' portfolio management decisions. This goal leads them to confine their purchases to better-known stocks with large numbers of shares outstanding. Otherwise, they face the risk that they will be unable to sell relatively large amounts of stock in small companies quickly because of limited trading volume in those issues.

Liquidity extends the concept of marketability to include the ability to convert a security to cash quickly with little or no loss of value. The best example of a liquid security is a short-term Treasury bill. Savings accounts are generally liquid, but a bank may limit the instant availability of funds in unusual circumstances. A demand deposit with a commercial bank offers complete liquidity, but it generally pays a very low interest rate, if any, and checks take a few days to clear. This might not seem important, but a check may not suit a business transaction that requires immediate cash.

To meet the need for liquidity, an investor should place a certain portion of available funds in short-term, liquid investments like Treasury bills, short-term certificates of deposit (CDs), or money market funds. Even these liquid investments require a week or so to convert to cash.

Tax Effects Investors should seek investments that minimize their tax burdens. Actually, this combines with rate of return goals into a general principle that an investor should look for the highest after-tax return from any investment, in either a growth or income portfolio. This remains important even when tax rates are low and capital gains enjoy favorable tax treatment as compared to ordinary income. Tax-exempt securities like municipal bonds might provide the highest after-tax income for a particular investor depending on his or her tax bracket, perhaps even outperforming growth stocks. Reinvesting tax-exempt income in still more tax-exempt investments may provide an excellent rate of return.

Since a taxpayer need not pay tax on a capital gain until he or she realizes it by selling the security that has increased in value, growth stocks provide a form of tax-free compounding. Many people reduce taxes by deferring income until after retirement when most fall into lower tax brackets. Income from certain legal trusts is taxed at a lower rate than other income, which can improve the return on these investments depending

upon the investor's tax bracket. Some tax-ded
similar performance.

Consider buying U.S. savings bonds
annually before taxes. The bondholder m
the bonds mature. Finally, IRS rules a
reduce the tax burden. Several of these
taxes and increase after-tax income.

Diversification Techniques

As mentioned throughout this text, successful investment and p management hinges on diversification. Rather than concentrating one capital in a single type of security, wise investors hold a range of individual assets within a broad mix of asset categories to reduce the risk of loss on any single investment. Careful diversification can reduce risk sharply, though it generally does require sacrificing some expected return. The reduction in the variability of portfolio returns can improve overall portfolio performance by increasing the return-to-risk ratio. Growth and income investors achieve diversification in different ways.

growth investor: An investor whose portfolio objectives emphasize long-term capital gains over current income.

Growth Investors and Diversification **Growth investors** seek primarily to generate long-term capital gains and growth of principal from their portfolios. They pursue short-term gains only as part of long-term strategies. They do not give much priority to generating current income since this also generates income tax liabilities.

A growth portfolio should include several common stock issues to earn the highest overall return with the lowest risk. An investor with a small amount of capital will find it difficult to hold round lots of sufficient numbers of stocks. Most investment professionals recommend holding a portfolio of between six and ten stocks, which would stretch a few thousand dollars too thinly. Instead, common stock mutual funds provide excellent diversification for portfolios of this size.

Even those who can afford the necessary stock purchases often fail in their efforts to time their transactions to take maximum advantage of market trends. To avoid this problem, a long-term investor can develop a dollar cost averaging strategy, as discussed in Chapter 14. Recall that this involves regular purchases of shares in a given set of stocks or stock mutual funds over a long period of time. By purchasing shares at varying prices, the investor pays an average of the long-term highs and lows. By effectively diversifying across market cycles, dollar cost averaging pays off by reducing the variability of portfolio returns.

Finally, investing for growth requires matching defensive and aggressive portfolio positions to market trends. If a market decline seems likely, selling stocks and investing the proceeds temporarily in short-term securities can reduce the portfolio's exposure to risk. These kinds of defensive securities

Defensive and Aggressive Portfolio Compositions

	$20,000 FUND		$100,000 FUND	
	AGGRESSIVE	DEFENSIVE	AGGRESSIVE	DEFENSIVE
Short-term debt	$ 2,000	$10,000	$10,000	$50,000
Equity	18,000	10,000	90,000	50,000
Number of securities	6–10	5	6–15	6–10

include short-term government securities, money market funds, and certificates of deposit.

If the market seems poised for a surge, a portfolio manager might buy stocks, leaving only 10 to 20 percent of the portfolio in defensive investments to meet liquidity needs. Exhibit 16.9 provides examples of defensive and aggressive portfolio alignments for growth investors with different amounts of capital. Benjamin Graham, the father of security analysis in the United States, has suggested that investors never have less than 30 percent of their portfolios in common stocks, and never have more than 30 percent in money market funds. As noted earlier, market timing is a risky strategy, so the actions suggested above are not for all investors.

income investor: An investor whose portfolio objectives emphasize current income over capital growth.

Income Investors and Diversification **Income investors** face different diversification problems than growth investors. Income investors need to balance goals of income maximization, risk minimization, and opportunities for future growth of capital to generate higher income as inflation reduces purchasing power. Reconciling these often-conflicting goals can severely test the skills of the best portfolio manager.

Short-term securities normally provide rather poor yields compared to longer-term issues. Concentrating exclusively on long-term, fixed-income securities normally will improve the portfolio yield, but fixed returns are subject to erosion by inflation, while shorter-term securities would allow regular reinvestment at current market rates. Also, rising interest rates will force the market value of long-term, fixed-income securities downward, creating a potential for capital loss.

High-dividend stocks also fluctuate in value in response to interest rate changes, but they offer the possibility of dividend growth, which fixed-income investments do not. For this reason, income investors should hold diversified selections of stocks that promise high and growing dividend yields over time. Combine this portion of the portfolio with a portion devoted to fixed-income securities to take advantage of their high current income payments and stable principal values.

If future prospects for the market seem uncertain, many investors maintain defensive positions that favor income growth. At a time when

EXHIBIT 16.10

Diversification for an Income Investor

Fixed-income securities	
1 year	10%
2–3 years	10
3–4 years	10
4–6 years	10
6–10 years	10
Common stocks, income and growth	50
Total	100%

interest rates were expected to rise, a wise portfolio manager would shift funds toward short-term, fixed-income securities. When interest rates peaked, he or she would buy long-term bonds or high-dividend common stocks to take advantage of low prices and high yields. Recognizing the difficulty of this kind of market timing, he or she might choose instead to employ dollar cost averaging and trust that gains will balance losses over the long term.

An example should shed more light on the problem. Assume that you are an income-oriented investor with $100,000 to invest. You fear that interest rates may rise. You might divide your portfolio equally between fixed-income securities and common stocks with high dividend yields. If common stocks seem overpriced, you might accumulate your stock funds in a reserve to purchase common stock later when the market corrects prices. As an alternative, you might make regular stock purchases in a dollar cost averaging strategy.

You might diversify the half of the portfolio invested in fixed-income securities as follows: one-fifth each in short-term securities (those maturing within one year), securities maturing in from two to three years, securities maturing in from three to four years, securities maturing in from four to six years, and securities maturing in from six to ten years. You would reinvest principal repayments you would receive as bonds matured based on market expectations at the time. Exhibit 16.10 illustrates this diversification approach.

Supervising a Portfolio

Every portfolio manager must devote considerable time and effort to supervision of the portfolio. After setting up the portfolio, he or she must constantly monitor and reevaluate it to make certain that the investments

portfolio supervision: Weekly or monthly sessions to monitor and reevaluate changes in price of portfolio securities.

perform as expected. This is **portfolio supervision.** It helps protect the portfolio from erosion of returns due to unfavorable price changes, and it allows the portfolio to take advantage of favorable price changes that will enhance returns in the long run. Both income and growth investors must devote substantial resources to this work.

This does not imply that anyone should trade shares every week. Monitoring portfolio performance on a weekly or monthly basis, even when it extends to include reviewing price changes of individual shares, does not make frequent trading necessary, especially when transaction costs from such a practice would themselves reduce portfolio returns.

Instead, portfolio supervision helps one to maintain awareness of the performance of individual shares and the general market climate. In particular, insight into current market conditions can help guide the timing of trades that the portfolio manager would make in any case.

As part of the portfolio supervision process, investors must continuously appraise companies to assess the risks and rewards of their common stocks. If a stock moves substantially above its expected price, the portfolio might benefit from a quick sale to realize profits. Of course, such a decision would require careful consideration of taxes. The portfolio manager could then reinvest the proceeds in other securities that offered greater potential.

Performance and Portfolio Measurement

portfolio performance measurement: Quarterly reassessment of portfolio returns in relation to investment objectives and performance of a market index.

Beyond supervision, a portfolio manager must complete a rigorous **portfolio performance measurement** process. Comparing the portfolio's return to that of a market index gives a good indication of relative performance. Although mutual fund managers reassess portfolio performance daily, most investors need to repeat this rigorous appraisal process only quarterly, provided that they maintain weekly supervision in order to avoid unpleasant surprises.

The process begins by finding price quotations for portfolio securities in *The Wall Street Journal.* Multiplying each stock's price by the number of shares the portfolio holds and then summing these individual values gives a total value for the portfolio. The value of the fund in relation to its cost reveals its return, and performance measurement requires comparing these figures to the corresponding figures for the end of the previous quarter.

Assume that a fund has a current value of $10,500, up from $10,000 at the end of the previous quarter. The portfolio has increased in value $500 over the quarter. Divide the $500 gain by the $10,000 original value to find the portfolio return for the quarter, 5 percent. This equates to a strong annual return of approximately 20 percent. To this, one must add the return due to dividend income. Also, one must subtract any additional capital contributions made during the period from the final value since these represent new investment funds rather than returns from previously invested funds. Performance measurement should gauge the performance of invested money rather than the overall growth of the portfolio from all sources.

Portfolio managers refer to two criteria to assess relative performance. First, they ask how much progress the portfolio made toward achieving its own objectives. If one expected the $10,000 portfolio to earn a 5 percent return during the previous quarter, then it achieved its objective. If one expected less robust performance, then it exceeded its goal. If the portfolio manager expected more than a 5 percent quarterly return, he or she should reevaluate the portfolio's composition carefully to judge whether it holds the right securities.

After assessing performance relative to objectives, the measurement process compares the same figures to those of the market. How does the performance of a particular portfolio compare with that of Standard & Poor's 500 Index? This comparison requires determining the value of the S&P 500 at the end of the current quarter less its value at the end of the previous quarter, then adding in dividends paid by stocks in the sample. Comparing this gain or loss to the index value at the end of the previous quarter reveals its percentage gain or loss, and this figure gives a market-based perspective on the percentage gain or loss on the portfolio. Unexpected differences between market and portfolio performance should lead to reexamination of each security in the portfolio to make sure that its return adequately compensates for the risk of holding it.

Establishing an Income Portfolio

A previous section discussed the objectives of income investors. To achieve these goals, income investors must construct carefully balanced portfolios of appropriate securities.

An income portfolio can be either conservative or aggressive. A conservative income portfolio generally concentrates on government bonds and the highest quality corporate bonds along with limited positions in high-dividend common stocks. In addition, a conservative portfolio will tend to hold debt securities with shorter terms to maturity than those in a more aggressive income portfolio. An aggressive income portfolio will hold more common stocks and corporate bonds, especially lower-rated bonds, and it will tolerate longer maturities in pursuit of higher yields.

Both conservative and aggressive income investors need think about future growth of income. To encourage this growth, they can spend less than the total income from the portfolio and reinvest the excess, or they can lean more toward common stocks to take advantage of expected increases in dividend payments.

Building a Conservative Income Portfolio

A very conservative income portfolio might hold a diversified mix of securities of the highest possible quality. Though its goals would emphasize safety, the returns from such a portfolio could still provide substantial income, provided the portfolio manager could avoid special problems and high income taxes.

An extremely risk-averse income portfolio might consist entirely of U.S. Treasury notes. These securities subject their owners to the risk of inflation because interest income on them does not increase with prices over time. On the other hand, their interest yields can be reasonably high. In the early 1990s an investor without much expertise could obtain a current cash yield from T-notes of approximately 8.4 percent. This portfolio would maintain liquidity and diversify by maturity date, while minimizing the number of securities in the portfolio.

Exhibit 16.11 shows a sample of such a portfolio that allocates approximately 20 percent of its capital to each of five Treasury note issues with maturities of two, four, six, eight, and ten years. Based on prices and yields reported in *The Wall Street Journal* on April 2, 1991, this portfolio would have had a current yield of 8.34 percent. Notice, however, that constructing a portfolio of real security issues raises practical problems that are not apparent in a hypothetical portfolio goal like investing $20,000 in each of five Treasury note issues. In April 1991 all of the notes in the chosen range of maturities traded at a premium so the portfolio manager would have had to pay more than $1,000 for each note. The reason they traded at a premium, of course, is that current market interest rates had fallen below the bonds' coupon rates.

This forces their yields to maturity below their current yields because the yield to maturity calculation amortizes the premium over the life of the note. To illustrate this difference, consider the FEB 2001 note with an 11.75 percent coupon rate. In April 1991 this note sold at a price of 124.56 ($1,245.60 for each $1,000 face value note). Together, this price and the high coupon rate gave a current yield of 9.43 percent ($1,175 for each $1,245.60 of current market value). The yield to maturity on this note, however, amounted to only 8.09 percent because that calculation reflects the fact that the notes would mature ten years later at their face value of $1,000 each. This gives each note an effective capital loss of $245.60 over its ten-year life. Therefore, the total return on the note, considering both the high coupon rate and the amortization of the capital loss, would be 8.09 percent per year over the ten years.

Altogether, the portfolio outlined in Exhibit 16.11 consists of Treasury notes with face values of $20,000 from each of five issues maturing at two-year intervals. The cost of the portfolio at April 1991 market prices would be $107,000. It would provide annual interest payments of $8,925, producing a current yield of 8.34 percent.

As these notes matured, the portfolio manager could reinvest the repaid principal to generate future income. Any change in interest rates would automatically affect the portfolio yield through this reinvestment process. The portfolio offers liquidity if the owner should need cash, and the near-term maturity dates reduce the possibility of substantial losses through yield

EXHIBIT 16.11

U.S. Treasury Note Income Portfolio, March 1991

DATE OF MATURITY	COUPON RATE	APPROXIMATE YEARS TO MATURITY	PRICE	DOLLAR AMOUNT[a]	CURRENT YIELD	ANNUAL INTEREST PAYMENTS	YIELD TO MATURITY
MAR 1993	7.125%	2	$100.28	$ 20,056	7.11%	$1,425	6.97%
APR 1995	8.375	4	102.69	20,538	8.16	1,675	7.59
APR 1997	8.500	6	102.78	20,556	8.27	1,700	7.91
FEB 1999	8.875	8	104.69	20,938	8.48	1,775	8.06
FEB 2001	11.750	10	124.56	24,913	9.43	2,350	8.09
				$107,000	8.34	$8,925	

[a] Dollar Amount = Cost to purchase $20,000 face value of note indicated

and price fluctuations. This portfolio of very high-quality debt securities offers a safe, steady stream of income and an excellent return of approximately 8 percent, ignoring any commissions on the purchase transactions. Ordinarily, this transaction cost would be relatively small.

Building a Quality Income Portfolio

To obtain a higher yield at a slightly higher risk, the portfolio manager could expand its investment boundaries beyond government securities to include high-quality corporate securities. Periodically, *The Wall Street Journal* publishes recent prices of new bond issues of various corporations. This requires more careful diversification among securities rated from AAA to A that vary in maturity from short term to intermediate term. Adding these corporate bonds to a portfolio will increase both current income and yield to maturity. This does require accepting additional risk, but diversification on the basis of quality rating and maturity can minimize the threat.

Exhibit 16.12 reflects a characteristic diversification pattern for such a fixed-income investment strategy. Although this portfolio is slightly more aggressive than one that limited itself to U.S. Treasury securities, it remains rather conservative, while still increasing cash yield by almost 0.5 percent per year. Additionally, since the calculations in Exhibit 16.12 reflect the values of par bonds, the yield to maturity matches the current yield, 8.76 percent per year.

This corporate bond portfolio would meet the diversification needs of an investor who wanted maximum current income together with highly secure principal. Note that the portfolio holds 20 percent of its capital in Treasury bonds with a ten-year average maturity. This sacrifices liquidity compared to the shorter-term Treasury notes to increase return. Another

EXHIBIT 16.12

Quality Income Portfolio, March 1991

	DOLLAR AMOUNT	CURRENT YIELD	CURRENT INCOME
Ten-year Treasury notes	$ 20,000	8.00%	$1,600
Six-year FNMA notes	20,000	8.50	1,700
Corporate bonds (AA-rated, ten-year maturities)	60,000	9.10	5,460
Total	$100,000	8.76%	$8,760

Yields are approximations based on representative bonds trading near par value at the end of March 1991.

20 percent of the portfolio is invested in six-year notes issued by the Federal National Mortgage Association, an agency of the U.S. government. The balance of the portfolio includes a mix of AA-rated corporate bonds with ten-year maturities that offer an average yield of approximately 9.1 percent if purchased at par.

Overall, the portfolio in Exhibit 16.12 would provide a yield of approximately 8.76 percent on a $100,000 total investment, so it would generate cash payments of $8,760 per year. The major risk of this portfolio comes from its lack of any type of protection against inflation. With only the effort necessary to flip through *The Wall Street Journal*, an investor could build a portfolio that would provide adequate diversification and a good yield without a great deal of risk. To meet the need for protection against inflation, the portfolio manager could diversify into high-dividend common stocks. The income payments from the common stocks might fall short of the current payments from the corporate bonds, but over time common stock dividends generally grow so they may ultimately provide higher rates of return than fixed-income securities, and the difference would offset inflation somewhat. In effect, this method sacrifices current income for future income, but it addresses the major disadvantage of a fixed-income portfolio. Over the last two decades interest rates have fallen and risen, but inflation has driven the general trend unmistakably upward.

Building Growth Potential into an Income Portfolio

Building a potential for capital growth into an income portfolio presents some challenging problems. The best solution to these problems involves buying good industrial, public utility, and transportation company stocks that pay high dividends, but still seem likely to continue to grow. American Telephone & Telegraph (AT&T) is a good example of a high-dividend stock that has increased in value over time, while still offering a high and fairly stable dividend yield.

Selecting an income stock requires more work than selecting bonds because the market offers a broader range of these securities from which to choose. Nonetheless, careful attention to *The Wall Street Journal* listings for trades on the New York Stock Exchange will reveal some stocks in growing industries that pay rather good dividends. Although the newspaper gives all the relevant data, the portfolio manager must analyze the data to verify that a particular company's dividend has grown over time and that current projections make continued growth seem likely.

Just reviewing the first part of the New York Stock Exchange Composite Transactions listings, a portfolio manager could compile an appreciable list of stocks that offer average current returns of 8 percent or higher with the possibility of substantial future price increases. Avoid public utilities that have not shown substantial past growth, however, since many of these firms have met serious difficulties in trying to increase their earnings, cover their interest charges, and increase their rates.

To improve the income from such a portfolio, its manager might mix in some long- and intermediate-term bonds. This would improve the current yield, while maintaining the possibility for growth to provide a hedge against inflation. Exhibit 16.13 shows a sample of this kind of diversification.

The portfolios under discussion have only illustrated a more complex process. The list of securities from which these samples came did not reflect every income-paying security available in the market. Establishing an actual income portfolio would require compiling a broader list of securities from sources such as Standard & Poor's, Moody's, and Value Line. A broker who has good research capabilities can provide invaluable assistance in this effort.

Protecting an Income Portfolio from the Tax Collector

High-income investors may want to consider building portfolios of municipal bonds in order to avoid federal income taxes on their investment income. Those who buy bonds issued in the states where they reside will enjoy an additional exemption from state income taxes. As it does for other types of securities, *The Wall Street Journal* lists current prices of actively traded tax-exempt bonds. Thinly traded bonds do not appear on these lists, however, but the brokers who sell them can provide information about current prices and yields. Most large brokerage firms have special municipal bond departments to provide information and trading access for municipal bond investors.

Constructing a municipal bond portfolio requires attention to similar diversification principles as those discussed for other types of portfolios. Spread capital among issues with varying ratings and terms to maturity, but avoid extending beyond ten-year maturities. Also, keep a 10 percent reserve in a tax-free money market fund to enhance liquidity since slow trading in municipal bond markets can restrict the availability of funds.

Diversification by maturities and quality ratings is as important to minimize risk in a tax-exempt portfolio as it is in a corporate bond portfolio

EXHIBIT 16.13

Balanced Stock and Bond Portfolio

Short-term securities	20%
Fixed-income securities:	
20 percent short-term	
20 percent intermediate-term	
divided equally among AAA, AA, and A securities	40
Income growth stocks	40
	100%

or any other kind of portfolio. The market for tax-exempt bonds may challenge the portfolio manager's resolve to find high yields in shorter maturities, and it may not offer municipal bonds in the desired quantity and maturities at all. Still, investors in high tax brackets sometimes need current income from their portfolios, and tax-exempt bonds can help them avoid surrendering this income to the tax collector.

Establishing a Growth Portfolio

Many long-term investors decide to postpone receipt of current income, whether to defer taxes or for other reasons, instead focusing their efforts on building up larger funds to support future consumption. To achieve this kind of capital growth, they invest in broad selections of growth stocks.

Growth As a Concept

The simplest definition of a growth stock identifies stocks whose earnings, dividends, and prices have grown faster than the overall market. Most growth stocks pay lower current dividends than income stocks; instead, the companies retain earnings to finance corporate growth that fuels strong price increases and, usually, higher total returns than other stocks.

Growth investors look for securities with histories of high growth in earnings that provide low but growing current yields. This combination helps ensure gains in the future. In addition, the low current income avoids potentially high taxes on dividends. They realize most of their returns in the form of capital gains on which they must pay taxes only when they sell the stocks and realize the gains. Current law taxes capital gains at a maximum rate of 28%.

Diversification with Growth Stocks

Building a growth portfolio requires a multistage process. This begins with a search for industries that appear to be growing. The portfolio manager identifies the dominant firms in such an industry, with special attention to the prospects for future growth of earnings and dividends. He or she selects a diversified sample of stocks issued by these firms.

This effort requires more information than the price, earnings, and dividend quotations that *The Wall Street Journal* can provide. The analyst needs historical information about company earnings growth from Standard & Poor's manuals, Standard & Poor's *Stock Guide*, and possibly from Value Line. Information from sources like these can give useful hints about securities that show good rates of growth in earnings and dividends, as outlined in earlier chapters.

A portfolio worth $100,000 or so should include stocks of approximately ten companies. Trying to diversify further by buying shares in more issues would not improve portfolio returns enough to compensate for the time required to analyze, manage, and measure the performance of the more diverse portfolio.

Timing Investments in Growth Stocks

Proper timing of stock purchases or sales requires maintaining some cash reserves to take advantage of outstanding temporary opportunities. Wise portfolio managers commit themselves in stages rather than thrusting all of their money into the stock market in a single plunge, and they select stocks that are bargains compared to the general level of the market.

After identifying attractive portfolio prospects, the investor must analyze the current market and his or her expectations for the future. This leads to a decision whether to maintain a defensive or aggressive position. For example, in early 1991 an investor would have faced worrisome threats from negative overall stock market returns in 1990 and a continuing recession in the United States economy. With such an uncertain outlook the investor would have hesitated to commit all of a portfolio's funds to the stock market. He or she may well have placed 30 percent or more of the available capital in a reserve invested in short-term securities to fund later stock purchases when market conditions seemed more appropriate. Despite the uncertainty, however, the portfolio manager would have committed some funds to stocks of growth companies he or she identified in the manner described above.

In fact, the stock market outlook is always uncertain. Even during an apparent boom, wise investors approach the market with caution and maintain adequate reserve funds. Such a fund can finance advantageous common stock purchases and provide some current income to cover costs and supplement growing dividends and capital appreciation.

a great deal of risk in pursuit of large returns, or defensive tactics, sacrificing some potential return to reduce risk. Wherever the portfolio falls in relation to these criteria, it must be diversified by industry, security, maturities of any debt securities, and cash.

After building a portfolio, its manager must supervise it and measure its performance. This requires a quarterly review of returns compared both to pre-established objectives and a market index like the S&P 500. Any securities that fail to perform as expected should be replaced quickly.

Meeting specific income and growth goals requires specially constructed portfolios. An income portfolio can generate current payments by either conservative or aggressive tactics. The most conservative income portfolios concentrate mainly on U.S. Treasury securities. More aggressive portfolios mix in corporate fixed-income securities and high-dividend common stocks in increasing proportions. Adding common stocks to an income portfolio accomplishes two important objectives: It provides cash payments that should increase in the future, and it offers some inflation protection through capital growth.

Growth portfolios generally concentrate mainly or exclusively on equity investments in the expectation of achieving higher total returns than income-oriented securities could provide. Growth portfolios nearly always offer much lower current yields than income-oriented portfolios, though. Shifting from income objectives toward growth requires a tradeoff; fixed-income portfolios generally offer only modest growth, while growth portfolios generally offer only modest income.

INVESTMENT MANAGEMENT CONCEPTS

1. Establish long-term goals and objectives.
2. Make security of principal top priority.
3. Diversify to reduce risk.
4. Diversify against all risks and try to maximize returns and minimize risk to maximize the return-to-risk ratio.
5. Measure portfolio returns quarterly in relation to returns on the S&P 500.
6. Trade infrequently, maintain a long-term perspective, and be selective.
7. Determine the weight of a particular security in a portfolio by its return and risk levels.
8. Even limited diversification can substantially reduce risk.
9. Select efficient stocks to construct portfolios.
10. Base investment decisions on the return and risk relationship of a security in a portfolio.
11. Plan an investment program to meet specific goals stated in terms of return and risk.

12. Manage a portfolio to achieve the highest possible return for an acceptable level of risk.

13. An income portfolio emphasizes current income, but must diversify against interest rate risk by balancing short-term securities against long-term securities.

14. An income portfolio remains subject to purchasing power risk.

15. A growth portfolio emphasizes efficient stocks that have the highest returns, the lowest risk levels, and the highest return-to-risk ratios.

16. Though it accepts more risk to generate larger returns, the growth portfolio must be diversified to reduce risk, as well.

17. Achieving a higher return requires accepting more risk. Within limits, as the number of securities in a portfolio increases, risk declines.

REVIEW QUESTIONS

1. List the assumptions of Modern Portfolio Theory (MPT).
2. Explain how the efficient frontier is determined using the Markowitz approach for a two-security portfolio.
3. Where does MPT suggest that one invest on the capital market line (CML)?
4. What are the strengths and weaknesses of the Markowitz techniques?
5. Explain how portfolio managers use the CAPM regression equation.
6. What assumptions do beta theorists make to solve portfolio management problems?
7. Explain each of the variables in the regression equation, $Y = \alpha + \beta X \pm \epsilon$.
8. Explain the use of the return-to-risk ratio $[(E_r - r_f)/\sigma_r]$ in building a portfolio.
9. Does the S&P 500 reflect activity in the entire stock market?
10. If a portfolio with a beta of 1.2 earns 18 percent when the market return is 15 percent, has it outperformed the market?
11. Explain why there is no one recipe for investment success.
12. List the goals and objectives of portfolio management.
13. Explain the difference between an income and a growth investor.
14. Explain the ways an investor must diversify. Why?
15. What is the difference between a defensive and an aggressive investor?
16. Why is portfolio supervision important?
17. Why should a portfolio manager monitor portfolio performance?
18. Distinguish between a conservative income investor and an aggressive income investor.

19. Should an income investor abandon any hope for capital growth?

20. What kind of investments would you favor if you were in the top tax bracket?

21. Discuss the process of building a growth portfolio.

SELF-CORRECTING PROBLEMS

1. Analyst Kennealy recommends two stocks for purchase, Clorox at a price of 60 and Procter & Gamble at 80, citing the following data on past returns (R), risk (σ_r), and expected returns (E_r):

	CLOROX	PROCTER & GAMBLE
1982	1.3%	−6.3%
1983	−0.1	3.8
1984	2.0	0.0
1985	−9.8	−4.6
1986	30.1	6.0
1987	69.3	42.8
1988	52.8	18.4
1989	−2.1	−3.1
1990	50.7	20.7
1991	37.7	24.2
Average return	23.1	10.2
σ_r	28.4	15.9
E_r	13.5	16.5

Which stock would you buy, if either? Why?

2. The uncertainty of these estimates leads you to consider buying both in equal amounts. What will happen to the portfolio expected return (E_r) and risk (σ_r)?

3. Since you might not minimize risk by holding 50 percent of Clorox and 50 percent of Procter & Gamble, you decide to change the weights to 0.7 for Procter & Gamble and 0.3 for Clorox. What happens to E_r and σ_r?

4. Financial analyst Hekman suggests that you replace Clorox with a drug company, Becton-Dickinson, which has the following return, risk, and expected return characteristics:

1982	−18.0%
1983	20.2
1984	−8.0
1985	19.4
1986	25.7
1987	−3.5
1988	4.1
1989	−14.9

1990	49.6%
1991	76.6
Average return	15.1
σ_r	30.1
E_r	22.0

What happens to return and risk when you combine these two securities in equal amounts?

5. You notice that Procter & Gamble has lower risk than Becton-Dickinson, so you decide to weight your portfolio 60 percent for Procter & Gamble and 40 percent for Becton-Dickinson. What does this do to the E_r and σ_r?

6. Assume you rely on your portfolio to contribute to living expenses. Rate each of the following investments in terms of its importance to your portfolio. Use a scale from 0 to 5, with 5 being the most important.

a. Risky growth stock
b. Cash
c. Short-term, tax-exempt bond
d. Growth stock
e. Long-term, tax-exempt bond
f. Income stock
g. Short-term bond
h. Medium-term bond

7. Suppose you will need to sell a portion of your portfolio to pay an obligation such as college tuition in the near future. In which investment option(s) listed above might you consider holding your funds?

8. Having determined your needs as an investor, whether for income, growth, or some other need, you now wish to assemble a diversified portfolio. What is weighting and how can it help you to structure your portfolio?

9. Why and how do changes in the tax code affect your use of municipal bonds or tax-exempt mutual funds?

Answers to Self-Correcting Problems

1. You should prefer Procter & Gamble for its higher expected return and lower risk.

	CLX + P&G	$\frac{\text{CLX + P\&G}}{2}$
1982	−5.0%	−2.5%
1983	3.7	1.8
1984	2.0	1.0
1985	−14.4	−7.2
1986	36.1	18.1
1987	111.1	55.6
1988	71.2	35.6
1989	−5.2	−2.6

	CLX + P&G	$\frac{\text{CLX + P\&G}}{2}$
1990	71.4%	35.7%
1991	61.9	31.0
Average return	19.0	
σ_r	18.0	
Weighted average E_r	15.0	

2. The expected return of 15.0 percent is lower than Procter & Gamble's, and the risk rises to 18.0 percent, higher than Procter & Gamble's. You would actually be better off with only Procter & Gamble.

3. The portfolio weighted 0.3 for Clorox and 0.7 for Procter & Gamble would perform as follows:

	0.3 CLX	0.7 P&G	TOTAL
1982	0.39%	−4.41%	−4.02%
1983	−0.03	2.66	2.63
1984	0.60	0.00	0.60
1985	−2.94	−3.22	−6.16
1986	9.03	4.20	13.23
1987	20.79	29.96	50.75
1988	15.84	12.88	28.72
1989	−0.63	−2.17	−2.80
1990	15.21	14.49	29.70
1991	11.31	16.94	28.25
Average return	17.0		
σ_r	16.0		

E_r 0.3 (13.5) + 0.7(16.5) = 4.05 + 11.55 = 15.6

E_r is 15.6 percent and σ_r is 16.0 percent. This combination is less attractive than Procter & Gamble alone. Better forget Clorox.

4. The Becton-Dickinson/P&G portfolio would give the following results:

	P&G 0.5	B-D 0.5	TOTAL
1982	−3.15%	−9.0%	−12.15%
1983	1.90	10.1	12.00
1984	0.00	−4.0	−4.00
1985	−2.30	9.7	7.40
1986	3.00	12.8	15.80
1987	21.40	−1.8	19.60
1988	9.2	2.1	11.30
1989	−1.6	−7.4	9.00
1990	10.3	24.8	35.10
1991	12.1	38.3	50.40
Average return	18.0		
σ_r	14.0		

E_r (11 + 8.3) = 19.3

The expected return increases to 19.3 percent from 16.5 percent for Procter & Gamble alone, and risk declines to 14.0 percent from Procter & Gamble's 15.9 percent. This is an excellent combination of assets.

5. The portfolio return and risk characteristics become:

	P&G 0.6	B-D 0.4	TOTAL
1982	−3.78%	−7.20%	−10.98%
1983	2.28	8.08	10.36
1984	0.00	−3.20	−3.20
1985	2.76	7.76	10.52
1986	3.60	10.28	13.88
1987	25.68	−1.40	24.28
1988	11.04	1.64	12.68
1989	−1.86	−5.96	−7.82
1990	12.42	19.84	32.26
1991	14.52	30.64	45.16
Average return	17.0		
σ_r	12.0		
E_r (9.9 + 8.8) =	18.7		

The average E_r decreases from 19.3 percent to 18.7 percent, but the risk declines to 12.0 percent from 14.0 percent. This raises the return-to-risk ratio from

$$(19.3 - 6.0)/14.0 = 0.95$$

for the equally weighted portfolio to

$$(18.7 - 6.0)/12.0 = 1.058$$

for the 60/40 portfolio. If you want minimum risk, get it with a 60/40 ratio.

6. As an investor who relies on investment income for living expenses, your selection should be based on stability and consistency of performance. Investment-grade private corporate bonds rated A or better and U.S. Treasury issues represent sound choices.

7. Requirements for cash needs should be considered when building an investment portfolio. You must balance your desire for a return on your money against the risk of short-term fluctuations in the price of the instrument you are holding. For example, it would not be wise to spend money you will need in three months on a 20-year bond. The price of the bond may decline just when you need to convert it to cash to pay your tuition. It would be wiser to hold the money in either a Treasury bill that would mature on or about the date of the cash payment, or to hold the money in a money market account.

8. As discussed in the chapter, no investor should expose his or her portfolio to risk solely due to small size. Varying the type and maturity of

the instruments held in the portfolio limits the effect that any given economic factor will have on the portfolio. You could buy short- or long-term debt securities issued by both government entities and private corporations rated from single A to triple A; each of these investments would respond differently to economic influences. By holding a variety you could diminish the effects of any single economic occurrence. The weight of each instrument in your portfolio depends on the risk and return characteristics you want to achieve. For example, increasing the weight of A-rated corporate bonds would increase your portfolio return due to their higher yields, but it would also increase the overall risk of the portfolio.

9. The advantages of tax-exempt securities come from their ability to improve the investor's returns by limiting tax exposure. A change in the tax code, such as the reduction in marginal tax rates that occurred in 1986, can change the advantage from holding municipal bonds. For example, an investor in the 50 percent tax bracket prior to the 1986 law would have sheltered 50 percent of the interest income from a tax-exempt bond as compared to another investment. If the current marginal tax rate is 28 percent, it means that the same investor now only realizes a 28 percent tax savings by holding a tax-exempt bond. Careful consideration of a municipal bond's tax advantages can assure that its after-tax return at least equals returns from other investment opportunities.

SELECTED READINGS

Amling, Frederick. *Investments: An Introduction to Analysis and Management*, 6th ed. Englewood Cliffs, N.J.: Prentice-Hall, 1989, Chapters 7, 21, and 24.

Andersen, Carl E., and James B. Ross. *Modern Mutual Fund Families & Variable Life: Tools for Investment Growth & Tax Benefits*. Homewood, III.: Dow Jones-Irwin, 1987.

Bouquet, Frank L. *Do-It-Yourself Mutual Fund Book*, 2d ed. Panorama City, Calif.: Systems Co., 1987.

Donoghue, William E. *Donoghue's Mutual Funds Almanac*, 23d ed. New York: Harper & Row, 1992.

Fabozzi, Frank J., ed. *Handbook of Fixed-Income Securities*, 2d ed. Homewood, III.: Dow Jones-Irwin, 1987.

Loeb, Marshall. *Marshall Loeb's 1992 Money Guide*. Boston: Little, Brown, 1992.

Merriman, Paul A., and Merle E. Dowd. *Market Timing with No-Load Mutual Funds: Low-Risk High-Return Investing with No Commissions*, rev. ed. New York: H. Holt & Co., 1987.

Renberg, Werner, and Jeremiah Blitzer. *Making Money with Mutual Funds: Investment Strategies to Beat the Market*. New York: John Wiley & Sons, 1988.

Ritter, Lawrence S. *The Role of Gold in Consumer Investment Portfolios*. New York: New York University Graduate School of Business Administration, 1984.

chapter 17

Managing Your Investment Portfolio

For three days at the end of December 1990 the members of the American Finance Association gathered in Washington, D.C., for their annual meetings and to celebrate the association's 50th anniversary. The highlight of the occasion was a gala dinner where more than 325 members gathered for a gourmet repast to honor past officers of the association and, especially, the three members who shared the 1990 Nobel Prize for economics.

Harry Markowitz won a share of the prize for his work on efficient portfolios, which allow an investor, by holding a diversified range of securities, to strike the best possible balance between risk and return. Besides the Nobel Prize, this work has earned Professor Markowitz wide recognition as the father of Modern Portfolio Theory.

William Sharpe shared in the Nobel Prize because he developed the Capital Asset Pricing Model (CAPM), which suggests a linear relationship between risk and return. This theory shows that, in conditions of equilibrium, portfolios with higher returns have higher risk levels, as measured by their betas. Recall from Chapter 11 that beta quantifies the relationship between the return on a security, or a portfolio, and the return on the market. This concept guides investors' efforts to create investment portfolios that suit their own individual needs.

Merton Miller, the third AFA member to become a 1990 Nobel laureate, helped develop the Modigliani-Miller theory, which states that the cost of capital for a corporation remains quite stable despite wide variations in the proportion of debt in its capital structure. Before this work, most scholars had thought that increasing the size of the low-cost debt component of a firm's capital would reduce the firm's overall cost of capital. Professor Miller's theory shows how the cost of both debt and equity capital rises as a firm uses more debt.

Together, these prize-winning authors have determined much about how theorists understand investing and financial markets, both as presented in this book and as used by finance professionals everywhere. In practice, they have guided all kinds of investors toward their financial goals, including the authors of the theories themselves. Professor Markowitz said that he would probably invest the money associated with the Nobel Prize; he did not know exactly where he would invest it, but he was sure that he would diversify.

Even the most renowned scholars must diversify their investments to achieve desired investment returns without accepting too much risk.

Introduction

Chapter 6 discussed investors' attitudes toward and tolerance for risk. Where an individual chooses to invest money depends on the amount of risk that he or she is willing to take. Those who are willing to take big risks in pursuit of big rewards will invest most of their money in common stocks or other risky assets. Those who do not like risk will invest most of their money in assets that provide fixed returns with the minimum possible variations in price. This attitude toward risk and return, or risk preference, develops from the match between the investor's personal situation and the investment choices offered by the marketplace.

An aggressive investor might decide to invest 80 percent of available funds in common stock, holding the remainder in U.S. Treasury bills or money market funds. How this goal is reached depends on how much money the investor has to invest and his or her idea of the best securities. Someone who had accumulated sufficient money would immediately begin considering which securities would best suit his or her needs. However, most young investors first need to accumulate enough money to achieve adequate diversification.

Bill, an aggressive stock investor with $5,000 to invest, could find that a single round-lot purchase would consume all of his capital. The entire portfolio would then suffer the ups and downs of that one issue, subjecting him to too much risk by modern portfolio standards. Instead of buying stock directly, Bill could invest $4,000 in a good common stock mutual fund and place $1,000 in a money market fund within the same mutual fund family. If his savings plan called for contributions of $500 a month, he would put $400 into the stock mutual fund and $100 into the money fund each month.

June, another aggressive stock investor, has accumulated $200,000 through judicious saving. Even if she follows the same portfolio composition guidelines (80 percent in common stocks and 20 percent in low-risk, liquid assets like short-term government securities or money market funds), she still has more options than Bill. For one option, she could use Bill's tactic of investing in stock mutual funds and money market funds. Her capital balance is large enough, however, to achieve sufficient diversification by buying $160,000 worth of common stock, investing the remaining $40,000 in money market funds. Now she must decide which common stocks to select.

Tactics of a Modern Portfolio Theorist

If she decided to follow Modern Portfolio Theory, June would invest in a broadly diversified list of stocks that would give her a total portfolio return that would match the return on the market. To absolutely assure herself of matching the market, she could buy the stocks that make up the stock market averages, the DJIA or the S&P 500 Index, matching the percentage of her available funds in each stock to the percentage of the market index's total value that each stock represents.

For example, IBM represents about 2 percent of the S&P 500 Index. This means that the total value of outstanding IBM stock equals about 2 percent of the total value of all the outstanding stock of all the companies in the index. If June were to invest 2 percent of her $160,000, or $3,200, in IBM common stock at a market price of about $90 per share, she could buy approximately 35 shares.

capitalization-weight method: A portfolio indexing method that multiplies share price by number of shares outstanding for each company in a market index, then sums these individual values to find a total value for the index. Dividing each company's value by the total index value gives each stock's percentage of the total index, which becomes the stock's percentage of the indexed portfolio.

This is the **capitalization-weight method** of portfolio allocation. June would sum the total market value of the stock of all the companies in the market, then divide the market value for each company's stock by the total value of the market to obtain each company's percentage of the total. She would multiply the amount of money she had to invest by the same percentage to find how much of her portfolio to allocate to each stock. Dividing this total investment in a stock by its market price per share would establish the number of shares of each stock to buy.

June makes these decisions because she assumes that she cannot beat the market, so she should simply join it. Unfortunately, if June were to spread her available money among all the stocks in the S&P 500 Index, she would buy just a few shares of each, which would run up large commission costs. As an alternative, she might buy shares in each of the 30 DJIA companies. Of course, she could save herself the trouble and buy shares in one or more mutual funds that follow the same policies.

Tactics of a Stock Picker

June may not accept the assumption of Modern Portfolio Theory that she cannot beat the market. Using analysis based on estimated return, expected risk, and estimated return-to-risk ratio discussed in Chapters 10 and 11, she may think that she can select stocks that will earn more than just the return on the market index. Even if she follows these feelings and decides to select individual stocks, June must diversify. Some people would suggest that she should put all of her funds in one stock and then keep an unflinching eye on that stock. Besides considerable strain on both her eye and her nerves, this would subject her to too much risk. If anything were to happen to the one stock, she would lose everything.

Naive Diversification Old-world traders might suggest that June should never put all of her tea in one ship and take the chance of it sinking, dragging her entire net worth to the depths with it. Instead, they would suggest that she divide the cargo with 10 percent in each of ten ships. If one ship were to sink, the profits on the other nine would keep her total net worth afloat.

naive diversification: A method of investing equal amounts in each of at least ten stocks to construct a portfolio.

This technique of **naive diversification** applies equally well to common stock investment. June would divide her available capital equally among at least ten stocks. Theory, backed up by practical experience, suggests that this number is a good rule of thumb to follow. Clearly, any individual investor must buy more than one or two stocks, but few can afford substantial positions in 20 or more. Buying shares in ten companies should give June adequate diversification by industry and company.

Efficient Diversification June may not want to bet her net worth on a rule of thumb, though. She can improve her portfolio's diversification without changing the number of stocks she buys by concentrating on the stocks that seem better and stronger. Rather than buying equal amounts of each stock, she would put more money in the stocks that seemed more attractive and smaller amounts in stocks that seemed less attractive. To develop a decision rule from this **efficient diversification** concept, she might allocate the same percentage of her portfolio to an individual stock as that stock's risk-to-return ratio represents of the portfolio's total risk-to-return figure. Assuming that the stocks that seemed stronger actually ended up performing better, this technique would maximize the return-to-risk ratio of her investment portfolio. For this extra return, she would owe Professor Markowitz some thanks, since the tactic arose from his work with efficient portfolios.

efficient diversification: A method of weighting stocks in a portfolio in proportion to their relative return-to-risk ratios to obtain the highest portfolio return-to-risk ratio.

If the old-world traders had known of Professor Markowitz's ideas, they would have concentrated their cargo in the fastest, largest, or safest ships with the best captains and crew. They would have entrusted less of their cargo to the smaller, slower, less well-protected ships with less able captains and crew, though those ships would still have to generate profits to remain in service. This efficient combination of ships would provide the strongest total fleet and the highest profits for the ship owners over the long term.

June must not suppose, however, that diversification can protect her net worth from all risk. Diversification can bring the risk level of the portfolio down only as far as the risk level of the overall market. Even a well-diversified portfolio of stocks will still suffer variations in prices and returns in response to changes in the balance between supply and demand in the market for stocks. June can completely avoid this risk only by avoiding stocks altogether. She should adjust the amount of stocks she buys to keep the overall risk of her portfolio within acceptable limits.

Investment Timing and Technical Analysis

Some investors think that they can predict changes in the balance between stock market forces and time their securities transactions to take the best advantage of these trends. Some of these investors actually do succeed in the age-old effort to buy low and sell high, but most of these speculators lose more often than they win over time. Over the years the market has left little doubt that most investors should follow the buy-and-hold principle.

Still, June and all other conservative investors should watch for the influence of the technical forces that drive short-term movements in the stock market. Both naive and efficient captains try to set sail at low tide and avoid charging into the middle of a storm.

This chapter will examine techniques by which an investor can most profitably manage a portfolio of securities. One method involves indexing the portfolio to capture the return of the market index. Further discussion will develop the ideas that underlie the effort to diversify both naively and efficiently. The chapter will conclude with an examination of some technical analysis methods by which an investor might squeeze a bit of extra return from securities transactions without adding risk. The discussion will use the Dow Jones Industrial Average to represent the overall stock market.

Assumptions of Modern Portfolio Theory

Modern Portfolio theory assumes efficient securities markets, as explained in Chapter 4. This means that all parties have equal access to information about security issues, the economy, and global events at the same low cost. Since this information affects investors' assessments of the value of a particular security, it determines the prices the market sets for securities. New information reaches the marketplace quickly and essentially costlessly, and the market responds by instantly adjusting prices to reflect the effects of events and revelations.

No general market participant can reliably predict events or newly revealed information, so no one can reliably predict the direction in which the constant flow of information will drive a security's price. A price established in a previous trade gives no suggestion of which direction the price might take at a given time. This critical assumption of modern portfolio theory implies that even informed, professional analysts cannot predict short-term changes in stock prices no matter how closely they watch the market or how much information they gather about a company or its trading history.

A top executive can often benefit from privileged access to unreleased information about his or her firm, buying or selling stock based on an understanding of the likely effect of soon-to-be-released news on the firm's stock price. Of course, this insider adds the risk of prison to the normal risks of securities markets, since federal law strictly prohibits insider trading.

Despite this limited exception, investors must understand and accept the efficiency of the stock market and abandon the fantasy that sifting through information about past prices can yield some nugget of information that will allow them to predict future prices. All investors develop estimates of many future values, but since everyone has the same ready access to these estimates, no one can expect to do much better, on average, than anyone else.

Investors who believe in Modern Portfolio Theory assume that they cannot beat the stock market. Instead, they build well-diversified portfolios of common stocks that should match the market's return and risks. Some investors manage to achieve higher returns than others, but they must buy stocks with higher risk than the market index. More risk-averse investors select stocks with lower risks and lower returns than the market. Modern Portfolio Theory assumes that all investors are risk adverse to some degree, requiring some additional amount of return to accept additional risk.

Once they give up the effort to predict future prices, investors see the wisdom of the buy-and-hold portfolio policy. They no longer try to profit by short-term trading, knowing that inevitable wrong guesses will almost certainly wipe out any gains from lucky guesses, and that the additional transaction costs of trading will reduce their returns even further.

Modern Portfolio Theory suggests that every investor follow the popular advice, if you can't beat them, join them. As the introduction mentioned, some extend this concept to its logical extreme and buy all of the stocks in a market index to assure themselves of keeping pace with market returns. The next section will discuss this practice, known as indexing, using the Dow Jones Industrial Average as an example.

Indexing with the Dow Jones Industrial Average

June, the rather wealthy stock investor mentioned above, could not buy shares in every stock in the market. Too many companies have issued stock. Instead, she would have to choose a group of stocks to represent the total market. The easiest way to do this is to buy the stocks tracked by a market index or average. Some professional mutual fund managers try to replicate the S&P 500 Index in their portfolios, but buying shares in 500 companies would strain the resources of an individual investor. The 30-stock sample of the Dow Jones Industrial Average makes it a much more likely candidate for **indexing.**

indexing: Dividing a portfolio's total value among stocks in the same proportions that those stocks represent of a market index to match portfolio return and risk to those of the index.

Calculating Portfolio Weights

The value of June's portfolio would not follow the DJIA exactly, however, unless each stock represented the same percentage of both the portfolio and the average. A given change in the price of a stock would affect June's portfolio more than it would affect the DJIA if the stock represented a larger proportion of her portfolio than its percentage of the total value of the stocks in the average. As mentioned in the introduction, matching the stocks' proportions in the portfolio to their proportions in the average requires the calculation of capitalization weights.

Exhibit 17.1 lists the 30 companies tracked by the Dow Jones Industrial Average. The first column lists the names of the companies followed by their stock symbols in the second column. The third column provides prices per share as of September 27, 1990, and the fourth column gives the number of shares outstanding for each company. Notice that American Telephone & Telegraph (with trading symbol T) has just over 1 billion shares outstanding. Multiplying its price of $31.50 per share by the number of shares outstanding gives the value of the company's outstanding stock of close to $35 billion. Find the total market value of each company in a similar manner.

Next, sum the total market value of all 30 companies: $533 billion. Finally, find each company's percentage of the total value of the average by dividing the market value of each company by the total market value of all the companies. AT&T, for example, represents 6.4 percent of the total market value of all the companies in the average. The two largest companies in the index are Exxon with 11.7 percent and IBM with 11.3 percent.

Determining each company's proportion of the total DJIA sample tells June how much money to invest in each company. She has $160,000 to invest in common stocks, so she should buy $18,720 worth of Exxon stock and $18,080 worth of IBM. She should invest the remainder of the money in each stock based on the percentages indicated in Exhibit 17.1.

To determine the number of shares to buy, June would divide the dollar investment in each stock by its price per share. Take another example. She should invest 0.8 percent of her portfolio, or $1,240, in Allied Chemical. At a stock price of about $29, she can buy only 44 shares. She should probably avoid such inefficient purchase units because these odd lots require excessive transaction costs. Analysis reveals that June would have to buy odd lots of several DJIA stocks, so in practice she would put this money in a mutual fund or simply ignore some of the smaller stocks in the DJIA to get the benefit of the smaller costs of round-lot transactions.

EXHIBIT 17.1

Market Value of the Dow Jones Industrial Average

COMPANY NAME	TRADING SYMBOL	PRICE PER SHARE 9/27/90	NUMBER OF SHARES (MILLIONS)	TOTAL STOCK VALUE (BILLIONS)	PERCENTAGE OF TOTAL INDEX VALUE
Allied Signal	ALD	$ 29.125	140.1	$ 4.08	0.8%
Alcoa	AA	62.750	86.9	5.46	1.0
American Express	AXP	21.125	438.2	9.26	1.7
AT&T	T	31.500	1,089.0	34.30	6.4
Bethlehem Steel	BS	12.000	75.7	0.91	0.2
Boeing	BA	40.875	346.2	14.15	2.7
Chevron	CHV	76.000	354.5	26.95	5.1
Coca Cola	KO	38.750	667.6	25.87	4.9
DuPont	DD	33.875	678.4	22.98	4.3
Eastman Kodak	EK	39.125	324.5	12.69	2.4
Exxon	XON	49.875	1,248.4	62.26	11.7
General Electric	GE	55.000	893.8	49.16	9.2
General Motors	GM	36.500	601.0	21.94	4.1
Goodyear	GT	17.750	58.2	1.03	0.2
IBM	IBM	105.375	573.7	60.45	11.3
International Paper	IP	45.125	109.0	4.92	0.9
McDonalds	MCD	25.875	358.5	9.28	1.7
Merck	MRK	74.125	391.4	29.01	5.4
3M	MMM	78.000	222.0	17.31	3.2
Navistar	NAV	2.625	251.3	0.66	0.1
Phillip Morris	MO	44.625	928.5	41.44	7.8
Primerica	PA	21.250	111.4	2.36	0.4
Procter & Gamble	PG	72.125	346.1	24.97	4.7
Sears	S	25.500	342.5	8.73	1.6
Texaco	TX	62.625	260.2	16.29	3.1
USX	X	31.625	254.8	8.06	1.5
Union Carbide	UK	14.250	143.2	2.04	0.4
United Technologies	UTX	43.875	120.3	5.28	1.0
Westinghouse	WX	27.750	291.6	8.09	1.5
Woolworth	Z	23.375	130.0	3.04	0.6
All DJIA stocks				$533.00	100.0%

Indexing a Larger Investment Portfolio

Exhibit 17.2 illustrates a $1 million portfolio of DJIA stocks that employs the weights calculated in Exhibit 17.1. This portfolio should provide the investor with the same return and risk characteristics as the market average. The larger portfolio value allows the investor to take round-lot positions in all of the stocks in the average.

EXHIBIT 17.2

Company Value As a Percentage of the Total Value of the Dow Jones Industrial Average

COMPANY NAME	TRADING SYMBOL	PRICE PER SHARE	WEIGHT (PERCENTAGE OF TOTAL)	VALUE IN PORTFOLIO[a] ($000)	NUMBER OF SHARES	DIVIDEND YIELD	ESTIMATED RETURN	RETURN-TO-RISK RATIO
Allied Signal	ALD	$ 28	0.8%	$ 8	275	6.7%	26.5%	2.8
Alcoa	AA	63	1.0	10	159	2.8	24.5	2.0
American Express	AXP	21	1.7	17	805	4.5	22.5	1.7
AT&T	T	32	6.4	64	2,032	4.4	18.5	2.1
Bethlehem Steel	BS	12	0.2	2	167	2.7	42.0	2.8
Boeing	BA	41	2.7	27	660	2.2	12.5	1.3
Chevron	CHV	76	5.1	51	671	4.3	10.5	1.1
Coca Cola	KO	39	4.9	49	1,265	1.7	12.5	1.3
DuPont	DD	34	4.3	43	1,269	4.5	17.5	1.6
Eastman Kodak	EK	39	2.4	24	613	4.8	25.5	2.6
Exxon	XON	50	11.7	117	2,346	5.2	10.5	1.3
General Electric	GE	55	9.2	92	1,673	3.6	22.0	2.0
General Motors	GM	37	4.1	41	1,123	8.7	36.5	3.7
Goodyear	GT	18	0.2	2	113	9.5	37.5	3.3
IBM	IBM	105	11.3	113	1,072	4.3	18.0	2.0
International Paper	IP	45	0.9	9	200	3.1	24.0	1.8
McDonalds	MCD	26	1.7	17	657	1.2	21.5	2.2
Merck	MRK	74	5.4	54	728	2.5	25.0	2.5
3M	MMM	78	3.2	32	410	3.4	16.0	1.5
Navistar	NAV	3	0.1	1	381	–	38.0	3.2
Phillip Morris	MO	45	7.8	78	1,748	3.3	21.5	2.0
Primerica	PA	21	0.4	4	188	1.7	24.0	1.8
Procter & Gamble	PG	72	4.7	47	652	2.3	13.5	1.4
Sears	S	26	1.6	16	627	7.9	25.5	2.2
Texaco	TX	63	3.1	31	495	5.3	8.5	1.2
USX	X	32	1.5	15	474	4.6	19.0	1.9
Union Carbide	UK	14	0.4	4	281	6.1	10.5	0.8
United Technologies	UTX	44	1.0	10	228	3.8	25.0	2.2
Westinghouse	WX	28	1.5	15	541	4.9	26.5	2.2
Woolworth	Z	23	0.6	6	257	3.4	23.0	1.8
All DJIA Stocks			100.1%	$1,000		4.1[b]	24.0[b]	

[a] $1 million portfolio.
[b] Weighted averages.

In fact, however, strict application of the portfolio percentages would result in only one even round-lot transaction (200 shares of International Paper). Practical application of capitalization-weighted indexing would require some compromises. The owner of the \$1 million portfolio would buy 500 shares of Texaco, 600 shares of Eastman Kodak, 700 shares each of Merck and Chevron, as so on. This would violate the strictly theoretical diversification guideline, but it would save the investor a lot of money in transaction costs, and a few shares one way or the other would not make much difference in overall portfolio performance. For simplicity the example will take the actual capitalization weights from Exhibit 17.2 without adjusting for round lots.

What return would this portfolio provide from dividends and capital gains? Since the amount of future dividends and, therefore, total returns depend on presently unknown decisions of company boards of directors, the investor can only estimate the total return. Exhibit 10.5 in Chapter 10 presented data on the expected returns from each of the Dow Jones Industrial Average stocks. To find the expected return from the DJIA, simply take a weighted average of the expected returns of the individual stocks. Exhibit 17.2 provides that information, estimating a return from 1993 to 1995 for the DJIA of 24 percent with a dividend yield of 4.1 percent. Unfortunately, this excellent return involves an element of risk since no one can guarantee that the stocks will actually realize the expected returns.

Selecting Stocks: Return and Return-to-Risk Ratio

Naive Diversification

As one common criterion, portfolio managers often select among a universe of common stocks based on expected return. Other things remaining equal, most investors want common stocks that provide the highest returns. Applying this notion to the Dow Jones Industrial Average sample, the investor would select the portfolio of common stocks listed in Exhibit 17.3. These 11 stocks had the highest rates of return and return-to-risk ratios of all the DJIA stocks. Following the rule of thumb mentioned in the introduction, the investor would have selected the ten best stocks, but four of the DJIA stocks (Westinghouse, Sears, United Technologies, and McDonald's) had the same return-to-risk ratio of 2.2, so any choice among them would be simply arbitrary.

The portfolio in Exhibit 17.3 is naively diversified, allotting 9 percent of the total portfolio value to each stock. This combination has an estimated annual rate of return of 30.0 percent for the period from 1993 to 1995. This return exceeds the total expected return from the Dow Jones Industrial Average by 25 percent (a 6 percent increase over the DJIA return of 24 percent). The return-to-risk ratio of 2.7 also compares favorably to the DJIA

EXHIBIT 17.3

Naively Diversified Portfolio of Dow Jones Industrial Average Stocks

COMPANY NAME	TRADING SYMBOL	PORTFOLIO WEIGHT	ESTIMATED RETURN	RETURN-TO-RISK RATIO
General Motors	GM	9%	36.5%	3.7
Goodyear	GY	9	37.5	3.3
Navistar	NAV	9	38.0	3.2
Bethlehem Steel	BS	9	42.0	2.8
Allied Signal	ALD	9	26.5	2.8
Eastman Kodak	EK	9	25.5	2.6
Merck	MRK	9	25.0	2.5
Westinghouse	WX	9	26.5	2.2
Sears	S	9	25.5	2.2
United Technologies	UTX	9	25.0	2.2
McDonalds	MCD	9	21.5	2.2
			30.0[a]	2.7[a]

[a]Weighted averages.

return-to-risk ratio, 1.86. Selecting fewer shares with higher returns seems to create a stronger portfolio.

Efficient Diversification

An efficiently diversified portfolio improves the expected return and return-to-risk ratio even further. Exhibit 17.4 lists the same stocks as Exhibit 17.3, but it weights them by return-to-risk ratio. GM's return-to-risk ratio of 3.7, for example, represents 12.5 percent of the total return-to-risk ratios for all of the stocks listed, so the portfolio would hold 12.5 percent of its value in General Motors stock.

Notice the return: It increases to 30.9 percent from 30.0 percent for the equally weighted portfolio. Efficient diversification increases the naively diversified portfolio's return by 3 percent, and the return-to-risk ratio increases by 3.7 percent.

This overall favorable effect makes the change seem valuable. If the estimates correctly predict the actual portfolio returns, efficient diversification appears to increase return while it reduces risk. Certainly all investors seek to combine these attributes.

June's Choice

Rather than merely mimicking the Dow Jones Industrial Average, June thought she could improve her portfolio's performance by selecting the ten

EXHIBIT 17.4

Efficiently Diversified Portfolio of Dow Jones Industrial Average Stocks

COMPANY NAME	TRADING SYMBOL	PORTFOLIO WEIGHT	ESTIMATED RETURN	RETURN-TO-RISK RATIO
General Motors	GM	12.5%	36.5%	3.7
Goodyear	GY	11.1	37.5	3.3
Navistar	NAV	10.8	38.0	3.2
Bethlehem Steel	BS	9.4	42.0	2.8
Allied Signal	ALD	9.4	26.5	2.8
Eastman Kodak	EK	8.8	25.5	2.6
Merck	MRK	8.4	25.0	2.5
Westinghouse	WX	7.4	26.5	2.2
Sears	S	7.4	25.5	2.2
United Technologies	UTX	7.4	25.0	2.2
McDonalds	MCD	7.4	21.5	2.2
			30.9[a]	2.8[a]

[a]Weighted averages.

DJIA stocks that seemed most attractive for investment. She weighted them by return-to-risk ratio to create the efficiently diversified portfolio in Exhibit 17.5.

The stocks June selected were dominant firms in their industries, and the industries selected had substantial growth potential. Even though the return-to-risk ratio was lower than the market portfolio, June's portfolio was well positioned to provide a superior return-to-risk. In addition, June thought that the undervalued stocks in her portfolio were better on average than the portfolio she could have selected by focusing solely on the return-to-risk ratio. Because we can never know for certain whether our forecasts will be achieved, there is merit to June's alternative approach to focusing exclusively on the return-to-risk ratio.

Emerging Portfolio Rules

A few rules for portfolio composition emerge from this discussion of diversification:

Rule One: From a list of acceptable stocks, select those with the highest expected returns and return-to-risk ratios.

Rule Two: Efficient diversification, allotting investment capital among stocks based on their return-to-risk ratios, results in the best combination of return and return-to-risk.

EXHIBIT 17.5

June's Portfolio of Dow Jones Industrial Average Stocks

COMPANY NAME	TRADING SYMBOL	PORTFOLIO WEIGHT	ESTIMATED RETURN	RETURN-TO-RISK RATIO
AT&T	T	10.8%	18.5%	2.1
Boeing	BA	6.7	12.5	1.3
Coca Cola	KO	6.7	12.5	1.3
Eastman Kodak	EK	13.4	25.5	2.6
General Electric	GE	10.3	22.0	2.0
Merck	MRK	12.9	25.0	2.5
Phillip Morris	MO	10.3	21.5	2.0
Procter & Gamble	PG	7.2	13.5	1.4
McDonalds	MCD	11.3	21.5	2.2
IBM	IBM	10.3	18.0	2.0
			20.1[a]	1.9[a]

[a]Weighted averages.

Rule Three: Selecting stocks based on perceptions of companies' investment characteristics can create a less desirable portfolio combination than trying to build an indexed, naively diversified, or efficiently diversified portfolio based on estimates of expected returns and return-to-risk ratios.

Rule Four: Investor demand can bid up the prices of the stock of an excellent company too far so that it sells at a low return-to-risk ratio. The stock of a less well-regarded company may tend to sell at a higher return-to-risk ratio and a lower price.

Market Analysis

market analysis: Evaluation of the stock market's current level based on its historical performance.

trend analysis: Analysis of market price and volume movements to predict future price levels based on supply and demand.

The effort to match portfolio performance to the performance of the market should include a **market analysis,** that is, an examination of the current level of the chosen market index in relation to its past history. This can help the investor protect the portfolio from plunging into an overpriced market and following it downward. If the market's current level seems unreasonably high, the investor might well save a few dollars per share and enhance portfolio returns by waiting until the likely correction adjusts stock prices downward. This kind of timing requires difficult decisions, and even some luck, but a sensitivity to **trend analysis** can improve returns without much additional risk. This does not imply abandoning a buy-and-hold investment policy in favor of short-term trading; instead, the investor seeks to take his or her long-term positions at the most opportune points in the market cycle.

After choosing the point at which to join the market's cyclical procession, an investor must analyze price trends for the stocks of individual companies. Individual common stocks follow the movement of the DJIA or S&P 500 Index more or less closely so different stocks can play different roles in an overall portfolio, even one that seeks only to match rather than to beat market performance. A careful assessment of trends in the share price of a particular common stock can help assure that other investors' enthusiasm for a good stock has not inflated its price above what the company's economic performance would justify.

Trend Analysis of Market Indexes

Examination of the monthly stock market averages from 1978 to mid-November 1990 in Exhibit 17.6 indicates a rising market trend over the entire period. Although the Value Line Composite index declined for most of 1990 and the DJIA declined in the last half of 1990, by early February 1991 both averages had recovered to rally close to the trend line.

During many years, however, the stock market defied this general upward trend and declined or remained flat. The DJIA declined in 1977, 1981 to 1982, 1983 to 1984, 1987, and 1990. The Value Line Composite, S&P 500, and NYSE Composite all followed similar patterns. Some of these market declines lasted as long as two years, but for every step backward the market took even more steps forward, although at an irregular pace.

What can the investor learn from studying the comings and goings of the market indexes? At any given time, a guess about the next short-term movement of the market could be right or wrong. Over the long term, however, the market shows a clear upward trend. This suggests that one can predict long-term movements much more easily and accurately than short-term movements, so the rational investor should choose to make long-term commitments to follow the market upward over time, rather than trying to react to every passing twitch in a market index. Certainly, one can seek to boost returns by timing those long-term commitments to take advantage of the market's current trend, but the overall goal should focus on buying securities to hold over time.

invest with the trend: A market timing method that ignores cyclical movements and tries to take advantage of the trend of the market for maximum growth.

In this effort to **invest with the trend** in the market, an investor must allow for the upward bias in the trend of stock prices. Establishing high and low price lines can give some guidance in judging this trend. When current prices approach a low price line projected from past data, the market is probably approaching a trough and preparing to rebound; when current prices approach a high price line, the market is probably relatively overpriced and set for a decline. For example, relatively high stock prices in 1987 and mid-1990 gave way to downward corrections that made stocks relatively cheap at the end of 1987 through 1988 and at the end of 1990.

EXHIBIT 17.6

Market Price Behavior

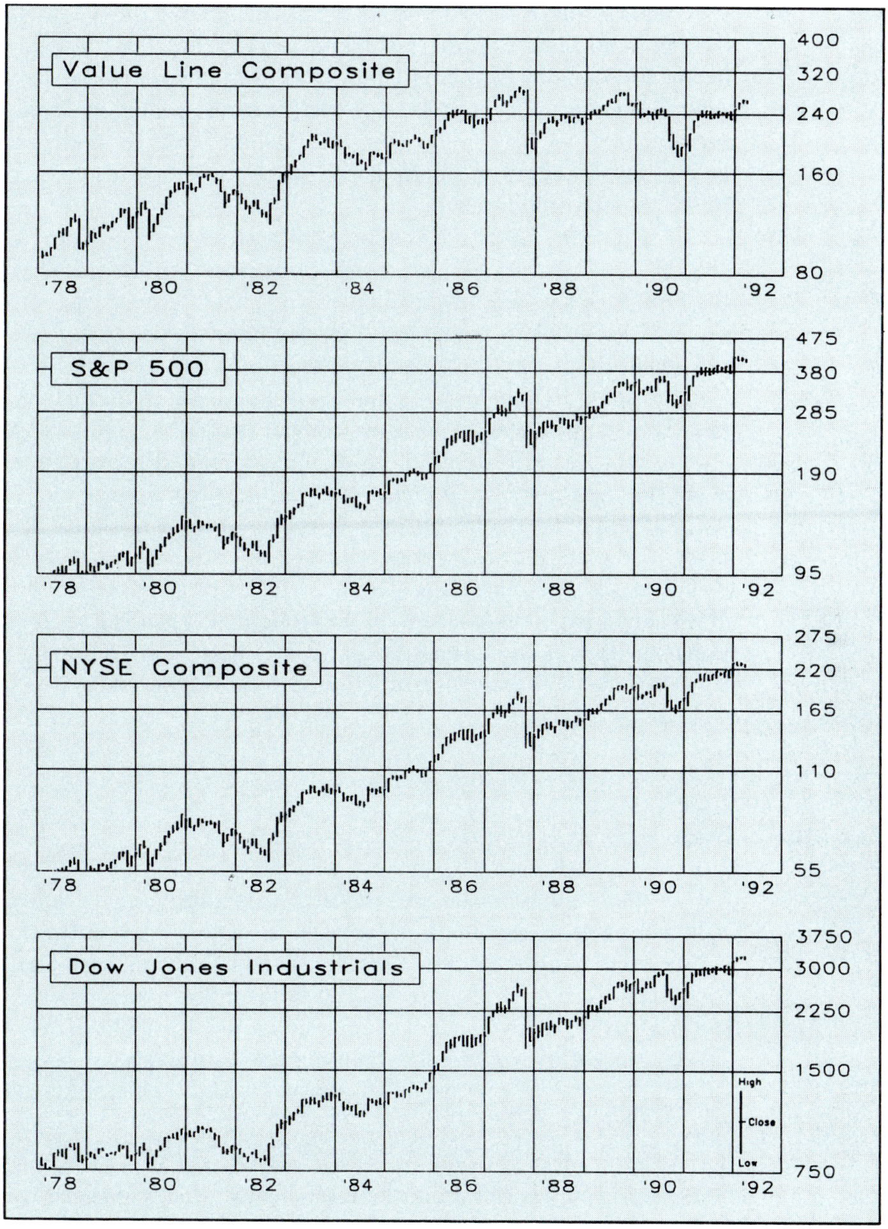

SOURCE: *Value Line Investment Survey*, March 20, 1992, p. 40. Copyright © 1992 by Value Line Publishing, Inc.; used by permission.

Prices rose again to excessively high levels in mid-1992, and many investors feared another correction.

Trend Analysis for Individual Stocks

Exhibit 17.7 illustrates the trends in prices for two different companies in the same industry. Illinois Tool Works stock began a positive upward trend in 1983. Watching the trend line over this period would have signaled several buying opportunities, but only one real selling opportunity in the summer of 1987. The market crash in October 1987 took the stock's price below its long-term trend line, and wise investors resumed buying the stock, with favorable results.

In contrast, Fansteel, Inc. stock has shown a downward trend since 1983. Even if an investor had bought this stock at its cyclically low prices, the investment would have produced no profits because each price rise fell short of the previous peak, and each decline took the price lower than the previous trough. Investors should avoid stocks like this one.

As a rule, then, investors should invest with the trends of both individual stock prices and market indexes. First, establish a realistic price range around this trend in which the stock should trade. The wise investor would avoid buying the stock, perhaps even selling shares he or she held, when its price approached the top of this range, since a decline becomes more likely as the stock rises closer to the top of its normal range. The investor would try to time purchases when the stock's price approached the bottom of its range, expecting an upward correction. Hold stocks while their prices remain within their normal ranges. All of these moves assume that taxes paid on gains will not change the outcome of the decision.

Dividend Yields and P/E Ratios in Portfolio Analysis

Two familiar financial indicators can supplement trend analysis to help the investor assess the relative level of the stock market: the price–earnings ratio and the current dividend yield. Previous chapters have used these data to suggest appropriate values for individual companies' common stocks. This section will adapt them to judge the level of the overall market.

In general, two principles should guide this analysis:

A high P/E ratio indicates a high stock market.

A low dividend yield indicates a high stock market.

These principles derive from the methods by which investors calculate the figures. When the market has bid up prices faster than company earnings have risen, those prices will begin to seem high and investors will begin to fear a correction. Since the dividend yield divides the dividend by the

EXHIBIT 17.7

Stock Price Behavior

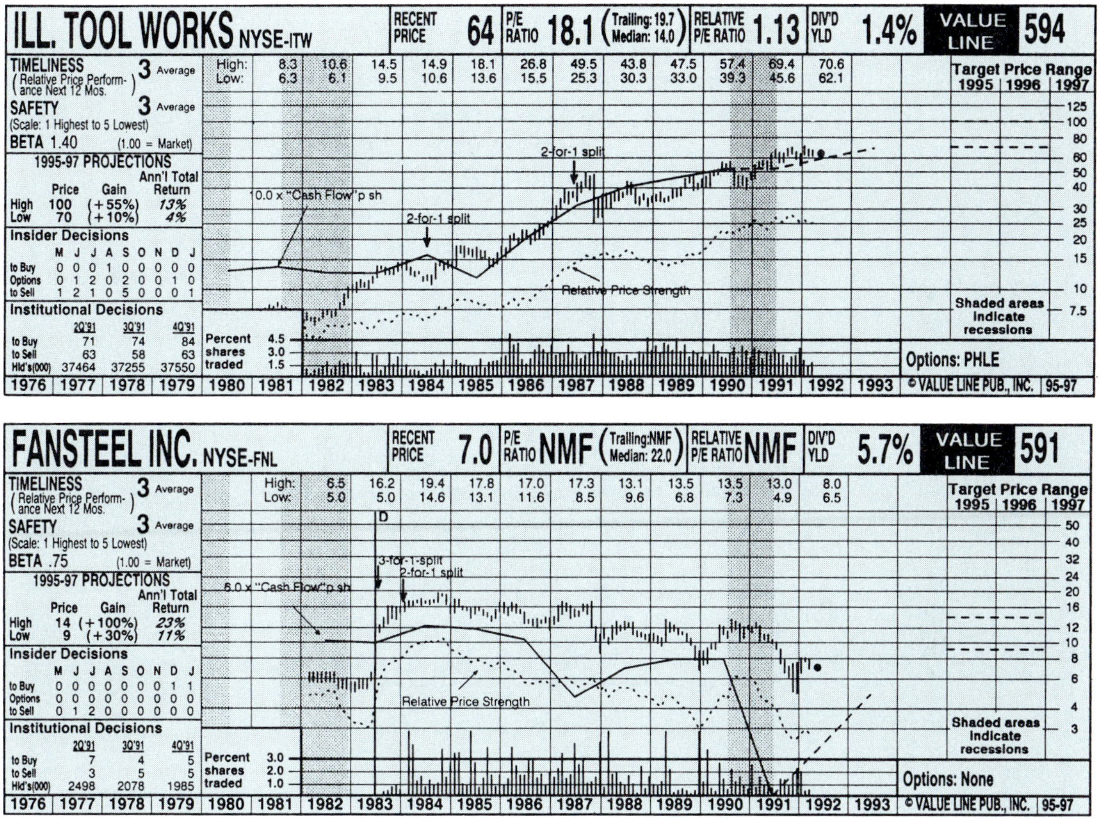

SOURCE: *Value Line Investment Survey*, April 10, 1991, pp. 591, 594. Copyright © 1991 by Value Line Publishing, Inc.; used by permission.

market price, a higher price gives rise to a lower dividend yield, which gives one more signal of an overpriced market that may soon fall.

To apply these rules, the investor must judge relative high and low levels for each indicator. Generally, experience suggests that a P/E ratio for the S&P 500 Index of 16 or higher would seem high, while a value in the 9-to-10 range would seem low. Most stocks have P/E ratios around 12. Exhibit 17.8 shows that the S&P 500 Index had a P/E of 25.25 in the last week of March 1992. One year earlier the S&P 500 had a P/E of 17.56, reinforcing the general impression that this level seemed high.

EXHIBIT 17.8

Market P/E Ratios and Dividend Yields

Indexes' P/Es & Yields

	Last Week	Prev. Week	Year Ago Week
DJ Ind.-P/E	57.2	58.0	16.8
Earns Yield, %	1.75	1.72	5.97
Earns, $	56.48	56.48	173.88
Divs Yield, %	2.86	2.80	3.46
Divs, $	92.43	91.82	100.87
Mkt to Book, %	242.69	246.86	228.32
Book Value, $	1331.52	1331.52	1276.19
DJ Tran.-P/E	Nil	Nil	77.6
Earns Yield, %	Nil	Nil	1.29
Earns, $	(d47.67)	(d47.67)	14.29
Divs Yield, %	1.41	1.36	1.67
Divs, $	19.44	19.44	18.53
Mkt to Book, %	175.51	182.38	146.74
Book Value, $	786.10	786.10	756.10
DJ Util.-P/E	13.4	13.6	17.2
Earns Yield, %	7.45	7.35	5.81
Earns, $	15.15	15.15	12.62
Divs Yield, %	6.84	6.75	6.46
Divs, $	13.91	13.91	14.04
Mkt to Book, %	131.58	133.45	140.41
Book Value, $	154.46	154.46	154.68
S&P 500-P/E	25.25	25.74	17.56
Earns Yield, %	3.96	3.89	5.70
Earns, $	15.98	15.98	21.37
Divs Yield, %	3.04	2.98	3.25
Divs, $	12.27	12.26	12.19
Mkt to Book, %	257.96	262.95	254.80
Book Value, $	156.42	156.42	147.26
S&P Ind.-P/E	28.44	29.01	18.27
Earns Yield, %	3.52	3.45	5.48
Earns, $	16.89	16.86	24.33
Divs Yield, %	2.65	2.60	2.84
Divs, $	12.73	12.72	12.62
Mkt to Book, %	315.70	321.49	305.64
Book Value, $	152.15	152.15	145.34

DJ latest 52-week earnings and dividends weekly file adjusted by the Dow Divisors in effect at Friday's close. S&P December 31 12-month earnings and indicated dividends based on Friday close. DJ and S&P book values latest available for FY December 1990 and 1989.

SOURCE: *Barron's*, March 30, 1992, p. 150. Reprinted by permission of Barron's,

An investor could also evaluate the increase in the market's P/E ratio over time. The one-year increase in the P/E of the S&P 500 from 17.56 to 25.25 amounted to an increase of almost 43.8 percent. This suggests that market prices increased 43.8 percent faster than company earnings. (In fact, total company earnings decreased, but the market still rose on the basis of expectations for future earnings growth.) At the time, an investor would have viewed this as evidence of an overheated market that would discourage immediate purchases.

Generally speaking, the overall market dividend yield would seem low at around 3 percent, a normal range might run from 4 to 5 percent, and 6 percent or above would seem high. Such a high dividend yield would suggest low overall market prices and a good time to buy common stock. A dividend yield of 3 percent or below would indicate high stock prices and a bad time to buy, but a good time to sell.

Exhibit 17.8 shows a dividend yield for the S&P 500 Index of 3.04 percent, which confirms the judgment based on the P/E ratio that the market was relatively high, creating a poor environment for buyers, but a good environment for sellers. The same conditions held during the previous year when the market dividend yield was 3.25 percent.

Basing investment decisions on interpretation of the market's P/E ratio and dividend yield can help the investor to judge market trends and time transactions to take advantage of them. This can prevent reductions in portfolio performance due to buying high and selling low.

Once again, however, remember that these techniques merely suggest appropriate times at which to make or adjust long-term commitments within a portfolio. Attempts to profit from short-term trading based on such indicators of market trends often actually reduce portfolio returns, especially after deducting high transaction costs. Anyone can easily find successful long-term investors; one seldom meets really successful short-term traders.

Still, some market participants disregard this advice and try to earn substantial rewards by taking large risks speculating on market trends. They have developed many elaborate techniques to predict these trends, all of which fall under the heading *technical indicators*.

Technical Indicators

Technical analysis assumes that the stock market has a life of its own, independent of the earnings and other influences on individual companies' values.[1] The overall market reacts collectively to information such as news about business and government just as an individual stock does. Technical analysts focus their efforts on assessing the position of the market, judging whether it is too high or too low, overbought or oversold.

Technical indicators or theories attempt to evaluate current and likely future movements of the market based on its own characteristic behavior rather than predicting changes due to fundamental information about individual stocks. This assumes that the movement of the market reflects all necessary information. As technicians often say, "the market discounts everything."

Some technicians, known as *tape readers,* concentrate on the ticker readouts and base investment decisions strictly on price and volume data for transactions on the New York Stock Exchange and the American Exchange. Chartists interpret and forecast market trends based on patterns of stock price movements. Most tape readers and chartists speculate rather than invest in the stock market.

Several principles underlie technical theory:

1. Market value depends solely on the interaction of supply and demand.
2. Supply and demand react to numerous forces, both rational and irrational, including the trades of fundamental analysts; investors' collective opinions, moods, and guesses; and simple, blind necessities. The market weighs and reflects all these factors continually and automatically.
3. Disregarding minor fluctuations in the market, stock prices tend to move in trends that persist for appreciable periods of time.
4. Trends change due to shifts in supply and demand relationships. No matter why they occur, evidence of these shifts appears sooner or later in the action of the market itself.[2]

Levy sums all of this up in the statement, "The basic assumption of technical theorists is that history tends to repeat itself."[3]

The market technician attempts to predict future prices based on past patterns of price changes believing in the dependence of successive price changes. As the discussion of efficient markets has explained, the fundamentalist believes that every price remains completely independent of every other price, depending solely on the intrinsic value of company earnings, particularly expected future earnings. This implies that the investor can reliably estimate future price only on the basis of fundamental information about the company that issues the stock.[4] This leads to the common value judgment that, "in fact, there is little justification for denying that properly performed fundamental analysis is superior to technical analysis."[5]

Though fundamental analysis may well give far superior trading guidance as compared to technical analysis, the investor should still watch technical market indicators rather than ignoring the insight these experience-based theories can give into short-term market movements. After discussing some popular technical market indicators, the chapter will reevaluate the efficient market theorists' random-walk hypothesis in light of technical analysis. This hypothesis states that past prices give no indication of likely near-term future prices because, statistically, each price remains completely independent of every other price. Clearly, this directly contradicts the premises that underlie technical analysis.

break out of the tops of their ranges (a breakout on the upside), this indicates that the market will move upward, and the technician accumulates stock to participate in the general market appreciation. If the averages break out of their trading ranges on the downside, the technician would expect the downward movement to continue and sell stock before its price fell any farther. Both averages must confirm such breakouts to give clear signals of market trends. If they give conflicting signals, the technician remains in doubt about the direction the market will take.

Success of the Dow Theory The Dow Theory successfully predicted the turn of the big bull market in the stock market crash of October 1929. The DJIA gave the signal on October 22, and the DJTA confirmed on October 23:

> On the late Charles H. Dow's well-known method of reading the stock market movement from the Dow Jones Averages, the 20 railroad stocks on Wednesday, October 23, confirmed a bearish indication by the industrials two days before. Together the average gave a signal for a bear market in stocks after a major bull market with the unprecedented duration of almost six years.[10]

In 1933 the DJIA signaled the end of the long bear market on April 10, and the DJTA confirmed the signal on April 24. In 1949 the Dow Theory signaled the end of the bear market that began in 1946, with the DJIA moving on August 1 and the DJTA following on October 10.

The Dow Theory has not always given such accurate signals, and even its proponents do not consider it infallible. Most advocates claim it will lead to the correct decision seven out of ten times, an excellent percentage in the uncertain investment markets. In addition, the Dow Theory gives a helpful gauge of the relative strength of the stock market and a useful barometer of business activity. Some evidence suggests that the Dow Jones averages move upward six months ahead of an upturn in the economy and move downward from three to six months ahead of economic declines.

To evaluate the predictive ability of the Dow Theory in modern times, consider the movements of the DJIA from 1985 through 1992 in Exhibit 17.10. In April 1987 the outlook for the market was uncertain. The DJIA had reached a new high, closing above 2,300 and giving a bullish signal. A downward movement seemed inevitable, but would it continue downward to signal a bull market, or rebound to reach a new high in the normal pattern for a secondary movement within an upward primary trend? To predict a bull market, the DJIA would have to move down past its previous trough at around 2,000. To indicate a secondary movement within a continuing bull market, The DJIA would have to turn back before this level and rise again through its previous peak of 2,334. The DJIA dropped below 1,800 at the beginning of 1988, confirming a bear market.

The market rebounded quickly, however, setting new record highs and giving strong bullish signals from late 1989 to mid-1990 when the DJIA reached 3,000. The average declined to 2,425, however, below its previous

EXHIBIT 17.10

Interpretation of Dow Theory from DJIA Movement

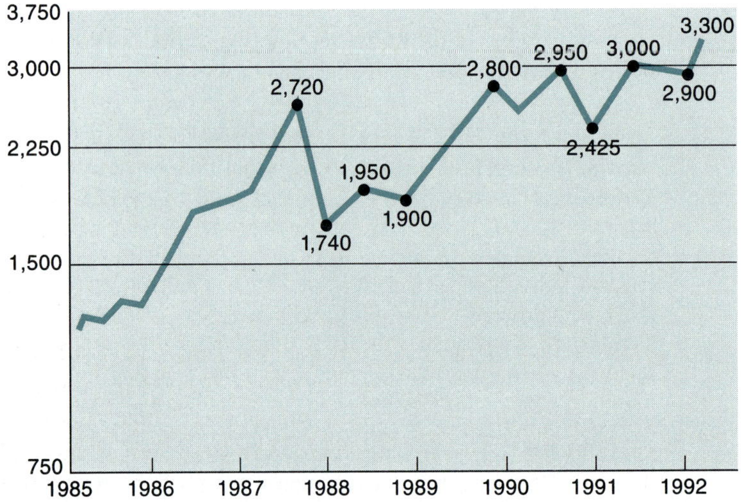

SOURCE: *Value Line Investment Survey*, April 3, 1992, p. 40. Copyright © 1992 by Value Line Publishing, Inc.; used by permission.

trough around 2,600 to indicate the first leg of a new bear market. Fortunately, the market rallied quickly once again and reached 3,300 by mid-1992.

Breadth Index

Some market participants have criticized the Dow Theory because it does not reflect the movement of all stocks in the market. The Dow Jones Industrial Average represents the movements of only 30 stocks in a market of thousands. Since few stocks move exactly in step with the Dow Jones averages, those averages give imperfect pictures of the true movements of the entire market. Some chartists follow the NYSE Composite Index, considering it a better guide to activity in the overall market.

breadth index: Net number of issues up or down as a percentage of total issues traded.

To develop a still more universal indicator, some market analysts use a **breadth index** to indicate changes in prices of all securities traded in the market. They calculate the breadth index by dividing the number of net issues that either advance or decline in price by the total number of issues traded. *The Wall Street Journal* and the Stock Market Data Bank can provide statistics to complete this calculation for trading on the New York Stock Exchange, the AMEX, and the NASDAQ system. For example, on

Tuesday, February 5, 1991, the NYSE handled trades in 2,075 different common stock issues. Of these, 1,151 companies' shares increased in price, 517 decreased, and 407 remained unchanged. The net advancing issues numbered 634 (1,151 minus 517), giving a strongly bullish breadth index of 30.55 percent (634/2,075).

Comparing such a breadth index with a moving average of breadth indexes for the previous 150 days gives a good indicator of a particular day's activity in relation to the long-term trend. As an alternative, an investor could compare a current figure with an average over some base year; many use 1982 data as a basis for comparison.

If the Dow Jones averages do not support the signals given by the breadth index, many analysts see technical weakness in the market, that is, they predict a market move in a direction opposite to the trend of the Dow Jones averages. If, on the other hand, the breadth index follows the movement of the Dow Jones averages, this indicates technical strength. In other words, parallel movement between the breadth index and the Dow Jones averages indicates a strong market trend, whether upward or downward; contrary movements in the breadth index and the Dow Jones averages suggests weak trends with no clear direction for the overall market.

The February 5, 1991, breadth index signaled strength, and the DJIA advanced 5.87 points. These indicators both showed strong potential for a rising market, so the technician would have concluded that the market was technically strong.

Volume of Trading

volume of trading: Number of shares traded, which can indicate the relative strength of a market trend.

The **volume of trading** in the market gives another guide to technical strength or weakness. Technicians review volume-of-trading statistics in the belief that an upward or downward movement that emerges from heavy trading represents a strong market trend, but a change of the same amount during thin trading shows only a weak market tendency that could easily reverse. Trading volume figures guide only very short-term perceptions of the market. Usually, they help only to confirm a change in the market's direction.

Assume that the stock market begins to rise after a period of decline. Investors hope this upward movement indicates that the market has changed its bearish course. They observe, however, that relatively slow trading produced the market rise. This indicates a technically weak market, so investors do not seriously expect a continued rise. If the upward movement had emerged from vigorous trading, investors could have assumed that a broad consensus of market participants supported an expectation of rising stock prices, so this would indicate a technically strong trend.

This gives no assurance, however, that the movement will continue upward. The broad market consensus has been wrong before. To guard against misinterpreting market signals, technicians generally review volume-of-trading numbers as part of an overall effort including other market indicators such as the Dow Theory. Still, history supports the importance of volume statistics. The Black Monday market decline on October 19, 1987, emerged from historically high volume, and high daily volume around 290 million shares accompanied the market rise during February 1991, confirming the strength of the upward rally.

Odd-Lot Volume and General Public Participation

Some technical analysts try to understand the kinds of traders who are buying or selling at a given time. Many believe that professional investors make astute, informed decisions, while the general public invests primarily based on emotions. This logic suggests that if professional investors dominate the stock market at a particular time, then any trend the market shows at that time should have technical strength. If these analysts see vigorous market participation by the general public, they interpret this as a sign of technical weakness. A sincere belief in the ignorance of the general public underlies these technicians' method. They think that naive investors wait too long for confirmation of trends and concentrate their purchases at the top of the market cycle when prices have peaked, bailing out only when the market has bottomed out. Investment managers who do this are known as *contrarians*. They buy when other investors are selling and sell when the general market is buying.

To judge the vigor of general public market participation, these technicians watch the quantity of odd-lot purchases and sales, assuming that only small investors buy odd lots, so a larger volume of odd-lot transactions should accompany greater public participation. They interpret any increase in **odd-lot volume** for either sales or purchases as a sign of technical weakness in a prevailing trend. *The Wall Street Journal* reports data about odd-lot transactions. On February 4, 1991, for example, investors bought 418,663 odd lots and sold 744,177. The excess of selling over purchases indicated that small investors doubted the technical strength of the rally.

odd-lot volume: A technical indicator of market strength that seeks to trade in the opposite direction from the general public.

In defense of the general public, history suggests that their participation in the market generally gives no valid indication of market weakness. Several studies have contradicted the assumption that the public buys at market peaks and sells at market troughs. Often they manage to invest with the trends, just like sophisticated professional investors.

Confidence Index

Some analysts watch *Barron's* **confidence index** as an indicator of technical strength or weakness. The magazine computes this index by dividing the yield on the bonds in its high-grade bond index by the yield on those in its intermediate-grade bond index. On February 4, 1991, for example, Barron's high-grade bond index yield was 8.88 percent, while the yield on the intermediate-grade bond index was 9.48 percent. Dividing 8.88 percent by

confidence index: *Barron's* index of the strength of market trends calculated by dividing the yield on high-grade bonds by the yield on intermediate-grade bonds.

9.48 percent gives a very high confidence index of 98.7 percent, confirming a strong upward market trend at that time.

Technicians base their use of the confidence index on the assumption that expectations for a strong market will lead investors to favor lower-grade bonds. When demand for lower-grade bonds increases, their prices rise and their yields fall. This run toward the lower-grade securities reduces the demand for high-grade bonds, so their prices fall and their yields rise. Together these forces diminish the spread between these yields, so high-grade bond yields represent a larger percentage of lower-grade bond yields.

The confidence index effectively measures this spread as an indication of market strength or weakness. Both a rising index and a value above 88 percent indicate unusual confidence in the market. A falling index or a value around 70 gives signs of depressed conditions and serious doubt about the strength of the market.

This index does not give perfect trading signals, nor does it suggest anything about the duration of the current market trend. As one component of a wider analysis, however, it can help the investor time forays into the market.

Short Sales As a Market Indicator

short sales: The sale of borrowed shares in anticipation of a price decline that would allow the investor to earn the difference between the selling price and the lower purchase price; the volume of such transactions can indicate relative market strength.

The volume of **short sales** (also called *short interest*) in the stock market gives technicians another indication of the strength or weakness of the market. An investor sells a stock short when he or she borrows stock from a broker and sells it, hoping its price will fall. The investor then repurchases the borrowed shares and returns them to the broker, pocketing the difference between the selling price and the lower repurchase price.

Short sales increase the supply of stock on the market, which tends to reduce prices. When short sellers repurchase borrowed shares, this tends to boost demand and increase prices. Some technicians believe that a large short interest in a rising market gives a particularly strong indication of strength for two reasons. First, the market has already absorbed additional supplies of stock, so investors need not fear dilution of existing demand due to new supplies of these shares. Second, if the market should begin to decline, short sellers will begin to buy, bolstering both demand and also supporting prices.

Outstanding short interest gives a strong technical indication of market strength in conjunction with a general theory of market movements such as the Dow Theory. Both *Barron's* and *The Wall Street Journal* publish data about outstanding short sales. For example, during the week of January 18, 1991, the NYSE handled total short sales of 98,697 shares. For the same period in 1990 investors sold 67,100 shares short. The higher figure during 1991 suggests a more bearish attitude among investors. On the other hand, some technicians would interpret this difference as a sign of stronger technical support for market prices during 1991, particularly since any

EXHIBIT 17.11

Point-and-Figure Chart

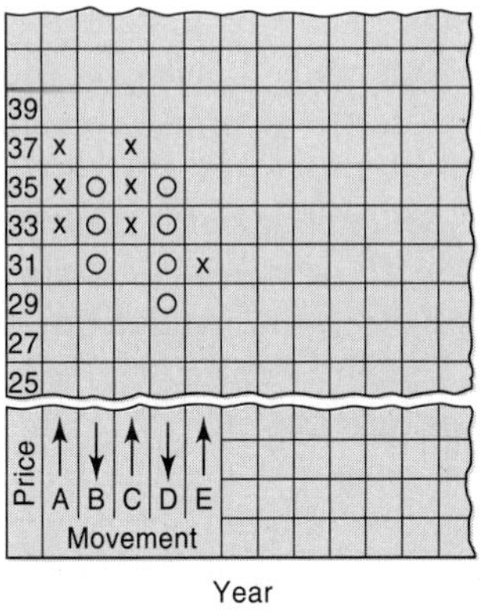

SOURCE: Frederick Amling, *Investments: An Introduction to Analysis and Management* (Englewood Cliffs, N.J.: Prentice-Hall, 1989), p. 565.

market decline would have generated stronger demand as short sellers repurchased shares and supported prices.

Point-and-Figure Charts

point-and-figure chart: A graphic device to indicate trends in stock prices to guide trading.

Many market technicians use **point-and-figure charts** to predict the extent and direction of market movements. To draw these charts, they place marks on ruled paper, as illustrated in Exhibit 17.11. In the exhibit, the numbers to the left of the marks represent stock prices in two-point ($2) intervals, but the technician can match the price-change intervals to the trading characteristics of an individual stock or market index in whatever units best suit the purpose of the chart. A long-term investor might keep a chart with five- or ten-point units, while a short-term trader might track one-point movements. To track a high-priced stock, five- or ten-point units may work best; a low-priced stock may require one-point or even smaller units.

Exhibit 17.11 shows an *X* in column A indicating an initial price of 33. When the stock moved up to 35, the technician added another *X* in column A, this logging went on as long as the price continued to move upward to reach 37. When the price declined by two points, the chartist recorded the change by placing an *O* in column B at 35, and subsequent *O*s at 33 and

EXHIBIT 17.12

Buying and Selling Signals on a Point-and-Figure Chart

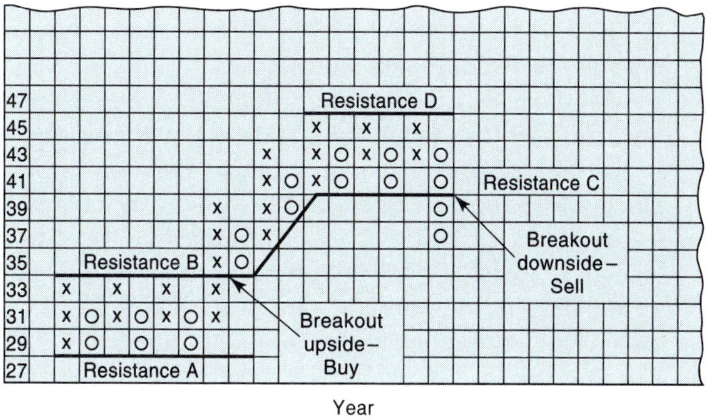

SOURCE: Frederick Amling, *Investments: An Introduction to Analysis and Management* (Englewood Cliffs, N.J.: Prentice-Hall, 1989), p. 574.

31 indicate a continuing downward trend. The point-and-figure chart gives no indication of the time required for the market to make these moves. It records price on the vertical axis and direction of movement on the horizontal axis. The chart moves to a new column each time the direction of price change reverses.

To interpret a point-and-figure chart's representation of market movements, look at Exhibit 17.12. While the market action bounces between the marks at A and B, the technician sees little indication of market action. When the price breaks out above the upper resistance mark B, the technician sees a bullish sign that would support a decision to buy. The price continues to move up, posting new highs on the chart, and each new low is higher than the previous low until it hits resistance mark D. The market bounces between two new resistance marks C and D, representing a new stable range. The price breaks out of this range when it drops below resistance mark C, giving a sell signal.

This explanation oversimplifies technicians' use of point-and-figure charts. In practice, however, these charts can give helpful guidance in interpreting market price movements and timing investments. Some investment advisory services, such as Dine's Technical Market Service, base their advice on point-and-figure techniques.[11]

SUMMARY

Investors must diversify to reduce risk in their portfolios, whether they invest 40 or 80 percent of their money in common stocks. Diversification reduces the variability of portfolio returns, but it does not completely eliminate price variability. Even a properly diversified portfolio will fluctuate in price. An investor who fears this risk can reduce the percentage of the portfolio invested in common stocks.

Methods of diversification depend on investment strategies. Modern portfolio theorists ignore any attempts at timing their purchases and sales to take advantage of market trends. They simply attempt to index their portfolios to include shares in the same proportions as those stocks appear in the index. Usually this requires matching the capitalization weighting of an index, which means allocating portions of the portfolio by total value rather than by numbers of shares or some other measure. To establish a total value of an index, the investor multiplies the share price of each company in the index by the number of shares of stock each firm has outstanding. Totaling the values for the individual companies gives the capital value of the index, and dividing each company's value by the index value gives the percentage that each company represents of the total index. The investor allots the same percentages of the total portfolio value to investments in the individual stocks to build a portfolio that will match the performance of the index.

Investors who think they can beat the performance of the index will select their own investments. These investors diversify either by investing equal amounts in each company (naive diversification) or by establishing percentages to invest in each stock based on some other method or their own judgment.

An experience-based rule of thumb suggests that investors hold at least ten common stocks. Many investors have achieved good results by weighting their investments in individual stocks by the efficient diversification method, dividing the total portfolio value among individual stocks in proportion to their return-to-risk ratios. This gives the portfolio the best possible risk-to-return ratio.

A few rules sum up the best approach to stock investment:

1. Select stocks with the highest rates of return and return-to-risk ratios.
2. Practice efficient diversification to give a portfolio the best return-to-risk ratio, at least above 1.0.
3. Watch for situations in which investors bid up the prices of excellent stocks above the appropriate levels; timid investors' fear of poorer-quality stocks can lead to underpricing relative to value.
4. Investors should seek to time their long-term commitments to take advantage of market trends.

Following the fourth rule, some investors complete market analyses to examine the trend of the market. These investors try to buy at the low point in a cyclical price pattern within the trend and to sell at the upper peaks in these patterns, both for the market and for an individual stock.

Dividend yield and P/E ratio analysis can help evaluate market trends. A higher P/E ratio indicates higher market prices and a poor time to buy. A lower dividend yield also indicates a higher stock market.

Technical indicators give investors more help in timing buy and sell decisions. The Dow Theory gauges the market's primary and secondary trends. The breadth index, trading volume data, and the confidence index all measure the strength of a current market trend. Some technicians watch data about odd-lot transactions as indicators of the general public's investment decisions, then take positions opposite to those of the public. High volumes of short sales signal overpricing in the market, but support during a falling market.

An investor can get help in constructing a portfolio from all of these methods, but they do not eliminate the need for patience. Long-term planning requires time to allow events to unfold.

INVESTMENT MANAGEMENT CONCEPTS

1. Select stocks with the highest returns and return-to-risk ratios.
2. Select a portfoilo of at least ten stocks that have the highest return-to-risk ratios, at least above 1.0.
3. Invest with the trend of the market.
4. In any attempt to time the market, try to buy at cyclical lows and sell at cyclical highs for each stock.
5. The stock market is overpriced when P/E ratios are very high.
6. The stock market is high when dividend yields are very low.
7. Base analysis of the level of the stock market on the Dow Theory.
8. A strong breadth index indicates a strong trend.
9. Large trading volume indicates a strong trend.
10. High odd-lot volume does not necessarily indicate weakness.
11. A high confidence index indicates market strength.
12. Many short sales indicate potential protection from falling prices when short sellers repurchase stock.
13. Point-and-figure charts can help identify trading opportunities.

REVIEW QUESTIONS

1. How does an investor's risk preference influence the composition of his or her portfolio?

2. How can risk management help an investor's portfolio performance?
3. How does timing affect security purchases?
4. For what term do the initials MPT stand?
5. How would the investor diversify using modern portfolio theory?
6. How can an investor construct a capitalization-weighted portfolio?
7. What principles guide security selection?
8. Explain the term *naive diversification*.
9. Explain the term *efficient diversification*.
10. How could an investor index a portfolio to the stock market?
11. What is an efficient market?
12. How do expected returns help investors construct portfolios?
13. How do return-to-risk ratios help investors construct portfolios?
14. Review some portfolio rules and explain how they affect investment decisions.
15. Why might an investor undertake a market analysis?
16. What does the investor hope to accomplish by investing with the trend of the market?
17. What is technical analysis, and how does it help investors make trading decisions?
18. How do technicians use the market P/E ratio and dividend yield to assess the level of the market?
19. What support might the Dow Theory offer for an investment decision?
20. What is a line movement in a stock market index?
21. How can the breadth index help simplify investment decisions?
22. How can the volume of trading help simplify investment decisions?
23. How can odd-lot volume help an investor determine the direction of the market?
24. How does *Barron's* calculate its confidence index?
25. How do investors use the confidence index to make investment decisions?
26. Why might a technician want to know the level of short sales?
27. Explain how to construct a point-and-figure chart.
28. How can a point-and-figure chart affect an investment decision?

SELF-CORRECTING PROBLEMS

The first part of the chapter introduced June, a relatively wealthy, aggressive stock investor. Exhibit 17.13 shows the portfolio of stocks she selected,

EXHIBIT 17.13

June's Portfolio Performance

COMPANY NAME	TRADING SYMBOL	AVERAGE DIVIDEND, 1991	PRICE, 9/27/90	PRICE, 12/31/91	GAIN (LOSS)	PERCENTAGE PRICE APPRECIATION	DIVIDENDS OVER FIVE QUARTERS AT 1991 RATE[a]	TOTAL GAINS FOR PERIOD	TOTAL PERCENTAGE GAINS (LOSSES) FROM DIVIDENDS AND PRICE APPRECIATION	PERCENTAGE RETURN, DIVIDENDS PLUS GAINS, 1991[b]
AT&T	T	$1.32	$ 31.500	$ 39.125	$ 7.625	24.2%	$1.65	$ 9.28	29.50%	29.90%
Boeing	BA	1.00	40.875	47.750	6.875	16.8	1.25	8.12	19.90	5.20
Coca Cola	KO	0.96	38.750	80.250	41.500	107.1	1.20	42.70	110.20	72.60
Eastman Kodak	EK	2.00	39.125	48.250	9.125	23.3	2.50	11.62	29.71	5.90
General Electric	GE	2.20	55.000	76.500	21.500	39.1	2.75	24.25	44.13	3.30
Merck	MRK	2.52	74.125	166.500	92.375	125.6	3.15	95.52	28.98	5.30
Phillip Morris	MO	2.10	44.625	80.250	35.625	79.8	2.63	38.25	85.75	5.10
Procter & Gamble	PG	2.00	72.125	93.875	21.750	302.0	2.50	24.25	33.60	8.40
McDonalds	MCD	0.37	25.875	38.000	12.125	46.9	0.46	12.58	48.60	30.50
IBM	IBM	4.84	105.375	89.000	(16.375)	−15.5	6.05	(10.32)	(9.80)	−21.20
DJIA										32.37
S&P 500										31.53

[a] Assumes same last quarter of 1990 dividend as for each quarter in 1991.

[b] *The Wall Street Journal*, January 2, 1992.

along with stock and market performance figures for 1991 obtained from *The Wall Street Journal.* June held the stocks from the beginning of the fourth quarter of 1990 until the end of 1991.

1. June put equal amounts of money into each stock, practicing naive diversification. What average return did she earn on the portfolio during 1991?
2. Had she followed modern portfolio theory, June would have invested in a capitalization-weighted portfolio of all of the stocks in the DJIA. What return would she have earned in 1991?
3. Did the stocks June selected match the profitability of the DJIA?
4. What total rate of return did June earn from her naively diversified portfolio over the entire holding period? What annual rate of return did she earn over this entire period?
5. If June had practiced efficient diversification, she would have weighted her investment in each stock in proportion to its percentage of the total return-to-risk ratio of the portfolio. What rate of return would she have earned in 1991? How would this return have compared to the return from naive diversification?
6. What total return would June have earned on an efficiently diversified portfolio for the entire five-quarter holding period? What annual rate of return would she have earned for this period?
7. Comment upon June's portfolio performance over the entire holding period compared to the DJIA and the efficiently diversified portfolio.
8. The P/E ratio of the S&P 500 Index totaled 22.71, and its dividend yield totaled 2.99 on December 31, 1991. What do these figures suggest about the level of the market?

Answers to Self-Correcting Problems

1. T	29.90	
BA	5.20	
KO	72.60	
EK	15.90	
GE	33.30	
MRK	85.30	
MO	55.10	
PG	8.40	
MCD	30.50	
IBM	(21.20)	
	Σ315.00/10	= 31.50 percent

The average return was 31.50 percent.

2. She would have earned the same return as the DJIA: 32.37 percent.

3. June earned slightly lower return than the DJIA. The difference was too small to be statistically significant, however, and since she earned a closely comparable return with fewer securities, her portfolio was more efficient.

4.

T	29.50
BA	19.90
KO	110.20
EK	29.70
GE	44.10
MRK	28.90
MO	85.70
PG	33.60
MCD	48.60
IBM	(9.80)
	Σ420.40/10 = 42.04 percent

The average return for the period was 42.04 percent, giving an annual rate of return of 42.04 percent/1.25 years = 33.63 percent.

5.

	RETURN		WEIGHT		PORTFOLIO RETURN
T	29.9%	×	10.8%	=	3.229%
BA	5.2	×	6.7	=	0.348
KO	72.6	×	6.7	=	4.864
EK	15.9	×	13.4	=	2.131
GE	33.3	×	10.3	=	3.430
MRK	85.3	×	12.9	=	11.004
MO	55.1	×	10.3	=	5.675
PG	8.4	×	7.2	=	0.605
MCD	30.5	×	11.3	=	3.447
IBM	−21.2	×	10.3	=	(2.184)
Return					32.550%

June would have earned an annual rate of return of 32.55 percent, slightly better than the return she earned through naive diversification, but the difference was statistically insignificant. Risk was lower, however, than that of the naively diversified portfolio, and efficient diversification provided a slightly better return-to-risk ratio.

6.

	RETURN		WEIGHT		PORTFOLIO RETURN
T	29.5%	×	10.8%	=	3.186%
BA	19.9	×	6.7	=	1.333
KO	110.2	×	6.7	=	7.383
EK	29.7	×	13.4	=	3.980
GE	44.1	×	10.3	=	4.542
MRK	28.9	×	12.9	=	3.728
MO	85.7	×	10.3	=	8.827
PG	33.6	×	7.2	=	2.419
MCD	48.6	×	11.3	=	5.492
IBM	(9.8)	×	10.3	=	(1.009)
Total					39.881%

June would have earned a total return for the period of 39.88 percent, and an annual return of 39.88 percent/1.25 years = 31.90 percent.

7. June's portfolio earned a slightly lower return than the DJIA earned, but she did it with a smaller number of securities and with less cash than she would have needed to match the entire DJIA. Efficient diversification would have provided a

slightly higher return than naive diversification with less variability. Statistically, this would have made no significant difference, however.

8. These data suggest the market was overpriced.

SELECTED READINGS

Butler, Robert E., and Donald Rappaport. *A Complete Guide to Money and Your Business*. Englewood Cliffs, N.J.: Prentice-Hall, 1987.

Cutler, Neal, et al. *Can You Afford to Retire?* Chicago: Probus Publishing, 1991.

Dattatreya, Ravi E., and Frank J. Fabozzi. *Active Total Return Management of Fixed Income Portfolios*. Chicago: Probus Publishing, 1989.

Dobbins, Richard, and Stephen F. Witt. *Portfolio Theory and Investment Management*. Oxford: Martin Robertson, 1983.

Donnelly, Austin S. *The Three Rs of Investing: Return, Risk, and Relativity*. Homewood, Ill.: Dow Jones-Irwin, 1985.

Mooney, F. Bentley, Jr. *Creating & Preserving Wealth*. Chicago: Probus Publishing, 1991.

Pond, Jonathan. *Jonathan Pond's Guide to Investment and Financial Planning: A Timely Reference for Improving Your Financial Life*. Englewood Cliffs, N.J.: Prentice-Hall, 1991.

Rubenstein, David H. *Invest for Retirement: A Guide to Financial Independence through Common Stocks*. New York: Free Press, 1981.

Chapter 17 Appendix

Utilizing the Return-to-Risk Maximizer

A personal computer program, written under the direction of author Frederick Amling, and called the Return-to-Risk Maximizer, has been used by the authors to help investors achieve efficient diversification of their portfolios. The investor's goal is to obtain a portfolio of risky stocks that has a return-to-risk ratio greater than 1.00 with a preference for portfolios that have the highest return-to-risk ratio.

In order to use the program, the investor must have a list of stocks acceptable as investments, an estimate of the expected annual returns for each for the next three to five years, and past annual rates-of-return for each acceptable investment. This information allows the computer program to calculate past average rates-of-return and the standard deviations of past returns used as a measure of risk.

Once an estimate of future expected return is determined, the program allows for the calculation of the return-to-risk ratio of each investment. The magnitude of the return-to-risk ratio helps in the selection process of the individual investments. Those investments with the highest return-to-risk ratio and those above 1.00 are most desirable.

The investments are combined into portfolios based upon the percentage of the total portfolio the investor wishes each investment to have. Usually the process begins with equal amounts being invested in 10 stocks. The computer calculates the expected return of the portfolios and the return-to-risk-ratios based upon the historic standard deviation of the portfolio.

The investor then varies the weights of each investment to achieve a combination that has the highest return-to-risk ratio. This is the optimum portfolio between return and risk. In theory and in practice, the investor should invest accordingly.

Exhibit 17A.1 shows the output of the Return-to-Risk Maximizer. The top half of the exhibit provides the expected return E_r, that is, the average

EXHIBIT 17A.1

Portfolio Determined by the Return-to-Risk Maximizer

Return Year (Y) = 1990

Current Risk-Free Return: 4.00%

NUMBER CHOICE:	EXPECTED RETURN E_r	RETURN-TO-RISK RATIO	SECURITY		10-YEAR AVERAGE RETURN	HISTORICAL STANDARD DEVIATION	RETURN (Y-9)	RETURN (Y-8)	RETURN (Y-7)	RETURN (Y-6)	RETURN (Y-5)	RETURN (Y-4)	RETURN (Y-3)	RETURN (Y-2)	RETURN (Y-1)	RETURN (Y)
151	26.50%	0.52	Magma Power	MP	8.41%	43.17%	−4.07%	44.25%	59.14%	8.90%	−31.99%	39.36%	52.76%	11.64%	−70.14%	−38.26
152	9.00	0.24	Mapco Inc.	MA	15.57	20.88	24.91	22.32	34.19	2.26	10.39	55.59	28.19	7.48	−0.73	−19.56
153	28.50	1.29	Pittson Co.	PT	−0.13	18.94	−5.31	−3.06	45.19	1.50	0.76	10.46	−8.56	−9.77	−11.50	−28.16
154	29.00	1.94	Westmoreland Coal	W	1.11	12.87	−9.33	15.08	15.32	−10.39	−3.19	8.05	−10.27	9.68	9.51	−23.81
155	29.50	0.98	Amax Inc.	AM	−3.14	26.15	−5.11	−6.32	26.82	−3.39	54.28	−7.46	−30.95	−17.13	−10.99	−33.15
156	14.50	0.39	Brush Wellman	BL	9.77	26.99	−15.96	−24.62	−3.03	−13.89	−0.58	−6.25	8.18	42.85	65.85	18.46
157	14.50	0.42	Cleveland Cliff	CL	3.56	25.16	15.57	−7.36	40.05	39.09	25.59	−29.56	−4.88	3.69	−2.08	−32.49
158	7.50	0.13	Cominco Inc.	CC	7.29	25.96	−1.70	−14.87	50.66	10.75	36.76	−3.32	−15.25	−19.15	37.24	−16.18
159	12.50	0.29	Great Northern Iron	GN	23.89	28.95	1.20	21.69	93.82	27.21	32.65	39.44	5.95	−0.74	−2.68	−2.29
160	14.00	0.36	Inco Ltd.	IN	10.50	27.89	18.33	−11.87	23.05	47.77	32.12	7.75	9.62	−25.46	45.37	−33.85

Portfolio

10-YEAR AVERAGE RETURN	HISTORICAL STANDARD DEVIATION	EXPECTED RETURN E_r	RETURN-TO-RISK RATIO	PORTFOLIO NUMBER	WEIGHTS STOCK MP	STOCK MA	STOCK PT	STOCK W	STOCK AM	STOCK BL	STOCK CL	STOCK CC	STOCK GN	STOCK IN	TOTAL
7.10%	14.08%	18.55%	1.03	1	10.00%	10.00%	10.00%	10.00%	10.00%	10.00%	10.00%	10.00%	10.00%	10.00%	100.00%
4.72	13.71	22.40	1.34	2	15.00	5.00	15.00	15.00	15.00	10.00	10.00	0.00	5.00	10.00	100.00
2.85	15.03	24.53	1.37	3	15.00	0.00	20.00	20.00	20.00	5.00	5.00	5.00	5.00	5.00	100.00
0.81	17.60	28.38	1.39	4	25.00	0.00	25.00	25.00	25.00	0.00	0.00	0.00	0.00	0.00	100.00
8.27	20.42	21.60	0.86	5	20.00	10.00	20.00	10.00	10.00	0.00	5.00	0.00	25.00	0.00	100.00
2.74	20.72	27.33	1.13	6	0.00	15.00	35.00	0.00	50.00	0.00	0.00	0.00	10.00	0.00	110.00
−0.41	18.94	27.10	1.22	7	0.00	10.00	35.00	0.00	55.00	0.00	0.00	0.00	0.00	0.00	100.00
−1.27	19.23	28.08	1.25	8	0.00	5.00	40.00	0.00	55.00	0.00	0.00	0.00	0.00	0.00	100.00
−1.06	19.33	27.90	1.24	9	2.00	6.00	30.00	2.00	60.00	0.00	0.00	0.00	0.00	0.00	100.00
−0.96	19.66	29.28	1.29	10	2.00	6.00	40.00	2.00	55.00	0.00	0.00	0.00	0.00	0.00	105.00

of the high and low return as estimated by *Value Line*. The return-to-risk ratio is calculated by subtracting the risk-free-rate of 4 percent from the estimated return and dividing by the historical standard deviation. The security is listed, along with its symbols, the historical standard deviation, and the annual returns from 1981 to 1990.

Notice in the exhibit that Westmoreland Coal has an expected return of 29 percent, a standard deviation of 12.89, and a return-to-risk ratio of 1.94 found by the operation

$$(E_r - r_f)/\sigma = (29.0–4.0)/12.87 = 1.94.$$

Other things being equal, this is an excellent ratio.

The lower half of the exhibit indicates the 10-year average return, the standard deviation, the expected return, and return-to-risk ratio of the portfolios derived from the percentage invested in the 10 stocks. The first portfolio is the one that invests equal amounts in each of the 10 stocks to the right, that is, the naive portfolio.

Actually, the naive portfolio is acceptable with a return-to-risk-ratio of 1.03 percent. However, number 4 offers a higher expected return and a higher return-to-risk ratio. Obviously this portfolio would be chosen.

The Return-to-Risk Maximizer allows the investor to determine what are the best alternative combinations of investments. It also allows the investor to determine what effect a purchase, a sale, or both of an asset will have upon the portfolio's estimated return and risk. This should help investors better manage their investments and make better investment decisions.

video cases

CASE 1: Investments in the Stock Market

Tim, who was a liberal arts major at the university had worked since high school and had saved a substantial sum of his money. Talking with Kim, his girlfriend, one Saturday afternoon, Tim admitted that he would like to invest his savings in something more profitable than a savings account, but that he didn't know much about other investments or investing. He told Kim that he had heard about the New York Stock Exchange but knew very little about what stocks were traded, how many shares were traded, who traded the shares, or how he could go about buying stock in a company. Tim had just bought a new Sony TV and wondered if he could buy Sony stock on the NYSE. He liked the product and thought it might be a good company in which to invest.

Kim told him that he should talk to a friend of hers who was a broker with a full service brokerage company. The friend, a woman she had known in her hometown, would be able to tell Tim about her brokerage firm and about placing an order.

Tim thought this to be a good idea. He told Kim that he didn't want to speculate but, rather, to invest for the long-term. Tim also confessed that he didn't know in what to invest: "I really don't know the difference between investment and speculation, and I don't know the difference between a stock and a bond, and I don't know about the different types of bonds," he said. Kim thought that her friend could help explain these things to him.

The next day Tim called the broker. The broker, Jean, told him about the differences between stocks and bonds, types of bonds, and the differences between speculation and investing. She also told him about the mechanics of placing an order.

Jean also advised him never to sell short (that was for speculators), not to buy on margin, and not to buy call options. She did indicate that he might become involved in these activities once he became more familiar with the stock market.

Jean told Tim that her job was to help him find investment opportunities, and that she would help him develop a program for future investments, no matter if he or she were bullish or bearish about the financial outlook.

After looking at the film, what do you think that Jean told Tim about the questions he asked?

CASE 2: The Bulls Meet the Bear

For 73 years the Soviet Union was organized and ran as a Communist state designed by Karl Marx. Vladimir Lenin and the Communist party overthrew the Czar of Russia, ousted the Russian royalty, confiscated all private property, and turned it over to the state. Henceforth, the 286 million people living in Russia operated on the principle "from each according to his or her ability, to each according to his or her need." The Communist party planned what was to be produced, how it was to be produced, for whom it was to be produced, and when it was to be received.

After a long succession of 5-year planning periods, the Communist system failed miserably. Since the symbolic Berlin Wall came tumbling down, Russia is now a country of its own and the Soviet Union is no more. A united Germany is in the process of being constructed with government-borrowed capital and an infusion of private capital from around the globe, including U.S. companies.

As you view the videotape *The Bulls Meet the Bear*, you realize that a new capitalistic system based on private property ownership and management is burgeoning in all countries that used to comprise the Soviet Union. More important, each citizen of the former Soviet Union has been issued vouchers representing ownership in private businesses. The country has changed completely from a state-owned nation to a place that has more individual share owners than any country on earth. People's capitalism is now in place, although it will take the next two decades to succeed and provide a profit to its owners.

Each Russian citizen must now learn what it means to save and invest. How would you explain these terms to Ivan and his friends? How would explain state ownership and contrast it to private ownership? Would it be easy for you to explain what an equity is, what an equity market is, and what the purpose of a stock exchange is? How would you explain that the prices of stocks are determined by the interaction of buyers and sellers and not by central headquarters? Before you define the word or concept of profit, you must define a legal system of ownership along with the law of contracts. How would you explain these terms as they are introduced in the videotape? How would you educate Ivan and his wife to work, save, own, be more productive, profit, and become wealthy in a free-market society? How would you convince them that it won't happen overnight and that they will have to work hard?

How will you tell them that they can invest their savings in real estate and drug companies in their country, just like the venture capitalists in the film? When they ask about attracting capital to their country, you can point to McDonald's and PepsiCo.

Explain how you motivate people in Russia to work for themselves without being told to produce a product or how to provide a business using their own capital. How do you convince them psychologically that they must be patient and work until they have wealth, but that it will take a long period of sacrifice before the fruits of their labor come to pass? How do you educate them to think like venture capitalists? In fact, how would you convince yourself and your fellow Americans of the same ideas?

CASE 3: America for Sale—Japan's Buyout Binge

Americans buy more goods and services from Japan each year than the Japanese buy from the United States. Consequently, more and more jobs are being created in Japan, and more are being lost in the United States. The problem is especially acute in the auto industry. Auto manufacturers in Japan have prospered, while U.S. manufacturers have suffered.

The scenario is not as simple as that, however. Japanese auto manufacturers *have* opened U.S. retail outlets and service facilities, creating U.S. jobs. They have also invested in auto production facilities in the United States that have provided jobs. But as the Japanese have expanded production facilities, U.S. manufacturers have closed facilities, as the tape will show. Perhaps the loss of jobs has not been as bad as it seems; nonetheless, there has been a shift away from U.S. ownership to Japanese ownership. This rankles many Americans.

Another problem relates to the trade deficit. The economically strong Japanese now have billions of dollars to spend and invest, and they have invested in the United States by buying buildings and companies. They have also invested in U.S. government securities. The Federal Reserve Board has followed a policy of "easy money" destined to stimulate the depressed U.S. economy, lowering interest rates. Lower interest rates have, in turn, caused the dollar to decline in value against the yen. That's the bad news for the United States. The good news is that this will make U.S. goods cheaper and more attractive to purchase. What America must do now is break down trade barriers to Japan and make products that the Japanese will buy from the United States.

In the tape *America For Sale; Japan's Buyout Binge*, you will learn about the problems discussed above with regard to Japan. You will learn that Japan invested almost $30 billion in the United States in 1990. You will learn that everyone else is now knocking on the Japanese door in order to enter and to sell their companies or products. You will learn that the Japanese have ties to almost 7,000 companies in the United States. The question raised is whether this is good for the United States. Should the Japanese own U.S. companies? Is this a political problem? An emotional problem? An economic problem?

The opinion is put forth that the Japanese might invest an additional $300 billion in the U.S. in the future, but that they are concerned about anti-Japanese sentiment. What do you think about these matters? Should we sell the United States to Japan? Should *we* invest in Japan? Should we buy American? What are the solutions to these critical issues?

CASE 4: Sensible Tax Planning

American statesman Ben Franklin once said that two things are sure in life: death and taxes. Tax evasion obviously is illegal, and schemes that promise great returns with minimal taxes, many based on land speculation, have earned a poor reputation in most people's view. Investment professionals, accountants, and financial planners can help you minimize your tax burden, however.

Explain the difference between tax shelters and tax fraud. Can you take advantage of existing tax laws to minimize your tax burden? One of the criticisms of existing tax laws is that dividends are taxed twice: once on the corporate level, and again on the individuals who receive them. Comment on this statement.

CASE 5: Investing to Eliminate the Retirement Income Deficit (RID)

Sadly, many people have financial problems when they retire. Although college students may scoff when told that saving for retirement should be of interest to them, the fact is that it should, indeed, be. Here are some little-known facts: (1) The savings rate in the United States is the lowest of any major industrialized nation. (2) The ratio of workers to retirees is now 3.3-to-1 and will fall to 2-to-1 after the year 2000. (3) The Social Security system is in serious trouble and is in danger of going bankrupt.

Retirees come to find they have less income in retirement than when they worked. How much money should you or you and your spouse have saved upon retirement? Given the present rate of inflation, if you anticipate retiring at age 65, how much should your portfolio be worth? Discuss the plans that you should make now to achieve this financial goal.

CASE 6: Mutual Funds As an Investment

Your friend Kim is considering investing in mutual funds and begins asking you the following questions: "What is the difference between an open- and a closed-end fund? What do the terms load and no-load mean?" Kim provides the following information and you are asked to advise her on investment alternatives.

	FUND A	FUND B
Front-end load fee	0	6.0%
Annual management fee	0.5%	0.2%
Rear-end load fee	0	0
Annual transaction costs	2.0%	2.0%
Return in past year	9.05%	9.54%

If both funds continue to perform as they have in the past year, which fund is a better buy for the short run? Which is better for the long run? Explain your answers.

CASE 7: Value-Oriented Investment

Find a good company with a depressed stock price, buy the stock, and then sell when the price appreciates. This is the best investment advice that exists, but finding bargains in the market is no easy task. After viewing the videotape in which Robert Torray outlines his approach to value-oriented investing, take his principles and try to apply them. Use standard reference materials such as *The Wall Street Journal, Value Line,* and other sources of information. Track the progress of the stock(s) you select through the semester, and compute your imaginary returns. Comment on why your investment strategies succeeded or failed, and what you would do differently the next time around.

Notes

Chapter 1

1. Frederick Amling, "A New Look at International Diversification—Asset Allocation That Pays," working paper, George Washington University, June 1991.

Chapter 5

1. "The Dow Jones Averages: A Non-professional Guide," Educational Service Bureau, Dow Jones & Company, Inc., 1992.
2. Ibid.
3. "How to Read Stock Market Quotations," rev. ed. Educational Service Bureau, Dow Jones & Company, Inc., 1989. Reprinted with permission.
4. "NASDAQ Bid & Asked Quotations," rev. ed., Educational Service Bureau, Dow Jones & Company, Inc., 1989. Reprinted with permission.

Chapter 6

1. *Stocks, Bonds, Bills, and Inflation Yearbook* (Chicago: Ibbotson Associates, 1989).
2. Gary P. Brinson, L. Randolph Hood, and Gilbert L. Beebower, "Determinants of Portfolio Performance," *Financial Analysts Journal*, July–August 1986, pp. 39–44.
3. See, for example, William F. Sharpe, "Integrated Asset Allocation," *Financial Analysts Journal*, September–October 1987, pp. 25–32.
4. See, for example, Lawrence S. Speidell, Deborah H. Miller, and James R. Ullman, "Portfolio Optimization: A Primer," *Financial Analysts Journal*, January–February 1989, pp. 22–30; and G. Fong, "An Asset Allocation Framework," *Journal of Portfolio Management*, Winter 1980.
5. William G. Droms, "Investment Asset Allocation for PFP Clients," *Journal of Accounting*, April 1987, pp. 114–118.

Chapter 12

1. R. C. Ibbotson, L. B. Siegel, and K. S. Love, "The World Wealth: Market Values and Returns," *Journal of Portfolio Management*, Fall 1985.

Chapter 16

1. Sidney Cottle, Roger F. Murray, and Frank E. Block, *Security Analysis*, 5th ed. (New York: McGraw-Hill, 1988).
2. Eugene F. Fama, "Efficient Capital Markets: II," *Journal of Finance*, December 1991.
3. Eugene F. Fama, "Efficient Capital Markets: A Review of Theory and Empirical Work," *Journal of Finance*, May 1970.
4. Harry M. Markowitz, "Portfolio Selection," *Journal of Finance*, March 1952, p. 89.
5. William F. Sharpe, "A Simplified Model for Portfolio Analysis," *Management Science*, January 1963, pp. 277–293.
6. Richard Roll, "A Critique of the Asset Pricing Theory Tests," *Journal of Financial Economics*, March 1977, pp. 129–176.
7. Edward M. Miller, "Counter Example to Random Walk," *Financial Analysts Journal*, July–August 1979, pp. 55, 56.

Chapter 17

1. See Robert A. Levy, "Conceptual Foundations of Technical Analysis," *Financial Analysts Journal*, July–August 1966.
2. Robert D. Edwards and John Magee, *Technical Analysis of Stock Trends* (Springfield, Mass.: John Magee, 1958), p. 86.
3. Levy, "Conceptual Foundations."
4. Ibid.
5. Ibid.
6. W. P. Hamilton, *The Stock Market Barometer* (New York: Barron's, 1922).
7. Robert Rhea, *The Dow Theory* (New York: Barron's, 1932); George W. Bishop, Jr., *Charles H. Dow and the Dow Theory* (New York: Appleton-Century-Crofts, 1960).
8. E. George Schaefer, "Hold Stocks for Final Market Upsurge," *Forbes*, December 1, 1962, pp. 38–49.
9. George W. Bishop, Jr., *Charles H. Dow: Economist* (Princeton, N.J.: Dow Jones Books, 1967).
10. *The Wall Street Journal*, October 25, 1929, p. 1.
11. Frederick Amling, *Investments: An Introduction to Analysis and Management* (Englewood Cliffs, N.J.: Prentice-Hall, 1989), pp. 565–574. Reprinted with permission.

Index